The Ottoman and Mughal Empires

The Ottoman and Mughal Empires
Social History in the Early Modern World

Suraiya Faroqhi

I.B.TAURIS
LONDON • NEW YORK • OXFORD • NEW DELHI • SYDNEY

I.B. TAURIS
Bloomsbury Publishing Plc
50 Bedford Square, London, WC1B 3DP, UK
1385 Broadway, New York, NY 10018, USA

BLOOMSBURY, I.B. TAURIS and the I.B. Tauris logo are trademarks of
Bloomsbury Publishing Plc

First published in Great Britain 2019

Cover design: Adriana Brioso
Cover images: [top] © Hermes Images/AGF/UIG/Getty Images;
[bottom] © Ayhan Altun/Getty Images

A catalogue record for this book is available from the British Library.

A catalog record for this book is available from the Library of Congress.

ISBN: HB: 978-1-7883-1366-7
ePDF: 978-1-7883-1873-0
eBook: 978-1-7883-1872-3

Typeset by RefineCatch Limited, Bungay, Suffolk
Printed and bound in Great Britain

To find out more about our authors and books visit www.bloomsbury.com and sign up for our newsletters.

To the memory of Nandita Prasad Sahai (1960–2013)

Contents

Acknowledgements

It is not easy to envisage a complex society such as the Ottoman from the vantage point of another polity, with which the viewer/author is but moderately familiar, as is true in my case where the Mughal world is at issue. The idea germinated during a series of introductory courses on Mughal history that I taught at Istanbul Bilgi University from 2014 onward. When in front of the class, I found that the best way of making the topic meaningful to the students (and to myself as well) was to step back and look at the manner in which the inhabitants of the Ottoman Empire approached a given problem, which albeit in a different shape, existed in the Mughal world as well. It was even more exciting to find that certain fundamental rules, with which Ottomanist historians are quite familiar, such as for instance the notion that the holders of tax assignments were responsible for law and order in the districts assigned to them, was not as central an issue in Mughal India, as it was in Ottoman history. The constant change from the familiar to the unfamiliar and back again, was one of the more stimulating experiences associated first with the classes that I taught and later with the writing of this book.

When preparing a study with a comparative slant, any author will accumulate even more debts than when he/she stays in his/her field of expertise. Afraid of omitting people whose aid has been crucial, I will proceed chronologically. Thus, for the beginning of this venture, I owe a debt of gratitude to Mustafa Erdem Kabadayı, now of Koç University, Istanbul, who in 2011 encouraged me to send a paper proposal to the congress of the Association of Indian Labour Historians of 2012. In this context, many thanks are due to Prabhu Mohapatra, Chitra Joshi and Rana Bihal, not only for graciously accepting an outsider at the congress that they had organized with admirable dedication, but for getting me in touch with Indian colleagues interested in the Mughal world as well. Moreover, in that same spring of 2012, Prabhu Mohapatra invited me to Delhi University, Vijaya Ramaswamy Krishnan to Jawaharlal Nehru University (JNU), and Najaf Haider to Aligarh Muslim University, where he introduced me to Irfan Habib and Shireen Moosvi. Furthermore, Sabyasachi Bhattacharya was kind enough to include an article of mine in the selection of congress papers that he made into an edited volume.[1] I have always felt that by this gesture, my colleagues showed their appreciation of the fact that from one sub-field of history to another, the struggles of working people had and have a good deal in common.

On this same occasion, I first met Bidisha Dhar, then a doctoral candidate waiting to defend her thesis on the embroiderers of Lucknow and now a faculty member at the University of Tripura; we have been friends ever since. In 2014, together with Tilottama Mukherjee, she arranged an encounter with students at Jadavpur University in Kolkota: It was impressive to see that the students continued to ask questions about Ottoman history until their professor decided that we must vacate the classroom. On that occasion, Lakshmi Subramanian invited me to the Centre for Studies in Social Sciences, housed in a building previously the home of Jadunath Sarkar, one of the great pioneers in modern-style historiography on the Mughals and their opponents.

As for the Istanbul side of the enterprise: By the spring of 2014, as noted I was bold enough to teach an introductory course on Mughal history to MA students at Istanbul Bilgi University, who patiently tolerated a professor who admittedly knew very little about the subject she had set out to teach. On the other hand, the experience of learning together was quite special, with students contributing articles they had located on the internet. I continue to cherish this memory.

Moreover, Aydın Uğur, then Dean of the Faculty of Humanities and Social Sciences at Istanbul Bilgi University, was willing to support a – for Istanbul – unprecedented venture: In the autumn of 2014, the university hosted a colloquium, which allowed Ottomanist and Indianist historians to get acquainted with each other. Thus, over twenty years after a group of scholars under the aegis of Tosun Arıcanlı had made a first attempt at getting a dialogue started we were able to repeat the venture, albeit on a far more modest scale. In the fall of 2015, the series of encounters proceeded at JNU in Delhi, with Ottomanists participating due to a generous travel grant from Istanbul Bilgi University. Moreover, when I became an emerita in the summer of 2017, this university hosted another Ottoman–Mughal conference, this time on historiography, so-to-say, as a retirement gift. For this gesture, I thank Bülent Bilmez and Gülhan Balsoy, past and present chairpersons, as well as Başak Tuğ, Murat Dağlı and for recent support, Mustafa Akay. Tunahan Durmaz has been of great help in the preparation of the Index.

As for myself, I got a further opportunity to establish connections with historians of the Mughal world, when the Centre for Historical Studies at JNU invited me and in addition, made me a fellow at the Jawaharlal Nehru Institute for Advanced Studies (JNIAS). Thus, I could teach a course on Ottoman social history during the fall (monsoon) semester of 2016. My thanks go to G. J. V. Prasad for the invitation to JNIAS and above all to Vijaya Ramaswamy and Najaf Haider for first inviting me and then coaching a newcomer in the academic customs and etiquette of an unfamiliar institution. In this context, I very much appreciate Professor Haider's co-teaching my course on Ottoman social history and handling the bureaucracy involved in recording student grades. Furthermore, listening to the various people speaking at JNU events was an amazing experience. Especially instructive was a lecture by Prachi Deshpande on the guru of Shivaji (d. 1680), the long-time opponent of Aurangzeb; and when attending a lecture by Romila Thapar, I became aware of Nandita Prasad Sahai, by that time unfortunately deceased, whose work has been a constant source of inspiration for the present study. In addition, my students were most impressive. For the most part, they had done their readings when they came to class; and two of them graciously helped me get to Jaipur when everything was in turmoil because of the 'demonetization', put differently the sudden lack of the paper money most often used in Indian everyday life (November 2016). In addition, I am grateful to Jiyoti Atwal, Nonica Datta and Sunil Kumar for their friendship and to Muzaffar Alam, Pius Malekandathil, Ranabir Chakravarty and once again Najaf Haider for supplying publications that I would not have found otherwise.

Apart from the scholarly interchanges at these different venues, it was a very special experience to see Fatehpur Sikri and the palaces of Agra Fort, as well as the Taj Mahal and Akbar's mausoleum in Sikandra. In Delhi, the Red Fort, Purana Kila and the eighteenth-century mausoleum of Safdār Jang (1754) gave me an idea of what Mughal (and Shēr Shāh's) buildings looked like, before and after the time of Akbar and Jahāngīr. I will never forget how Arif Bilgin (Sakarya University, Turkey), after attending a colloquium at JNU, with me braved the autumn pollution of Delhi to visit the mausoleum of Safdār Jang and the Red Fort. Without these encounters with people and monuments, I could not possibly have undertaken this project.

As for their reading of various chapters and comments on the same, I am most grateful to Elif Akçetin, Shadab Bano, Giancarlo Casale, Rishad Chowdry, Lester Crook, Stephen Dale, Richard Eaton, Jane Hathaway, A. Azfar Moin, Harbans Mukhia, and Sanjay Subrahmanyam, in addition to the author(s) of the anonymous comments received through the publisher I. B. Tauris. My special thanks go to Giancarlo Casale, Lester Crook, Richard Eaton, and Jane Hathaway for their patience in reading the entire manuscript.

In addition, Ibn Haldun University, where I now teach, allowed me a lot of free time for writing this book. For this gift of quality time, a rare generosity these days, I thank my department chair, Halil Berktay, as well as my other colleagues in the History Department. Of course, none of these generous people is in any way responsible for the errors and imperfections that doubtless remain.

Suraiya Faroqhi
Istanbul, September 2018.

A Note on Spelling and Transliteration

I have spelled terms and names from Ottoman Turkish according to the rules of modern Turkish; however, first names appear as 'Ahmed' or 'Mehmed' rather than as 'Ahmet' or 'Mehmet'. Words commonly used in English appear in English spelling. For Persian terms and names, I have employed the transliteration used by the *Encyclopaedia of Islam*, 2nd edition, leaving out diacritical marks except those denoting long vowels: 'ā', 'ī', 'ō' and 'ū'. The names of dynasties (Bahmanis, Mamluks, Safavids, Sharifs and others) appear without any diacritical marks. The spelling of Hindi personal names follows that of the secondary sources in which I have found them.

Geographical names that have become current in English appear in English spelling. All other terms follow the *Collins World Atlas: Reference edition* (2017).

Figures

All photographs have been taken by the author

(a) Aqueduct passing through the Thracian town of Kavala in Northern Greece, ascribed to Sultan Süleyman's one-time friend and grand vizier Makbul ve Maktul İbrâhim Paşa (aka Pargalı, d. 1536), who did in fact establish a pious foundation in this town. The recent rediscovery of İbrâhim Paşa's grave has made this long-deceased dignitary once again newsworthy. (b) A *bauli* or underground water source, with an access way embellished by elaborate architecture and once frequent in Northern India. Today, these structures only function as 'touristic' sites and therefore their conservation can be difficult. This *bauli* is part of the Bara Imambara in Lucknow, opened in 1784 and despite its late date, chosen for its good state of preservation. (c) The public fountain of Emin Efendi in Samakov/Bulgaria; the donor was the head of the sultan's kitchen, who probably had some connection to this small town. Built around 1660, the fountain has no inscription but shows signs of later restoration. As the construction of (nearly) cubic buildings to house fountains is an eighteenth-century fashion, perhaps the present shape of the fountain is due to a later restoration. Note the arrangement for watering animals and the attached birdhouse. Compare: (Machiel Kiel, 'Samakov', *Diyânet İşleri İslâm Ansiklopedisi*, https://islamansiklopedisi.org.tr/samakov, accessed on 19 September 2018) 147/148/149

14. **Trade supplying artisans**: Mosque in the Koza Hanı of Bursa (perhaps built 1490–1). In the centre, there is a fountain with a small mosque on top. The name means '*han/khān* of the cocoons'. The names of *han*s changing frequently, it is unclear when people adopted this name. In the 1970s, the Koza Hanı was in fact a wholesale market for fabrics and silk cocoons. Today the complex is a shopping centre selling silks, and the courtyard a favourite for tea and recreation. 208

15. **Ministering to the comfort of artisans and other townspeople**: the public bath (built in 1645) attributed to Cinci Hoca (d. 1648) in the Anatolian 'museum town' of Safranbolu/Turkey, where traditional crafts persisted into the 1970s and 1980s. Without ever completing his madrasa studies, Karabaşzade Hüseyin Efendi, born in Safranbolu, became famous for his presumed familiarity with the spirit world. Ministering to the psychologically challenged Sultan İbrahim (r. 1640–8), he managed to become an army judge (*kadıasker*) and amassed an enormous fortune, from which he may have financed this building. 214

16. **Fabrics drying on the banks of the river Gomti**, in Lucknow: traditionally, Lucknow has been famous for its textiles, and although today the city is best known for its heavy industry, the city's embroiderers, both men and women, produce work that is in considerable demand, both within India and abroad. 218

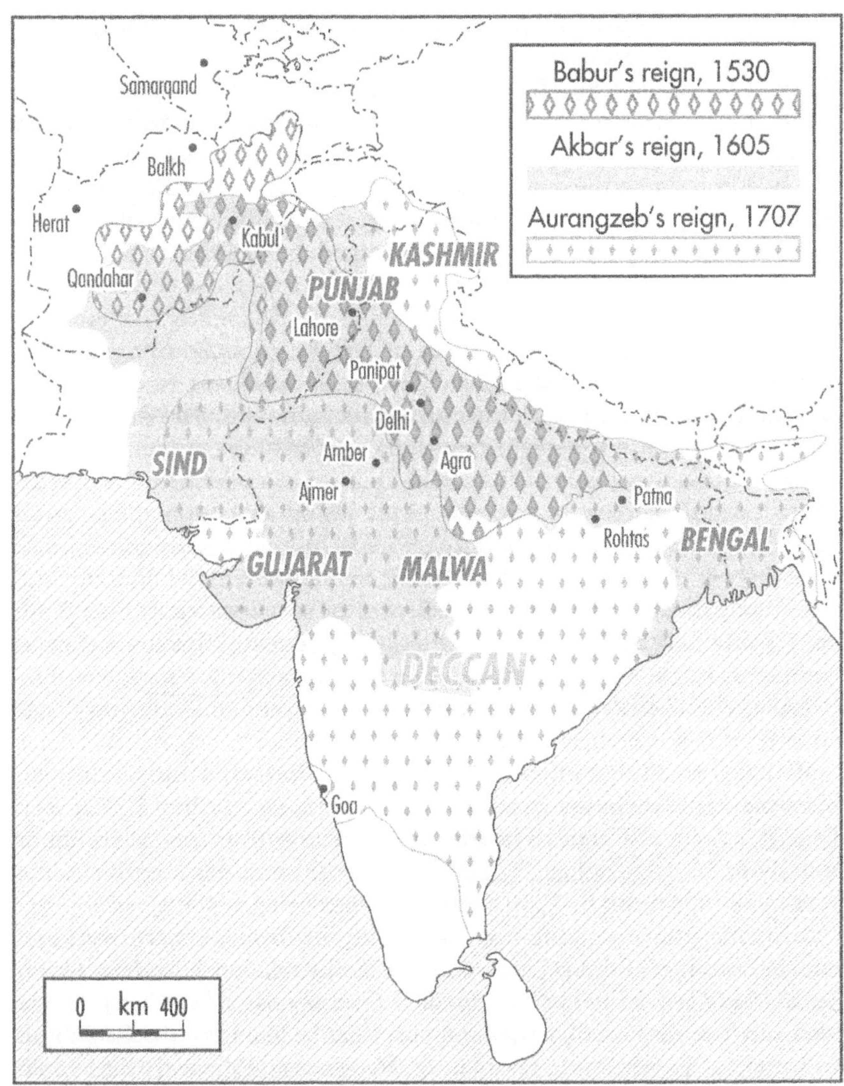

Map 1 Map of India, reproduced from Catherine B. Asher, Cynthia Talbot, *India before Europe* (Cambridge, 2006) p. 117. © Cambridge University Press 2006, reproduced with permission

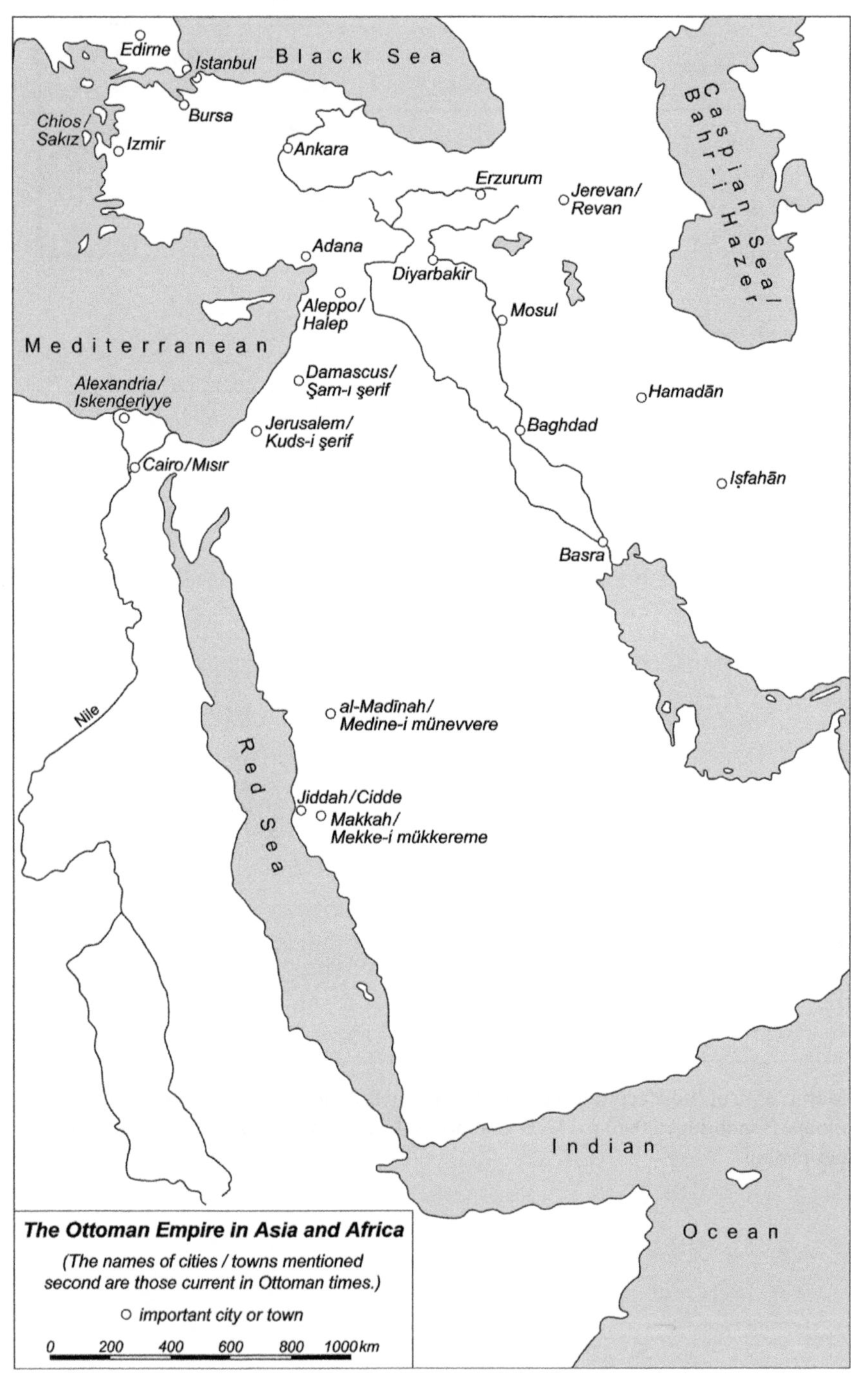

Map 2a The Ottoman Empire in Asia and Africa

Map 2b The Ottoman Empire in Europe

Introduction

In the present work, we attempt a confrontation of the societies governed by the Ottoman and Mughal (in Turkish usage: Baburi) empires of the sixteenth, seventeenth and early eighteenth centuries. Differently expressed, we survey the social – and to a lesser extent economic and political – features shared by the two empires, and at least as importantly, we highlight the differences.

There are good reasons for bringing together the two societies; for only by comparing a given empire with others of a similar type, will we see what is specific about the polity of our concern. Otherwise, at least when dealing with the Ottomans, we easily succumb to the temptation of viewing the political, religious or artistic activities and attitudes widespread in Istanbul or Cairo as typical of all major Islamic empires. Certainly, this temptation is less relevant to historians of South Asia. In this case, too, however, by avoiding comparison, we risk ignoring the range of options from which rulers, elites and artists of the 1500s to 1700s might choose, and the more limited possibilities available to members of the subject populations. In this manner, we hope to promote a wider vision of human life and historical possibilities.

While the subject populations are our chief concern, we cannot approach the lives of these people without examining the writings produced by the officials running the two empires. For the curation of the vast majority of surviving sources is the work of serving or former office-holders, who – like all authors – have brought their own concerns and assumptions to bear on the documents or chronicles produced. After all, in both the Ottoman and the Mughal worlds, even activities seemingly remote from official preoccupations, such as poetry, were often a means of gaining recognition at the court of a sovereign. In turn, such appreciation could influence the progress of an official career.[1] Therefore, to our misfortune, we can never approach Ottoman or Mughal subjects in a direct fashion; for the most part, we can only access their reflections in a – seriously distorting – mirror.

Moreover, early modern Ottoman and Mughal sources depict the relevant societies as consisting almost exclusively of males; and this pre-selection very much limits our vision. Given the silence of the sources, women of necessity remain in the background of our analysis; for despite all the efforts to locate sources, which historians have made – and continue to make – women have entered into Ottoman and Mughal writings only under special circumstances. We will include them wherever possible.

In this situation, when aiming for a study of 'ordinary people' we need to adopt an indirect approach, adjusting our focus toward the interface between the Ottoman and

Mughal governing apparatuses on the one hand, and on the other, the taxpaying subjects in town and country.

Given this game of mirrors, the present effort at confrontation and/or comparison, which seems quite straightforward at first glance, is in reality, much more complicated than it appears. As Jeroen Duindam has said, in a different context, apparent similarities may hide underlying differences and immediately visible differences disguise underlying similarities.[2] Even a rapid glance will show that this statement is valid for the Ottoman and Mughal settings. A large tax grant to a high-level Ottoman dignitary (a *has*) somewhat resembles the *jagīr* that rewarded the commanders and administrators serving the Mughal emperor. At the same time, Mughal officials did not much emphasize the notion that the emperor was the ultimate owner of all agricultural lands, an understanding fundamental to the Ottomans' official conception of tenure. Despite this difference, however, neither Mughal nor Ottoman peasants owned their farms in the sense that they could handle them according to their personal preferences, including the abandonment of cultivation. However, it seems that insulated by their castes and clans, Mughal peasants were less dependent on the *jagīrdār* receiving their dues than was true of their Ottoman counterparts (see Chapter 8).

In the context of world history: Empire building by Mughals and Ottomans

The present enterprise is part of a broader concern with the history of empires, which has interested historians of Europe for many centuries already. There is an extensive literature attempting to gauge the impact of the Roman Empire on medieval but also on nineteenth- or twentieth-century Europe, a concern apparent already in the 1700s if not earlier and continuing down to the present day.[3]

Other historians have approached empire studies in a comparative mode. Thus, a historian of the Roman Empire set out to show that this polity was not in any way a precursor of nineteenth-century style modernity, in the sense that some of his colleagues liked to maintain. Basing his comparison on an impressive array of secondary studies concerning the Mughal Empire, Peter Bang presented the Roman polity as a social, political, and economic formation very much in line with the world empires that emerged all over Eurasia from the third century BCE down to the 1800s.[4] In the view of the present author, the Ottoman Empire would have served Bang's purposes just as well or even better, as for several centuries the sultans ruled the eastern section of the Roman world and thus dealt with similar geographical and environmental constraints. However, Bang may have wanted to show that the parallels highlighted were *not* the result of similar physical environments and perhaps even long-term political traditions. While the Roman and Mughal empires were distant from one another in terms of geography and political culture, the constraints of empire building and maintenance of rule in environments of limited wealth and slow communications might result in rather similar formations. Traditions and ideologies were perhaps less determinant than material constraints.

In a different vein, scholars working in the Ottoman world of the fifteenth to eighteenth centuries – Kâtib Çelebi (1609–57) is a prime example – have studied Islamic empires and dynasties. At the same time, few Ottoman Muslim intellectual figures working before the 1850s have shown a sustained interest in the Roman, Chinese, Japanese and other empires outside of the Muslim world. As an exception, we may refer to the conquests of Alexander, the Macedonian king (356–23 BC) in the Greek world and the Achaemenid Empire, whom authors working in Islamic contexts seem to have regarded as an 'honorary Muslim'. Probably, it is not by chance that one of the first authors to write about the Ottoman sultans framed his account with stories about Alexander.[5]

In the world of today, the rise and dissolution of major empires during the last century or so has caused historians to review similar polities, which flourished in the past. Thought-provoking examples include the collapse of the Ottoman Empire and the 'peace to end all peace' that followed it.[6] In particular, the wars, massacres and expulsions accompanying and following the last years of the Ottoman Empire have become the subject of much research and controversy. In addition, historians have studied the fall of the Tsarist Empire, its re-emergence under Soviet rule and its dissolution in the 1990s, or else the disappearance of the British Empire in the decade after World War II, to say nothing of the challenges to the American informal empire that we are currently witnessing. On the Indian side, domination by the British Empire and the violence that accompanied it, but also the hostilities among the 'successor states' of India and Pakistan have encouraged historians to take a closer look at the past: To what extent did the legacies of Mughal and British domination determine the paths taken by India and Pakistan?[7] Quite often, researchers will violently disagree about the after-effects of polities passed into history some decades or centuries ago. In these choices, allegiance to a given nation state may be important but other considerations come into play as well. Whatever the situation, historical and/or archaeological research is the precondition sine qua non for any sensible discussion.

When surveying current debates about royal rule, we find that Jeroen Duindam's recent study of ruling dynasties active between the fourteenth and eighteenth centuries CE has foregrounded the Ottoman and Mughal rulers quite prominently. In Duindam's analysis, these monarchs take their places beside the emperors and shoguns of Japan, the Ming and Qing emperors of China, the Austrian Habsburgs, Louis XIV of France (r. 1643–1715), and a variety of Sub-Saharan African kingdoms.[8] Other dynasties enter the scene on an ad hoc basis. Duindam's study is particularly relevant for our project because this author does his best to avoid grand narratives such as 'the rise of the West' or 'the great divergence', which in the opinion of the present author, historians should sidestep, at least for the time being. Duindam also treats religion and culture as factors among others, instead of making them into prime movers, in the fashion that was widespread in the mid-1900s and which once again, many authors prefer today.

Instead, Duindam concentrates on similarities and differences in the political field, apparent when examining the tension between the person of the emperor/sultan/king or other royal on the one hand and the demands of his – or more rarely her – office on the other. In his second chapter, Duindam studies the position of the ruler among members of his extended family, including the question of succession, together with the problems that this event has always entailed.[9] A third chapter deals with royal courts. But for our purposes, the most relevant part of the discussion comes at the end; for in the fourth and last chapter, Duindam deals with the 'interface' between the ruler and those sections of the subject population about whom the author has found evidence. A similar problematic inspires the present study.

To take up a formulation of Farhat Hasan, we regard the Ottoman and Mughal governing apparatuses as engaged in constant conflicts with a broad range of social groups. Some of the latter were insiders to the ruling elites at various levels, while others remained (more or less) outside of these charmed circles.[10] Therefore, the interface between the governing apparatuses and the societies they attempted to control is necessarily fuzzy, as some social actors claimed positions of authority, with others sharply contesting this claim. Moreover, power balances were constantly shifting, so that a person or group of actors, whom we may call small-scale rural power-holders, might within a few decades emerge as kingmakers or even kings. However, problems of this type are common to all social historians of early modern empires.

In the Ottoman world, the theoretical distinction between the servitors of the sultans (*askeri*) and the taxpaying subjects (*reaya*) was clear-cut, but due to the incessant struggles that Farhat Hasan refers to, realities on the ground were often unclear. In the Mughal orbit, the interface between members of the governing apparatus and the subject populations is even more difficult to analyse because representatives of the central government intersected with caste and community leaders in a variety of ways.

Questions of time and place

We begin with a clarification of terminology. While calling both the Ottoman and the Mughal realms 'empires', we reserve the term 'emperor' for the Mughal monarch and refer to the Ottoman rulers as 'sultans'. If one assumes that 'sultan' designates a regional power while the Ottoman monarch obviously was a ruler of far higher status, this terminology is open to challenge. On the other hand, it has the advantage that, at a glance, the reader knows to whom we are referring. From another perspective, the term 'Mughal' is problematic, as it invites confusion between Mughals and Mongols.[11] However, as 'Mughal' is so widespread, especially in Indian historiography, presumably this risk is not too great. As for the alternative term 'Timurid' it is mainly familiar to scholars while the other alternative, namely 'Baburî' is only in use among Turkish speakers. With respect to geography, we follow Indian custom and sometimes call the space occupied by today's India, Pakistan and Bangladesh 'the subcontinent' for short, with South Asia being an alternative designation.

Ottoman history programs in Turkey often consider the period between the late 1400s and early to mid-1800s as the 'modern' age, with many specialists preferring the term 'early modern'. While – as in other historiographies – there are ongoing disputes among Indian historians about periodization, many scholars – and university programs as well – distinguish between four periods, called ancient, medieval, modern and contemporary. Seemingly, many historians regard the founding of the Delhi sultanate in the late twelfth century CE as an acceptable beginning for a new period, which the historian may call medieval.[12] During this period immigration into India was significant, with Central Asian Turks an important component of the migrant population, and specifically of the ruling group. In addition, newcomers arrived from

Iran and today's Afghanistan in the 1200s, often as refugees from Mongol attacks. At times, the Delhi sultanate's power reached far into the south, temporarily incorporating a large part of Peninsular India as well.

Some historians regard the years around 1500 as the beginning of a new period: Thus, Sanjay Subrahmanyam uses the expression 'early modern' for the years from about 1500 into the eighteenth century.[13] Catherine Asher and Cynthia Talbot have used the same term in their history of Mughal and non-Mughal India. These two authors stress that they focus on 'India before Europe', and thus not on European interventions – the arrival of the Portuguese in 1498 is not at issue here. Even so, they consider that the increasing number of interregional interactions throughout the subcontinent justify viewing the sixteenth to eighteenth centuries as decidedly post-medieval or early modern.[14] This view nicely coincides with Joseph Fletcher's conclusion that, between 1500 and 1800, societies all over Eurasia showed common characteristics including among others, population growth, accelerating social change, and the increase of towns and commerce.[15] These views support our present assumption that both the Ottoman and the Mughal empires were part of an early modern world.

In 1526, Bābur (r. 1526–30), a descendent of Timur/Tamerlane (1336–1405), conquered the last Delhi sultanate then ruled by the Lodi dynasty. We begin our discussion with this conquest, which for our purposes, begins the early modern period. By contrast, scholars favouring a 'long' medieval age may prefer to view 1526 as beginning a subdivision of the 'medieval' time-span, namely the Mughal period (1526–1739, alternatively 1526–1857). The Mughal emperors ruled a gradually increasing part of India from 1526 to the early 1700s, and the empire lasted, at least on paper, until the formal British takeover in 1857. However, the disintegration of the empire was already underway when in 1739, the Iranian ruler, Nādir Shāh Afshār (1698–1747) raided Delhi and carried off much treasure, including the so-called 'peacock throne'. This date may mark the end of the epoch in which the Mughals dominated India.[16] During the last section of the early modern period, often called 'transitional' (1739–1857), the Mughal Empire, which at the death of Aurangzeb (r. 1658–1707) had encompassed almost the entire subcontinent, seriously contracted. After 1739, the Mughal Empire was only a regional kingdom along the banks of the Yamuna and the Ganges, which furthermore continued to lose power, while the political impact of the East India Company (EIC) increased. Mughal dissolution became especially marked after the Company's victory in the battle of Plassey (1757), which resulted in the territorial control by the EIC of the rich province of Bengal, formerly a premier possession of the Mughal Empire.

To limit the area under investigation, already enormous, we focus on the realm as it was around the year 1600, when Akbar's reign was about to end.[17] In the Northwest, the Mughals controlled Kashmir and Kabul. While the Himalaya range was roughly the northern border, the empire extended eastward to encompass Bengal with the Ganges and Brahmaputra deltas. The southern border was the most complicated, as by 1600, the Mughals had begun but not completed the conquest of the Deccan. Thus, Berar and Gujarat were already part of Akbar's empire, but Ahmadnagar, Bijapur and Golconda were still separate polities under their own sultans.

It is more straightforward to define the temporal and spatial limits of the Ottoman domain under discussion here. As Bābur displaced the last dynasty of the Delhi sultanate in 1526, we begin our analysis at about the same time. Coincidentally, the Ottoman armies began their conquest of Hungary in 1526 as well, winning the battle of Mohàcz. Conquering Hungary took several decades. However, by the mid-sixteenth century the empire had almost reached its maximum extension on the North Western front, or to put it differently in Central Europe. During the seventeenth century, the Ottomans gained some additional territory from their Habsburg and Polish rivals, and conquered the previously Venetian island of Crete. However, Crete was the only permanent addition, as the Habsburgs mostly recovered their lost territories in 1699, when the sultans had to give up almost all of Hungary. Otherwise, there were no further losses before the later 1700s; or, to be more precise, the Ottomans reconquered Iraq, briefly lost to the Safavids (1639), and in addition retrieved Belgrade, which the Habsburgs had occupied for a few years (1718). Our analysis will focus on the 'central lands', namely Western and Central Anatolia as well as the Eastern Balkans. Egypt and Syria will enter the picture too; however, it is illusory to claim that we can cover the empire in its totality.

It seems a good idea to end the Ottoman discussion in 1768. In this year, Sultan Mustafa III (r. 1757–74) entered the war against Russia, when the intentions of the Russian, Prussian and Habsburg rulers to partition Poland had become apparent. The first of these partitions occurred in 1772. While the Ottoman recovery of Belgrade from the Habsburgs (1739) took place in the same year as Nādir Shāh's attack on Delhi, ending the discussion in this year probably gives the reader an overly optimistic slant on Ottoman history, while ignoring the challenges, which the empire had to face shortly afterward. Following the comparatively prosperous mid-century, the sultans' realm entered into a series of massive crises, and in the late 1700s, it seemed on the verge of dissolution.[18] All predictions to the contrary however, the Ottoman dynasty held out just as long as did its Habsburg and Russian rivals.

Inter-empire contacts

Apart from comparisons, we will upon occasion discuss the contacts between subjects of the Ottoman sultans and the denizens of the Mughal Empire, following up the 'encounters' that as Sanjay Subrahmanyam has suggested, were part of the histories of all Eurasian empires.[19] However, our sources on important aspects of this relationship, including Ottoman–Indian commerce, are not very ample. Therefore, the discussion of encounters is quite short, even if inter-empire contacts surely were closer than our limited documentation records.

Historians including Yakup Mughul, Naim Rahman Farooqi, and Salih Özbaran have studied Ottoman intervention in the Red Sea and Indian Ocean as a reaction against Portuguese aggression and as a means of protecting the pilgrimage routes to Mecca.[20] This latter concern was paramount first for the Mamluk sultans of Egypt and Syria, and after 1517, for the Ottoman rulers when the conquest of Egypt made them into the overlords of the Hijaz. More recently, Giancarlo Casale has adopted a wider perspective, inspired by the rapidly growing integration of the Ottoman world into the study and teaching of world history.[21] He has suggested that quite apart from the protection of the spice trade and the religious-cum-political legitimacy concerns highlighted by previous researchers, Selim I (r. 1512–20) and Süleyman (r. 1520–66) – and particularly their admirals – were out to explore the wider world and make a place for the Ottomans in overseas territories.

If this hypothesis gains general acceptance, the concerns of mid-sixteenth-century Ottoman leaders resembled those of the commanders serving the Spanish and Portuguese kings. In consequence, historians should not regard the Ottoman Empire as a land-based polity for which the navy and maritime warfare were incidental. At least in the eyes of a certain faction at the sultan's court, headed by the long-lived grand vizier Sokollu Mehmed Paşa (1506–79), expansion in the Indian Ocean region was a significant component of empire building. However, in the last quarter of the sixteenth century, after the murder of Sokollu, Ottoman priorities changed, and with the decline of Portuguese power in the 1600s, Ottoman sultans no longer attempted to chase away the Portuguese and – perhaps – acquire territory on the western coasts of India.

On the other hand, in the reign of Akbar (r. 1556–1605), there was considerable inter-empire tension when the Mughal ruler seemingly attempted to establish a presence in the Hijaz, allowing a high-profile pilgrimage to Mecca on the part of several prominent palace women. The latter remained in the Hijaz for several years, much to the discomfort of the Ottoman authorities.[22] Presumably, Akbar's move involved courting the Sharifs that governed the holy city of Mecca, autonomous but recognizing the Ottoman sultan as their suzerain.[23] Under Jahāngīr (r. 1605–27) and Shāh Jahān (r. 1628–58) the builder of the Taj Mahal, the two empires occasionally exchanged ambassadors; and there were further embassies in the early 1700s.

Non-Mughal venues for contacts between Ottomans and Indians include the Bahmani sultanate (1347–1527). The Bahmanis had close commercial links to the fifteenth-century Ottoman realm, and members of the local elites often travelled to the Hijaz, under Ottoman control after 1517.[24] Even more important were the immigrants into India who arrived from the Ottoman realm, settled in Gujarat and at times controlled the city of Surat, later the major Indian Ocean port of the Mughal Empire. In the mid-1500s, these immigrants, mostly known as Rumi, strongly supported the interventions of Ottoman sultans and viziers against Portuguese attempts at controlling navigation in the Indian Ocean.[25]

While the late 1700s are outside of the period treated here, noteworthy Ottoman–Indian contacts occurred in this period as well, namely when the ruler of Mysore/Deccan Tippu Sultān (d. 1798) sought Ottoman aid in his struggle against British encroachment.[26] However, during those years, Sultans Abdulhamid I (r. 1774–89) and Selim III (r. 1789–1807) were embroiled in both domestic and inter-empire conflicts, so that intervention in remote Peninsular India, which would have surely resulted in a confrontation with Great Britain, was not a practicable possibility.

Situating the problem: The politics behind historiography

As noted, many if not most authors of surviving early modern texts served, or had served in the bureaucracies of their respective rulers. Therefore, we largely have to construct our account on documents and narratives intended to stabilize the rule of

Ottoman sultans and Mughal emperors. As our purpose obviously differs from the aims of these authors, we need to read them 'against the grain' whenever possible. Given these and other difficulties, the present project is more modest than Duindam's enterprise is. While his work encompasses a large number of dynasties, we concentrate on just two of them, asking questions about the manner in which the texts and images produced by and for the Ottoman and Mughal court elites reflected the concerns of the relevant subject populations.

In both cases, the polities at issue had come into being by the conquest of a well-established agricultural territory by Turkic armies. Turkic migrants had been present in Anatolia since the later eleventh century and their numbers had much increased during the 1200s, because at that time many inhabitants of Central Asia fled from the Mongols, whose empire building often involved brutal attacks on the autochthonous populations. When the Ottoman dynasty in the early 1300s became visible to chroniclers, its members and adherents were thus no strangers to Anatolia. However, as Turkish-speaking Muslims whose scholars used Persian as a literary language, they differed profoundly from the local inhabitants, mostly Greek-speaking Orthodox Christians and Armenians, marginalized over the long term, by conversion to Islam.[27]

Large-scale out-migration by warrior communities from Central Asia had reached India in the 1100s as well, probably due to the same reasons as in the Anatolian case. Thus, in 1526, the presence of Turkic and Muslim warriors founding sultanates in northern India was no novelty; and some of these rulers encouraged the composition of chronicles in the Iranian palace style.

In 1398, the Delhi sultanate had been the victim of a major raid by Timur/Tamerlane, who massacred the population of Delhi. At least indirectly, Bābur's memoirs indicate the author's awareness of this traumatic event and his attempt to distance himself from it.[28] Even so, long after the Mughal dynasty had founded a large Indian empire, its representatives – at least in certain contexts – continued to identify as descendants of Timur and Genghis Khan. By contrast, the authors writing about the early Ottoman dynasty certainly had no reason to glorify the still largely pagan Mongols of the late 1200s and early 1300s; nor did chroniclers writing in the fifteenth century see any reason to praise Timur's victory over Bayezid I in 1402. However, educated adherents of the early Ottoman project were part of the same 'Persianate' tradition of rule that the Mughals used as a source of inspiration; and thus, notions of good government were quite similar as well.[29] In addition, differently from the Safavid rulers of Iran, who dealt with an overwhelmingly Muslim population and might even develop ambitions to convert the entire population to Shiite Islam, Ottoman and Mughal elites, throughout their respective histories, accepted the existence of many non-Muslims among their subjects.

Despite these points of contact, for a long time Ottomanists regarded the empire ruled by the sultans as a state formation sui generis, which had little in common with either its western or its eastern neighbours.[30] This 'isolationist' view made sense for people who viewed the Ottoman Empire, and particularly the nineteenth-century avatar of this long-lived polity, as an 'ancestor' of the Republic of Turkey, by now nearly a century old. At the same time, once the Ottoman archives had become available, from the 1940s onward and – more significantly – in the closing years of the twentieth century, Ottomanist historians mainly focused on the empire's internal history; for researchers soon became aware that they had known very little about urban or provincial life before the opening of the archives. For many researchers working during the last quarter of the twentieth century, the domestic history of the Ottoman Empire thus had a clear priority, although this preference did not completely exclude relations with the outside world.

Whenever the latter were at issue, the conquest of principalities, kingdoms and sultanates in the Balkans, Anatolia and finally the Arab lands took centre stage, followed by the integration of these new acquisitions into an empire that profoundly changed character as it grew.[31] Historians concerned with economic relations rather than politics might look beyond the Ottoman borders because they wished to chart the process by which the empire, or at least some of its provinces, suffered 'incorporation' into the 'world economy' dominated by the industrializing powers of Europe and at a later stage, North America.[32] Historians of literature and painting, by contrast, looked toward Iran, as Iranian culture, both in its Timurid and its Safavid incarnations, made a profound impression on the people creating Ottoman palace culture. As for Japan, this ancient empire began to interest first Ottomans and then Ottomanists after the Japanese victory in the Russo-Japanese war (1904–5): The dissident 'young Turks' of the period considered Japan an example they hoped to emulate.

Thus, both Turkish and Japanese scholars have published on late Ottoman history.[33] By contrast, other world empires have remained in shadow. The number of Ottomanists concerned with Russia is still limited; and China until quite recently was completely outside the world as imagined by historians of the Ottoman domain.

In today's Turkey, there is some tension between the historians' vision of Ottoman history and a 'popular' view, which currently has strong support in governmental circles as well, and which focuses on the greatness and glory of the Ottoman sultans and the benisons they bestowed on humankind in general. Even among professional historians, there are many who assume that the Ottoman state represented Islamic justice and morality, playing down abuses as rare and uncharacteristic.[34] However, at present debates about such matters are mostly the affair of journalists with an interest in history and historians appearing in television programs and/or widely diffused print media. When writing for fellow professionals, few historians focus on Ottoman glory and morality.

Matters are somewhat different when it comes to India. Here, the fact that the majority population is Hindu but the rulers and elites in power for centuries before 1857 were largely Muslim is an issue that sparks heated political debate. Even remote periods such as the Delhi sultanate (1206–1526) and the Mughal Empire (1526–1857) are not exempt from political uses. Recently, exchanges have become even more polemical, since the current government apparently sees itself as representing Hindu values often equated with 'national' ones.

At the same time, quite a few historians teaching in elite Indian universities take issue with claims and policies of that kind.[35] It is in fact quite probable that their concern with the possible political implications of their work has made them more attentive to the uses and abuses of sources than is true within the somewhat less politicized Ottomanist community.

Ottoman–Mughal connections and the long shadow of Marshall Hodgson

Viewing matters from a different angle, the reader soon notices that in comparative studies dealing with the Ottomans, Safavids and Mughals the Ottoman perspective remains under-represented. Marshall Hodgson, the pioneer who inspired scholars and teachers to take an interest in this type of comparison, was a world historian, working on what he used to call the region between Nile and Oxus. Hodgson mainly studied the religion and culture of what he had labelled as the 'Middle Period' of Islamic history, thus concentrating on the period before about 1500; he was definitely not an Ottomanist. Stephen Dale and Douglas Streusand, who have written on the 'three empires' as well, have made their reputations as historians of India, and specifically of the Mughal Empire.[36] Muzaffar Alam and Sanjay Subrahmanyam, Naim Rahman Farooqi and most recently Gagan Sood, who all have shown interest in the Ottoman world, are principally historians of India as well.[37] Only Ali Anooshahr falls into a different category, combining a comparative orientation with a strong interest in the founding periods of both the Ottoman and the Mughal empires, while Central Asia is one of his major concerns as well.[38] Surely, the time has come to complete the picture and attempt a comparison from the perspective of the mature Ottoman Empire, and this is the aim of the present study.

Hitherto, scholars viewing the Ottoman and Mughal empires in a comparative mode have often included the Safavid polity of Iran (1501–1722).[39] There are many arguments in favour of such a proceeding. Firstly, albeit in varying degrees, all three empires used gunpowder weapons to a significant extent, although only the Ottomans specialized in cannon and musket warfare. Secondly, the Ottoman, Safavid and Mughal empires were contiguous, so that discussing all three of them together results in a study covering much of South and West Asia, with Egypt, North Africa and the Balkans 'thrown in'. Thirdly, historians will find it attractive that the Safavid and Mughal dynasties flourished and lost power at about the same time.

As a fourth reason for including the Safavids, the observation of Iranian political culture can make us aware of phenomena existing in the Ottoman and Mughal orbits too, but to which we may not have paid sufficient attention. Rudi Matthee's study of the seventeenth-century Safavid Empire, for example, provides much 'food for thought' when the author discusses the lack of interest of the last two shahs in military matters – surely an issue relevant to the mid-eighteenth-century Mughal emperor Muhammad Shāh (r. 1719–48) as well. Furthermore, the ferociously divisive factions at the Safavid court made it impossible for provincial office-holders to concentrate on their jobs, because they needed to counteract the innuendos by which their enemies might make their positions untenable. These observations bring to mind the representatives that in the 1700s, Ottoman magnates routinely entertained in Istanbul as well, although these people probably dealt more with the gains or losses from tax farms or the complaints of overtaxed provincials, than with rumours of possible treason. In a similar vein, a Safavid governor of Qandahar once handed over the city to a Mughal commander because he feared execution, probably due to another court intrigue.[40] The problem of elite morale that Matthee has thus raised is surely of interest in the Mughal and Ottoman contexts as well.

Despite the advantages of a tripartite comparison, there are good reasons for focusing on merely the Ottoman and Mughal cases. Hodgson and Dale have written general histories with a strong focus on high culture, Anooshahr has discussed the socio-political role of literature in the self-fashioning of Islamic rulers, and Streusand has approached tripartite comparison as a political and military historian. By contrast, the present author deals with the interaction between elites and societies, with a strong emphasis on the latter. Thus, this study focuses on the growth and contraction of cities and urban systems, merchants active in domestic and foreign trade, and craftspeople both organized and unorganized. In addition, it includes the men and women that contemporary elites probably considered 'marginal', such as female members of the subject classes, servants, and slaves. To deal with this multitude of issues in two rather different societies, both characterized by the coexistence of different religions, already requires a good deal of space. An attempt to discuss three societies in some depth would have resulted in a book too voluminous for most publishers – to say nothing of the fact that for an Ottomanist, obtaining even a limited degree of familiarity with a single non-Ottoman empire is already enough of a challenge. Whenever the opportunity has presented itself, I have thus opted for the scrutiny of details, viewed as closely as possible. If this procedure means sacrificing breadth of coverage, so be it!

As noted, the starting point for scholars today attempting to compare the Ottoman and Mughal empires is the third volume of Marshall Hodgson's classic *The Venture of Islam*. Admittedly, Hodgson (1922–68), who had spent much of his life teaching in Chicago and interacting with locally based historians and anthropologists, had left his magnum opus incomplete at the time of his death; and it fell to his friends and students to prepare it for publication.[41] Despite the lack of polish that Hodgson would surely have given his work had he lived long enough, his notion of an 'Islamicate' culture has been and is still very influential. By this term, historians denote an environment in which Islam predominated although non-Muslims including Christians, Jews and Hindus might be strong minorities – or even the majority.

Hodgson wrote at a time when the Ottoman archives were accessible only to a very limited extent, and in any case, archival studies were not his main interest. For this author as a practising Quaker, the role of religion in developing individual consciences and inculcating social responsibility was a key issue. From that perspective, Hodgson emphasized the significance of sharia-mindedness, a worldview that could bind elite and non-elite people together. Following a line of reasoning opened up by his academic teacher Gustav von Grunebaum, Hodgson was interested in global cultural trends, an orientation which today's readers may find somewhat one-dimensional, at least where *The Gunpowder Empires and Modern Times* are at issue. Well informed on ongoing research, however, Hodgson did not assume that the differences between Islamic empires were of little importance in comparison with their common features, especially religion; he was far too careful a scholar to make such claims. Nor did he believe, as older colleagues had been inclined to do, that the Ottomans destroyed the prosperity of the lands that they conquered; Hodgson pointed out that quite often, the opposite was true.[42] Similarly, while discussing the problems inherent in eighteenth-century decentralization, he readily acknowledged that some provincial magnates were closer to the populations they ruled than the sultan's officials had ever been.[43]

At the time when Hodgson was writing his magnum opus, only a few of İnalcık's articles had appeared in English; in the 1970s and 1980s these works were to give non-Ottomanists a sense of what Ottoman subjects were doing when they were not thinking about religion or moral responsibility, but making a living or simply enjoying life. After all, in 1968 İnalcık had not yet relocated to Chicago – we may speculate about the interchanges that could have taken place between these two scholars had Hodgson only lived some ten years longer. As this discussion never occurred, the image of Ottoman society as presented by Hodgson is very much a general overview, in the sense favoured by von Grunebaum, without the attention to individual cities, guilds, books or buildings which today we expect from an account of Ottoman culture and society. However, Hodgson's claim that, in comparison to Iran and the Mughal Empire, Ottoman culture encouraged its representatives to be very cautious about philosophical or intellectual novelties retains some validity.[44] Even so, we now know more about Ottoman 'non-conforming spirits', who were out of line with the conservative tendencies of their contemporaries, than was possible in the 1950s or 1960s. Evliya Çelebi (1611–after 1683) comes to mind first, but Şanîzâde (d. 1826) is a strong candidate as well.[45] Pressures to conform were certainly strong, but Ottoman society did produce its own brand of people ready to explore their physical and cultural environments.

Both in the Ottoman and in the Mughal realm, palace culture was a feature that Hodgson admired, but about whose elitist character he had misgivings. He had encountered the Mughal variety of this culture, including Akbar's palace of Fatehpur Sikri, during a post-doctoral year in India. Any scholar from abroad could easily encounter some of the major works of Ottoman and Mughal architecture, while the arcana of miniature painting were less accessible – and even on a major example of architecture such as the Ottoman palace, the work of Gülru Necipoğlu and Leslie Peirce was still far in the future. It is thus not surprising that Hodgson, otherwise so careful, was quite ready to attribute the woes of the empires to 'harem intrigues', presumably on the part of eunuchs or palace women.[46]

Intriguingly, despite the high esteem that Hodgson's work enjoyed, Ottomanists and Mughal historians before the year 2000 did not produce many tripartite or 'two-empire' studies with a comparative slant. While in the late 1980s and early 1990s, a number of conferences did bring together Ottomanists and Mughal historians, the researchers involved did not publish most of the resulting contributions in a single venue, and thus the enterprise had limited impact.[47] Only a few scholars, with Sanjay Subrahmanyam perhaps the most committed, continued to stress that historians might learn something from Ottoman–Mughal comparisons. By the new millennium, however, reviving interest in world empires induced several historians to take up the challenge involved in such comparisons.

In 2006, Subrahmanyam published an important article confronting the empires of the Spanish Habsburgs, Ottomans and Mughals, with a revised version appearing in 2018.[48] After examining the Iberian and Mughal empires, Subrahmanyam took a long hard look at the economic and commercial situation of the Ottoman world as depicted by Halil İnalcık. He concluded that the latter had overestimated the importance of

Ottoman dirigisme, which many Ottomanists would probably call a 'command economy'. Even more remarkably, and gratifying to the present author, Subrahmanyam argued that İnalcık had exaggerated the role of Islamic institutions – presumably the pious foundations (*vakıf, evkaf*) in Ottoman economic life. In this context, Subrahmanyam pointed out that, if proceeding just a single step further on the road indicated by İnalcık, the historian would arrive at the assumption that Islamic institutions impeded capital formation, and thus were responsible for the lack of economic development in the Ottoman territories.[49]

The logic is impeccable, although surely İnalcık had never intended such a claim. However, by viewing Ottomanist statements from the critical distance made possible by a close study of the Mughal Empire, Subrahmanyam encourages his readers to reopen an old question: Were Islamic institutions as hostile to economic development as some authors tend to think?[50] If they were not, what explanations can we offer for the fact that the market economy, Ottoman style, did not lead to capitalism? Following Çizakça and Kenanoğlu, the present author would opt for the force of the political opinions held by the Ottoman central elite, inveterately hostile to social groupings that its members found difficult to control. Elite policies thus impeded capital formation at least in the central provinces. However, other responses are surely possible.

Turning to the political and cultural spheres, Subrahmanyam points out that, while the Ottomans never tried to force the vast majority of their Christian subjects to convert to Islam, the Mughals were more successful in ensuring that non-Muslim, Hindu elites acquired a stake in the imperial enterprise, thus establishing a political culture that promoted supra-regional unity.[51] This issue will resurface in the course of the present study.

In a volume that appeared in 2010, Stephen Dale has jointly discussed the three major Islamic empires. Apart from works on the South Indian community of the Mapillas and Indian merchants active on Russian territories, this author has written major works on Bābur's autobiography and Ibn Khaldūn, thus engaging with socio-economic history as well as the resurgent genres of cultural historiography, biography included.[52] The author defines *The Muslim Empires of the Ottomans, Safavids, and Mughals* as a guide for students.[53] However, he by far transcends this modest aim, for he has produced a panorama of cultural history appealing to specialists as well. Confined to a single chapter, economic issues take a back seat, so that the book at times reads like a modern version of Hodgson's work, much enriched by the research undertaken in the nearly forty years elapsed since the publication of *The Gunpowder Empires and Modern Times.*

The authors' choices in terms of time result in further resemblance between the works of Hodgson and Dale: Both authors do not end their accounts in the eighteenth century, as is true – for instance – of the present study. Therefore, they have to deal with the aftermath of empires and the nostalgia for past glories, an issue featuring prominently in Turkey's political culture today. On the other hand, Dale does not focus on the religious-moral impetus so characteristic of Hodgson's work, nor does he share the interest of his predecessor in systematizing the periodization of political and social change. Even so, Dale too focuses on explicating the dilemmas confronting present-day Muslims to an American or European audience.

A brief glance at the 'Table of Contents' shows that cultural history is the main concern: Dale discusses the legitimacy of rulers in addition to the cultures they fostered, devoting about one third of the text, to poetry, art and, especially in the Iranian context, philosophy and mysticism as well. Moreover, the author confides that he would have liked to dedicate more space to architecture and gardens, the favourites of Mughal royalty and nobility, and especially of Bābur.[54] Of particular interest for our present purposes is his discussion of the personal and political use to which Sultan Süleyman put his knowledge of Persian-style versification.[55] For the uses of literature in real life are a complex question, which Ali Anooshahr had taken up just a year before, although the latter author has defined his work partly in opposition to Stephen Dale's biography of Bābur.[56]

Among the authors discussed here, Anooshahr is unusual because he is willing to focus on two rulers that few (if any) historians have regarded as having something in common, namely Bābur and the Ottoman sultan Murad II (r. 1421–44 and 1446–51). In line with current concerns with 'self-fashioning', Anooshahr suggests that medieval Islamic historiography provided not only ways of describing past deeds and events, but models for future conduct as well. Thus, when Bābur found himself campaigning in the Ganges-Yamuna plain, the history of Mahmūd of Ghazni provided a first 'script' for his own conduct, for which he later substituted some of his own writings. As long as Anooshahr discusses Bābur's self-fashioning, the latter's diary provides an incontestable textual base. More hypothetically, this author points out that the words of the anonymous historian of the Islamic-cum-heroic campaigns (*gazavat*) of Murad II resonate with Bābur's own 'script'. Of course, the difficulty is that we do not know if Bābur had ever heard of this text – and if he had heard of it, what the lines of communication may have been.[57] While we will gladly follow Anooshahr in leaving this matter undecided, it is important to remember that texts, including chronicles, not only reflected reality but might furnish models for heroic and religiously sanctioned conduct as well.

Warfare as a literary subject and a means of 'self-fashioning' brings us to the most recent attempt at treating the Ottoman, Safavid and Mughal empires together, namely the work of Douglas E. Streusand, another member of the Chicago school of comparative historians. While Streusand starts out from the approaches pioneered by Hodgson, he has thoroughly assimilated the work of his former professor Halil İnalcık. While Streusand's monograph concerns the Mughal conquest of India, in the tripartite comparison attempted in his second book, the author has paid much attention to Ottoman expansion, with İnalcık's article on 'Ottoman methods of conquest' seminal to his thinking.[58] Streusand resembles Hodgson in that he claims to address his work to (advanced and intelligent) undergraduates, but differently from Hodgson he is as good as his word. For while the present author thinks that much of Hodgson's discussion is intelligible only to readers after considerable preparation, Streusand has put a great deal of effort into making his text as accessible as possible, particularly by the long 'chronologies' that in reality, discuss the political histories of the empires under study. Moreover, as a professor at a military institution, Streusand has paid much attention to the tactics and technologies of warfare, once again building on the work of İnalcık for the Ottoman world and that of Jos Gommans for the Mughals. In a different vein, the author has focused on Mughal views of kingship in the time of Akbar and his successors, thus discussing military history not as a self-contained field but as part of the structures of imperial rule. While in the study undertaken here, military history gets short shrift, Streusand reminds us that we must keep the military basis of Ottoman and Mughal rule constantly in mind.

Outlining the present project

As noted, we begin our discussion in 1526, when Bābur won the first battle of Panipat and Sultan Süleyman began the conquest of Hungary. However, this choice does not imply the claim that the two monarchs stand for the same stage in the histories of their respective dynasties. As Ali Anooshahr has explained *in extenso*, in the tripartite scheme of dynastic history favoured by medieval Islamic authors, Bābur was the 'founder king', in the Ottoman realm, parallel perhaps to Murad II. Süleyman by contrast stood for the maturity of an Islamic empire, in which the monarch ensured justice and presided over the conquests of subordinate 'warriors for the faith', but without necessarily taking the field in person.[59] However, despite the inspiration derived from Duindam's work, the present study focuses not on dynasties but on elite–commoner interactions. Therefore, we do not emphasize questions of dynastic rise and decline.

In the first chapter, we discuss written sources. Both Ottomanist and Indianist historians in the last few decades have paid renewed attention to what authors of the past actually said, what they could say given the literary models available, what kinds of lessons they wanted their readers to take away, and often most importantly, what they left unsaid. Given this knowledge, and with all due caution, we may then try to read between the lines, searching for information about interactions between officials and ordinary people. Moreover, since the history of the archives is markedly different in the Ottoman and Indian contexts, we will briefly discuss the problem of storing and accessing documents as well. It is worth remembering that officials composing documents in some ways conformed to the same rules as chroniclers, for they too worked according to established models. Thus, the image of events that they recorded was not a simple reflection of realities on the ground, and for that very reason, the voices of the underprivileged often remain hidden. Our attempts to make them audible are deeply problematic, but they are worth making nonetheless.

The second chapter deals with visual records: Both Ottoman and Mughal patrons normally sponsored work inspired by Iranian-style arts of the book. However, in addition Mughal – and Iranian – grandees ordered large-scale wall paintings showing people and animals, a genre known to Ottoman art lovers – if at all – through the booty that army commanders brought back from Iranian campaigns.[60] As for the interface between Ottoman elites and non-elites, miniatures showing the wedding and circumcision festivities of 1582 and 1720 are the most helpful, as they depict the floats through which Istanbul artisans showcased their daily work in front of sultans Murad III (r. 1574–95) and Ahmed III (r. 1703–30). On the Mughal side, the miniatures made in the entourage of Akbar are especially valuable. After all, this ruler liked to attend construction sites in person and commissioned miniatures depicting him in this activity, amidst the workpeople building a fort or palace. In addition, scenes of daily life often appear in the backgrounds of pictures focusing on religious or literary topics, and the frequency of this type of artwork permits us to interpret it as a historical source. When establishing the dominant artistic conventions, however, we soon come up against limits set by the rules of a given atelier. Thus, we do not know what information about the denizens of the working world the painters have sacrificed, for the sake of aesthetic appeal, gravitas or decorum.

In the third chapter, the focus is on the way in which Ottoman sultans and Mughal emperors established and secured their rule, through their armies and, in the Ottoman instance, through a navy that in the mid-1500s, was the most powerful in the Mediterranean. Once a region was under the sultans' rule, the Ottomans often built fortresses to secure their new acquisitions, both in the territories conquered from the Safavids in Eastern Anatolia and in the Northwest, near the border with the Austrian Habsburgs in Hungary. In the Mughal world, castles seem to have had a rather different function; they were the strongholds of especially Hindu Rajput princes that the Mughals set out to conquer, often with much bloodshed. Akbar, Jahāngīr and Shāh Jahān also fortified their palaces in Agra and Delhi. To conclude, certain Mughal miniatures allow us at least a vague impression of the role of masters and labourers in the building trades. By contrast, Ottoman patrons were much more reticent on this issue.

In the third chapter, we discuss the notion of the 'gunpowder empire', often used for both polities, although Ottoman commanders mustered more enthusiasm about firearms than their counterparts in the Mughal world ever managed to do. In this context, we introduce the anti-Mughal rebellion of the Marathas and their efforts to found a Hindu kingdom in Peninsular India: Evidently, under certain circumstances, the commanders of Maratha war bands easily found large numbers of raiders willing to fight for them. Then, the discussion turns to the challenges to Mughal power posed by neighbouring polities; in particular, the emperors' military preparedness had to impress the Portuguese Estado da India and the English and Dutch trading companies as well. However, these foreigners remained of limited political importance as long as the Mughal Empire was securely in place.

Armies consist of soldiers, often modestly paid and eager to supplement their income by booty. In the 1400s, Ottoman sultans and commanders required military service from peasant-soldiers, and in the Balkans from nomads too; however, the latter had lost their tribal affiliations at an early date. In the 1500s, Ottoman officialdom, now eager to draw a sharp line between the taxpayers and the privileged servitors of the sultans, phased out these peasants and nomads as regular combatants, although the men at issue might become guardsmen. From the late 1500s to the end of the period under study, sultans and especially grandees of various types hired so many mercenaries from among the subject population that soldiering became a source of livelihood for significant numbers of villagers, particularly in Anatolia. The men recruited in this fashion had certain affinities with the peasant-soldiers that were part of the Mughal and Maratha armies, although the Ottomans did not find their soldiers in the loosely controlled borderlands of the empire, as was widespread in the Indian context.

The fourth chapter takes up a problem confronting both Ottomans and Mughals, namely the post-conquest legitimization of rule. For this purpose, both elites highlighted the power and glory of the rulers through ceremonies, festivities and the display of valuable objects. Rulers might enjoy special appreciation when providing visual and auditory experiences to people whose daily lives were otherwise monotonous and full of toil. Ceremonies and festivals were especially prominent in the Indian world, but we do not have much information on the role that the Mughal emperors, their grandees and individual artists played in the organization of festivities. By contrast, the Ottoman archives retain an enormous documentation on the 'nuts-and-bolts' of organizing such events, including occasional protests of urban artisans and traders against the high costs of celebrations. After all, even if 'on paper' the sultan or a high official footed the bill, the money ultimately came from the scanty resources of urban and rural taxpayers.[61]

Sufis and dervish saints, sometimes close to the ruling elite and sometimes conspicuously aloof, had a role to play in the legitimacy of most early modern Muslim empires. Quite often, these men mediated between the varieties of Islam practised at the Ottoman and Mughal courts on the one hand, and on the other, the Muslim – and sometimes non-Muslim – subject populations. In both empires, Sufism opened up spaces for the arts, especially poetry and music. Where Mughal–Ottoman encounters were at issue, the 'new style' Naqshbandī/Nakşbendi dervishes known as the Mujaddidiya, founded by an Indian religious figure, drew numerous adherents among the Ottoman elite of the eighteenth century.

On a different plane, the policies adopted by sultans and emperors toward their non-Muslim subjects were part of their legitimacy quests as well. A major issue, on which the two governments differed profoundly, was the demand for payment of the poll tax (*cizye/jizya*), which Ottoman non-Muslims always had to defray but which was intermittent in the Mughal orbit: Akbar abrogated, and Aurangzeb reinstated it, while after this ruler's death abrogation and reinstatement followed one another at a rapid pace. In Mughal India, circumstances surrounding payment of the *jizya* might give rise to questions of honour and respectability, as complaints from Hindu taxpayers often emphasized the aggressive behaviour of the collectors. By contrast, reinstituting the *jizya* probably enhanced Mughal legitimacy in the eyes of certain Islamic scholars.

While for the rich Mughal exchequer, the *jizya* was of minor significance, for the less well-endowed Ottoman treasury, the *cizye* was a major source of income especially when it came to financing the wars against the Habsburgs (1683–99, 1715–18). Individuals rather than communities became liable for payment, so that officialdom could reach down to the individual taxpaying family. We may wonder whether in the Mughal realm as well, demanding the *jizya* was a means of keeping track of the non-Muslim population.

When recruiting future servitors for the ruler, language was a potent device. Sometimes, knowing or not knowing a given language was crucial for a young boy aspiring to rise into a particular section of the elite. In the 1400s and 1500s, for instance, the sultans did not recruit boys as potential janissaries, who already knew Turkish, presumably because they had access to information that the elite wished to withhold. On the other hand, the mastery of Ottoman Turkish in the sultans' realm, or Persian fluency in Mughal India, was a prerequisite for entry into the bureaucracy. If a boy with the necessary language skills entered officialdom, his gratified family must have often viewed the ruler as a legitimate source of status and livelihood.

In India, Hindus could attend a madrasa and acquire fluency in Persian and a polished style 'in school', an option unavailable to would-be entrants into the Ottoman ruling apparatus.[62] As far as we know, in the Ottoman world it was unlikely for the son of a peasant to enter a madrasa and later make a brilliant career as a scholar-official; moreover, no Christian or Jew ever attended a school of this type. As Ottoman non-Muslims were unlikely to make places for themselves in the governing apparatus unless they converted to Islam, they had less motivation to learn Ottoman Turkish than did Hindus when it came to mastering Persian.

In the fifth chapter, the focus is on markets and small towns, substantial port cities, and large capitals as well. In both empires, roadside stops and customs offices attracted buyers and sellers. In both venues, villages might turn into towns when overall population grew and opportunities for trade increased. In the Mughal Empire and the post-Mughal principalities, as well as in the Ottoman realm, officials attempted to found markets, for as tax-takers they needed to convert grain dues into money, thus promoting the exchange of goods for cash. However, villagers and townsmen needed to regard the newly established markets as useful, or the latter remained empty.

Port cities flourished and declined partly because of natural factors, namely the availability of deep water close to the coast, necessary for the unloading of large ships. By contrast, ports declined when nearby rivers had silted up so much that large vessels could no longer access them. Political conditions played a role as well. Thus, Cambay lost out to Surat because the latter port enjoyed the protection of the Mughals; and at a later stage, Surat suffered from the dissolution of Mughal power in Gujarat.[63] In this instance at least, imperial power usually protected merchants from the depredations of robbers, officials and subordinate princes. Izmir, by contrast, owed its florescence at least in part to the limits that seventeenth-century conflicts in Anatolia placed upon the sultans' control of the new urban site. Relative remoteness from the attentions of the central power certainly attracted foreign merchants, although we should not exaggerate the 'incorporation of the Aegean coast into the European-dominated world economy' during the seventeenth or even the early eighteenth century. Settlements where official control was less intense attracted Ottoman merchants and artisans as well. Unfortunately, we cannot clearly determine when royal power was a source of security and when the demands of its officials destabilized the region, causing taxpayers to flee.

As for capital cities, the situation in the Ottoman and Mughal empires differed profoundly. While in the 1300s and 1400s, the sultans had moved their seats several times, in the second half of the fifteenth century, the government finally settled in Istanbul and apart from an interruption of about fifty years in the 1600s, remained in this city until the end of the empire in 1923. By contrast, the pre-eminence of Delhi was less clear-cut; as in the sixteenth and early seventeenth centuries, there was competition from Lahore and Agra, the latter including the nearby palace, mosque and mausoleum compound of Fatehpur Sikri. Delhi became the uncontested Mughal capital only with the founding of Shāhjahānabād (today: Old Delhi) in the mid-1600s.

The demand generated by the rulers' palaces stimulated trade, although with respect to Istanbul, we should not overestimate the resulting commercial opportunities. After all, Ottoman taxpayers had to supply many goods and services at below-market prices, or even without payment of any kind, in lieu of taxes. Even so, Istanbul artisans joined revolting soldiers in 1703, when it seemed that the sultans might permanently transfer their capital to Edirne. After all, the palace and central administration employed many people who had to buy necessities in the urban market. The serious difficulties of Istanbul during the first fifty years of the Republican period (1923 to the 1970s) may indicate the value of the market generated by government employees and investments.

In the Mughal Empire, the nexus linking palace and marketplace seems to have been stronger, although the emperors and many subordinate princes could procure high-quality goods outside of market channels. However, gold and silver were available in India in far larger quantities than in the Ottoman milieu. Thus, there was much more money in circulation in Shāhjahānabād or Agra than in Istanbul, a situation that helped sizeable numbers of Delhi and Agra inhabitants to make a living by means of the market.

Individual traders, the focus of Chapter 6, remain elusive in both empires; in the Ottoman world, their accounts have survived in the archives mostly when the owners had died leaving debts to the treasury, and officials confiscated the delinquents' inheritances. However, in Cairo around 1600, there was an exceptional trader, who for reasons remaining unknown had most or perhaps all of his transactions recorded by the local qadi. From Nelly Hanna's study, there emerges a merchant with business connections to both Venice and India, and who sometimes even cooperated with traders professing a different religion.[64] Apparently, business skills were the principal qualification that a junior merchant needed to become and remain a partner of the redoubtable Ismā'īl Abū Taqiyya. Moreover, it is noteworthy that this successful trader avoided involvement with the governing apparatus. Evidently, in Cairo around 1600 this was possible. In Istanbul, by contrast, such a merchant might not have been able to avoid investments in tax farming and the confiscations so often resulting from this line of business.

Close-up views of Indian merchants are not frequent either, but we possess the unique example of a seventeenth-century minor trader, a Jain, who specialized in jewels and precious stones. While this man proclaimed the importance of keeping silent about successful business deals, his open discussions of his many failures, and how he managed to survive them, provide incomparable insights into seventeenth-century North Indian business life.[65]

Indianist historians have studied local merchants working for the export market, whose activities have entered the records of their Dutch, English or French business partners. Ottoman archives seemingly contain few records concerning Ottoman subjects active in the export business; but Armenian merchants in close contact with Izmir, selling cotton in eighteenth-century Amsterdam have left records in the archives of that city. Moreover, Ottoman merchants trading in Central Europe have left traces in eighteenth-century Vienna or Hungary, mostly a Habsburg possession after 1699.[66] Until very recently, historians used to think that eighteenth-century Ottoman traders in Europe were all non-Muslim. While this observation is true for most venues, recent research has shown the occasional involvement of Muslims as well.

No city without craftspeople: and in Chapter 7, artisans working for the courts of the two empires permit interesting comparisons. After all, the Ottoman archives contain significant evidence on people servicing the palace, as highly skilled artists or practitioners of very humdrum trades. As for the Indian context, the Hindu principality of Jaipur, long in close contact with Agra and Delhi, has left us with a sizeable amount of evidence on the artisan servitors of the princely court, a major source covering elite and artisan interactions.

Migrating craftspeople invite comparison as well. In Mughal India, the frequent movement of the emperors must have caused many artisans to follow, as the imperial court contained their best customers. Furthermore, in the late seventeenth and early eighteenth centuries, dislocations caused by the Mughal-Maratha wars must have caused numbers of craftspeople to move house as well. In a different vein, droughts often increased the price of basic foodstuffs, so that there remained very little money disposable for the purchase of craft products. Under such conditions, migration was often a precondition for survival.

In seventeenth-century Anatolia, artisans must have migrated along with other town dwellers, when previously prosperous places like Amasya were shrinking to half their sixteenth-century size.[67] Presumably, Istanbul was a preferred destination for all migrants, artisans included, as the presence of the sultans and their soldiery kept the city – though not necessarily the suburbs – safe from bandit attacks. Among the artisans attracted by İzmir, we find Jewish woollen weavers, refugees from Salonika, where a slack market for locally woven woollens, combined with large-scale textile deliveries required by the janissaries, placed many weavers in a nearly hopeless situation.[68] Once again, many artisans fled to a city where the taxes were lower and the chances of finding customers seemed better.

All townspeople depend on the countryside for their food, and the growing, marketing and taxation of food crops dominates Chapter 8. In both the Ottoman and the Mughal contexts, tax registers reflect what officials thought that peasants could pay as taxes. In the Ottoman case, such records are numerous and indicative for the 1500s but less helpful for later periods. In the Mughal instance, sixteenth-century documents are available largely – though not exclusively – through the account that Abū'l-Fazl 'Allāmī (1551–1602) has left of them.[69] Even so, enough evidence survives from principalities once subject to the Mughals – and retaining Mughal modes of taxation – that we can discuss the control of agricultural land and the role of what we might call the rural gentry as a power intermediate between the central administration and the peasantry.

In the Ottoman Empire, the central government during the 1500s exercised relatively tight control over these intermediaries. In the late seventeenth and throughout the eighteenth century, by contrast, there was significant decentralization. Even so, the central government retained some control over its appointees, and differently from the Mughal polity of the 1700s, magnate autonomy did not result in the central government's complete withdrawal from its more outlying provinces.

In the Ottoman world, the sultans' officials refused to recognize the control of large landholders over 'their' peasants by sultanic law, though tolerating the de facto powers of local magnates. This issue is inseparable from the sultans' claim to eminent domain over all fields and meadows in their empire, allowing their subjects the ownership only of shops, houses and gardens. In Mughal India, peasants apparently had relatively secure control over their fields although they could dispose of them only within certain limits. In addition, local power-holders known as *zamīndārs*, in addition to the village community, hedged in the rights of even the wealthier landholders.

Peasants in the Mughal Empire and its 'successor states' were often more involved with the market than their Ottoman counterparts were, because apart from needing cash for their taxes, at least in certain areas, peasants wove cotton cloth on a part-time basis. Travellers through Mughal India often commented on widespread rural poverty, but present-day historians profoundly disagree about the value of these testimonies. Even so, nobody denies the miseries suffered during famines, typically caused by the late arrival or scantiness of the monsoon rains. Under such circumstances, the widespread monetization of the economy increased the likelihood that peasants might fall into debt, with their wives and children becoming servants in wealthier households. Prominent families, sometimes with connections to princely courts, might adopt the posture of life-saving – and exploitative – patrons.

In the ninth and last chapter, we take a brief look at people, who in the opinion of their contemporaries, counted as marginal, with women outside elite circles the largest group at issue. It may sound like an exaggeration to include all females of the subject class in this category; and where the Ottoman world is at issue, there is now an important range of studies showing female agency, with women attempting to exit from marginality and act as legal subjects, exercising some control over their possessions and married lives.[70] However, as the work of Nandita Prasad Sahai, on eighteenth-century Jodhpur, and the study of Madeline Zilfi, on Istanbul during the 1700s and early 1800s, have shown, non-elite women encountered formidable barriers. Frequently they even had trouble asserting their rights as free people, although Ottoman husbands could not legally sell their wives, as was sometimes possible in Jodhpur.[71] Zilfi's work has shown that in Istanbul wealthy men easily acquired slave concubines, who could be formidable competitors to freeborn spouses and determine the 'climate' in the harem of a rich man. However, many slave women were simply servants, maids-of-all-work in middle-income households; or else they began life in the Ottoman world as little girls, raised as servant-companions to their age-mates from elite families.

Youngsters handed over by their usually very poor parents to a family of somewhat more extensive means, the so-called *beslemes*, at a later stage of their lives, might have trouble proving their free status if their employers wanted to sell them as slaves.[72] In India, servants were often both males and females born into lower castes, not slaves but forced to provide service because of their lowly status. The Mughal and post-Mughal governments rarely intervened in matters concerning caste hierarchies.

As studies of both the Ottoman and the Mughal/post-Mughal worlds have demonstrated, we cannot possibly conceptualize social structure without close attention to the gender divide. In Ottoman Istanbul, from the mid-seventeenth century onward, male slaves apparently became rare outside of the palace. Slaves working for the Ottoman elite and some middle-ranking families were now frequently female. Gender discrimination divided society in its entirety, although elite women might enjoy protections unavailable to their non-elite counterparts. In consequence, non-elite females suffered, not only because of elite demands with which their men-folk had to comply as well, but in addition they were subject to the pressures of their male relatives. Poets often express such fundamental realities of social life more readily than historians are likely to do: Nazım Hikmet (1902–63) once referred to the Anatolian peasant women of the 1930s, who in the mind of a contemporary rural male had a right to their food only after the oxen had received their fodder.[73] We might thus group together poor women and animals as beings that could remain alive only through unremitting toil and service. However, this is an extensive topic, which would take another book to explore.

Part One

Approaching the Sources

1

Texts in Context: Relating Primary to Secondary Sources

This chapter and the following one deal with methodologies. We begin with the complications that appear when scholars try to understand a given piece of writing: Is it really the work of the supposed author, and what were his/her probable intentions? How do we tease out the meanings that the author may have intended, but did not clearly spell out? To what extent do genre conventions determine what an author could or could not say, and is there evidence of the latter's attempt to transcend these boundaries? How do historians locate the sources of use to the questions they set out to answer, and what kinds of social or political constraints determine the records, which they can – or cannot – see?

On one level, textual criticism spells out the biases inherent in a text, and this endeavour may appear as a search for 'objectivity'. At the same time, no such search is ever 'completely innocent'. Rather, political, social or cultural assumptions determine, often without the knowledge of the researcher, which sources or assumptions are subject to critique, and which remain in the shadow, unexamined. These issues confront historians of all times and places, but we will here focus on the specific problems with which Ottomanists and historians of the Mughal Empire have to contend. The present chapter closes with a major issue of common concern between the two scholarly communities, of special significance given our concern with the interface between rulers and ruled: How have historians of the twentieth and twenty-first century conceptualized Ottoman and Mughal societies? What kind of a place have they assigned to the subject populations, and which primary sources have they particularly emphasized?

The medieval setting: Adopting Islam, the Persian language and a new script aesthetic

The Turkic conquest of Northern India and the Turkish and – later Ottoman – expansion into the Mediterranean world were not isolated phenomena. Rather, these two processes were part of a 'migration of peoples' beginning in the eleventh century, and speeding up in the 1100s and especially in the 1200s, when the Mongol conquests changed the entire political map of Eurasia. In both cases, the Turkic conquerors introduced Islam into a land inhabited by non-Muslims. At least in Anatolia, this population was apparently sparse and over the later Middle Ages, the immigrants imposed their religion, Islam, and their language, today called 'Old Anatolian Turkish' (Eski Anadolu Türkçesi), the latter appearing in the Arabic script during the 1300s. Only in the Balkans did most of the conquered population remain Christian and continue to speak Greek or a Slavic language, although at least in certain regions, Turkish-speaking Muslims immigrated in significant numbers and local people, especially in Bosnia, converted to Islam. In Northern India, settlement was presumably denser at least in the Ganges-Yamuna plain, and while conversions to Islam were frequent too, the majority of the population continued to believe in varieties of the religion today called Hinduism.[1]

In both cultural areas by the 1200s, Persian was the language of the elite and of written culture. In Mughal and post-Mughal India, this language continued to hold a central position over the centuries. By the 1500s or 1600s, the institutions and practices of the Mughal and Ottoman governments had quite a few common features, and this fact is apparent from the terminology, which was Iranian.[2] Even so, in the Ottoman world, Anatolian Turkish became the dominant language of administration already in the fifteenth century if not earlier, both Arabic and Persian serving for specified purposes as well (see Chapter 4). In the central Ottoman lands, the two 'classical' languages of the Islamic world remained important vehicles of scholarship and *belles lettres*, although by the 1500s, everyone claiming membership in the governing elite needed to be familiar with Ottoman Turkish, by now containing many Arabic and especially Persian loanwords. In the Arab lands, conquered by the Ottoman sultans after 1516, Arabic remained the dominant language.

Given the common Turco-Iranian background, certain problems of source criticism are common to the Ottomanist and the historian of medieval/early modern India.[3] In both cases, after all, the composition of court chronicles in the Iranian style became current only after Turkic conquerors had established sultanates of some size and power. Ottoman literati and their counterparts from the Delhi sultanate and later, the Moghul Empire eagerly adopted the writing of chronicles (*tarih*). This endeavour was part of Iranian-style palace culture, but in the sultans' realm, people 'domesticated' these histories by mostly writing in Ottoman Turkish.[4] In the Indian orbit, by contrast, the language of these texts was always Persian. After the standard invocations of the Deity and the Prophet Muhammad, these chronicles dealt with purely political matters, campaigns and conquests occupying centre stage. News from the monarch's court, including the appointment or loss of office on the part of high-ranking dignitaries was another favourite topic, perhaps because the prospective readers of these works were people who, successfully or not, aspired to official employment.

While Iranian-style historical writing was thus a 'cultural bridge' between the three empires, this issue to date has not aroused much scholarly interest, and therefore, the history of Ottoman chronicle composition appears largely as an 'internal affair' of the sultans' realm.[5] Moreover, before the eighteenth century, Orthodox and Jewish subjects of the empire did not produce many works that included the history of their own times. Thus, we may even regard the composition of Ottoman chronicles during the 1500s and 1600s as an activity typical of the – largely palace-educated – Muslim elite.

In both cultures, calligraphy was a highly esteemed art, in which an accomplished scribe and producer of official documents needed to be proficient. The most distinguished Iranian calligraphers were familiar to connoisseurs in seventeenth-century Northern India, while even the most famous Ottoman representatives of this art did not necessarily occur in reference works compiled in South Asia.[6] Thus, despite numerous parallels, the writing and reading publics of sultanate and Mughal India on the one hand, and the Ottomans on the other, did not establish many close relationships. In eighteenth-century Istanbul, the popularity of the Müceddidi version of the Nakşbendi dervish order, which had originated in Northern India although the order itself was of Central Asian foundation, was one of the few exceptions proving the rule.[7] Historians trying to read, understand, and evaluate 'their' primary sources need to work within these parameters.

Establishing what a text is, and what it is not

Source criticism can mean different things to different people. Firstly, as noted, there is the traditional task of finding out whether the text at issue is what it claims to be, in terms of author, time, and place of composition. Wherever retrievable, the intent of authors, editors and copyists is at issue too. We adopt a broad understanding of 'source criticism', expanding the notion to include the search for 'new' sources, either materials not previously used or else the combination of sources rarely considered together. Thus, in the Ottoman and South Asian contexts, few scholars have tried to combine written sources and archaeological finds.

However, the story does not end there, as in different times and places, people have undertaken source criticism with a wide variety of 'background considerations' in mind. Ottomanist historians can come up with a striking example, concerning the introduction to the early nineteenth-century chronicle of Şânîzâde Mehmed Atâullah Efendi (d. 1826). Apart from his historical work Şânîzâde was a medical man and, at one time, qadi of the pilgrimage town of Eyüp/Eyüpsultan, today part of Istanbul.[8] Ottomanists have known for a long time that Şânîzâde knew European languages including Italian, Modern Greek and French.[9] Moreover, he seems to have had contacts among educated Armenians, who may have helped him with translations. Whatever the sources of Şânîzâde's information, Edhem Eldem has found out that the introduction to the chronicle, an indispensable component of formal Ottoman prose, is a somewhat watered-down – and unacknowledged – translation of a text by Voltaire. For present-day historians, it is noteworthy that in the late 1700s and very early 1800s, some Ottoman religious scholars were curious to explore texts about which contemporary European intellectuals were thinking as well. Visibly, and contrary to what many people have assumed, not all the men with madrasa (*medrese*) training limited their concerns to Islamic divinity and law.

More immediately relevant to the present world is Eldem's concern with Şânîzâde's self-censorship, for which the watering-down of Voltaire's text is a prime example. Attitudes of this type being pervasive in twentieth- and twentieth-first-century Turkey, in Eldem's view, authors including Şânîzâde are often so concerned with the negative reactions to which their statements may give rise among readers – and non-readers – that they avoid saying what they really want to say. However, as Şânîzâde died in exile in a provincial Anatolian town, perhaps he was not cautious enough … and more recent parallels come to mind quite readily. If, on the other hand, we want to define the critical work that Eldem has performed on Şânîzâde's text, we can say that this twenty-first-century scholar has proven what the introduction is not, namely Şânîzâde's original formulation, and what it is in reality, namely a translated and truncated version of a text by Voltaire.

Intertextuality: Politically motivated, at least on occasion

Not all intertextual connections involve suspicions of plagiarism; and in any case, historians have come up with more or less widely recognized rules covering the citation of sources only in the 1800s and 1900s. As long as chronicles remained a major historical source, the authors of recent works quoted extensively from those of their predecessors. Sometimes such – more or less accurate – quotations served to accredit the author. As Sonja Brentjes has pointed out, the famous Roman author Pietro della Valle (1586–1652) larded his account of travels to the Ottoman Empire, Iran and India with quotations from authors of antiquity. Della Valle intended these quotes to impart authority to his text and help in getting the work past the papal censors.[10]

Della Valle had enjoyed a thorough classical education, and he must have known the books from which he quoted. However, some writers cited authorities that they had not consulted. Thus Meşkure Eren, now over fifty years ago, showed that Evliya Çelebi (1611–after 1683) mentioned quite a few texts, which he had not seen, and omitted others that he had in fact used.[11] Motivation in this case remains unclear.

Since the 1950s, but especially in recent years, finding out which Ottoman chronicler used which sources has become a topic of some interest. When engaging in textual criticism, scholars of the last century or so have often dwelt on the chronicles covering the early years of the Ottoman principality on the one hand, and the murder of Osman II. (r. 1618–22) on the other. For in the early years of the Republic of Turkey these two topics had become part of a political discourse legitimizing 'nation' and 'modernity'. Due to this 'overlay' of politics, recent scholars have sometimes enlivened their exercises in textual criticism by focusing on the interplay between 'history' and 'historiography'.

The earliest years of the Ottoman Empire, from about 1300 to the middle of the fifteenth century, pose a special problem, for very few attempts at writing the history of the Ottoman dynasty antedate the reign of Mehmed the Conqueror (r. 1451–81). Nor do the sources written by Byzantines and other outsiders have much to say at least about the – still emergent – Ottoman principality of the early to mid-1300s. One early text of some importance, probably written by Yahşi Fakih, whose father had been the imam of Sultan Orhan, has not come down to us. However, the well-educated and long-lived dervish Aşıkpaşazade (1400–after 1484) has used this text as a major source; and by comparing Aşıkpaşazade's account with early sixteenth-century chronicles, textual students have even tried to figure out which sections may be actual quotations

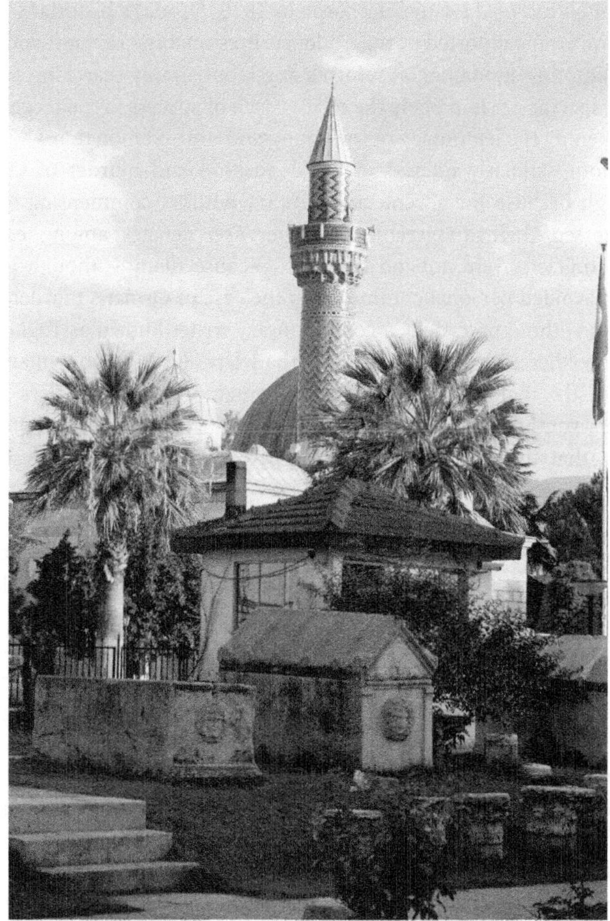

Figure 1 The beginnings of the Ottoman Empire: the mosque of the Çandarlızade in İznik/Turkey: a rare building from the early Ottoman period. Known as the Green Mosque due to its tilework, this structure is a foundation of the chief judge and later grand vizier Çandarlı Kara Halil Paşa (1378–91). The sarcophagi in the foreground stand in the garden of the Iznik Museum.

from this mysterious but fundamental source of Ottoman historiography, perhaps composed in the early 1400s.[12]

As for the 'Ottoman tragedy' of Osman II, present-day historians have started out with the observation that early republican historiography regarded the janissaries of the 1600s, 1700s and early 1800s as 'corrupt', mainly because after about 1600, they so often failed to win victories. Therefore, historians working during the early decades of the Republic of Turkey viewed Sultan Osman's attempt to raise another body of troops from Anatolia that should have competed with the janissaries and perhaps sidelined them, as an early attempt at modernizing the military and therefore, a kind of prelude to the final abolition of the janissary corps in 1826.[13] Today's historians tend to view this contention as unsupported by the evidence. Presumably, Osman II and his advisors were not attempting fundamental reforms at all, but simply searching for an ad hoc solution of a specific crisis, namely the relative lack of success in the recent war against Poland, weakening the legitimacy of the young and untried monarch.

Furthermore, scholarly interest in the deposition and murder of Osman II has remained high because the seventeenth-century authors commenting on this event openly expressed their disagreements. Otherwise, debates among early modern Ottoman chroniclers were not too frequent, because many – though by no means all – of them avoided personal comments. In the case of Osman's murder, however, an event hitherto without precedent, a contemporary writer known as Tuğî defended the actions of the soldiers, mostly janissaries, who had deposed the young sultan. Apparently, Tuğî reflected the majority opinion among contemporary chroniclers, namely that Osman in his youthful inexperience had listened to the wrong advisors. Even so, a minority felt that the soldiers had overstepped their bounds and deserved severe punishment.

Other studies involving intertextuality focus on chronicles of the later sixteenth to nineteenth centuries. In the recent past, historians have studied the narrative and archival sources consulted by the principal authors of Ottoman chronicles, focusing on the manner in which writers including Mustafa Âlî (1541–1600) or Ahmed Cevdet (1822–95) used these materials. Such research has often been part of the preparation for critical editions, but individual monographs on some of the principal writers are available as well.[14] Not all attempts at 'debunking' key tenets of early republican historiography have resulted in studies of intertextual relations among narrative sources. In other cases, historians with this aim in mind have concentrated on archival materials, which may tell a story rather different from that relayed by the chronicles on which an older generation of Ottomanists had mainly relied.[15]

Historians of South Asia also engage in source criticism to debunk views of historical persons and/or events that have become part of the scholarly and/or public consensus, including school textbooks. Thus, just as in the Ottoman case, the relevant discourses may acquire political relevance many centuries after the events at issue. The discussion concerning the biography of Aurangzeb (r. 1658–1707) by Jadunath Sarkar is a prime example. Sarkar had focused on the attempt of this emperor to rule as a strictly Islamic monarch and felt that by engaging in what the author regarded as fanaticism, Aurangzeb had profoundly alienated his Hindu subjects. For decades now, historians have questioned and criticized this claim.[16] The issue is of current importance because some commentators view this alienation as a prelude to the Hindu–Muslim conflicts that have been disrupting life on the subcontinent down to the present day.

In this context, Rajeev Kinra has compared the writings of his 'hero', the Hindu, gentlemanly scribe and Persian-language litterateur Chandar Bhan (about 1600–after 1666) to the statements of a slightly later author, named Shēr Khān Lōdī, who had included Bhan's biography in a text completed in 1690–1.[17] Kinra's investigation begins with the association of this Hindu scribe and official with Prince Dāra Shukōh (d. 1659), the eldest son of Shāh Jahān (r. 1628–58) and for a while, the latter's heir apparent. Dāra

Shukōh had a reputation for his profound interest in Hindu philosophy and mysticism. He had some important works in this field translated from Sanskrit into Persian, and even wrote on related subjects in person. However, in the struggle for the throne, he lost out against Aurangzeb, and the latter had him executed for heresy.

Rajeev Kinra has tried to explain the astonishing fact that while Chandar Bhan had served two Mughal emperors with distinction, Shēr Khān Lōdī took up an anecdote that one of his litterateur predecessors, writing in 1682, had invented for reasons remaining obscure. According to this tale, incidentally unrecorded during Bhan's lifetime, Dāra Shukōh had introduced this Hindu literary man to Shāh Jahān, and Chandar Bhan had committed the major *faux pas* of reciting a poem that a Muslim might consider offensive. Shēr Khān Lōdī has even gone out of his way to render the story more pointed and 'political'. However, Kinra stresses that in all likelihood, the real-life monarch would have been enough of a literary connoisseur to take the poem in his stride.[18] Sharp criticism of the prince, by now long dead, would have made 'political' sense since Aurangzeb, Dāra Shukōh's arch-enemy, was now on the throne.[19]

The inventions of these two seventeenth-century litterateurs are significant for us because, similar to the discussion of the murder of Osman II by Tezcan and Piterberg, Kinra highlights the current political relevance of his work. After all, quite a few writers have faulted Shāh Jahān and especially Aurangzeb for having abandoned the inclusive religious policies of Akbar (r. 1556–1605) and thus instituted a government that alienated the Hindu majority of their realm. In this context, some authors have depicted Dāra Shukōh as a last forlorn hope for a form of rule that both Hindus and Muslims might have accepted. Comparable to the Ottomanists who have debunked the supposedly 'army-reforming modernity' of Osman II, Kinra is at pains to show that instead of religious tolerance, down-to-earth matters were at issue. Presumably, Dāra Shukōh's defects as a politician and a soldier rendered him unacceptable to many members of the Mughal nobility.[20]

Regardless of seventeenth-century politics, the tragedy of Dāra Shukōh gained twentieth- and twenty-first-century relevance because in the 1800s and 1900s, the machinations of British colonial administrations deepened Hindu–Muslim hostility and the ultimate result was the partition of 1947, with all its disruption and bloodshed. Kinra's source criticism thus sets out to debunk a set of myths, by showing that even near-contemporary sources were capable of spreading invented stories, the author suspecting that career considerations of Chander Bhan's detractors may have been at issue. In addition, Kinra stressed that neither Shāh Jahān nor Aurangzeb were as hostile to Hindus as has often been claimed.[21]

Unearthing 'invisible' content

Source criticism may also involve teasing out the 'invisible' contents of a given text; in some instances, by 'invisible' we mean implications that the author wanted to conceal, and which he hoped that only an informed minority of his readers would figure out. In the Ottoman context, an author writing for instance in the 1500s, might have wished to hide his sympathy for certain heterodox dervishes, whom the central authorities were persecuting at that time. In other cases, the information of interest to present-day historians is not immediately discernible, simply because the early modern author considered this information too ordinary for relaying. Even so, allusions may have crept in which present-day scholars are struggling to understand.

To use an example from medieval Indian history: when Sunil Kumar examined the literary construction of the chronicles of the Delhi sultanate (1192–1527) in detail, he wanted to find out what information these texts contained beyond the obvious accounts of wars, conquests and palace intrigues.[22] Kumar set out to establish the relationships between the more successful among the immigrant Turkic rulers, the princes that made up the next generations of royals and the current – and past – rulers' military slaves. In so doing, Kumar hoped to come closer to the process by which the Delhi sultans formed a polity that was remarkably stable, even though the ruling dynasties changed quite frequently.

On a deeper level, Sunil Kumar questions certain facile generalizations, such as the blanket assumption that the invasion of the Turkic Muslims liberated many of the local poor from the constraints of the caste system and thus facilitated both urbanization and Islamization. Muhammad Habib (1895–1971), and some of his followers of the Aligarh school, had adopted this view in an attempt to counter the claim of colonial historians that the invasion of Turco-Muslim armies and subsequent Islamization had been merely destructive of Indian culture.[23] Moreover, this latter claim is also central to present-day Hindu nationalists; and while Kumar is sceptical about the defensive discourse of Muhammad Habib, he even more emphatically uses source criticism to demolish a set of historical myths concerning the inherent destructiveness of the Islamic conquest with respect to the culture of pre-Islamic India. The title of a collection of articles edited by the same scholar concisely states the issue: *Demolishing Myths or Mosques and Temples?*[24]

Supplementing the palace chronicles, today's historians of the Delhi sultanate rely on inscriptions, which admittedly are not very numerous, either. However, in certain cases, they are virtually the only written source available. Incidentally, the study of inscriptions has been just as central to the researchers concerned with the various principalities that emerged in Anatolia between the eleventh and fifteenth centuries; for, apart from the Seljuks and belatedly the Ottomans, few of these princes seem to have sponsored court chronicles. On the other hand, inscriptions adorning mosques and other pious foundations are numerous, and gravestones with inscriptions have survived in appreciable numbers as well. Between the 1930s and the 1970s, Ottomanists thus wrote a fair number of monographs based on this material and dealing with minor Anatolian principalities.[25] Historical toponyms have become the subject of study too, as they provide information on the settlement of Turkish tribes after 1071.[26] As usual, historiography being the work of the victors, there is not much information about the reactions of the conquered peoples remaining on site.[27]

Troublesome tropes and fictitious histories

At first glance, many chronicles seem very factual, if perhaps rather dry. However, on close investigation, surprises may occur: In the Indian case, several historians have dwelt on the story of the temple of Somnath, near the Gujarat port of Viraval, destroyed by Mahmūd of Ghazni (971–1030), whose royal court was in today's Afghanistan.[28] Sultan Mahmūd had raided the temple, probably about 1025–6, for the rich booty in votive offerings that it contained; and the gold and silver his warriors carried off financed conquests in Central Asia. Seemingly, establishing an empire on the subcontinent was not part of Sultan Mahmūd's political agenda.

However, the chronicles recounting this event probably served as models for later writers, who commemorated the conquests of various rulers of Delhi in the twelfth and thirteenth centuries. In these texts, we find rather repetitious tales of derring-do involving several monarchs and their commanders, who supposedly destroyed the temple of Somnath, killing some 50,000 infidels in the process. However, Romila Thapar has pointed out that archaeologists excavated the temple site in the early 1950s, before prominent sponsors, against the protests of Jawaharlal Nehru, had an entirely new building put up on the site; yet the excavations have not yielded any evidence of numerous medieval destructions and rebuilding.[29] Apparently, local sponsors rebuilt the temple after Sultan Mahmūd had returned to Central Asia. However, it seems to have decayed fairly soon, and in the late 1100s a much larger building replaced it. Seemingly, the new temple did not suffer much destruction from a Delhi sultanate army that, however, did raid it in the late thirteenth century.[30] Thus, the most likely explanation for the unrealistic claims of the chroniclers is that the destruction of Somnath had become a trope, by which the authors of Persian-style chronicles meant to express the Islamic zeal of the rulers they were in the business of celebrating. We can only hope that no 50,000 infidels ever lost their lives in these attacks.

No one will claim that destruction of temples never occurred, but quite often they were due to princes competing with the patron of the sanctuary at issue, and the destroyers might in fact be non-Muslims, likely favouring a different variety of 'Hindu' belief. Quite often, people closely associated the religious potency of the image that they carried off, with the good fortune and legitimacy of the deposed ruler. In this case, appropriation and removal symbolically expressed victory over a rival. A non-Muslim Indian king might well destroy a temple built by his defeated competitor, and possibly certain medieval Muslim sultans could have shared at least some of the underlying assumptions. If this reconstruction of medieval political views is at all realistic, religiously inspired iconoclasm was only part of the story.

Even so, Richard Eaton has documented eighty instances of temple desecration by Muslim rulers and commanders for the period beginning in 1192, when the sultans of Delhi founded an empire, to the year 1760, when the Mughal Empire was clearly on a downward spiral.[31] Certainly this number is far from insignificant; and it is noteworthy that Bābur (r. 1526–30), Humāyūn (r. 1530–40, 1555–6), and Akbar completely refrained from such acts. However, as Eaton has rightly pointed out, even when such gestures became quite frequent under Aurangzeb, most temples remained in place; and usually, only those structures that the Mughal emperor connected with real or suspected rebellions became victims of desecration.

Why is this issue so important? For a variety of reasons, during the last thirty years or so religious and/or political sectarianism has been on the increase the world over. As noted, in 1947 the partition of former British India into a largely Muslim state, namely

Pakistan, and a largely Hindu polity, namely India, took place amid a great deal of violence and bloodshed. As an outcome, there has emerged what Sanjay Subrahmanyam has called 'a veritable grievance industry', which in India is directed not only at Pakistan, but at the large Muslim minority that continues to live in the country as well.[32] As Subrahmanyam remarks, some of the resentment involved may have come to the surface in reaction to the 'official stance' current in Indian historiography shortly after Independence, namely that the different religious and ethnic communities inhabiting the subcontinent had lived mostly in peace with one another before the advent of British imperialism. By contrast, the current discourse highlights the fact that tensions between Muslims and non-Muslims were common enough in the pre-colonial period as well. While conceding this point, scholars who wish to keep this 'grievance culture' from becoming all-pervasive often stress that social class and sometimes tensions between rival occupational groups were also tinder that might ignite and result in a riot – outwardly religious but which, in actual fact, mostly had worldly motivations.

Thus in a very careful and critical study, Najaf Haider has discussed a conflict that started out in the Gujarat city of Ahmadabad in 1714, with a Hindu townsman enthusiastically celebrating the spring festival of Holi. This feast involved – and often involves even today – spouting paint over passers-by.[33] A well-placed Muslim victim took offence, and the complaint went all the way to the by now not very powerful Mughal court in Delhi, which favoured first one side and then the other, according to whichever faction currently had the ear of the emperor. Yet in the end, locally important people, and not the ruler, decided that the time had come to make peace. As Najaf Haider has pointed out, many people chose the side that they happened to take by criteria that had nothing to do with religion, including loyalties to a patron and even commercial gain.

As for the relevance of these debates to Ottomanist historiography, it is noteworthy that Sanjay Subrahmanyam himself brings up a pertinent example, namely the monograph by Katherine E. Fleming on the power-holder Ali Paşa of Yanya/Joannina (1740–1822). 'The Muslim Bonaparte' as he is called in the title of Fleming's book, happened to dominate what is today northern Greece at the time of the 1821 Greek uprising in the Peloponnesus, Moldavia and Wallachia.[34] Fleming relays how the Greek participants in conferences where she presented her findings could only view her as being 'for' Ali Paşa, and thus anti-Greek and by implication pro-Turkish, or else critical of this figure and therefore favouring the Greek side; and her tale of black-and-white oppositions has struck a sympathetic chord with Subrahmanyam. Surely this story does not stand alone; the older members of the Ottomanist profession will remember how in 1989, shortly before the collapse of 'bureaucratic socialism' in Bulgaria, the regime (as yet) in power whipped up a nationalistic frenzy against the Turkish minority, forcing many of these people to leave the country. In this campaign, the government mobilized certain historians, although the best-regarded Bulgarian academics mostly managed to remain aloof.

Similar cases of historical research misused for political purposes occurred in other places as well. At times, social class rather than religious and/or ethnic communities were at issue. Thus both in the 1940s and again in the 1970s, the important historian Mustafa Akdağ (1913–72 or 1973) was in political difficulties, likely at least in part because of his insistence that in the late 1500s, when the Ottoman Empire was at the height of its power, ordinary people were living rather difficult lives. Probably his interest in sixteenth-century student rebels in Ottoman madrasas, whose protests – barring error – no one but Akdağ has ever investigated, further contributed to the distrust of the powers-that-be. Presumably, because of such concerns, Turkish officials and journalists decried Akdağ as a 'leftist' at a time when Cold War politics made many people view even social democrats as a danger to the state.[35] The South Asian debate surrounding the 'demolition of mosques and temples' is thus a subject that many Ottomanists will find congenial.

Fictions[36] in the archives

When reading the works of historians studying archival documents, the methodology involved in teasing out less-than-obtrusive meanings differs from that developed by scholars dealing with narrative accounts. In the Ottoman instance, the scarcity of archival sources from the reign of Mehmed the Conqueror (r. 1444–6, 1451–81) makes life difficult for historians. The first coherent series of tax registers (*tahrir*), for several decades the main primary source used by twentieth-century Ottomanists, dates to the reign of the Conqueror's son Bayezid II (r. 1481–1512).[37] However, 'the great leap forward' in documentation only occurred in the reign of Sultan Süleyman (r. 1520–66), when the financial bureaucracy became a specialized branch of Ottoman administration; and the late 1500s are one of the best-documented periods in pre-nineteenth-century Ottoman history. In the 1600s, by contrast, the number of documents in the central archives increased at a modest rate, if at all, perhaps because between the mid-1600s and 1703, the court spent most of its time in the Thracian town of Edirne. Archival materials may well have perished when the court moved between the two cities. Once the sultan had re-established himself in Istanbul, however, both officials and documents multiplied; moreover, we can expect further important discoveries once the cataloguing of eighteenth-century archival records is more or less complete.

Ottoman documents being so numerous, and in addition covering the empire from the Abyssinian coast of the Red Sea to Crimea, from Baghdad to Algiers, and from Tabriz to Vienna, twentieth-century historians for decades went through a veritable honeymoon with the archives, and by implication the long-dead scribes who had produced them. Certainly, there were good reasons for this predilection, but many scholars remained unaware of the 'blind spots' which this orientation involved, especially with respect to women, children, and other 'marginal people'. For quite some time, historians accepted these gaps as unavoidable evils.

Therefore, it took some time to delimit the coverage of Ottoman archival records, and even longer before scholars began to think about the possible meanings of the gaps that they observed. Heath Lowry was one of the first to point out that for reasons that we cannot always discern, a scribe may have copied sections of a given *tahrir* from its predecessor. If possible, we therefore have to study the tax registers of a given locality not singly but in sequence.[38] At times, the recording officials may have had trouble getting the locals to respond to their queries, and on occasion the latter had some good fun at the expense of the probably frustrated scribes questioning them in the name of a remote sultan.[39] There were officials honest enough – or with good enough personal connections – to write down that they had not been able to collect any useful information. Less courageous, or less favoured by powerful friends, others preferred to gloss over the problem. We will not always find out why there are gaps in the available archival documentation, but it is important to pose the question nonetheless.

Historians with a concern for legal history, moreover, have shown that the court records of the Islamic judges (qadi), often the main – if not the only – source for the social historian of the sixteenth and seventeenth centuries, are not as easy to interpret as might appear at first glance. Boğaç Ergene has shown that the costs of turning to a qadi court could be substantial, and the preference of Islamic religious law for witness testimony as opposed to written documentation must have made many litigants, especially those of limited means, hesitant to turn to the courts.[40] What could poor people do if a crucial witness had moved out of their town or even just of their town quarter? Unable to track down the man whose testimony could decide their case, they likely relied on informal mediation, which rarely made it into the registers.

Other scholars, those with a feminist bent, have pointed out that given the limited rights accorded to women in the qadi's court and in society as a whole, well-placed males may have used legal fictions, perhaps to the disadvantage of females. Thus the court cases in which a woman paid her husband to divorce her (*hul'*), quite frequent already in the late 1500s, may sometimes have been due to the initiatives of propertied women, wishing to terminate their marriages. In other cases, by contrast, husbands who had tired of their wives may have pressurized the women into making applications for *hul'*; in this fashion, the ex-husband saved the money that he would have had to pay to his ex-wife if he unilaterally divorced her, as Islamic law permitted him to do.

These considerations show that even archival documents do not necessarily contain the truth, the whole truth, and nothing but the truth. Sometimes, when the historian is lucky, he/she may be able to track down the fictions that the sultans' tax paying subjects and officials entered into the records; and as more and more historians examine the conventions involved in the writing of court documents, some hitherto undiscovered fictions shall probably come out into the open.[41] In many cases, however, the background story may be impossible to retrieve; but we must never forget that simply repeating the claims of the documents investigated will not produce a satisfactory result.

Yet, for several decades avoiding mere summaries of the official records at issue was a golden rule easy to preach but difficult to implement. Once the great registers assembled by Ottoman scribes had become accessible, scholars needed to spend much time and effort on familiarizing themselves with scripts often difficult to decipher. Learning the peculiarities of Ottoman bureaucratic language, tabulating the data collected and perhaps mapping them or turning them into graphs are time-consuming tasks as well. Often it was difficult to progress beyond this stage, particularly since many researchers had spent so much time on these basic issues that little energy remained for anything more sophisticated.

During the last twenty years or so, however, the manner in which Ottoman scribes produced and archived documents has become much clearer. Quite a few scholars now emphasize that, while the archives are very rich we should not necessarily take the claims of the sultan's officials at face value. This statement may at first sound banal, but given the near-religious value assigned to 'the state' in much of current discourse in Turkey, it makes sense to stress the point.

As archival records from the Mughal period have not survived in large numbers in Delhi or Agra, it is more difficult to figure out if petitioners and/or officials have produced fictional accounts – after all, it is by comparing documents with one another that historians can track down such artifices. Yet from the later seventeenth century onward, archival documents have survived rather better, including the many letters of Aurangzeb. Shireen Moosvi has been especially assiduous in tracking down and publishing such 'forgotten' documents in commented English translations, thus making them accessible to scholars from other fields.[42] In a limited number of regional principalities, especially of Rajasthan, in Jodhpur, Jaipur, and elsewhere, eighteenth-century documents have survived in sizeable numbers.[43]

However, in some cases at least, the reader of recent Mughal historiography may suspect that certain claims made by Akbar's officials are somewhat exaggerated. Supposedly, the centralized record-keeping of Akbar's financial expert Tōdar Mal had ensured that the imperial apparatus reached down to the ordinary taxpayer, thus penetrating the 'hard shell' of village or regional societies whose aristocrats had previously collected local dues and paid them to the Mughal treasury as tribute.[44] Here the Ottoman example is worth pondering: Most Ottoman peasants did not form caste-based groupings and thus were presumably more accessible to government intervention. At the same time, even if officials worked conscientiously, registration was never without significant gaps. Given these findings, we may wonder whether the access of Mughal finance officials to the village level was as successful as claimed, or if any successes achieved were of long duration. As Nandita Prasad Sahai has memorably stated, 'The crucial question is not whether the state aspired to be absolute but whether it could actually accomplish its ambitions'.[45]

As noted, Ottoman historians begin from the premise that archival documents, generated by the sultans' officials, are usually believable. In the South Asian context, however, few historians will accord English, Portuguese, Dutch, French and other non-Indian documents a similar level of credibility. As Indian archives permitting historians to check the claims of European officials are so often non-existent, some researchers have turned to a very close analysis of the one-sided documentation that has in fact survived. In her recent book on piracy in the coastal waters of Western India, Lakshmi Subramanian has reminded us that the researcher must begin by determining the purpose for which governors, company directors and their scribes have put together the currently available archive.[46] Admittedly, the events highlighted by Subramanian took place some sixty years after the cut-off point of the present study, but because of its methodological interest, this work can be an inspiration to Ottomanists as well.

Investigating the genesis of an archive may involve considerable research into the backgrounds of the responsible officials, feasible in Subramanian's case because the period covered is short, the number of British report writers limited, and the latter often left both official and private papers that may have reflected dramatically divergent perspectives. Most intriguingly, Subramanian has 'teased out' the fact that some of the pirate leaders had claims to feature as marginal Rajput warriors and thus even as martial heroes. Apparently, this fact appealed to several of the British authors who have produced the surviving records – not coincidentally, these men were often Scots and imbued with the culture that had produced the romantic novels of Walter Scott (1771–1832).[47] Notions of derring-do have thus found their way into the archives of sober military men.

Constituting archives and permitting access – or perhaps rather not

While Subramanian thus 'problematizes' archives, Ottomanists tend to view the existence of the Ottoman central archives as a given. Rather, they focus on the emergence of specialized administrations in the course of the 1600s and 1700s, which developed their particular forms of record-keeping.[48] On one level, this approach makes sense, as official Ottoman repositories date back to the fifteenth century. At the same time, non-official collections of documents are rare, and only the archives of certain dervish lodges are accessible to historians – at least if luck favours them.[49] However, in Mughal India and in the sub-Mughal principalities of the eighteenth century, only a part of the writings produced by a variety of administrations have ended up in the rulers' archives, many other documents remaining in the homes of the senior officials once responsible for their production.

With time, these documents passed to the heirs of the original holders; by the 1920s and 1930s, when history writing in the modern, nineteenth-century mode became a concern of Indian historians, the question of who would get access to which documents became a matter of serious concern.[50] The struggle for document access involved several parties: On the one hand, there was the British colonial government, which controlled the documents that its officials had received or created since 1857, when the British government formally took over India as a colony. In addition, the government held documents acquired from diverse sources since the mid-1700s, when the East India Company had taken over the administration of Bengal, and later on of other formerly Mughal provinces as well. Allowing or not allowing Indian scholars access to these documents was clearly a political decision, in which official apprehensions about the growing Indian independence movement played a significant role.[51]

At the same time, many documents being in the possession of persons who had inherited or purchased them, accessibility depended upon the attitude of the owners, who might be members of princely families. Some of these men were wealthy, highly educated and interested in history, to the point of financing the publication of significant selections of the archives they controlled. Furthermore, at least the Bombay colonial government once allotted money to such a project as well.[52] Other owners of documents however, saw the items in their possession merely as a potential source of money. Therefore, historians attempting to establish research-oriented archives 'from scratch' had to find the funds needed for document acquisition, with all the haggling and personal or political pressures that this enterprise involved.[53] In addition, the collectors of documents, often not trained historians, might have a major interest in the prestige of certain communities and/or families. Nation building was a concern too, so that establishing historiography in the positivist sense of the term in the nascent academic world of India contended against powerful competitors.

Fundamental questions of source reliability, which go far beyond the 'archive question' are more often in the foreground in Mughal or post-Mughal history than is true of the Ottomanist context. Given regional pride, some scholars were willing to accept records that a positivistic-minded historian would have rejected. Thus, the doyen of Indian historians Sir Jadunath Sarkar (1870–1958) and his lifelong friend Govindrao Sakharam Sardesai (1865–1959) profoundly disagreed on the reliability or unreliability of sources concerning the life and activities of Aurangzeb's opponent King Shivaji (d. 1680). Moreover, as the study by Prachi Deshpande – and a quick glance at the internet – show, contestation over similar issues continues to the present day.[54]

To my way of thinking, the constitution of archives in early twentieth-century India, of which Dipesh Chakrabarty has provided a riveting account, can be 'food for thought' for Ottomanists as well. It is worth reflecting on the small number of private archives in the Ottoman world of the 1600s and 1700s. Even if we admit the loss of much material because of wars, migrations, and expulsions, it is still noteworthy that in often war-torn India, where moreover the climate drastically endangers the survival of documents, local princes and dignitaries managed to hang on to significant quantities of archival records. Did perhaps the central government play a more determinant role in the Ottoman orbit? Perhaps Ottoman local notables had less motivation to preserve their records than was true of many sub-Mughal and post-Mughal princes. Possibly, the 'statist' bias of many Ottomanists, often criticized in the recent past, is the consequence of a long tradition, going back far beyond the establishment of the Republic of Turkey. While I cannot answer these questions, they are worth thinking about nonetheless.

Combining multiple sources, and thereby 'inventing' new ones

In the Ottoman world, as in sultanate, Mughal and post-Mughal India, source criticism has thus been both an academic and a political concern; and locating hitherto unused or under-used historical sources has been part of the scholarly-cum-political project. Where modern-style Ottomanist historiography is at issue, politics were certainly of importance: About a century ago Mehmet Fuat Köprülü (1890–1966), one of the 'founding fathers' of our discipline, aimed at establishing the Ottoman Empire, and the Republic of Turkey as well, as legitimate polities with an original cultural tradition. Thus, the first generation of historians active in the Turkish Republic wanted to show that the Ottoman Empire was not the creation of 'barbarians', whose rule European colonizers and their Balkan nationalist allies could demolish with justification.

Above all, this project of legitimization required a reliable source basis. However, when Köprülü and his contemporaries debated the genesis of the Ottoman polity, they soon came up against the paucity of sources. As noted, in the fourteenth century no Ottoman author had ever written a chronicle; and even in the early 1400s, attempts to commemorate sultans Osman, Orhan and Murad I (r. 1362–89) were as yet quite simplistic, and the same observation applied to Bayezid I (r. 1389–1402), the vanquished opponent of Timur (1336–1405). It bears repeating that Ottoman chronicle writing

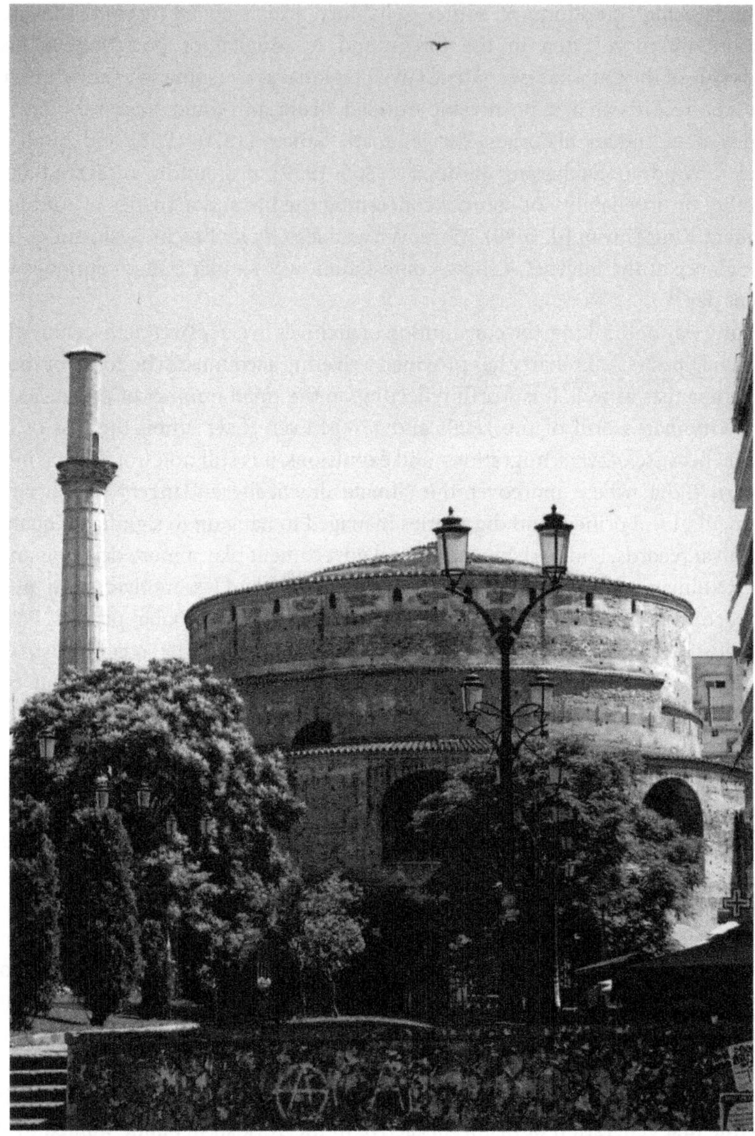

Figure 2 A Byzantine church recycled: the Rotunda in Thessaloniki, Greece. Originally part of the palace of the Roman emperor Galerius, this building became a Christian church around the year 400, when the new users sponsored a mosaic decoration still partly in place. Converted into a mosque in the 1500s, long after the Ottoman conquest, it includes the only minaret standing in today's Salonika.

only came into its own after about 1470, a hundred years and more after the events that the authors purported to describe.

To the present day, we have not resolved many of the problems resulting from this situation. At least, the source basis is somewhat broader than it was in the 1930s or 1940s, mainly because scholars have looked more closely at Late Byzantine sources and materials in Italian and Balkan repositories. Among the sources shedding a few rays of light on Ottoman expansion in South Eastern Europe, the memoirs of the long-lived Byzantine emperor John VI Cantacouzenos (about 1292–1383) are particularly important, the royal memorialist having recorded his alliance with Sultan Orhan, to whom he even married his daughter.[55] Interestingly, the Ottoman chronicles, written after the end of Byzantium, ignore this wedding and the military support given by Orhan to his father-in-law.[56] Other historians have studied the text in which a Byzantine clergyman bemoans the conquest of Salonika by the Ottomans in 1430: Melek Delilbaşı has studied this lament and translated it into Turkish.[57] In addition, the Athos monasteries contain a number of documents relevant to Ottoman history; for in the later Middle Ages, the leaders of quite a few of these communities concluded that the Byzantine emperor could no longer protect them. Some of these monasteries therefore acquired the protection of the sultan and – in their turn – were able to protect Balkan aristocrats seeking a secure place for their persons and property.[58]

Figure 3 The beginnings of the Ottoman Empire: entrance to the tomb complex of Hacı Bektaş in Hacıbektaş, Turkey. Located on the road from Ankara to Kayseri, this lodge put up pilgrims to the saint's grave as well as passing travellers. Today it is a museum, but the shrine is a place of pilgrimage as well. Restored in recent decades, the complex retains many inscriptions commemorating donors who lived in the fifteenth to the nineteenth centuries.

More recently, Thomas M. Bohn, Adrian Gheorghe and Albert Weber have published the Ottoman and Balkan sources on the prince Vlad Dracul (1428/31–1476/7), who gained and lost the principality of Wallachia several times over and fought in quite a few campaigns against Sultan Mehmed the Conqueror.[59] Moreover, the Venetian archives contain a certain amount of material relevant to early Ottoman history, as the Serenissima controlled Crete from the early 1200s onward, and the governors of the island sent home regular reports, some of which survive. As for the Venetian treaties with the princes of Aydın and Menteşe studied by Elizabeth Zachariadou, they are in a roundabout way also relevant to early Ottoman history. After all, the sultans conquered the territories ruled by these dynasts, lost them due to the defeat of Bayezid I at the hands of Timur in 1402, and then reconquered them in the course of the fifteenth century.[60]

In addition, the Genoese archives are relevant to fourteenth- and fifteenth-century Ottoman history; for the Republic of Genoa possessed a number of fortified towns on or near the Black Sea coasts, until Mehmed II conquered them all in the later 1400s. Moreover, the town of Galata, across the Golden Horn from Constantinople, and in the late thirteenth to early fifteenth centuries the imperial city's commercial hub, was also a Genoese possession until 1453, when the town council submitted to the Ottoman sultan.[61] Also, until 1566 the Genoese occupied the island of Chios, a few kilometres from the Anatolian coast, and their tribute payments to the sultans have left a paper trail in the city's archives. Using both Latin and Ottoman documents, Kate Fleet has shown the economic underpinnings of Ottoman expansion in Mediterranean trade, for which the Genoese connection was of some importance.[62] Other documents relevant to early Ottoman history survive in the archives of the tiny city-state of Dubrovnik: first a Venetian possession, later at least nominally subject to the kings of Hungary, and finally – until 1808 – a polity subject to the sultans.[63] Yet other sources were the work of the Hospitaller Knights, based for a while in Bodrum/Petrum on the Anatolian coast and engaged in constant corsair warfare against the Ottomans. All these archives have interested scholars, although presumably there are still unknown/unstudied documents hidden away somewhere.

Ottoman sources by contrast do not say very much about the early sultans' conquests in the Balkans or the Mediterranean coastlands. Even so, these men do document the connections of fourteenth- and early fifteenth-century sultans and aristocrats with a variety of dervish saints, with Fuat Köprülü pioneering the use of these legends (*menakıbnames*) by historians.[64] A series of studies by Ahmet Yaşar Ocak, Rıza Yıldırım and others have demonstrated that we cannot mine these stories for 'facts' relevant to the lives of late medieval personages. After all, these texts often had circulated orally for centuries before somebody wrote them down.[65] Sometimes the work of these latter-day recorders is datable, for instance when they wrote in a rhetorical style in vogue at the end of the nineteenth century. However, in a few cases, we do have manuscripts going back to the 1600s or even earlier times. Moreover, where the buildings of a lodge are medieval at least in part, the findings of architectural historians are of interest too.

Combining the study of *menakıbnames* with architectural history is helpful because quite a few saints' legends explicate the foundation history of a dervish lodge in existence at the time of writing. Put differently, they contain scraps of a 'mythological history' of the relevant buildings. The vita of the popular Central Anatolian saint Hacı Bektaş is a good example of this tendency. Likely, the saint lived in the second half of the thirteenth century and had no contact whatsoever with the earliest Ottoman rulers. However, by the reign of Bayezid II, the lodge may well have enjoyed the sultan's patronage, perhaps because the monarch and/or his advisors assumed that the Bektashi dervishes might convince the 'wild and woolly' holy men of Anatolia that integration into the Sunni community had now become necessary.[66] Other grants-in-aid for additions to the dervish lodge came from the Malkoç-oğulları, long since domiciled in the Balkans but seemingly anxious to maintain contact with their province of origin.[67] In the *menakıbname*, there appear the names of several Anatolian saints with whom Hacı Bektaş supposedly established contact, and whose feats as miracle-workers he easily surpassed. Perhaps the sheikhs of the lodge believed, or wanted their listeners/ readers to believe, that the relevant sheikhs had accepted the supremacy of their own patron saint. Thus, combining the study of texts with architectural vestiges left by dervish sheikhs can help today's historians view the Islamization of Anatolia and parts of the Balkans in ways substantially different from the 'history of conquest' as detailed in chronicles. While the study of *menakıbnames* goes back some ninety years and that of medieval Anatolian architecture further still, the combination of the two sub-fields and their source materials is something of a novelty.

Historians of medieval and early modern Delhi have used their sources in similar ways. Thus behind Sunil Kumar's analysis of the sultanate chronicles we can discern, *en filigrane* so to say, a project of writing the social history of this city, which, admittedly with some interruptions, has been the capital of major Indian polities for over a thousand years.[68] In a recent article, Pius Malekandathil has highlighted the fact that when in 1192, Qutb al-Dīn Aybak had conquered the Rajput-governed settlement located in the south of present-day Delhi he apparently had no qualms about establishing his military apparatus on a site that had previously housed a Hindu ruler.[69] However, Aybak's successors during the 1200s, 1300s, and 1400s frequently moved their fortress-palaces, occupying a series of proximate locations, all in the southern sector of today's metropolis. Apparently, the reasons for these costly and at first glance incomprehensible moves lay in the apprehension of a newly established ruler with respect to the clients and especially the ex-military slaves of his deceased predecessor. The new sultan therefore built a separate fortified residence staffed with his own men, relegating the partisans of the dead sultan to the periphery of his capital. As for the townspeople, these moves made their lives difficult because they might not only lose customers, but also needed to organize their own defence at a time when attacks by rival contenders to the throne were quite frequent. Some of the fortifications built by the successive dynasties of the Delhi sultanate are extant, and so is the monumental mosque of Delhi's first Islamic rulers featuring a widely visible minaret known as the Qutb Minar.

Combining architectural and textual studies has also been helpful when working on the mausoleums and graves of Indian Muslim saints. Such studies can be quite difficult, as many buildings and the graves even of prominent people often do not possess identifying inscriptions, so that only hypothetical identification is possible. In any case, from the late twelfth century onward, the elites governing Northern India were usually

Muslims and venerated representatives of Islamic mysticism (Sufis), while these masters of spirituality were alive – and after their deaths as well. Canopies of stone often honoured the most frequently visited sites. Delhi contained (and contains) a number of such mausoleums, which contributed to urban stability; for even when the sultan had come to reside elsewhere, pilgrims continued to visit Sufi graves, which never moved. In the last centuries of Mughal existence, after the end of the period discussed here, the figurehead emperors often inhabited the southern Delhi district of Mehrauli, near the grave of a famous dervish saint.

As in medieval and early modern Anatolia, the adherents of holy persons who had lived under the Delhi sultans sometimes glorified their spiritual masters through accounts of their saintly lives.[70] In the medieval Anatolian milieu, only urban saints such as Mevlana Celaleddin Rumi (1207–73) and some of his successors in the Mevlevi order of dervishes wrote down their teachings, often in poetic form, or one of their adherents undertook this job on their behalf. By contrast, the authors of certain Anatolian saints' legends, perhaps working in villages or small towns, displayed these holy men as miracle workers fighting unbelievers and on occasion, other saints as well. Irène Beldiceanu Steinherr has suggested that one of these heroic figures, on record as Seyyid Ali Sultan aka Kızıl Deli, was identical with one of the early Balkan conquerors who founded a dervish lodge after retirement from fighting.[71] As for the 'fathers' (*babas*) who guided immigrant nomad groups into Anatolia, none of their teachings have come down to us, and the same observation applies to the early conquerors of the Balkans later considered holy.

On the other hand, many Indian texts dealing with holy men focused on the actual teachings of the sheikhs. Evidently, many inhabitants of fifteenth-century Northern India had an understanding of the veneration of Sufi saints that differed from that of their Anatolian contemporaries, and the writings recording the memory of Indian holy figures placed a greater emphasis on verbalization than seems to have been typical of medieval Anatolia. Given the scarcity of evidence, it would be hazardous to attempt an explanation.

Constructing socio-political histories: A matter of common concern

After discussing methods and principles, we now turn to their practical application, discussing the construction, by historians active during the last few decades, of syntheses reflecting the Ottoman and Mughal polities. Remarkably, historians of Mughal India have shown more interest in Ottoman history than Ottomanists have directed toward Indian developments, although a few younger historians in Turkey are now about to broaden their perspectives.[72] Ever since the early 1990s, Indian historians such as Sanjay Subrahmanyam, Farhat Hasan, or Ruby Lal have been reading secondary literature on the Ottoman Empire and using this historiographical knowledge in their own work.[73] Thus, Ruby Lal's monograph on the female relatives of the early Mughal emperors frequently refers to the study of Leslie Peirce on the Ottoman imperial harem, incidentally making the differences between the two institutions obvious even to the casual reader.[74] It is difficult to give a reason for the more circumscribed outlook of Ottomanists; perhaps we should simply say that the historiography of Mughal India is more sophisticated in methodological terms.[75]

Situating the Ottoman social formation

In constructing comprehensive histories of the Ottoman and Mughal realms, scholars in both these fields have provided instructive examples of the interplay between historical sources and present-day historiographical concepts. In the Ottoman environment, studies of urban and rural societies began in the late 1940s and early 1950s, when archival documents first became accessible in significant quantities. Historians such as Ömer Lütfi Barkan (1903–79) and Halil İnalcik (1916–2016) were intent upon showing that the Ottoman Empire, at that time defunct for only a few decades, had been a polity with a developed system of land tenure and a promoter of infrastructure and inter-continental trade, the latter issue being particularly prominent in İnalcık's work.[76] Given these achievements, there was thus no basis to the claim that 'the Turks' had spread destruction wherever they went, a figure of speech widespread in the nationalist discourses of the states recently emerged on formerly Ottoman territory.[77] At the same time, it would be unfair to assume that among the first generation of scholars active in the Republic of Turkey, *laudatio temporis acti* was the dominant concern. On the contrary, many scholars of the 1960s and 1970s were genuinely enthusiastic about the potential of Ottoman archival documents for the construction of an Ottomanist historiography comparable to that created by French and British historians working on the medieval and early modern periods.

In their very different ways, during the late 1960s and the 1970s, Ömer Lütfi Barkan, Serdar Divitçioğlu (1927–2014), Huricihan İslamoğlu, Çağlar Keyder, and Halil Berktay all participated in the debate concerning the position of the Ottoman socio-political formation when viewed in a Marx-inspired perspective.[78] Was it a feudal society that in the twentieth century was mutating into capitalism, or was it a social formation of a completely different kind, which would not of its own accord ever become capitalist? In Turkey, historians, economic historians and economists situated the Ottoman polity in a variety of ways. A conservative secularist, Barkan claimed that the empire was a formation sui generis, not comparable to European medieval societies, although he conceded that the early Ottoman Empire had included 'pockets' of serfdom. Berktay viewed the Ottoman social formation as feudal, albeit as a special variety of feudalism in which 'the state' largely took the place of European-style lords in the collection of surpluses from peasants operating their own farms.[79] Divitçioğlu saw the Ottoman social formation as a variety of the Asiatic Mode of Production (AMP, in Turkish: ATÜT), while İslamoğlu and Keyder only explored this option at the beginnings of their respective careers.[80]

From the historian's viewpoint, this debate, which should have been fruitful, was deeply problematic because it soon became a mixture of incompatible concerns. After all, a purely political question, concerning the alliances that the Turkish Left was to form – or not form – during the 1970s, intersected with a specifically historical problematic, namely the debate concerning the transition from feudalism to capitalism, at that same time a major issue discussed by historians of late medieval and early modern Europe. In the later 1970s moreover, Ottomanist historians including Halil İnalcık became very much interested in the work of Immanuel Wallerstein and explored the place of the Ottoman Empire in the 'world economy' as envisaged by Wallerstein, and in different terms by Fernand Braudel as well.[81]

Some Turkish authors of the 1960s and 1970s vehemently deplored the 'Levantinization' of local intellectual life. By this term, they meant the adoption of (historical) models developed in Europe and the United States. By contrast, the academics participating in the feudalism–AMP debate had mostly received their degrees from major Western universities; and they were anxious to insert Ottoman history into the expanding sub-discipline of world history. Scholars working with Wallerstein's model of core and periphery, and the place of the Ottoman Empire in it, had often studied, for longer or shorter periods, in the Anglophone world as well.

Whatever the merits or demerits of this so-called 'Levantinization', the relevant discussions had a long-term positive effect on the status of Ottoman history; for most of the discussants mentioned above stated their positions not only in Turkish but in English or French as well. They thus contributed toward making Ottoman history into an accessible field, whose representatives asked questions that occupied people in other sub-fields as well, while for several decades, as Rifa'at A. Abou-El-Haj never tired of stressing, Ottoman studies had developed in none-too-splendid isolation, as an arcane discipline accessible only to a few specialists.[82] Ottomanist contacts with world history at first were probably unintended but still of major significance. As Karl Marx put it, albeit in a different wording, people make history, but rarely the history they intend to make.[83]

A major problem that the participants in the feudalism versus AMP debate frequently encountered was the scarcity of detailed studies based on primary and especially archival sources. It was thus not rare for people with a philosophical or social science education to theorize while using insufficient data. However, to some extent the gap in concrete knowledge filled up during the following years.

Extant mostly since the late 1400s, the Ottoman registers known as *tahrir* or *tapu tahrir* – ideally – enumerated all taxpaying adult males, and given the greater accessibility of town dwellers, were probably most comprehensive when it came to the urban world. Using these materials, from the 1950s and 1960s onward historians produced a spate of urban studies focusing on Anatolian towns and on Istanbul as well, although the capital had only occasioned lists of pious foundations but no registers of taxpayers.[84] These works foregrounded population in addition to craft- and trade-connected activities such as weighing silk, grain and fruit, or else dyeing cloth, as all these activities had left traces in the tax records. Moreover, whenever the registers of local qadis were available, historians tried to link the traders and craftspeople whose disputes surfaced in this documentation with the data recorded in the *tahrir*s. In the process, they made some strange discoveries, finding out that the monetary values of different crops recorded in the *tahrir*s for purposes of tax assessment did not coincide at all with market values. Additionally, a few detailed lists of administratively imposed prices (*narh*) gave information on goods traded especially in Istanbul, an intriguing parallel to the price list recorded by the fourteenth-century historian of the Delhi sultanate Ziyā al-Dīn Baranī.[85] Buildings meant to serve trade and crafts appeared in the documents establishing pious foundations (*vakfiyye, vakıfname*) and perhaps more importantly, in the annual accounts, which the administrators of those foundations that received grants from the sultans had to submit with greater or lesser regularity. At least some of these accounts survive in the Ottoman archives.

Writing urban history proved most productive when a sizeable city was a site of lively trade. Thus, Bursa, the earliest Ottoman capital that even after the transfer of the seat of government to Edirne and Istanbul remained the premier city of Anatolia, was the darling of Ottomanist historians. Writing about small towns was much more difficult because the qadi registers, if even they survived, often did not say very much about local trade and crafts, perhaps because in such places, quintessentially urban activities took second place to the cultivation of gardens and fields. These studies showed that, in the course of the sixteenth century, Anatolian towns and markets grew in size and numbers, but stagnated or even contracted after about 1580 when military rebellions and/or banditry hampered trade and caused the flight of peasants and townspeople.[86]

Recently, Mehmet Kuru has provided a new explanation for this crisis, entering the variable of climate into the discussion. Kuru has shown that mid-sixteenth-century population growth took place mainly in Central and Southeast Anatolia, where a period of relatively abundant rainfall allowed a spectacular expansion of rural and urban settlement.[87] When drought struck in and after 1590, inaugurating a long period of low rainfall, people fled the area, young men joining the military or perhaps the military rebels known as the Celalis.[88] Alternatively, refugees settled in the coastal regions of Anatolia, where rainfall remained sufficient for agriculture – the shores of the Aegean had not been so attractive when rainfall was ample all over the peninsula. The rise of İzmir, insignificant during the sixteenth century and today the third-largest city of Turkey, was thus not only due to the expansion of European trade in the Eastern Mediterranean, for which İzmir became one of the major venues, but also a consequence of large-scale migration, as drought and bandit attacks drove people from their homelands.[89]

Situating the Mughal Empire

With respect to the Indian context as well, during the 1970s and 1980s historians debated whether 'feudalism' was a useful category for the historian attempting to situate, within a world historical context, relations between the Mughal elites, the governmental apparatus and the 'ordinary' taxpaying population. Harbans Mukhia discussed this issue in the same *Journal of Peasant Studies* to which historians interested in categorizing the Ottoman socio-political system contributed as well.[90] Mukhia concluded that in Indian societies, disputes focused on the distribution or redistribution of the agrarian surplus rather than on the redistribution of the means of production, including land and capital. There was thus no room, socially and politically speaking, for the rise of a bourgeoisie making money out of trade, office holding and the putting-out of raw materials to dependent craftspeople. Given the absence of a strong bourgeoisie, it was impossible to establish capitalism and successfully challenge the established elites deriving their wealth from the control of land and peasants – to say nothing of the fact that the same elite controlled the means of coercion as well.

At the same time, communalism – or put differently, the tense relationship between socio-religious communities, Hinduism and Islam in particular – has played a major role in the conceptualization of Indian and especially Mughal history. This issue is central in part because for decades, British imperialist authors had legitimized colonial rule by promoting the notion that British government had instituted the rule of law, and thus protected the Hindu majority from the centuries-long exactions of their Muslim overlords. Given tense intercommunal relations, when it came to designing the post-colonial regime of the subcontinent, members of the Muslim elites were unwilling to live as a minority in a secular republic, founding Pakistan as a Muslim state. At the same time, many Hindus increasingly came to regard Indian Muslims as a source of trouble and disruption.

These issues have had consequences for historiography: As Mukhia has pointed out, communalism involves the assumption that religion has an 'overarching importance' in the social life of – for instance – the Mughal world.[91] Paradoxically, Hindu, Muslim, and British historians of the early twentieth century often enough shared this assumption. In Mukhia's view, the only way out of this impasse is to focus on completely different issues, especially those relevant to the non-elites. Both Mukhia and Habib, and younger scholars such as Mayank Kumar too, have thus promoted the study of technologies available to peasants and artisans, the organization of farms and workshops and especially, of ecological constraints including droughts, floods, deforestation and the (un)availability of water for irrigation.[92] Thus, historians gain the possibility of viewing religion as one issue among several and can avoid seeing all of history only within the constraints of the communal perspective.

In the Mughal context, scholars engaged in enterprises of this kind have had to compensate for the loss of the large-scale imperial registers once serving the collection of the land tax. Apparently, the latter were very precise, but they have come down to us only through the account of Abū'l-Fazl 'Allāmī (1551–1602), chief advisor and friend of Akbar.[93] Most of the data recorded by Abū'l-Fazl concern the years around 1595, so that his work does not cover those regions that the Mughals conquered only in the seventeenth century. With respect to rural production, Irfan Habib has authored what remains the standard discussion of Abū'l-Fazl's agricultural data.[94] Sure to arouse the envy of many Ottomanists, the information given by this single source is detailed enough to permit discussions of trade in agricultural products and the relationship of peasant producers to the market, questions on which Ottoman documents provide only limited information. Furthermore, the data made available by Abū'l-Fazl permit us to visualize the people on whose actions the survival of a peasant household ultimately depended. These persons include the village community and its representatives, the local power-holders cum revenue collectors (*zamīndārs*), and at least indirectly, the nobles to whom the emperor had assigned the major revenue sources (*jagīrs*) located in the region. An expert in financial management, Abū'l-Fazl has treated the mechanics of revenue collection with particular competence.

Ottomanists reading the work of Irfan Habib will find certain affinities with the analysis of sixteenth-century Central Anatolian village life by Huri İslamoğlu İnan.[95] However, while Habib has devoted an entire chapter to rural uprisings, the Ottomanist scholarly tradition until recently has paid very limited attention to acts of rebellion, in which nomads and semi-nomads were more active than peasants seem to have been. For Habib, the discussion of rural oppression is the prelude for his analysis of peasant participation in rebellions against the Mughals. However, he does not posit that peasant uprisings brought down the ruling dynasty. Even less, does he claim an incipient class-consciousness on the part of the rebels, emphasizing instead the close connections between insurgent peasants and *zamīndārs*. Even so, it is worth noting that Habib terminates both this chapter and the book as a whole with a quote from the Persian poet Sa'dī (d. *c.* 1290) about the oppression that the rulers of Iran visited upon their subjects and the ultimate – and complete – demise of these tyrants.[96]

In his study of the provinces of Awadh and Punjab in northern India during the early 1700s, Muzaffar Alam has dwelt on widespread agrarian uprisings as well; and he agrees with Habib that the latter were the work of *zamīndārs* with peasant followings often connected to their leaders by ties of clan and caste. In addition, Alam and Habib have both stressed that these rebellions for the most part had limited ambitions, mainly the aggrandizement of the often small-scale territories controlled by the relevant group of rebels.[97] The dissolution of the Mughal Empire thus had little to do with the uprisings of poverty-stricken rural dwellers, although as noted, the latter certainly rebelled upon occasion. While many peasants lived in abject poverty, their *zamīndār* leaders typically had accumulated enough resources during the seventeenth-century prosperity of Awadh and Punjab to purchase armaments including muskets. Similar to what happened in the Ottoman world around 1600, local gunsmiths made handguns available to their customers, and the attempts of the rulers to prevent this from happening were at most temporarily successful.[98] On the other hand, the entrenchment of the *zamīndārs* by caste and clan ties to the peasantry that they controlled was a characteristic of Indian social structure without parallels in the central Ottoman provinces.

Another important difference between the two societies was the limited importance of pious foundations (*vakıf, evkaf*) in Mughal India: in the Ottoman Empire by contrast, these institutions, large or small depending on the resources of the donors, collected significant shares of agricultural revenue and transferred rural surpluses to the towns and cities. In addition, *vakıfs* provided numerous urban services, from mosques and madrasas to covered markets and water supplies. In the Mughal world, on the other hand, Muslim religious and charitable ventures often received finance directly from the imperial budget, and the central government appointed its own officials to oversee accounts. Thus, in the 1660s, Aurangzeb sent Chandar Bhan Brahman, whom we have already encountered, to administer the money that the central government provided for the running of the Taj Mahal, the burial place of Shāh Jahān and the site of an important mosque.[99] Some Muslim religious, educational and charitable undertakings functioned with the help of grants-in-aid (*madad-i ma'āsh*) assigned by the Mughal rulers. Moreover, in the late 1600s and early 1700s the holders of such grants established in Northern India, whom we may compare to Ottoman administrators of sizeable *vakıfs*, held positions of authority because local claimants to power sought out their support for purposes of legitimization.[100] Even so, these Indian figures apparently did not have as dominant a presence as the administrators and/or beneficiaries of major pious foundations in the Ottoman world.

A very provisional conclusion

What can we learn from this discussion of Ottomanist source criticism and its counterpart in the historiography of the Mughal Empire? Furthermore, what do the findings imply for our study of the interfaces, where elites and non-elites came into contact?

As a starting point, reading these two historiographies in tandem highlights the attention we have to pay to literary tropes and requirements of genre. The story of Mahmūd of Ghazni and the temple of Somnath as analysed by Richard Eaton, Sunil Kumar, and Romila Thapar shows that literary tropes may dominate not only poetry, but chronicles as well. Ottomanists may not find this information easy to digest. How many tropes, as yet undiscovered, may lurk in Seljuk or early Ottoman chronicles, and to what extent were later authors imbued with a different ethos, namely that of reporting 'the facts and nothing but the facts'? At the same time, the tale of Somnath shows that crosschecking with the results of other disciplines, especially archaeology, is essential. If no excavation had taken place in Somnath, we would still believe that the structure had gone through numerous destructions and extensive rebuilding during the medieval and early modern periods.

Indian historians are moreover very cognizant of the destructive potential inherent in 'communalism', in politics but also in historical research. Reading the work of scholars like Najaf Haider or Rajeev Kinra, it soon becomes apparent that seventeenth- or eighteenth-century authors might gossip about rivals whom they wished to marginalize, perhaps because of professional jealousy. Other reasons were at issue too, including the notion that only the members of a given community had the right to intervene in certain debates. Sadly, this way of thinking is still current in our day.

For a long time, these issues did not play much of a role in the thinking of Ottomanists; for after all, differently from the situation in the Mughal Empire, non-Muslims, unless they converted, had very little access to the scribal culture of the elite.[101] Dialogues between educated Muslims and non-Muslims were thus not very frequent, although they did happen on occasion. Thus, the 'inter-cultural' conversations between Hindus and Muslims, which currently arouse a great deal of interest among Mughal historians, have very few parallels in the Ottoman world.

Historians, including the Ottomanist variety, tend to follow the 'drift' of their sources, and this tendency is especially obvious when we examine contacts between elites and non-elites. People who were not Turkish-speaking Muslims were of limited interest to the Ottoman elite, and the concerns of these people remained on the margins of chronicles and archival documents, if they occurred at all. Twentieth- and twenty-first-century historiography frequently operated in the same manner. Remarkably, this lack of interest even applied to the Arab world, although this region was of great importance for the Ottoman centre: Egyptian taxable wealth was a significant addition to the treasury and the legitimacy of the Ottoman monarchs strongly depended on their well-advertised role as protectors of Mecca and Muslim pilgrims.

Presumably, in this matter, many historians of the recent past have followed the inclinations of the reading public in Istanbul and Ankara, whose members have customarily shown little interest in the Arab world. Despite important exceptions, now fortunately increasing in number, few Ottomanists have been comfortable with Arabic sources and few historians of the early modern Arab world have used the Ottoman archives. While this situation is now changing, for decades many Ottomanists were inclined to leave the Ottoman Arab provinces to specialists on the Arab world, who in their turn often showed little interest in the Ottoman capital, Anatolia or the Balkans. *Mutatis mutandis*, similar observations have applied to other non-Turkish-speaking subjects of the sultans.

Yet now that the historical experience of Arabs, Orthodox Christians, Armenians, Jews, and Kurds has become part of the overall narrative of Ottoman history, the question of 'concealed communalism' will likely appear more often on the Ottomanists' agenda. After all, promoting the concerns of the community to which a given author belonged may well have been part of the 'hidden agendas' of both Ottoman Muslims and non-Muslims. When reading chronicles, hagiographies and even archival documents, it is worth keeping such possibilities in mind.

However, not only written sources pose problems for historians to analyse and if possible resolve. The interpretation of pictures can be just as difficult; and in the following chapter, we tackle the attitudes of Ottomanist and Indianist historians when dealing with the world of images.

2

The Trouble with Imagery[1]

Calligraphy, drawings, paintings, and sculpture can all be helpful to the historian, although many patrons and makers had intentions other than conveying historical information. In the Ottoman context, sculpture was largely absent, while calligraphy had the highest status because of its relevance to the Quran. Calligraphy, whether by local masters or by esteemed artists from Iran and Central Asia, was highly valued at the Mughal court as well, where the names and achievements of these masters entered the written record.[2] At the same time, India possessed a long sculptural tradition, usually linked to the different varieties of Hinduism, with which certain Mughal rulers engaged, at least occasionally. For they might have the doors of their palaces decorated with large elephants, a sizeable terra cotta model of this animal surviving in New Delhi's Purana Kila archaeological museum.[3] Otherwise, however, the Mughal emperors did not much favour sculpture in the round, as opposed to reliefs.

As for drawings and paintings, often on paper, Ottoman painters and artists intended these works to impart information, especially on geography and/or recent history, while at the same time glorifying the sultan and his viziers. Apparently, this type of artwork served to instruct junior members of the sultan's court in the conduct expected from an Ottoman gentleman, with aesthetic enjoyment involved as well.[4] In the case of Mughal miniatures, the aesthetic aspect seems to have been more prominent: At least that is a possible explanation for the many elegant images of beautiful harem ladies doing their best to please handsome princes, attended by servitors dressed scarcely less magnificently than the principal figures.[5] In both empires, the painting of flowers – and, among the Mughal elite, whimsical depictions of animals both real and imagined – may have served primarily for aesthetic enjoyment.[6]

When analysing these works of art for historical purposes, we approach them in a manner closely akin to the procedures discussed in the case of written work. To figure out what we can learn from Ottoman or Mughal depictions, we first have to establish who the patrons were, and second, if possible, find out something about the painter(s). This task is easier in the Mughal case than in the Ottoman art world, because in Agra, Delhi or Lahore, artists were more likely to sign their paintings. In addition, we attempt to find out the aims that patrons were pursuing when they commissioned a given piece of art. All these questions are the province of art historians, so cooperation between history and art history is therefore indispensable.

Both Ottoman monarchs and their counterparts in the Mughal realm sponsored imagery. However, unlike what we have observed in the world of text, when it comes to pictures, the differences between the Ottoman and Mughal cases by far outweigh the similarities, despite the Iranian inspiration so clearly evident in both.

In Anatolia and the Balkans before the immigration of Muslim Turks, images seem to have been in limited supply, although the accidents of survival make any broad claims very risky. While the Byzantine court of the fifth and sixth centuries CE sponsored an abundance of both religious and non-religious painting and mosaics, the works known from the eleventh century onward are manuscript illustrations, almost all of them religious, and the icons and wall paintings decorating churches. A few furnishings decorated with mostly religious images have come down to us as well. In Asia Minor, Byzantine church decoration survives mostly in the caves of the Central Anatolian region of Ürgüp and Göreme, provincial sites far from the capital. In the Balkans, many of the more important churches have once served as mosques and thus lost their imagery. Moreover, in Istanbul during the Ottoman centuries, Byzantine churches not transformed into mosques typically decayed; and in these cases too, the painted decorations are gone even though the walls may still be standing. Thus, presumably, the imagery that the Turkish immigrants into Anatolia encountered was all but exclusively religious; and they must have felt no motivation to engage with it. Antique statuary was exceptional, as certain Seljuk dignitaries had no hesitation about reusing it.

When beginning in the late 1400s, we encounter the first Ottoman illustrated manuscripts, the models were courtly and Iranian, and no Anatolian or Balkan input is visible. By contrast, Mughal painters drew on a long tradition of painting, largely but not exclusively connected with Hindu religious practice. Moreover, when the emperor resident in Delhi could or would no longer fund lavishly illustrated books, quite a few of the Indian princes that had formed independent polities during the first half of the eighteenth century became patrons of miniature painting. Presumably, as traditions of painting had existed all over the subcontinent for a very long time, the patronage of a single court, however rich, was much less decisive than in the Ottoman orbit.

The ambiguities inherent in Ottoman painting

It is certainly possible to use aniconic paintings as historical sources; but most historians are not too well versed in the study of such abstract imagery and therefore, prefer to work with depictions of living beings and material life. Ottoman artists invented decorations that were floral in a naturalistic mode, floral yet strongly stylized, or else completely abstract. Such pictures were mostly miniatures included in books and albums sponsored by the sultans' court; palace decoration on walls and ceilings contained very few depictions of people or animals. In the Topkapı Palace, we only find a few small images of this kind, hidden away in large tile-work compositions.[7]

In the thirteenth century, royal customs had been quite different; the Seljuk sultans when residing in Konya and nearby Kubadabad on Lake Beyşehir, both in southern Central Anatolia, had certainly used tile-work featuring human and animal figures in their palaces, and they even sponsored sculptures of animals and fairy-like creatures 'in the round'.[8] In this milieu, as noted, it was also quite common to reuse antique statuary.[9] While surviving Seljuk sculptures are today in museums, a nineteenth-century engraving shows that some of them had originally decorated the Konya city walls, soon afterward torn down as part of an urban renewal project.

In their time, these sculptures of the Anatolian Seljuks, whether original or re-employed, were highly visible. But few if any texts tell us what Ottoman observers thought of this rather extensive use of figurative imagery by rulers, to whom the earliest Ottoman princes had once owed allegiance, at least if we trust the claims of some late fifteenth-century chronicles.[10] On the other hand, it is worth noting that Ottoman power-holders never destroyed these holdovers from pre-Ottoman times.

Nor do we know whether Ottoman literati ever discussed the de facto rejection of human and animal figures in Istanbul palaces, if not confined to the pages of a book. There may have been debates of this kind, whose details escape us: After all, Evliya Çelebi (1611–after 1683) noted that even in the mid-1600s, connoisseurs visited the decoration of a Safavid pavilion from the royal palace of Tabriz, brought to Istanbul by an Ottoman commander some time before the author's birth.[11] Now Safavid works meant for palaces, as opposed to mosques, very often displayed images of people and animals; and we can surmise that the paintings on view in the Bosporus pavilion, likely of exquisite quality, contained images of this kind.

In books and albums, images featuring people and animals survive in significant numbers, so that a section of the Ottoman elite surely appreciated them. However, a famous episode recounted by Evliya Çelebi featured a man from the town of Tire in Western Anatolia who had acquired a painted manuscript at auction and then disfigured the miniatures by rubbing out the faces it contained, because he considered this artwork objectionable from a religious point of view.[12] However, the pious buyer tried to bilk the auctioneer of his fee, who complained to the local governor. When the latter saw the damage, he made the owner pay a supplementary sum, in part to defray auction costs, and then had him ignominiously chased from his court. Evliya did not explain why he thought that the man was blameworthy, apart from the fact that he apparently belonged to the followers of the 'fundamentalist' scholar Kadızade Mehmed (d. 1635), whom Evliya heartily despised. Perhaps socio-political status was also at issue: The palace-educated author may have considered that an ordinary subject had no business judging whether books made for the elite were or were not permissible. Some of the surviving illustrations in Ottoman manuscripts do indeed show smudged faces; but often we do not know whether the damage was accidental or deliberate.

Some reticence toward figurative painting was present at the Mughal court as well. Ebba Koch has drawn attention to a passage written by Abū'l-Fazl (1551–1602), in which he acknowledged that the work of European painters could lead people from a concern with mere appearances to a higher truth. Even so, the author emphasized the prime importance of writing/calligraphy in conveying 'the experiences of the ancients'.[13] However, the Mughal emperors did not ban figurative painting from their court, even though later rulers did not continue the active interest of Akbar (r. 1556–1605) Jahāngīr (r. 1605–27), and Shāh Jahān (1628–58).

The patrons of Ottoman illustrated manuscripts

In the Ottoman world, the florescence of figurative painting was closely connected with the interest of the current sultans. A lengthy line of rulers who sponsored painting and/or the arts of the book, including miniatures, began with Mehmed the Conqueror (r. 1451–81). After the death of this monarch, there was a hiatus of some forty years. However, courtly interest resumed with Süleyman the Lawgiver/the Magnificent (r. 1520–66) and his successors Selim II (r. 1566–74), Murad III (r. 1574–95), Mehmed III (r. 1595–1603), Ahmed I (r. 1603–17) and Osman II (r. 1618–22). After that, sultanic patronage for miniature painting was rare and only revived, briefly but intensively, under Ahmed III (r. 1703–30). Moreover, in the second half of the eighteenth century, oil painting became fashionable in palace circles, a development that further narrowed down the possible clientele for miniaturists.

In the 1600s, many of the miniatures produced were either single-leaf paintings that buyers could later incorporate in albums, presumably intended for less affluent purchasers within or outside the palace milieu.[14] Other miniatures of those years were rather modest sketches, with little colour or even only in black-and-white. These pieces, sometimes known as the work of bazaar painters (*çarşı ressamları*) quite frequently appealed to European diplomats and other well-to-do visitors, who wanted mementoes of a stay in Istanbul.[15] Albeit in an artless manner, these miniatures showed scenes from urban life, including shops, markets, and the inside of a caravansary, scenes that court artists very rarely depicted.

In a recent study, Nathalie Rothman has argued that an experienced dragoman serving the Venetian ambassador (*bailo*) may well have commissioned a set of such seventeenth-century miniatures, today in the Museo Correr (Venice), which show an Istanbul fire among other genre scenes. Perhaps the dragoman had intended these images for the instruction of his successor(s).[16] Furthermore, Hans Georg Majer and Tülay Artan, historians of Ottoman art and society, have both suggested that, when no court patronage was forthcoming even established miniaturists might work for this kind of market. Apparently, there is no reason to draw a sharp line between 'high' or courtly and 'low' or bazaar art.[17]

Ottoman non-royal persons commissioning local artists to illustrate books were quite rare; one of the exceptions concerned late sixteenth-century Baghdad, where small, illustrated books perhaps went to a clientele of well-to-do urbanites.[18] Whenever viziers sponsored illustrated manuscripts, they ensured that the decoration was more modest than that of copies intended for the sultan, even if the text was identical.[19] In addition, Ottoman elite but non-royal figures in the 1500s were in the market for illustrated volumes 'made in Shiraz', where manuscripts of good but not royal quality were commercially available; today many of these works are in the Topkapı Palace Library.[20] Otherwise, the sultan might commission illustrated manuscripts, or else highly placed palace personnel had books decorated for presentation to the monarch. Remarkably, most of the many magnates and powerbrokers controlling the Ottoman provinces in the 1700s and early 1800s do not seem to have been very bookish; and even less did they buy illustrated manuscripts. The remarkable Ali Çelebi, who in the late 1500s assembled a large library in the border fortress town of Buda (today:

Budapest), seems to have had few successors.[21] Many seventeenth-century viziers, whose estate inventories featured numerous manuscripts, favoured Qurans in the calligraphy of famous masters, rather than illustrated volumes.

Commissioning paintings: Ottoman artists

In the late 1400s, Mehmed II had invited the Venetian painter Gentile Bellini (1429–1507) to work at his court, and produce a portrait of the sultan. Bellini received royal largesse, which he brought back to Venice.[22] Probably, the sultan commissioned medals from Italian artists including Costanzo da Ferrara as well, the manner of remuneration often remaining unknown. Some Ottoman figures including Sinan Bey also painted royal portraits; this artist may have been a court personage. From the 1520s onward, the registers of artists and artisans working for the sultan (*ehl-i hiref defterleri*) record the names of the people to whom the sultan paid a salary, so as to have them available when needed (see Chapter 7). It is difficult to say whether these people ever accepted outside commissions, unless palace patronage failed. On the other hand, they often presented their work to the sultan as 'gifts' and received the ruler's largesse in return. Thus, all manner of informal solutions must have been possible.

In the early years of Sultan Süleyman's reign, the artists brought to Istanbul by the monarch's father Selim I (r. 1512–20), as part of his booty from Safavid Tabriz, were still a significant presence, although shortly after his enthronement, Süleyman had allowed people who wished to do so to return to their homes. Ottoman bureaucrats kept registers of the *ehl-i hiref* well into the eighteenth century, but quite often the most illustrious artists do not appear in them.[23] Some miniaturists may have worked in the time that official business left them: the painter Osman active in the early 1600s even ended his career as a pasha.

Others may have had private resources and worked for the palace only when invited for a specific project: Perhaps the outstanding artist Abdülcelil Levni (d. 1732–3) fell into this category. We do not know much about the manner in which this painter made a living. As he wrote poetry too, he must have had a literary education and probably came from a family with some resources.[24] As a young man, Levni had studied with Musavvir Hüseyin, one of the very few distinguished miniaturists of the late seventeenth century.[25] Levni also trained students, some of whom collaborated on a famous festival book, commissioned by Ahmed III to commemorate the circumcisions of his sons. However, none of these painters seems to have equalled the creativity of the master.

Patronage and artists in the Mughal world

While as noted, India already possessed a highly developed painting tradition when the Mughal court began to sponsor illustrated manuscripts under Akbar, it was the court of the latter, which intensively promoted the encounter with Iranian art. After all, the Timurid style was an Iranian creation; and Bābur and his family were proud of their descent from Timur (1336–1405). In the mid-1500s, quite a few painters trained in the Iranian style were already at hand; among others, the distinguished painters Mīr Sayyid ʿAlī and ʿAbd al-Samad had joined Humāyūn (1508–56) when he was still in Kabul and then followed him to Delhi.[26] While Humāyūn died only a few months after his return to India, and thus had little occasion for art patronage, his successor Akbar continued to encourage artistically trained migrants from the Safavid Empire, in difficulty once Shah Tahmāsp (r. 1524–76) had dissolved his painting workshop. In addition, certain grandees of Akbar's court set up their own ateliers; ʿAbd al-Rahīm Khān-i khānān (1556–1627) especially made a name for himself by his lavish patronage. We can debate whether this decentralization of patronage was simply due to the superior wealth of the Mughal elite, whose members had always disposed of resources unmatched elsewhere.[27] Or else, did perhaps differing political structures require different rules of deference that Ottoman and Mughal elites followed when confronted with their respective rulers?[28] We might surmise that the Mughal court appreciated competition among artists and patrons, while the Ottoman sultan saw himself not as the ultimate arbiter but as the only patron. However, at this point it is best not to speculate.

Apart from Iranian and Central Asian immigrants, the imperial Mughal workshop also employed local artists; and differently from the usual Ottoman practice with respect to painters, not all of these people were Muslims.[29] We know the identity of many artists because as noted, quite a few of them signed their work, sometimes adding the names of their fathers. This custom carried over into some of the courts of princes subordinate to the Mughals, so that documentation survives on the eighteenth-century artists who made the reputation of Jaipur as a centre of painting.[30] Some of these artists continued to practise their craft for many generations. Thus, in present-day Jaipur, there is still a family of painters whose ancestors had once served the Mughal court.[31]

Many artists probably worked in the imperial workshops (*kārkhānas*); some historians of Akbar's palace in Fatehpur Sikri near Agra have identified such a building, but in the absence of written sources, it is impossible to be sure.[32] Most miniatures were the work of more than one person; typically, there was one senior designer aided by one or more junior artists, the latter being often responsible for the colouring and/or the details considered less significant. After completion, the more important volumes passed into the imperial library, where they were subject to periodical inspections. Specialists have collected the thousands of inspection notes that the officials undertaking these tasks have left us, and art historians have used the greater or lesser frequency of such inspections as indicators of the growing or declining popularity of certain prominent illustrated manuscripts, in the eyes of the current emperor.[33]

Akbar and his son Jahāngīr were both connoisseurs of painting. Jahāngīr even prided himself on his ability to recognize the work of individual painters at a mere glance; and for this ruler, collecting seems to have been part of his royal persona. On one of his many portraits, he appears above the image of a Christian holy person, perhaps because the piece at issue had just entered his collection.[34] These two rulers thus took an active role in selecting the books to be illustrated and the painters that were to work on them. Moreover, from their collections they sometimes provided examples, which they wanted their painters to study. As a result, there were artists in the imperial workshops familiar, not only with Iranian and Central Asian painting

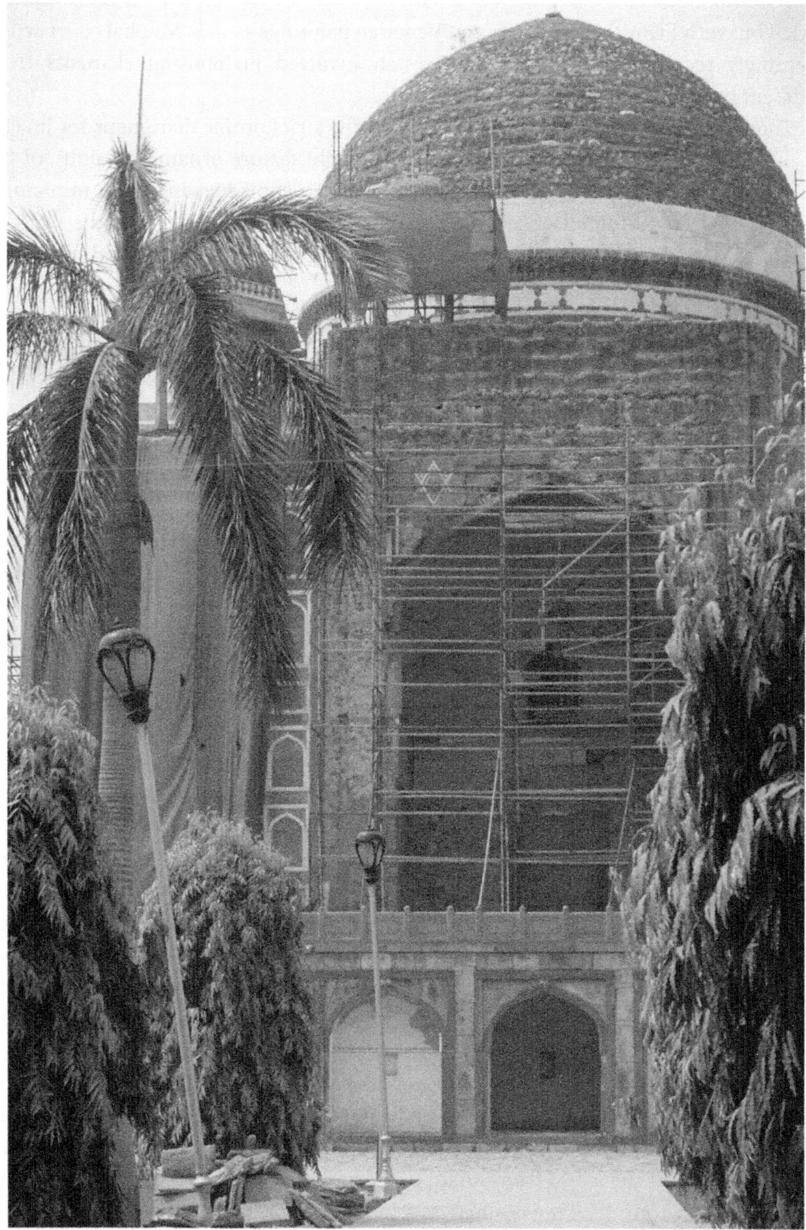

Figure 4 Patrons of art: ʻAbd al-Rahīm Khān-i-khānān (1556–1627). Tomb of ʻAbd al-Rahīm Khān-i Khānān (1556–1626) in Delhi, near the tomb garden of Humāyūn. ʻAbd al-Rahīm Khān-i Khānān was the son of Bayrām Khān, who had been Akbar's tutor during the first years of his reign. After a failed rebellion, Bayrām Khān received a royal pardon and permission to perform the pilgrimage to Mecca, but an enemy murdered him before he could do so. The emperor had his son ʻAbd al-Rahīm raised at court, where he became one of the most senior and loyal nobles and a great patron of the arts (Asher and Talbot 2007, pp. 144–9).

styles, but with Flemish engravings and Venetian paintings as well. Mughal court artists seemingly received commissions that often involved juxtaposing elements from different painting traditions.

Thus, the portrait of an emperor, painted in the strict profile de rigueur for images of this kind according to Mughal convention, might feature ornamental putti, of the kind favoured in Renaissance artwork. Some of the people viewing these miniatures seemingly wished to emulate Jahāngīr's connoisseurship, by discerning the work of different painters of previous generations that an eighteenth-century artist might cite in his work.[35]

The practice of donating artwork to foreign rulers enhanced the impact of Mughal art. Thus, there survives an illustrated copy of Sa'dī's *Bustān*, on which Shāh Jahān (r. 1628–58) had noted that he had destined it as a gift to the British king.[36] Gifting paintings was customary at the courts of minor princely families as well. The transferrals of some of this artwork are on record, so that we can reconstruct how artistic models must have travelled. At the court in Jaipur, images showing the emperor Aurangzeb (r. 1659–1707) were important enough for painters around 1900 to copy them, long after the demise of Mughal rule.[37] By contrast, while the Ottoman sultans received illustrated manuscripts as royal gifts from Iran, for the time being there is not much evidence of their making such gifts in return.

Commissioning miniatures: A survey of favourite subjects

In terms of topics, a small group of manuscripts sponsored by the Ottoman court featured images of Islamic religious figures, including depictions of the life of the Prophet Muhammad.[38] As for 'secular' topics, the Iranian custom of illustrating the 'classical' epics found favour among Ottoman patrons. When working in this genre, Istanbul miniaturists adhered rather closely to the Iranian courtly model. 'Romantic' epics, in which it was not a priority to correctly render scenes from everyday life, served for the enjoyment of wealthy and well-educated dignitaries, while Firdausi's *Shāhnāma* provided the inspiration for texts glorifying the Ottoman sultans. Morphed into mythical figures, Sasanian kings appeared in images promoting them as exemplars of royalty.

When it came to depicting the more recent past, miniatures showing court life in the palace and on campaign were favoured subjects, in addition to the royal hunt. In the mid-sixteenth century, Süleyman the Magnificent and his advisors projected a gigantic history of the world from Adam to the lifetime of the current ruler. While not all volumes have survived, we do possess a long series of miniatures featuring the life and heroic deeds of this successful and long-lived sultan.[39] In the later 1500s, when Murad III had given up leading his armies in person, high officials took to sponsoring illustrated accounts of single campaigns. Thus, the sultan could see on the pages of a book what he had not experienced in real life.[40] At the same time, these illustrated volumes served as promotional material for the various commanders, who often ferociously competed for the favour of the monarch. While unique and frequently kept in the palace treasury, rather than in the various pavilions serving as receptacles for

Figure 5 Patrons of art: the mosque of Mihrimah Sultan (1522–78), daughter of Sultan Süleyman and Hürrem Sultan, near the gate of Edirnekapı, which at that time was the limit of the city. Even today, the building, set on a bluff, dominates the skyline. A second mosque of the same princess is located on the waterfront in Üsküdar.

other books, these volumes nonetheless were shown to courtiers and, as noted, to the sultan's pages as part of their education.

Different from his father and grandfather, Mehmed III did participate in an Ottoman campaign in Hungary, although his commanders provided actual military leadership. To celebrate the victory gained at Meszökeresztes/Haçova, the sultan commissioned a miniature with a topic rare in Ottoman iconography, namely his triumphant return into Istanbul.[41] His successor Ahmed I sponsored miniatures too, collected in an album now called after him; and as this sultan was much interested in hunting, he or his courtiers commissioned miniatures referring to this activity. A set of images depicting different types of horse bears the name of Ahmed I as well.[42] As for Osman II, the young sultan and/or his advisors ordered a collection of miniatures, which were to help him understand and navigate the difficult political situation of the early 1600s.[43] Unfortunately, the young sultan did not have enough time to profit from this advice.

At the Mughal court, Akbar, when still in his teens began a very ambitious project, namely an illustrated copy of the adventures of Hamza, a relation of the Prophet Muhammad, to whom later legends attributed all manner of adventures and derring-do. The project directors were the Iranian artists Mīr Sayyid ʿAlī and ʿAbd al-Samad that had come to India with Humāyūn, but they had a large number of assistants.

Akbar's biographer Abū'l-Fazl claimed that Daswanta, another participant in this project, had come to the ruler's attention through the graffiti that the – probably – still very young boy had left on the walls of some building or other. Contemporaries were particularly impressed by the large size of the *Hamza-nāma* paintings; their claim that the images were about a square metre in size is somewhat exaggerated, but only slightly so. While the exact dates of inception and completion remain elusive, the project probably began in the late 1550s and was complete around 1572–3.[44] It consisted of fourteen 'volumes' (probably, in fact, boxes in which the officials in charge had stored the paintings); for while literary sources refer to 'volumes', the surviving paintings do not show any evidence of past bindings. However, as only about one tenth of the 1400 paintings once in existence have actually come down to us, it is wise to avoid categorical statements.

Other major projects involved the illustration of the memoirs of Bābur (r. 1526–30), whose conquests had established the Mughal dynasty in India; furthermore, the translation of the *Mahabharata* into Persian (*Razm nāma* or 'Book of War'), ordered by Akbar, featured lavish imagery as well. Under Jahāngīr and Shāh Jahān, royal interest apparently shifted to individual paintings placed in elaborate frames of coloured paper, which in turn might contain images of people or animals telling their own stories but in hues more subdued than were those of the central image. Such artwork found its place in albums – unfortunately in later times, profit-hungry dealers mostly disassembled these creations, works of art in their own right. However, different from the Ottoman case, in Agra or Lahore the motive for preferring individual sheets of paper was apparently not the desire to make paintings accessible to dignitaries of limited resources. Rather, royal albums perhaps allowed the emperor to exercise his connoisseurship in painting and calligraphy without being 'distracted' by lengthy pages of ordinary text.[45]

Imagined women on the pages of real books

Ottoman royal women never appeared in miniatures; nor were there any female painters, at least as far as we know. Matters were somewhat different in India, where 'in principle' royal women were to remain invisible as well. In a seventeenth-century miniature, however, there appeared a woman artist called 'Chiteri the lady painter', shown while drawing the portrait of a highly placed woman, seated in the harem of a nobleman.[46] We also possess portraits of a few royal women, including Jahāngīr's consort Nūr Jahān, perhaps based on the work of artists such as Chiteri – we do have a few names of female painters but their work only survives in exceptional cases.[47] Other images doubtless were fantasies by artists who had never seen the ladies depicted. The status of these paintings thus resembled that of the portraits of Hürrem Sultan/Roxelana (d. 1558) or Süleyman's and Hürrem's daughter Mihrimah Sultan, (1522–78), both the work of Venetian painters to whom the appearance of these two royals must have been a complete mystery.[48] It bears remembering, however, that even fantasy portraits of Ottoman women were always the work of European artists and never of Istanbul painters.

In the Ottoman world, females mostly appeared in the illustrations of literary texts, which by definition did not show the real world, in miniatures depicting the life of the Prophet Muhammad, in pictures showing the adventures of seventeenth- and eighteenth-century urbanites, in addition to a few eighteenth-century single-figure images. Some of the latter were the work of Abdülcelil Levni, who must have known the work of the Iranian painter Rizāyi 'Abbāsī (about 1565–1635); Levni did indeed identify some of his male figures as Iranian.[49] As for the women that he depicted, some of them were (probably) Iranians as well. We may wonder where and how the painter had obtained his models; perhaps they had come to Istanbul as war captives.

As for love scenes, they were quite rare in Ottoman imagery, although in the early 1600s we find a picture of a prince served by females in a garden. Perhaps this painting functioned as the illustration of a Persian literary text, a genre permitting the depiction of women. However, in the course of the century, the 'love interest' apparently became more widespread.[50] A century later, by the end of the eighteenth century, females appeared more frequently and in more varied contexts: for instance, in a picnic scene, often reproduced these days, situated in a garden near the summer palace of Sadabat.[51] A more risqué image showed two men spying on a group of young women once again in a garden, and a few more or less pornographic images appeared as well.[52] Historians still struggle to interpret this trend, which coincides with the increased interest in personal life that appears in seventeenth- and eighteenth-century literature as well.

Favoured by the elites: Portraiture in a courtly ambience

In courtly circles, series of portraits showing Ottoman sultans, as individual images made by Venetian artists and their Istanbul followers, or else as part of a genealogy of the ruling dynasty, began to appear in the second half of the fifteenth century. However, once Mehmed the Conqueror had died in 1481, this undertaking lapsed, as Bayezid II (r. 1481–1512) did not share his father's tastes. Once the court of Sultan Süleyman revived the project, however, there was once again considerable interchange between the sultan's ateliers and Venice, where the workshops of Titian and Veronese, among others, received commissions for portraits of the sultans and a few high-ranking Ottoman dignitaries.[53] The grand vizier Sokollu Mehmed Paşa (d. 1579) even ordered – and received – a portrait of Sultan Süleyman from Venice; and the Danish artist Melchior Lorichs, who had visited Süleyman's court when accompanying a Habsburg embassy, left a portrait of this sultan that probably served as a model for certain Ottoman miniaturists.[54] In the second half of the sixteenth century, there was thus a period in which courtly portraiture in Istanbul, and pictorial art in general was very cosmopolitan, responding to ideas and challenges from both East and West.

Royal portraiture existed in the Mughal domain as well, but the emphasis was different. First of all, portraits were much more numerous and varied; in the case of Akbar, there are not only ceremonial images, but others that show him in a pensive mood, perhaps to depict his concern with religious and intellectual issues.[55] The motif of the emperor visiting a holy man and listening to his teachings, which appeared in Akbar's time, was to become popular among seventeenth-century Indian rulers and princes, perhaps because it resonated with the reverence that people showed to men considered holy, often but not necessarily Muslims. By contrast, it is hard to even imagine an Ottoman sultan in that position, who at most might appear as a host to religious scholars. Other paintings showed Akbar's prowess as a sportsman, capable for instance of taming a furious elephant. In the Ottoman context, a famous miniature showed Selim II as a marksman, when he was still the heir apparent.[56] Jahāngīr commissioned numerous portraits, showing him as a hunter, but also as a diplomat asserting his supremacy over Shah 'Abbās I of Iran (r. 1588–1629). In other portraits, the emperor appeared as an archer, taking aim at the severed head of his – supposedly – slain enemy Malik 'Ambar (1548–1626), whom Jahāngīr never managed to capture.[57]

In both Istanbul and Agra or Delhi, sultans and emperors appeared either in action scenes, or else in courtly gatherings (in the Mughal context: *durbar*) in which nobles and servitors of the court, grouped according to their places in the hierarchy, gathered around the monarch. The Ottoman palace, by contrast, only had such gatherings depicted on a few special occasions. Thus, the Ottoman court did not celebrate wedding feasts of the kind that allowed Mughal princes to appear in public in all their finery. Ottoman princes did not marry and in the rare cases that a sultan did so, he did not have this event celebrated in public. A few exceptions confirmed the rule, including the wedding of Sultan Süleyman to Hürrem/Roxelana, probably in 1534.[58]

On an everyday level, from the mid-sixteenth century onward, the ageing Sultan Süleyman no longer appeared in public very frequently, apart from Friday prayers and military campaigns.[59] Following Süleyman's example, his successors Selim II and Murad III were but exceptionally visible in public; in fact, Murad III moved his official residence to the imperial harem, so that even the grand vizier saw him but occasionally, and communication could often take place only in writing. Apparently, the ruler's inaccessibility enhanced his imperial aura. These practices differed profoundly from those of the early Mughal emperors, who appeared on the balcony of their palace (*darokha*) every single morning, so that their subjects could see them – and quite often, a crowd gathered for just this purpose.[60]

In miniature paintings, Ottoman sultans typically sat on a throne, perhaps alone in a chamber, perhaps accompanied by a few pages. Sultans with claims to be warrior heroes, such as Osman II or Murad IV (r. 1623–40) might appear on horseback. Images of the royal hunt typically showed the monarch riding an often elaborately decorated horse.

Depictions of Ottoman sultans receiving foreigners, including ambassadors, were quite rare. Often reproduced, a sixteenth-century miniature shows the Hungarian nobleman John Zapolya (1487–1540) bareheaded and prostrate before Sultan Süleyman; however, there are few images showing European ambassadors postdating the mid-1500s.[61] From that time onward, portraits of European envoys at the Ottoman court were always the work of painters employed by the relevant dignitaries, and thus unofficial from the sultan's point of view. Exceptionally, the ambassadors attending imperial circumcisions appeared in two Ottoman illustrated festival books, unobtrusively in the account of the 1582 festivities and more prominently in Levni's miniature, when they enjoyed the shows of 1720.[62] While Iranian diplomats appeared in Ottoman miniatures showing courtly receptions and festivities, such images were not very common either. Envoys from the Mughal court made only a fleeting appearance in Ottoman chronicles and, as far as presently known, they did not feature in any kind of artwork. Foreign rulers, including King Louis of Hungary (d. 1526) and the shah of Iran, only appeared when on the battlefield, usually if defeated and/or dead.

By contrast, there are two paintings showing Ottoman dignitaries appearing at the Mughal court, one of them in a rather Italianate style.[63] Moreover, the miniatures showing Jahāngīr as universal emperor, who – in the world of the imagination – embraced a decidedly smaller and weaker Shah ʿAbbās, have no parallels at the Ottoman court. From the images presently available, the viewer comes away with the impression that, when imagery – rather than text – was at issue, the sultans avoided scenes that depicted them as being in contact with the supernatural.[64]

Ottoman miniature painters did not often show their rulers in naturalistically painted landscapes, strongly stylized settings being the rule. If rulers and courtiers demanded realistic depictions, they usually preferred images of fortresses, especially those conquered from the Habsburgs in Hungary.[65] By contrast, at the Mughal court, Shāh Jahān's eldest son Prince Dāra Shukōh (1615–59), for example, appeared as a hunter of Indian gazelles (*nilgai*) in a highly atmospheric landscape.[66] On occasion, at least Jahāngīr and Shāh Jahān were so much interested in the depiction of landscape that they permitted the latter to compete with the princely presence for the attention of the viewers.

In general, however, the Mughal emperor and his nobles appeared with the required formality, usually in quarter- or pure-profile. Under Shāh Jahān the constraints placed upon painters working in the imperial atelier became especially stringent. Even so, the court continued to be interested in natural phenomena; and artists tried to reconcile the conflicting demands of courtly hierarchy and realistic landscape by relegating the latter far into the background.[67] Design ideas from European maps, engravings, and perhaps miniature paintings on copper helped Mughal artists to bridge these contradictory demands. After Shāh Jahān's deposition by his successor Aurangzeb, imperial interest in painting much decreased and the courtly painting workshop soon closed. However, some artists who had known the emperor continued to depict him in portraits. In some of the latter, he appears as an old man. We do not know whether the artists had artificially aged the monarch's features or whether they had actually observed him in his later years.

However much they might emphasize hierarchy, the Mughal court painters generally showed the noblemen surrounding the emperor as very diverse human types. One way of avoiding monotony was to depict these men as being of varying ages and physical types. India was – and is – home to people of many different skin colours and facial configurations, and even the highly formalized durbar paintings of Shāh Jahān's time do not attempt to hide this fact of life. By contrast, Levni, even if he also introduced some variety into the faces of the participants in the 1720 parade, put much more stress on the fact that these people shared the unifying quality of being the sultan's servitors. While showing that the Chief Black Eunuch Beşir Ağa (d. 1746) was definitely an African, Levni at the same time played down the personal features of his model. Especially when the artist depicted two court eunuchs together, the viewer might regard them merely as dark-skinned gentlemen. Being eunuchs, they evidently lacked moustaches, a fact that allowed the painter to show their brilliantly red lips.[68] As for the differences between, for instance, a Tatar from Crimea, an inhabitant of Bosnia, and an Egyptian, seemingly the court did not regard them as worthy of depiction. Hypothetically, we may thus claim that the artists serving the seventeenth-century Mughal rulers enhanced the emperor's prestige by showing humankind in its diversity paying homage to his grandeur by submitting to the discipline of the *durbar*. For the Ottomans, by contrast, at the sultan's court official rank was of primary importance, and the differences between human beings counted for little once they all served the monarch.

It is hard to say whether these differing styles of depicting ethnic difference had ideological implications for eighteenth-century viewers, or whether the whole matter is of interest mostly in a present-day context. In addition, it is worth investigating why both the Ottoman and Mughal courts promoted artists who liked to emphasize the passage of time: In some images, long-lived rulers such as Sultan Süleyman and Akbar or Aurangzeb appeared not as timeless icons but as young and, later on, elderly men.

A favourite at court: Cartography as a fine art

In the cartographical work of Piri Reis (d. 1553) and Matrakçı Nasuh (about 1480–1564), we may observe a phenomenon which, for want of a better word, we may call 'Pan-Mediterranean' cosmopolitanism in the service of Ottoman maritime expansion. Piri Reis was an admiral of the Ottoman navy who seemingly lost his life after an unsuccessful campaign in the Gulf of Basra, undertaken when he was probably in his eighties.[69] He produced two world maps, for which, as one of his sources, he used a map by Columbus that has not come down to us. Apparently, a captive Spanish sailor provided Piri Reis with explanations. The maps only survive as fragments, but the section showing America is extant in both of them.[70] In addition, Piri Reis produced a highly original atlas of the Mediterranean conceived as a set of portolan maps (two versions from 1521 and 1526). While much of this work depended on personal experience, the author was familiar with the relevant work of Italian map-makers as well, adorning his maps with vignettes of port towns, some of them part of the Christian world.[71] As the mass of practical information on anchorages and water supplies suggests, the author had originally intended his book for practical seamen. As later copies became ever more luxurious, however, it seems that Ottoman dignitaries, who had never been at sea, favoured this book for their libraries. On the other hand, Fikret Sarıcaoğlu has pointed out that, in certain manuscripts marginal notes cluster during the seventeenth-century war with Venice over Crete. They may have served as 'updates', at a time when much of the practical information conveyed by the original was way out of date.[72]

As for land routes, the mathematician, artist, chronicler, courtier and sportsman Matrakçı Nasuh (about 1480–about 1564) developed the genre of the army itinerary, normally a simple list of stopping points on the way to the front, into a separate artistic genre. However, this creation never became very popular among later patrons. The artist adorned the principal towns on the route taken by Sultan Süleyman's army marching toward Baghdad with vignettes of their most significant buildings, strongly stylized but still permitting the viewer to distinguish the place depicted from all other localities. Particularly striking is the double-page miniature-cum-city map depicting Istanbul, which shows the city before the Süleymaniye (1557), the Sultan Ahmed Mosque (1617) or the Yeni Cami/New Mosque (1660s) had re-defined the Istanbul silhouette.[73] Matrakçı Nasuh also showed that in the early reign of Sultan Süleyman, urbanization outside the Byzantine walls was still quite limited. To the north of the Golden Horn, Galata, today one of the city's hubs, was still a very small town. Neglected by Matrakçı, settlement on the Anatolian shore was even less significant.[74] Nasuh's 'trademark' was his ability to combine geographical information and painterly appeal.

In the seventeenth century, the Ottoman scholar Kâtib Çelebi (1609–57) had, with the help of a former priest converted to Islam, produced a translation of the Dutch *Atlas Minor*, which he appreciated because it provided information absent from the Islamic geographical literature.[75] After Kâtib Çelebi's death, work on his world geography *Cihân-numâ* ('showcase of the world') continued: A map of Anatolia, drawn by Migrediç of Galata came out in the printed edition of the *Cihân-numâ* (1732), a publication by the scholarly printer İbrahim Müteferrika (1674–1745). In the early eighteenth century, an Ottoman map featured the name of Sultan Ahmed III, who was probably the patron.[76] Moreover, in 1803 a full atlas of the world appeared in print in Istanbul, the first of its kind available to readers of the Islamic world.[77]

By contrast, maps were of less interest at the Mughal court: when the English ambassador Thomas Roe (1581–1644) presented a recently published atlas to the Emperor Jahāngīr, the latter returned it after a while, with the explanation that the scholars at his court were unable to read it.[78] Irfan Habib's work on Mughal cartography thus discusses the production of just one expert cartographer, Sādik Isfahānī, who in 1647 produced the first atlas covering India in several sheets, and who discussed the perennial problem of determining longitude. At the same time, the terrestrial globe did feature in artwork produced for Jahāngīr, but as a sign of world domination rather than as a means of ordering geographical information. The monarch appears while standing on such a globe, clearly identified as a depiction of the earth, on which India is prominent.[79] Asserting world domination in such a manner was unknown in Istanbul. We can thus assume that, despite a visible interest in the aesthetic aspect, the Ottoman elite was more concerned with maps as practical tools.

However, other Indian potentates developed a sustained interest in map-making. The accounts of the manuscript workshop of the Rajput court of the Kachhwaha dynasty in Jaipur, which in many ways had assimilated Mughal civilization, are extant from the late 1600s to the mid-1800s, demonstrating the importance of map-making in this sub-imperial venue.[80] The cartographers-cum-artists working in Jaipur have left us a number of city maps. One of them shows that the central, walled section of the 'new town' of Jaipur, founded in the early eighteenth century, featured a regular pattern of intersecting streets, which incidentally has survived to the present day. In some cases, the artists working for the Jaipur court of the 1700s sought a happy medium between depicting a courtly scene and showing the layout of, for instance, the princely polo grounds. In other cases, however, patrons and artists opted for maps pure and simple.

Thus, when in the mid-1730s the local prince had his new capital of Jaipur inaugurated, the locality became the subject of a map, which reflects realities 'on the ground' well enough for a present-day visitor to recognize the road to the former princely residence of Amber Fort. In this case, the explanations are in Persian; by contrast, one of the Jaipur princes also commissioned a map of the Red Fort, the Mughal palace in Delhi. He must have received permission to measure the palace grounds. In this case, the explanations on the map are in Devanagari, an Indian script much used today. Perhaps following the model of the Iranian garden carpets, a superb example of which, dating to the seventeenth century, is in the Albert Hall Museum of Jaipur, local artists also produced maps of the gardens of various noblemen.[81] We may wonder whether this interest in maps was a peculiarity of the Jaipur princes, or whether perhaps in eighteenth-century Delhi, cartography had achieved a higher status than it had possessed in Jahāngīr's time.

Of some interest to monarchs and grandees: Plants and animals depicted

Certain animals were the favourites of Ottoman or Mughal patrons, who might therefore commission pictures that showed not any horse or falcon, but a particular creature. In the Ottoman palace of the early seventeenth century, the most famous example was that of Sisli Kır, a grey horse with spots, which belonged to Sultan Osman II and died even before its youthful owner; the sultan had a gravestone erected that has survived to the present day.[82] Moreover, a miniature shows the sultan riding this animal. Osman's father Ahmed I had also been fond of horses and hounds, the archetypical hunting companions; and artists prepared a book for his perusal featuring images of different kinds of horses, both real and imaginary.[83] Other animals appeared not because they were anybody's favourite, but perhaps as reminders of mortality, including birds of prey attacking antelopes and crows pecking at an exhausted horse while the creature was still alive. In certain instances, the border between existing animals and creatures of the imagination was probably permeable.[84]

There was never any religious objection to the depiction of flowers, and in the later 1500s, there had been quite realistic Ottoman images of hyacinths, tulips, roses, carnations and prune blossoms, depicted on tile-work. Ottoman flower-painting on paper, by contrast, came into its own only during the 1700s. Perhaps patrons became interested because in this period, there was a notable sociability connected with the growing of tulips; and competitions allowed cultivators, from both elite and non-elite circles, to show their gardening skills.[85] Some of these aficionados wrote books and booklets about the aesthetic evaluation of tulips, including tips on how to achieve high quality although the bulb was unpromising. In 1725–6, Ahmed III even issued an edict limiting the prices of most of types of tulip, while permitting that very few specimens could sell at high prices.[86] Certainly, the more far-reaching claims about the Ottoman elite's hedonism and delight in European-style novelties during the so-called Tulip Age (1718–30) are largely mythical. However, there is no reason to deny that before the catastrophes of the Russo-Ottoman war (1768–74) members of the Ottoman elite valued certain kinds of tulips and to some extent, roses and hyacinths as well. Sometimes, depictions of these flowers embellished a text, while at other times, they appeared for their own sake as items of beauty and delight.[87]

In manuscripts made for the Mughal court, artists depicted plants and animals as well. Horses, and especially elephants, might have notable parts to play in a hunt or battle scene. Moreover, some creatures could become the 'heroes' of separate paintings. While Bābur had not commissioned any illustrations for his famous memoir, he had mentioned animals striking his fancy often enough to encourage courtly interest in later times. Especially Bābur's great-grandson Jahāngīr often noted remarkable animals in his own memoirs; and he encouraged Ustād Mansūr, whose reputation was/is due to his paintings of animals and flowers. Another painter, whose 'Persianate' animal drawings date to the same period, was Abū' l-Hasan b Aqa Rizā Jahāngīrī; perhaps he was the artist to whom we owe an impressive drawing of two pigeons highlighted by slightly coloured wash.[88] As for Mansūr, around 1621 he painted a tulip accompanied by a butterfly, the latter creature being something of a rarity in Mughal miniatures. Som Prakash Verma has identified the flower as the variety known as *tulipa clusiana*. Admittedly, the latter is a Mediterranean plant not attested for the Himalaya or Kashmir, where other types of tulip were and are native. Who knows, perhaps this tulip had been a gift from a traveller who had visited the Mediterranean?[89] On the other hand, the red tulip painted by Mansūr had broad petals, which first took the shape of a chalice and, at a later stage of its development, opened out to form a star; it was thus very different from the long, narrow, and extremely pointed petals favoured by Ottoman growers of the eighteenth century.[90]

Not especially favoured, but present nonetheless: Scenes from non-elite lives

As noted before, in 1582 Sultan Murad III had his son – and later successor – Prince Mehmed circumcized in a festival that lasted for some fifty days. He then sponsored a 'festival book' that highlighted an element of the celebrations, which was then still a novelty, namely a huge parade of Istanbul's artisans, complete with floats depicting some of their workshops.[91] Between the late 1500s and early 1700s, the sultan's court frequently organized artisan parades to celebrate the circumcisions of princes and the initiations and conclusions of military campaigns. However, only verbal descriptions reflected these events, some in prose and others in verse. It was only in 1720, when Ahmed III had celebrated the contemporaneous circumcisions of several of his sons, that a sultan once again commissioned illustrated festival books. Both manuscripts depicting the festival of 1720 featured processions of artisans, in addition to the well-known parades of palace dignitaries.[92]

Admittedly, even these three illustrated festival books showed floats enhancing a festive procession, rather than everyday scenes in the urban marketplace. Unfortunately for the present historian, miniatures featuring 'real' shops, however stylized, were quite rare occurring mostly in the works of the so-called bazaar painters. Painters working for a courtly public usually depicted them when illustrating literary texts such as fables and stories.[93]

In the Mughal setting, everyday scenes including people at work might occur when the artist had to present a momentous event with all the detail surrounding it. Thus when depicting the birth of a prince he might show the nurses taking care of mother and child, or the cooks preparing food soon to be served to well-wishers. A depiction of a construction site might show masons, stonecutters and other workpeople, sometimes as 'background figures'.[94] Such depictions of people at work were common enough for Syed A. Nadeem Rezavi to devote an article to the manner in which painters serving the Mughals depicted 'middle class professionals'.[95] Furthermore, as emperors, princes and their suites frequently appeared on elephants, Mughal imagery contained quite a bit of information on the caretakers responsible for these valuable animals.

Illustrated volumes made by and for Ottoman Christians

For Ottoman Christian communities, the eighteenth century was often a time of commercial expansion and prosperity.[96] Patrons became more numerous, and with increasing literacy some of them developed an interest in the arts of the book. While we concentrate on manuscripts and early printed works embellished with illustrations, pictures in books might relate to other kinds of images, especially icons used in church services. Sadly, it is impossible to discuss this issue in a brief introduction.

Orthodox printed books of the early modern period, with or without illustrations, often came from Venice, where the book market was lively. Printing in sixteenth-century Greek, as opposed to the classical idiom studied by scholars, was feasible in Venice, since the Venetian colonial possessions (*stato da mar*) held a significant number of Orthodox subjects, at least before the Ottoman conquest of Crete (1645–69).[97] Printers could thus be sure of a certain number of customers. In some few cases, these Venetian publications reached the Ottoman Empire too, where printing was a fairly late arrival. Among the Orthodox, history books in particular were in very short supply before the eighteenth-century princes of Moldavia and Wallachia began to promote scholarship, often in Rumanian, which became a written language at about this time.[98] In part, the scarcity of printed books had an 'ideological' reason, as many Orthodox churchmen thought it best to copy holy texts by hand, according to tradition. At certain times and in certain places, printing moreover was in bad odour as the creation of 'Latin heretics', and particularly of the Venetians, whose domination of Crete many Orthodox profoundly resented.

Even so, these concerns did not result in a complete rejection of printing. On the contrary, the work of Olga Gratziou has shown that the long coexistence of printed and hand-copied books meant that the scribes producing illustrated and illuminated manuscripts had frequently seen printed materials.[99] Thus, quite a few typographical details, in addition to the layout in which book designers presented Byzantine-style imagery, would have been unthinkable if the scribes had not known contemporary printed books.

Among Armenians, manuscript illustration went back into the Middle Ages as well, with the late thirteenth and early fourteenth centuries an especially productive period. Printing, the making of woodcuts and engraving became important art forms only during the 1700s. Although early printed books were not cheap, they probably aimed for a broader public than did manuscripts. After all, hand-painted volumes were part of church inventories and mostly inaccessible to the laity, while printed works could – in principle – be the property of anybody with the necessary money.[100] However, until the mid-1800s, in some places the underpaid work of monks was so cheap that their products competed with early printed books, which, due to their size and cost, must have often been unavailable outside of churches and monasteries.

At least, ecclesiastical use is probable in the case of a huge volume that Grigor Marzvanec'i designed and printed in Istanbul. This artist was probably born in the 1660s and had an association with the town of Merzifon in Northern Anatolia, although his early years remain largely unknown.[101] In 1706, Marzvanec'i trained as a scribe and miniature painter before going into printing, published a work bringing together the lives of the saints mentioned in the Armenian liturgy (*Synaxary*), which he embellished with many woodcuts. Grigor was in fact one of the pioneers of a novel type of woodcut, in which the artisans, preparing a slab of wood for the artist to work with, cut it out of the tree trunk vertically rather than horizontally. This technique allowed the manufacture of large images, because the diameter of the tree trunk employed no longer determined the maximum size of the woodcut. In addition, the wavy grain of the wood appearing in a vertical cut affected the work of the artist, in a fashion that differed from the impact of the concentric design typical of a horizontal cut. As for the artistic designs, Armenian printers for some time had been seeking inspiration in the work of the Flemish engraver Christoffel van Sichem; and Grigor continued to work in this tradition. Nor was the artist from Merzifon the only person printing lavishly illustrated Armenian works in Istanbul; for he had a competitor and former associate who, under circumstances remaining unknown, managed to appropriate Grigor's workshop and all the material it contained. However, by the 1730s, and shortly before his disappearance from the records, Grigor had rebounded and was once again printing lavishly illustrated works for church use.

The story of Armenian image-making in Cairo was quite different, as here the small Armenian community often interacted with the much larger Coptic congregations. These contacts are apparent, for instance, in the cooperation of the icon painter Yuhanna al-Armānī (d. 1786), an Armenian with an unspecified connection to Jerusalem, with his older colleague and probable teacher Ibrahīm al-Nasikh (active by 1732, d. 1785). The latter, who was a Copt, worked as a calligrapher and illuminator of manuscripts, which is why he enters the present chapter.[102] Apparently, Ibrahīm introduced the novelty of signing his name to the icons that he painted, perhaps a transferral of a custom already existing in manuscript production; for scribes and miniaturists had been signing their works already in earlier years.[103]

At the same time, the designers ornamenting religious works by means of woodcuts in Istanbul shared one important feature with their fellow Christian artists in Cairo: These men were trying to make a living through their work. On the other hand, as noted, in earlier centuries monks and priests supported by their churches wrote and painted manuscripts for pious purposes, and thus they were largely indifferent to the market value of their work.[104] Moreover, the appearance of professional Christian artists in Istanbul and Cairo seems to support assumptions about the overall expansion of markets and market culture during the eighteenth century, in the Ottoman world as elsewhere.

Paintings executed for and by Ottoman Christians apparently drew inspiration from Byzantine and local, Orthodox or Armenian, traditions, with designs from Western Europe and Italy mainly reaching the Ottoman lands through woodcuts and prints. By contrast, while artwork from the sultan's court had a notable impact on textiles produced by/for Ottoman Muslims, and on liturgical fabrics used by Orthodox churchmen too, we cannot discern any impact of miniatures on the artwork of Ottoman non-Muslims. Presumably, these works remained inaccessible as they rarely left the palace.

By contrast, works executed in the workshops (*kārkhānas*) of Hindu princes more or less tightly subjected to the Mughal emperors were frequently quite close to the paintings sponsored by the imperial court in Delhi, Agra, or Lahore. This resemblance was due to the migrations of illustrated manuscripts, which quite frequently found their way from imperial ateliers to those belonging to non-imperial Indian dynasties. Members of the Kachhwaha family, first of Amber and from the early 1700s onward, domiciled in Jaipur, were avid collectors of artwork from the Mughal court.[105] To the present day, this princely family owns a lavishly illustrated manuscript of the *Razm-nāma* or 'Book of War', the Persian translation of the 'Mahabharata' sponsored by Akbar's court. Accepting Mughal over-lordship after Akbar's victories, the Kachhwahas had adopted key elements of imperial palace culture.[106]

For our purposes, the Jaipur venue is so apposite because the collections of these princes, developed over the centuries, are still largely in place. They are on view in two local museums, and many examples have been studied and published. Art historians have documented the arrivals of paintings that came as gifts from the Mughal court, which inspired local artists over the centuries, and in addition, the gifts arriving from both Hindu and Muslim kingdoms of the Deccan and elsewhere. Furthermore, the Jaipur court employed artists who had trained at the Mughal court. These men must have been looking for alternative employers when the constant struggles of Mughal princes for the throne and the contraction of the empire into a regional kingdom sharply reduced the amounts of money that the Delhi court could spend on artistic patronage.

At the same time, the manufacture of high-quality goods in Amber and Jaipur court workshops has left a substantial paper trail; and this is an extraordinary piece of good fortune as the survival of archives in India has so often been problematic.[107] Sumbul Halim Khan has found that the various princely workshops produced mostly for the imperial court, which demanded gifts of luxury goods from the nobility. Producing illustrated manuscripts was the responsibility of the Chitragarh or Suratkhana, which was a venue for map-making. Originally, this institution had dealt with textiles destined for painted and printed decoration. However, the men responsible ultimately placed textile embellishments and map-making in two separate ateliers.[108]

In South Asia, large-scale paintings on paper and textiles, meant for the decoration of walls, were widespread at princely courts, and the ruler and his courtiers were favoured subjects of depiction. As these wall decorations have no parallels in the Ottoman world, we focus on illustrated manuscripts, and in this context, single page-images of smaller size are of considerable interest. Frequently, the owners had them framed in elaborately ornamented paper and then bound them together in albums (*muraqqa'*). The latter were indeed manuscripts, albeit of a temporary sort: Collectors could easily disassemble the images and dispose of them individually. In addition, eighteenth-century painters working for the Jaipur court produced conventional illustrated manuscripts as well; the two major ones depicted the struggle of the goddess Durga against demons, one of the latter taking the shape of an elephant. The painter Ghasi, one of the most important participants in this large-scale collaborative project, had visibly studied imperial Mughal miniatures of buffaloes and elephants. Religious concerns evidently did not preclude the use of models made for an Islamic court, even in paintings focusing on Hindu beliefs.[109]

Conclusion: The broader appeal of Mughal artwork in India

With the exception of the so-called bazaar painters' work, Ottoman miniatures made between the late fifteenth and the mid-eighteenth century were a nearly exclusive privilege of the sultan's court. Only in certain provincial venues and above all in the later 1600s and the eighteenth century, when the court was losing interest, could a well-to-do urban clientele access such artwork. Certainly high-ranking courtiers commissioned illustrated books, but in most cases, they intended these volumes for presentation to their monarch. Somewhat exceptionally in the sixteenth century, certain Ottoman dignitaries purchased Shiraz miniatures for their own delectation; and these volumes ended up in the palace libraries due to the frequent confiscations of the possessions belonging to disgraced or deceased dignitaries. Apparently, Ottoman subjects, if in the market for decorated volumes or even individual pages, preferred calligraphy and the abstract illuminated headings that provided a splash of colour to the written page.[110]

This close connection between the palace and the art of the miniaturist determined the choice of topics: While the illustrations of Iranian romantic literature remained popular, the *Shāhnāma* also provided a model for highlighting the martial prowess of the Ottoman sultan. Ottoman miniaturists received their most ambitious commissions in the 1500s, when the court of Sultan Süleyman wanted his royal person as well as his ancestors depicted as part of the divine plan for humankind. Later monarchs such as Selim II and Murad III might feature as conquerors not through their personal achievements, but due to the victories gained by pashas campaigning in their names. Portraiture was a prerogative of the sultan and a few high officials, including the chief admiral Hayreddin Barbaros, and certain holders of religious-cum-juridical office; occasionally the artists received permission to include self-portraits. Such artwork also served to impress the viewers, all connected to the sultan's court in one capacity or other, with the antiquity and legitimacy of the Ottoman line.[111]

The Mughal palace sponsored royal portraits in abundance, but though courtly hierarchies were elaborate, the rulers did not view portraiture as a royal prerogative. On the contrary, Akbar even sponsored an entire album, now unfortunately lost, whose very aim it was to record the members of his court and nobility.[112] Moreover, this custom spread to 'sub-Mughal' Indian courts, both Muslim and Hindu, which had accepted the canons of Mughal palace painting. We thus possess many male portraits from Northern Indian venues, typically in strict profile, set against a little-differentiated background, but showcasing the garments and jewellery characteristic of the high ranks enjoyed by these personages.

While there was no known contact with the 'costume books' made in the early modern Ottoman world – first by Europeans and then by Abdülcelil Levni – the similarities between the two genres are still striking. Present-day scholars have thus studied ceremonial dress and even the role of certain monarchs – including Akbar – in inspiring courtly garments and inventing entirely new clothing terminology.[113] We may wonder whether these collections of full-length portraits also served as guides to instruct junior members of the Moghul and princely courts in the etiquette which they would need to follow – and, on the other hand, whether certain novelties first adopted by high-ranking members of the hierarchy perhaps could be models for younger and less prominent men.

A major difference between the two painting cultures was thus the fact that Ottoman painting was almost exclusively a palace prerogative, sponsored by certain sultans and not by others. The canons of this art did not spread to the empire's non-Muslims, who remained attached to local traditions and at a later stage, engaged with European artwork, especially with prints. By contrast, even when Aurangzeb had closed the royal ateliers, their style was familiar outside the imperial milieu and painters continued to work in the Mughal style, albeit for other patrons, who might well be Hindus.

Tentatively, we may postulate that, at least in the realm of figurative painting, the Mughal court was more concerned with the creation of a culture that was 'Persianate' in character and acceptable to the elite of the non-Muslim majority of the Indian population. Perhaps the imperial court considered painting as a factor that could tie the elites of different ethnic and religious backgrounds together. Formidable religious and linguistic diversity was a challenge to the ruling groups of both empires, to say nothing of the often hostile terrain. In the following chapter, we will delineate how the Ottoman and Mughal elites coped with the broader political – and indeed military – issues involved in managing their empires.

Part Two

Running Two Empires: Diversity and Disagreement as Political Problems

3

Geopolitical Constraints, Military Affairs and Financial Administration

While geopolitical constraints, military affairs and administration are the principal subjects of 'normal' history books, we will not focus on these matters for their intrinsic interest. Rather, issues of this type serve as indispensable 'background information' for the real topic of our study, namely the interface between the Ottoman and Mughal elites, on the one hand, and the societies that they ruled, on the other. After all, the structures within which ordinary people lived out their lives – or died early deaths – originated in conquest, and while power elites changed, the fact of domination was perpetual. Put simply, people work, if lucky acquire some property, pay their taxes, and die.[1] However, these activities take on very particular colourings, depending on the socio-political system within which a given man or woman needs to operate.

The present chapter is an overview of the sources of power available to Ottoman and Mughal elites in their Eurasian environment, focusing on borderlands and geopolitical constraints. This undertaking involves a lengthy *tour d'horizon* surveying the major opponents of sultan and emperor, with in addition, a rapid glimpse of their allies. As there can be no conquest without soldiers, the composition of the relevant armies is a major focus of interest. In the second section, we foreground sultanic and imperial households as power centres. For, wherever the official capital might be, Ottoman sultans and Mughal emperors depended on the soldiers actually present in the ruler's camp or palace. As the third step, we explore the different meanings that twentieth- and twenty-first-century historians of the Ottoman world and Mughal India have attributed to the notion of conquest.

Since the maintenance of rule depended on the extraction of taxes, channelling revenues to the military and administrative apparatuses will occupy the fourth section of our discussion. In this context, we need to approach the thorny question of whether the Ottoman and Mughal administrations worked so 'efficiently' as to appropriate all resources not required by the producers for their subsistence, or whether a certain amount of 'slack' remained for members of the subject populations to develop their own business affairs. For this purpose, we survey the rules of good government intended to limit the exploitation of the taxpayers, sometimes effective and sometimes not. These issues will resurface in later discussions of town formation, trade, crafts and village life (Chapters 5–8).

On the borders of empire, the sultan's opponents – and, occasionally, his allies

The empire's north western borders: Ottomans and Habsburgs in conflict

In the two hundred years up to 1526, Ottoman rulers and elites had expanded their empire over the entire Balkans; and in the battle of Mohács (1526), an Ottoman victory, the last king of medieval Hungary Lajos II (r. 1516–26) lost his life. In the following decades, the formerly Hungarian province of Transylvania (today part of Rumania) emerged as a principality subordinate to the Ottoman sultan, while most of central Hungary became an Ottoman province, administered by a governor-general or *beylerbeyi*.[2] A small but rather densely populated section came to be part of the territories ruled by the Habsburg archdukes of Austria, whose capital of Vienna the Ottoman armies besieged but failed to take (1529). By mid-century, the border between the Ottoman Empire and Catholic Christendom thus passed through central Hungary, with a significant part of today's Croatia within the Ottoman domains as well.

Presumably, the sultans' armies did not advance any further into Central Europe because the Habsburgs of Vienna, while controlling only a small territory with limited resources, could count on the support of their cousins ruling Spain. For in 1516, Charles V, Burgundian and Habsburg on his father's side, had taken over the kingdom of Spain from his mother, a daughter of the royal couple Ferdinand of Aragon (r. in Castile 1479–1504) and Isabella of Castile (r. 1479–1504), whose marriage had first brought the kingdom of Spain into being. From the early 1500s onward, the kings of Spain had access to the enormous silver resources of Mexico and Latin America, which they largely spent on European wars. In addition, from 1519 onward, Charles V ruled the Holy Roman Empire as well. Despite religious-cum-political division into Catholics and Protestants, which was to tear the polity apart during the Thirty Years War (1618–48), the mostly German princes whose loose alliance formed the empire worried enough about a possible Ottoman attack on their own territories, that they supported the defence of the Habsburg domain.[3]

By the mid-eighteenth century on the other hand, the sultans had lost most of their conquests in Hungary in the war of 1683–99, in which the Ottoman sultan Mehmed IV (r. 1648–87) and his grand vizier Kara Mustafa Paşa (d. 1683) had, for the second time, attempted to conquer Vienna (1683). Differently from what had happened to earlier coalitions of European princes, the Habsburg alliance with the Polish king John III Sobieski (r. 1674–96) held up, and Habsburg commanders advanced far into the Balkans.[4] In the Peace of Karlowitz (1699), the Ottomans retained only Temeşvar (lost to the Habsburgs in 1716) and Belgrade, the former border fortress of the medieval Hungarian kingdom, which Sultan Süleyman had taken in 1521. While Belgrade too became a Habsburg possession in 1718, a short Ottoman–Habsburg war in 1739–40 returned the city to the sultan's domains. In the later eighteenth century, military conflict between the two empires became rare, except for the war of 1788–91, from which both sides drew little benefit, with Russia the principal winner.

In the far north: Sultans and tsars in imperial competition

On the empire's northern frontiers, by 1526 the sultans' control was unchallenged. The conquests of Mehmed II (r. 1451–81) and Bayezid II (r. 1481–1512) had turned the Black Sea into an Ottoman domain, as the Tatars of Crimea had accepted Ottoman suzerainty in the fifteenth century. Admittedly, in this period, the khans were not as closely dependent on the Ottoman sultan as they were to be in the seventeenth and eighteenth centuries, when the tsars of Muscovy (and later of Russia) expanded southward and put pressure on the khans, to whom they had previously paid tribute. However, already by 1569, the Russian conquest of the khanate of Astrakhan had the sultans concerned about the security of the pilgrimage route from Central Asia to Mecca, prompting a major campaign against the forces of the tsar. Unfortunately for Ottoman war aims, the sultan's commanders thought they could only dislodge the Russians if there was a canal connecting the Don and Volga rivers, which however did not materialize. According to Akdes Nimet Kurat, poor planning was responsible for this failure.[5]

While, in the sixteenth century, contacts with the grand princes and later the tsars of Muscovy were intermittent, a further confrontation occurred in the mid-1600s, when the Ottomans were party to a conflict involving the Crimean Tatars and their opponents the Cossacks, some of whom owed allegiance to the kings of Poland-Lithuania, and others to the tsars.[6] An early eighteenth-century conflict with Peter I (1672–1725) over Russian navigation in the Black Sea, at that time an Ottoman lake, ended with a victory of the sultan.[7] Possibly this success gave Ottoman monarchs and viziers an overly optimistic view of their military strength when compared to the resources that the tsars could muster, once the latter had mobilized the enormous Russian supplies of timber and water power.

Remarkably, the government of the tsars in the mid-eighteenth century invited the Ottoman ambassador Şehdi Osman Efendi to a 'guided tour' of the armaments factory at Tula, where the diplomat noted that apart from the blacksmiths, all the workers used waterpower. The Russian authorities even gave the ambassador samples of the Tula factory's work to take back to Istanbul, and Şehdi Osman Efendi dutifully recorded these facts in his embassy report.[8] However, apparently his superiors did not fully understand the implications of these novelties.

By the mid-1700s, the southward expansion of the Russian Empire was thus the principal threat to the continued existence of the Ottoman Empire. In the 1780s, shortly after the period covered in this study, Catherine II (1729–96, r. 1762–96) even projected the dismemberment of the sultans' domains, with certain parts of the Balkans to become kingdoms governed by her relatives under Russian tutelage. She even discussed her plans with the Habsburg emperor Joseph II (r. 1780–90). While specialists still argue whether the empress was serious about this project, or perhaps rather not, the sheer fact that a major ruler aired such intentions shows the diminished position of the sultans among European rulers.[9]

In concrete terms, the Peace of Küçük Kaynarca (1774) dissociated Crimea from the Ottoman Empire, the first step toward Russian annexation in 1783. The tsars could now send ships into the Black Sea.[10] In the late 1700s and early 1800s, the Russian

Empire developed what is today the southern Ukraine as a major grain producer, and the new town of Odessa became a commercial hub. At least in the long term, these changes compromised Ottoman interests. For people with commercial capital and experience were a precondition for trade to flourish; and in their search for such merchants, preferably of the Orthodox faith, the Russian authorities attracted Ottoman Greeks, who thus took their material and immaterial assets outside the sultans' domains. By the early 1800s, many Greek merchants active in the tsars' domain were to become proponents of a Greek national state.[11]

In addition, Crimea, lost between 1774 and 1783, had been one of the regions supplying grain to Istanbul. For Ottoman Istanbul this loss was especially dire as frequent Ottoman–Russian wars, between 1774 and 1914, so often destroyed harvests in Wallachia, Moldavia and Eastern Bulgaria. Thus, the bread of Istanbul came to depend on political conjuncture, and at the end of the eighteenth century the insecurity of the food supply was a major source of urban unrest.[12] Furthermore, the Ottoman armies, previously quite well supplied, suffered as well. By the last quarter of the eighteenth century, just beyond the limits of the period under consideration, a vicious circle had come into being: As the armies could not count on regular provisioning, they preyed on the civilian population, thus compromising future harvests and supply lines. Furthermore, given the increasing presence of the tsars in the minds of the empire's Orthodox people, a constant lack of security induced previously loyal subjects of the sultan to hope for Russian intervention.[13]

To sum it up: in the mid-1700s, the Habsburgs were a secondary – though still serious – opponent of the sultans, while Russian southward expansion was the most direct threat. Thus, the Ottomans' major competitors were two land-based polities, certainly not at the forefront of contemporary commercial and technological progress. It is therefore not realistic to make deficiencies in military technology the only factor threatening Ottoman survival, although by the later eighteenth century these defects certainly contributed to the empire's difficulties. As we will see, the transformation of the Ottoman standing army of the sixteenth century into an urban militia, combined with reliance on mercenaries, was the major reason why, during the 1700s, the sultans' soldiers found it increasingly difficult to win battles against professionalized Russian armies. At least this opinion seems widespread among today's historians.

Mediterranean coastlands: France as a (temporary) ally, and Venice as a defeated opponent

On the European scene, the king of France was a major political player, significant to the Ottomans because of his enmity to the Habsburgs. King François I (r. 1515–47), unsuccessful competitor of Charles V for the imperial dignity, after a major defeat (Pavia 1525) against the latter sought an alliance with Sultan Süleyman (r. 1520–66) to end the encirclement of his territories by the Spanish and Austrian Habsburgs.[14] In 1543–4, military commanders in the service of the French and Ottoman monarchs, with the famous admiral Hayreddin Barbarossa (d. 1546) representing the sultan, undertook a joint attack against Nice/Nizza, then a possession of the dukes of Savoy, allies of Charles V. While the two rulers did not undertake any further common campaigns, Christine Isom-Verhaaren has shown that, at the time, adherents of the French king did not view the Franco-Ottoman alliance as unusual or scandalous – although partisans of the Habsburgs promulgated the opposite view.[15] Throughout the next 150 years, an informal anti-Habsburg alliance between France and the Ottoman Empire remained in place, disturbed mainly during the Ottoman–Venetian war over Crete (1645–69) when the French king, while ostensibly neutral, allowed some of his nobles to volunteer their services to the Venetian side.[16]

By the mid-eighteenth century, the conflict between the Habsburgs and France had lost much of its raison d'être, as the new Spanish monarchs were now closely related to the French royal family. With encirclement by the Habsburgs no longer a concern, a major reason for French diplomats to support the Ottoman dynasty had disappeared, although the court in Versailles continued to view the sultan as a force that might prevent the tsars from becoming a Mediterranean power.[17] However, the Ottoman defeat in the Russo-Ottoman War of 1768–74 must have shown all interested parties that Tsarina Catherine II had far stronger armies at her disposal.

As for the Mediterranean Sea, throughout the fifteenth and sixteenth centuries, the sultans' navies were highly successful against the scattered Venetian possessions on the coast, known as the Stato da Mar. By 1526, most previously Venetian strongholds were in Ottoman hands, Cyprus followed in 1570–3 and Crete, as noted, between 1645 and 1669.[18] Already by the mid-1500s, three quarters of the Mediterranean coastline were largely under Ottoman over-lordship, as small Muslim polities on the North African coast either submitted to the sultan or became part of his empire in the course of Ottoman–Spanish naval wars. Despite Ottoman expansion, however, the north western section of the Mediterranean, including the Italian principalities, Southern France and Catalonia, all of which received abundant rainfall and possessed highly productive agricultures, never became part of the sultans' domain.

Even so, by the second quarter of the sixteenth century, Ottoman naval supremacy was apparent, especially after the victory of Preveza (1538) won by Hayreddin Barbaros against the combined fleets of Spain, Genova and Venice. In the Eastern Mediterranean of the late 1500s, only Crete, a few Dalmatian towns and the strongly fortified island of Corfu/Kerkyra remained in Venetian hands. Already in an Ottoman–Venetian war fought from 1499 to 1503, the advance troops (*akıncı*) of Bayezid II had entered Friuli, taking many prisoners and killing those that they could not carry off.[19] Throughout the many Ottoman–Venetian wars, however, the continuing naval strength of Venice apparently dissuaded the sultans from attacking the city proper. By the mid-1700s, the last-ditch attempt of Venice to conquer the Peloponnesus had failed (1715), and the city's merchants had largely withdrawn from trade with the Eastern Mediterranean. Even so, information channels remained open, due to Jewish merchants active in Aleppo, who frequently reported to the Serenissima.[20]

The Ottoman Empire encountering the European-dominated world economy

Viewed in a commercial context, by the mid-1700s, Ottoman 'incorporation into the European-dominated world economy' had begun, although the process was in its early stages and became a major issue mainly after the end of the Napoleonic Wars (1815).

In this sector, French activity was most significant, as British merchants had largely left Ottoman ports when after the fall of the Safavids (1722), Iranian raw silk became difficult to obtain; and Bengal silks were cheaper and more abundant.[21] While for eighteenth-century British merchants, the Eastern Mediterranean thus was marginal, French merchants bought a variety of goods in Izmir, Salonika and Syria, and therefore the decline of the Iranian silk trade affected them less.[22] In addition, Ottoman domestic traders largely freighted French ships, the so-called *caravane maritime*.[23] For that reason, the balance of payments was favourable to France, although the sale of French woollens, while substantial, did not balance the exports of Ottoman cotton and angora wool. Moreover, in wartime, French traders illegally exported grain as well.

In addition, the sultans' domain differed from India, in that there was no local banking sector comparable to the sophisticated businesses of Surat and other cities in the Mughal realm. In consequence, money transfers, for instance by Ottoman provincial administrators needing to send regular contributions to the central treasury, became a profitable branch of activity for French merchants. In consequence, financial circuits in the Ottoman Empire of the later 1700s came to be under the control of French capital.[24]

While European traders active in the Ottoman world enjoyed important privileges in the form of tax exemptions and the right to consular jurisdiction, they never possessed towns over which they exercised political control. While Izmir, Salonika or Aleppo might be home to numbers of people subject to foreign rulers, the regular administrative structure, with its qadis and tax farmers, remained in place. Only on the western edge of the empire was there an exception to this rule: The town of Dubrovnik, from the late Middle Ages until the intervention of Napoleon, remained a mini-republic paying tribute to the sultan, with the town itself off limits to the sultans' officials. However, while an important commercial centre in 1526, by the mid-eighteenth century Dubrovnik and its trade were of modest significance.

The Ottomans at their eastern and southern borders

Judging from the extant narrative and archival documentation, once Selim I (r. 1512–20) had conquered Eastern Anatolia, Egypt and Syria, the sultans and their officials usually prioritized expansion in the Mediterranean and Central Europe. Presumably, acquisitions along the western borders had priority because these regions were less mountainous and received more rainfall, therefore producing more revenue than provinces in the Caucasus or Northern Iran. While the sultans' armies might conquer North Western Iran as well, they never could maintain themselves for any length of time.

At the eastern borders of the Ottoman lands, the dissolution of the Aq Qoyunlu Empire after 1490 resulted in a lengthy conflict between Bayezid II and the Safavid dervish sheikh Ismāʿīl (r. 1501–24), who declared himself shah of Iran in 1501–02. The latter ruler had strong support among the nomads and semi-nomads of Anatolia, marginalized by the sedentary bureaucratic and military apparatus that the Ottoman sultans had established from the time of Mehmed the Conqueror (r. 1451–81) onward. Thus, Sultan Selim fought against a foreign ruler and in addition, against his own subjects, many inhabitants of Anatolia falling victim to the ferocity so common in civil wars.[25] In 1514, Selim's victory at Chāldirān established the border between Ottoman Eastern Anatolia and Safavid Western Azerbaijan; by contrast, Iraq, previously a Safavid possession, only came to be part of the Ottoman Empire after a campaign of Sultan Süleyman's in 1533–6.[26] If we disregard a short interlude in the early 1600s, this province remained within the Ottoman borders until the Great War.

For our purposes, the southern borders of the Ottoman Empire are especially significant as, in this region, subjects of the sultans and people owing allegiance to the various Indian sultanates quite often encountered one another. Ottoman concern with the Indian Ocean was largely a consequence of the post-1498 Portuguese threat to the Red Sea and the Holy Cities of the Hijaz, which the Mamluk sultans could not defend on their own, as the lack of timber in Egypt made it almost impossible to build a navy of ocean-going ships. Ottoman–Mamluk cooperation on this issue, while briefly attempted, failed quite soon. Moreover, after Selim I had conquered Syria and Egypt, patronage over the Hijaz fell to the Ottomans, as the pilgrimage to Mecca, a religious obligation of all Muslims with the necessary resources, was only viable if the Holy Cities had access to Egyptian grain. In the mid-1500s, the Ottoman navy attempted to dislodge the Portuguese from the coast of Western India; while this attempt failed, the sultan's captains did prevent the recurrence of the Red Sea raids that Portuguese captains had undertaken on several occasions.[27]

Other encounters resulted from the activities of less highly placed persons. Halil İnalcık has found records in the Bursa qadi registers of traders serving a vizier of the Bahmani sultanate, who sold goods on commission in this great trading city and even in the Balkans (see Chapter 6).[28] In a more political vein, the Ottoman sea captain Seydi Ali Reis, and Portuguese documents as well, claimed that Ottoman Turks established in the Indian port city of Surat were preparing an Ottoman takeover.[29] In addition, the sultanate of Atjeh on the northern tip of Sumatra established relations with the sultan in Istanbul, asking for and receiving firearms to facilitate the struggle against the Portuguese.[30] However, in the later sixteenth century, Ottoman sultans and viziers concentrated on war aims closer to home and largely abandoned the Indian Ocean.

Ottoman involvement in the Red Sea and Indian Ocean had a commercial aspect as well. In the sixteenth century, the importation of spices, especially pepper, was a major branch of intercontinental trade. Not only European consumers, but Ottoman subjects of some wealth as well, consumed significant quantities of this condiment, some of the pepper in fact originating in India. In the fifteenth century, the Mamluk sultans had made the spice trade into a monopoly of the ruler, probably to compensate for the losses in population and revenue caused by the Black Death and other epidemics of the time. For a while, Mehmed the Conqueror apparently hoped to reroute the spice trade away from Egypt and through the Ottoman central lands. However, this proved unfeasible, and after the conquest of Egypt and Syria in 1516–17, the spice mart of Alexandria in any event became part of the Ottoman Empire.

In the early 1500s, the attempts of the Portuguese to cut off the spice trade with the Red Sea and the Gulf of Basra caused a commercial-cum-political crisis in Egypt and in Venice, both centres of pepper distribution. However, by the 1530s it had become clear that the Portuguese were unable to monopolize supplies, and the Mediterranean pepper trade revived. It remained a flourishing activity until the beginning of the seventeenth century, when the Dutch did establish monopoly control over the pepper trade with Latinate Europe. The sultans' territories, by contrast, continued to receive supplies through Yemen.[31] Ottoman interest in controlling overseas trade routes was apparent in the mid-1700s as well, but as by that time the spice trade had lost most of its importance, the Red Sea and Basra routes were of significance mainly for the importation of Indian cottons and Yemeni coffee.

Mughal expansion and contraction in the subcontinent, between 1526 and 1739

A *tour d'horizon* of the Mughal borderlands

Bābur had arrived in India from Afghanistan, where he had been ruling a kingdom whose centre was in Kabul, and the surrounding region mostly remained part of the newly established Mughal Empire. The Lodi dynasty, overthrown by Bābur in 1526, originated from Afghanistan as well; but the sultans had long been resident in Delhi, where a number of their mosques and mausoleums are extant. Perhaps for this reason, Bābur, and especially his son Humāyūn, seem to have appropriated the city as a royal centre, although these two emperors, constantly at war, were but rarely in residence.

On the North Western frontier, the Mughals soon encountered the Safavid monarchy, established but a few decades before Bābur's arrival in India. Bābur had enjoyed Safavid support, and his son Humāyūn found refuge at the court of the shah when ousted by his rival Shēr Khān/Shāh; he reconquered his kingdom with the help of Iranian reinforcements. Thus, until the late 1500s it was difficult for the Mughals to deny the Safavids a position of superior prestige. However, by the early 1600s, Akbar's son Jahāngīr (r. 1605–27) no longer saw matters in the same light.[32] Border tensions often involved Qandahar, today in Afghanistan, with the heavily fortified town changing hands several times during the seventeenth century. A map drawn up by Jos Gommans has suggested that while Kabul lay within the radius of 1200 km that armies departing from Delhi could reach, and return from, within a year, Qandahar lay just outside of this charmed circle.[33] Seemingly, however, both Safavids and Mughals acquired or lost the fortress, not necessarily through any major military effort, but due to a variety of political circumstances.[34]

Even so, between 1649 and 1709, Qandahar remained in Safavid hands; but at the latter date, the Ghilzai Afghans were becoming a strong regional force. In the early 1700s, after the shah's court had not reacted to repeated complaints against the misdeeds of the locally stationed Safavid soldiery, the Ghilzai revolted and, in 1722, conquered Isfahan, precipitating the fall of the ruling dynasty. In Qandahar, the Afghan tribesmen remained in control until 1729, when dislodged by Nādir Shāh. Qandahar was still part of the Iranian Empire in 1739, when the shah raided Delhi, ending the period that we discuss here.

Further to the north, the Mughals in the 1640s tried to expand into Central Asia. Apparently, to enhance his imperial legitimacy, the emperor Shāh Jahān (r. 1628–58) attempted to retake the lands that Bābur had once ruled, before the Uzbeks had forced him to try his fortune in India.[35] In the mid-1640s, a struggle for the throne between the Uzbek ruler Nazar Muhammad Khān and his son presented the Mughal emperor with a chance to intervene, perhaps to keep the then resurgent Uzbek Empire divided among several pretenders to royalty.[36] However, the army, though commanded during the later stages of the war by the assiduous campaigner and later emperor Prince Aurangzeb (r. 1658–1707), was unable to proceed beyond Balkh, as supply problems and harsh winters caused huge numbers of casualties. Thus, despite the superior quality of Mughal artillery, the Uzbek heartlands with the capital city of Bukhara remained outside the reach of Shāh Jahān and Aurangzeb. Moreover, there was an obvious disproportion between, on the one hand, the enormous amounts of money spent on the northern campaigns and, on the other, the rather modest revenues which the Mughals, if successful, could have collected from this territory.[37] Clearly, the enterprise was a prestige project, with human and material costs a secondary matter.

For the most part, the Himalayas were the northern frontier of the Mughal Empire, despite the conquest of Kashmir, first undertaken in 1589, and occasional campaigns reaching as far as Tibet. While Mughal texts focused on the natural beauty of the Kashmiri landscape and its enhancement by officially sponsored gardens, by the 1600s the manufacture of shawls had become a major economic activity for artisans and merchants domiciled in the Kashmiri capital of Srinagar.[38] Further to the east, the dense forests and swamps formed by the combined Ganges and Brahmaputra deltas limited Mughal expansion. Bengal in 1526 was still an independent sultanate, one of the remnants of Afghan political control that had encompassed most of Northern India before the arrival of Bābur, and once again during the Iranian exile of Humāyūn. Mughal conquests in the region began in the 1570s, when the current sultan Da'ud Karranī, already a tributary subject of the emperor, refused to continue payments.[39] Akbar began his campaign by the conquest of Bihar and its central city of Patna. Afterward, Tōdar Mal, later famous for his reform of the Mughal revenue system, defeated the Afghan ruler in a field battle, and Bihar, Bengal and Orissa officially turned into provinces of the Mughal Empire. In reality, Mughal rule only began in 1576, after Da'ud had lost his life in a second confrontation. Local unrest continued, however, and only in 1602 was Akbar able to establish his authority in the city of Dhaka, while it took until 1613 for the Mughal Empire to control the entire province.[40]

Despite the agricultural and industrial wealth of Bengal, the Mughal emperors did not try to prevent outsiders from establishing themselves in the territory, as long as the newcomers remained loyal subjects. Centralization was unfeasible in many places, as local magnates that had controlled large swathes of territory over many years did not easily accept Mughal over-lordship.[41] While imperial armies drove 'unofficial' Portuguese settlers out of the Bengal town of Hugli for having forcibly converted Muslim slaves to Christianity, the emperors tolerated the Dutch and English merchants settling in the Ganges delta, mainly to buy the cotton fabrics for which the region was famous.

When after the death of Aurangzeb the emperors in Delhi no longer controlled their regional representatives, the governor of Bengal set up a semi-independent principality centred in Murshidabad, where Mughal ideology and institutions continued to operate as a source of legitimacy for the de facto ruler known as the *nawab*. However, by the mid-1700s, attacks by warriors from the ethnic community of the Marathas, based in the Nagpur region (1742–51) destabilized the principality, facilitating a takeover by the East India Company (EIC), which had established a small settlement called Calcutta, today Kolkota, already by the 1690s.[42] In 1757, when Mughal central control had largely disappeared, the EIC intervened militarily against Sirāj al-Davla, the current semi-independent Mughal governor.[43] An elaborate intrigue allowed the Company's commander to win the battle of Plassey, and the resulting increase in power made possible the total conquest of Bengal during the 1760s and 1770s.

Due to the complexities involved, we cannot neatly limit the discussion of the southern border of the Mughal Empire to the years between 1526 and 1739. When Bābur died in 1530, his kingdom included Rajputana, Bundelkhand in the south, and Jharkhand in the southeast.[44] However, Mughal domination was not very secure, and only in the initial years of Akbar's reign did the current prince of Amber from the Kachhwaha dynasty, Bihar Mal, begin the long association of certain Hindu princes of Rajputana with the Mughal court.[45] In those years, Akbar's governor of Mewat had supported a competitor of Bihar Mal, apparently with the intention of joining Amber to the lands directly ruled by the Mughals. However, Akbar preferred to gain the support of the Rajput princes as a counterweight, both to his various competitors descended from Bābur, and to a group of princes (*mīrzās*) ensconced in the southern section of Gujarat and who, by Central Asian standards, had a stronger claim to rule. For while the *mīrzās* were descendants of Genghis Khan (1162–1227) on their fathers' side, the family of Bābur was part of this lineage only, when we take maternal descent into consideration. After all, Bābur's paternal ancestor Timur (1336–1405), had married, among other wives, a princess descended from Genghis Khan. However, Akbar defeated the *mīrzās* and obtained the submission of the Rajput princes of Mewar and Marwar. The latter principality first became part of the Mughal crown lands, but Akbar ultimately reinstated a prince of the local dynasty, tied to the imperial court by the marriage of a female relative with Prince Salīm, later the Emperor Jahāngīr.[46]

In the early years of the Mughal dynasty, the province of Gujarat, a crucial possession in later times, was still outside the borders of the realm, being under the control of the Ahmadshāhīs. Akbar conquered this territory in 1572.[47] By contrast, the attempts of this ruler, and later of Jahāngīr, to conquer the Nizāmshāhī kingdom failed for many years, even after the submission of the capital city of Ahmadnagar in 1600. For Malik ʻAmbar (1548–1626), an ex-slave and later a powerful military leader of Ethiopian background, organized a strenuous resistance, in alliance with the Bhonsla, a Maratha princely dynasty. Only ten years after the death of Malik ʻAmbar in 1636, the Mughals annexed at least part of the Nizāmshāhī kingdom, the remainder going to the sultanate of Bijapur.[48]

By the late seventeenth and early eighteenth centuries, Aurangzeb had expanded Mughal control far into the southern Peninsula. However, the Deccan conquests – such as they were – remained extremely insecure due to the kingdom contemporaneously established in the western Peninsula by the Maratha warrior Shivaji Bhonsla (1627–80).[49] Shivaji's family had risen to prominence in the sultanate of Bijapur, but by the 1650s and 1660s, Shivaji was raiding the fortresses of his supposed overlord and plundering Mughal territory as well. Two spectacular attacks targeted the rich and unfortified city of Surat (1664 and 1670), as the Mughal governor could or would not defend it.

As noted in the Bengal case, Maratha bands sometimes went on plundering raids in the Peninsula too, from which they brought back enormous booty and in places virtually stopped caravan trade. Elsewhere however, the money collected from certain towns and regions to buy off plunder turned into 'regular' taxation by the Marathas. Aurangzeb went to war against Shivaji; and after the Raja Jai Singh Kachhwaha (d. 1667) as a commander of Mughal troops had taken the major fort of Purandhar (1665) on behalf of the emperor, Shivaji had to submit and pay homage at Aurangzeb's court, from which however, he escaped the following year.[50] In 1674, Shivaji crowned himself, in a highly publicized ceremony that emphasized Hindu, as opposed to Indo-Iranian features. After his death, members of his family took over a compact state bordering the western coast of the southern Peninsula: For Shivaji had soon realized that demanding tribute from ships, including those transporting Mecca pilgrims, was an efficient way of filling the treasury.[51] In 1680 the town of Pune, later the centre of the Maratha government, still lay on the border of the lands ruled by Shivaji.

Aurangzeb spent the final decades of his life in unending campaigns in the Deccan. The first was against his son Prince Akbar, who apparently had attracted noblemen thinking that the emperor was needlessly antagonistic against the sultanates of Bijapur and Golconda. In addition, these dissidents were sceptical of the rising influence of Muslim religious scholars, and opposed the reintroduction of the *jizya*, the discriminatory tax against non-Muslims that Akbar had abolished. However, as Prince Akbar and Shivaji's son and successor could not agree on a common strategy, the rebellion fizzled out, with the Mughal prince taking refuge at the Safavid court.[52] Afterward Aurangzeb conquered Bijapur (1686), Hyderabad/Golconda with its diamond mines and the recently established Maratha principality. By 1689, this process was complete.

However, these campaigns did not pacify the southern borderlands, as the Maratha raids continued, now in a decentralized fashion. Excelling in hit-and-run warfare, the Marathas made the Mughal conquest of major forts, such as Jinji in the South Eastern Peninsula, seem almost irrelevant. Typically showing compact blocks of territory, the maps depicting the borders of the Mughal Empire thus hide the fact that the emperor's governors might control cities and fortresses but could not protect the taxpaying subjects from plunder and extra-legal taxation. By about 1700, in some areas there were two tax-taking regimes, namely the Mughal governors on the one hand, and the representatives of Maratha rule on the other.[53] In that sense, the empire was only an 'upper layer' of political control; and when Mughal central power weakened during the wars between the various candidates for the throne following the death of Aurangzeb (1707), a 'second layer' of governors and imperial princes intervened, instituting regional polities. In a sense, the EIC was one of the more successful contenders for regional lordship, having accumulated political power during the lengthy period when Aurangzeb devoted most of the empire's huge revenues to the conquest of the Deccan.

The European-dominated world economy in its Portuguese and English guises, arriving in South Asia

In India, the dissolution of the Mughal Empire, already in the early 1700s, spelled trouble for local communities. Apart from accelerating the integration of Indian textile producers and bankers into the European world economy, the power vacuum resulting from Mughal retreat facilitated the takeover of the EIC, which mutated from a commercial company to a predatory quasi-state. Where 'threats from the West' were at issue, the Mughal Empire was perhaps in a more precarious position than the Ottomans were, because the power differential between the Mughals and the small European settlements on the Indian coasts for a long time masked potential threats. After all, Om Prakash has pointed out that down to the mid-1700s, local rulers and particularly the Mughals viewed European traders – apart from the Portuguese, generally considered a nuisance – mostly as useful generators of revenue.[54]

While the Mughals never built a navy, Ottoman seaborne intervention in the Indian Ocean sharply limited Portuguese options. Given the Ottoman presence, the Portuguese could not acquire any bases in the Red Sea, and after a few decades, their control of Indian Ocean shipping turned out to be patchy as well. As noted, from the 1530s onward, the spice route through the Mediterranean revived in consequence, with a corresponding crisis in the fortunes of the Portuguese overseas empire in India and elsewhere.[55] The principal Portuguese settlement in Goa declined to a small colony with limited commerce, partly because of the dissuasive effects of the aggressive missionary efforts of the Portuguese-sponsored Inquisition among local Christians. In addition, the Spanish Habsburgs' anti-Jewish policies prevented the influx of capital belonging to 'New Christians', of Jewish extraction, who sometimes practised their former faith in secret and avoided places where the Inquisition was powerful.[56] In brief, Goa decayed because of changes in the political and commercial ambiance, to which the Portuguese government never found a satisfactory response.

As for the British and French commercial companies, active in the subcontinent since the seventeenth century, the dissolution of the Mughal Empire after Aurangzeb's death allowed them to engage in vicious competition for commercial – and political – supremacy.[57] These struggles were part of a global rivalry, fought out in Central European theatres of war but in North America, the Caribbean and Mediterranean Seas, as well as in India. Overall, the British were the winners, although they lost their North American colonies in the American War of Independence (1775–83). In the Indian setting, this political conjuncture facilitated the victory of the EIC, which increasingly abandoned the trade which royal British privilege had granted to the merchants, who had formed it. Against sharp criticism by competitors denied a part of the spoils, the company – as stated – turned into a state-like organization, with its own army, generals, and particularly ships usable in warfare. In 1759, just twenty years after Nādir Shāh's attack on Delhi, the Company intervened in the rivalry between different post-Mughal contenders for the resources of the major port of Surat, taking over the fortress protecting the city in the so-called 'castle revolution'.[58] A few years later, the EIC appropriated the revenues of the rich province of Bengal.[59] This latter takeover allowed the British to push out their Dutch rivals, who had previously been very active in the exportation of Bengal textiles. As Om Prakash has put it, this was the time when coercion took the place of commercial negotiation in this province, with the pattern repeating itself on the western, Gujarati coast as well.[60]

Rulers and their armies: Recruiting military manpower within the empires and without

Continuing a pattern established under the Delhi sultanate, Mughal rule was noteworthy because of the role that outsiders to India played in its establishment. Bābur arrived with a war band from Central Asia, and throughout the period discussed, a large section of the military-cum-administrative elites continued to come from Iran, Central Asia or, albeit to a much lesser extent, Afghanistan. These people arrived as large- or small-scale military entrepreneurs, or else as people with literary and administrative skills. Typically, the newcomers became part of the household either of an established elite figure or else of the emperor himself.

Immigrants from Central Asia benefited from the fact that throughout their reign, the Mughal emperors continued to emphasize their Timurid origins: Put differently, even though at least seventeenth-century emperors quite often had Indian mothers, descent from a Central Asian conqueror was part of the self-image of the dynasty.[61] However, in the early stages of Mughal rule, Bābur carefully played down the connection. He must have known that Timur's massacres of the Delhi population were still very much present in local social memory, not only among the Hindus but among the Muslims as well.[62]

On the other hand, Ottoman self-definition was quite different. Although the ancestors of the Ottoman sultans had immigrated into North Western Anatolia as well, this migration remained largely undocumented and undated. Once in power, the sultans never denied their descent from petty local dynasts, first noticed by chroniclers around 1300 and, supposedly, subject to the Anatolian Seljuks. As remote ancestors, however, chroniclers serving the early Ottomans claimed the prestigious Turkic clan of the Kayı and the biblical figures of Esau and Japhet.[63] Furthermore, compared to Mughal practice, the outsiders that the Ottoman rulers incorporated into their military elites were limited in number. There were the 'elite slaves' from the lands to the north of the Black Sea, who became part of the Mamluk establishment that in a much altered fashion, the sultans permitted to re-emerge in Egypt after the conquest of 1517. In fact, the Mamluks of Ottoman times so strongly differed from their medieval antecedents that Jane Hathaway regards the Mamluk establishment of the 1600s and 1700s as an entirely new organization.[64] In addition, at certain times, other elite slaves, often Abkhazians (Abaza), came to Istanbul to enter palace service, as military men who might become commanders.

Paradoxically however, most 'elite outsiders' of the fifteenth and sixteenth centuries came not from foreign lands at all but from within the Ottoman Empire, namely from the Christian rural population, culled for the service of the sultan through the so-called 'levy of boys' (*devşirme*). Islamized and acculturated, these men served mainly in the army as musket-bearing janissaries and as cavalry in the service of the palace, with a small minority gaining promotion into the governing elite.[65]

Early references to this practice date to the late 1300s, although given the scarcity of documentation, we cannot exclude that it had existed at an earlier time. Draftees had no choice but to become Muslims, regardless of what their wishes may have been. We know very little about the reactions of these youngsters; presumably, those who found this demand unacceptable tried to abscond, but we cannot tell how many succeeded in doing so. In the late 1500s, we find some of these young soldiers attending ceremonies at the dervish lodge of Seyyid Gazi (Eskişehir), which the central government considered deviant and tried to abolish, probably without much success. Perhaps this cult eased the transition.[66]

Moreover, the drafted boys became the sultan's *kul*, meaning that they were dependant on the monarch just as if they were his slaves. In the 1300s and 1400s, *devşirme* boys – and thus the janissaries that emerged from them – were slaves of the sultan in the narrow sense of the term, although this was no longer true from the 1600s onward, when the administration phased out the *devşirme* and most janissaries had been born as Muslims. Scholars of the sixteenth century – and those of the twentieth too – have argued whether or not this practice was consonant with Islamic law, which grants the non-Muslim subjects of a Muslim sultan the right to retain their freedom and their religion. Sa'deddin, a famous religious scholar of the late 1500s, emphasized the 'missionary' value of the *devşirme*: He estimated that in the – roughly – 200 years of its existence, the institution had produced over 200,000 converts to Islam.[67]

From the military viewpoint, the janissaries were important because they were the first standing infantry in Europe, wearing uniforms, receiving quarterly pay, and subject to a discipline that by the 1500s, included training in the use of firearms. However, the powerful esprit de corps of this group might work against the sultan: In the winter of 1514–15, Selim I (r. 1512–20) had planned to winter in Karabagh to be ready for a new anti-Safavid campaign in the following spring. Given the protests of the janissaries, however, the sultan had no alternative but to return to Istanbul.[68] Until the late 1500s, the janissaries remained an elite troop, but from that time onward, the need for masses of soldiers to fight against Habsburgs and Safavids made the government recruit large numbers of men, whose pay became almost symbolic. As the soldiers now needed to earn a living, the transformation into an urban militia of part-time artisans and traders was a matter of time, mostly complete by about 1700.

By contrast, military slavery and *a fortiori* the levy of boys were unknown in the Mughal Empire, although the former had existed in the Deccan between the fifteenth and seventeenth centuries. Even more importantly, a clear-cut distinction between the sultans' tax-exempt servitors (*askeri*) and the tax paying Muslim and non-Muslim population (*reaya*), a fundamental feature of Ottoman political organization well into the 1700s and beyond, did not exist in the Mughal Empire. Moreover, the Mughals were quite ready to include immigrant tribal leaders together with their followers into their armies, a proceeding that the Ottomans tended to avoid.[69] Only in the border provinces of Eastern Anatolia, local potentates might recruit their fellow tribesmen; but these contingents rarely participated in the long-distance ventures of the Ottoman central army.

Entry into Mughal service was possible for any person with a suitable number of armed followers on horseback, who might present himself before the emperor. If the latter considered his credentials suitable, the newcomer received an official rank (*zāt*) and a revenue assignment (*jagīr*) that went together with the obligation to provide a certain number of cavalry soldiers.[70] Always payable in money, *jagīrs* underwrote the expenses of the men assigned offices (*mansab*), with the ruler able to change both offices and *jagīrs* at his pleasure. Office-holders had to submit warhorses for the emperor's inspection, preferably imports from Arabia or Central Asia but good-quality local breeds as well. Mughal dignitaries received *jagīrs* of enormous size when compared to the tax assignments (*timar, dirlik*) of Ottoman assignees, known as *sipahis*.[71]

When mustered, Ottoman *sipahis* had to appear together with their armed servitors, whose number depended on the size of the grant assigned. Many *sipahis* with small grants might appear in person but without fully armed servitors.[72] Similar to Mughal practice, the Ottoman administration often re-appointed *sipahis* to localities at some distance from their previous holdings, to prevent these tax-takers from 'putting down roots'. In most places, forming local ties was difficult in any case, as the *timar*-holders were often absent on campaign and thus unknown to the peasants, with the exception of a few *sipahis* staying home to collect taxes and convey the proceeds to the army.[73] On the Hungarian borders, however, the government tolerated long tenures and even permitted sons to succeed their fathers, probably to compensate for the risks involved in life on the frontier.[74] Even if not stationed in the borderlands, however, some *sipahis* retained their holdings over lengthy periods; after all, they were responsible for keeping the peace and thus needed to establish a presence in the localities from where their revenues originated.

Sipahis who did not show up when called were liable to lose their assignments. When prices increased dramatically in the late 1500s and early 1600s, this matter became a political problem, as *timar*-holders who felt that they could not afford further campaigns on the remote Ottoman–Habsburg frontier did not appear at the muster and lost their *dirliks* as a result.[75]

By contrast, holders of Mughal *jagīrs* spent much of their time at court, although at times they visited the places where their revenues originated. When attending court in Delhi or Agra, they enjoyed a luxurious lifestyle. The central administration changed their assigned revenue sources every few years, to prevent the transformation of *jagīr*-holders into local magnates. Only long-established princes that had accepted Mughal suzerainty and received the so-called *vatan jagīrs*, retained the same holdings over the generations, similar to the Eastern Anatolian lords with comparable privileges in the Ottoman–Safavid borderlands. Most *jagīrs* were much larger than Ottoman *timars*, which produced less than 20,000 *akçe* in revenues or even than most *zeâmets*, whose revenues oscillated between 20,000 and 100,000 *akçe*.[76] Probably most similar to the Mughal *jagīrs*, the richest tax grants known as *has*, produced over 100,000 *akçe*; they benefited the highest echelons of the Ottoman bureaucracy and members of the sultan's family. The nobles of the Mughal Empire had to provide much larger numbers of cavalry soldiers and horses, than did the modest contingents recruited by the holders of *timars* and *zeâmets*. For the foot soldiers directly paid from the coffers of the central administration, whose role was central in Ottoman armies had only a small part to play in Mughal warfare.

Different from *timar*-holders, but similar to the beneficiaries of the largest Ottoman grants (*has*), the assignees of *jagīrs* did not collect their revenues in person. As people with financial resources bid for tax-farming contracts (*ijāra*) to collect these dues, *ijāra* in the Mughal world was an integral part of the functioning of many *jagīrs*: The tax farmers, according to their contracts, paid the *jagīr*-holding nobles. Thus, in the Mughal orbit, short-term tax farming was not an alternative to the assignment of tax grants to members of the military and administrative apparatuses, as was common in the Ottoman Empire until the seventeenth century. While Ottoman *sipahis* appeared at the muster with small numbers of men, the *jagīr* holders had to pay for large contingents, and thus the money economy was more intrusive in the sixteenth-century Mughal Empire than in the Ottoman orbit.

On the lower levels of military recruitment too, differences were profound. In India even before the arrival of the Mughals, in areas with only a short agricultural season, young peasants, who had grown up using arms, sought employment as soldiers with a locally established, tax-collecting dignitary (*zamīndār*) or any other military entrepreneur active in the region at issue. Some of these young men returned to their villages when the agricultural season began, while others became professional soldiers for a few years or even their entire lives. Any prince (emperors included) needed to hire people from this 'military labour market'.[77] For if he did not, jobless soldiers might enter the service of a rival, apart from the robberies and other disturbances they were likely to commit.

Ottomanists have encountered a comparable phenomenon not in the centrally managed army, which consisted of the sultan's servitors and the *timar*-holding cavalry in the provinces, but among the mercenaries (*levent*) that from the late 1500s onward augmented the armies in wartime and hired themselves out to local grandees when the sultans no longer needed them.[78] As for the peasant warriors (*yaya, müsellem*) of the 1400s and early 1500s their situation was different, as they had received landholdings to cultivate, recorded in the official tax registers: They paid few taxes but served in the army. However, in the late 1500s, the government abolished these units, perhaps because they were difficult to categorize as either servitors of the sultan or else as peasant taxpayers. *Yaya* and *müsellem* were thus not part of a 'military labour market' offering their services to the highest bidder. On the other hand, the men who followed the 'marcher lords' (*uç beğleri*) cooperating in the conquest of the Balkans while only loosely subordinate to the sultan, may well have resembled their Indian counterparts. Unfortunately, we know very little about their recruitment.

If Gommans's observations are correct, the Mughals throughout their reign used the marches at the edge of their empire as sources of military recruitment. By contrast, the Ottomans mostly rejected this option at an early stage. Instead, they tried to transform the marches into centrally governed provinces as soon as possible. Even when recruiting soldiers, they thus built a polity whose base was in the agrarian heartlands.[79] Exceptionally, in the Anatolian border provinces close to Iran, long-established princes supplied manpower mostly for local backup, while the borderland of Bosnia with its largely islamized population provided military men to defend the even more exposed provinces of Hungary.

The local magnates (*ayan*, or if Christian, *kocabaşı*) that from the later 1600s onward, controlled significant sections of the Ottoman Empire as lifetime tax farmers and employers of mercenaries, at first glance resembled the *zamīndārs* of India, but once again, the similarity was superficial. For, differently from many *zamīndārs*, Ottoman magnates in many cases did not have any familial or clan ties with the people from whom they collected taxes. Thus, the soldiers they recruited were not necessarily local men. Moreover, while the Mughal government recognized the legitimacy of the *zamīndārs* despite trying to curtail their power, the Ottoman central authorities of the years around 1600 tended to assume that *ayans* and *kocabaşıs* had illegitimately inserted themselves between the ruler and his 'poor subjects' (*reaya fukarası*). The authorities regarded this situation as highly problematic, though perhaps unavoidable. To counterbalance the power of these magnate interlopers, the sultans continued to view the peasants as their own tenants, choosing to ignore their de facto dependence on the *ayan*.[80]

Later on, in the eighteenth century, certain local power-holders might develop a cooperative – and indeed – symbiotic relationship with the Ottoman central government. While in Mosul for instance, these local elites controlled a large share of the resources available in town and countryside, the governor, a central appointee who might establish close ties to these elites, increased his administrative powers as well. As part of this compromise, local power-holders financed the food supply of the army contingents that Mosul contributed to the sultan's campaigns. In addition, they procured funds for the recruitment of troops.[81]

From a military perspective, the *ayan* thus were an important source of recruitment and war finance. While the monarchs could not directly force the *ayan* to appear at the muster, failure to supply the numbers of men demanded often resulted in the deposition and execution of the delinquent magnate. Brought together from distant places for a single campaign, these provincial units served together with the regular contingents of soldiers, who qualified as the ruler's servitors.

Admittedly, the Ottoman army fighting the Russo-Ottoman war of 1768–74 had very little in common with the standing army of the 1500s. For in the late sixteenth century, Ottoman commanders required large numbers of infantry soldiers, not only for campaigns, but in addition, to garrison the larger cities as well. Sultans and viziers increased the number of janissaries, gunners and other military men, who remained on the payroll even after the wars with the Habsburgs and Safavids had come to a provisional end. During those years, numerous currency devaluations decreased the pay of the soldiers, who thus needed to supplement it by crafts or trade (compare with Chapter 7).[82] As a result, the number of semi-militarized urbanites with some political force increased, limiting the power of the sultans. On the other hand, the urban militias stiffened by mercenaries of divergent origins found it more and more difficult to win victories, especially against their Russian opponents, whose soldiers served for many years and regarded military drill as a – doubtless unfortunate – routine.[83]

In the Indian context, emperors and other power-holders might find that victory on the battlefield eluded them because their opponents had offered money to the commanders of certain units who might then abandon the battlefield. The most notorious case involved the British winning the battle of Plassey (1757), 'with its foundation of spies, lies and betrayal', but the tactic had been in use for centuries.[84] After all, as noted, commanders at every level needed to recruit soldiers from the military labour market, and if the mercenaries thus hired assumed that the personage for whom they were fighting was likely to lose, they might negotiate a change of sides.[85] If, by contrast, the emperor was in a strong position, a rebellious prince or *jagīrdār*, who had found refuge in one of the many fortresses dotting the Indian countryside, might watch his army melt away without being able to halt the process. Tribal contingents too might abandon the commander they had promised to serve if the latter did not meet their expectations.

At the same time, the Mughals especially during Aurangzeb's campaigns in the Deccan were unable to muster sufficient forces against the Marathas, who, although Shivaji had lost his kingdom on the western coast of the Peninsula and died in 1680, organized marauding expeditions deep into Mughal territory. In the Ottoman case, the fall of an *ayan* usually meant that the sultan took back the territory he had governed – at least temporarily. By contrast, Mughal victories against the Marathas very often did not result in the imperial government's assumption of full control over the lands once ruled by the defeated opponents. Lower-level power-holders often remained in place and the emperor needed to placate them. While the conquest of a territory thus meant different things in the two empires at issue, Ottoman and Mughal commanders might experience certain comparable problems too; for in both cases, mercenaries might ravage the areas they supposedly protected.[86] For Ottoman taxpayers of the years after 1600, the presence of looting mercenaries must have often been a novel problem; for as far as we know, discipline among the *timar* and janissary armies of Sultan Süleyman's time had been strict, and complaints about soldiers robbing the taxpayers were not very frequent.

Military technology

While both the Ottoman and the Mughal armies used guns and gunpowder, the manner of use differed significantly. In the early modern period, the Ottoman armies rapidly focused on firepower, adopting not only cannons and gunpowder, but in addition, the tactics permitting commanders to make optimum use of the firepower newly acquired. Thus, the use, in field battles, of an arrangement of carts chained together and defended by soldiers armed with pikes and handguns had been a successful innovation of the fifteenth-century Hussite resistance against royal power in Bohemia. By 1444, the Ottomans had encountered this technique apparently in its Hungarian avatar, as they used the term *tabor*, derived from the Hungarian term for the arrangement, alternatively known as *Wagenburg*.[87] In the early 1600s, moreover, during the Long War against the Habsburgs (1593–1606), the janissaries employed volley fire, put differently, several lines of musket bearers relaying one another so that the unit as a whole continued to fire although every single line had to step back and reload. European army commanders knew this technique as well, although it only came into effective use by the 1620s. Thus, it is quite possible that the Ottoman armies had pioneered this technique; and as Günhan Börekçi reminds us, the absence of evidence on this score does not mean that Ottoman priority is an impossibility.[88]

In India, soldiers from the Ottoman world, known as Rumi had a reputation as expert gunners, and were thus much in demand. When Seydi Ali Reis, stranded in India in the mid-sixteenth century, decided to return to Istanbul overland, he must have taken into account that he had only a few men left. Presumably, in the competitive environment of Western India, the missing soldiers had found rulers offering them good pay. As for the Mughal context, gunpowder weaponry certainly was part of the formidable arsenal, which served Akbar to win an empire. Even so, the central force was – and remained – cavalry armed with swords and lances, and among Mughal rulers, only Akbar showed a sustained interest in the technology of gunpowder weapons.[89] In the seventeenth century, Mughal artillerymen were often foreigners, Europeans appearing most often in the sources. Rumi soldiers must have served the Mughals as well but, to our frustration, we know very little about them.

Royal courts and capital cities as centres of power

From the second half of the fifteenth century onward – and thus by 1526 – Istanbul was the recognized seat of the Ottoman sultanate.[90] At that time, the sultans had recently conquered Egypt and Syria (1516–17), and thus they had come to rule over the core lands of the Islamic world. Even so, the sultans treated the newly acquired provinces as prestigious possessions, rather than as centres from which they intended to govern. Remarkably, no reigning sultan ever performed the pilgrimage to Mecca, although viziers and royal women might do so – after the conquest of 1516–17 no Ottoman sultan ever visited the Arab provinces.

Whatever the importance of controlling Cairo, Mecca, and Istanbul, for an Ottoman monarch of the 1500s holding his palace and capital was less crucial than controlling his household, with its thousands of attached infantry and cavalry troops.[91] Even so, by 1566, the newly enthroned Selim II (r. 1566–74) had trouble accepting this fact of life. After the death of Sultan Süleyman under the walls of Szigetvar, the new monarch showed little inclination for an autumnal trip to Hungary to meet his father's funerary procession and assert his presence as the new sultan, in front of the army and the many dignitaries who had accompanied Süleyman on his last campaign. Apparently, Selim II considered it sufficient that he had sat on the throne in Istanbul and received declarations of loyalty and submission from those few dignitaries present in Istanbul at that time. Encouraging Selim II to set out nonetheless, the grand vizier Sokollu Mehmed Paşa (d. 1579) explained in a letter that, only by being physically present could the new ruler take over the household he had just inherited. In the end, Selim II accepted this argument and met his returning army halfway.[92]

In the Mughal case, it was even more valid to claim that the centre was wherever the emperor had established his household. During the reigns of Bābur and Humāyūn, the newly emerging empire had no fixed capital city (see Chapter 5). Even after the founding, first of Fatehpur Sikri in the later 1500s, and then of Shāhjahānabād a few decades afterward, many emperors did not spend much time in their official residences. Thus, Akbar was an assiduous campaigner, and so was Aurangzeb. Both emperors led their armies in person, and particularly Aurangzeb travelled from Afghanistan to the southern Deccan, with the dignitaries and commanders, who were part of the imperial household of necessity following their sovereign. In the end, Aurangzeb died far away from Delhi, in the peninsular city of Ahmadnagar. By contrast, the emperors who ruled the contracting Mughal Empire after 1707 normally resided in Delhi and, just like the contemporary Ottoman monarchs of the time, did not often lead or even accompany their armies.

Thus, the Mughal Empire in its stage of florescence conformed to the pattern known from the post-Seljuk principalities of later medieval Anatolia, ruled from wherever the prince and his army happened to be. However, after the death of Aurangzeb, holding Delhi was a crucial marker of imperial sovereignty, and apart from the booty, Nādir Shāh (1688–1747) doubtless occupied and plundered the city for just that reason. As for the Ottomans, while never repudiating the assumption that the sultan and his household were the centre of the empire, over time they tended to place more emphasis on the symbolic role of Istanbul and the Topkapı Palace as a source of imperial legitimacy. In practical terms, by contrast, the monarch's household as a power base declined in the 1600s and 1700s, as the attendant military men became a reason for perpetual worry: In the period discussed, seven out of fifteen Ottoman sultans lost their thrones due to rebellions on the part of the soldiers stationed in Istanbul.

Deciphering the meaning of the term 'conquest'

Both the Ottoman and the Mughal empires were products of conquest. In the Ottoman case, the model of conquest and incorporation created by Halil İnalcık is still valid, at least in part: If the sultan had defeated a given prince, the latter often received an appointment to govern his former territory under the over-lordship of the Ottoman sultan.[93] In the next generation, however, the son of the defeated prince did not inherit his father's principality. Rather, the monarch would send him to govern a province often remote from his father's former lands. Thereby, the young man's membership in an ex-princely family was largely irrelevant, and the territory at issue became a new Ottoman province.

Admittedly, this model is valid in some places but not in others, as only certain ex-principalities mutated into provinces. Thus, although the Tatar khan of Crimea had become an Ottoman vassal in the fifteenth century, his domains never turned into a 'regular' part of the empire, although admittedly, in the early 1700s the khans had less room for manoeuvre with respect to the sultan than their fifteenth-century predecessors had enjoyed. In a similar vein, the principalities of Moldavia and Wallachia remained subordinate domains and never became ordinary provinces. Certainly, the governors sent by the eighteenth-century Istanbul administration, Orthodox aristocrats residing in the Istanbul area of Fener/Phanar, and thereby known as Phanariots, could not act as semi-independent princes. Thus, they sharply differed from their sixteenth-century predecessors, members of the Wallachian and Moldavian aristocracies, who often had revolted in alliance with outside potentates. Despite their increased dependence on the Ottoman centre, however, the sheer fact that the governors of these territories were always Orthodox Christians shows that the sultans never made the two principalities into ordinary provinces, for only Muslims could serve as *beylerbey*s.

A fortiori, the Ottoman sultans never made the Hijaz, controlled by a dynasty known as the Sharifs and claiming descent from the Prophet Muhammad, into a province of the empire.[94] Frequently, the nearest governor general officiated on the opposite shore of the Red Sea. In the late 1500s, furthermore, the sultan used the person responsible for collecting revenues from the port of Jeddah as his principal representative in the area, although the latter, known simply as *emin* or official-in-charge, did not rank as a governor general.[95] While the central government could depose a ruling Sharif, until the end of the empire in 1922–3 the sultan always appointed another member of the dynasty as his successor. This situation allowed certain Sharifs a considerable amount of political leeway, including occasional defiance of the sultan's orders.

Once a sultan of the 1400s and 1500s had decreed the institution of a province (*beylerbeylik*) divided into sub-provinces (*sancak*) and districts (*kaza*), he normally ordered the compilation of a tax register (*tahrir, tapu tahrir*). Even so, from the late 1500s onward, such registers came to be rare because the revenues demanded from the subjects were no longer the result of administrative calculations, but rather of competitive bidding by tax farmers. Exceptionally, in the 1600s and early 1700s, new *tahrirs* introduced Ottoman officialdom to recently conquered provinces such as Crete (1645–69), Podolia (1672) and the Peloponnesus retaken from the Venetians in 1715.[96] In the 1400s and 1500s, arable lands and pastures in a newly instituted province became the property of the sultan (*miri*), the cultivators being tenants who enjoyed security of tenure as long as they worked the land and paid their taxes. However, with respect to the island of Crete, newly conquered in the mid-1600s, the administration decided to regard the cultivators as the owners of the land they worked.[97] The reason for this change is unclear; perhaps the sultan authorized it because not all religious scholars accepted the category of *miri* land as legitimate.

If the pre-Ottoman rulers had been Muslims, such as the Karaman dynasty in Central Anatolia whose territory Mehmed the Conqueror annexed in 1471, it was customary to record at least the most important pious foundations established under the ex-rulers in the *tahrir* and thereby accord them legitimacy.[98] Only in the first half of the nineteenth century did Mahmud II (r. 1808–39) claim that certain pre-Ottoman foundations were illegitimate, thereby abrogating the privileges accorded by a long series of his predecessors.[99]

Even in provinces formerly ruled by Muslim princes, the Ottoman sultans might order the transferral of people considered a potential danger to places where they had no prior attachment (*sürgün*). Sometimes the monarch aimed at settling loyal subjects, Muslim or non-Muslim, in a newly conquered province. *Sürgün* families were unable to leave their assigned places, although they did not become slaves. It is unclear when and under which circumstances administrators and neighbours became willing to forget this disability, and the *sürgün* turned into ordinary subjects. Over time, this latter outcome was apparently normal. By contrast, in Mughal India we do not often encounter the wholesale transfer of populations that the Ottoman sultans – and the Safavid shahs as well – used as a means of consolidating their rule.

In territories formerly ruled by Christian princes, the Ottoman sultans did not have much commitment to precedents; and at least in some places, the peasants benefited, for instance from the abolition of serfdom.[100] However, early advantages might soon evaporate if the sultan increased taxes to pay for further campaigns.[101] When Byzantine control over South Eastern Europe disintegrated, some monasteries, especially those on the Athos Mountain, negotiated the conditions of their submission and despite official suspicions, documented around 1600, that the monks might have helped Christian pirates and corsairs, the Ottoman authorities never occupied the mountain.[102]

As for the preservation and repair of Christian churches, everything depended on local circumstances; in some places and at some times, such projects do not seem to have encountered much opposition.[103] In other instances, the opposite was true. The head tax collected from non-Muslims (*cizye*) being a major source of revenue, the Ottoman authorities had no interest in forcing people to convert, conversions happening on the initiative of individuals, families, and villages or town quarters. There was only one exception to this rule: As noted, the boys drafted through the *devşirme* could not avoid conversion.

Jewish youngsters were exempt from the *devşirme* as Ottoman officials wanted rural boys, and the Jews were town-dwelling artisans and traders. Mostly, Jewish authors of the early modern period were very favourable to the sultans' rule.[104] For even though anti-Semitism certainly occurred among Ottoman subjects too, being a member of a protected non-Muslim religion was a status greatly superior to the degradation, eviction and occasional pogroms that Jews suffered throughout early modern Europe. Paradoxically, the Alevis of today, Muslims whom the authorities of the time called Kızılbaş, were the only religious community for whose members the Ottoman conquest meant acute danger, at least in certain places and at certain times. For the sultans' officials regarded them as non-Sunni heretics, and in addition, as adherents of the shah of Iran, one of the main adversaries of the sultans (see Chapter 4).[105]

The Mughal Empire was a product of conquest as well. Tapan Raychaudhuri has pointed out that the nobility was ever eager for new acquisitions: Even when Shāh Jahān was willing to recognize the sultanates of Bijapur and Golconda as tributaries, his nobles pushed for conquest and in the end, had their way.[106] While Raychaudhuri emphasizes the role of simple greed, imperial office-holders also had to worry about keeping their soldiers supplied. After all, the latter only received minimal pay and, when on campaign, hoped for booty – even if this hope did not always materialize. In the Ottoman world at least, similar concerns explain why the soldiers might pressure the sultan to go to war.[107]

In practical terms, the Mughal conquest had a meaning that differed strongly from the implications of its Ottoman counterpart: Local aristocracies that the sultan could or would not uproot certainly existed in the cities of the Arab provinces, or even in the Lebanese Mountain, but they were weak or even non-existent in the Balkans and Central Europe.[108] By contrast, in Indian conquests – and the Mughals did not expand much beyond Kabul or Bengal – *zamīndār*s of one kind or another were always present. Moreover, the emperors never insisted on the ownership of all fields and pastures, so that the conquest did not mean a complete revamping of the system of land tenure; the emperors simply wished to collect as much revenue as possible. Typically, the kings and nobles of defeated kingdoms, which, as the rise of Shivaji in Bijapur indicated, had often turned into 'hollow shells' long before Aurangzeb's annexation, demanded 'compensation' for their brand-new loyalty in the form of *jagīr*s. Sometimes, the demand of the defeated dignitaries was so insistent that shortly after a conquest, it was, paradoxically, hard to find sufficient resources for new *jagīr*s.[109]

There is large body of studies on the decline of *jagīr*s in the later seventeenth and early eighteenth centuries, impossible to summarize in a few sentences: for example, Satish Chandra has suggested that the entrenchment of lower-level power-holders (*zamīndārs*), on whose cooperation the central government often relied, undermined the loyalty of many *jagīrdārs* to the emperor. At the same time, this policy alienated the more prosperous peasants as well, who now no longer looked to the emperor as a protector from exploitative power-holders.[110] This development prepared the dissolution of the empire into principalities, often ruled by dissident former governors and *jagīrdārs*.

As the Mughal Empire derived its revenue mostly from the enormously productive agriculture of Northern India, the *jizya* was not a major resource for the Mughal treasury: After all, Akbar abolished it without causing any major upheaval in imperial finances. As Harbans Mukhia has stressed, Mughal rulers – apart from Akbar – defined their empire as a Muslim polity, and especially Aurangzeb wished to rule according to the precepts of the sharia.[111] Even so, the emperors did not enforce any mass conversions, and there was no equivalent to the Ottoman custom of converting *devşirme* boys by administrative fiat. If in the Mughal world, people received an order to convert, it was quite often a form of punishment, an alternative to execution – and Akbar had doubts on the sincerity of enforced conversions.[112] In the Ottoman context, not the central government but local people and administrators might force an individual to convert: Perhaps a young non-Muslim had inadvertently used a formula indicating adhesion to Islam, or else made disparaging remarks about the dominant religion. In such cases, conversion might be an alternative to execution as well, although such events were probably rare.[113]

Given the numerous wars of conquest throughout the period under discussion, enslavement was a common phenomenon in the Mughal Empire. As for the Ottoman armies, when they advanced in non-Muslim territory, they sometimes carried off huge numbers of slaves. As the fifteenth-century chronicler Aşıkpaşazade (*c.* 1400–*c.* 1485) recorded, individual soldiers not only sold their captives, thus turning them into slaves, but also might receive slaves from the sultan in recognition of their services.[114] Once Ottoman rule was in place, by contrast, the sultans' subjects were not in danger of enslavement by the established authorities, unless, as non-Muslims, they had rebelled. However, illegal enslavement was another matter (see Chapter 9).

Collecting revenue

From the perspective of the Ottoman and Mughal elites, the subject population existed for the sole purpose of providing the taxes and services demanded by the ruler. To conceptualize the resulting political system, Marshall Hodgson has suggested the term of 'military patronage state', by which he meant a political organization that placed the resources of the subjects, and indeed their lives, entirely at the disposal of the military elite and the monarchs emerging from within the latter.[115] Next to the sharia, these potentates invoked specific dynastic laws with greater or lesser intensity.

Originally referring to flocks, the term *raiyyet/reaya* in the Ottoman world and *ra'īyatī* among the Mughals indicates that – in the eyes of the elites – the taxpaying population resembled animals, raised for their wool, milk and labour power. Interestingly, in the Ottoman world of the 1700s this term, originally in use for subjects of whatever religion, came to denote the non-Muslims exclusively. Perhaps the increasing emphasis on the Islamic character of the Ottoman Empire and the informal acquisition of political rights by Muslim town dwellers through their affiliation with the military or paramilitary corps had something to do with this change of terminology; it is impossible to be sure. For the Muslims, the Ottoman bureaucracy of the time began using the term 'İslam'.

In the late 1400s, and throughout the sixteenth century, many of the taxes payable by Ottoman villagers and townsmen were on record in the *tahrirs*; and these documents retained a considerable normative force even under the changed conditions of the eighteenth century. The tithes demanded from crops were a principal revenue source, collected in money only if, for instance, fruits or vegetables were likely to spoil (compare with Chapter 8). Silver being in short supply, Ottoman peasants might complain if required to pay in coin; and in a cash-poor economy, marketing the *timar*-holder's grain was not always an easy task either. Cash was *de rigueur* for market dues and the payments demanded for the possession of a farmstead. Many of these dues never reached the central treasury, as the government had assigned them to *sipahis*, local officials and administrators of pious foundations (*vakıf*), who consumed them on the spot.

As for the central treasury in Istanbul, it collected the tributes of subordinate polities such as the princes of Moldavia and Wallachia and the city government of Dubrovnik. In addition, after 1526 the central treasury received payments that the Habsburg emperors owed the sultan for their possession of a small strip of Hungary. The 'kings of Vienna', as Ottoman officials called them, only stopped remitting this tribute in the seventeenth century.[116] Until the Ottoman conquest of Cyprus in 1570–3, Venice paid tribute for its possession of the island. Furthermore, the governors of Egypt and Yemen – as long as the latter country was part of the empire – made annual payments (*irsaliye*) to Istanbul, as the sultan had never instituted any *timars* in these provinces. Given the proverbial productivity of Egypt, it was a major setback for Ottoman finances when, from the late 1600s onward, the Mamluks, who had appropriated the local tax-collecting mechanisms, reduced the *irsaliye* and stopped regular contributions to the financing of the annual haj caravan.[117] Moreover, the central provinces contained numerous revenue sources designated as *has*, many of which accrued to the treasury unless the sultan appropriated them for his own use. As noted, the *cizye* was a major source of income as well, as a sizeable part of the rural Balkan population remained Christian even though the towns, limited in number and size, mostly had Muslim populations. As there were few converts to Islam in Hungary, this province, in Ottoman hands between the mid-1500s and 1699, produced a significant amount of *cizye* as well.

By contrast, in India, where the export of cotton cloth and pepper brought in substantial amounts of bullion, tax collection was normally in cash, although sharecropping occurred as well (see Chapter 8). In the later sixteenth century, the Mughal authorities collected taxes based on information gathered by special agents recording crop yields, market prices and cultivated lands.[118] Taxes differed according to the crop planted, with villagers possessing some resources focusing on the more lucrative commercial crops. Probably, these Mughal documents contained more accurate information than their Ottoman counterparts did, if only because Akbar's aide Tōdar Mal (d. 1589) insisted on uniform weights and measurements. By contrast, Ottoman *tahrirs* contained only vague information on the extent of cultivated land, and the prices on record for agricultural products, used in the assignment of *timar*s, by the late 1500s were far lower than market prices. Probably given widespread tax farming, officials had little interest in updating this information (see Chapter 8).[119] As noted, in the Mughal orbit, holders of *jagīr*s might farm out the taxes they received to so-called *ijāradār*s, although the emperors frequently expressed reservations against tax farming.[120]

To collect and distribute revenues, both the Ottoman and Mughal empires developed sophisticated financial organizations. In the Ottoman case, the survival of a very large proportion of the archives from the mid-sixteenth century onward permits the reconstruction of the history of the financial bureaucracy. Evidence is very scanty for the time preceding the 1450s, when Mehmed the Conqueror began to move his administration to Istanbul. However, a surviving register fragment from the 1430s shows that at that time already, an organization was in place whose servitors could traverse a recently conquered province and record individual households.[121] Before the mid-1500s, the office of the *defterdar*, responsible for these surveys and referred to in a law-book attributed to Mehmed the Conqueror, was probably quite small. Around the mid-sixteenth century, however, a specialized financial bureaucracy emerged, becoming increasingly elaborate over time. The sultans often appointed provincial *defterdar*s, who were to approve the expenditures of the governors and thus limit the power of the latter.[122] Over time, especially in the eighteenth century, the number of offices concerned with administering particular sources of revenue grew steadily. Thus, the registers produced by the central accounting office or *Başmuhasebe*, first founded in the early 1600s grew steadily in scope and importance: The relevant officials checked the accounts of the numerous and varied offices spending the sultan's money.[123]

Thus, the gradual 'phasing out' of the *timar*, and its replacement at first by short-term, and after 1695 by lifetime tax farms (*malikâne*), did not lead to a contraction of the financial bureaucracy, for the central government was anxious to maintain control over its tax farmers. Therefore, the sultan's officials closely supervised the bidding for tax farms, and the relevant records are a major source for the Ottomanist historian. Moreover, the person acquiring a *malikâne* needed to pay a large sum of money before he could start managing his new acquisition. These revenues went into the central treasury, and so did the annual payments due from such a tax farm.[124]

Intriguingly, in the 1700s, a time-honoured practice occasioned a novel layer of bureaucracy. Ottoman officialdom had always assumed that the commands of a sultan were no longer valid once the latter had lost his throne, by death or by deposition. At least in the mid-1500s, the Mughals seemingly had had a similar arrangement. For Seydi Ali Re'is, who had visited Humāyūn in Delhi and finally received the monarch's permission to embark on the long journey home, recorded that when Humāyūn died before the Ottoman admiral had actually set out, officials told him that the deceased emperor's permission was now no longer valid.[125] However, it is unclear whether the death of Humāyūn had rendered his permission invalid, or whether the decisive factor was the new emperor's command forbidding travel to Kabul and Qandahar. The Ottoman visitor was to wait until Akbar gave him a new permit, which Seydi Ali Re'is received only after a period of waiting.

We do not know whether the Ottoman sea captain had witnessed a routine or else an exceptional practice. In the Ottoman world, however, the commands of a dead

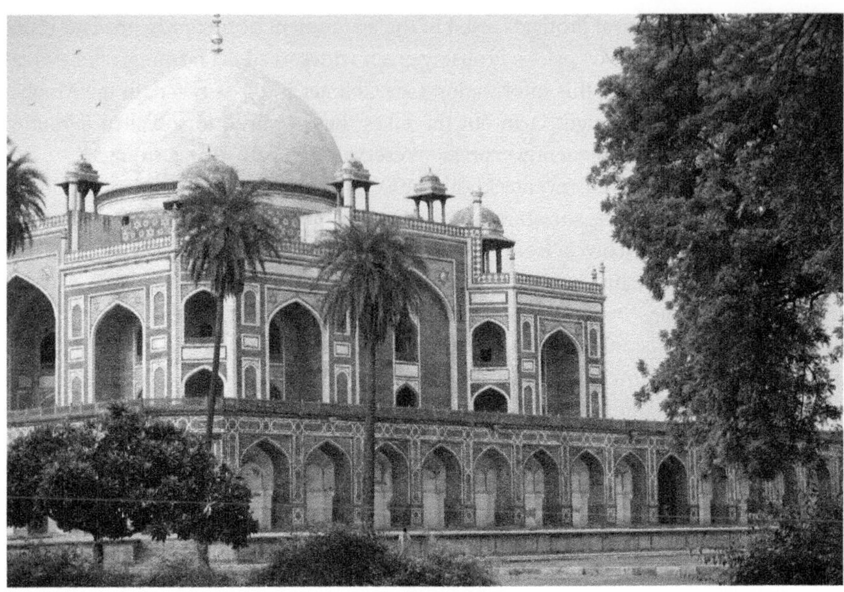

Figure 6 The mausoleum of Humāyūn in Delhi: an assertion of power and piety. Akbar and Humāyūn's widow Hamīda Bānū Begam had this structure built after Humāyūn's death in 1556. The enormous tomb garden is not far from the grave of Nizām al-Dīn Awliyā, much venerated to the present day.

sultan always needed confirmation by his successor. Thus, people holding large and small privileges had to present their documents in Istanbul soon after the new sultan had ascended the throne. If lucky, they received an official confirmation. In the 1700s, officials of the central administration began to systematize this practice, compiling enormous registers of all the documents confirmed after a given sultan had begun his reign. Probably, this enterprise was part of the bureaucratic mechanism by which the Ottoman authorities attempted to keep track of what happened in the provinces, even if local notables/magnates had taken charge of everyday administration. While not all these confirmations dealt with financial affairs, a large percentage did record exemptions from certain taxes or at least their reductions, thus benefiting individuals, families or villages. Keeping track of privileges accorded by previous sultans was thus, at least in part the responsibility of the financial bureaucracy.

In the last few years, Turkish archivists have catalogued enormous numbers of previously unknown financial records. Thus, Ottomanist scholars can now discern how the financial administration followed up on individual projects, from repairs to remote border fortresses to festivities in Istanbul and Edirne, celebrating the circumcisions of the sultans' sons. It is still too early to say to what extent these newly accessible records will change the findings of the 'classical' studies of Ottoman finance administration, mostly published in the 1980s and 1990s.

While the Mughal emperors maintained enormous cash reserves – Akbar's treasury at his death in 1605 supposedly contained 522.4 million florins – the nobles of the empire accumulated money as well, usually millions of rupees. The holdings of deceased noblemen went to the treasury; in that sense, the situation of these dignitaries resembled that of the sultan's *kul*. Even so, Aurangzeb warned his officials that they should only collect whatever was due to the state. While this injunction probably implied that many zealous servitors of the emperor confiscated whatever they could find, it is still notable that the monarch did not assume that everything owned by his nobles was his by right.[126] Usually, the emperor decided whatever portion of the inheritance he wanted to return to the family of the deceased; this arrangement resembled Ottoman practice, where the heirs of a dead dignitary normally received a portion of the estate as well. A royal monopoly might become a source of additional revenue: In 1631, the emperor Shāh Jahān reserved the trade in indigo for his own person, which he then leased out to tax farmers. Admittedly, this attempt at monopoly did not last for very long.[127]

In addition to legal exactions, there were many illegal levies. Not only European merchants, whose prejudices make their testimonies questionable, but Indian traders too complained about the rapacity of local governors, likely to use physical abuse in order to extract revenue. The seventeenth-century jewel merchant Banarasidas recorded that when Akbar died (1605), everybody in Jaunpur hid his wealth because the future seemed so insecure, and he told stories of traders fleeing from certain dignitaries infamous because of their exactions (compare with Chapter 6).[128] Quite often, provincial governors demanded loans from merchants that they never returned, or else lent money at usurious terms to unwilling borrowers. Collectors often used legal taxes such as road tolls as occasions for extortion; apparently, the problem became so intractable that Aurangzeb at one point abolished these dues altogether, although it is hard to say to what extent local power-holders obeyed his command.[129] In his old age, this same monarch wrote that he regretted not having provided protection to his subjects, and the numerous illegal extortions, of which he was well aware, doubtless were heavy on his mind.[130] However, Aurangzeb's unending wars in the Deccan and his notorious lack of success in ending the Maratha raids had nullified a significant advantage enjoyed by taxpayers under his predecessors, namely short campaigns with manageable costs and relative peace in the central provinces.[131]

Despite these drawbacks, the high rate of profit usually gained from luxury trades allowed certain merchants to survive and even prosper; and if Aurangzeb really hoped that the extra dues, which he demanded from Hindus, would make them incapable of continuing in business and thereby induce conversion, he was unable to realize his ambition.[132] Whether the emperor really had such hopes is, however, questionable; for the source for this story is Niccolao Manucci, a purveyor of bazaar gossip and thus not a very reliable witness.[133]

Revenue collection, without thought for the consequences? The 'circle of justice' and the meaning of *wajabi*

As the previous discussion has shown, both in the Ottoman and the Mughal worlds, the administrators of imperial finances needed to square the circle, namely collect as much revenue as possible while allowing at least some of the 'poor subjects' enough reserves to maintain and occasionally even expand their businesses. In the Ottoman world, during the stressful campaigns especially of the later 1700s, this consideration often fell by the wayside.[134] However, in times of relative peace, certain trades and traders managed to prosper. Thus, following a trail opened by Halil İnalcik, we can construct a parallel to the argument made by Tapan Raychaudhuri: In times of peace, or at least when campaigns were short, Ottoman as well as Mughal rulers needed wholesale merchants with ample capital as purveyors of goods. Whenever convenient, both monarchs took the concerns of such traders into account.[135]

On a more general level, members of the Ottoman elites often reiterated their commitment to the 'circle of justice', a concept derived from Mesopotamian and later on, Iranian thinking about royal rule. Stripped to the essentials, this reasoning stated that royal power depended on the military, and there could be no army without the necessary financing. Finances could only come from the taxpaying subjects, who could only deliver if prosperous enough to do so – or perhaps more realistically, if not so impoverished that they fled. At the same time, prosperity depended on the justice of the ruler, so that the circle began and ended with him. Appearing frequently in Ottoman political thinking, this notion with all its ramifications has recently become the subject of a full and instructive monograph by Linda Darling.[136]

Princes learned from their preceptors that it was both their duty and their self-interest to protect their subjects from excessive exploitation. Moreover, once on the throne, princes soon discovered that the most likely exploiters were their own governors and the military men who served the latter. At least in the second half of the sixteenth century, when Ottoman sultanic commands become numerous, we frequently find the monarchs advising their governors to use moderation, threatening them with dire penalties if they exploited the sultan's subjects to the point that the latter fled in desperation. After all, given the availability of sparsely settled borderlands, flight was a 'way out' open to peasants in both the Ottoman and the Mughal empires.[137] Sultan Murad III (r. 1574–95) at one time even forbade local administrators (*ehl-i örf*) to send their armed men into Anatolian villages, where these mercenaries were likely to collect taxes by force and mayhem. He later went back on this concession, probably because tax collection without some type of threat proved very difficult.[138] However, even the failed attempt to remove the tax-collecting soldiers from Anatolian villages shows that the sultan realized that the *ehl-i örf* were highly oppressive, and his legitimacy depended on supporting the peasants against them. This chain of events certainly reminds the reader of Aurangzeb's regretful admission that he had failed to protect his subjects.

Analogous concerns dominated relations between rulers and ruled in Akbar's empire; this monarch constructed a discourse on legitimacy that posited him as the paterfamilias of his household, which he equated with the empire.[139] In the eighteenth-century Indian principality of Jodhpur, whose Rajput (Rathor) chiefs became independent kings once Mughal power in the region had receded, we encounter a different but related discourse encouraging the ruler to moderate his demands. While most of the relevant documents date to the later 1700s, it makes little sense to disregard them for that reason alone. After all, the time lag is minor, the surviving archive large, and we have the great advantage of referring to the pioneering analysis by Nandita Prasad Sahai.[140] This author has emphasized that, while armed force and oppression characterized the relationship between rulers and ruled, other concerns entered the equation too. For paradoxically, the rigidities of the caste system as lived in this region gave the members of lower castes some bargaining power: If for example, the flayers of dead animals deserted a given locality, the resident members of higher castes would have to make do without leather goods.

Moreover, in this region perpetually threatened by drought, migration was often unavoidable, so that it was not a very difficult decision for the oppressed members of lower castes to try their fortune elsewhere. The situation thus resembled that prevailing in Anatolia around 1600, where the peasants were surprisingly mobile as well.

Therefore, the Rathor kings of Jodhpur had reason to moderate their demands; and at least in the world of political theory, the rules of '*wajabi* or appropriateness' operated in a manner resembling the limitations that an Ottoman ruler needed to take into account. If sultans, kings and emperors wanted to collect taxes, they had to provide their respective subjects with possibilities to make a living; and this concern was behind the generous sponsorship of luxury goods, buildings and other works of art. Even Aurangzeb, who otherwise spent his revenues mainly on military campaigns, once arranged for a lavish court festival at least partly to give merchants a chance to sell the costly textiles, in which they had invested but for which they had not found any customers because of persistent warfare.[141]

Conclusion

Both the Ottoman sultans and the Mughal emperors defined themselves as ruling by conquest, and once established in conquered territory, they had to stabilize their rule. In terms of personnel, monarchs and elites adhered to the notion that the new regime could and should find reliable supporters outside of locally established aristocracies. From the mid-1400s onward, the Ottomans were quite successful in assimilating and/or removing the latter, typically placing the sultans' own men in positions of power.

Until the late sixteenth century, the sultans' men came from a group of people living within the empire but of humble non-elite backgrounds. These 'inside outsiders' were former Christian peasants converted to Islam and given a military upbringing, especially the top levels defining themselves as the sultan's loyal slaves (*kul*) and making this self-image into a major part of their identity. Incidentally, the ethos of faithful service remained strong even when in the 1600s high office-holders often were the descendants of other dignitaries and thus not 'outsiders' in any meaningful way. When Mehmed IV. (r. 1648–87) sent a messenger to Belgrade, with orders to execute his grand vizier Kara Mustafa Paşa after the latter's failure before Vienna (1683), members of the vizier's household volunteered to defend him, but the dignitary himself refused the offer.[142]

As for the Mughals, they made no systematic attempts to remove military men of Indian background from the levers of power. On the contrary, especially Akbar integrated Hindu Rajput warriors into his system of rule and into the army, and even the convinced Muslim Aurangzeb had a Hindu Kachhwaha prince command several of his campaigns. For many of the highest positions, however, the Mughal emperors favoured outsiders arriving from Iran and Central Asia, who sometimes formed separate factions and allowed the ruler to balance one against the other. Remarkably, the Mughal emperors avoided the precedent set by the Deccan sultanates, namely the purchase of African military slaves (*mamluks*) as the ultimate outsiders: We do not know the reasons for this decision. Furthermore, soldiers were available in the 'military labour market' that was a special feature of the Indian ambience. While this system of checks and balances was mostly efficient, there was no equivalent to the loyalty ethos of the *kul*, which many members of the Ottoman military-administrative establishment showed toward the ruling dynasty, even when their own lives were at stake.

Given their role as conquerors, Ottoman sultans and Mughal emperors demanded unconditional obedience. Even so, military power was not enough, and discourses concerning the 'circle of justice' and the need for – even minimal – compliance with the demands of appropriateness/*wajabi* show that Ottoman and Indian monarchs needed to justify their rule toward an array of different constituencies. The latter included elite and non-elite persons; and Muslims were certainly the preferred audience for any discourse concerning the monarch's legitimacy. However, at least in the Indian case, non-Muslim addressees were important as well. Furthermore, holding a vast empire together made it necessary to adopt one or several languages emblematic of rule, and to regulate access to this language on the part of the monarch's subjects. Therefore, legitimacy and language will occupy us in the following chapter.

4

Legitimizing Monarchic Rule Amid Religious and Linguistic Diversity

While empires, including the Ottoman and Mughal varieties, were the products of conquest, military might did not suffice for the endurance of rule. On the contrary, justifying the government of a given potentate in 'merely political' terms, or more importantly, in a discourse derived from religion, was a condition sine qua non for the success of the monarchy at issue. Proceeding from the actions of the elites to the interface between rulers and ruled, which will occupy us in the following chapters, we now discuss worldly advantage and religious beliefs in the legitimization strategies favoured by the Ottoman and Mughal monarchs. By this formulation, I do not mean to say that rulers and officials cynically used religion to bolster their own status. In most cases, they probably believed in the righteousness of their claims. Even so, for a present-day historian, living in a realm of 'post truth', it is impossible to be sure when and where conviction took second place to political advantage. After all, we cannot see into the hearts of the living, and *a fortiori*, we cannot claim to know those of the dead.

In early modern societies, including the Ottoman and Mughal varieties few people separated the 'religious' from the 'political' realms. Moreover, both in non-religious and in religious legitimization strategies, several motifs and strands of opinion came together. The present discussion begins with down-to-earth concerns, such as the expectation that a given ruler will ensure at least minimal security on the roads. We then proceed to the question of whether, in the seventeenth and eighteenth centuries, the legitimization discourse current in the Ottoman realm foregrounded motifs that differed from those in favour during the 1400s and 1500s. If legitimacy devices changed little and the basic motifs of this discourse remained similar, are we justified in assuming that the Ottoman polity remained substantially the same over several centuries? Or else, may similar legitimization strategies be compatible with different regimes? In both the Ottoman and the Mughal worlds, the notion that a just ruler must protect his subjects from injustice is important, so that there is a marked resemblance between the two legitimizing discourses – however, a similar emphasis on justice prevailed in medieval and early modern France as well.[1] In the Indian world of the 1500s and early 1600s, the emphasis on political harmony was perhaps stronger than it was in the Ottoman orbit.

Turning from concrete 'performance' to more general issues, we discuss the prestige of the two dynasties as descendants of famous rulers, and focus on the conditions under which a monarch was accessible to members of the elite and the population in general. We then turn to the role of presumed 'inherent sanctity or holiness', which Muslim and Hindu rulers, and Christians as well, occasionally invoked. The work of Azfar Moin has shown the centrality of such beliefs for the Mughal dynasty in the sixteenth and early seventeenth centuries.[2]

It bears remembering that, as Jeroen Duindam has shown, many dynasties have claimed supernatural sanction, although monotheistic religions typically oblige rulers to be prudent when positioning themselves with respect to the Deity and the heavenly court.[3] If certain rulers – and the authors serving them – decide to go further in highlighting their links with the supernatural, they may claim that the empire in question closely precedes the end of time, usually without specifying when exactly they expect the Last Judgement. Eschatological claims enjoy special favour among the adherents of heterodox versions of Islam, although under especially difficult circumstances, people who define themselves as right-thinking Sunnites may express an interest as well. By contrast, emphasizing the protection of the pilgrimage to Mecca is a discourse commanding the adherence of all Muslims, and both the Ottoman sultans and the Mughal emperors have used it to strengthen their respective versions of legitimacy.

On a different level, we need to figure out how non-Muslims fitted into the legitimizing ideologies of the Ottoman and Mughal elites. This issue is of special importance in South Asia, where the majority population always remained non-Muslim. However, even in the Ottoman Empire, where from 1517 onward, the population was mostly Muslim, and legitimizing discourses largely addressed this constituency, Christians and Jews remained sizeable minorities whose allegiance the sultans needed to retain (see Chapter 3).

Apart from inclusion – or else exclusion – based on religion, the legitimacy of the Ottoman and Mughal dynasties required the acculturation of at least a few members of 'their' subject populations, prior to employing these people in their respective governmental structures. Accordingly, we discuss the arrangements by which at least samplings of the linguistically diverse populations subject to the two monarchies became part of the military and/or the bureaucracy. In this context, language plays a central, integrative role: Persian in Agra and Delhi, and Ottoman Turkish in Istanbul. In the concluding section, we focus on the social consequences of these more or less successful incorporations.

Political advantages as legitimizing factors

We begin with a mode of interpretation which is deliberately anachronistic. For as noted, focusing on 'naked' political advantage divorced from religious and ceremonial considerations was probably a way of thinking foreign to most inhabitants of early modern empires. However, even if denizens of the Ottoman and Mughal realms saw things differently, as historians of the twenty-first century we may include considerations derived from present-day experience of empires both past and present. To begin with the Ottoman world: For several centuries, the sultans succeeded in legitimizing their rule rather well, even among their Christian subjects in the Balkans and Hungary. Had the opposite been true, and given the proximity of Spanish-controlled Southern Italy and the Austrian Habsburgs a few kilometres from Ottoman Budin (today: Budapest), there should have been many anti-Ottoman rebellions in the Western Balkans and Hungary. Such revolts did not often occur, partly due to the dissuasive effect of Catholic princes in South Eastern Europe forcing their Orthodox subjects into conversion to Catholicism.

Another factor strengthening the legitimacy of the sultans was the possibility for outsiders, sometimes of very modest backgrounds, to enter the governing elite and thus climb the ladder of socio-political status. In the Ottoman world, social mobility was often easier to achieve than in the rigidly stratified societies of early modern Europe, where socio-political ascent, in the best of cases, took several generations.[4] A few people must have migrated to Ottoman territories with such considerations in mind. More frequently, men who had arrived in the Ottoman Empire as captives opted for the acceptance of Islam and a 'career open to talent'.[5] Especially in the formative period of the Ottoman Empire until the mid-fifteenth century, a lower level of taxation and the absence of serfdom further helped to make Ottoman rule acceptable to the Christian peasantries.[6] Thus, the first major anti-Ottoman uprising in the Balkans only occurred in the late 1600s, when a sizeable section of the Serbian population sided with the Habsburg emperor, whose invading armies had taken Belgrade and for a short time even Nish.[7] Under the leadership of their spiritual head, many of these Habsburg partisans withdrew with the regular imperial armies and about 1700, settled on the territory of the emperor as peasant-soldiers. However, this event was quite exceptional. Even in the late 1800s, a century after the end of our analysis, Bulgarian anti-Ottoman rebels were often unable to mobilize the local peasantry: The consequence was rapid defeat.[8]

In the Indian context as well, villagers, traders and merchants of different religions must have seen advantages in accepting Mughal power. Firstly, as noted (see Chapter 3), the Mughal conquest often left established landholders (*zamīndārs*) in place, and even noble supporters of the previous regimes easily transferred their allegiances from the sultans of Ahmadnagar, Bijapur, Golconda or Bengal to the Mughal emperor. Evidently, the Sunni–Shiite divide, a major constituent of official identity in Safavid Iran and the Ottoman Empire, was not as potent in India. People with strong loyalties to their clan and caste leaders may thus often have felt that little had changed, and they could live with whatever changes had occurred. Moreover, in areas where no military operations were in progress, the Mughal emperors enforced a degree of security on the major trade routes. Admittedly, Francisco Pelsaert, who in the 1620s travelled in northern India, as a merchant working for the Dutch Vereenigde Oostindische Compagnie (VOC), claimed that Jahāngīr was a 'King of the plains or the open roads' because his writ did not run beyond the major cities and caravan routes.[9] In isolated and forested territories, the empire's forces were normally absent. However, the panic that the jewel merchant Banarasidas (1586–1643, see Chapter 6) described as having occurred in his hometown of Jaunpur after Akbar's death in 1605, indicates that a strong central power was a precondition for the welfare of traders. Otherwise, they could expect the aggressions of local power-holders eager to grab their property. Thus, the legitimacy of the Mughal emperors rested in part on the security they provided, from 'ordinary' robbers and from money-grabbing officials as well.

Similar to the Ottoman situation, subjects of the Mughal emperors from modest backgrounds could enjoy successful careers, at least if they were lucky. Certainly, studies in the 'collective biography' of Mughal dignitaries have shown that possessing fathers and grandfathers once prominent in imperial service was a definite career advantage. Mughal nobles thus vaunted the quality of being a *khānazād*, which meant that really, or putatively, they had enjoyed education in the imperial palace.[10] However, this situation did not exclude talented individuals, especially from careers in the military, where, as noted (see Chapter 3) immigrant soldiers of fortune might arrive with their retinues and gain acceptance in the imperial armies. The existence of a 'military labour market' facilitated the rise of men with organizational talents as well, as these people could enter the service of the prince offering the most advantageous conditions. Moreover, differently from Ottoman custom of the fifteenth to seventeenth centuries, there was no hard-to-cross boundary between 'servitors of the ruler' (*askeri*) and ordinary subjects (*reaya*). This factor must have boosted mobility even further, although at the highest level, there was a 'ceiling' unknown in the service of the sultans in Istanbul, namely the accession to the nobility, often difficult as the candidate needed to hold a tax assignment of impressive proportions, in addition to high official rank.[11]

Despite this limitation, the wealth of northern India and the high tax revenues of the Mughal emperor attracted many would-be members of the elite from Central Asia and Iran. By contrast, in the Ottoman world, apart from a trickle of Sunni Iranian migrants only the North African provinces recruited significant numbers of men from outside the empire's borders.

'Stability', 'socio-political change', or else 'decline'? Debating Ottoman rule and society

Subjects of the Ottoman sultans, or those of the Mughal emperors, could enjoy political advantages of any kind only if an established system of rule functioned with some efficiency. The latter might remain stable over a lengthy period or else change, often quite rapidly. In the 1950s and 1960s, many Ottomanist historians thought that sultans and viziers in the second half of the fifteenth century developed a system of government, which *mutatis mutandis* remained unchanged until the nineteenth century. Only from the 1820s onward, at a time transcending the limits of the present study, Mahmud II (r. 1808–39) and his successors profoundly overhauled state structures, adopting a policy that we can call 'modernization to save the state'.

Historians of the period following World War II believed that before the crisis of the late 1700s and early 1800s, which occasioned the intervention of Mahmud II, Ottoman society did not change very much either. In the 1960s and early 1970s, Halil İnalcık described this society as 'traditional'.[12] In the thinking of İnalcık, who dominated the Ottomanist world during several decades of his long and productive life, the persistence of traditional Ottoman society – and the methods of governing it – were flexible concepts, which allowed him to include the 'decline' of the empire after a century and a half of florescence. By the later 1590s, the 'classical age', as envisaged by İnalcık, had already run its course.[13]

In later work, İnalcık elaborated on the factors that in his opinion had made the political system of the 'classical age' unviable, especially an urgent need to transform military organization. For as hand-held firearms became widespread, attacks by cavalry soldiers financed through tax assignments (*timar*-holders, *sipahi*s, see Chapter 3) were less decisive than they had been during the 1400s.[14] However, once the overhaul of the army was complete, Ottoman government and society needed to cope with 'footloose' mercenaries, out of a job when either the sultan's army, or the high-level official who had hired them, had no further need of their services. Apart from the robberies that these men often committed, they required payment in cash; and backed up with the firearms acquired when on active service their demands were an extra burden on the peasantry. Despite this crisis, by the mid-1990s İnalcık apparently envisaged Ottoman society as stable, although the proliferation of firearms, and the need for cash to pay mercenaries, remained significant factors in the crisis of empire that in his earlier publications he had regarded as symptoms of 'decline'. By the end of the twentieth century, however, the latter motif seemingly disappeared from his thinking.[15]

References to 'Ottoman decline' had been widespread long before the history of the empire became an academic discipline, as they already occurred in the writings of Ottoman authors working about 1600 and in the books of European contemporaries as well.[16] As primary sources for the 'decline paradigm' that became a prominent element in their conception of Ottoman history, Ottomanist scholars normally used literary works belonging to the so-called advice literature that proliferated in the years before and after 1600. These texts have attracted close study ever since Bernard Lewis had dubbed them 'Ottoman observers of Ottoman decline'.[17]

As a policy to counteract 'decline' as they perceived it, the seventeenth-century authors of 'advice literature' often recommended a return to the practices of Sultan Süleyman and his predecessors, advocating the employment of military men supported by tax grants (*timar, zeâmet*) as opposed to mercenaries (*levent*). Furthermore, these authors criticized the tendency of the sultans of the post-Süleymanic age to not lead their armies in person, to say nothing of the vituperation that some of them heaped on palace women exercising a degree of political power.[18]

While up to the 1980s these judgements were part of standard Ottomanist historiography, around 1980 a number of scholars began to express their doubts. While Ottomanists mostly (but not always) conduct their debates in a low key, this non-confrontational style should not disguise significant differences of views and evaluations. In particular, Rifa'at A. Abou-El-Haj has pointed out that we cannot regard the authors of the 'advice literature' as reliable witnesses always doing their best to tell the truth. Rather, the texts that they produced served the vicious and often deadly infighting among courtly factions trying to gain the sultan's ear. At times, one of the competitors advocated the adoption of a given policy and denigrated its alternatives. Perhaps more frequently, an author tried to secure employment, for his own person and for members of his faction, often a difficult proposition.[19] Among Ottomanists, 'historicizing the advice literature' thus has limited its credibility, and from the late

1980s onward many, though by no means all, scholars tend to speak of a 'transformation' of Ottoman rule rather than of its 'decline'.

In this perspective, the next step was to assume that around 1600, the entire Ottoman political system changed character. Central rule weakened, while groups that had not shown much independent political initiative in earlier times now took on a more prominent role. In the provinces, tax collection provided occasions for patronage. Enriched by the fees and gratuities offered by clients, collectors of taxes and dues might become notables and later on, even magnates.[20] In the capital, decentralization meant that the servitors of the sultan could rebel, enforcing the execution of viziers and the resignation of sultans – less frequently, the deposed monarchs might lose their lives as well. The loyalty of the *kul*, much vaunted and highlighted (see Chapter 3), concerned the dynasty as a whole, rather than any individual sultan.

Analysing these changes, Baki Tezcan has concluded that we should posit the early seventeenth-century emergence of a new and different system of Ottoman rule.[21] Firstly, the role of the sultan changed: Between the early 1600s and the re-establishment of absolutist rule by Mahmud II, the Ottoman sultan certainly remained a key figure, without whose presence the empire would likely have collapsed. Some sultans participated in the governing of their empire. However, even if they did not do so or intervened but intermittently, the business of government continued, handled by a coterie of palace figures and viziers, including the powerful Köprülü household, in office most of the time between 1656 and 1702.

Secondly, as noted, the soldiers stationed in the capital, by this time closely connected to Istanbul's Muslim merchants and artisans, enforced changes of personnel, often with the support of discontented religious scholars. Tezcan has concluded that the widening of the circle of decision makers was significant enough to warrant the term 'proto-democratic'.[22] It is too early to say whether this latter term will become part of current historiographical discourse. Jane Hathaway has suggested the term 'participatory', which in my opinion fits the situation better.[23]

Moreover, a periodization assuming a hundred and fifty years of 'florescence' (*c.* 1450 to *c.* 1600) followed by more than three centuries of 'decline' (*c.* 1600–1923) is an unsatisfactory solution. We may decide to end the period of 'decline' with the administrative reshuffling of the Tanzimat (1839–76), which is a dubious proposition given the foreign interventions and territorial losses that occurred during the later nineteenth century. Furthermore, the disproportion, in terms of duration, between 'florescence' and 'decline' is far too large, even with that modification. The present author thus assumes that a first system change took place when Mehmed the Conqueror (r. 1451–81) established a regime in which slave-like officials (*kul*) served the monarch in many important offices. A second regime change occurred in the beginning of the seventeenth century, and the reassertion of absolute power by Mahmud II in the 1820s may feature as a third epochal change.

However, Rhoads Murphey, the author of an important book on Ottoman court ritual and sultanic legitimacy, has proposed what seems to be a very different interpretation of this set of observations. At first glance, the reader may gain the impression that Murphey has reverted to the older view of an Ottoman socio-political system that remained constant between the late 1400s and the Tanzimat.[24] At the same time, however, Murphey makes allowance for the conquest of the Arab provinces in 1516–17, which significantly changed dynastic traditions.[25] Moreover, he agrees that the seventeenth-century regulation of the sultanic succession by seniority was a corollary of the demise of the monarchs' military role, who no longer commanded their armies in person.[26] In Murphey's perspective, this set of changes is not evidence of decline. He makes a further strong point when stressing that the disruption caused by the mid-sixteenth-century struggle of Süleyman's sons for the throne probably had posed a more serious threat to the survival of the empire, than the limited political competence of several palace-bound sultans was to do in the 1600s. Thus, Murphey's interpretation seems to differ more in nuances than in principle from the idea that the seventeenth-century Ottoman Empire went through a comprehensive regime change.

Even so, Murphey assumes that the means of expressing sovereignty and thereby legitimizing the Ottoman sultan remained constant throughout the centuries, all the way to the Tanzimat.[27] The sultan became a legitimate ruler by means of the conquests that he made, and in later years the campaigns that he ordered and in which he sometimes participated. Admittedly, by the end of the period treated here, this source of legitimacy had vanished.

Other legitimizing features included the protection that the monarch provided and his visibility in public venues as well. In Murphey's perspective, the withdrawal of Abdűlhamid II (r. 1876–1909) into the isolation of Yıldız Palace, so that people only saw him during his brief visits to the neighbouring mosque, indicated the profound mutation of sultanic legitimacy in the second half of the nineteenth century.[28] Murphey has thus stressed public visibility and accessibility, as a precondition for a style of rule that Ottoman subjects seemingly regarded as benevolent. In this perspective, the withdrawal of rulers such as Murad III (r. 1574–95) into the harem should have undermined the sultan's legitimacy. For an absent sultan could not protect his subjects, as a proper paterfamilias should do. Mustafa 'Âlî (1541–1600), a scholar and courtier with a very poor opinion of Murad's political and personal capacities, accused the sultan of a deficient sense of responsibility.[29] Perhaps the sultan's withdrawal into the depths of his palace contributed to this loss of prestige.

Victory in war, protection of the taxpayers against excessive exploitation by the elite, in addition to regular appearances of the ruler before his subjects were thus important in Ottoman legitimacy discourses. These issues were central to Mughal imperial legitimacy as well.[30] Barring error on the part of the present author, Mughal historians of the twentieth and twenty-first centuries seem to regard stability and/or mutation of the political system as less important problems than their Ottomanist colleagues tend to do. The reason is quite trivial: After all, the Mughal Empire dissolved in the course of the eighteenth century, after having existed for slightly over 200 years. By contrast, the Ottoman sultans remained on the throne for over six centuries and, despite a dramatic loss of power during the 1800s, managed to avoid the division of their realm among the colonialist powers.

Given this state of affairs, Ottomanist historians want to know what types of adjustment the sultans and governing elites undertook, knowingly or sometimes unconsciously, which permitted the empire to survive until the end of the Great War. As noted, there is widespread agreement that the restoration of sultanic absolutism from the 1820s onward was in fact a regime change, while a different version of absolute rule had prevailed in the late fifteenth and throughout the sixteenth centuries, when the sultans were at the apogee of their power. Whatever one may think of the current debates, clearly the position of the Ottoman sultan, in his official discourse and in his practices as well, has turned into a significant subject for reflection.

'Harmony' and 'protection of the subjects' as legitimizing discourses

In the Mughal context as in the Ottoman world, early modern arguments promoting imperial legitimacy emphasized the role of the monarch as a protector of his subjects. Especially in the Mughal realm, the emperor appeared as a paterfamilias enjoying legitimacy because everywhere in the Mughal realm, the family was under the – hopefully benevolent – rule of the father, to whom his wives, concubines and sons obediently submitted.[31] Abū'l-fazl 'Allāmī (1551–1602) especially felt that his patron and hero Akbar had achieved a high level of familial harmony in the vast empire that he had conquered. In this perspective, the notion of 'universal peace', put differently tolerance of all religions and belief systems, which the author promoted with the emperor's encouragement, removed the legitimacy of the latter's rule from religiously imposed limits, including the sharia.[32]

'Universal peace', however, had no validity when it came to the imperial succession. Open succession to the throne meant that princes might go to battle, most memorably the sons of Shāh Jahān during the illness of their father in the 1650s. The sons of a long-lived ruler sometimes staked their claim to the throne even during the lifetime of their father. As Akbar survived into his sixties, a long life by the standards of the time, he had to contend with the rebellion of his eldest son Salīm, the later emperor Jahāngīr, who seemingly feared Abū'l-fazl's influence enough to have him murdered. However, as Harbans Mukhia has expressed it, Mughal courtiers avoided mentioning divisions within the imperial family as long as they could – and sometimes beyond that limit.[33]

In the Ottoman world, rulers and their ideologues were less inclined to claim 'universal harmony', least of all when the succession was at issue. Ottoman authors freely admitted that according to the rule established by Mehmed the Conqueror, the prince who defeated his brothers in the struggle for the throne killed the latter for the sake of maintaining 'world order' (*nizam-ı alem*). Throughout the sixteenth century, the rule of an Ottoman monarch thus began with bloodshed within the family, of major proportions as the young sons of defeated princes might lose their lives as well. Seemingly, public protest against this procedure only erupted when the victims were both very numerous and very young, as happened when Mehmed III (r. 1595–1603) ascended the throne. As Mustafa 'Âli put it, Murad III had once again shown his irresponsibility by fathering many sons destined for an early death.[34]

Ottoman princes who rebelled usually targeted their brothers and half-brothers, rather than their fathers. In the Mughal world, by contrast, Akbar and Aurangzeb both had to contend with rebellious sons wanting to replace them, to say nothing of Shāh Jahān, who after his deposition by Aurangzeb ended his life as his son's prisoner. Therefore, the rebellion of Prince Selim, later Selim I (r. 1512–20), who did dethrone his father Bayezid II (r. 1481–1512) was a special case. On the one hand, Selim had violated the respect that any Ottoman subject, whether elite or commoner owed to his/her father. On the other hand, his victory over Shah Ismāʿīl (1514) and his conquest of the Mamluk Empire (1516–17) made him into a heroic figure at least to people close to the dynasty.[35] In the mid-1600s, almost one and a half centuries after the event, Evliya Çelebi (1611–after 1683) was conscious of this ambiguity, recounting an urban legend according to which Sultan Bayezid, being a saint, had forgiven his son, foreseeing that the latter would rule for (merely) eight years.[36]

The prestige of the dynasty in the Ottoman and Mughal worlds

By the sixteenth century, the Ottoman dynasty already could look back upon a history of over two centuries, having outlasted the Anatolian Seljuks, the Ilkhans, and the Aq Qoyunlu. Thus, the longevity of the dynasty was a legitimizing factor all by itself. In the palace milieu, by the mid-1500s it had become popular to commission illustrated volumes featuring portraits of all the sultans, beginning with Osman I (r. *c.* 1299–1324) and Orhan (r. 1324–62). In later periods such commissions of dynastic 'collective portraits' (*silsilename*) expanded to include all rulers down to the time of composition.[37] Most of the older sultans had never been the subject of portraits and therefore, the images depicting them were products of the imagination.[38] However, there survive portraits of Mehmed the Conqueror, Süleyman and certain other rulers from the late 1500s onward, painted during their lifetimes, so that for instance, we can still recognize the characteristic features of Mehmed III.[39] Most illustrated books including the *silsilenames* remained in the palace library and thus were inaccessible to outsiders; but inmates of the palace including young pages, training for future careers as military men and administrators, could see some of these manuscripts as part of their education.[40] As images probably made a profound impression on people raised in a largely non-iconic environment, viewing these portraits probably contributed to the reverence for the dynasty that was an enduring characteristic of the Ottoman elite.

Propagandists of the Mughal emperors emphasized that their rulers' conquests were legitimate, because these monarchs were merely repossessing territories once occupied by their ancestor Timur, during his brief and bloody raid of the Delhi sultanate (1398–99). Admittedly, Bābur, once arrived in India, seemingly abandoned Timur as a legitimizing role model.[41] In the context of the late twentieth century, moreover, the economic historian Tapan Raychaudhuri (1926–2014) remained unconvinced by ideological justifications of any kind, stressing ordinary raw greed as a motivation of conquering rulers and their soldiers.[42] In the Ottomanist context, it is uncommon to ascribe such 'low' motives to any sultan. After all, while the Mughals do not play a major role in the present-day legitimization of either India or Pakistan, the Ottoman rulers and their conquests have a significant share in the legitimization of the Turkish state to its citizens.[43] Mehmed the Conqueror especially has become a heroic symbol, giving his name to bridges and universities, and even to intra muros Istanbul as a whole, now officially called Fatih. Moreover, in recent years the veneration of Selim I has become part of official and semi-official discourse as well.

Given local memories, Bābur's downplaying of the Timurid connection, once he had arrived in India makes very good sense.[44] In the later 1500s by contrast, Timur's massacres had presumably receded into the past and in palace circles at least, celebrating Timurid ancestry was no longer controversial. After all, certain Ottomans concurred; when Mustafa 'Âlî referred to Timur's destruction of the first Ottoman Empire, founded by Bayezid Yıldırım (r. 1389–1402) he noted that Timur was a 'lord of the conjunction' and thus, predestined to rule.[45] Princes opposing him therefore had only themselves to blame if Timur destroyed their polities and decimated their subjects.

The monarch's presence, visible or invisible

Although Rhoads Murphey has regarded the sultan's visibility as an integral part of his legitimacy, it bears remembering that from the reign of Sultan Süleyman onward, the Ottoman ruler mostly resided in the Topkapı Palace harem, inaccessible to outsiders.[46] When the monarch appeared, reverent silence being *de rigueur*, communication was possible only for the very few courtiers and officials that the ruler wished to receive. Certainly, these customs changed in the 1700s, when the sultan spent time in seaside venues where he could not only view but was accessible to viewers as well. Moreover, just after the period treated here, Abdűlhamid I (r. 1774–89) and Selim III (r. 1789–1807) sometimes visited the markets of Istanbul in disguise. While we know about these forays from the writings of the two sultans, surely contemporary denizens of Istanbul were aware of the royal presence too.[47]

Making the ruler visible was more significant in the Mughal case, for according to Indian tradition and especially in Akbar's time, both grandees and subjects expected to catch a glimpse of the emperor in the morning. For this viewing ceremony, the outer walls of fortified Mughal palaces typically featured decorated balconies (*darokha*), at considerable height so as not to compromise security. Furthermore, Mughal palaces contained two courtyards, one for large and another for small gatherings. Regularly, grandees of the empire needed to attend meetings presided over by the emperor, known as durbar, and leaving them without permission was a challenge to the ruler's authority. Thus, when the defeated Shivaji appearing at Aurangzeb's palace (1666), felt that the monarch had slighted him in front of the entire court, he left the assembly – according to some sources after a fainting fit.[48] If the latter account is true, Shivaji may have feigned sickness in order to avoid burning his bridges, making known his defiance by leaving the durbar but keeping open the possibility of reconciliation. Attending the monarch in his palace, taking one's place in the court hierarchy and viewing the imperial presence all signified that the attendee accepted the paramount position of the Mughal emperor.

'Inherent holiness' as a legitimizing device in the Ottoman world

In the present survey, we can only present a greatly simplified discussion of the religious roles ascribed to Ottoman sultans and Mughal emperors. Differently from their Safavid rivals, Ottoman rulers never claimed descent from the Prophet Muhammad, preferring to emphasize their practical services to the cause of Islam. However, courtiers or former courtiers might claim that the Deity had singled out the Ottoman house for special grace. Thus, Mustafa 'Âli claimed that by heavenly favour, the sultans' palace never suffered from plague although this disease was common enough in Istanbul. Furthermore, no member of the dynasty had ever become a heretic, a remark probably meaning that no prince had ever shown Shiite leanings.[49]

It is hard to say which sultans, apart from Bayezid II (1481–1512), Selim I (r. 1512–20), Süleyman (r. 1520–66) in his younger years, and Murad III (r. 1574–95), enjoyed special religious status in the eyes of – at least – some of their subjects. As the religious role of Selim I, and the dreams of Murad III, have but recently become subjects of study, perhaps other Ottoman monarchs tried to project a similar image, enterprises which still escape the notice of historians.[50] Whatever claims certain sultans may have made, it is worth remembering that in the 1400s and early 1500s, the Ottoman court had allowed special signs of mourning at the funerals of deceased sultans. However, in the later 1500s and the seventeenth century, these customs disappeared and it became the norm to treat the sultan's funeral just like that of any dead Muslim. In the Ottoman context, few sultans posed as millennial sovereigns with numinous qualities, in the Safavid or Mughal sense of the term, and those that did so had limited audiences.[51]

Even so, the Ottoman sultans enjoyed great veneration, documented especially by the silence surrounding their public appearances, when pages and courtiers served their ruler without uttering a word. Foreign ambassadors frequently commented on the large numbers of people who played their part in courtly rituals while mostly communicating in sign language. Obviously, 'behind the scenes' palace folk might act differently, and as a former page to Murad IV (r. 1623–40) Evliya Çelebi did record some of his witty and amusing interchanges with the young monarch.[52]

At the same time, the difficulty of communicating with palace-bound Ottoman sultans must have impeded information flows. At times, the sultan only knew what his courtiers and viziers chose to tell him. Thus, the veneration as an icon of Ottoman rule accorded to the sultans of the 1600s and 1700s compensated for their loss of political power and initiative at least in part. Put differently, the enlarged political base among the soldier-artisans of Istanbul may have increased the sultans' legitimacy; and the latter was effective enough to compensate for climatic disasters, long wars that were not always victorious, and devaluation of the currency pauperizing people with fixed incomes. Sometimes legitimacy crumbled, but never enough to make soldiers, artisans and religious scholars combine to overthrow the dynasty.

Inherent sanctity, moreover, was not a privilege of ruling dynasties. In both the Ottoman and Indian contexts, certain men (and a minute number of women) claimed holiness because of their commitment to mystical Islam (*tasavvuf*, Sufism). In the Ottoman world, people sometimes regarded holy men as beings in harsh competition with one another, and even with current rulers. Thus, their vitas focused on the hostility these types of competition might generate. When, seemingly in the late 1400s, unknown authors put together the core of the vita of Hacı Bektaş, who probably had lived in the second half of the thirteenth century, they included a story about the saint entering Anatolia from Khorasan, using the metaphor of a dove pursued by birds of prey.[53]

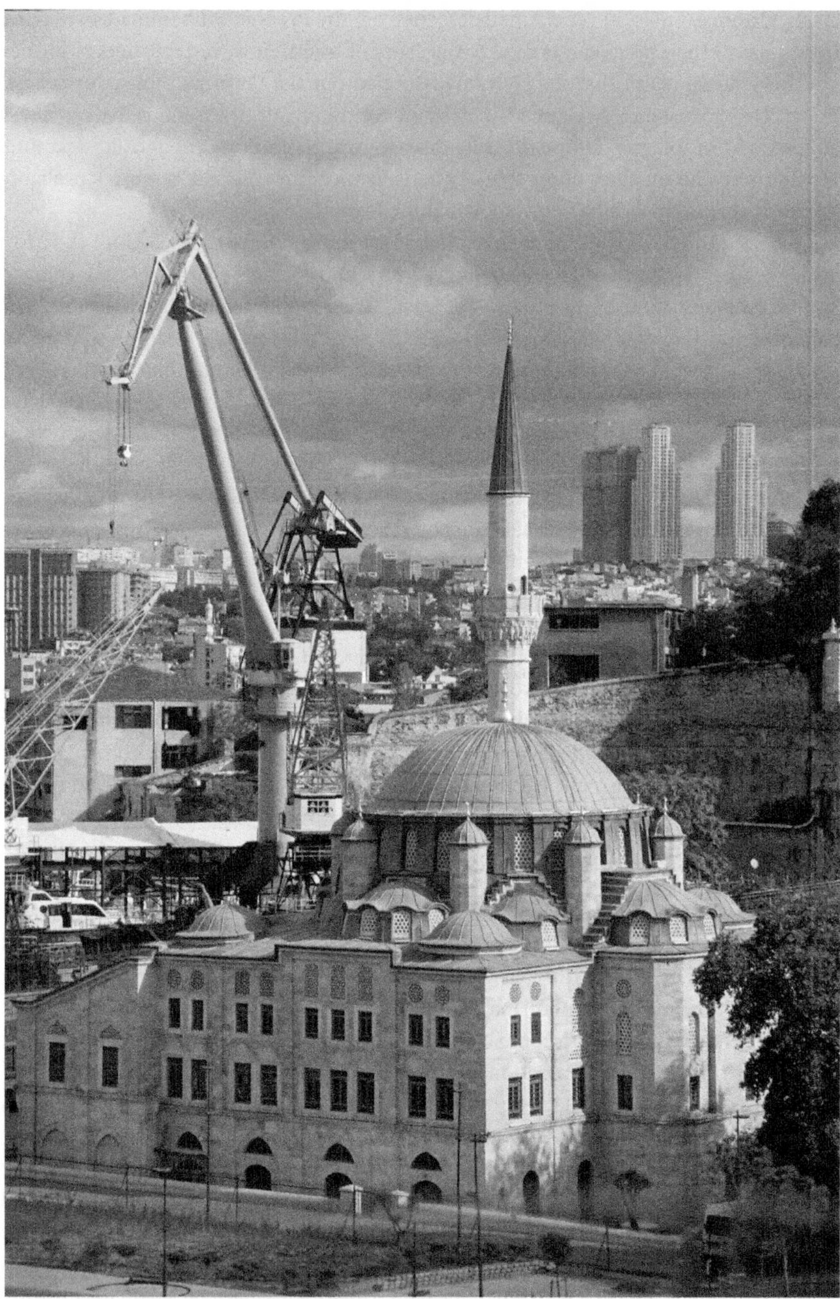

Figure 7 Legitimization by mosque building: the mosque of Sokollu/Sokullu Mehmed Paşa (d. 1579). Located between the wall of Galata/Istanbul and the dockyards of Kasımpaşa, this building is one of the many works of the famous architect Sinan (985/1577–8). (Semavi Eyice, 'Azapkapı Camii', *Diyânet İşleri İslâm Ansiklopedisi*, https://islamansiklopedisi.org.tr/azapkapi-camii, accessed 19 September 2018).

Moreover, in the late fifteenth century, when a dervish known only as Küçük Abdal (the small/younger dervish) wrote the biography of his deceased master Otman Baba, he made the latter claim 'real' supremacy over the Ottoman lands, thereby the saint aspired at least in the spiritual realm, to a position above the sultan.[54] However, by the 1500s, such claims apparently had become inacceptable. While the author(s) of the vita of Demir Baba, probably a contemporary of Sultan Süleyman, claimed that the monarch honoured the saints, as a pious ruler should do, the holy man himself appeared as a faithful servitor of the sultan and in no way as the latter's rival. However, the saint might still claim to be the superior of an Ottoman pasha, serving as the 'real' representative of the deeply religious Sultan Süleyman.[55]

When the sultans' empire was in its early stages, holy men of possibly heterodox beliefs and practices had an impact upon the courtly elite, which their successors did not often enjoy in later centuries. However, even in the heyday of their prestige, in the fourteenth and fifteenth centuries, the holy men of Anatolia and Rumelia did not exercise extensive political power: There was thus no parallel to the rise, in the former realm of the Aq Qoyunlu, of the Safavid Sufi Ismāʿīl to kingship as Shah Ismāʿīl I (r. 1501–24).

'Inherent holiness' as a legitimizing device in the Mughal world

Religiously based legitimacy was especially relevant in South Asia, where ever since the late twelfth and early thirteenth centuries Muslim princes, often recent arrivals from Iran and Central Asia, had governed small but growing populations of Muslims, while the majority populations adhered to the cults of Vishnu, Shiva and Durga. When the sultanate of Delhi ruled Northern India, the blessing of the caliphs in Baghdad helped to establish the newcomers as legitimate rulers, and by the early 1200s, many Indian Muslims considered the caliphs numinous figures although the latter lacked political power. Even more remarkably, in South Asia Muslim elites continued to invoke these iconic figures even after the Mongols had killed off the last caliph residing in Baghdad (1258).[56]

In the empire of the Mughals, an important dervish sheikh might greatly impress emperors, princes and courtiers with his spiritual powers and thaumaturgy. Even so, such a personage had less scope for independent action than had been true at the time when, for instance, pre-Mughal Bengal was a frontier territory whose Islamization was only just beginning. There might even be an implied competition between saints and monarchs for legitimate rule, certain authors claiming that kings could only hold power because a given Sufi saint had granted them the right to do so.[57] If – as is likely – such beliefs were widespread in the Ottoman orbit as well, it is easier to understand why Murad III – though an unlikely candidate – tried to establish his claim to sainthood.

As for Bābur (r. 1526–30), the founder of the Mughal Empire, he did not make any claims to saintliness, and freely admitted that he had drunk alcohol before repenting, a few years before his death. By contrast, Bābur's son Humāyūn (r. 1530–40 and 1555–56), invoked the power of a variety of Indian holy men, and more dramatically the planets, even selecting his clothes in an effort to harness the power of these heavenly bodies to his own – rather unstable – rule.[58] Bābur's grandson Akbar at least in later life did claim high religious status in his own right. After all, in 1579 he decreed that, in matters on which Muslim religious scholars had not arrived at a clear decision, henceforth his own word was to be law.[59] The model for his relationship with favoured courtiers was that of a Sufi master with his disciples. This arrangement allotted Akbar a great deal of power and responsibility, for contemporaries accepted that a man teaching the mystical way had absolute authority over his disciples. Thus, the cult known as the *dīn-i ilāhī* was not a religion in the normal sense of the term, but an order whose members pledged their undivided loyalty to the emperor, to whom they promised if necessary, even to sacrifice their honour and abandon their families.[60]

The semi-divine qualities that Akbar attributed to himself were not acceptable to a number of his courtiers, and in his unofficial and oppositional chronicle, al-Badā'ūnī (1540–*c.* 1615) expressed his disapproval of some of Akbar's innovations including the prohibition of cow slaughter.[61] For in so doing, Akbar had arrogated to himself the right to forbid a practice permitted by the consensus of Muslim religious scholars, with the aim of satisfying his Hindu subjects, who considered the killing of cows a major sin. While al-Badā'ūnī lost Akbar's favour for his continued adherence to established Sunni Islam, he does not seem to have suffered any punishment. Other religious scholars received invitations, or rather commands, to perform the pilgrimage to Mecca and not return without official leave to do so.[62] As far as we know, this manner of politely disguising banishment was not in common use at the Ottoman court.

Figure 8 Proximity to the ruler as a legitimizing device: one of the windows of the tomb adjacent to the mausoleum of Humāyūn. The occupants are unkown, but must have been close to the emperor; popularly known as the Tomb of the Barber.

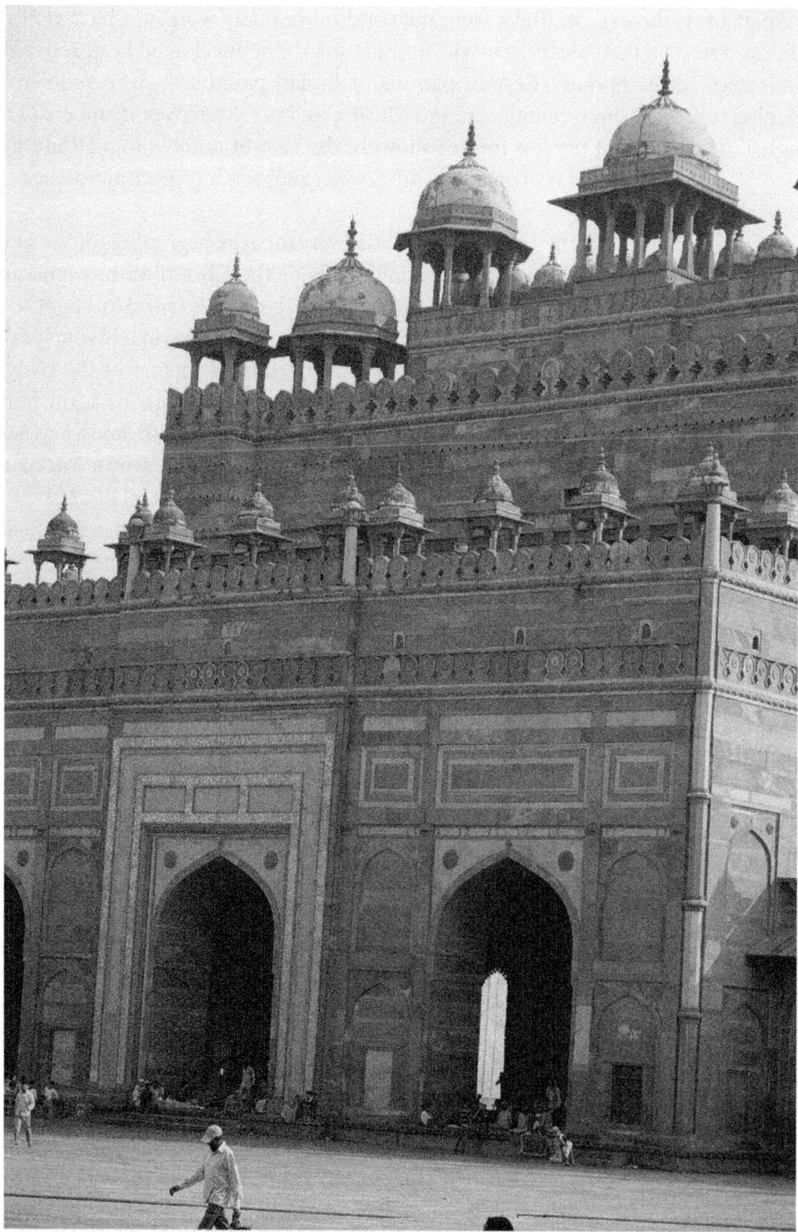

Figure 9 Legitimization through reverence to a holy man: Mosque and tomb complex in Fatehpur Sikri/India. The courtyard of the mosque and tomb complex, by which Akbar honoured the Chishtiyya sheikh Salīm, who had predicted the birth of a son to the monarch, at that time still without an heir. Akbar sent a pregnant queen of his to give birth in the house of the sheikh (1571) and built the palace of Fatehpur Sikri in an adjacent location (Asher and Talbot 2007, pp. 144–9).

Apart from the dynasty, there were men and more rarely women, whose claim to holiness rested on their ascetic lifestyle. In India such 'renouncers' had been active and visible ever since antiquity. Certain patrons of Indian painting had no problem in grouping together Hindu renouncers and Muslim ascetics. Moreover, members of the Mughal dynasty might possess images showing the visit of a noble to a Hindu holy figure, in which the dignitary appeared with few servitors, as a respectful watcher and listener.[63]

Major Sufi hermitages had operated in India ever since the beginnings of the Delhi sultanate and perhaps even earlier. Especially Sufis of the Chishtiyya order became revered saints, whose tombs people visited for the blessings (*baraka*) supposedly emanating from these sites. Some of these places of pilgrimage were in outlying locales, such as the town of Bahraich on the river Saryu, a northern tributary of the Ganges, today close to the Indian border with Nepal.[64] This place became famous as the burial site of a supposed nephew of Sultan Mahmūd of Ghazni (r. 998–1030), known as Salār Mas'ūd/Ghāzī Miyān.[65] It remains unclear whether Ghāzī Miyān, whose nickname indicates that he was a Muslim warrior-for-the-faith, ever existed in real life. His oldest vita bears the date of 1620, written in Persian by 'Abd ul-Raḥmān Chishtī, a Sufi sheikh of the lodge of Rudauli. Ghāzī Miyān may have been a product of the imagination, as contemporary chronicles recording the life of Sultan Mahmūd know nothing of a nephew by that name.[66] Though never considered a saint – rather the opposite – Mahmūd's son Mas'ūd may have inspired the story, merely through his name.[67] Already toward the end of the thirteenth century, the Delhi poet Amīr Khosrav alluded to a gravesite in Bahraich, admittedly without naming the saint. Fifty years later, the traveller Ibn Battūta (1304–68/69 or 1377) visited Ghāzī Miyān's grave together with the current sultan of Delhi, a pilgrimage indicating high official esteem.[68]

We do not know how and why Ghāzī Miyān, who in the hagiography of 'Abd ul-Rahmān Chishtī appears as a staunch Muslim warrior, in locally produced ballads on record since the late 1800s, became a much more ambiguous figure. On the one hand, nineteenth- and twentieth-century ballad singers made him enter Benares/Varanasi, smashing some idols and converting others to the Muslim faith.[69] On the other hand, the bards depicted Ghāzī Miyān as a young hero who left his wedding night incomplete in order to protect the local shepherds and their cows; the saint suffered martyrdom while still wearing his nuptial ornaments.[70] Thus, these men completed the 'Indianization' of the originally Afghan warrior, which had already begun in the story told by 'Abd ul-Rahmān Chishtī. In the nineteenth and twentieth centuries, the grave was a site of pilgrimage for Hindus and Muslims, and to a more limited degree, it attracts visitors of both religions even today.[71]

However, as Shahid Amin insists, it is not sufficient to stress the confluence of Islamic and Hindu beliefs surrounding this figure. At the same time, the stories about Ghāzī Miyān and his supposed grave point to significant conflicts within the population of South Asia, in past centuries and today as well. Thus, the story of Ghāzī Miyān's attacking the Benares temples reflects a profound opposition between the representatives of the two major religions practised in the area. An additional 'split' is due to gender inequality. Women without surviving sons, trapped in a profound misery inflicted by their husbands and families, often visited – and probably in some instances continue to visit – the 'cow protector's' grave, to escape the pauperization and humiliation that threaten women in their situation. It would not make sense to erase these contradictions, to use the Marxian term, for the sake of constructing a 'peaceful' account, although the latter may seem appropriate in a context of current – and increasing – Hindu and Muslim exclusivism.[72]

Eschatology in Mughal and Ottoman legitimizing discourses

In the Ottoman context, the Deity might assign a given monarch a role in His plans for the latter-day history of the world. According to certain Ottoman authors, the Last Judgement was at hand, with the conquest of Constantinople in 1453 and later on, the Islamic millennium of 1000H/1591–92 as fatidic dates.[73] Recently, Erdem Çıpa has shown that petitioners addressing Selim I claimed to have seen this ruler in their dreams, together with the Prophet and major Islamic saints. Apparently, these people considered it appropriate to associate the conquering monarch with these heavenly figures, and to strengthen their case and ensure the success of their petition, they often engaged in 'prognostication after the event'. One such person, obviously an educated man, even validated his account by referring to a book of dream interpretation by a respected author of the Abbasid period.[74]

After 1520, during the early reign of Sultan Süleyman, a soothsayer named Haydar Remmal was active at the Ottoman court. This man persuaded a number of courtiers and perhaps the sultan as well, that Süleyman's conquests were to spread Islam all over the world, thus preparing humankind for the end of time.[75] A religious scholar named Mevlana Isa made similar claims, which fit in with the millenarianism that during the sixteenth century was common to several Eurasian civilizations.[76] However, once Süleyman reached middle age and his sons began to fight for the succession, this discourse receded into the background. While Haydar Remmal remained at court, his predictions now focused on worldly issues.

Sanjay Subrahmanyam has pointed out that the millenarian expectations observed in Western and Central Europe, as well as in the Ottoman Empire and Safavid Iran, appeared in northern India as well. Sayyid Muhammad Jaunpūrī (1443–1505) claimed to be the Mahdī, a figure preceding the Last Judgement, and for a while, he had adherents at the court of the sultan of Gujarat, about 1500 still an independent ruler.[77] While Jaunpūrī's enemies ultimately pushed him out of the royal court, Sunni scholars continued to read his works with appreciation long after his death. Moreover, at one time Akbar sponsored a multi-author chronicle, known as the *Tārīkh-i Alfī*, which in its title referred to the year 1000, a figure with obvious millenarian implications.[78] However, while Azfar Moin regards the reign of Akbar as suffused in millenarian expectations, Subrahmanyam appears to think that these tendencies – while certainly in existence – excited only a limited number of people for a limited amount of time. Thus, for instance, Akbar soon lost interest in the *Tārīkh-i Alfī*. Perhaps quite a few intellectual figures in both the Ottoman and Mughal worlds concurred with Mustafa 'Âlî, who first considered the possibility that the end of the world might be close, and then decided against it.[79]

Sunni Islam and the pilgrimage to Mecca as legitimizing factors

As noted, the Ottoman and Mughal dynasties were both Sunni Muslims and shared in the Iranian and Central Asian traditions of legitimate empire. The Ottoman sultans occasionally called themselves caliphs of the Islamic world, although there seems to be no truth to the story that Selim I had the last scion of the Abbasid dynasty invest him with the caliphal dignity.[80] However, the latter title gained in significance during the years following the end of our study in 1774. For while the Ottomans lost Crimea in that year, the Ottoman–Russian peace treaty conceded that due to his quality as caliph, the sultan would remain the spiritual head of the tsars' new Muslim subjects. In consequence, the caliphal dignity came to play a major role in late Ottoman diplomacy. In India during the colonial period, the Ottoman caliphate even became a Muslim rallying point.[81]

In sixteenth-century India, by contrast, probably very few people believed in the caliphate of the Ottoman sultans. At the same time, Akbar 'came perilously close to declaring himself as Caliph of the eastern Sunni domains'.[82] In the end however, he did not take this step. There was a certain amount of Ottoman–Mughal rivalry in the Hijaz, where Akbar seemingly wished to establish a presence, when he granted several women from the imperial family their ardent wish to undertake the pilgrimage. The lengthy stay of these royal females in Mecca caused concern in Istanbul.[83] Remarkably, while a considerable amount of documentation on the 'women's pilgrimage' is available in Indian sources, Ottoman officialdom had very little to say about the matter, perhaps because in the sultans' perspective, any interference by a foreign prince in the affairs of Mecca and Medina was profoundly unwelcome. Even so, writing about the early 1670s, the notoriously irrepressible Evliya Çelebi recorded the existence of a Qādirī dervish lodge supposedly set up by Akbar, which housed all Indian *fukara*.[84] Apart from dervishes, the author may have intended ordinary poor pilgrims.

As a reason for Ottoman reticence, we need to bear in mind that, in the period under study the sultans focused on their role as protectors of the pilgrimage and 'servitors of the two holy sites' (*hadimü 'l-harameyn*). In this quality, they took responsibility for the security of the pilgrims on their travels through the desert, a proceeding that necessitated substantial gratuities to the Bedouins living close to the pilgrimage routes.[85] For if the latter did not receive the money and/or goods, agreed upon after arduous negotiations, they might attack the pilgrim caravans, as happened several times during the later 1600s and especially the 1700s.[86] In addition, the protection of the pilgrims involved supplying mostly Egyptian grain to the year-round inhabitants of Mecca and Medina. After all, the Hijaz produced little food, and only the timely arrival of this Egyptian supplement filled the markets of the Holy Cities and allowed the pilgrims to feed themselves.

As a counterpart, the sultan received religious legitimization: He had the caravan accompanied by a litter known as the *mahmal*, which was sometimes empty and sometimes contained a Quran.[87] While primarily a political symbol inherited from the Mamluk sultans, for many Muslims this item took on a religious quality as well, showing once again the close connection between religion and politics characteristic of many early modern polities.

Religious legitimacy derived from the protection of the pilgrimage had an ecumenical aspect as well. Put differently, the Ottoman sultans needed to transcend the Sunni–Shiite divide which at least until the late sixteenth century (and sometimes beyond) was a major element of their legitimizing discourse. After all, in the sixteenth century, the Ottoman and Safavid dynasties had resuscitated the ancient division between Sunnis and Shiites as a means of making the difference between their respective regimes more sharply visible. Certain religious scholars on both sides might even say that the opponents were heretics so execrable that their claim to be Muslims was unacceptable.[88] Perhaps, however, this discourse was mostly 'war propaganda'. By contrast, in peacetime the Ottoman sultans needed to accommodate Shiite pilgrims, although they sometimes did so with a very bad grace.[89]

Muslims and non-Muslims in legitimizing discourses

While the Ottoman Empire by 1526 held a Muslim majority, there were enough non-Muslims remaining, especially in the Balkan countryside, to make the legitimization of the sultans' rule in the eyes of their non-Muslim subjects into a worthwhile object of study. Orthodox clergymen active in the Ottoman Empire might propound that the Deity had given the sultans dominion over Christians as atonement for the sins of the latter. In addition, many Orthodox persons, especially if monks might feel that being subjects of the sultan was preferable to acknowledging the pre-eminence of the Pope, as they would have needed to do if governed by a Catholic sovereign.[90]

Among Jewish rabbis of the sixteenth century, the Ottoman sultans were often very popular because they allowed Jews to settle in their domains and live their lives without the molestations so common in Latinate Europe (see Chapter 3). Writing in what was still Venetian Crete Elia Capsali (*c.* 1485–90 to after 1550) thus commemorated, not only the Ottoman conquest of Constantinople (1453), but that of Syria (1516), Egypt (1517), and Rhodes (1522) as well.[91] Capsali particularly appreciated that the Ottoman conquest of Jerusalem allowed Jews to access the Holy Land without undue difficulty, and therefore he regarded Selim I (r. 1512–20) as a charismatic figure. In addition, the defeats of Christian nations in Capsali's perspective implied that the Messiah would soon emerge and save the Jews from their often very difficult position.

In a different vein, certain Muslim religious scholars were willing to allow that a non-Muslim king, who practised justice, was acceptable as a ruler.[92] On a less elevated level, Evliya Çelebi pointed out that the Habsburg emperor Leopold I (r. 1657–1705), while incredibly ugly, was a clever man who liked an honest if unflattering opinion. Moreover, the area between the Ottoman frontier and Vienna supposedly was prosperous, and this fact reflected well on the ruler.[93] Thus, under special circumstances, a non-Muslim king might enjoy some legitimacy in the eyes of an Ottoman author. Even so, many if not most men of religion opined that Muslims could not live according to their religion if the ruler was not a Muslim.

Furthermore, Ottoman officials and religious scholars maintained that the sultan owed it to his Islamic legitimacy to hold on to any lands that had once been part of the Muslim world. Therefore, Ottoman authorities found it difficult to accept the principle of *uti possidetis* when making peace on the Habsburg front, as this might mean that lands previously conquered by the sultan might return to the infidels.[94] In this respect, Turkic customs came into play as well: A vizier might refuse any territorial concessions because the sultan had an inalienable right to any lands on which the hoofs of his horse had trodden. In addition, religious scholars might teach that the sultan could break a peace treaty with a non-Muslim ruler, to reconquer territories once under Muslim authority.[95] At times, even the graves of Muslim holy figures located on what was now infidel territory might become a *casus belli*. Thus, one of the arguments for abrogating the peace with Venice in 1570 and conquering the island of Cyprus was the claim that the infidels had disrespected the grave of a relative of the Prophet Muhammad, who reputedly had died on the island during the first stages of the Arab conquest.[96]

In the vision of certain Mughal palace circles, Timur the conqueror was not only a revered ancestor but a saintly figure as well. Intriguingly, from the mid-1500s onward, a sizeable number of Hindus were willing to live with such Timurid ideologies, loyally serving not only Akbar but Shāh Jahān and Aurangzeb as well.[97] Reproducing a motif favoured at the Mughal court, certain miniatures sponsored by the Kachhwaha princes of Jaipur documented the cohesion of the Mughal dynasty, by placing the emperors in a circle comprising not only Bābur and his descendants, but Timur as well.[98]

The charisma that courtiers and officials attributed to the current Mughal monarch sometimes had a basis in standard Islamic thinking, but at Akbar's court in particular, Abū'l-fazl developed mystical speculations, of which many Muslim religious scholars did not entirely approve or which in certain instances, they stridently rejected. Abū'l-fazl wanted to see Akbar as the 'Perfect Man', directly connected with Adam, a saint according to Islamic understanding. Through this link to the first stages of creation, Akbar became a semi-divine figure, above allegiance to any particular religion. Therefore, transcending the division between Muslims and non-Muslims, he could claim the entire world as his domain.[99]

Languages: Means of integration and exclusion in the Ottoman world

Most empires adopt one official language, or at the most two or three. How elites and non-elites handle the fact that they often do not understand one another without a special effort is an important aspect of the interface between the two groups, and thus a central object of the present study. Moreover if, as noted, both Ottoman and Mughal political figures felt that the monarch gained legitimacy by being accessible to the complaints of his subjects, the 'language question' has relevance to sultanic/imperial legitimacy as well.

We begin with a few general considerations: People do not choose their native language, and usually continue to use it throughout their entire lives. If sufficiently motivated, however, they may push it into the background of their consciousness, and work hard to put more practically useful and/or more prestigious languages in its place. Moreover, the adoption of written communication may necessitate a change of languages. Thus in the 1700s, speakers of Albanian wrote in Ottoman Turkish, Greek or Italian, as Albanian was not yet a written language. We may wonder whether for people who wrote often, the language in which they composed their texts ultimately took precedence over their native language, which they may have regarded as uncouth.

Many people learn to handle the languages or dialects used among the people that they need to address. In cosmopolitan cities such as Istanbul around 1700, ethnic/occupational dialects of Turkish abounded and might become a subject of mockery.[100] Under pressure, some of the people targeted by jokes and criticism became experts in manipulating their linguistic heritages according to the occasion. Ottomanist historians have tended to leave such matters to socio-linguists, but perhaps the time has come to communicate across discipline boundaries.

In both Ottoman and Mughal realms, people eager to enter the elites had to learn Ottoman Turkish in one instance and Persian in the other, and learn these languages well. In the sultans' realm, a good knowledge of formal Ottoman was the condition sine qua non even for middle-level service in the Ottoman bureaucracy. As nobody spoke this language at home, and it was not a subject of madrasa studies either, students had to learn Ottoman Turkish from tutors, and this requirement must have excluded the vast majority of Turkish-speaking Muslims from both official and literary prestige. On the other hand, people thoroughly familiar with formal Ottoman might decide to write in a language close to educated speech, as Evliya Çelebi and certain eighteenth-century poets chose to do.[101]

Ottoman multilingualism and its discontents

Until the early sixteenth century, the Ottoman chancery had used a variety of languages, including Old Serbian and Greek, when writing to rulers beyond the western borders of the empire.[102] However, by the 1520s, the use of foreign languages ceased and Ottoman Turkish became the standard language of correspondence. The servants of foreign rulers receiving official Ottoman communications thus needed to employ professional translators (*tercüman* = dragoman). In the last twenty to thirty years, these people have attracted a good deal of scholarly attention because of the now widespread interest in mediation and mediators between groups and political setups that, at first glance, seem to be completely alien to one another.[103]

During the second half of the sixteenth century, many Ottoman merchants traded in Venice, and quite a few Italian or Slavonic-speaking ex-merchants and ex-captives with language skills worked as official and non-official translators. Typically, the latter found employment as brokers for Ottoman merchants, forbidden to do any business in Venice without such control-cum-mediation.

The Ottoman chancery employed dragomans as well.[104] In the sixteenth century, these men were quite often converts from Italy, Hungary, or the Germanies. By the 1600s, local Orthodox Christians might hold this office, as very few Muslims born in the Ottoman world before the mid-nineteenth century had studied European languages. In addition, the French, Venetian, or English embassies present in Istanbul from the 1500s onward hired increasing numbers of local dragomans.

When viewed from the ambassadors' perspectives, the employment of these men was a liability. Being subjects of the sultan, they did not enjoy diplomatic immunity and when under pressure, might reveal the secrets of their employers to Ottoman officialdom. For this reason, at least the Venetians and the French during the 1600s and 1700s trained young subjects of the relevant states to take over this employment; and by the later eighteenth century the Habsburg rulers used the same method. Ebubekir Ratib, when ambassador in Vienna, visited the relevant school in 1792 and found the students' performance quite acceptable.[105] However, it was not easy to monitor the studies of young candidate translators, especially during their practical training in Istanbul. Thus, despite complaints, quite a few dragomans of Christian or Jewish background continued to work for European embassies throughout the eighteenth century.

From the sultan's point of view, the problem was no less serious. It was customary to exempt the employees of foreign embassies from a variety of taxes including the poll tax (*cizye*). This privilege made even a nominal employment as a dragoman very attractive for non-Muslim traders; moreover, embassies strapped for funds actually sold these positions. Particularly in the 1700s, quite a few dragomans did not do any translating, and often did not even know the languages from which they supposedly translated.[106]

While the numbers of tax-exempt fictitious dragomans were probably not as high as scholars had once assumed, the exemptions still posed a serious problem to the Ottoman exchequer, which in the late 1700s was in serious difficulties due to pressing military needs. In addition, it was an infringement of the sultan's prestige if his non-Muslim subjects could so easily escape their obligations. Only in the 1800s, long after the period treated here had ended, did Sultan Mahmud II attempt to solve this problem by creating privileged Muslim and non-Muslim traders, whose exemptions would, or so the sultan hoped, enable them to compete with European merchants. However, by that time the 'dragoman problem' no longer had any connection to translation and mediation. Rather, it had become an aspect of the process, by which the Ottoman Empire of the late 1700s and early 1800s became part of the periphery of industrializing Europe.

Arabic and Persian: Extensively used, but over time largely replaced by Ottoman Turkish

In the Ottoman world, the overwhelming majority of documents was thus in Ottoman Turkish, but the use of Arabic and Persian was significant as well. Documents instituting pious foundations (*vakfiyye, vakıfname*) were often in Arabic, although by the 1700s, *vakfiyyes* in Turkish had become numerous too. In the late fifteenth-century qadi registers of Bursa, entries in Arabic were common, but in the course of the 1500s, Turkish became dominant and the registers from other towns of Anatolia and the Balkans were mostly in that language as well.[107] However, as late as the seventeenth century the scribes compiling the registers of Istanbul's qadi courts wrote certain texts in Arabic. We do not know the reasons underlying this choice, probably because we do not yet possess a full list of the Arabic texts present, for example, in the Istanbul or Bursa qadi registers.[108]

In the Arab provinces, where Arabic was the native language of the scribes, official documents composed in this language predominated by far. However, at least in Damascus certain scribes mixed in Turkish words, perhaps because at least some complainants and defendants used this language.[109] Commands from the sultan were always in Turkish and since the scribes entered them into the registers 'as is', even volumes otherwise in Arabic contained a number of Turkish texts. We do not have much information on how the court scribes handled this type of multilingualism: Occasional misunderstandings must have been part of life especially since the classical Arabic that the judge had studied in the madrasa differed significantly from the spoken language of plaintiffs and defendants. It seems however that these issues have attracted less attention than the problems posed by the dragomans.

In the 1500s, inscriptions on public buildings were often in Arabic, even in Turkish-speaking cities including Istanbul and Bursa. These inscriptions ornamented mosques and madrasas, often in exquisite calligraphy and if appearing on tile-work, enhanced by a deep blue background. We may assume that this artwork impressed people even though for the most part, they could not understand the texts. While gravestones from the fifteenth to seventeenth centuries only survive in small numbers, the usually short and formulaic inscriptions are mostly in Arabic too.[110]

However, customs changed from the eighteenth century onward. In one of the oldest surviving cemeteries of Istanbul, inscriptions written before *c.* 1750 are very rare, but in the later 1700s, gravestones, now often inscribed in Turkish, became more elaborate and were more likely to survive. Presumably, a larger number of people could now honour their deceased relatives by setting up gravestones in their memory.[111] Similar tendencies toward lengthier Turkish texts appear in the inscriptions identifying eighteenth-century pious foundations, smaller but more numerous than their sixteenth-century counterparts had been. Placed in locations of easy access, for instance, on public water fountains, Turkish verse inscriptions brought current literary fashions to a broadening Istanbul public.[112]

At least to some extent, Persian was in use in the Ottoman financial administration. In the documents compiled by accounting bureaus, certain formulas appeared that readers could decipher if knowledgeable about financial practices, linguistic sophistication not being a requirement. The basic features of Ottoman financial administration went back to the accounting manuals used by the scribes of the Mongol Il-khāns governing medieval Iran, which the officials serving the early Ottoman sultans must have known very well.

Much more important, however, was the use of Persian as a language of literature and elite culture. Selim Kuru has shown that until the second half of the sixteenth century, Ottoman literati were still struggling to master the refinements of Persian poetics, compiling dictionaries and anthologies, and producing translations and calques of Iranian literary works. Encyclopaedias of poets including sample verses were popular as well.[113] Given these means of instruction, an educated Ottoman admiral might be proficient in Persian literature. In the mid-1500s, the one-time naval commander Seydi Ali Reʿis, returning home overland after losing his ships in the Indian Ocean, claimed to have mastered the art of Persian versification well enough to gain the appreciation of Safavid literati. He even maintained that when on Iranian territory, a timely poem in praise of ʿAlī, the son-in-law of the Prophet Muhammad, had saved him from likely death as a spy. Whatever the truth of the story: the sheer fact that the author included it in his travelogue shows the high prestige of Iranian literature in the eyes of educated Ottomans.[114] In this context, it is noteworthy that these people did not identify Persian as the hallmark of the Safavids whom, on the contrary, at least some members of the Istanbul elite regarded as 'uncouth Turks'.[115] However, when in the later 1500s, Sunni refugees from the Safavid realm became serious competitors for senior positions in the scribal hierarchy, the well-known historian and litterateur Mustafa ʿÂlî voiced his misgivings, even to the point of doubting the loyalty of the recent arrivals to their new overlord the sultan.[116] A thorough evaluation of the manner in which educated Ottomans related to Iran, on the model of the studies focusing on English or French views of the Ottoman Empire, is not yet available.[117] However, as cultural historians have noted, in Istanbul Iranian art and literature remained a source of inspiration throughout the period studied.[118]

On the other hand, Persian did not gain many devotees in the Ottoman Balkans: Among the many Ottoman period manuscripts surviving in today's Bulgaria, Arabic as the language of religion prevailed (81.5% of the total), followed – at a distance – by Ottoman Turkish (14.7%).[119] Persian manuscripts were very few (3.8%). Apparently, in this provincial setting, few people had an interest in the frequently non-religious sophistication that readers might gain from Persian literature.

What do we know about the linguistic customs of the Turkish-speaking non-elites? By the 1700s, Istanbul inhabitants of some means used the gravestones of their deceased relatives to assert family status and sophistication. Mostly, these stones featured snatches of poetry in Ottoman Turkish, perhaps augmented by snippets of information about the life of the deceased. As eighteenth-century gravestone inscriptions were longer than had been customary earlier on, these texts had an increased use value as status markers among people who were not very prominent, but might fancy themselves as having connections to the palace elite.[120]

Apart from gravestones and the records of local qadis, Ottoman non-elite subjects living before the mid-1800s and possessing some property and/or education have left records of their doings mainly through their numerous petitions, some of them concerned with sensitive questions such as violence against women. Admittedly, this material does not allow us to retrieve the 'voices' of the people who submitted their claims and complaints to the sultans' officials.[121] For the vast majority of petitioners, professional petition writers were indispensable intermediaries, for even if literate on a certain level, most people did not know formal Ottoman Turkish and the rules of composing a proper document in this language. Many negotiations in the qadis' courts took place orally, in the Arabic and Turkish vernaculars, although the scribes did not record these statements verbatim. We know even less about the mediators that helped Bulgarian peasants or Armenian artisans to bring their claims to court. Despite a degree of flexibility, the fact remained that elite and non-elite people used different languages and/or dialects; but the standardized format of court documents made little or no allowance for the ensuing difficulties.[122]

Mughal multilingualism

The use of Persian as a means of securing imperial cohesion

In terms of language, communication between educated Ottomans and their Mughal counterparts should have been easy, as they had presumably read the same texts of classical Persian literature when in school. Writers living under the Delhi sultanate mostly used Persian, and the Mughals continued this literary tradition. While Bābur (r. 1526–30) had still composed his famous memoirs in Chaghatay Turkish, the following generation had already switched to Persian, even including female royals. Akbar's aunt Gul-Badan Begam probably wrote her court chronicle in Persian.[123] 'Persianized' culture – to adopt the term often used by historians of Mughal India – involved the use of Persian even in the everyday lives of the Mughal elite.

Given the lengthy history of Persian in Northern India, the incoming Mughal rulers, without any special effort, found Persian speakers in sizeable numbers. After all, long before the Mughal conquest, the sultanates of Gujarat and Golconda had become home to significant numbers of Iranians.[124] Thus, the decision of the emperor Akbar to conduct imperial administration exclusively in Persian did not mean the introduction of a language foreign to the subcontinent. Given this policy, the knowledge of Persian expanded, as now modest village officials had to understand the orders of the central government written in this language, and compose their own documents in Persian as well, doubtless with much effort.

Moreover, the imperial administration took the view that the standard of pronunciation and spelling was to be that prevalent in Khorasan, thus rejecting specifically 'Indian' varieties of Persian.[125] Ex officio, the imperial elite thus took sides in a literary dispute about the 'correct' way of writing in Persian, encouraging authors to avoid non-Persian loanwords, including those of Arabic origin. In the eyes of government officials, standardization over large expanses of territory was a major merit of Persian, which made it preferable, for instance, to the many variants of Hindavī in use in Northern India.[126] Intriguingly, some historians of literary style have noted that Turkish stylistic peculiarities occur in the Persian written by Indians, perhaps due to the linguistic heritage imported by Bābur's court.[127] Throughout, knowing or not knowing Persian differentiated people with even a modicum of education from the majority of the empire's subjects.

Mughal relations with Iran and the Persian language had an everyday, personal aspect as well, since immigrants from Central Asia and Iran continued to enter the Mughal nobility throughout the period under study. The Iranians were especially prominent in the early stage of Mughal rule, after Humāyūn had regained his throne with Safavid support in 1555.[128] The Mughal emperors encouraged Iranian immigration because in this way, they hoped to balance the impact of other court factions including the Central Asians. Thus, Akbar's court sent out veritable 'talent scouts', who were to find prominent Iranian authors and encourage them to relocate to India, offering generous subsidies for the cost of moving.[129] As for the migrants, some of them were likely uncomfortable in seventeenth-century Iran, where the predominance of Shiite religious scholars often made life difficult for dissidents. In addition, the much greater resources of the Mughal nobility permitted a more generous distribution of patronage.[130]

Persian poetry: Teaching it, composing in it, and using it as a stick with which to beat one's rivals

Ever since the Delhi sultanate, Indian literary figures had written Persian prose and poetry, a tradition continuing under the Mughal emperors. Since from the later sixteenth century onward, writing good Persian was an absolute requirement for entrance into the Mughal elite, and as noted people could learn the requisite skills in the madrasa, we find Hindus attending these institutions. Focused on the training of future administrators, such schools taught mathematics, revenue management and accounting. In Bengal at least, wealthy Hindus even sponsored such schooling to open administrative careers to local youngsters. At the earlier stage of Persian language acquisition, the teachers were often immigrants from Iran; but at a later stage, local Muslims and Hindus took over and educated new generations of pupils.

However, it is worth noting that the 'Indianization' of Persian literature resulting from these efforts was objectionable to certain authors, who – in conformity with official attitudes – praised the 'purity' of Persian and dwelt on the supposed inability of non-Iranians to excel in this pursuit. Literary figures working in Iran particularly disapproved of the inclusion of Hindavī words in the compositions of their Indian colleagues. Professional competition between scribes of Iranian and non-Iranian backgrounds was at issue here, comparable to the conflicts previously evoked by Mustafa 'Âlî.[131]

To a person aspiring to high rank in the Mughal world, even as a revenue administrator, composing Persian texts was a distinct advantage. The Hindu Chandar Bhān (d. 1662–3), who used the evocative sobriquet of Barahman (Brahman) as his literary alias, acquired a reputation for his Persian prose. As Rajeev Kinra has shown, while this master in the art of composing elegant letters was alive, nobody questioned his eminent stature.[132] Only after his death did certain literati start rumours that Chandar Bhān had been ignorant of palace etiquette, and had therefore committed a major faux pas in the highly regulated world of Shāh Jahān's court. According to Kinra, this polemic was a means by which Chandar Bhān's detractors proclaimed their own superiority over a fellow author, who was not a native speaker of Persian and in addition a Hindu.[133] We may wonder whether, given occasional tensions between the Mughals and the Safavids, the loyalty of Iranian immigrants to the Mughal emperor was ever in question.

Despite such tensions, in South Asia the familiarity with major texts of Iranian literature, beginning with Firdawsi's *Shāhnāma*, established links between educated people inhabiting different provinces, similar to the familiarity with Shakespeare's major plays current in the English-speaking world and beyond. In addition, Persian was the language through which interested Muslim gentry could access Hindu religious scriptures, philosophical discourses and *belles lettres*. For Akbar had commissioned a series of translations from Sanskrit into Persian, an enterprise continued by his great-grandson Dāra Shukōh (d. 1649). Cooperation between the adherents of different religious and cultural traditions was a precondition for the success of this undertaking. For Hindu scholars with a thorough knowledge of Sanskrit texts and traditions did not normally know Persian, and courtly litterateurs with a command of Persian stylistics, usually Muslims, had no Sanskrit.[134] The only language common to the two groups was Hindavī, around 1600 a spoken rather than a written language. Thus, the two groups of authors cooperated, sometimes voluntarily and sometimes rather less so, in conformity with the emperor's orders.

As Persian was the common language of the sophisticated world, quite a few words passed from this language into Hindavī, the common ancestor of today's Hindi and Urdu. As Muzaffar Alam has expressed it: 'Yet Hindavī was first Persianised before its entry into the charmed circle of the Mughal echelons'.[135] As for present-day Turkey: Despite twentieth-century attempts to replace Arabic and Persian loanwords with Turkish neologisms, a sizeable number of words remain common to Modern Turkish on the one hand and Urdu or Hindi on the other. They are mostly of Iranian origin. As for the variant of Bengali spoken in India, linguists have determined that about 2,500 words of Persian origin are currently in use.[136]

'Persianized' culture was thus a major strand in the prestige and legitimacy of the Mughal monarchs, and this legitimacy long outlasted the dissolution of the empire in the mid-eighteenth century. Muzaffar Alam has highlighted a controversy that, in the 1800s, involved a prince governing the polity of Hyderabad in the Deccan and a high official active at the court of the latter, recently arrived from Northern India. The newcomer had suggested replacing Persian by Urdu, the Hindavī-based, 'Persianized' language of the Mughal camp. This suggestion made the prince very angry, as he regarded Persian as a symbol of the victory of the Muslims, who had 'conquered this land by the sword'.[137] Thus, long after Mughal rule had dissolved, this prince, who governed a polity on the margins of the Mughal world, regarded the use of Persian as a symbol of Muslim victory and legitimate dominance. However, as in these matters, nothing is ever without ambiguity, for Muzaffar Alam the great advantage of Persian to the Mughal elite was exactly its openness to non-sectarian content. While certainly associated with Islamic power, this language permitted its elite users to project an identity that at least to a certain degree, remained separate from religion.[138]

To conclude

Quite a few legitimacy discourses in the Ottoman and Mughal orbits show what one might call a family resemblance. In both polities, it was the duty of the ruler to protect his subjects, and in his old age, Aurangzeb regretted that he had not fulfilled this essential obligation.[139] While the image of the ruler as a paterfamilias writ large is more appropriate to the Mughal context, the protection that the sultan claimed to grant to whomever invoked it, is an enduring motif of Ottoman legitimacy discourse as well. Moreover, in quite a few cases, the sultans did protect outsiders seeking refuge, although their empire did not systematically replenish its elite from foreign parts, as was the custom in the Mughal realm.[140]

In the Ottoman Empire, legitimization discourses changed slowly, although we should not exaggerate the conservatism of the elite. By 1720, an Ottoman ambassador might describe his ruler as an administrator reconstructing his war-damaged realm, rather than as the customary military hero.[141] Moreover, legitimacy discourses, being discourses, can be somewhat separate from the actual functioning of a given polity. Thus, at least to the present writer, a slow change in legitimacy discourse can be compatible with contemporaneous regime change; and, apart from the foundational period of Mehmed the Conqueror, the Ottoman Empire experienced such regime changes both in the early 1600s and in the early to mid-nineteenth century. As for the Mughal orbit, official legitimization discourses in the time of Akbar differed strongly from those of Aurangzeb, although only a century separated the two rulers. Seemingly, present-day historians of the Mughal Empire have not discovered regime changes comparable to those observed in the Ottoman world. However, the question remains open.

To a considerable extent, the similarities between the two empires are due to the shared traditions of the Muslim Turkic kingdoms of Central Asia. Accordingly, both dynasties defined their rule as based on conquest, preferably of territories inhabited by infidels. Admittedly, in practice both monarchs fought and annexed Muslim principalities as well. In the Ottoman case, rulers and officials might claim to promote Sunni right belief against Shiite 'heresy'.[142] In the Mughal world, by contrast, sectarian arguments, if formulated at all, do not seem to have been much in favour. Enlarging the Mughal Empire by conquering neighbouring polities, even if ruled by Muslims, apparently did not need any special justification. In both realms, some rulers claimed special sanctity, as a being of near-divine status in the case of Akbar, while the Ottoman sultans Selim I, Süleyman and Murad III associated with holy men from whom they desired blessings, and perhaps hoped to acquire some supernatural status as well. However, we cannot be sure: It is impossible to look into the hearts of people, be they living or dead. . . .

At Sultan Süleyman's court, a few soothsayers following an Islamic line of thought were welcome, at least for a while, and they suggested that the ruler might take on an eschatological role. By contrast, Akbar's claims to sanctity had an Islamic base only to a very limited extent, for apparently, Zoroastrianism was a more significant inspiration for the sun worship that this emperor adhered to in his later years.[143] At present, it seems that the notion of sacred kingship was more acceptable in India, where various forms of Hinduism tend to blur the difference between gods and human beings.[144] By contrast, this difference is fundamental to Islam, even though some mystics accept that a few chosen men are so saintly that they transcend the limits of ordinary humankind.[145] Admittedly, historical studies highlighting the claims of certain Ottoman rulers to privileged communication with the world of the divine are still in their beginnings. Perhaps there were more rulers wishing to appear in contact with the supernatural than we had hitherto assumed.

The elites of both empires defined the polities they ruled as Islamic, but the meaning of that statement varied over time. Perhaps the intention of Aurangzeb, who wanted to reconstruct the Mughal Empire as a polity fully consonant with Islamic law, came closest to the policies of Sultan Süleyman or Mehmed IV (r. 1648–87); particularly the latter – after all, Aurangzeb and Mehmed IV were near-contemporaries. Both rulers promoted conversion to Islam more intensively than had been the custom among their predecessors, particularly in Mughal India.[146] We may see Aurangzeb's re-introduction of the *jizya* in the same context; after all, the revenues the treasury gained from this source were less significant in the Mughal than they were in the Ottoman Empire. However, if Aurangzeb intended to establish a totally Muslim elite similar to what had long been in place in the Ottoman orbit, his options were limited. For since it was his major aim to conquer the Deccan, he needed the cooperation of Rajput warriors, many of whom might be Mughals in culture but had little inclination to change their religion.

Both the Ottoman and Mughal empires promoted the use of an imperial language, and in the sultans' domains, Turkish became the standard idiom, not only of command and administration, but of poetry and historiography as well. As for Ottoman Christians and Jews, Turkish terms seemingly entered mostly their everyday vocabularies, rather than the formal languages written by clerics and rabbis. Balkan food culture contains many dishes derived from the Ottoman culinary repertoire; and despite attempts at 'language purification' in late nineteenth- and early twentieth-century Bulgaria and Greece, many food-related terms derived from Ottoman Turkish continue in use to the present day. At the same time, there is no parallel to the enduring impact of Persian on the subcontinent, promoted by the Mughal policy of including Hindus in the administration and even the military without prior conversion, as well as the teaching of Persian in the institutional framework of the madrasa. Apparently, Ottoman Turkish did not become part of the sultans' legitimization discourse in quite the same intensity, as Persian seems to have done, even in post-Mughal Bengal or Hyderabad.

For reasons that we do not yet fully understand, Mughal legitimacy was an enduring force, and many Hindus became 'culturally Mughal' and remained faithful servants of the empire, even under a self-consciously Islamic ruler such as Aurangzeb. Comparable phenomena are less frequent in the Ottoman realm, but they did occur. Thus, an Orthodox Phanariot dignitary named Stephanos Vogorides (1780–1859), even in the age of nationalism, staunchly maintained his loyalty to the sultan throughout his long life. In his autobiography, this personage baldly stated that, if the Deity had intended him to side with the Russians, He surely would have caused him to be born in Russia.[147]

Throughout, it seems that the Ottoman sultans and their elites engaged less intensively with the intellectual worlds of their non-Muslim subjects than was true in South Asia. If an Ottoman non-Muslim wished to have elite figures take his ideas seriously, conversion to Islam was the first step. Perhaps matters would have developed differently if after 1481 the successors of Mehmed II (r. 1451–81) had followed his example, showing an interest in Greek philosophy and Renaissance art. However, counterfactual history not being part of our present project, the following chapters will leave the world of the elites and focus on towns, merchants, artisans, and agriculturalists, with at least a sidelong glance at the people, whom the elites had relegated to the margins of society.

Part Three

'Ordinary People' in Business and at Work

5

Towns and Cities

In the third section of our study, we will embark on a *tour d'horizon* of the interfaces between the Ottoman and Mughal – or post-Mughal – governing apparatuses on the one hand and, on the other, the relevant tax paying populations. Wherever the available documentation permits, we envisage these relationships from the perspectives of Ottoman and Mughal subjects, looking at the relevant interface 'from the bottom up'.

The first chapter in this section contains a discussion of Ottoman and Mughal/post-Mughal towns and cities, in which we briefly introduce the chances of, and impediments to, urbanization due to natural conditions. Secondly and just as briefly, we consider the modest population densities necessary for any urban development. The following and rather longer section deals with the manner in which Ottoman sultans and Mughal emperors promoted pre-existing towns – or in one exceptional case, a newly founded settlement – to function as royal capitals. When the seats of sultans and emperors were at issue, the elites of both empires developed ideas about town planning. Unfortunately, we do not know what the subjects of both monarchies thought when ordered to relocate. Did they look forward to increased opportunities or did they resent the inconvenience of moving? We just do not know.

Where available, maps are a prime source. By the eighteenth century, the Kachhwaha princes, Hindus by religion but culturally close to the Mughal court, documented both older cities and their newly founded capital of Jaipur (1727) in large and elaborate city maps.[1] For this reason, and due to the ready adoption and adaptation of Mughal artistic conventions in this well-documented principality, we dwell on Jaipur more often than readers might expect. While this town was not in the narrow sense of the term, a Mughal city, it is defensible to use it as a stand-in.[2]

By contrast, Ottoman rulers and elites were less interested in mapping towns and generally articulated their understanding of good government through the issuing of imperial commands and, at the local level, the decisions of the qadi courts. These and other documents regulated who might do what in any given place.

After a brief discussion of fortifications and gardens, as well as their role in town formation, we introduce cities that were centres of caravan or riverine trade. In the Arab world, the three examples that first come to mind are Aleppo, Damascus and Cairo. We focus on Aleppo, while recognizing that it is impossible to discuss the research concerning these great cities in any detail. As a large commercial city in Northern India that was neither a capital nor a seaport, Patna is a good example, because quite a few visiting merchants, unfortunately mostly foreigners, have recorded their impressions.

In the next section, a very specific variety of settlement, namely those towns and cities associated with deep-water harbours, will occupy centre stage. Numerous monographs have demonstrated their great commercial and political significance in both the Ottoman and the Mughal orbits. Certainly, not all ports have become major players in the commercial world. However, in the Ottoman Aegean and in Western India, some of the smaller harbours invite study as well, for they served as feeders, channelling goods to their successful competitors the large-scale ports. Or else, they functioned as outlets for the modest production of their respective hinterlands. Small centres existed on land routes as well, on which good fortune has sometimes preserved documentation.

Linguistic similarities indicate that the urban cultures of the two empires shared certain features. The term used for a small town of the Indian world, namely '*qasbah*' is comparable to the '*kasaba*', which in both Ottoman and Modern Turkish denotes a small town. By choice or by command, townspeople lived together in urban wards, which both in the Ottoman Empire and in Mughal India, went by the name of *mahalle* and *mahalla*. When subjects of one monarch visited the cities dominated by the other, they would have found their way without too much trouble.

Though dealing with the sixteenth to eighteenth centuries, we must keep in mind that Anatolia and the Balkans, as well as certain parts of India, had all been urbanized regions long before the Ottomans or the Mughals appeared on the scene. Thus, many Anatolian towns go back to Hellenistic and Roman times, even if in intervening periods from the ninth to the twelfth centuries, they were no more than fortified villages. While in some parts of the Balkans, urbanization was more often medieval than Roman, the territory of today's Greece, once part of the Ottoman domains, has towns going back several centuries before the Common Era. Where Northern India is at issue, we often do not have much information on urban life before the Delhi sultanate, which began in the late twelfth century, temples being almost the only surviving structures.[3] However, around 1200, the first of the numerous settlements comprising the Delhi of today was in place.

In both the Mughal and the Ottoman worlds, the founding of new towns was the exception rather than the rule. On the other hand, especially in the Indian orbit, evidence on recently founded towns, or on those that emerged from obscurity between 1526 and 1740 is often more ample than what we possess on more established settlements. The present discussion reflects these imbalances.

Preconditions: The possibilities and limitations imposed by nature

As everywhere in the world, Ottoman and Mughal towns each had a history of their own, with local conditions playing a significant part. İzmir, Istanbul and Salonika owed their prosperity to natural harbours that sheltered ships against most – though not all – contrary winds. In the interior provinces, bridging a river might promote the growth of a small town, as happened to Osmancık in North-central Anatolia when a stone bridge crossing the capricious Kızılırmak River facilitated caravan trade.[4] In a different vein, the port town of Balat on the Aegean coast of Anatolia lost importance when the nearby river Menderes brought in quantities of stones and earth, moving the delta westward and silting up the harbour.[5]

In the Indian world as well, the vagaries of the Indus, Ganges, Yamuna, and other rivers contributed to the growth and decline of towns. The city of Patna, known to non-Indians mainly through its rice, depended on the Ganges and Yamuna for trade connections to Agra, Allahabad, and Varanasi/Benares; and the concentration of commercial centres near the two rivers promoted overland trade as well, especially to Central and Western Asia. To the east, river transport linked Patna to Bengal and Orissa. English merchants discovered the natural advantages of this inland port already in the early 1600s, recording the speed by which the waters of the Ganges flowed, allowing them to bring merchandise eastward very quickly, while the same circumstance slowed down upriver travel.[6] In a different vein, the prosperous port of Khambhat/Cambay in Gujarat lost out to Surat after 1620, among other things because a tidal bore – put differently, a wall of water that could rise in a few moments – put ships at risk. While this natural phenomenon, and the shifting sandbanks in the river, were not the only reasons for the seventeenth-century decline of the port, they did play a significant role.[7]

Preconditions: A certain level of population density

In addition to natural advantages and the support of rulers, the emergence of towns required a certain level of population density. If there were not enough agricultural producers around, the surpluses in the hands of peasant or nomad families were insufficient for town formation. In both the Ottoman and the Mughal contexts, it was after all a major role of towns and cities to function as markets for local crops (compare Chapter 6). Peasants could themselves sell their produce, as was the custom in many places in Mughal India. In the post-Mughal ambiance, merchants wishing to profit from commercializing peasant dues needed these markets as well, especially where crop sharing was a significant mode of revenue collection.[8] After all, crop sharing meant that revenue collectors found themselves holding significant amounts of grain, which they had to convert into money. In the Ottoman context as well, the *timar*-holding *sipahis* needed to market, or have their peasants market, the grain tithes that were the backbone of the Ottoman taxation system. Once again, there would not be any purchasers for these grains if populations were very sparse, as is apparent from the sixteenth-century tax registers of the Central Anatolian sub-province of Bozok (today: Yozgat). In this area, where there were few villages and most of the locals made a living as migrant sheep breeders, no major towns existed in the 1500s; and the first urban centre of some importance emerged only at the beginning of the nineteenth century.

In the Indian context, forested areas might not possess any towns at all; and given the lack of documentation, historians have tended to neglect these sites. On the other hand, the work of Chetan Singh has shown that in situations of scarcity, forest resources permitted the survival of rural populations and by extension, saved the lives of townspeople.[9] At the same time, the western part of Rajasthan despite its dry climate and nearness to the Thar Desert contained a significant number of market towns, although the area as a whole had a small population. Some of these towns served for the marketing of goods produced by migrant herdsmen, such as wool and butterfat; in addition, the dry climate facilitated the production of salt, which pastoralists purchased in large quantities.[10] The salt trade was lucrative enough to interest the British: Once the latter had secured political control, the authorities instituted a salt monopoly that put large numbers of local people out of work.[11]

Imperial intervention: Promoting capital cities

Natural conditions apart, imperial policies had an impact upon urbanization – positive or negative. Although natural harbours were available on the Aegean coast of sixteenth-century Ottoman Anatolia, coastal towns were quite small, and on the western Black Sea of the 1500s, town formation remained limited as well. Scholars have plausibly linked this situation with the sultans' policy of reserving agricultural products from areas accessible by sea for the consumption of the army, the court, the navy and the population of Istanbul.[12]

After all, the army consumed large quantities of food and fodder, the navy needed cotton and hemp in addition to foodstuffs, and the court acquired not only luxuries but also modest foodstuffs and clothing for its numerous servitors. The capital city contributed to the functioning of the empire by artisan production and commerce, and its inhabitants enjoyed privileged access to meat and grain, due to the perennial concern of officialdom that food scarcities might cause urban rebellions. In addition, after the Ottoman conquest in 1453, Istanbul benefited from the many commercial buildings sponsored by Mehmed the Conqueror (r. 1451–81) and Bayezid II (r. 1481–1512), including two covered markets, both still in use.[13] Intending to make Istanbul into a great Islamic metropolis, control the trade routes and stage the glories of their empire, these two monarchs made great efforts to attract merchants and artisans to Istanbul.[14] For a couple of decades, the success of this enterprise was doubtful: The city was largely empty because of the upheavals accompanying the conquest, and it was probably not clear to Anatolian families with some disposable money whether commerce would ever revive. In addition, some of the new inhabitants had come because the sultan had promised them freehold housing, and when the monarch changed his mind, assigning the houses to the foundation of the Aya Sofya (Haghia Sophia) mosque-cum-madrasa instead, there was considerable discontent.[15] Some people must have left because of this disappointment; in addition, a plague epidemic decimated the city's inhabitants shortly afterward.[16]

However, by the 1470s, Istanbul was once again a large city of 16,324 households, although we have no information on average household size and therefore cannot estimate urban population with any confidence. Only rough estimates are possible; in the earliest years of Istanbul's existence as an Ottoman and Islamic city, many households must have contained sizeable numbers of slaves, not included in the count because they were the property of their masters.[17]

In the period studied here, the Ottoman capital did not move: Istanbul was the residence of the sultans although certain rulers appreciated the abundance of game near Edirne and regularly went there to hunt. Visits to Edirne were part of sixteenth-century court protocol, as the sultans regularly visited the former capital in a ceremonial proceeding known as the *göç-i hümayun* or 'imperial migration'. This official interest prompted the grand vizier Rüstem Paşa (d. 1561), son-in-law to Sultan Süleyman, to construct a two-storeyed business-oriented structure (*han*) with accommodation for traders in two courtyards, a building that is still a notable feature of the Edirne city centre.[18] During the 1500s and 1600s, moreover, certain sultans commanded or at least accompanied military campaigns, usually in the Balkans, an activity which occasioned residence in Edirne and thus temporary absence from the capital. Only during the second half of the seventeenth century did it seem, for about fifty years, that the court might permanently settle in this Balkan city. However, the protests of the soldiers and artisans of Istanbul forced the recently enthroned Sultan Ahmed III (r. 1703–30) to return to the established capital.[19]

Before Istanbul became the seat of the sultans in the third quarter of the fifteenth century, and on occasion even afterward, the early Ottoman capital of Bursa attracted some official attention. For in the 1500s and 1600s, the Topkapı Palace kitchen in Istanbul depended on supplies from Bursa, with the disaffected former sultans' palace now serving as a workshop.[20] Moreover, merchants and artisans benefited from the stock of commercial buildings established in the past, when Bursa had been the capital, quite a few of these business-oriented structures surviving to the present day. The 'old covered market', today known as the Emir Hanı, is already on record in a foundation document dated to 1360, when Bursa was the principal residence of Gazi Orhan Bey (d. 1362), arguably the person who placed the emergent Ottoman principality 'on the map'.[21]

As for Istanbul, there are so many examples of pious foundations supported by business-oriented structures that we can only cite a few examples among many. Thus, the grand vizier Rüstem Paşa built a mosque decorated with exquisite tiles right in the centre of the Istanbul business district, situated on an elevated terrace over the hurly-burly of the market street. This arrangement allowed artisans and traders a few minutes or hours in which to concentrate on the spiritual side of life. The same vizier had a caravansary constructed in Galata, the port of Istanbul, still in use as a business venue.[22] A few years later, the current grand vizier Sokollu Mehmed Paşa (d. 1579) patronized not one but two Istanbul mosques, one of them located on the Golden Horn, adjacent to the Galata walls on one side and the naval arsenal of Kasımpaşa on the other (see Fig. 7). A number of shops, landing places for boats and a double public bath, with separate structures for men and women, provided revenue to Sokollu's pious foundation. In addition, the grand vizier intended the substructures of his new mosque to contain storage spaces, whose users provided further rental income.[23] Away from Istanbul, the structures producing revenue for Sokollu's Istanbul-based and other charities included some shops in addition to a large (and still operative) public bath located in the centre of Edirne.[24]

However, by the later 1500s, the pious foundations of the capital did not always work in the way the founders had planned: The acid but observant author Mustafa 'Âlî (1541–1600) remarked that the public kitchens supposedly serving food doled out soup inedible even for poor madrasa students. Supposedly, the latter visited these soup kitchens in order to meet their friends but fed the 'grub' to the dogs.[25]

Thus, from an early stage the Ottoman sultans preferred a fixed capital city attracting substantial investment in building stock, not only in the city proper but also on the major roads connecting Istanbul with provincial and border destinations. By contrast,

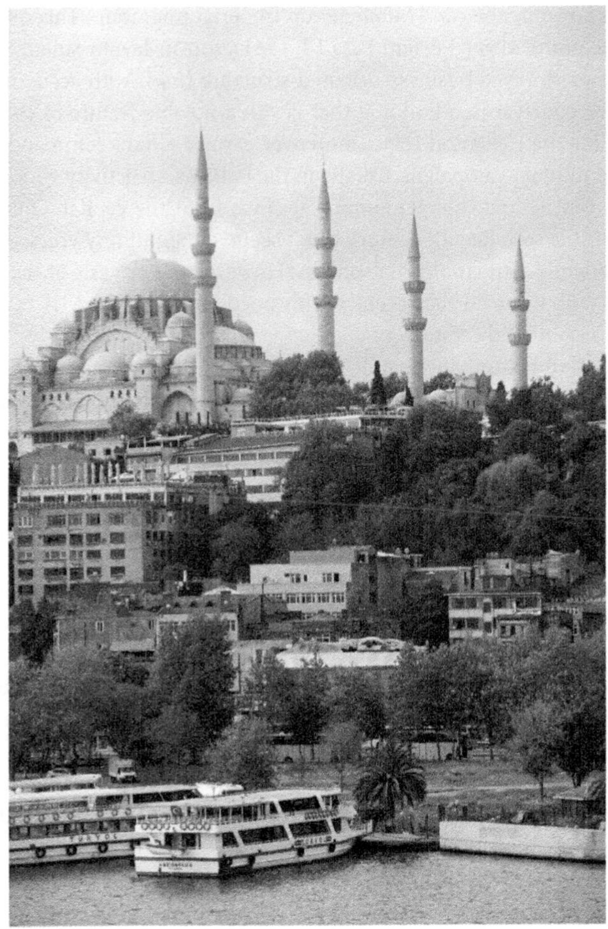

Figure 10 A mosque complex contributing to the emergence of an imperial capital: The mosque of Sultan Süleyman, built by the architect Sinan between 1550 and 1557. In his memoirs, which Sinan dictated to a friend long after Süleyman's death, the architect reported that his enemies had misled the sultan; and these calumnies led to a confrontation in which Süleyman implicitly threatened him with imprisonment or death. However, Sinan bested his critics by finishing the construction on time.

before the Ottomans became the sole rulers of Anatolia, the princes governing the polities of Aydın or Menteşe in the western peninsula had not necessarily lived in a single capital, but moved between the more important towns of their respective realms. This pattern seems more germane to the migrations of the Mughal emperors, who certainly ruled from Delhi and Agra more often than from anywhere else; but in addition, Akbar experimented with the new 'custom-built' city in Fatehpur Sikri and resided in Lahore for many years. Moreover, in the case of Aurangzeb (r. 1658–1707), campaigns in the south of the subcontinent took up so much time that the ruler did not live for very long in his ostensible capital.

Even so, Mughal rulers and their relatives invested in the commercial infrastructure of their capital cities. An important feature, for which we do not find any parallels in Ottoman palaces, is the construction of a shop-lined street (*arasta*) within the palace compound. Inspired by Iranian models, this feature has survived very well in the mid-seventeenth-century fortified palace of Shāh Jahān (r. 1628–48) in Delhi, known today as Lal Qila or Red Fort. Here the shop-lined street connects the main entrance gate to the hall where the emperor gave public audiences (*divān-i ʿāmm*).[26] We do not know whether in the seventeenth century, these shops housed only artisans employed in the imperial workshops. If so, the men at issue would have been reminiscent of the Ottoman artists and artisans working for the sultans (*ehl-i hiref*), whose shops were sometimes in the first courtyard of the palace, but for whom no monarch had ever ordered a special street.[27]

Throughout, Akbar's palace-cum-residence in Fatehpur Sikri, Agra, and Old Delhi or Shāhjahānabād are the most accessible examples of the support provided by Mughal rulers for commercial transactions in their respective capitals. Apparently, the compact *bedestans* that marked most towns of any significance in Anatolia and the Balkans were not much in favour, and in Mughal cities, patrons preferred shop-lined streets resembling Ottoman *arastas*. An elaborate version of this design might have two such shop-lined streets crossing one another at right angles; the crossing might then become a plaza, where presumably street traders waited for customers.[28] Caravansaries were an integral part of Mughal capitals as well, as apparent from the ruins of these structures still visible in Fatehpur Sikri.[29] Such buildings were numerous in Shāhjahānabād as well.[30]

In Agra, sources of information on commercial potential include the tax records of the late sixteenth century diligently summarized by Abū'l-Fazl, who has noted the premier status of the city as a capital of the Mughal Empire. In addition, Agra gained commercial importance because of its mint.[31] Descriptions of the Taj Mahal (see Fig. 11) at the time of its completion in the mid-seventeenth century indicate its position with respect to the city centre, and accounts in Persian, made for early British colonial administrators, help the reader to visualize the city as it was at around 1800.[32] Most importantly, the eighteenth-century Agra map preserved in the museum of Maharaja Sawai Man Singh II contains evidence concerning not only the tomb gardens and riverfront palaces, but documents commercial sites as well.[33] Research on the Taj Mahal has shown that, originally the forecourt contained bazaar streets, no longer extant. Beyond the outer gate, known today as Sirhi Darwaza, there were four caravansaries grouped around a plaza, similar to the arrangement observed in Fatehpur Sikri. Today the caravansaries have mostly disappeared although the gates remain.

Even though the Taj Mahal is at some distance from Agra Fort (see Fig. 12), which was the city centre, by the 1700s the perimeter walls included both sites. Thus, by the middle of the seventeenth century, the city should have held at least two commercial districts. In Agra, the beaux quartiers bordered the river Yamuna, which thus became the most elegant thoroughfare of the city. As the riverside was so full of gardens, palaces and tombs, it does not seem that Agra's waterfront could have had a large space dedicated to the loading and unloading of ships, although perhaps this mundane activity took place at the bend of the Yamuna, next to the walls of Agra Fort. Given the demands of the Mughal palace, it would

Figure 11 Agra: The Taj Mahal: This is the funerary monument built in 1632–47 by Shāh Jahān for Mumtāz Mahal (d. 1631), his favourite wife. In 1666, Aurangzeb had his father, already dethroned for several years, buried in the same location (Asher and Talbot 2007, p. 194).

Figure 12 Agra: One of the entrances to Agra Fort: Mostly built on the orders of Akbar, with additions by Jahāngīr, this massive building was the central structure of the city. Imperial patronage made a previously insignificant town into one of the great cities of the sixteenth- and seventeenth-century world.

have made sense to locate at least a small river port in this very spot. The layout indicates that the Mughal emperors had at least part of the city built according to detailed plans, perhaps devised by architects after consultation with the principal noblemen. Apparently, the ancient Hindu planning principle that a city should resemble a bow together with its bowstring played a role in the design of Shāhjahānabād, even though the emperor was emphatically Muslim in his public persona. In addition, Aniruddha Ray has suggested that the Islamic notion that a city was comparable to the body of a man, with the palace functioning as its head, was an important consideration as well.[34]

Public baths (*hammam*) were a feature of Mughal cities, and especially of their capitals, as they were in the Ottoman world. Albeit in a ruined state, they survive in appreciable numbers in Fatehpur Sikri.[35] A typical structure contained a dressing hall, a hot room, a cold room and latrines. Thus, these buildings were not as elaborate as some of the larger Istanbul baths were. Some of the latter, including Sokollu's foundation, encompassed separate buildings for men and women. The many charities of Hürrem Sultan (d. 1558), wife of Süleyman the Magnificent, included a double *hammam* of impressive size, located between Aya Sofya and the Sultan Ahmed Mosque: Today, after many vicissitudes, the building once again serves its original purpose.

Figure 13a Towns needed ample water supplies, with monumental structures marking their existence in both the Ottoman and the Mughal realms. Aqueduct passing through the Thracian town of Kavala in Northern Greece, ascribed to Sultan Süleyman's one-time friend and grand vizier Makbul ve Maktul İbrâhim Paşa (aka Pargalı, d. 1536), who did in fact establish a pious foundation in this town. The recent rediscovery of İbrâhim Paşa's grave has made this long-deceased dignitary once again newsworthy.

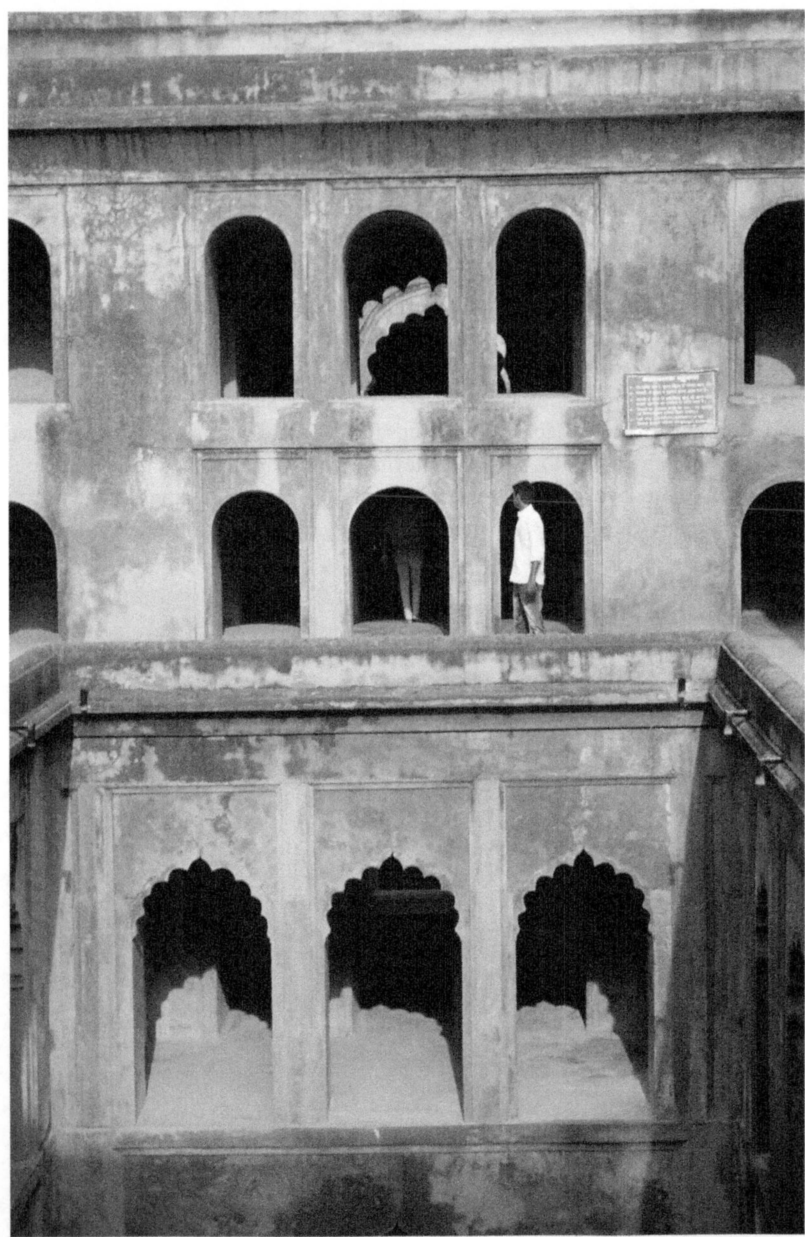

Figure 13b Cities needed ample water supplies: A *bauli*, or underground water source, with an access way embellished by elaborate architecture and once common in Northern India. Today, these structures only function as 'touristic' sites and therefore their conservation can be difficult. This *bauli* is part of the Bara Imambara in Lucknow, opened in 1784 and, despite its late date, chosen for its good state of preservation.

Figure 13c Towns needed ample water supplies: The public fountain of Emin Efendi in Samakov/Bulgaria; the donor was the head of the sultan's kitchen, who probably had some connection to this small town. Built around 1660, the fountain has no inscription but shows signs of later restoration. As the construction of (nearly) cubic buildings to house fountains is an eighteenth-century fashion, perhaps the present shape of the fountain is due to a later restoration. Note the arrangement for watering animals and the attached birdhouse. Compare: (Machiel Kiel, 'Samakov', *Diyânet İşleri İslâm Ansiklopedisi*, https://islamansiklopedisi.org.tr/samakov, accessed on 19 September 2018).

Imperial intervention: Promoting pilgrimage centres and commercial venues

In the Hijaz, the region encompassing the two great pilgrimage centres of Mecca and Medina, the Ottoman sultans promoted urbanization by pious foundations serving the needs of the numerous pilgrims. While no sultan ever went on the haj, the Ottoman rulers enabled large numbers of people to discharge their religious obligations by underwriting, through pious foundations in Egypt and other Ottoman provinces, the expenses of transporting grain, usually from Egypt, across the Red Sea. During the pilgrimage season, merchants could thus sell food to the pilgrims, which, given the very limited agricultural possibilities of the Hijaz, would have been nearly impossible without such official support.[36] Incidentally, in this realm, Akbar (r. 1556–1605) apparently tried to compete with the sultans, albeit on a modest level; for the Ottoman traveller Evliya Çelebi, who visited Mecca in 1672, noted that there was a shelter for Indian pilgrims established by the Mughal emperor and located in a lodge of the Qādirī dervish order (see also p. 124). Admittedly, we have no other source mentioning this building, nor does Evliya record the origin of his information. It is even more difficult to verify his claim that the lodge of the

Mevlevi dervish order (*mevlevihane*), located on the outskirts of Mecca, had originally been the foundation of a dervish from Lahore named Muhammad, who with the permission of the head of the Mevlevi order, had for a while officiated as the head of this institution.[37] Whatever the truth, Evliya's remark documents that he – and probably other knowledgeable visitors to Mecca as well – believed that Akbar and other prominent people from India had built dervish lodges and provided charities for poor pilgrims.

In the Mughal Empire too, Muslim and non-Muslim places of pilgrimage were numerous, and both categories enjoyed official support. In his earlier years, Akbar had established his capital of Fatehpur Sikri because of the pilgrimage that he had undertaken to the lodge of a well-known Sufi saint of the Chishtiyya dervish order (see Fig. 9). A mosque, a mausoleum, and a large structure functioning as a gateway are extant today, and so is a part of town bearing the name of the dervishes in question.[38] At times, non-Muslim places of pilgrimage enjoyed imperial protection too; in particular, Jain visitors to the court of Akbar waxed enthusiastic about the favour that this ruler showed to their principal sanctuary.[39] In Varanasi/Benares, long part of the Mughal realm, Rajput, Jat, and Maratha grandees financed temples, with the Rajputs focusing on the divine figure of Ram while the Marathas concentrated on Shiva.[40] Occasionally, a Mughal dignitary helped to fund the rebuilding of a Hindu temple, while a Hindu prince might provide finance for a mosque, hoping to attract Muslim traders or gain prestige at the Mughal court. Comparable gestures were rare in the Ottoman world; and those that we know of date mostly to the 1800s.

However, there was some official challenge to 'inter-religious' patronage: Aurangzeb had ensured that Islam and Mughal over-lordship over Varanasi remained ever present in the pilgrims' minds, of whatever religion, by sponsoring a mosque with widely visible minarets.[41]

With respect to non-Muslim pilgrimages, the Ottoman sultans sometimes played the role of arbiters, ensuring that sectarian rivalries did not prevent all Christians from praying at the Church of the Holy Sepulchre in Jerusalem.[42] After all, the sultans' officials collected dues from Christian or Jewish pilgrims, so that it made sense to allow the presence of all bona fide visitors. However, the money needed for the upkeep of this and other pilgrimage sites always came from within the communities using the places of worship at issue.[43] Rulers from outside the Ottoman sphere might take on an active role as well: When it came to repairing the Church of the Holy Sepulchre, French kings or at a later date Russian tsars, often provided the necessary funds. Given the political disputes of the times, obtaining the sultan's permission for such repairs could become a complicated diplomatic issue.

Outside of capitals and pilgrimage places, in localities of no particular religious significance, rulers could favour the development of a city, by once again supplying spaces suitable for commercial exchanges. In Ottoman Anatolia, certain viziers and women of the court erected many such buildings: The *han* built on the orders of Silâhdâr Mustafa Paşa in 1636 is extant in the centre of the settlement that was once Malatya and is today Battalgazi.[44] In Anatolian towns, princes learning the art of government at 'miniature courts' sometimes sponsored covered markets or *bedestans*; this happened for instance in Larende (today: Karaman) when Prince Cem (1459–95), a son of Mehmed the Conqueror, resided in this town.[45] Mahmud Paşa (Angelovič,

d. 1474), grand vizier to Mehmed the Conqueror, and in some quarters venerated as a saint after his execution at the hands of the sultan, built a covered market in Ankara, today the home of a museum of Anatolian antiquities.[46]

In addition, both Ottoman and Mughal elites furthered facilities catering to travellers on major routes, especially those connecting important provincial centres to the relevant capitals. As a counterpart to the *han* of Silâhdâr Mustafa Paşa, there remains the caravansary built on the orders of Jahāngīr's queen consort Nūr Jahān. According to the British traveller Peter Mundy, the establishment bearing her name possessed many arches and domes entirely built of stone. In a locality called Chaparghat, the same author reported a similar but probably even more elaborate structure, with four towers at the corners and twenty-one gates.[47] These buildings must have been much larger than typical Ottoman caravansaries, which normally had very few entrances and but rarely featured towers.

Projecting and conceiving the city: Town quarters and streets in the Ottoman world

As for intervention in urban layouts on the part of the ruling power, the Ottoman Empire differed from Mughal India. Before the mid-1800s, Ottoman sultans might have royal foundations occupy a hill or a waterfront to make them visible from afar, but did not impose a plan that regulated streets or street crossings. Nor did most sultans attempt to decide which buildings might line the shores of the Bosporus and the Golden Horn, unless they – or a member of the governing elite – wanted to set up a pious foundation in a space previously inhabited by non-Muslims; in that particular instance, unceremonious removals were common.[48]

Moreover, in the years before and after 1800, well after the end of the period discussed here, Selim III (r. 1789–1807) commissioned lists of properties located on the Bosporus, which had become a favoured summer residence for members of the elite and wealthy people in general. These documents made it possible to monitor whose villa was where, and to ensure among other matters, that rich non-Muslims did not commission houses too close to those belonging to Muslim members of the elite. As Ayşe Kaplan has expressed it, in the eighteenth century the expansion of Istanbul and a greater interest on the part of the city's inhabitants in the pleasures of life had led to a blurring of the lines between different social groups. By contrast, in the crisis of the years before and after 1800, Selim III and Mahmud II (r. 1808–39) tried hard to re-establish these boundaries.[49]

City maps of Istanbul and the principal provincial cities were rare before the mid-nineteenth century and, where they did occur, often the work of foreigners. However, some spatial planning could occur even without a prior mapping. Thus, for example, the Ottoman elite of the sixteenth to nineteenth centuries assumed that Muslims and non-Muslims should inhabit separate town quarters (*mahalle*s), with Muslim quarters often named for the mosques that were the centres of local life. Quite often, members of the governing elite wished to ensure that no mosque had too small a congregation for efficient functioning. In certain cases of this kind, non-Muslims received the order to sell their houses and move, so that there would be a sufficient number of Muslims living near the mosque. These commands, if fully obeyed, profoundly changed the layout of the city. Likely, in certain cases mutations of this kind had more worldly reasons as well, such as securing desirable real estate for a locally influential figure.

Christian churches and Jewish synagogues by contrast did not always give their names to adjacent town quarters. For in some places, the authorities when ordering registers of urban taxpayers simply grouped all Orthodox, Armenian, or Jewish non-Muslims together, so that their sites of worship did not appear in the records. In practice, 'religiously mixed' *mahalle*s did occur at times, because the site in question was in the process of transiting from non-Muslim to Muslim or vice versa. However, there were some cities, particularly Ankara, where 'mixed' living persisted over the centuries.[50]

Perusing the lists of Ottoman shop-lined streets (*çarşı*) often occurring in the foundation documents of larger mosques and madrasas, we find further examples of spatial planning without the use of maps. For it was customary to have artisans congregate in streets specific to their trades, which then took the name of the guild whose members worked there. This practice facilitated both tax collection and the mutual monitoring of artisans practising the same craft, while allowing customers to more easily compare the qualities of the goods on offer. However, sometimes artisans set up shop outside the street assigned to their craft, and occasionally even gained an official permission to do so. We should therefore not assume that no artisan ever practised his trade outside the street occupied by his guild.

Shops in the *çarşı* being quite small, most artisans probably lived in houses separate from their places of work, although given the lack of transport, they probably clustered in places close to their respective *çarşı*s. Ottoman taxation lists before the nineteenth century did not feature street addresses, so that we cannot make firm claims. Even so, the custom of separating workplaces and dwellings seems to have been dominant during the sixteenth and seventeenth centuries.[51] In the late 1700s and early 1800s, by contrast, records detailing the whereabouts of Istanbul artisans do show that quite a few men lived in their shops. Probably, they were either not yet married or else recent migrants to the city; some of these people may have been apprentices or journeymen obliged to guard their masters' shops at night.

Planning the city: Town quarters and streets in the Mughal world

As noted, a tendency toward formally planning the physical layout at least of capital cities was more apparent in the Mughal world, including not only the areas directly governed by the emperors but certain sub-Mughal principalities as well. Most information is available on Fatehpur Sikri: Beginning in 1571, Akbar had the city constructed as his capital on the site of a pre-existing village, next to the lodge of a greatly respected sheikh of the Chishtiyya dervish order.[52] However, already in 1585, the emperor abandoned the site, although recent archaeological work and a careful perusal of written sources reveal that the town remained a commercial and carpet-weaving centre for quite some time afterward; it did not deteriorate nearly as fast as previous scholars had assumed. While Akbar's son Jahāngīr claimed that the local water supply was insufficient for a large city, the historian-cum-archaeologist Syed Ali Nadeem Rezavi rejects this argument and considers that political tensions obliged Akbar to seek out the safety of the strong walls of nearby Agra Fort (see Fig. 12).[53] Whatever the truth of the matter, by the late nineteenth century both Akbar's palace and the urban facilities built upon his orders were in ruins; and since that time, a large part of Fatehpur Sikri has been a site of archaeological investigations and the starting point for acrimonious disagreements as well.

Scholars have concluded that the camp city, the model of which Bābur had brought with him from Central Asia, was the origin of city planning in Fatehpur Sikri, although this model was not of any importance in Agra or Delhi. In Fatehpur Sikri, the rectangular garden structure favoured in Iran and popularized in India by the Mughals played a secondary but significant role. A surviving sketch of a Mughal encampment shows that the central area was the domain of the emperor and his immediate family, with the tents of the princes and nobles located in a 'second zone'. Even further away from the centre, on the corners of the encampment, were the markets and other service areas. In the case of Fatehpur Sikri, the planners used the geographical features of the site to indicate socio-political hierarchy. Thus, the palace and its appurtenances lay on a high ridge, while the common people had to be content with housing on a lower level. Furthermore, the Timurid tradition decreed that a north-south axis should be the backbone of any imperial camp, with the ruler facing south when appearing before his subjects for the daily ceremonial viewing that was an attribute of royalty in India. The orientation of the ridge, which as noted was the site of the central sections of Fatehpur Sikri, allowed the builders to fulfil these requirements of royal ritual.[54]

In the secondary literature, when historians discuss connections between the imperial camp and urban structures, there seems to be a subtext that repays a brief look. On the one hand, the link to Central Asia and the Timurid tradition implied by the nexus between army camp and settled town is important for historians such as Rezavi, even though the latter strongly rejects any implied association with the ruler's patrimonial household.[55] After all, the Mughal dynasty continued to stress its Central Asian origins throughout its existence, and immigrants from Central Asia were a significant part of the governing elite. However, the historian Tanuja Kothiyal has emphasized that the camp-inspired model was but one of the many different types of town present in India, and that other urban forms were far more permanent. In this manner, she inserts Mughal town planning into a broader 'Indian' context, thus de-emphasizing the importance of what many people still view as a military and 'foreign' model.[56]

In a similar vein, Fatima Imam stresses that when Aurangzeb abandoned Shāhjahānabād to be close to the southern localities where he constantly campaigned, the city did not turn into an empty shell, as one might expect if it had been merely the 'service area' of the imperial camp. Certainly, there was a decline in population, but in the late 1600s, Shāhjahānabād remained a sizeable city.[57] Apparently, the issue of urban permanence (and its opposite) crops up so frequently because many historians of Mughal India strongly reject the assumption that Mughal cities somehow were not 'real' cities at all but temporary agglomerations without urban lives of their own.

Comparisons with London or Paris in terms of population size further stress the need to see Mughal capitals as being part of a category that for want of a better term, we might call 'pre-industrial' capital cities. In this context, it is worth remembering that Fernand Braudel has commented quite extensively on the loss of urban initiative when the princely states of fifteenth- and sixteenth-century Europe subdued previously autonomous towns, especially those that they had chosen as their capitals.[58]

Interestingly, Ottomanist historians have no particular objection to viewing the ruler's household as a core and starting point of political organization. On the contrary, for the last few decades, they have constantly emphasized that from the seventeenth century onward, the households of grandees in towns and countryside competed with the sultan's palace as a training ground for future administrators and military commanders.[59] Moreover, in harmony with the 'statist' preoccupations of Ottomanists in the 1970s and 1980s, when the interest in urban monographs was at its height, many studies of Anatolian towns foregrounded the administrative structure, to such an extent that in some cases, merchants and artisans appeared almost as an afterthought. While currently 'statism' is less dominant than it used to be, the role of grandee households and the concern of provincial power-holders with the promotion of towns through pious foundations continue to be concerns of current historiography.[60]

While, for our present purposes, the Mughal palace is of secondary importance, we need to concentrate on the commercial areas nearby, because the shops and markets were what made a settlement into a city. Rezavi has pointed out that the commercial sectors of Fatehpur Sikri did in fact lie in the corners of a long rectangle surrounding the palace, although admittedly the northern section had only one market, while there were four to the south of the palace.[61] Even more suggestive is another map, which shows the entire city in the shape of a long rectangle, traversed by the principal streets connecting the main city gates.[62] Roughly speaking, these major thoroughfares divide the city into nine contiguous rectangles, although one of these streets instead of being more or less straight follows a curve resembling a bow.[63] As another irregularity, a diagonal street cuts through one of the rectangles, so that, instead of nine there are ten functional zones.

Some of the rectangles had identifiable functions; thus, certain zones mostly contained gardens and pleasure pavilions, which we can connect to aristocratic residents present at Akbar's court. Unsurprisingly, the palace compound is at the centre of the grid, surrounded by offices and service structures.[64] Moreover, in the sixteenth century, there was an artificial lake bordering one of the long sides of the rectangle in which Rezavi (and his predecessors) have inscribed the city. By now, this lake has mostly dried up. As there was no space for much building on the side of the rectangle bordered by the lake, the denizens of the palace on the ridge must have enjoyed an unencumbered view of the water and its setting.

Rezavi has especially focused on the offices of the many functionaries needed for the running of court and empire, as well as the dwellings insofar as remnants subsist. While the hovels of the poor have usually disappeared without leaving any traces, Rezavi has provided a view of a Mughal capital that is far more comprehensive than is possible in Agra or Delhi, cities where continuing growth and rebuilding have obliterated a large part of the earlier structures. While Fatehpur Sikri is not typical of Mughal capitals, we happen to know more about this site than about many others.

The city of Shāhjahānabād, but even more dramatically the new town of Jaipur, featured parallel streets and crossings at right angles, which are clearly apparent even today.[65] In addition, a map of Jaipur, showing the city when it was brand new, survives in the palace museum. Although both cities followed designs imposed by their princely founders, the two rulers at issue emphasized different features. In Shāhjahānabād, strong fortifications protected the palace, situated on a spur over the Yamuna; the structure thus could serve as a citadel. Even so, thick walls and complicated gateways did not keep out Nādir Shāh in 1739, to say nothing of Ahmad Shāh Durrānī in 1757 or the British a century later. However, perhaps the deficiencies in leadership and training of the late Mughal armies were so glaring that the defensive qualities of the citadel were of little significance.

Situated on another hill, the great mosque was the second dominant feature on the skyline of Shāhjahānabād. In Jaipur by contrast, not religious buildings but the enormous palace of the prince, with its many courts and a high freestanding façade are the most prominent structures. Apparently, defence was not a major concern of the eighteenth-century Kachhwaha princes; for they had deliberately moved from their castle town of Amber, situated on a high hill and surrounded by strong walls, to a site on the nearby plains: For the most part, the walls of Jaipur probably served administrative rather than military purposes.

Fortifications

With a few exceptions, in Ottoman lands only cities that had 'inherited' walls from previous regimes, such as Diyarbekir, Konya, and particularly Istanbul, featured constructions surrounding the entire built-up area, or at least most of it. Town walls constructed in Ottoman times might protect settlements close to the frontiers, such as (Old) Van, near the border with Safavid Iran.[66] In Western and Central Anatolia, by contrast, only Ankara, and perhaps the Aegean town of Aydın Güzelhisar, boasted walls of Ottoman construction surrounding most of the settlement. In Ankara, this was a local endeavour, undertaken when around 1600 the inhabitants had suffered spoliation by the military rebels known as Celalis, and wished to avoid further damage to their property.[67]

Away from the borders, in what Ottoman sources sometimes called the interior lands or *içel*, the only urban fortification was typically a citadel (*kale*), within whose walls there might be a few town quarters, together with accommodations for soldiers. High-level administrators might reside in these protected places as well. In eighteenth-century Cairo, the governor sent by the authorities in Istanbul lived on the citadel hill and could not easily leave it, so that lower-level military men controlled a sizeable section of urban life. Many citadels relied largely on the natural defences supplied by steep and rocky hills, in some places reusing the early medieval walls of the minuscule fortress towns that occupied the sites of many defunct antique settlements of Western Anatolia. As the areas enclosed by these medieval mini-towns were so small, the covered markets and caravansaries of the Ottoman period lay close to but outside of the citadel walls, as obvious from the layout of well-studied cities like Bursa or Ankara. A few towns had no defences at all.

In Mughal cities, city walls delimited the urban territory, which people entered through gates that were often very ornate. In Shāhjahānabād and in Fatehpur Sikri too, these gates often bore the names of the towns, which the traveller could access by the roads starting at these places. Apparently, it was common for major Mughal cities including the capitals to possess walls suitable for defence; by contrast, Istanbul and Edirne were unfortified, with the Byzantine walls of Istanbul serving as administrative boundaries only. As for the palace compound, Gülru Necipoğlu has pointed out that the walls encircling it were non-functional in military terms even at the time of construction, being so thin that a few cannon shots would have sent them tumbling down.[68] They thus delimited the palace grounds and kept out a few rebellious soldiers, and in addition, the battlements may have served as a decoration. With due caution, we may thus assume that while Mughal emperors expected attacks on even the centres of their power, this concern was not relevant in the Ottoman context. In fact, no such attack ever occurred: Even the Allied occupation after World War I (1918–23), long after the period studied here had ended, did not entail any fighting in or near Istanbul.

Gardens and summerhouses

In Ottoman towns many houses did not have large gardens, although the ubiquitous courtyards might contain a few bushes and trees. Even the sultan's gardens, which were extensive, were often at some distance from the palace, the shores of the Bosporus being a favourite location.

In compensation, the major towns of Anatolia and the Balkans often had a 'green belt' of gardens and vineyards surrounding them, now mostly swallowed up by urban sprawl. These gardens produced fruit and vegetables that people preserved for the winter. Many families built more or less elaborate summerhouses in these garden zones, an arrangement that allowed the owners to leave the congested inner cities during the summer, when the danger of infectious disease was most serious. From the women's point of view, it was an additional advantage that the families living on neighbouring garden plots often were real or presumed relations. Therefore, females were under less pressure to stay indoors and conceal themselves from the regard of men.

In the vicinity of the Ottoman capital, gardens and vineyards were semi-public sites of amusement as well. Already by the mid-1600s, many Istanbul males were in the habit of visiting the seashore to socialize and have fun. According to the travelogue writer Evliya Çelebi (1611–after 1683), even sultans liked to visit the seaside and its gardens, and he claimed that Selim II (r. 1566–74) spent time in a Bosporus village where he could get good food to go with his wine.[69] Female outings for pleasure appear mainly from the eighteenth century onward, although quite possibly such trips occurred in earlier times too, but went unrecorded in the scantier documentation of that time. As for the early eighteenth century, Sultan Ahmed III (r. 1703–30) spent large spans of time in Bosporus villas belonging to members of the royal family. In addition, he built himself a summer palace by the banks of a stream situated in an elaborate garden inspired by Iranian models, with perhaps a few French-style decorations added on. In these venues, the sultan was more of a presence to the inhabitants of the capital than he could have been if staying behind the walls of the Topkapı Palace.[70]

Gardens played a very prominent role in Mughal towns as well. Bābur (1483–1530), the founder of the dynasty never built a palace in his newly conquered kingdom, but ordered the construction of a number of gardens to which he gave poetic names, above all the 'Eight Paradises', established in Agra, as yet a very modest settlement.[71] In later capital cities including Agra and Fatehpur Sikri, formal gardens, organized in geometrical patterns and thus different from the more informal 'landscape gardens' favoured by the Ottoman elite, played a significant role in shaping the urban layout.[72] Both in Agra and in Fatehpur Sikri, gardens were places for cultivating, not only ornamental plants but vegetables and fruit as well; and at least as important, they served as places where the elites enjoyed life. Later monarchs and members of the imperial family, as well as dignitaries of less elevated status built themselves pavilions in extensive gardens organized in completely symmetrical fashion. After the deaths of the owners, these sites often became tomb gardens. In the ideal case, walkways and straight canals/water channels divided the rectangular garden into four smaller rectangles, with the pavilion-turned-mausoleum either set in the centre or if the garden was close to the river, in a location near the water's edge.[73] In addition, it became customary to surround the gardens with walls interrupted at regular distances by often elaborate gates. It is an intriguing question whether tomb gardens were ever accessible to people not part of the households of the deceased, but special arrangements surely allowed the visitation of graves belonging to people that locals considered holy, and from whose visitations they expected to obtain blessings.

Caravan and riverine cities

In the Ottoman world, large cities situated at some distance from the sea and operating as centres of interregional or inter-empire overland commerce were quite numerous, especially in the Arab provinces. When Selim I (r. 1512–20) conquered the Mamluk Empire, and his son Süleyman (r. 1520–66) took Iraq from the Safavids, the old Islamic centres of Aleppo, Damascus, Cairo and Baghdad became Ottoman provincial cities. Especially the work of André Raymond has however shown that 'provincialization' did not mean that these cities decayed.[74] On the contrary, the relative peace that the sultans ensured promoted trade, at least in some periods and in certain regions. Certainly, the sultans and their governors focused on Istanbul and the routes leading toward the city, with the connection to the Hijaz an object of special solicitude. Even so, they promoted pious foundations supported by business-oriented structures in the established caravan cities as well, especially in Aleppo.[75] Due to space constraints, we will concentrate on this city; however, similar discussions are possible concerning Damascus and – of course – Cairo.

In the seventeenth century, Aleppo was a focus of the inter-empire trade in raw silk. This meant that in the *hans* of the city, Armenian merchants subject to the shah of Iran and resident in New Julfa near Isfahan, marketed raw silk, which largely belonged to their ruler. The purchasers were merchants associated with the English Levant Company, in addition to private traders from Venice and elsewhere. When studying this trade and its impact upon the Ottoman polity, Bruce Masters has concluded that the urban elite of the city directed its investments toward lifetime tax farms, real estate, and *soi-disant* pious foundations that benefited mostly the family of the founder.[76] Some members of the elite certainly traded. However, their orientation was toward the security of a diversified portfolio, rather than toward the more risky investments that might have made them competitive with the European merchants, whose presence became more intrusive during the 1600s and 1700s.

In addition, Aleppo served as a hub of regional trade, soap made from local olive oil being in considerable demand. After investigating the registers of small-town Syrian qadis, Antoine Abdelnour has therefore pointed out that even though eighteenth-century Aleppo suffered from regional unrest that drove people from the countryside into the shelter of the city the latter continued as a commercial centre.[77] Thus, the Ottoman–Iranian trade in raw silk, which disappeared in the early 1700s due to the wars surrounding the demise of the Safavid dynasty – in addition to the competition of Chinese and Bengali silks – was less important for Aleppo's urban prosperity than scholars had previously assumed.

At the same time, seventeenth-century Aleppo had a reputation for its elaborate commercial structures, unfortunately, it is hard to say how many of these buildings have survived the current civil war. The Nuremberg merchant Wolffgang Aigen, who lived in Aleppo between 1656 and 1663, recorded with admiration that the *hans* of the city featured ashlar masonry, running water and small mosques. In the most important business streets, covered with vaults for protection against the sun, varieties of textiles were on sale, both Indian cottons and the European fabrics, which Aigen recorded with special care. In addition, the author recorded the presence of coffee, a popular mood enhancer that had not yet reached European consumers.[78] In the mid-seventeenth century, the so-called New Han even contained a coffeehouse, where patrons could enjoy their beverage while watching the passers-by.[79] While in seventeenth-century Istanbul, the sultans sometimes forbade the consumption of coffee, the inclusion of a coffeehouse into a pious foundation indicates that this prohibition was of limited validity in Aleppo.

Given the key role of the Ganges, Yamuna and their many tributaries in Northern India, a commercial city was largely a place where merchants arrived by boat. Patna had been a major settlement in antiquity but declined in medieval times. However, by the early 1500s, Shēr Shāh established his capital in this locality, which soon overtook an older town in the vicinity. Urbanization in this area depending on the frequently changing course of the Ganges, Patna's good fortune was that by the 1500s, the river was much closer to the settlement than had been the case in antiquity. Although in the Mughal period beginning in 1574, Patna was only a provincial capital, lively urban growth continued. The location of the city on the route from Delhi and Agra to the rich province of Bengal provided an additional advantage, although at certain times the prominence of the Portuguese established in this province probably limited the opportunities available to Patna merchants.[80]

The English traveller Ralph Fitch, who has provided a late sixteenth-century description of Patna, commented on the size of the city and the active trade in cotton, cotton cloth, sugar and opium, which traders supposedly conveyed to Bengal.[81] When discussing this statement, Aniruddha Ray has expressed his doubts, as these goods were traditional products of Bengal too and it is hard to see why Patna should have supplied them. Ray thinks that Fitch may have referred to goods destined for export via one of the Bengal ports, but perhaps the English visitor had simply made a mistake and meant that these goods arrived from Bengal. By the late 1590s, the revenue data compiled by Abū'l-Fazl indicate that cash crops including silk, opium and sugar had become prominent in the region, thus augmenting possibilities for traders. In the 1620s, Francisco Pelsaert stressed that Patna had moreover become a silk mart of significance, while local weavers wove a coarse variety of muslin. In addition, by the early seventeenth century Dutch and English merchants had established themselves at some distance from the city, buying saltpetre, an essential ingredient of gunpowder, which they refined and exported through Bengal. Several emperors prohibited these sales but revoked their prohibitions within a year or two, so that the trade continued.

Apart from commerce with the English and Dutch, an English visitor of the later 1600s mentioned overland links by caravans circulating between Patna and Iran, Georgia and the lands of the Tatars.[82]

Foreigners visiting Patna before about 1670 did not have much to say about the building fabric, stressing the prevalence of simple mud huts. However, the Dutch traveller Nicolas de Graaf, who saw the city in the 1670s, mentioned the existence of fine houses and temples in addition to the normal accoutrements of an Islamic city.[83] Artisans had settled in a large shop-lined street, and Ray has concluded that these people used raw materials from the countryside to manufacture goods that merchants then traded downriver.[84] It would seem that when Patna's trade expanded, the city attracted investments by the Mughal elite, and the settlement was still prosperous when Mughal control unravelled in the early eighteenth century. In the 1740s, however, at the time when we end our study, locally established Afghans, the (ex)-Mughal governor and the Marathas were at war in the region, which must have ended the prosperity of Patna, at least for a while.

Lasting for over a hundred years, the success stories of these two cities show that, in the seventeenth century merchants in both empires arranged for profitable domestic and export trade, involving European merchants whenever that seemed practical. In both cases, they cared less about the buildings in which their trade took place, leaving construction to members of the elite. In fact, Masters has opined that in the case of Aleppo, elite figures were far too optimistic in their assessment of commercial potential.[85] Seemingly, such miscalculations did not happen in Patna.

The promises and dangers of the sea

The Ottoman Empire had very long coastlines, in the Black Sea, the Aegean and the Mediterranean, to say nothing of the Red Sea to which Indian ships delivered spices and cotton textiles, thus making the fortunes of Cairo traders. As for the Mughal Empire, before the conquests of Aurangzeb in the later seventeenth century access to the Indian Ocean was available in Gujarat, while possession of Bengal and Orissa allowed the Mughal emperors to collect customs duties from trade in the Bay of Bengal. In the present context, we focus on Gujarat because of the large number of available studies and the high rate of urbanization in this former sultanate turned Mughal province.[86]

Unlike the Ottomans, the Mughal emperors did not invest heavily in naval construction, but they often freighted trading ships. In addition, a variety of more or less autonomous communities, established on the western coasts of the subcontinent, made a living from maritime trade until the British dislodged them in the late 1700s and early 1800s.[87] Local merchants and regional princes, the latter loosely subordinate to the Mughal governor or – from the later 1600s onward – to the Maratha rulers, were the main actors in the commercial field.

While differing when it came to the assertion of naval power, in the commercial sector the maritime policies of the two empires resembled one another; for the elites of both empires had little interest in the seaborne trade of their subjects. While the Ottoman navy dominated the eastern part of the Mediterranean, building ships for commercial use did not enjoy much official support. By the 1700s, many Muslim Ottoman merchants trading within the Mediterranean had even come to prefer the services of French or Italian shippers.[88] Moreover, apart from some investment in the spice trade, the Ottoman sultans did not often participate in maritime ventures.

As for the Mughal emperors, the rulers and members of their households invested in maritime cargoes far more often than the Ottoman palace did; in particular, royal women freighted ships to the Arabian Peninsula. Sometimes the emperor in person intervened: At one point, Shāh Jahān decided that a ship belonging to a member of the dynasty should go not to Jeddah but to Mocha; apparently, merchants had advised the emperor that the Jeddah market was already saturated.[89] However, when the export trade of the empire's subjects was at issue, the emperor, similar to his Ottoman counterpart, showed almost no interest.

Thus, in both realms, the port towns were sites in which foreign merchants came to exercise significant power, although we should not project backward into the seventeenth century conditions applying to the late 1700s or even the 1800s (see Chapter 6). In this context, it makes sense to compare Izmir and Surat, although Surat was by far the larger city: The population supposedly ran to about 200,000 during the Mughal period, while optimistic estimates for İzmir in the late 1600s only reach about 90,000.[90]

In addition, Surat is of interest to the Ottomanist as, in the sixteenth century, this city housed a number of Rumis; a term, which in India denoted inhabitants of Anatolia and the Ottoman realm in general.[91] These people show up in Portuguese sources as strong partisans of the Ottoman sultans and opponents of the Portuguese. However, it is a piece of bad luck for the historian that as Ottoman involvement in Indian Ocean affairs petered out after the 1580s, Portuguese authors active in India lost interest, and other sources do not often record the activities of the Rumis.[92] Given the close trade relations of Surat with the Arabian Peninsula, some resident Rumis must have traded with this region, and as the Ottoman sultans of the sixteenth century recently had added Yemen to their territories, there may have been some plans to establish an Ottoman 'bridgehead' in Surat. However, the Mughal conquest of Gujarat in 1572–73 ended all projects of this kind.[93]

Both Surat and İzmir were ports with substantial hinterlands, in which European merchants purchased goods for exportation, imports being relatively limited. In Surat, the cotton fabrics of Gujarat were the principal export, while Izmir traders supplied British, French, Dutch and Venetian exporters with Anatolian products such as raw cotton, some cotton yarn/cloth, angora wool and fabrics made from this latter material. In addition, especially British merchants purchased large quantities of Iranian raw silk brought in by caravan traders.

While the manufacture of cloth was a specialty of Surat and the suburbs of the city, Izmir's artisans concentrated on the local market and did not work for export. After all, raw materials made up a large share of Izmir's trade and were available in the countryside, while those manufactured goods that attracted the interest of exporters typically came from places like Ankara or Manisa. Certainly, Izmir did not have merchants with the enormous resources and business contacts of Virji Vora or 'Abd ul-Ghafūr (see Chapter 6). However, some seventeenth-century Anatolian merchants did profit from export trade; such as, for instance, Imamogli/İmamoğlu from Ankara, who with his commercial gains acquired large expanses of land that he drained and converted into gardens.[94] As happened in other settings as well, a successful trader thus turned himself into a landholder.

In both cities, English and French merchants appeared during the seventeenth century, although Izmir and the Aegean coast in general had a long history of medieval trading relations with Italian cities. In the case of Izmir, there has been some discussion about the impact of English and French commerce upon the local economy, with Daniel Goffman assuming that already in the 1600s Izmir had become a stamping ground for European traders, over whom the sultan could exercise but limited control. However, the recent work of Merlijn Olnon has shown that the situation was not so simple: in the second half of the seventeenth century the powerful vizier family of the Köprülüs managed to reassert a significant degree of control over the city's commerce by means of a large pious foundation. Located near the harbour, the latter included storehouses where exporting merchants needed to deposit their wares, and thus the latter could no longer 'get away' without paying customs duties.[95] As Ashin Das Gupta has observed, the decline of Surat and the takeover of the local fort by the British, were largely a consequence of the dissolution of the Mughal Empire in the early eighteenth century.[96] As Ottoman central power adapted more successfully to the changing international situation, the sultans' officials retained a greater degree of control over the activities of foreign merchants. Where İzmir was at issue, this re-assertion of central control had an impact upon the buildings of Izmir's core area; i.e., the storehouses forming part of the Köprülü foundation. Unfortunately, because of earthquakes and fires, the structures put up by this influential dynasty of viziers disappeared long ago.

Historians of the Gujarati coast have often stressed that it is not sufficient to look at the major ports.[97] The smaller harbours, including even the 'forgotten' ones, are worthwhile objects of study too, partly because they act as 'feeders' for the larger commercial nodes and partly because they may have been more important in the past, and thus their fortunes allow us to reconstruct regional history. In the case of Gujarat, scholars have studied Khambhat/Cambay, in the Middle Ages the prime port of the region.[98] Furthermore, apart from the premier port of Surat, places such as Gogha, Gandhar, Broach, Rander, and Ghandevi all have had their periods of florescence. Presumably at certain times, merchants profited from the remoteness of the (supposedly) paramount powers, first the Mughals and their governors of Gujarat and later on, the Maratha rulers.[99]

In the İzmir region, smaller ports included Kuşadası, in the Middle Ages known as Scala Nuova by the Italian traders doing business there. In addition, some traffic passed through Foça, in the thirteenth to fifteenth centuries a frequent stop for Genoese shippers. After all, the nearby Şaphane Dağı supplied aluminium sulphate or alum, a mineral, which dyers used to clean wool before dyeing it. In the fifteenth century, when İzmir was – at the time – a very small place, the port of Ayasoluğ near the ruins of Ephesus and the modern town of Selçuk was popular among both local and Italian traders. However, before the seventeenth-century rise of İzmir, the most important harbour was on the island of Chios/Sakız; and, at least in the 1400s, the principal port of this island was not a feeder but a competitor for İzmir, the Genoese controlling the locality until the Ottoman conquest of 1566. Thus, the rise and decline of ports, with one or the other controlling the bulk of maritime traffic and the others acting as feeders or (temporarily) disappearing altogether, is a feature shared by the Gujarati and Aegean coasts.

Small towns on overland routes

Small towns did not just emerge near waterways, but along land routes as well. While in this study, we focus on those places that had come into being before the 1770s, most present-day Anatolian small towns are of a more recent date. Urbanization on the grassroots level became significant in the 1800s, when voluntarily or not, former nomads and Muslim refugees from the Balkans settled the interior of Anatolia, large sections of which had been nearly empty after people had fled the droughts and military rebellions of the years before and after 1600.[100]

In the Anatolian context, sometimes a caravansary became the nucleus of a township. Thus, the modern town of Kadınhanı, to the north of Konya, has taken its name from the local caravansary, while nearby Argıthan (now part of Ilgın, but earlier on an independent township) seemingly emerged around a caravansary built in the 1700s, whose strong walls discouraged marauders.[101] In Thrace, on the European side of the Bosporus, where the road from Istanbul to Edirne crossed a small river, the grand vizier Sokollu Mehmed Paşa built a mosque, two caravansaries and a market, which turned the previously insignificant stopping point into a sizeable town, today known as Lüleburgaz. Very often, Ottoman official attempts to develop road stops into supply markets for travellers were thus quite successful.[102]

Even so, failures were on record too. Thus, Sultan Selim II (r. 1566–74) ordered the construction of a sizeable pious foundation in the settlement of Karapınar in the Konya region, which took on the name of Sultaniye after the donor; and people who settled in this locality received tax breaks. However, after a short while, there were complaints that the new settlers spent only short stretches of time in the locality, and the tax register recorded an official threat that people who failed to fulfil their obligations would lose their tax exemptions. Apparently, the town was unattractive because winds in the dry steppe sometimes caused moving sand dunes, a source of discomfort otherwise unknown in Anatolia.[103] Over the centuries, however, Karapınar did turn into a modest town, the name Sultaniye being no longer in evidence. To help outsiders distinguish the place from the numerous other Karapınars of Anatolia, the name of the settlement now includes that of Konya, the provincial capital.

In the dry areas of eighteenth-century Western Rajasthan, there was not much permanent settlement either; but, despite the decline of the centralized revenue-collecting apparatus of the Mughal Empire, practices first developed by this bureaucracy spread to the increasingly independent Hindu principalities of the region. To the efforts of the accountants serving the princes of Jodhpur and Bikaner, we owe information about the regional and local roads that by the 1700s served some of the camel caravans that had deserted the imperial highways.[104] Along these roads, princes placed checkpoints, or police posts, known as *chowkis*; mainly, the officials in these places collected transit dues (*rāhdārī*) while, if everything went well, providing some security as well. In certain respects, these *chowkis* resembled Ottoman *derbends*, where pass guards recruited from the local populations were responsible for the security of caravans but sometimes made common cause with the robbers that they should have suppressed. In Western Rajasthan, former bandits sometimes became guardsmen, enjoying daily or weekly payment for their services; in addition, tribal chiefs and hard-to-control nobles could take responsibility for guard posts against a share in road taxes. However, when none of these solutions was workable, merchants might pool their money to hire 'mercenary bands' for the protection of rural markets. In addition, a uniquely Indian solution was available: Traders could hire members of certain castes, known as Charans (bards) and Bhats, the killing of whom made the murderer into an outcaste. If apprehended, he would suffer the death penalty; but an additional deterrent was the threat of the Charans and Bhats to commit suicide in the presence of the culprit if they could not save the goods that they had promised to protect.[105] Merchants might thus mobilize the moral and religious scruples of local robbers to protect their goods.

Rural markets, known as *mandis*, often came into being near checkpoints. C. S. L. Devra has placed *chowkis* at the bottom of the urban and commercial hierarchy, with *mandis* a step higher; the latter allowed local men and women to market the goods that they had produced.[106] If the environment continued to be more or less peaceful and there were no major famines or epidemics, such *mandis* might turn into *qasbahs* or small towns; in the opposite case, the market disappeared.

With good arguments in favour of their position, both Ottomanists and scholars dealing with the Mughal Empire assume that while peasants could afford to buy only very few manufactured goods, the taxes that they paid were the precondition for urbanization of any kind. The goods produced and traded by urban dwellers in part served the everyday consumption of their fellow townspeople. If the goods produced were of higher value, they went to the governing elite and also, albeit to a lesser extent, to prosperous merchants and men of religion.

To effect the transfer of goods from the rural to the urban world, an administrative apparatus was necessary, made up of people whom the monarchs rewarded by allowing them a share of incoming taxes. In addition, the household members associated with these privileged tax-takers served their masters by performing some of the work involved, while expecting to obtain at least a livelihood – and sometimes, a share in their masters' power as well (see Chapter 3).

Ottomanists have tended to accept this state of affairs – more or less – as a given; while among Indianists there has been more debate on whether we should consider towns and cities as parasitic upon the countryside. With some qualifications, Irfan Habib has endorsed the latter view, while Rajat Datta has argued that matters were more complicated.[107] From Datta's point of view, although peasants could not buy many urban goods, the demand for agricultural products generated by nearby towns induced the villagers to increase production, and even if the state apparatus creamed off much of the surplus, some of it remained in the hands of the villagers. A layer of prosperous rural dwellers might thus come into existence. Put differently, villages near a town or city should have had a slightly higher standard of living than settlements in outlying locations. However, if the monarchs' tax-taking apparatus was 'too efficient' the peasants might merely need to work harder without obtaining any benefits.

In conclusion: Urban hierarchies

In this chapter, we have differentiated between capitals, both permanent and temporary; major commercial centres, often found on seashores and rivers; and small towns serving as markets for agricultural produce.[108] Ottoman official parlance distinguished Istanbul as the seat (*paytaht*) of the sultans. Delhi sometimes appears as the Dār ul-Khilāfa or seat of the caliphate, and the latter title distinguished seventeenth-century Shāhjahānabād as well.[109] Among port cities, the case of Ottoman İzmir has aroused much interest largely because of historians' concern with the history and prehistory of 'incorporation into the world economy'. As for Surat, the advent of colonialism, especially visible in commercial centres, has made the city into an attractive focus of research, perhaps with the city's phenomenal recent growth acting as a further source of inspiration.[110]

In addition, in the Indian case, Surat continues to fascinate because of the concern among scholars with the formation of a Gujarati identity encompassing both Hindus and Muslims, which presumably is a reaction against the high incidence of communal riots in the otherwise wealthy and educated state of Gujarat.[111] Likely, observers from the Ottoman and Mughal court milieus were less concerned with port cities than historians are today, given the advantages of hindsight.

As scholarship on Gujarat focuses on the region as a whole, historians have become interested in small and 'forgotten' port towns, which are part of the picture as well. This focus is comparable to the current interest of Ottomanists and Mediterranean historians in the Aegean port towns that were of some prominence in the Middle Ages before silting and malaria made them unviable. However, these Aegean ports were rarely if ever 'feeders' for İzmir and often must have been competitors. Remarkably, the question of 'feeder' ports has only attracted historians working on Istanbul.[112]

At the same time, Ottomanists and historians of Mughal India share a concern with small towns serving as markets for tax grains; and they have noted the tendency of such settlements to establish themselves in places where caravans stopped and paid dues. After all, scholars in both sub-fields agree that, in an empire whose revenues came mainly from agriculture, markets were an essential means of transforming produce into money; and, while not all markets turned into towns, many of them did so. There are thus good reasons for taking a closer look at trade; for this reason, merchants and their business practices will be the topic of the following chapter.

6

Investigating the Business of Merchants

When exploring the Ottoman and Mughal Indian commercial scenes, source criticism is – once again – the starting point; for, especially in this area, the analyses of historians studying the Mughal Empire are of great interest to Ottomanists. Given two very different source bases, we begin by examining the production and preservation of the relevant records and the challenges that they pose to historians on either side of the Indian Ocean. The next step involves a comparison of the activities and organization of merchants in the Ottoman and Mughal realms; in both polities, the trade in grain and other agricultural products was a field, in which merchants interacted with the governmental apparatuses, sometimes a dangerous experience. Moreover, in Mughal India, a certain amount of information is available on the jewel trade, a matter on which Ottoman records do not say very much.

The next step takes us into the heart of the matter, namely a closer look at what we know – and more significantly, what we do not know – about imported Indian textiles used in the Ottoman world. While our sources are not ample, they do reflect the popularity – and affordability – of many Indian textiles in Ottoman markets. As no trade can flourish without transportation and money, a review of these matters shows why the wealthiest among Indian merchants were much more significant figures than any of their colleagues trying to make a profit in the Ottoman Empire. We conclude by discussing the reasons for Mughal commercial prosperity in the late 1500s and throughout much of the seventeenth century, which by far surpassed the more modest growth of domestic and inter-empire trade observed in the sixteenth-century Ottoman world.

Primary sources from the Ottoman world

For both the Ottoman and Mughal worlds, the secondary literature on merchants, markets and trade is vast. In the Ottoman archives, we find customs records and documentation concerning bids for tax farms, the latter often involving revenue sources such as customs duties, obviously dependent on trade. Moreover, where the sixteenth century is at issue, the tax registers (*tahrir*) tell us something about the locations of markets and fairgrounds; for the users of these facilities paid tolls to a person or institution to whom/which the sultan had assigned the ensuing revenue. Unfortunately for today's historians, Ottoman officials of the 1600s and 1700s rarely compiled registers of taxable markets and fairs.

When comparing Anatolian records from the early sixteenth century to similar sources from the 1570s or 1580s, it becomes clear that the population growth typical of those decades resulted in increased commercialization. Apart from villages turning into small towns, which by definition possessed markets, commercial exchanges took place in the open countryside as well, with enough turnover to make taxation worthwhile.[1] The attempts of traders to avoid these imposts sometimes have generated additional paper trails.[2] Commercial partnerships have entered the official record too, especially if problems occurred and the – soon to be – ex-partners asked the qadi to preside over the final settling of accounts. Partnerships often did not last very long. With respect to certain popular types of commercial association, Islamic law required dissolution when one of the partners died. However, other types of partnership could continue, now involving the heirs of the deceased. Many merchants of the Ottoman world seemingly preferred short-term partnerships, which their heirs might decide to renew or not renew. Admittedly, it is hard to say whether these often extremely shrewd businessmen knowingly decided to forgo the benefits of long-term investment.[3]

Very few sets of data allow us to follow the business of an individual Ottoman merchant over a lengthy span of time; yet an extraordinary historian like Nelly Hanna has unearthed the – just as extraordinary – business life of a trader named Ismā'īl Abū Taqiyya, of Syrian background but an inhabitant of Cairo in the years before and after 1600. This man differed from his colleagues by his willingness to document his business deals in the office of one of the Cairo qadis, leaving about 1,000 commercial records at the time of his death. Admittedly, Ismā'īl Abū Taqiyya was special in other ways as well: for example, he was no great believer in the principle, widespread in his time, of choosing close relatives as business associates. On the contrary, he was willing to form commercial societies with 'strangers', including even non-Muslims upon occasion.[4] These contacts gave him a network stretching from Venice to India.

In the registers of urban judges (qadis) we find a significant number of references to commercial cases. Unfortunately, for the central districts of Istanbul these archives only begin in the early seventeenth century, with a large gap in the mid-1600s. For Salonika, another commercial metropolis, records survive only for the 1600s and 1700s, and with very few exceptions, the archives of the qadi in charge of the Aegean metropolis of Izmir have all gone missing. Moreover, the commercial content of the qadi registers is substantial only in the major towns, where the scribes serving the local court had to write out and preserve records of debts and partnerships. However, even in smaller places, where sellers and purchasers rarely had their deals put down in writing, researchers will probably find information on patterns of money lending, seemingly ubiquitous in a cash-poor environment.

Further information comes from tax-farming records; until 1695, these arrangements were normally short-term (*iltizam*) but, after this date, many tax farmers purchased the right to collect certain revenues for a lifetime – an arrangement known as *malikâne*. If the holder of such a tax farm made an extra payment, he might even transfer the revenue source to his sons. If short-term, tax-farming records are of interest mainly if surviving in series; for they make it possible, for instance, to chart the rise and decline of a tax farm covering customs duties. If matters proceeded according to plan, the ups and downs of yearly customs revenues represented the rise and decline of the trade that passed through the relevant collecting point.

If, however, the customs duties at issue were part of a lifetime tax farm, the annual revenues would normally exhibit little change. By contrast, when the holder of a *malikâne* died, the Ottoman exchequer, before entering upon a new contract, auctioned off the tax farm at issue; and bidders were normally aware of the earning potential of the customs duty or market tax collected in a given town.[5] In such cases, it was the 'entrance fee' (*muaccele*) that indicated the value that bidders attached to the tax farm; for the present-day researcher, the growth or decrease of this sum of money serves as a proxy for the changes in the relevant dues, as evaluated by potential tax collectors.[6] Therefore, rather than focusing on merchants, Ottoman documents reflect the perspective of the tax-takers, who for the most part, regarded trade as merely one source of revenue among others. Even so, these records have the great advantage of being of Ottoman – rather than of foreign – manufacture; in the central provinces of the Mughal Empire, equivalent documents have but rarely survived. For the Indian context, we possess comparable records mainly where principalities such as Jodhpur or Jaipur are at issue, dependent on the Mughal emperor but largely autonomous in domestic affairs.[7]

In the Ottoman world, merchant accounts commonly ended up in the archives because of confiscations – seemingly, very few businessmen followed Ismā'īl Abū Taqiyya's example in depositing their papers in the qadi's office. Unpaid dues quite often resulted in seizure by the Ottoman central administration.[8] While confiscations of merchant fortunes became more common in the late 1700s, when unsuccessful wars emptied the sultan's treasury, some confiscated merchant papers date to the 1760s and are therefore relevant to the present study.[9] Incidentally, in the early eighteenth century, merchants in the (formerly) Mughal province of Gujarat suffered similar kinds of extortion, when governors in need of cash confiscated the resources of merchants, brokers and bankers.[10]

Foreign traders active in the Ottoman world

Non-Muslim Ottoman subjects might leave traces in the archives of the foreign states where they did business. Thus, historians studying Armenian and Orthodox traders active in the eighteenth-century Netherlands, or Orthodox merchants from present-day Northern Greece doing business in Hungary will mostly turn to Dutch or Hungarian archives, rather than to the long-destroyed records that may once have existed in the hometowns of the merchants at issue.[11]

In addition, British, French and Dutch traders, doing business on Ottoman territory, have left great quantities of records, some of which have been the fulcrum of interest for over 100 years.[12] In consequence, even scholars primarily interested in European trade, rather than in the Ottoman polity where the foreign merchants conducted their business, have moved away from commercial history in the narrow sense of the term. Thus, some historians of European trade in Izmir and Istanbul have focused on banking, a matter gaining importance in the second half of the eighteenth century, when these two cities became part of European commercial circuits.[13] Others deal with the social context of trade, a set of topics that previously had attracted only limited interest. Such investigations focus on the personal connections established by traders among themselves and with the intermediaries that served them.

As a fine example, we can refer to the work of Marie Carmen Smyrnelis, who has studied the French community in Izmir as recorded not only by the local French consulate, but also by the scribes of the Izmir church of St Polycarpe, where French Catholics and people associated with this community worshipped and received the sacraments. Her study particularly focuses on the links established or confirmed through intermarriage, the assumption of responsibility for a child through god-parentage, as well as guarantees securing the loans contracted by a trusted friend. In addition, the documentation studied by Smyrnelis permits the reader to follow the more-or-less French, or more-or-less Ottoman identities of the men and women concerned; for, contrary to assumptions current in the age of nationalism, such identities were not stable at all, but changed according to need and circumstance.[14]

With the aid of sources generated by the English Levant Company, which functioned from the late sixteenth to the early nineteenth century, other historians have studied the social milieu that British traders created in Istanbul, Aleppo, or once again in Izmir. For this purpose, some private archives of family firms in Britain have proved very useful. Frequently, the correspondents were relatives by blood or marriage; therefore these texts may include personal impressions and concerns. Thus, the people who made sales and purchases – or else failed to do so – come into direct view. In this context, Ralph Davis has produced a pioneering work, first published in 1967, focusing on early eighteenth-century Aleppo; at the time in question British merchants in this city were not doing too well and ultimately returned home.[15] For once Iranian raw silk was no longer of much interest to European customers, and the wars in Iran connected to the fall of the Safavids had significantly reduced supplies, British merchants partially withdrew from Mediterranean trade. They were to make a comeback in the late 1700s; but soon afterward the Revolutionary and Napoleonic wars put another – albeit temporary – stop to their business, which only resumed after the defeat of Napoleon in 1815. In a recent study of the Levant Company, James Mather has also focused on the manner in which successful British merchants – and other travellers – viewed the Ottoman sultan's power, and the domains over which he ruled.[16]

Fewer studies concern the Dutch presence; perhaps because, when Dutch trade was at its apogee in the mid-1600s, the importation of spices and cottons from the lands that today form part of India and Indonesia by far overshadowed Mediterranean trade. Even so, the Dutch Republic started to send ambassadors to Istanbul in 1612, and Dutch traders lived in Izmir, sometimes over several generations. The Istanbul embassy generated a significant archive, including post-mortem inventories written in a mixture of Dutch and Ottoman Turkish, which permit a glimpse of the material environment inhabited by the people close to the ambassadors and their families.[17]

Records on trade in the Indian context

In the Indian context too, merchant records are at a premium, although we do possess a unique autobiography, penned in the seventeenth century, by a Jain trader with literary ambitions and wide-ranging religious interests.[18] A vast archive and a diary document the life of an eighteenth-century businessman, closely associated with the French governor of Pondicherry; unfortunately for our present purpose, the activities of this trader, named Ranga Pillai, took place mostly outside the geographical locus of this book.[19] In addition, individual businessmen sometimes surfaced in the surviving documents because of their troubles with Mughal dignitaries and tax farmers in charge of internal customs and tolls. In extreme cases, traders as a group might flee a city where money-hungry administrators operated unchecked.[20] Princely archives, where they survive, thus contain some evidence on merchants petitioning for the redress of such grievances.

How did the assignees of imperial revenue sources, known as *jagīrdārs* in the Mughal world, come up with the cash needed for their households and military campaigns? In the Mughal Empire, peasants and their headmen were responsible for marketing the – usually large – share of current crops payable as taxes.[21] Specialized grain merchants might take part in the process as well. In addition, tax farming was quite widespread, although many authors of the Mughal period pointed out the damage that taxpayers were likely to suffer.[22]

Marketing, of grain was more widespread in Northern India than in the Ottoman world, as the Mughal emperors had not instituted any equivalent to the petty cavalry soldiers (*sipahi*) receiving tax grants (*timar*), partly payable in kind (see Ch. 3). In the Ottoman world, this intake of grain fed the grantees and their households, bypassing the money economy to a certain extent.[23] In Mughal India, by contrast, cavalrymen were part of the retinues of princes and noblemen, who maintained their households out of the cash revenues that the emperor had assigned to them, in the form of large tax grants (*jagīrs*).[24] At least in principle, it was therefore not possible to circumvent the market; for, especially after the reform of the revenue system under Akbar, tax payments to the Mughal treasury had to be in cash, which many tax farmers acquired through sales in urban markets.

Tax farmers were even more necessary for revenue collection if the system in use 'on the ground' was crop sharing, as was sometimes the case especially in sub-Mughal principalities – and, though less obviously, also in certain domains ruled by the central government.[25] For in such instances, the peasants did not market their own crops, and it was the exclusive responsibility of the tax farmer to convert agricultural products into cash.[26]

While local sources are thus very helpful to the commercial historian, much of the documentation on Indian trade comes from the archives of European states and trade companies. While merchants from the Mediterranean world had done business in India ever since Roman times, it was only after the Portuguese sea captain Vasco da Gama had reached the southern Indian port of Calicut in 1498 that the Portuguese king and his commanders – for the first time – established a direct connection between a European polity and India. Conquest, both real and projected, in addition to attempts at monopolizing the trade in spices destined for the European market, generated a large number of documents. At first, the Portuguese attempted to ruin the trade of Muslim merchants in the Indian Ocean and when that proved impossible, they settled for the collection of 'protection money', inventing the so-called *cartazes*. Issued to non-Portuguese shippers, these licenses promised 'protection' against the Portuguese authorities themselves, a classical example of a protection racket. As a counterpart, the holders of *cartazes* had to pay customs duties in a port controlled by the Portuguese; the documents were valid as long as the holders did not deviate from the routes and goods specified in them. As the Mughal Empire did not build a significant navy, even members of the imperial dynasty when engaged in trade or pilgrimage might acquire Portuguese *cartazes*.[27]

In the following centuries, all European companies active in the Indian Ocean issued such 'letters of protection', and certain Indian princes with domains on the ocean shores soon followed their example.[28] In the 1600s, the emperors tried to oblige the British, Dutch and French commercial companies to protect the ships of Mughal (elite) subjects against piracy. After all, freebooter sea captains supposedly subject to European states had reputations as especially dangerous robbers.[29] In Surat, which for the Mughals was a commercial centre and a link to the holy city of Mecca as well, political tensions often originated from the unwillingness of the Portuguese authorities to provide the *cartazes* required, or else from the difficulty of finding armed ships, whose captains were able and willing to suppress piracy.[30]

Portuguese activities in the area thus generated a significant archive. The latter expanded yet further when the king permitted the Inquisition to install a tribunal in Goa, a town on the western coast of the southern Peninsula, which the Portuguese had conquered and made into the centre of their political, commercial and religious activities. The Inquisition was to ensure the adherence to the Roman Catholic faith of all people once baptized and inhabiting the realm controlled by the Portuguese in Asia, known as the Estado da India, with the Inquisition judges turning 'heretics' over to the secular arm for punishment. In the relevant court records, we find information, not only on trade but also on many aspects of social life, which might have become commercially relevant. Admittedly, these archives focus on Peninsular India, and are therefore but marginally relevant to the topics covered here. Furthermore, by the 1600s, the religious and cultural intolerance of the Portuguese regime had alienated a great many people, local Christians included. Thus, competing Dutch and English traders, who both appeared in India at about that time, found business partners without much difficulty.[31] In this early period, after all, neither the Dutch nor the British had much interest in spreading their religion.

In the early seventeenth century, traders from the emergent Dutch Republic established a chartered monopolistic company, the Vereenigde Oostindische Compagnie (VOC), based in Amsterdam, which sought and soon obtained a de facto monopoly in the spice trade with Europe, completely supplanting the Portuguese in this business. Apart from the spice trade, which took place on the islands now comprising Indonesia more than in India proper, the Dutch merchants focused on the purchase of silk and cotton cloth in addition to in reeled silk, demanded by the emerging European silk manufactures of the 1600s. Known as 'factories' in the language of the times, the Bengal trading posts were subordinate to a Dutch official known as 'governor', resident in a settlement on the island of Java that the Dutch called Batavia, on the site of present-day Djakarta. In consequence, the Dutch merchants active in Bengal during the seventeenth and early eighteenth centuries, reported both to Batavia and to the VOC office in Amsterdam, generating an enormous archive in the process. The latter is particularly important as in the late 1600s and early 1700s, the Dutch 'kept tabs' on their competitors by compiling records of the ships anchoring in Bengali ports, regardless of ownership or destination. In his numerous works, the economic historian Om Prakash has analysed the statistical information contained in this collection.[32] Prakash is thus in the fortunate position of dealing with a series of figures documenting the trade passing through a given Bengal port, with customs duties, tolls, or lists of ships in transit functioning as proxy figures – Ottomanists have only limited quantities of comparable documents at their disposal.

The French Compagnie des Indes, based in the port of Pondicherry on the shores of the Bay of Bengal, has also produced an appreciable archive, mainly for Southern India. For our present purposes, it is important that the French presence in the subcontinent was part and parcel of the Anglo-French rivalry which, in the 1700s, was a determining factor in European politics. Moreover, these conflicts often 'spilled over' into the relevant factories on Indian territories.

Doubtless, the most encompassing archive, and the most indicative for trade, is that of the East India Company (EIC); but the historian using this material encounters a set of rather intractable problems. In the 1700s, the British company increasingly became a state-like formation, which dominated, not only newly formed towns such as Bombay, Madras and Calcutta (today: Mumbai, Chennai and Kolkota), but also waged war – particularly against Tipu Sultan of Mysore (d. 1799) and the Marathas, a loose confederacy of principalities dominating much of Central and Southern India. The Third Maratha War, concluded in 1818, allowed the British to control a large stretch of territory, after, in 1759, they had already taken over the castle of the important trading city of Surat.[33] Moreover, in Bengal the Company had become a territorial power even earlier. After all, the 1757 victory of Plassey against the prince (*nawab*) of Bengal allowed the Company a freedom of action that for a long time, it did not possess in Gujarat. In this latter region, a large number of more or less autonomous local princes confronted the British after the near-disintegration of Mughal power structures.[34] The documentation generated by the Company during the eighteenth century thus deals with commerce only to a limited – and decreasing – extent. However, in the period studied here, the 1600s and early 1700s, the administrators of the EIC in London still often opposed the political and military ventures promoted by their subordinates in India, as these enterprises necessitated large expenditures that cut into profits. Even after the mid-eighteenth century, opposition against the Company's empire building was strong enough to result in a trial for abuse of power of Robert Clive, one of the people that had established Britain's control over Bengal (1772). However, the case ended with an acquittal.[35]

The differing perspectives of outsiders and insiders

Thus, many records concerning Indian trade approach merchants, trade goods and relations with local manufacturers from a very specific perspective, determined by the attitudes typical of European capitalists of the early modern variety. This issue is familiar to Ottomanists as well, but for the period covered by the present study, probably of less importance; for as noted, in the work of Ottomanist historians, the accounts of the British Levant Company do not stand on their own as historical sources. The same observation applies to the records generated by Venetian or Genoese merchants trading in the Ottoman lands and the Dutchmen appearing on the sultans' territory in the early 1600s, or else to the documents preserved in the Marseilles Chambre de Commerce. On the contrary, present-day researchers try to link non-Ottoman sources with Ottoman evidence, although the differing perspectives involved frequently make the task rather difficult. While Ottomanists continue to struggle with this problem, at the present stage of research, sources of non-Ottoman origin are no longer the commercial historian's principal resource, as they had been in the 1960s or 1970s.

Studying European archives, in conjunction with their Ottoman counterparts, makes special sense when historians focus on Izmir, in recent decades a popular topic. However regrettable the absence of qadi registers, we do possess Ottoman records from the mid-1600s listing the owners of business-related structures (*han*) and an attempt at recording local properties liable to taxation. Probably part of the same project of intensified tax collection, these records usefully complement the data that foreign merchants and consuls have compiled on the rather small town quarter where they conducted their business, the so-called Street of the Franks. The Dutch historian Merlijn Olnon has ingeniously combined these two records with a document through which the current grand vizier established a major urban pious foundation (*vakfiyye*). Thus, he has compensated, to a significant extent, for the absence of the qadi registers.[36]

That said, it is hard to claim that the state-centred records created by the sultan's bureaucracy are easy to use by historians of trade. Thus, for example, tax-farming records often do not encompass just a single source of revenue, but amalgamate two or even three such items, with some of the revenues included in the 'portfolio' not necessarily relevant to commerce. Even worse, quite often the 'portfolio' farmed out to a given moneyed man may change from one year to the next; if such procedures are at all frequent, the commercial historian will not be able to draw any valid conclusions. However, by locating archival sources that do lend themselves to analysis, and by adjusting the questions asked to the potential of the source examined, historians have used Ottoman sources with some frequency and success. Thus for example, the seventeenth- and eighteenth-century customs duties of the important trading city of Erzurum, close to the Iranian border, are extant in a format that allows the researcher to draw conclusions concerning the trade between Anatolia and the realm of the late Safavids.[37]

Differing political contexts are responsible for the differences between Ottoman and Mughal recording practices. Certainly, between the late 1500s and the 1760s, the Ottoman Empire went through a series of political and military crises, which resulted in widespread decentralization. However, few provincial magnates attempted to set up principalities of their own; on the contrary, most of them seem to have regarded the sultan in Istanbul as a continuing source of legitimization, in whose absence rival power-holders might readily challenge the revenue rights of a given tax farmer.[38] As a result, the empire remained in place despite the control of local power-holders 'on the ground'. By contrast, the Mughal Empire contracted quite rapidly after the death of Aurangzeb in 1707, and the high office-holders who had previously represented Mughal power in Lucknow, Gujarat and Bengal, but also smaller potentates such as the princes of Jodhpur, ruled their domains more or less independently.

This 'splitting up' of earlier concentrations of power must have been one of the reasons why fewer bureaucratic records survive from the Mughal Empire and many of its 'successor states' than is true of the Ottoman world; and, for this reason, the perspectives of outsiders are of greater importance to scholars working on India than is true of Ottomanists. In the Ottoman world, the sultan's officials tried to counteract centrifugal tendencies by promoting correspondence not only with local administrators, but also with those people among their 'ordinary subjects' that possessed the financial and social resources to petition the central authorities and thus keep the latter more or less informed of what was happening in remote provinces. Complaints focused on moneylenders and the excessive interest they charged, or on trade and pilgrimage routes made unsafe by robbers. Certainly, these records concern individual events and often we cannot place them in series, but have to interpret them item by item. No historian will deny the defects of such anecdotal evidence; but in the end, scholars cannot create any data but only analyse and interpret whatever they can distil from the primary sources.

Despite the limitations outlined, over time the task of Ottomanist historians may become less arduous than we may think today. From the mid-1500s to the early 1800s, the enormous series of 'Registers of Important affairs' (Mühimme Defterleri) contains significant amounts of commercially relevant information. From the mid-1600s onward, we can glean interesting texts from the so-called Şikâyet Defterleri (registers of complaints), supplemented from the mid-1700s on by the even more voluminous Vilâyet Ahkâm Defterleri (registers of commands sent to the provinces). If these series should ever become machine-searchable at least in part, it might become feasible to bring together all references to bridge and market tolls, trade fairs, and other topics that have attracted the attention of the sultans' officials. If such a project materializes, we may obtain a much more complete picture of Ottoman domestic trade than we have hitherto dared to hope for.

Ottoman merchants at their business

Before the 1990s, Ottoman merchants often had a bad press because many – though not all – historians assumed that trade was a specialty of non-Muslims while Muslims were generally farmers, military men and administrators. At the same time, in much of the secondary literature, non-Muslim merchants did not feature as subjects of the sultans, but as subservient allies of British or French traders, whose activities only disrupted the orderly functioning of the Ottoman administration. In addition, certain observers regarded Christians and Jews as 'unfair competitors' of Muslim merchants; for as they saw it, the networks established by non-Muslims prevented outsiders from gaining a share of the trade.

When viewing matters in this perspective, scholars must have often drawn inspiration from the nationalism of the late nineteenth and early to mid-twentieth centuries. For from the second half of the eighteenth century onward, many non-Muslims did react first to the often-inequitable taxation policies of the time, and later, after 1839, to the centralization drives of the Ottoman government. By 'opting out of the system' and becoming protégés or even subjects/citizens of foreign governments, they obtained advantages inaccessible to their Muslim competitors. At an even later stage, after 1908, the government of the Committee for Union and Progress (İttihad ve Terakki) regarded the creation of a Muslim bourgeoisie as a major task; and this endeavour presupposed the elimination of non-Muslim traders from the core lands of the Empire and later on, from the territory of the Turkish Republic as well. Given this political project, today largely complete, it made sense to denigrate Ottoman commerce of the seventeenth- or eighteenth-century variety as a destabilizing factor. We may call this set of political-cum-scholarly assumptions 'the nationalist paradigm in commercial history'.

However, today many researchers do not subscribe to these assumptions; and, indeed, some of them stress the factual errors inextricably connected with this paradigm. Firstly, already in the 1960s, Halil İnalcık had pointed out that Muslim merchants were not at all rare in – for instance – fifteenth- and sixteenth-century Bursa; on the contrary, at that time they were the dominant group. Moreover, as the customs registers of Caffa/Kefe/Feodosia show, in the late 1400s Muslim traders controlled most of the Black Sea trade as well. İnalcık demonstrated, moreover, that the Ottoman conquest of the coastlands of the Black Sea by Mehmed the Conqueror (r. 1451–81) and Bayezid II (r. 1481–1512) resulted in Genoese merchants withdrawing from the area. Ottoman subjects, for the most part Muslims, took their places.[39]

As for the sixteenth century, Maria Pia Pedani Fabris, Tommaso Stefini, and Cemal Kafadar have shown that Muslim merchants, from Bosnia but also from Central Anatolia, visited Venice, the one major European port where they could trade without too many difficulties.[40] Furthermore, Daniel Panzac's studies of eighteenth-century French consular records have made it apparent that while the means of transport were often in the hands of French or Italian shippers, the merchants freighting these ships were usually Ottoman Muslims.[41] Thus, until the early to mid-1800s it was not realistic to claim that Muslim subjects of the sultans shied away from trade, particularly when such business necessitated prolonged contacts with 'infidels'. On the contrary, such encounters must have been commonplace, for instance when an Ottoman–Muslim merchant made a contract with a French shipper to have his goods delivered in a distant Mediterranean port, and perhaps visited the local French consulate to have the contract validated. Presumably, some Muslims found such contacts unacceptable, but they did not determine the attitudes of the business community as a whole.

Dealing in grain

Furthermore, there were branches of Ottoman trade that did not involve contact with western merchants at all. Admittedly, we have no figures enabling a global evaluation of internal trade. However, piecemeal evidence concerning markets, caravansaries and shop rents shows that cities like Aleppo, Ankara, Bursa, Diyarbekir and Sarajevo were not just places where outsiders made sales and purchases among themselves, but where local merchants catered for local consumers as well. As André Raymond has shown, the geographical expansion of sixteenth-century Aleppo, the prosperity of the city at that time and its rapid revival after the crisis of the early 1600s were largely due to trade with Iran and India.[42]

In particular, the grain trade was a major branch of business, especially where supplying the capital city of Istanbul was at issue. Merchants wishing to invest in this business seem to have functioned in a 'grey zone', between serving the sultans on the one hand and trading in the narrow sense of the term on the other. Put differently, it is often not clear to what extent these men could legitimately attempt to make a profit, as opposed to receiving payment for services rendered. Merchants who proposed to deal in grain that they planned to sell in the Istanbul market received a certificate from the office of the Istanbul qadi (see Chapter 3), which specified exactly where they were to purchase the quantities recorded in their document, at prices determined by the Ottoman administration, which very often were way below market value.[43] They then had to deliver the grain to the shippers whose job it was to carry it to Istanbul, and finally settle accounts at the public weighing scales of Unkapanı, in downtown Istanbul. The paperwork required by such deals gives us an idea of how officialdom expected the system to operate. However, we do not know very much about the manner in which traders secured the required grain from cultivators, who frequently must have been unenthusiastic about parting with their crops.

As for the Indian context, eighteenth-century records from the dependent principality of Jaipur – which, as noted, conformed closely to regulations known from the Mughal centre – inform us about the activities of rural merchants. These men purchased grain or butterfat from the producers and thus provided rulers with taxes in cash, making a profit from the transactions (see Chapter 8). The officials of the prince could certainly coerce merchants into buying agricultural goods, by forbidding private grain trade until the wheat or rice belonging to the government had found purchasers. They even exacted a special due from those traders who refrained from dealing in tax grain.[44] Even so, there was a basic community of interest between tax collectors and traders, and turning food crops into cash required cooperation between these two sets of people.[45]

Ottoman traders: Vitality and limitations

In addition, Ottoman merchants purchased imported Iranian goods, an activity that involved contact with other Muslims, albeit Shiites that admittedly, certain sultans tended to consider damnable heretics. In consequence, quite often Armenian traders subject to the shah, rather than Ottoman merchants, imported raw silks and woven fabrics into the sultans' domains; but Muslims engaged in Ottoman–Iranian exchanges as well.[46] Moreover, for historians that do not subscribe to the 'nationalist paradigm in commercial history', there is no reason to assume that before the advent of nationalism, non-Muslim subjects of the sultan were anything but Ottoman traders.

Despite the commercial vitality that studies of Ottomanists have made visible, in Istanbul the preponderance of the sultan's government made it difficult for traders to conduct large-scale business for any length of time. Certainly, the economic historians Murat Çizakça and M. Macit Kenanoğlu disagree with the claims of their colleague Timur Kuran, who has proposed that, as Islamic law required the dissolution of partnerships at the death of any one partner, long-term capital formation could not take place, or at least had to overcome very serious impediments.[47] As Çizakça and Kenanoğlu have emphasized, certain forms of partnership were available in Islamic law that did not require such dissolution. Even so, the fact remains that, differently from Cairo, in Istanbul long-standing commercial partnerships were rare. Çizakça and Kenanoğlu seem to think that the political climate, rather than Islamic law per se, inhibited long-term capital pooling in trade or manufacturing, as particularly investments in tax farming were often more profitable than money placed in trade. In consequence, whatever capital was available tended to move into a non-productive sector, where in addition, the risk of confiscation was significant.

At the same time, enterprising Ottoman subjects suffered from the tendency of the sultan's government to overburden successful enterprises with severely underpaid deliveries to the armies in times of war, a demand that often wiped out whatever capital the owners had managed to accumulate.[48] These troubles, however, affected manufacturers more seriously than traders; and therefore we discuss them in Chapter 7.

Given these difficulties, many Ottomanists assume that the sultans' attempts to ensure ready supplies, outside of market constraints, for the army, the navy, the palace and the inhabitants of Istanbul, made it difficult for Ottoman merchants to invest in the growth of their businesses. Even more importantly, the sultans and the elite that served them probably had an interest in preventing the emergence of a group of wealthy merchants and manufacturers who might challenge the power of the monarch and his bureaucracy. In distant cities, especially Cairo before the late 1700s, it was easier to keep a business alive and in family hands.

In the eighteenth century, the situation became even more complex since, as noted, commerce was an occupation open to people of all faiths. However, the strong commitment of the Ottoman court to Sunni Islam, in conjunction with the sultans' loss of prestige in Christian lands after the treaty of Karlowitz (1699) may have induced the Istanbul government to lose interest in the welfare of Ottoman merchants venturing abroad, by this time mostly Orthodox Christians. In the 1500s and early 1600s, the situation had been different, and Muslim and Jewish merchants running into trouble in the Adriatic could count on the support of sultans and viziers. By contrast, their eighteenth-century counterparts doing business in Central Europe seem to have been 'on their own' as soon as they had crossed the Ottoman border. Often enough, these men secured protection by becoming Habsburg subjects.

In Mughal India: Jewel traders and others

Turning to commerce in the Mughal territories, it is by a piece of good fortune that we possess the versified life story of a seventeenth-century merchant from Jaunpur, written by the 'hero' in person toward the end of his career; and we use this unique opportunity to approach trade in Northern India from the perspective of a local participant. Banarasidas (1586–1643) was a jewel merchant, poet and Jain scholar-cum-religious reformer, who possessed a circle of acquaintances with whom he could share these interests and accomplishments. His work provides some first-hand information on the conduct of business during the reigns of Akbar, Jahāngīr, and Shāh Jahān.

Banarasidas came from a merchant family. It was, however, a family with a difference; for his father Kharagsen (d. 1616), while trained in the jeweller's craft, in his youth had attempted a career in the revenue administration of Bengal. While Mughal officials did not hesitate to recruit non-Muslim scribes, and did not demand conversion to Islam as a precondition for a successful career, Kharagsen's spate as a bureaucrat quickly ended with the death of his patron. He returned home to join the family business, trading not only in gold and silver, but also in pearls, rubies and 'the dust of precious stones'.[49] It is intriguing that this early list does not include diamonds, although in the seventeenth century the Indian sultanate of Golconda held the only major mines of white diamonds in the entire world.[50] However, by the time Banarasidas had grown into a schoolboy, Kharagsen did deal in rubies, coral, and diamonds as well.[51] In a manner that would resonate with historians of the Armenian trading community of New Julfa/Isfahan, Banarasidas stressed that his father and the latter's business partner enjoyed a relationship built on mutual trust and understanding.[52]

After Banarasidas had acquired basic literacy and numeracy, the older man expected the adolescent to join the family business. It was a source of frequent quarrels that Banarasidas had little interest in this enterprise, preferring religious learning and poetry instead. In the realm of literature he was successful, and later generations of scholars have celebrated the text he has authored as 'possibly, the first autobiography in an Indian language'.[53] Presumably, in making such a claim historians exclude the writings of the two Mughal rulers Bābur (r. 1526–30) and Jahāngīr (r. 1605–27) because one is in Turki and the other in Persian. Whatever the considerations involved, it is true that the Jain merchant Banarasidas did not have any access to these courtly writings and needed to find his own method of telling his life story.

As noted, the author's talents lie more in the realm of religious thought and literature than in trade or accounting. In consequence, while he impresses today's readers by originality, he has included less information on business practices than we might expect. This omission was deliberate, as Banarasidas consciously avoided discussing those business deals in which he had been successful and mainly highlighted his failures. We do not know whether this behaviour was due to modesty or else to the hope of keeping competitors away. Differently from the story of Ismāʿīl Abū Taqiyya as pieced together by Nelly Hanna, the account of Banarasidas' trading activities thus appears as a story of limited successes and some egregious failures, partly due to the inclination of the author and his friends to enjoy the pleasures of life and thereby dissipate the gains that should have increased their capital.

Yet some of the business disasters that Banarasidas referred to had political causes and were not the author's fault. As jewellers possessed cash, bullion, and precious stones, they were at risk whenever there was a military conflict. The author recorded that his family had to flee their hometown when he was still quite young, because the Mughal commander of Jaunpur had certain local jewellers flogged in order to seize their money. Once released, the victims conferred with their colleagues and as a result, all of the town's jewellers decided to leave. A second such flight became necessary in 1600, when war between Akbar and his eldest son Salīm (later: Jahāngīr) seemed imminent, and the governor had prepared the town for battle against the rebellious prince. Typically, Banarasidas provided some 'human details', when he described how the merchants asked the governor whether they should stay or flee, and the beleaguered dignitary only replied that he fully expected to lose his life in that confrontation – which in the end, however, did not take place.[54]

Banarasidas traded in both fabrics and precious stones. We may assume that at one stage of his career, his knowledge of textiles was limited, for he recorded having acquired low-quality cloth that at first he was unable to sell and on which he lost money when finally he got rid of it. However, this misfortune did not deter him from trying again, this time focusing on cloth made in Jaunpur, where presumably he knew manufacturers and dealers.[55] As a mainstay of his business, Banarasidas mentioned pearls, unfortunately without recording where they had come from, perhaps from the Coromandel Coast or else from the region of Kachh, to the north of Cambay and Surat.[56] Sometimes, the border between trade goods and personal belongings was permeable, as Banarasidas once referred to pearls that he kept in an amulet, but which at a later date, he preferred to sell.[57] In addition, he quite often mentioned the dust of precious stones, in which his father had also traded, but once again, without telling his readers to what uses jewellers put this material.

As for business techniques, while occasionally referring to *hundi*s, or letters of credit, which were in wide usage throughout the commercial world of India, Banarasidas mostly used simple, direct contacts, attending what he called 'the marketplace' in person. At times, he established partnerships with friends, one of which, at a later stage, was to cause him a good deal of trouble.[58] The author did not hesitate to note that at one time in his life, he unsuccessfully tried to hide from his wife that he had absolutely no capital left. When she found out the truth, she helped him by secretly procuring funds from her natal family.[59] However, the author apparently did not make this woman into his official 'sleeping partner'. Taking into account that scholars have applied the term 'pedlar' to many merchants without much justification, in the case of Banarasidas it is appropriate to describe him in this fashion. When times were hard, he even turned to non-commercial ventures like the public reciting of religious texts.

On the other hand, seventeenth-century India contained people who may have been among the richest merchants in the world; but they did not write about their lives and dealings, the latter being on record only in the archives of the EIC or the VOC. One of the most famous examples is Virji Vora (*c.* 1585–1670), established in the Gujarati city of Surat, who was a Jain like Banarasidas and the latter's contemporary as well; but there the similarity ends.

Surat had come to prominence when the Mughal emperor Akbar had conquered the region and his government began to use the city as the empire's principal port.[60] Benefiting to the full from the resulting advantages, Virji Vora became a wholesaler on an imperial scale. As the British merchants who were then beginning to patronize Surat soon found out, he was able to purchase all the pepper available in a given local market, so that whoever wanted this commodity could buy from no other source. The British merchants in Surat might try to avoid situations of this kind, but Virji Vora was capable of buying up several accumulations of commercial stocks, one after the other; he thus prevented any sales to which he was not a party.[61]

Virji Vora did not specialize in any single commodity. On the contrary, the commercial historian Makrand Mehta has shown that this wholesaler bought opium and cotton locally, to exchange them for spices in Southeast Asia, or else he used these goods to acquire quicksilver, lead and coral, in deals with Dutch and English merchants frequenting the port of Surat. In addition, he acted as a banker, especially to EIC merchants, who could only take limited supplies of bullion out of England and thus upon arrival in India, needed cash to begin the trade cycle from which they made their profits. Given the scale of his business, Virji Vora could demand payment in the coin of his choice, and if he wanted something else than the rupees normally used in commercial transactions, he could demand an extra bonus on account of having accepted these rupees – although the latter were legal tender in the entire Mughal Empire.

Another representative of the Jain commercial world under the rule of Akbar, Jahāngīr and Shāh Jahān was Shantidas Zaveri (*c.* 1585/90–1659), a jewel merchant like Banarasidas, but a far more successful one. Shantidas' base was in the Gujarat capital of Ahmadabad, which was not only a centre of textiles production but also of jewellery. Shantidas resembled Banarasidas in his interest in promoting the Jain religion; but as he was a far richer man, he could act on a grander scale. In 1625, he had sponsored the construction of a Jain temple in his home city; and when, twenty years later, Prince Aurangzeb (r. 1658–1707), at that time the governor of Gujarat, had the temple defiled, Shantidas enjoyed enough influence with the emperor Shāh Jahān to receive permission to rebuild it, apparently with funds granted for the purpose.[62] While Jain religious literature typically was the work of monks, the merchant Shantidas donated money for the preservation of manuscripts and encouraged the production of new religious texts.[63] In addition, he engaged in a certain amount of politicking, taking sides in the disagreements between different Jain sects; once again, Banarasidas had engaged in similar behaviour, albeit on a much smaller scale.

In late seventeenth- and early eighteenth-century Surat, the dominant figure was 'Abd ul-Ghafūr, an Indian Muslim merchant whose trade supposedly equalled that of the entire EIC; and the twenty ships that he owned varied in size between 300 and 800 tons. In the years around 1700, pirates like the infamous William Kidd and others caused great damage to Indian shipping including the trade of 'Abd ul-Ghafūr personally. In response, the latter organized a movement against the Dutch trading in Surat, in order to force them to compensate the Muslim merchants for their losses. However, as he made no effort to include the numerous Hindu traders also active in the city, the merchant coalition that he built ultimately unravelled; nor was he able to secure the unqualified support of the Mughal governors. The Surat merchants and their Dutch competitors ultimately reached a compromise; but the conflict dragged on until 1714.[64]

What do we know of the religious and cultural patronage extended by Ottoman merchants? If Muslims, they might institute pious foundations (*vakıf, evkaf*) to serve the people of their hometowns, especially through schools or public fountains. In Cairo, certain important merchants even constructed mosques, some of which existed in the 1970s and hopefully are extant today. Moreover, certain merchants who had built commercial structures (*wakala*, the equivalent to the Ottoman-Turkish *han*), presumably at a later stage in their lives turned over their property to pious foundations.[65] Unfortunately, many of the documents recording such charities do not specify the professions of the donors. Therefore we often cannot highlight the people who had made their money by trade, especially if the founders were females from commercial families. Orthodox traders of the 1700s sometimes donated silver ornaments to their churches, on which they might have their names inscribed. As these gifts became more frequent in the 1700s than they had been earlier on, we may assume that growing commercialization particularly in the Balkans, allowed more traders to demonstrate their wealth through generous charitable gifts.

Jewish merchants often showed their munificence by sponsoring synagogues; as an example we might mention the Ahrida synagogue in Istanbul, which went back to the fifteenth century. However, its present-day shape is due to a restoration undertaken in the late 1600s.[66] Given the difficulty of tracking down merchant donors, it is hard to say whether, among these non-elite figures, there were people comparable to Shantidas in terms of wealth and charity. While most of them probably operated on a much smaller scale, we can only hope for the results of future research.

Ottoman and Indian merchants: Trade and politics

Ottoman merchants normally formed partnerships, with a certain preference given to family members – but as the life story of Ismāʿīl Abū Taqiyya shows, this rule had exceptions. The senior merchant provided the financing by means of a contract, often of the *mudāraba* variety, stipulating that the junior partner, who did the travelling but might not have invested any capital, would receive a pre-determined share of the profits. Unless he blatantly disregarded the instructions of his senior, the junior partner was not liable for losses due to storms, piracy, robbery and other misfortunes.[67] If business was good, the junior after a number of trading trips might accumulate enough capital to become a senior investor in his turn.

Where the Ottoman world is at issue, we have very little evidence of large-scale organization, for instance in commercial guilds. It is likely that in Istanbul or Bursa, guilds (see Chapter 7), were a form of organization popular among shopkeepers, rather than among wholesalers. Probably in terms of mentality, shopkeepers were closer to artisans than to merchants with far-flung connections. However, in eighteenth-century Cairo, the situation was different. Here we do find *shāh bandar* or heads of a merchant guild, whose close relations with the dominant military establishment allowed them real power, even though in the perspective of the Ottoman elite, these men were part of the subject population.[68] We do not find any evidence among Ottoman long-distance traders of the elaborate 'trade councils' through which the Armenian merchants of the Isfahan suburb of New Julfa enforced contracts and behaviour deemed appropriate for a member of this privileged group.[69] Occasionally, the Ottoman qadi decided commercial disputes, even among non-Muslims; but as the relevant records are not very numerous, dispute resolution through informal mediation must have predominated.

Though little documented, these informal mechanisms must have been quite effective. For the limited capital of many traders made sales on credit into a necessity, a home truth of which British merchants 'on the spot' in Izmir or Aleppo tried to convince their 'seniors' forming part of the Levant Company, often with little success. For the most part, debtors must have paid up.

The dominant form of organization was thus the family firm, with the junior travelling members mostly tied to their capital suppliers through the *mudāraba*. In addition, merchant communities played a crucial part. Members of such expatriate groups of traders, who might be Greek Orthodox or Armenians established in

Amsterdam, or else Greeks operating in the Habsburg cities of Trieste and Vienna, for several generations retained a separate religious and ethnic identity. Attendance at their respective churches was a requirement, and often these traders continued to wear their characteristic costumes.[70] Within the Ottoman world of the eighteenth century, Syrian Catholics became a wealthy group of 'immigrant' traders, although they travelled no further than Egypt: After 1730, a sizeable number of people from this community had left northern Syria in order to escape the conflict between the newly formed Catholic group and the Orthodox patriarch of Aleppo. Specializing in the importation of French textiles, in which they became the much-feared and detested competitors of the *Marseillais*, from 1769 onward, one Syrian Catholic after the other farmed the Egyptian customs dues. This position gave the incumbents a de facto leadership of this wealthy merchant community and an informal but sometimes powerful influence within the ruling elite as well.[71]

At the same time, among some merchant groups there is evidence of multiple identities: Thus, one of the wealthiest exporters of red cotton yarn from Ottoman Thessaly to eighteenth-century Vienna translated his family name into German and retained this form (Mavros/Schwartz) even after building an elaborate house in his native town of Ambelakia/Greece.[72] Sometimes, Thessalian merchants assimilated to the Habsburg context because of pressure from the government of Maria Theresa (r. 1740–80) and Joseph II (r. 1780–90). In other instances, they probably wanted to ensure the security of their contracts, as if necessary, the authorities in Vienna or Trieste would enforce agreements recorded under their auspices.[73]

As apparent from the story of Banarasidas, in the Indian world, family firms were popular as well.[74] Beyond membership in a trading family, caste played a role in determining who would become or remain a merchant. Most traders admitted belonging to the Vaisya caste group, the third in the hierarchy recognized by Hindus, although some groups claimed association with the more highly regarded warrior caste group known as the Kshatriyas, who held the second rank after the Brahmins.[75] However, it was common enough for sub-castes to re-define their allegiances to a major caste group.

In the northwestern region of the Mughal Empire, the city of Multan, today in Pakistan, was the starting point for the business trips of several merchant communities including Muslims, Jains, and Hindus.[76] Once they had left the Mughal confines, caste solidarity played a special role among the latter. These merchants-cum-moneylenders were active in the Afghan territories, in the Uzbek khanate and in Russia; in the 1500s and 1600s, they procured an appreciable share of the silver used in the minting establishments of the Mughal emperors.[77] As in other such communities, the principals (*sah* or *shah*) provided their junior travelling partners with funds, often assuming responsibility for the junior's families as well – in due course the principal merchant would deduct the expenses of the wife and children of his travelling associate from the share of the profit accruing to the junior.[78] This measure ensured the protection of the dependents while the head of the family was away for months or even years. At the same time, as Sebouh Aslanian has pointed out, the junior merchant was more likely to provide satisfactory service if his family would bear the repercussions of any infraction that he might commit.

The Multani traders covered a wide area, combining trade and banking while providing financial services even in Moscow. Their importance in the – by now former – Russian capital was especially palpable when in the early 1700s, a widow from a Hindu family established in the city was to be ceremonially killed following the death of her husband. When the tsar refused permission, the entire Hindu community left the city, and the expected loss induced the ruler to permit the killing. Moreover, a similar event recurred even in the late eighteenth century.[79]

Among the different Multani merchants, the trading caste of the Khatris was especially successful, due to the patronage of the Mughal emperors, whose policy included the promotion of trade with Central Asia. The Uzbek khans supported this trade as well. In certain cases, the emperors even entered into partnerships with Multani merchants. However, once established, merchants often prospered on the strength of their own abilities and connections, even at a time when the Mughal Empire was already disintegrating. By contrast as noted before, the Ottoman sultans only in the 1400s and 1500s had showed a serious interest in promoting or protecting Ottoman traders; and to the present author's knowledge, none of the sultans freighted ships for overseas trade, as was common enough among Mughal emperors, nobles and even royal women.[80]

According to our present knowledge, there were not many Indians who in person visited the Ottoman central lands for purposes of trade; while Indian dervishes gained a great following in eighteenth-century Istanbul, we only find a few scattered references to merchants.[81] However, textiles 'made in India' regularly reached the Ottoman lands, and enough silver went in the opposite direction to seriously upset eighteenth-century Ottoman dignitaries.[82] Mostly, Indian textiles arrived in Cairo by the mediation of local traders, who sent their agents to Mocha or Jeddah and then handled the distribution of these goods in the Ottoman Empire.

At the same time, Armenian travelling merchants, not necessarily affiliated with their more famous colleagues of New Julfa near Isfahan, started out from Istanbul and Izmir to link the Ottoman world with Poland and the Netherlands. Moreover, as we have seen, Iranian merchants, often Armenians but sometimes Muslims as well, imported Iranian silks into the Ottoman lands. It would be interesting to find out how Muslim merchants, both Ottoman and Iranian interacted with their Armenian counterparts, both Julfan and non-Julfan, when they all happened to do business in Istanbul; but, at present, we know very little about such contacts.

Ottomans and Indians in contact: Importing Indian goods

This rapid survey of merchant behaviour introduces us to the traffic that more than any other connected the two empires: namely, the importation of Indian cotton and silk fabrics into the Ottoman world. The demand for these textiles, in addition to spices, had a lengthy history, as the relevant commerce had flourished in Egypt long before the Ottoman conquest of 1517. Due to the studies of textiles specialists at the Ashmolean Museum in Oxford and the Victoria & Albert Museum in London, it has become apparent that Indian cotton prints were already reaching Egypt in the eleventh century;

and seemingly, the trade intensified after the Mamluk takeover in the mid-1200s. As the Oxford textiles scholar Ruth Barnes has expressed it, '. . . the archaeological evidence shows that Indian textiles. . . were commonly traded to Egypt by the thirteenth and fourteenth centuries, and that they were not only in use in metropolitan centres, such as Fustat, but had a wide distribution'.[83] It is intriguing that the archaeological record summarized by Barnes seems to have yielded but a few items dated to the period after 1600, while there are a number of cottons that could have arrived either in Mamluk or in early Ottoman times.[84]

Certainly, the author emphasizes that once the European trade companies became involved in the cotton trade, Egypt continued to import Indian cottons; but she does not discuss why these fabrics show up so rarely among archaeological finds. In part, this gap may be due to the abandonment of the medieval port of Quseir al-Qadīm, where dating the finds through their context is possible. As for the later period, scholars can only work on finds from the Cairo suburb of Fustat, whence many textiles finds supposedly originate, but where it is impossible to reconstruct the context. In the eyes of archaeologists and textiles experts, Quseir finds thus have had precedence, with an automatic bias in favour of the older pieces. Even more speculatively, one might think that Ruth Barnes and her collaborators, when confronted with the daunting task of selecting a few pieces for carbon dating among the enormous collection awaiting study, did not show much interest in pieces that looked like the seventeenth- or eighteenth-century fabrics well documented in collections such as that in the Victoria & Albert Museum. Instead, the team may have preferred textiles with designs that seemed older; but this assumption is quite speculative.

Most remarkably, in the second half of the nineteenth century, India's connection with the Middle Eastern market revived; and particularly cottons of modest quality, presumably meant for the everyday use of ordinary people showed a significant increase.[85] We need to supplement this archaeological evidence by the written documents from Cairo, which André Raymond has analysed. Beginning in the late 1600s, this material consists of post-mortem inventories recording the goods of important Egyptian merchants. While these people certainly traded in Indian textiles, Raymond has not been able to unearth any details.[86] Moreover, Ruth Barnes has already pointed out that we know very little about the extent to which Indian merchants engaged in this trade.[87] Raymond has opined that Cairo merchants rarely went beyond Jeddah, but it is not very clear whether the Indian goods available in this port had transited through the Arabian Peninsula or arrived from the subcontinent by boat. At least, these findings support the notion that the spheres of Indian and Ottoman merchant communities overlapped in the Red Sea coastlands. In any case, the existence of numerous large ships carrying Indian pilgrims to Mecca – and of the fair of Mina/Muna, at which the hajjis relaxed once the stressful pilgrimage was complete – make it seem likely that significant quantities of Indian cottons arrived in Jeddah by the maritime route.

Outside of Egypt, very few Indian cotton fabrics have survived in the Ottoman world, although in the 1700s, and after the revival of the Indian industry in the late nineteenth century, such textiles must have been common enough. There are many reasons for their disappearance, one of them the relative lack of interest on the part of Ottoman elite families before the late 1800s in preserving items for which the current generation had no immediate use. If still in satisfactory condition, such pieces might rather become hand-me-downs for the use of slaves and other menials.[88] Cotton textiles were especially at risk, as many items were of modest quality and intended for daily use, a situation that made their preservation unlikely. In addition, the many wars, flights, migrations and spoliations from which the inhabitants of the (former) Ottoman lands suffered between 1870 and 1950 must have resulted in further losses of property.

As for ethnographical museums in Turkey, which might have functioned as repositories, their establishment typically dated to the last ninety years or so, when most Indian cottons once present in the empire had already disappeared. Moreover, outside of a few premier museums in Istanbul, interest in 'non-Turkish' artefacts remained limited. Turkish museums with a textiles focus, normally due to the commitment of private collectors, came into existence only in the 1980s or 1990s. While the collections of the Topkapı Palace contain some Indian textiles, in Istanbul or Ankara there is nothing comparable to the Calico Museum of Ahmadabad, or the textiles collection exhibited in the Crafts Museum of New Delhi.[89]

Given the scarcity of Indian cotton cloth made in the 1400s to 1700s, and surviving in the former Ottoman territories, we depend almost exclusively on written sources, both narrative and archival. These topics have attracted the attention first of Halil İnalcık and later of Gilles Veinstein.[90] The seventeenth-century travelogue writer Evliya Çelebi (1611–after 1683) has claimed that, in the later 1600s, Egyptian linen did not last very long, but perhaps this deficiency was due to the fineness of the fibre.[91] If this claim is valid – but we have no way of knowing – the durability of many Indian cotton fabrics should have been a competitive advantage. Ottoman–Indian trade was by no means limited to the lands forming part of the Mughal Empire; for in the late fifteenth-century qadi registers of Bursa, İnalcık has found evidence of three agents sent by Mahmūd Gāwān, vizier to the Bahmani/Bahamani sultanate in the Deccan between 1466 and 1481. Arriving for the first time in 1466 and once again in 1479, these men were to sell the goods entrusted to them by their master, with textiles a prominent item.[92] A further and larger group of traders appeared in 1481, the year in which Mahmūd Gāwān was killed. Some of these agents later travelled from Bursa to the Balkans; but apparently the Ottoman records have nothing more to say about them. In any case, the presence of these businessmen shows that Indian textiles had a market in Bursa by the last quarter of the fifteenth century; and, as it is unlikely that Mahmūd Gāwān had sent out agents without knowing whether they would find customers, we can assume that by the mid-1400s there was a market for Indian textiles in the Balkans as well.

İnalcık returned to Ottoman–Indian trade around 1980, but at this time there was a concern with current affairs that had been absent in his earlier works. At the time when İnalcık was writing his later article, Turkey's government had accepted neo-liberal principles and dismantled the combination of state and private investment that for several decades had sustained an economy founded on import substitution and in many cases, the protection of domestic producers by high tariff walls. As local manufacturers were now about to lose this protection, İnalcık worried that the – relatively – high wages earned by Turkish workers might prevent the textiles produced in Turkey in the 1980s from being competitive in the world market.[93] İnalcık also subscribed to the notion that 'in the East' all wages were miserably low.[94] However, in recent years, Prasannan Parthasarathi has argued against this position. According to Parthasarathi, the high mobility of Indian handloom weavers secured them a wage that did not differ much from the payment received by their counterparts in England, which admittedly was very low as well (see Chapter 7).[95] In this perspective, deepening misery and a return of disillusioned weavers to agriculture were features of the colonial period only, and not of the 1600s or early 1700s.

Ottoman consumers and Indian prints

İnalcık's survey has pointed to a phenomenon that we tend to associate with the much more recent work of Prasannan Parthasarthi, Giorgio Riello and Maxine Berg, namely the imitation of Indian cotton cloths by English manufacturers, which the latter then might market in the Middle East.[96] This point is probably more important to present-day researchers than it was to İnalcık's colleagues in the 1970s. After all, scholars involved with post-colonial studies, which only entered the historical mainstream with Edward Said's famous book, have often made the point that inventiveness in design and production was not a European monopoly.[97] On the contrary, particularly in the textiles realm, successful industrialization involved learning from China and India. A few years after İnalcık, the Japanese scholar Katsumi Fukasawa made a similar point, who emphasized that ornamenting textiles by block-printing was an Indian invention, widely practised in the seventeenth century, and that European manufacturers, similar incidentally to their Iranian and Ottoman colleagues, learned this technique from their Indian models.[98] Seemingly, some French manufacturers were especially adept imitators. For when the ambassador of Sultan Selim III (r. 1789–1807) to France visited Parisian workshops between 1806 and 1811, he highlighted the techniques by which manufacturers produced prints of good quality, connecting the individual imprints on a roll of cloth in such a manner that the transitions from one stamping to the next remained invisible.[99]

Perhaps due to the special interest of French manufacturers in Indian cotton printing, the most valuable data on Indian fabrics imported into the Ottoman Empire, as well as their local imitations, comes from French sources. After all, Marseilles merchants, during the heyday of this trade in the eighteenth century, were active purchasers of Ottoman cotton, cotton cloths, and angora wool. Katsumi Fukasawa has provided further detail on this important but neglected issue, highlighting the role of Aleppo as a textiles market.[100] Apparently, quite a few Indian traders entered the Ottoman lands from Basra and Baghdad; with the latter city, many Aleppo traders had established close ties, after Bandar 'Abbas had lost favour because of the long wars in Iran that accompanied – and later followed – the demise of the Safavids. At least in part, however, manufacture for the Ottoman market seems to have taken place not so much in Gujarat or Bengal, as in Indian territories further south and outside of our present concern. Masulipatnam, on the Coromandel Coast and later the English colony of Madras (today: Chennai), were especially prominent, and so was the French settlement of Pondicherry. According to a French estimate of the late 1700s, the

Istanbul market, despite the many crises of this war-torn period, every year purchased Indian goods, for the most part cotton textiles, worth five million *piastres izelotes*. While a sizeable share of these *piastres* or *guruş* paid for fine muslins suitable for turbans, painted and printed cottons were also in demand.

Ottoman sources also reflect the widespread use of Indian textiles. Thus, around the year 1700, the decedents of Damascus studied by Colette Establet, who were on the whole of very modest property, still were quite likely to own a few Indian fabrics, rather than the French textiles that merchants from France were trying to popularize at just this time.[101]

Already by the beginning of the eighteenth century, the Ottoman official historiographer Mustafa Naima was voicing his misgivings about the vogue of Indian goods.[102] Naima worried about an issue that had been of concern to the rulers of Mediterranean countries from time immemorial: Namely, that Indian merchants demanded payment in gold or silver, as the Mediterranean region offered few goods marketable in India. At the same time, bullion was indispensable for waging wars, a situation that explains the reticence of Naima and other eighteenth-century figures vis à vis Indian trade.

In response to the growing difficulty of obtaining 'the real thing', Ottoman manufacturers emulated Indian cotton, with the weavers of Aleppo, Ayntab (today: Gaziantep) and Diyarbekir being particularly successful. However, quite a few of these fabrics were relatively coarse and heavy, so that wealthy subjects of the sultan may well have continued to prefer the Indian originals. On the other hand, Fukasawa has found that these 'imitation Indian' cottons had a market among French traders, especially the *chafarcani* 'made in Diyarbekir', ornamented with white flowers on a red or violet background. Due to French purchases, a number of samples survive in Marseilles repositories. For French merchants trading in Aleppo, this fabric was attractive because of its handsome colour; and, as in northwestern India a fabric known by the same name had been in use for some time already, the model for the Diyarbekir variety was probably Indian and may have transited through Iran. Perhaps Armenian traders, well established in Bengal since the late 1600s and migrating to India in sizeable numbers during the eighteenth-century crises in Iran, continued to trade between their present and former homelands and thus played a role in diffusing *chafarcani*s to Iran and eastern Anatolia.[103]

The means of transport

It is intriguing that, where the Ottoman domains are concerned, relatively few studies deal with the mobility of traders. However, as in the early modern period, goods only travelled if there were people to accompany them, the number of sometimes wealthy and often quite modest merchants proceeding on caravan routes and sea-lanes must have been appreciable.[104] According to traditions established by the Anatolian Seljuks (1081–1307, with strong regional variations), on the principal roads the Ottomans constructed further caravansaries, often called *han*. On the whole, Ottoman *han*s were utilitarian and did not show the monumentality and grandeur of their medieval predecessors; even so, in some places, a *han* functioned as a fort and became the nucleus of a town (see Chapter 5).

Especially in the Balkans from the later sixteenth century onward, travelling merchants attended fairs, sometimes associated with the festivals of the patron saints of local churches. Much of the available information comes from the fact that high-level Ottoman dignitaries appropriated the spaces where these fairs took place, converting them into revenue-producers for the pious foundations that they had instituted in Istanbul and elsewhere. Therefore the relevant account books sometimes contain information on the dues payable by merchants and the places from which the latter had come, the goods traded, and the physical appearance of the fair venue. Incidentally, both in the Ottoman world and in eighteenth- to nineteenth-century Jodhpur, a variation on the term *bisat* designated those sellers who did not have stands of their own, but simply spread out their wares on the ground.[105]

Transportation in the Ottoman world took place on the backs of camels, mules and packhorses, with wagons important in those parts of Anatolia and the Balkans where the roads made their use practicable.[106] In Syria and Egypt, camels had completely displaced the carts and wagons that had been in use in Roman times, as the animals did not require paved roads. However, in Anatolia there were problems that balanced the advantages of camels; for only hybrids of dromedaries and Bactrian camels could survive the rain and cold of winter, or travel on the steep mountain paths that caravans had to negotiate in certain parts of Anatolia and the Balkans. Furthermore, being a hybrid, the combination of dromedaries and Bactrian camels degenerated quite rapidly, requiring hybridization often enough to make the process quite costly. While camels were in occasional use in Byzantine Constantinople, and immigrant nomads from Anatolia employed them to transport goods needed by Ottoman armies campaigning in South Eastern Europe, they did not play the preponderant role in the Balkans that they had acquired in Syria or Egypt. Thus, the hopes of the sixteenth-century Habsburg ambassador Ogier Ghiselin de Busbecq, who wanted to acclimatize camels in Central Europe, did not lead to any practical result.[107]

In consequence, transport facilities were highly variable: some entrepreneurs, especially in Anatolia, were nomads and semi-nomads who hired out their camels to merchants. Packhorses were in use as well; and mules served especially in hilly terrain. When commercial opportunities expanded in the eighteenth-century Balkans, some muleteers managed to make the transition from working for others, to trading on their own account.[108] As for maritime transport, in the 1700s there were trading vessels owned by Ottoman Greeks, who prospered especially because Franco-British wars frequently prevented the voyages of their competitors, the owners of transport ships domiciled in Southern France that many Ottoman passengers and trade goods used during peacetime. By contrast, few Ottoman Muslims were active in maritime transport.

In the Indian context, commercial transportation by nomads or semi-nomads has become a subject of study, particularly with reference to the Thar Desert, which is located to the west of Delhi and close to the frontier with Pakistan. However, little 'solid' data on transport is available for the period before the late nineteenth century; put differently, scholars have to largely rely on colonial ethnography, data collected after

1947 by officials of the Republic of India, and oral traditions as well. The desert occupies much of the land that in Mughal and post-Mughal times formed the princely territories of Jaisalmer, Jodhpur and Marwar. Particularly, the inhospitable climate of Marwar induced many inhabitants of a mercantile mentality, both Jain and Hindu, to emigrate and make a living by trade or money lending in other parts of the subcontinent.[109] In the late 1800s, Marwaris often served the holders of the remaining *jagīrs* and lent money to peasants. However, it is difficult to determine to what extent they had carried on these same activities in past centuries and to what extent trade and money lending in this region were 'novelties' of the colonial era. As incomes from agriculture were – and remain – unpredictable, the inhabitants of this area raised bullocks, which carried the goods made for instance in the productive region of Punjab, to the markets of distant regions.[110] Time and again, observers recorded the huge caravans of bullocks, often owned by people known as Banjaras, who moved around with their families and herds, playing a key role in commercial transport.[111]

Money matters

In both the Ottoman and Mughal contexts, a range of data produced by local officials, which would allow the historian to reconstruct economic conjectures, is not very common – and for our present purposes the records of European trade companies, put together with the needs of these outsiders in mind, are of limited utility. Even so, both Ottomanist historians and their colleagues working on the Mughal Empire have located and used written documents concerning coinage, as well as surviving coins, to reconstruct the monetary history of the two polities. In addition, the evidence on builders' wages that a team led by Şevket Pamuk has put together makes it possible to follow the changing wages of trained and untrained workers in the construction sector, and compare the results with those of the many early modern European cities, for which scholars have undertaken similar studies.[112] However, as the Indian evidence does not seem to have yielded any data on builders' wages, we focus instead on a problem amenable to comparison, namely the consequences of the cheapening of silver worldwide, subsequent to the Spanish conquest of Latin America.

When the historian Ömer Lütfi Barkan published the first Ottomanist study on this issue in the 1970s, he accepted that the 'quantity theory of money' dominated price formation and thereby economic life. Put differently, if the amount of silver in circulation increased, prices necessarily rose, and Barkan thought that the silver imported into the Ottoman world through trade resulted in enormous price increases that made the Ottoman state apparatus largely non-functional.[113] However, when in the 1990s, Şevket Pamuk revisited the question using a much broader source base, he significantly modified these conclusions. Firstly, Pamuk stressed that the amount of silver in circulation was not the only factor promoting inflation. Certainly, economists have disagreed on the question whether population increase, which the Ottoman tax registers document for the sixteenth century, can result in inflation, namely when food supplies, expanding less rapidly than the consuming population, push upward the prices of grain and other basic foodstuffs. Whatever the outcome of this dispute, given the growth of Anatolian rural markets apparent from sixteenth-century taxation lists, it is probable (though not provable) that money circulated more rapidly than had been true in earlier periods, and this increased rapidity promoted inflation as well.[114] Urbanization, which the sixteenth-century Ottoman tax registers clearly reflect, is another factor increasing the volume of transactions and thus the velocity of circulation.

While there is no direct way of measuring this crucial variable, Pamuk has proposed a number of indicators suggesting that this factor was indeed responsible for a sizeable part of the price increase. After all, the Ottoman exchequer of the years before and after 1600 instituted a novel slew of taxes known as *avarız-ı divaniyye*, largely payable in money. Taxpayers could only earn enough cash to pay these new taxes if they sold growing quantities of agricultural and manufactured goods, resulting in a more rapid turnover of the coins circulating in the market.[115]

Secondly, Pamuk pointed out that, while Barkan had distinguished between prices in current coin and prices in grams of silver, he had underestimated the degree to which the sultans of the time had debased the currency. Put differently, while Barkan knew about the 'debasement factor' he had too readily attributed price increases to the quantity of circulating silver alone. This fact of life became especially obvious when Pamuk focused on the 1700s, a period not covered by Barkan. For as numismatic evidence shows, this period saw a second spate of inflation, with debasement the main culprit. Furthermore, both Barkan and Pamuk have stressed that the growing demand for cash, and the resulting debasement of the currency, was due to the need for larger armies to fight against the Habsburgs and Safavids. Monetary instability was thus only in part due to the influx of silver, and as happened in seventeenth-century European polities too, the Ottoman sultans were spending more on warfare than the economy of their empire was able to sustain.

Debasement was the consequence of a 'silver famine', which ironically, was the consequence of the importation of silver pushing up prices. Certainly, some silver mines operated in the Ottoman Balkans and in Anatolia; however, their productivity was moderate, and frequently, mining became uneconomical after American silver had entered the empire in large quantities.[116] While before about 1750, the Ottoman balance of trade with European countries remained favourable, the economy lost silver because as noted, much of the Mediterranean carrying trade was in the hands of Italian and French shippers. In addition, silver flowed to Yemen, after the 1630s no longer part of the empire, to pay for the consumption of coffee by Ottoman subjects. Imports of silk from Iran, and of spices and textiles from India, added to the eastward outflow of bullion. Especially in wartime, specie was thus in very short supply; and it made sense to use peasant deliveries in kind, in the shape of tithes or *avarız*, to feed campaigning armies.

In the late 1500s and early 1600s, the Ottoman Empire was not the only polity to experience inflation due to a growing abundance of silver. Rather, Spain was the *locus classicus* of this problem, and the impulse to investigate this type of inflation came from historians of early modern Spain, beginning in the 1930s with Earl Hamilton. Thus, historians of the Mughal Empire came to ask whether inflation of this type occurred in India as well. The question was timely, as after all a share of the silver that the Spaniards had extracted from the New World transited through Latinate

Europe and the Ottoman Empire to pay for Indian spices and fabrics. Moreover, while a sizeable part of the specie arriving in the Ottoman lands thus did not remain there for very long, the Mughal Empire was self-sufficient, apart from a limited import trade in high-quality horses.[117] While silver entering the subcontinent did not usually leave it, Mughal sources do not contain the litanies of complaint about budget deficits and debasement of the currency that are so familiar to Ottomanists.

Irfan Habib has solved this problem at least in part by pointing out that, until the very late 1500s the Mughal currency used in daily life, as well as for revenue payments, was not a silver coin like the *akçe* but a copper coin known as a *dam*.[118] In consequence, the sixteenth-century cheapening of silver did not affect the Mughal economy and revenue collection at all. However, by the first half of the seventeenth century, the growing availability of silver did induce the administration to gradually replace copper by silver coins, a process diligently recorded by Irfan Habib and his collaborators. For everyday transactions, the mints began issuing coins worth a fraction of a rupee and in the long run, copper coins became rare, although they never completely disappeared. The Mughal Empire thus 'avoided' the period in which silver inflation was most serious in the Ottoman Empire, namely the late 1500s and early 1600s.

As for the later seventeenth century, it is worth noting that the Mughal domains never suffered from the 'price revolution', although the influx of silver into the territories of the Mughal emperor was far larger. For, as noted, over the centuries merchants from Western Asia, and later from Europe, who did business in India, could only sell small quantities of goods from their own countries. Therefore, payment in gold and silver was the normal procedure. Bullion in-flows into the Mughal Empire increased dramatically once American silver had entered European commercial circuits. On the other hand, as Om Prakash has pointed out, there was no significant increase in the Indian price level and, *a fortiori*, no rampant inflation.[119]

An older generation of scholars had suggested that this difference was 'culturally' determined: Much of the imported bullion never entered monetary circuits, as people transformed it into jewellery and hoarded it as savings for an emergency, or donated artefacts in gold and silver to Hindu temples. While, as we have seen, the trade in jewels was indeed a thriving concern, probably more so than in the contemporaneous Ottoman Empire, the 'moral' judgement that historians have attached to this phenomenon was often quite 'orientalist' in tone.[120] Put differently, these historians claimed that Indian owners of wealth did not 'rationally' invest their money in agricultural improvements or manufacturing, and thus were responsible for missing the opportunity to industrialize and successfully compete with European societies.

However, Om Prakash has pointed out that hoarding and the constitution of treasuries were not the only reasons why the Mughal Empire, and the principalities subject to it, avoided a bullion-induced inflation. According to his argumentation, prices will increase when the stock of bullion in a given society grows, but the aggregate quantity of goods in circulation does not, or at least not at the same speed; for in that case, a larger number of coins will correspond to a more or less static quantity of goods, and price hikes are inevitable. Shireen Moosvi and Najaf Haider have also argued that the large volume of commercial transactions, in part due to the need to pay taxes in cash, sustained an urgent demand for money. As demand was so high that bankers created 'bank money' by making possible the transfer of bills of exchange, the money supply evidently did not exceed demand, and thus, there was no inflation either in the late sixteenth or in the seventeenth century.[121] In a similar vein, Om Prakash has suggested that because of the increased demand for Indian products, especially textiles, in Western Asia and later in Europe as well, the manufacturing sector grew quite rapidly.[122] As manufacturing expanded 'in lock-step' with the growing supply of gold and silver, the result was a balance between circulating goods and bullion that did not change very much; and therefore, Mughal India did not experience the inflation that so dramatically upset existing equilibriums in the Spanish and Ottoman empires.

After all, in a non-capitalist economy, we can view inflation as a growing supply of silver chasing a stagnant or slowly growing supply of goods; if the volume of goods increases as fast as the available silver stocks do, there should not be any inflation.[123] By contrast, Tirthankar Roy has opined that, as the share of exports was tiny when compared with the size of the economy of seventeenth- or early eighteenth-century South Asia, the incoming amount of silver was too small to make any difference to the local money supply. The reader may object that, even if the annual amount of incoming silver was tiny, the cumulative effect should have been important, since only small amounts of silver ever left the subcontinent. In addition, perhaps it is necessary to account for significant regional differences, as Muzaffar Alam has pointed out that in the Northern provinces he has studied taxes increased during the 1600s in tandem with inflation.[124]

Economic expansion and its limits

Ottoman tax registers of the sixteenth century provide only indirect evidence concerning the expansion of arable land, and as agricultural technology did not change very much in the period at issue, this expansion is at the root of commercial and artisan prosperity. Akbar's officials, by contrast, had received instructions to carefully measure taxable lands (see Chapter 8). Therefore, we know that in the late 1500s, and during the seventeenth century, when Ottoman population growth was ebbing, the expansion of arable land in Bengal and Bihar, recently conquered by the Mughal emperors, was impressive indeed. When Mughal agriculture and the revenue derived from it expanded, the money economy expanded too, as all office-holders received their incomes in cash. Moreover, the business managers of highly placed nobles lent money to merchants engaging in long-distance trade and shipbuilding. While merchants, even very rich ones, did not become part of the Mughal elite, the involvement of nobles in trade must have made them more sensitive to the needs of merchants – at least, if they did not develop the 'robber mentality' that, as Banarasidas has so graphically recorded, merely caused the traders to flee. Thus, revenue derived from village farms fuelled commercial expansion. As John Richards has summarized the situation: '... the Mughal system encouraged both a deepening level of monetary usage as well as more intense linkages between the locality, the state, and the larger economic worlds beyond'.[125]

In the Ottoman world, incidentally, the linkage of villagers and elites with the market, mediated through the agency of the state, was probably less profound and widespread than it was in the Mughal ambiance. Firstly, we have seen that in the Ottoman lands, tithes were largely payable in kind, so that the tax-takers, rather than the peasants took this grain to market. Secondly, many members of the elite disapproved of their colleagues engaging in trade, considering that the sultans' subjects should earn money without competition from privileged office-holders.[126] Even so, such elite investors existed, but in limited numbers. Even more importantly, the Ottoman Empire exported only a limited quantity of manufactured goods in high demand, and thus the expansion of the empire, while it certainly promoted trade, could not generate a level of commercial growth comparable to that of the Mughal world.

In a different perspective, the sixteenth- and seventeenth-century prosperity of the Mughal Empire was due to the flexibility of weavers and merchants working for export. If these people had not expanded their output to respond to increased demand for Indian textiles in the Ottoman world, Latinate Europe, eastern Africa and Southeast Asia, unit prices would have increased and given the importation of silver by European commercial companies, the Mughal Empire might well have experienced the silver-induced inflation that made life difficult for Ottoman wage-earners and the exchequer alike.

In conclusion: 'Incorporation into a capitalist world system'

As a major result of this survey, the differences between merchants who were subjects of Ottoman sultans and those who owed allegiance to the rulers of the Mughal Empire have become clearly visible. While a number of Indian regions, including Gujarat, Bengal and certain coastal regions of the Indian Peninsula specialized in the exportation of cotton textiles, the Ottoman lands exported mostly agricultural products and some semi-finished goods such as yarn and leather. By contrast, textiles 'ready for the tailor' such as the Anatolian cotton goods sold on the northern shores of the Black Sea, the mohair fabrics of Ankara going to Venice and the Bursa silks sold to Poland or Russia were not goods for a mass market, and their cultural importance did not necessarily translate into economic value. We thus do not find merchants who organized textiles manufacture for export by selecting certain weavers as business partners and granting credit to the latter. In the agricultural milieu, however, it was common enough for Ottoman traders to give loans to peasants and then acquire their crop at a previously fixed price (*selem*), although many Islamic jurists were wary of the practice.[127]

Moreover, at the present state of our knowledge it does appear that in Mughal Bengal and Gujarat, the role of middlemen traders (*gomashtas*) and others serving foreign companies dwarfed the volume of business transacted by the often non-Muslim traders who sold their purchases to French, British and Dutch merchants active in Izmir.[128] Even so, it would be helpful if we could devise a way of comparing the business of the Syrian Christians in late eighteenth-century Cairo with the trade of their Bengali or Gujarati counterparts.

Today, quite a few historians of Mughal India have moved away from the earlier assumption that the appearance of Portuguese, Dutch, English and French merchants in the sixteenth and early seventeenth centuries was an unmitigated disaster for local economies and societies. Rather, scholars such as Om Prakash, and Ghulam Nadri to mention a member of the younger generation, assume that there was a difference between the sixteenth and seventeenth centuries on the one hand, and the 1700s and 1800s on the other.[129] In the earlier period, the silver brought into the country by foreign traders and the increasing demand that they generated especially in the textiles sector, promoted an expansion of economic life. However, in the later centuries, when especially the East India Company grew into a territorial power, the trend soon reversed. Once the EIC had become a political and military force, immigrant 'country traders' of British background established their businesses in the (former) Mughal domains, side-lining Indian merchants. Weavers' pay, which *mutatis mutandis* had previously been comparable to that of handloom weavers in England, declined dramatically in consequence.[130] As Prakash put it, the relationship passed from 'Market-determined to Coercion-based', put differently, from negotiation to the use of force.[131]

It would seem that the rapid contraction of the Mughal Empire in the first half of the eighteenth century was the principal factor causing the mutation of trade relationships into colonial domination, with the economic regression this changeover implied. As Shireen Moosvi has memorably pointed out, compared to the situation in the late 1500s as recorded by Abū'l-Fazl 'Allāmī, significant indicators, especially in urban manufacturing, showed that by 1900, the economy of Northern and Central India was somewhat below the level characterizing the last years of Akbar's reign.[132] It would be far more difficult to make a similar diachronic comparison for the Ottoman world; but we need to remember that manufactured imports did not compete with Ottoman products before the late 1700s, and in many cases only after 1830. As Mehmet Genç has shown, in the eighteenth century difficulties in manufacturing were quite often due to the peculiarities of Ottoman war financing, rather than to the competition of imported goods.[133] In a sense comparable to what Indian historians have found in the case of the Mughal domains, we need to differentiate carefully between periods and geographic spaces if we want to discern which damages were due to European interventions and which difficulties had purely local causes.

In fact, the focus of quite a few recent works on trade in the Mughal or formerly Mughal domains concerns either particular regions or else specific social groups; and this interest surely explains, at least in part, why certain historians of the eighteenth century do not think that everything that happened in this period was necessarily catastrophic. This attitude is especially apparent among historians focusing on Bengal or Gujarat, as particularly in the latter region, certain Indian merchants might do quite well even after the British had established political control.[134] Business historians have focused on such successes, as apparent especially in certain volumes forming part of the series recently put together by Gurcharan Das. Some of the contributors are deliberately 'hard-nosed': Put differently, they treat the trade in opium, not as the major crime we would consider it today, but as one way among others to make a profit, no matter the millions of Chinese who suffered.[135]

Probably, the best-known proponent of this view is Tirthankar Roy, who has gone so far as to suggest that business historians may view the resources which Great Britain extracted from India in the roughly two hundred years of colonial dominance as having been mostly 'idle treasure' in the hands of princes and magnates. In any case, Roy asserts that these resources were not available for investment.[136] Obviously, this argument ignores the fact at least some of this 'idle treasure' remained in the hands of its owners even under the British regime, while poor weavers or modest salt traders bore the brunt of colonial exploitation. More intriguingly, Roy has proposed that historians should regard these sums of money, enormous as they were, as a kind of 'payment for service'. For Roy, the service at issue is the business, industrial and academic infrastructure, which partly emerged during the colonial period, and greatly progressed after 1947. This infrastructure has enabled Indian businessmen – and incidentally scientists as well – to become a major presence in today's world.[137]

Evidently, this perspective is impossible to adopt for a scholar looking at commercial relations as practised in the colonial period when viewing the matter from Delhi, Lucknow or Agra. However, presumably it appears less outlandish to people who look at the world while working out of Mumbai, the former Bombay. In the latter city, certain world-class enterprises owned by Indians started to operate already in the late 1800s, and some wealthy entrepreneurs began to invest in the city's infrastructure at that time as well. However, these debates, while beginning with events such as the British takeover of Surat castle in 1759, on the whole are relevant to the period after 1760 and thus not of immediate concern to this study.

Even so, it makes sense to ask whether these discussions may be relevant to the historian of Ottoman trade as well. At first glance, it seems that in this field, the divergence is so wide that Indian debates are only marginally useful for Ottoman commercial historians, if only because the Ottoman state apparatus was much more resilient and the empire lasted so much longer. While 'incorporation into the European-dominated world economy' certainly occurred in the Ottoman context as well, whatever happened in Istanbul or Izmir always occurred with the input and sometimes with the consent of Ottoman officialdom. Given the weight of the bureaucratic apparatus, Ottoman merchants were thus never in a position to play the role of a Virji Vora, an 'Abd ul-Ghafūr, or an Arjunji Nathji (*c.* 1680–1760).[138] To date, business history is an underdeveloped sub-field in Ottoman history; and few Ottomanists have tried to reconstruct the careers of individual Ottoman merchants. Nelly Hanna and İsmail Hakkı Kadı thus form some of the few exceptions to this rule.[139] It seems that quite often, Ottomanists will assume that European sources contain information only about European traders. However the advances made by Indian business historians show that this view is overly pessimistic; and it makes sense to search for Ottoman merchants documented in both Ottoman and non-Ottoman records.

Many Indian merchants became rich because they organized the production of cotton textiles; put differently, they managed to dominate local artisans, albeit within certain limits. Relations between Ottoman artisans and traders were rather different, if only because once again, the bureaucratic apparatus had a more significant input; the following chapter deals with this issue.

7

Early Modern Crafts in the Ottoman and Indian Orbits

In studies of Ottoman history, artisans often appear as the victims of the changes imposed by early modern European capitalism, as it impinged on the Mediterranean world.[1] Certain artisans, especially the woollen weavers of Salonika, did indeed lose their markets already in the 1600s, although most of their colleagues did not feel the effects of European economic expansion before the late eighteenth century, after the end of the period at issue here. Other historians have viewed Ottoman craftsmen as devoted servants of the sultans that the governing apparatus could move around like pieces on a chessboard. Though largely unseen, their labour in manufacturing guns and gunpowder, weaving sailcloth, or building fortresses and mosque complexes enabled the monarchs to pursue ambitious state building projects from Yemen to Hungary.

By contrast, the present chapter highlights what Ottoman craftspeople had in common with their colleagues working in the vastly different political context of the Mughal Empire. Put differently, we will be sceptical about regarding artisans merely as victims of capitalism and servants of the sultans. In large empires, where market transactions were crucial although they did not dominate human relations, we may expect certain similarities in political structures and elite attitudes toward artisans and the work of the latter. At the same time, grassroots Indian societies differed profoundly from their Ottoman counterparts; and the similarities observed are especially remarkable for appearing in such varied contexts. Within these parameters, we 'tease out' the similarities and differences between the artisan worlds of the Ottoman and Mughal empires, including sub-Mughal principalities where appropriate.

From the work of Eugenia Vanina on Indian artisans between the thirteenth and eighteenth centuries, which focuses on comparisons with medieval and early modern Europe, the present author has learnt a good deal although the aims of this chapter are different.[2] Firstly, Vanina, a specialist on India has extensively used the work of foreign travellers such as Francisco Pelsaert (1590–1630), Jean-Baptiste Tavernier (1605–98) and François Bernier (1625–88), the latter author having attempted comparisons of French and Indian socio-political structures from his own philosophical perspective. While the limits and dangers of Bernier's thinking are obvious today, he and his commercially minded traveller colleagues have relayed information on artisan production unavailable in any sources produced in the Mughal Empire. The observations of these authors thus form a vital link between seventeenth-century Europe and the Mughal orbit.

By contrast, the Ottoman subjects that spent time in Surat or Delhi have not left any descriptions of the artisan world, and the same thing applies to the dervishes and traders from India that visited the Ottoman Empire for pilgrimage or trade. Linkages on the personal level, which surely facilitate comparative approaches, are thus difficult to find although they must have existed. Especially in late eighteenth-century Lucknow, there must have been a connection to the Ottoman capital, or else it would be hard to explain the existence of the monumental 'Roomi' Gate (1784), supposedly inspired by Istanbul models.[3]

Secondly, Vanina covers the subcontinent as a whole and not just Northern India, and she has chosen a far longer period as well. For the present project, her conclusion that Indian artisan technologies did not change very much between the sixteenth and eighteenth centuries, allows us to avoid this topic. Moreover, this proceeding makes good sense, as artisan technology in the early modern Ottoman orbit has not excited much scholarly interest.

Both in the Ottoman world and in Mughal India, women were a small minority among skilled workers, although they might labour in the preparatory stages of, for instance, textiles production. Particularly, spinning was often women's work. In the Ottoman context, female apprenticeships must have been rare, although they occasionally occurred in sixteenth-century Bursa, where we encounter at least one young girl entrusted to a woman who was to train her as a silk weaver.[4] Furthermore, around 1700 skilled female Orthodox embroiderers likely worked for their churches; in eighteenth-century Thessaly (Northern Greece) there was even a guild consisting only of women, with recruitment a family affair.[5] However, such cases were exceptional, and the norm was for women to receive no special training. In eighteenth-century Jodhpur, Nandita Prasad Sahai has found artisans refusing to teach women craft-skills, as upon marriage, females would take their capabilities to a potentially rival household.[6] Given this situation, we will assume that the gender of artisans was male and call them 'craftsmen' upon occasion.

In the present inchoate state of comparative studies, we avoid all speculation as to how the similarities between Ottoman and Mughal artisan life, observable in certain instances, may have come into being. If we try to explain the genesis of artisan practices in the Ottoman or Mughal worlds by reference to the medieval artisans of Samarkand, Isfahan or Kabul, we risk trying to elucidate one 'unknown' factor by means of another, which remains largely unknown as well. To avoid this trap, we treat the roughly two and a half centuries between the early 1500s and about 1770 as an entity in and of itself, without referring to artisan pasts or futures. Dealing with the craftsmen of two very different social and political worlds whose documentation presents formidable challenges, is difficult enough – without compounding the problem through speculation.

Our investigations begin with a discussion of the attempts of Indianists and Ottomanists to picture 'the economy' of the relevant regions during the sixteenth century, and particularly the place that artisans must have occupied in it. In the second section, craft workshops producing manufactured goods for the ruler and his palace, both in the Ottoman world and in South Asia, occupy centre stage, followed by the difficult question of artisan remuneration. Evaluating the incomes of artisans is difficult because in the Ottoman and even more so in the Mughal world, the data are very 'spotty', and conclusions thus remain very tentative. Next, after briefly introducing the role of castes and sub-castes in the Indian craft context and of artisan guilds in the Ottoman world, we proceed to a treatment of the 'moral economy' which in different yet comparable ways, functioned in early modern Central India and in the core provinces of the Ottoman Empire. As the next step, we show how artisans might migrate in order to protect their livelihoods, even if the respective governmental apparatuses might wish them to stay in place. To conclude, we discuss a methodological issue, explicating the reasons why 'oral history' is of great importance in the study of Indian craft, while Ottomanists concerned with the period before about 1900 have shown only limited interest.

After having touched upon the traders' approach to artisan production (see Chapter 6), we now return to this issue, but this time to visualize the perspective of craftspeople. Often we discover the concerns of these men and women only by reading 'between the lines' of our sources. In the non-capitalist market economies of the Ottoman and Mughal empires, some artisans sold directly to the consumer, especially if demand was largely local. Usually, weavers working for export needed to turn to merchant intermediaries, but exceptionally, Jean-Baptiste Tavernier recorded that the weavers of Benares/Varanasi in the mid-1600s sold many of their products directly, even to foreigners.[7] Given divergent economic interests, relations between artisans and merchants were contentious more often than not, and presumably we know less about artisans because the winners write history and the craftsmen were often the losers.

The sources: The fleeting traces of artisans

In both worlds artisans formed a sizeable part of urban populations, especially of the largest cities; and, albeit to a lesser degree, they were present in certain villages as well. Even so, literary documentation involving these people is quite rare. As exceptions, we may mention the *fütuvvetnâmes*, often pre-Ottoman treatises reworked in Ottoman times, which discussed the virtues an artisan should cultivate, often in the context of popular Sufism. There is evidence that literate artisans copied out these texts, and probably read them to their illiterate colleagues. At least in certain towns including eighteenth-century Sarajevo, artisans wishing to qualify as masters had to show that they knew the precepts contained in this literature.[8] Very occasionally, saints' legends (*menâkıbnâme*), set in an artisan milieu, have come down to us as well.[9]

Although losses due to fire and neglect have been considerable, Ottomanist historians dealing with artisans have the enormous advantage of large surviving archives, some of them produced by the central government and others, more significant for our purposes, by local judges (qadis). However, the documentation shows a heavy bias in favour of Istanbul; and thus, historians have sometimes made general statements that apply to the capital and perhaps a few large cities, but probably not to the multitude of artisans working in small towns.

Produced wherever the judges officiated and thus closer to grassroots realities than other kinds of documentation, the registers even so remain the work of the qadis' scribes, composed according to established bureaucratic formats. These registers contain copies of orders sent by the central administration, thus serving as administrative handbooks for provincial judges; but, at the same time, they contain claims and counter-claims, including disputes about presumed poor workmanship or the activities of artisans not recognized by their respective guilds. In addition, the archives of the judges comprise inventories of the estates of deceased persons, which may cover those artisans with enough property for their descendants to have an inventory compiled.[10] In addition, when artisan guilds brought their differences not to the qadi but to the sultan's court, the result, at least in the 1700s, was often a registration of guild rules (*nizâm*, later often: *nizâmnâme*), which usually did not enter the records in uncontested situations. Often found in the court records but sometimes in separate manuscripts too, there are short registers of administratively decreed prices (*narh*), which sometimes include specifications concerning the quality of certain goods. They thus provide information about the practices, licit and illicit, customary among the artisans of major Ottoman cities.[11] Lists of artisans and artists working for the sultans' palace have survived as well and become the subject of several monographs and text editions.[12]

By contrast, given the scarcity of archives in Mughal India, historians frequently have concentrated on archaeological and literary evidence. In addition, miniatures, sponsored not only by the emperors but by princes under Mughal suzerainty as well, sometimes show artisans at work, although such lowly people are rarely the centre of attention.[13] At least, miniatures are much more common in Mughal India and the sub-Mughal and post-Mughal principalities than is true of the Ottoman world.

Indianist scholars often focus on Jaipur, a Rajasthan principality subject to the Mughal emperors since the sixteenth century, whose archives have survived better than the collections located in Delhi or Agra, where losses due to warfare have been very high. Sumbul Halim Khan has analysed a sizeable quantity of evidence concerning the local court workshops (*kārkhānas*) of the late 1600s and the entire eighteenth century.[14] This evidence is especially precious as no comparable documents survive for the core lands of the Mughal Empire, although we know from literary sources that the emperors enjoyed the manufactures of extensive court ateliers. According to Abū'l-Fazl, almost one hundred such workshops were active in Akbar's time. The same author has provided a list of the textiles most popular at the Mughal court, with prices appended.[15] At the same time, the palaces of Agra and Delhi used craft products brought in from the provinces, although it is hard to say whether these items had arrived as gifts or else through marketing circuits.[16]

Nandita Prasad Sahai, another connoisseur of Rajasthan, has studied petitions by eighteenth-century craftspeople to the Rajput rulers of Jodhpur. Unfortunately, she died before she could use her great talents to the full.[17] Jodhpur had become largely independent when the Mughal Empire dissolved during the 1700s, but suffered seriously from Maratha raids. Local merchants, who often doubled as tax farmers, lost money because of these attacks and passed on their losses to the less well-placed artisans from whom they collected dues. Petitions that the craftspeople presented to their rulers frequently reflect their distress.

Moreover, as Indian artisans produced many goods for export, certain European visitors have recorded their observations concerning craft products, especially silk and cotton textiles. Of special interest is the travelogue of the French trader Jean-Baptiste Tavernier, who visited India several times between the 1640s and the 1660s. While specializing in precious stones, particularly diamonds the author attempted to develop overall French trade in India, so that he paid much attention to the textiles available in places such as Cambay, Burhanpur, Sironj and Bengal. As an intriguing extra, he moreover warned prospective buyers about the peculiar demands of – for instance – the French or Polish markets in which they might try to sell these fabrics.[18] While textiles made for export certainly were only a small part of total Indian production, Tavernier's observations are a valuable addition to the small stock of information at our disposal.

In addition, there are the archives generated by the British colonial power, which for instance in Bengal go back to the mid-1700s and contain significant information about the manner in which the East India Company (EIC) controlled local artisans. Dutch archives have moreover yielded information on weavers in Bengal. In the seventy-odd years between Indian independence and the present day, these documents have become the object of intensive scrutiny, of a type to which Ottomanists have not often subjected the documents on which they work. This difference is probably part of a broader set of attitudes: While using the caution that is part of their training, most Ottomanists do not view the government of the early modern Ottoman Empire as a hostile entity whose every move requires careful watching. Or else, if they do, as may be the case among certain historians in the Balkan world, they often lack the familiarity with Ottoman documents that would permit the critical examination that we can observe among many Indian historians.

Probably, the numerous registers documenting the tax obligations of the Mughal emperor's subjects contained as much information on artisan/market taxes as their Ottoman counterparts do, and perhaps even more. However, we mostly know these records from references in chronicles and other literary works, while the originals have long since disappeared.[19] For the period of Mughal florescence, the most important source is the third volume of Abū'l-Fazl 'Allāmī's (1551–1602) account of the reign of Akbar (r. 1556–1605).[20] After covering the history of Akbar's reign in two volumes, Abū'l-Fazl, trusted companion of the emperor, produced a detailed statistical account of the Mughal realm. Detailing revenues and the sources from which they had originated, most of the relevant figures seemingly date to 1595–6.[21] While most imperial revenues came from agriculture, craft-based taxes were significant enough to leave a certain number of traces. This documentation has permitted Shireen Moosvi to produce a large-scale statistical study of the Mughal economy, in which urban and rural crafts have a role to play.

The long shadow of Abū'l-Fazl 'Allāmī

In addition, Moosvi has undertaken a comparison of Abū'l-Fazl's data with those recorded by the officials serving the full-blown British colonial empire around 1900, thus assessing the impact of colonialism on the Indian revenue sources and economy. The results of this comparison are a major contribution to one of the 'big questions' in Indian history, namely in what manner and to what extent colonial rule held back economic development (see Chapter 6). In our present context, however, we deal only with her evaluation of late sixteenth-century domestic demand for craft products. In this context, we need to remember that historians of the Mughal world, more than their Ottomanist counterparts, have emphasized the very unequal distribution of income among the population. They have thus debated whether, and if applicable to what extent, people of limited income could purchase craft products, a question to which hitherto Ottomanists have not paid much attention. However, a highly unequal distribution of income characterized the Ottoman world as well; and, as Colette Establet has pointed out in a recent article, many Damascenes of the years around 1700 lived in rooms that were virtually empty.[22]

If we were to attempt a global study of the Ottoman economy similar to that undertaken by Moosvi, and establish the place of artisan incomes within it, we would have to bring together the contents of a rather large number of tax registers, preferably from the reign of Sultan Süleyman (1520–66). Nobody has ever attempted such a synthesis; and admittedly, there are good reasons for holding back. After all, in the Indian case, all the available figures come from a single text, namely the statistical overview produced by Abū'l-Fazl and/or his secretariat, and the sources on which these people constructed their account are no longer available. However, in the Ottoman case, the researcher can assess the reliability of the summary revenue accounts (*icmâl*) produced by sixteenth-century officials, at first glance the most convenient source for overall assessments. Unfortunately, they contain quite a few errors.[23] Incidentally, Moosvi has made a similar observation where the calculations of the secretariat of Abū'l-Fazl are concerned – but, as noted, there is no alternative and consequently the whole issue is of limited importance for her work. By contrast, Ottomanists will need to gather the requisite data from the long and detailed (*mufassal*) registers that are the sources of the *icmâl*s, surviving for some provinces but not for others. Therefore, the statistics resulting from such an enterprise will always be 'spotty'; and the researcher will soon ask him/herself whether the results repay the effort. This foreknowledge must have contributed to the reticence of Ottomanists, who normally have focused on the data that the tax registers provide for individual provinces or even cities, fleshing out the data by information from the records of the relevant qadi's courts, in addition to tax-farming documents.[24]

Secondly, the Ottomanist historian has to cope with the fact that for the most part, the sixteenth-century tax registers of Egypt do not survive. Unfortunately, for the historian, Egypt was however one of the central government's major sources of revenue. Certainly, Stanford Shaw has estimated Egyptian revenues with the help of documents in the 'Registers of Important Affairs' (Mühimme Defterleri) and other archival and literary sources. In addition, André Raymond, Nelly Hanna, Michel Tuchscherer, Nicolas Michel, and Alan Mikhail, among others, have devoted their careers to the in-depth analysis of the urban and rural economies of the Nile valley.[25] To sum up the problem, the *tahrir*s of sixteenth-century Anatolia and Rumelia to some extent allow an overall evaluation, but for that period, including Egypt into our consideration is highly problematic. On the other hand, we have more data on Egypt for the 1600s and 1700s, but no usable sources for the central provinces. For this reason alone, any attempt to determine the place of artisans in the Ottoman economy will be highly speculative and if constructing a parallel to the impressive work of Shireen Moosvi, we will inevitably come up with 'guesstimates' instead of more or less reliable statistics.

In this context it is worth noting that in the early 1970s, Bruce McGowan estimated sixteenth-century rural incomes in areas today belonging to Serbia, using the concept of 'economic wheat equivalent' in order to compare incomes from a variety of agricultural and non-agricultural activities.[26] However, while this article, which *mutatis mutandis* proceeded in a fashion comparable to Moosvi's work, attracted a good deal of attention when it first appeared, it concerned a rural area whose crafts were of limited importance. Nobody seems to have attempted comparable work on an area where crafts and manufacture were prominent.[27]

In certain instances, Moosvi has had to resort to hypothetical budgets and other estimates generated in the colonial period. This proceeding implies the assumption that certain basic facts-of-life involving non-elite working people did not change that much between the late sixteenth and the late nineteenth centuries. As certain scholars have dwelt extensively upon the major changes that colonial rule brought about, we cannot be sure that this premise is indeed true. On the other hand, it is very difficult to proceed in our quest if unwilling to make that assumption; for in that case, we will be unable to even estimate the sixteenth-century demand for urban products in town and country. Taking account of all these caveats, Moosvi has concluded that the income of the urban working population of Akbar's realm amounted to about one fifth of the earnings of the rural-cum-urban population as an aggregate. Allowing for lower prices in the countryside, Moosvi then suggests that the urban population – crafts and menial services combined – amounted to about fifteen per cent of Akbar's subjects as a whole. Moosvi's one-time mentor Irfan Habib had suggested an even higher percentage, close to seventeen per cent.[28] By early modern standards, Akbar's realm thus enjoyed relatively high levels of urbanization; and the same thing applied to artisan production, especially if we 'factor in' the observation that a large number of Indian artisans lived in villages.

In a sense, Moosvi's work recalls a point once made by Fernand Braudel, namely that we need to construct the 'big picture', in his case the model of the Mediterranean economy, and that for this purpose we often must rely on statistics that are less than perfect, but at least provide an order of magnitude.[29] Today, the territories ruled by Sultan Süleyman in the mid-1500s form about twenty states, whose historians have usually focused on the history of the nation state that they inhabit, with the Ottoman period often enough the 'poor relation'. While many Ottomanist historians today are aware of the dangers of concentrating too narrowly on a specific region, language barriers combine with national history concerns in discouraging the plans for broadly based studies of the kind undertaken by Shireen Moosvi. If such projects were to enter the Ottomanist agenda at some time in the future, a group effort along with the appropriate funding surely would be necessary. Perhaps a time will come when Ottomanist historians will once again feel the attraction of the 'big questions', and then Moosvi's work will be worth revisiting.

Relating Ottoman crafts to the Indian situation: Court workshops

As apparent from Sumbul Halim Khan's work, Indian princes, not only the Mughal emperors but in addition, major dignitaries including governors and subject princes, organized production in workshops that brought together artisans of high quality. Ottomanists will find Halim Khan's study particularly intriguing because in the 1500s, the Ottoman court sponsored a 'design office' (*nakkaşhane*) as well. For the sixteenth, seventeenth and eighteenth centuries, a series of palace-based records survives, listing the different corps of artisans/artists working for the sultan, including the payments allotted to these men. Occasionally, the scribes added bits of personal information: In the 1520s, artists/artisans that Selim I (r. 1512–20) had brought back from his campaign against Shāh Ismā'īl of Iran (r. 1501–24) were a prominent presence, in addition to islamized inhabitants of the Balkans, probably often drafted for the service of the sultan through the levy of boys or *devşirme*. Slaves in the narrow sense of the term (*esir, üsera*) seem to have been rare, although the Iranians brought in by Selim I could only leave when after the death of this monarch, his successor gave them permission to do so. Officially speaking, these exiles must have been in banishment (*sürgün*).

Located at least for a while in a former Byzantine church, from about 1500 onward, the *nakkaşhane* produced designs that with some adaptation, decorated a diversity of objects including silks, faience, manuscripts, and leather bindings for books.[30] Using designs on (more or less well) dated items, Ottomanist art historians have thus constructed a sequence of fashionable designs, which succeeded one another in the course of the sixteenth century.[31] Unfortunately, as we do not know very much about the transmission from design office to workshop, we usually cannot say whether a given design spread because of an official command to employ it, or whether patrons close to the court eagerly copied *nakkaşhane* models because they could thus show off their closeness to the reigning monarch. In some cases, however, a chain of palace bureaucrats clearly transmitted the wishes of the sultan.[32] As for the opinion of educated Ottomans concerning this arrangement, any general statement is impossible. However, there survive the acidic comments of Mustafa 'Âlî (1541–1600) in his *Counsel for Sultans*, to the effect that the gilders, painters and decorators in the sultan's employment were far too many and it would be a good idea to transfer them all to the Palace cavalry.[33]

For the most part, the products of Indian palace workshops (*kārkhāna*), did not enter the market. Eugenia Vanina has provided a convincing explanation to the question of why Mughal and sub-Mughal potentates instituted *kārkhānas*. For artisans with little capital, working on their own, it would have been impossible to spend time and money on high-quality products for which demand was limited.[34] Independent artisans could only survive if turnover was high, prices low and quality therefore modest. In luxury production where rapid turnover was impossible, only the protection of a patron enabled the artist/artisan to produce works of high quality; an observation that François Bernier had already recorded in the 1600s.[35] In addition, the *kārkhānas* often included weapons manufactories, where the production process was a regulated sequence of activities undertaken by specialists, incidentally similar to the cannon foundry (*tophane*) of Ottoman Istanbul.[36]

At the same time, Sumbul Halim Khan has pointed out that the accounts of quite a few *kārkhānas* contain the prices of the finished products, and so did the accounts of the textiles workshops serving Akbar's palace. Apparently, it is unclear whether officials produced these records of monetary values to control the manufacturing process and ensure efficiency, or whether perhaps some items did reach the market, by transactions that remained unrecorded.[37] In certain contexts, members of the Mughal dynasty patronized artisans not otherwise connected to the palace by buying their goods. In fact, it would have been impossible to pay the tribute of Bengal in current coin if there had not been an extensive elite demand for the cloth of this province in Delhi and in Agra. After all, purchasers in the capital had access to the silver that the Bengalis lacked. Thus, the imperial court and high-level aristocrats did not just consume the products of their own *kārkhāna*s, but entered the market as well.[38]

Other links of the *kārkhāna*s to the marketplace came about because the emperor and his dignitaries, as well as subordinate princes, purchased the raw materials needed by their workshops in the open market, and paid wages to the non-slave artisans working for them. In Jaipur, records of revenues and expenses have survived. However, it bears remembering that these documents concern a subordinate state governed by a Hindu prince under Mughal suzerainty – rather than a province directly controlled by the emperor. Furthermore, these records cover the period from 1683 to 1843, when the Mughal Empire was in crisis and later, in the course of dissolution. Therefore, it would be hazardous to assume that the results derived from the Jaipur records are valid for the *kārkhāna*s of the Mughal emperors as well. Even so, these records have the great virtue of being available in the original.

In Jaipur, certain artisans/artists received their pay according to the work performed, while the most outstanding masters, including those 'imported from the Mughal court' had monthly salaries.[39] In this venue as well, the product was non-commercial; and once again, wages, salaries and the purchase of raw materials linked the administration of the Jaipur *kārkhāna*s to the market.

*Kārkhāna*s ensured the training of the next generation of artisans, as masters employed in these workshops brought in their sons as soon as they were old enough to work. As Mika Natif has shown, in the highly specialized atelier producing illustrated books, artists often positioned themselves with respect to the masters whose works they had studied with close attention, adopting certain features of their models, with the aim of surpassing the latter in skill and invention.[40] However, the princely *kārkhāna*s were not alone in training future masters, as in ordinary shops and workshops as well masters usually trained their sons to take their places. Perhaps the most important contribution the *kārkhāna*s made to the supply of available goods was, quite simply, the enormous quantity of items that they produced, from highly decorated cannons to textiles, maps to palanquins.[41] Presumably, the princes or dignitaries commissioning this work retained some of it, as apparent from the collections extant in the Town Hall and Maharaja Sawai Man Singh II Museum in the City Palace in Jaipur. Other items went as gifts to foreign courts, where some pieces of Jaipur provenance are still in existence.

In addition, the officials responsible for the relevant storehouses, probably with some regularity, got rid of items that the sponsor of the *kārkhāna* did not wish to keep. Some of these goods became gifts to retainers; or else second-hand dealers purchased them for resale. We may thus posit a circulation of objects that did not enter the market when new, but which might do so at a later stage of their existence. Moreover, even if an item only circulated within the gift economy, it still contributed, in its own way, to the supply of goods available to the better-off Indian townspeople, thus promoting consumption. Given the large amount of goods involved, we may thus posit that next to the market economy, there existed a redistributive mechanism involving not just food grains or money, as common in other systems of this sort, but items of manufacture as well.

Mostly, *kārkhānas* employed artisans working for wages. In some venues, a foreign company might operate *kārkhānas* of its own, as the Dutch East India Company (VOC) did in Kasimbazar from the mid-seventeenth to the early eighteenth century: Here, the company hired 'master reelers', presumably men with some capital and experience in silk-reeling, who in turn employed workmen to reel raw silk under their supervision.[42] Sometimes, provincial governors forced people to work for them as *corvée* labourers, within their own workshops or in the homes of the relevant artisans.

In the Ottoman world, goods manufactured in official workshops circulated as well, but on a much smaller scale. As an example, we may refer to the 'robes of honour' (*hil'at-i fahire*), which not only the sultan, but his appointees in the provinces as well, distributed to a sizeable selection of people that the government considered 'deserving'.[43] Some of the recipients of such robes had their possessions confiscated within a few years, and the textiles once again belonged to the sultan, who could then decide on a new round of circulation. Moreover, especially those recipients that were comparatively poor may well have sold their robes after a few years. Thus, items made for non-commercial purposes, partly remained within the 'gift circuit' and partly entered the market.

On the other hand, production in Ottoman court workshops was more limited than what their Indian counterparts turned out; and we have almost no evidence of persons apart from the sultan setting up such establishments. In the late 1500s and early 1600s, the imperial workshops employed some 700 to 900 artisans, with an exceptional increase to 1451 persons in the year 1596. Afterward, the number decreased to the level that had been normal in the preceding years.[44] After the middle of the seventeenth century, however, there was a precipitous drop; and from 1698 until the abolition of the institution in 1796, only about 230 artisans worked as *ehl-i hiref*. Presumably – but to date evidence is lacking – in the later period the Ottoman palace must have acquired luxury goods from artisans working for the market as well. Viewed in this perspective, the sheer number of Indian *kārkhānas* and the scale of their production mean that the redistribution of manufactured objects in the Mughal Empire by far surpassed comparable types of circulation in the Ottoman world. While the courts of the Mughal emperor and the princes that had accepted his rule certainly consumed large quantities of luxury objects, recent scholarship has stressed that some of these items arrived by means of the market and ultimately left the palaces, re-entering commercial circuits.

Relating Ottoman crafts to the Indian situation: Artisans' incomes

Historians have derived a certain amount of information on the incomes and expenses of Ottoman artisans from the lists of administratively decreed prices (*narh*), often on record in the registers of the local judges. In many provincial towns, these lists only contained basic foodstuffs and materials, but in the larger centres, especially in Istanbul, manufactured goods including implements used by artisans might make it into the record as well. Thus, certain price lists featured trays for the preparation of baklava and large kettles of the type used in dye-houses, with cooks and dyers presumably the principal users.[45] In some cases, the officials compiled lists of all the inputs that went into the production of a given manufactured item, assuming that the remuneration of the artisan should amount to one tenth of the money that he had spent on his work.[46] Occasionally, the profit margin might be even lower; however, ten per cent seems to have been a common rule-of-thumb. When the work was difficult and/or of high quality, the market inspector (*muhtesib*) might permit a margin of twenty per cent. Perhaps we should take this low level of remuneration as an indication that raw materials and intermediary goods were so expensive that the sultan's officials felt that they could not allow the artisans higher remuneration without endangering the interests of the governing apparatus. We may also hypothesize that in seventeenth-century Istanbul, a time and place comparatively well documented, the supply of trained artisans was large enough for competition to push down the rates of pay. By contrast, we do not know what percentage the craft masters had received in the early 1500s, when presumably competition had not been quite as stiff. In the sultan's ateliers, as noted, artists and artisans received a daily wage, which the late sixteenth-century author Mustafa ʿÂlî considered far too high: Seemingly, in the 1580s, masters received five to ten *akçe* per day, in addition to payments for the material used and bonuses when the work was complete.[47]

We have only a very general notion on how Ottoman officials determined prices. In principle, they should have regularly conferred with the heads of craft guilds to adjust prices to the local supply and demand; for when the gap between administratively decreed prices and those current in the market became too large, 'black markets' were likely to emerge. Even so, we cannot be sure that the price lists were always up-to-date, particularly since the registers of Istanbul judges, our principal source for this key question of urban craft history, have survived only in part. In the 1600s, some religious scholars objected to the promulgation of officially decreed prices because they maintained that buyers and sellers should be free to make their own decisions; but the influence of these learned men remained limited and administratively decreed prices survived into the war economies of the twentieth century.[48]

Due to the efforts of Ottoman officialdom, we have a reasonable amount of evidence on the wages and purchasing power of Istanbul construction workers, both skilled and unskilled, for the two and a half centuries between about 1520 and 1770. Measured in grams of silver, and thus adjusted for devaluations, the wages of unskilled labourers changed very little, while those of skilled workmen were somewhat more variable.[49] In the mid-1600s, there was a major crisis leading to a sharp drop in the wages of the skilled, which then recovered and briefly even reached an all-time high. After 1670, however, we observe a declining tendency interrupted by a short recovery around 1760–70. In terms of purchasing power as well, unskilled labourers experienced little change in the quarter millennium under investigation, while the purchasing power of qualified workmen decreased in the early 1500s but 'took off' after 1750, toward the end of the period studied.

With the caveat that Istanbul prices are not representative of the empire as a whole, Şevket Pamuk has concluded that in the early 1500s, Istanbul builders' wages were not much different from those obtained in other European cities, but that the standard of living was lower due to a higher price level. The gap between Istanbul and major European cities 'widened after the Industrial Revolution but less than one might have expected'.[50] From this viewpoint at least, historians can justify the customary emphasis on comparisons between the Ottoman and European worlds: Istanbul was a city of South Eastern Europe, and at times probably the largest city of the Mediterranean world. Unfortunately, for the early modern period, we do not possess any family budgets from the Ottoman orbit. Nor do we have any detailed information on the manner in which Indian artisans spent their money, whether employed in construction or in other crafts.

Apart from the *kārkhānas* discussed by Vanina, where a few data on payment are on record, much of the available information on artisans and their pay concerns Southern India, Gujarat and Bengal.[51] In these regions, the British, Dutch and French companies documented the amounts of money spent on textiles purchases, as well as the conditions under which production and payment took place. However, we do not know how large – or rather, how small – were the payments collected by the producers, and how much the middlemen kept for themselves.

In the 1600s and 1700s, the fabrics produced by Indian artisans found a ready market in the Ottoman world.[52] Quite often, the imported fabrics were cheaper than similar Ottoman products. As noted, Halil İnalcık has assumed that the low payments received by Indian artisans were the reason for this commercial success (see Chapter 6). However, more recently Prasannan Parthasarathi has come to a different conclusion: as we have seen, because of the lower level of prices in pre-colonial Southern India, local handloom weavers had a standard of living similar to that of their British counterparts, even though the payment was low when expressed in current coin.[53] As we have no data on the pay received by Ottoman weavers, we cannot go beyond hypotheses.

The social organization of crafts: (Sub-)castes and guilds

Ottoman artisans in the period under study organized in large and small guilds. By now, there is an extensive literature on artisan guilds in Istanbul and several larger provincial cities, including among others, Aleppo, Ankara, Bursa, Cairo and Sarajevo.[54] In India, by contrast, artisans belonged to castes and sub-castes, which in turn were divisions of the four major caste groupings (*varna*) recognized by Hindus, which Susan Bayly has described as: 'the fourfold scheme of idealised moral archetypes'.[55] In principle, these were the Brahmins or mediators with the world of the divine, the Kshatriyas or kingly warriors, the Vaishya or farmers, herdsmen and merchants, and the Shudras or servants. Degrees of ritual purity differentiated the castes; and the system included so-called untouchables as well, relegated to the lowliest jobs.

Even so, while the *varnas* occurred in ancient scriptures, a caste society was not prevalent in many parts of India before the eighteenth century or even the colonial period. After all, under Mughal rule, much of the country was under forest, and the people establishing communities in these areas knew very little about caste purity or pollution. State formation – even if the rulers were Muslims – thus often went together with the spread of caste distinctions, and colonial rule dramatically speeded up the process. As Susan Bayly has memorably put it: '... far from being a universal feature of "traditional" Indian life, caste in this form, as an array of ritually based schemes of ritual hierarchy, sprang in large part from the relatively recent experiences of colonial "modernity"'.[56]

For the artisans of the Mughal and post-Mughal world, the decisive organizations were not the overarching *varna*s but myriads of lower-level castes and sub-castes.[57] While people belonged to these groupings (*jati*) from birth and could only marry people with whom their caste or sub-caste permitted *connubium*, the status of many *jati*s in the Mughal or post-Mughal world was not set in stone. If the opportunity presented itself, castes or sub-castes might claim a higher status than they had previously enjoyed, especially if their wealth had grown. Put differently, with the spread of markets groups that had made gains might legitimize them by defining them as caste privileges. Or, people who saw their position threatened might claim caste privilege as a means of self-defence.[58]

In other contexts, individuals might try to make their neighbours accept that they belonged to a higher caste than previously assumed. Such endeavours must have had a chance of succeeding if the person in question moved to a locality where his family was unknown, or else if he could show extraordinary success, which made people believe that as his achievements showed, he 'must be' of a higher caste. Only during the colonial period did the compilation of official records, which normally included information on the caste and sub-caste to which an individual belonged, make such mobility far more difficult.

Certainly, Ottoman subjects too were born into social categories, which defined how they could – or could not – organize their lives. Firstly, a male child from a family rendering service to the sultan (*askeri*), even in the modest position of an artisan, inherited this status if he followed his father's trade, becoming a privileged *askeri* artisan, rather than an ordinary tax paying subject (*reaya*). Secondly, as in Mughal India, many artisans learned the crafts of their fathers or uncles and ultimately inherited the shops of the latter. In both places therefore, the practice of certain crafts might become hereditary. On the other hand, Ottoman guilds did not formally limit their members' choice of marriage partners. Admittedly, it was probably common for young artisans to marry the daughters of their senior colleagues, especially since Islamic law stressed that marriage partners should be from families considered social equals. However, on the marriages of artisans, and on the apprenticeships of their sons as well, early modern Ottoman documents are almost totally silent; and so complete is this silence that Ottomanist researchers recognize that they are missing something only when they look at the situation from a Mughal, medieval European, or other 'foreign' vantage point.

While Ottoman artisan guilds might possess Muslim, Jewish or Orthodox religious sanction, guilds of mixed faiths existed as well, especially in Istanbul. Guilds were thus not 'secular' in the modern sense of the term, but their religious character receded into the background, to a greater or lesser extent according to the time and the locality. We may assume that, in mixed guilds the members interacted in myriad ways, not all of them approved by the government. Admittedly, these inter-faith organizations became less frequent by the nineteenth century, when rivalling nationalisms and identity politics, in which religion/denomination played a major role often induced artisans to set up single-faith guilds. Sometimes, the non-Muslim artisans might secede because in a common organization, they needed to defer to their Muslim colleagues; and people who had enriched themselves in the mid-eighteenth-century 'mini-boom' were no longer willing to accept such subservience.[59]

Ottoman guildsmen certainly watched their fellows to ensure religious conformity; and, if Muslims, they reported men who did not attend communal prayers to the Islamic judge or market supervisor (*muhtesib*). In the case of Christians and Jews, similar types of community vigilance were common as well. However, there does not seem to have existed any organization comparable to the caste/sub-caste councils (*panchayat*), which could in extreme cases, throw an offender out of the organization

Figure 14 Trade supplying artisans: Mosque in the Koza Hanı of Bursa (perhaps built 1490–1). In the centre, there is a fountain with a small mosque on top. The name means '*han/khān* of the cocoons'. The names of *hans* changing frequently, it is unclear when people adopted this name. In the 1970s, the Koza Hanı was in fact a wholesale market for fabrics and silk cocoons. Today the complex is a shopping centre selling silks, and the courtyard a favourite for tea and recreation.

into which he had been born and thereby end his existence as a social being.[60] Certainly, Ottoman guilds could terminate the membership of an artisan, but such events were rare – and historians have debated whether perhaps some guildsmen expelled a (former) colleague because they had begun to consider him as a merchant and thereby, as a – possibly wealthy – outsider to the life of the guild.[61] Furthermore, churches and Jewish communities could ban people from participating in the religious services of the community to which they had previously belonged; and this punishment could be disastrous for the men affected – women being very rarely at issue. In the Ottoman world, guilds, religious communities, and state officials thus cooperated in securing artisan conformity.

We need more research before we can decide whether a *panchayat* could be more effective in enforcing artisan compliance than this cooperation of separate organizations with differing though interlocking memberships. As the *panchayat* was a single body of men with jurisdiction over both craft issues and others that modern researchers would consider 'religious', an individual craftsman confronted with influential peers active in this council might have had less room for manoeuver than an Ottoman artisan in the same position. Moreover, the escape routes that conversion to Islam might offer to the accused/defendants in court cases were not generally available in the Indian world, as to some extent, castes continued to be a fact-of-life even after conversion to Islam or Christianity.

The moral economy of artisans

As direct statements do not survive, Ottomanists as well as Indianists have to use indirect approaches when trying to elucidate the mentalities and expectations of seventeenth- and eighteenth-century artisans. In some periods, and in some regions of South Asia, textiles seemingly appeared as carriers of purity and/or pollution, and artisans sometimes featured as 'clean' or 'unclean' according to the activities they engaged in.[62] However, there were so many regional variations that generalizations are hazardous. In the Ottoman world, concerns about pollution seemingly were less pervasive than they were in the subcontinent, as long as people adhered to the ritual purity defined by Islamic law. In some circles, there were concerns about non-Muslims not being as careful about cleanliness as Muslims were, but many Istanbul Muslims did not object to eating bread from the numerous Armenian bakeries of the city. In the Ottoman as in the Mughal orbit, pious Muslims, if male, avoided silk, while there was more flexibility when women were at issue. In both venues, some people compromised by using cotton–silk mixtures, called *mashru*, or 'permitted', in the subcontinent.[63] If the weave ensured that the wearer's body touched only the cotton, there was no reason to forgo the sheen of silk; however, we do not know how many craftsmen could have afforded even *mashru* clothing.

In our search for artisan mentalities, illiteracy is the major barrier. Even when petitioning in his own name, a 'typical' artisan must have turned to a professional petition writer who knew – or believed that he knew – what was appropriate in a given situation (see Chapter 4).[64] However, such limitations did not prevent artisans from bringing up issues that they considered important. Thus, we find eighteenth-century Jewish druggists/perfumers in Istanbul complaining about their Muslim colleagues, who supposedly had conspired to drive them out of business.[65] As for the sultan's government, its members did not automatically favour the Muslims but might suggest a compromise, in which the dominant concern was apparently that all artisans legitimately established in the city should be able to make a living. Thus, even if artisan petitions did not reflect the unmediated voices of their authors, these men expected that sultans and viziers would seriously consider their grievances. Even 'second-class subjects', such as Christians and Jews, made similar assumptions.

In analysing the petitions of low-caste artisans labouring in Jodhpur, Prasad Sahai has made use of a concept that with some variation, is familiar to Ottomanists as well, namely the assumption that the ruler and his officials would abide by the requirements of *wajabi* or 'appropriateness'.[66] In the Ottoman milieu, the 'circle of justice' should have guided the behaviour of the ruler. According to these two related key concepts, the prince needed to respond to the complaints of his 'poor subjects', artisans included, at least to some extent. As Ottoman political wisdom put it, the ruler needed military power, which he could only secure if he had money. As noted, this money could only come from the taxes of his subjects, the latter being able to pay only if treated with (a modicum of) justice. In this context, justice meant the defence of poor artisans and peasants against oppressors, especially members of the governing apparatus. As Ottoman authors writing on political affairs knew very well, this type of justice was the precondition for raising an army and retaining or extending political power.[67]

Artisan migrations

In Jodhpur, complying with *wajabi* was the Indian equivalent of the Ottoman principle of extending protection to subjects in accordance with the circle of justice. At least in part, the ruler had to satisfy the demands of his 'poor subjects', invariably connected with the need to secure at least a modest livelihood.[68] Or else, given a sparse population, the prince might find himself governing empty expanses that produced no revenue. Jodhpur craftspeople were highly mobile, incidentally resembling some of their eighteenth-century Anatolian contemporaries. Inhabitants of Ottoman Anatolia rarely left the sultan's domains altogether, but commonly fled the province controlled by a governor or tax farmer known as particularly rapacious. In the Jodhpur context, the king might have trouble finding replacements for the people that had fled; for in Western Rajasthan, the area covered by the extant documentation, drought and famine were almost everyday occurrences.[69]

Incidentally, Prasad Sahai's finding, that the Jodhpur rulers promoted archival records to obtain a better overview of the available human and material resources, will strike a chord in the Ottomanist as well. As noted, in Rajasthan, it was a matter of retaining men and women in a setting of labour scarcity. In the eighteenth-century Ottoman Empire as well, and especially around 1800, the sultans' officials extended record-keeping to hitherto unknown levels.[70] However, the motivation was quite different, as the Ottoman elite had come to worry about the great size of Istanbul, which supposedly made the city difficult to govern. The sultan and his officials thus planned to get rid of certain categories of inhabitants rather than seeking to retain them, as seems to have been the case in Jodhpur. Even so, by early modern Indian standards, the population of the Ottoman Empire was very moderate, but the 'statistical gaze' of the sultans' servitors did not reach much beyond the capital city with its 400,000–500,000 inhabitants.[71] Despite their posturing, both governments could control artisan mobility only to a very limited extent.

In the South Asian context, the mobility of weavers helped to protect their incomes; especially in the South, a major producer of cotton cloth, weavers moved to escape warfare and the famines that became rather frequent during the 1700s – in the Indian Peninsula and in Rajasthan as well, the latter were often due to monsoon failures.[72] Given the Indian climate, the decision to move was perhaps less costly than it would have been in Anatolia or the Balkans, although even in the world of the Eastern Mediterranean, artisans might decide to migrate. In many parts of India, after all, heating was unnecessary and houses did not need the solid walls that, in Anatolia or the Balkans, kept out the winter cold – at least to some extent. Other crises that pushed Indian weavers out of their habitats came about because the supplies of raw cotton and foodstuffs on which they depended arrived on poor roads, traversed by bullock carts. A disturbance anywhere along these lengthy routes might result in weaver communities running out of food or raw material.[73]

Moreover, mobility provided South Asian textiles artisans with an advantage in their dealings with foreign merchants. Most weavers needed advances from the local traders placing orders as intermediaries for the European trading companies. When circumstances intervened that made fulfilment of the contract difficult, the weavers might decamp, returning the money if possible but sometimes retaining it. Therefore, Indian merchants who had taken the risk of guaranteeing cloth deliveries to exporters quite often lost their money.

Artisan migrations of this type played an especially important role in the textile-exporting centres of Gujarat and Bengal, where already in the 1600s merchants found it difficult to control the quality of cloth delivered.[74] In response, the EIC took measures to impede weaver mobility in the settlements under its control, especially in Mumbai/Bombay and Chennai/Madras. Despite this disadvantage, when under extreme pressure because of constant warfare between the Mughal emperors and their Maratha opponents, textile-manufacturing communities took refuge in these foreign-dominated ports, despite the loss of earnings and personal independence that such a move might involve.

By contrast, where artisan migrations in the Ottoman world were at issue, state initiatives were of prime importance. From the fifteenth century onward if not earlier, the Ottoman administration had on occasion transferred some of its subjects to reinforce the sultan's domination. Officials might assign artisans – and other inhabitants of the central Ottoman lands – to (re)populate, for example, a newly conquered city which the authorities wanted to develop and/or whose established populations they wished to control.

Moreover, the great building projects that have become an Ottoman 'trademark' necessitated the employment of large numbers of craft specialists, often from distant locations, who might or might not be willing to undertake the work assigned to them. Drafting artisans for such enterprises thus became another way of controlling the urban population. In the sixteenth century, the construction of the large pious foundation complexes of Sultan Süleyman (r. 1520–66) mobilized numbers of artisans from the building trades, and enlarging the sultans' palace would have required immigrant workers as well.[75] This policy of mobilizing and transferring workingmen re-emerged during the eighteenth century; by now, the repair of border fortresses was of even greater importance, especially on the contested border with the Russian Empire.

At the same time, voluntary migration, especially to Istanbul, did occur; it was already a subject of concern to the administration in the late 1500s. However, after the rebellions of 1703 and 1730, in which Istanbul-based soldiers doubling as artisans played key roles, preventing migration into the capital city became a virtual obsession of the sultans and their servitors. Roadblocks sprang up on access routes; people returning to home after a trip to a nearby town might have to provide witnesses testifying to their residence in the city. At times, officials were so paranoid about possible migrants that they were willing to violate the Ottoman version of *wajabi* rules. For in the 1700s, new commands made it difficult for provincials to access the sultans' palace and the offices of the grand vizier, where they would have normally presented their petitions – after all, petitioning was a major resource of the 'poor subjects' attempting to secure 'justice' and a livelihood.[76]

Ottoman records thus highlight migrations, either commanded by the sultans' officials or else population movements that the government tried to prevent. By contrast, officials de-emphasized migrations caused by natural calamities. Even so, recent studies have shown that such migrations occurred quite frequently, particularly after the long droughts from which Anatolia suffered in the late sixteenth and early seventeenth centuries. While people frequently abandoned towns and villages in Central Anatolia, the port town of Izmir, insignificant in the 1500s, by the late seventeenth century had mushroomed to become one of the largest cities of the Ottoman Empire (see Chapter 5). Artisans were part of this migration, especially the Jewish woollen weavers from Salonika whose specialty craft was in crisis.[77] While the extant records often do not reflect 'spontaneous' migrations of the subject population with any accuracy, now that many historians have abandoned the state-centred perspective typical of the older Ottomanist historiography, migrations comparable to those witnessed in India do come into view.

Artisans working for exporting merchants

While the markets of the subcontinent absorbed a sizeable share of local textiles, the activities of Indian merchants in promoting export, put differently in organizing artisans to produce cottons and silks for European markets, have generated a sizeable amount of contemporary documents and modern research as well.[78] Our present focus being the Mughal Empire as it was in 1605, we highlight the provinces of Gujarat and Bengal, both conquered by Akbar in the 1570s and traditional sources of export textiles.

In Bengal, which in the terminology of the 1600s and 1700s included the present-day Indian states of West Bengal, Bihar and Orissa, in addition to the independent republic of Bangladesh, many artisans producing everyday goods lived in the countryside, where both raw silk and high-quality cotton were available. Local artisans had a long tradition in producing both luxury textiles and items for the 'ordinary' market.[79] The finest cottons were the work of Dhaka weavers; they were so expensive that the Dutch exporters, active in Bengal since the early 1600s, did not carry them. Thus, the manufacturers and merchants must have intended these delicate textiles for the turbans of Indian elites, mainly those connected with the Mughal administration. Certain artisans specialized in the working of gold, silver and silk yarns into cotton textiles to produce brocades, mainly of floral designs, popular especially in Poland and Muscovy. In addition, specialized artisans produced embroidery, which Om Prakash has likened to the *chikan* textiles still made in today's Lucknow. In general, Bengal was less prominent in the field of everyday cottons, and focused on silks and silk–cotton mixtures.

Among the sophisticated cotton–silk mixtures available in Bengal, often striped and chequered, Ottomanists will note the presence of *alacha*, which must have some connection to the 'mixed' or 'striped' fabric known as *alaca* available in Ottoman markets.[80] In Bengali commercial terminology, *alacha* was 'a bright coloured striped silk fabric'; and in Ottoman parlance, stripes were a typical feature of *alaca* as well.[81]

As noted, while some artisans worked on their own behalf, most of them did not have the capital needed by a manufacturer hoping to produce a type of cloth only demanded in distant markets. Vanina's argument explaining the popularity of princely *kārkhānas* is valid here as well: If the exporting merchant refused to accept the goods on offer, the weaver and his family would have starved.[82] Therefore, manufacturers accepting advances had to follow the samples received from exporting merchants. We may wonder how experienced masters, accustomed to create their own designs, reacted to impositions of this kind.[83]

In Gujarat, merchant–artisan relations apparently were easier on the weaver than they were in Bengal. At least by about 1700, security concerns had prompted many Gujarati textiles producers to relocate to Surat, the largest city in the province, and their capacity for negotiation may have improved as a result. In this location, the existence of capital-supplying intermediaries did not necessarily mean that the weavers were poverty-stricken. Demand for Gujarati products was high, especially in the Arabian/Ottoman market. In consequence, even in the late 1700s and early 1800s, well after the end of the period treated here, weavers could work for more than one merchant and the factors of the EIC were not (yet) in a position to dictate prices. Presumably, this situation benefited local merchants more than artisans. However, the EIC, while acquiring political power in Gujarat after 1750, found it more difficult to dominate the local artisans than to control weavers in Bengal or Peninsular India.[84]

In the Ottoman world, the relationship between artisans and traders collecting manufactured goods for export has not often entered archival documents, largely because European traders focused on raw cotton, raisins, leather, or sometimes – against the sultan's commands – on wheat and barley. However, even though the

Figure 15 Ministering to the comfort of artisans and other townspeople: the public bath (built in 1645) attributed to Cinci Hoca (d. 1648) in the Anatolian 'museum town' of Safranbolu/Turkey, where traditional crafts persisted into the 1970s and 1980s. Without ever completing his madrasa studies, Karabaşzade Hüseyin Efendi, born in Safranbolu, became famous for his presumed familiarity with the spirit world. Ministering to the psychologically challenged Sultan İbrahim (r. 1640–8), he managed to become an army judge (*kadıasker*) and amassed an enormous fortune, from which he may have financed this building.

exportation of manufactured goods was far less important in the Ottoman context than in India, it did exist. In the eighteenth century, towns and villages in Thessaly produced red cotton thread for the use of weavers in the Habsburg Empire, while tanners in villages of today's Bulgaria sold part of their output to merchants trading with Vienna and Buda.[85] In addition, Ottoman silk textiles found markets in Poland, some of them produced specifically for the Polish market.[86] Ottomanists concerned with crafts and trade will need to pay more attention to merchant–artisan relations, hitherto neglected because Ottoman luxury production is typically the province of art historians.

Craft history and ethnography

The last section of this chapter is concerned with methodology. After gaining independence in 1947, the Republic of India through the relevant ministries collected significant amounts of data on traditional crafts, and sometimes sponsored the publication of reports. Textiles became a focus of interest, with a view toward increasing responsiveness to market demand and in consequence, the survival of the craft at issue. Even today, handicraft products play a significant role among the goods available on the urban – and export – markets of India, as a visitor to upmarket chains of Delhi clothes stores will soon realize. While foregrounding present-day conditions, late twentieth-century reports and related studies sometimes shed light on older artisan technologies as well; for as Irfan Habib has shown, the textiles sector has changed very slowly – even though, if we consider not decades but centuries, technical changes were dramatic.[87]

On the other hand, in the Republic of Turkey, there have been but a few social historians interested in ethnography, and only a few ethnographers with historical interests. The number of historians concerned with textiles production is smaller still. As one of the few exceptions, we might mention Halil İnalcık, one of the 'founding fathers' of Ottoman history, who has collected textiles and published his collection.[88] Doubtless, this relative lack of interest results at least partly from the fact that in Turkey handicraft production for export or broad domestic markets is not an issue, apart from the niche market catered for by specialized 'gift shops'.

Furthermore, in the Indian context, researchers on craft history can go back beyond the last seventy years or so, a proceeding that Ottomanists can rarely emulate. Once India had become a British colony in the full sense of the word, from the 1860s onward, the colonial authorities attempted to tailor local economies according to British needs and the demands of the British consumer. For this purpose, officials produced numerous records, which the authorities intended to use for increased taxation as well. The aims of the colonial government involved destroying certain crafts and remodelling others according to the demands of the world market. At the same time, local skilled artisans, such as the embroiderers producing the work known as *zarduzi* and *chikan* recently studied by Bidisha Dhar, built intricate hierarchies of skill, experience and prestige in an attempt to retain self-respect and pride in their work.[89] Historians will ask to what extent the social organization of nineteenth- and early twentieth-century artisans continues practices going back to the Mughal period. Admittedly, in many cases, the question will remain unanswered, although some anthropologist-historians have discovered intriguing continuities.

Dealing – for instance – with the popular and festive culture of silk weavers, metalworkers and woodworking artisans inhabiting the city of Banaras, the social anthropologist Nita Kumar has focused on the period from the 1880s to the 1980s.[90] In these specialties, even in the late 1900s many sons followed the trades of their ancestors, thereby continuing a textiles tradition already on record in the early and mid-1600s.[91] Silk weaving had declined in the later 1800s but recovered after Indian independence, with tourist and pilgrim demand keeping the market buoyant. On the other hand, by the late twentieth century the manufacture of metalwork in small workshops was in crisis; once again, this was an ancient craft, as Francisco Pelsaert, writing in the 1620s, already had mentioned Banaras as a place where craftsmen produced copper dishes and other household goods used by Hindu families.[92] As Kumar noted, the manufacture of wooden toys, which played a significant role in the Banaras economy of the 1980s had an antecedent 'in Mughal times' as well; but as the sources she had used dated to about 1900, it is hard to judge the reliability of her statement from this material alone.[93] An older source is however available, going as far back as the mid-1600s, for Jean-Baptiste Tavernier recorded that parts of the coloured gum lac acquired in Bengal and Pegu served for the decoration of wooden toys, which the local people – presumably of eastern South Asia – liked very much.[94] Unfortunately, Tavernier did not specify where these artisans worked, in Banaras or somewhere else.

In addition, historians of the Indian world emphasize folk songs, proverbs and other products of 'unwritten literature' more often than Ottomanists do, as they regard these productions as an access to the otherwise voiceless world of the subalterns. This view makes sense because in India, such texts quite often entered the written record during the 1800s, well before similar materials attracted the attention of collectors working in the sultans' domains. In the Ottoman world, interest in such issues only emerged much later, in the very last decades of the sultans' rule and particularly in early Republican Turkey. As a result, almost no testimonies collected by oral historians and relevant to the artisan world refer to events and situations known from the early modern period.[95]

Even so, we do possess a few ethnographic and/or economic studies relevant to artisans, particularly the extensive and richly illustrated synthesis by Henry Glassie.[96] Among monographs, the work of Halûk Cillov, Heidemarie Doğanalp Votzi and Claudia Kickinger is important.[97] Published in 1949, the doctoral thesis of Halûk Cillov, an economist who later became a well-known statistician, covers a period when the inhabitants of outlying Anatolian towns and villages still used quantities of hand-woven cottons, which were substantially cheaper though of lower quality than machine-woven items. While Cillov concluded his study with a few reflections on whether the government should protect hand weaving, these considerations were a minor part of his work.

Unlike the Indian setting, with its emphasis on commercial viability in the world of today, field studies of Ottoman traditional crafts often set out to record working conditions of the past, before they disappear not only from practical life, but from memory as well. Thus Doğanalp Votzi, who in the 1980s interviewed the last artisanal tanners working in the Western Anatolian town of Safranbolu, has shown that under propitious circumstances, it is possible to combine written sources with the oral history of a craft.[98] Apart from tanning technologies of the recent pre-industrial past, the author has recounted the memories of older artisans, which went back to the early 1920s. These men remembered that, before the Turco-Greek exchange of populations in 1923–4, there had been a small number of Greek artisans active in the trade; and pointedly, some of the former Safranbolu tanners told the author that since the Orthodox were 'little people', it had been customary to allow them privileged access to the local market. Presumably, the Muslim tanners had seen themselves as the more successful craftsmen who, for moral reasons, assisted their weaker colleagues. Thus, allowing the Orthodox tanners to sell their goods first would have been a form of charitable assistance.

In conclusion

In the Ottoman artisan world of the sixteenth to eighteenth centuries, guild organization was pervasive, at least in the larger cities. We do not know whether the sultans imposed these organizations in newly conquered provinces. It is, however, quite intriguing that guilds appeared in Cairo or Jerusalem in the 1500s and/or 1600s, while they apparently had not been on record in the Mamluk sultanate (1250s to 1517).[99] Even so, as our evidence on Ottoman guilds comes from a limited number of sizeable towns, we do not know to what extent guild organization gained a foothold in smaller localities. In any case, since the exportation of manufactured items from the Ottoman lands was always very modest, when compared with the Indian export trade, guild elders in the sultan's lands seem to have negotiated with rival guilds, obstreperous members of their own organizations, or else the sultan's officials. Bargaining with merchants acquiring goods for export was of much less significance.

Interestingly, sources on Indian artisans provide only limited information on the prices of goods fixed by the sovereign and valid, at least in principle, in all the markets of a given city. Not that the terminology was unknown: We may wonder whether the prices of textiles and jewels recorded by Abū'l-Fazl merely documented what the palace had paid, or whether the prices were normative in intent as well. In the case of building materials, however, Abū'l-Fazl specified that Akbar had had the prices recorded in order to prevent fraud. Therefore, these data were clearly normative, and resembled their Ottoman counterparts, although we do not know whether administratively determined prices were the rule or the exception.[100] In Bengal too, data on *nirkh*s were sometimes on record. However, the rulers normally confirmed the prices that the vendors had set and seemingly did not spend much energy on enforcement.[101] In Istanbul, by contrast, officially fixed prices were extremely common, the government continually stressed the need to enforce them, and in less elaborate form, they were present in provincial towns and cities as well. At the same time, the Ottoman elite acquired fewer manufactured goods from court artisans than was true of the princes and office-holders operating *kārkhāna*s in the Mughal Empire and its successor kingdoms. If we allow ourselves a bit of speculation, we may even assume that because *kārkhāna* production was widespread, the Mughal emperors did not regard the administrative control of market prices as crucial to their economic interests.

Secondly, the major difference between the Ottoman and Mughal artisan worlds lay in the structure of society-at-large. For Indian artisans, belonging to a given caste or sub-caste defined, at least in most cases, what kind of work they would undertake, whom they would marry, and in which neighbourhood they would live. Ottoman guilds had fewer constraining powers; however, they had the support of established religious communities and if needed, of the governmental apparatus as well. We cannot be sure, however, that these three institutions together equalled the influence exercised by a well-organized caste or sub-caste.

In practice, arrangements in the urban marketplaces of the Mughal Empire often were more flexible than caste rules allowed for. Certain castes/sub-castes gained in wealth and managed to transform worldly riches into increased social status. In the weaving sector, moreover, lower castes sometimes received offers to 'aid' members of higher castes during a surge in demand; and underprivileged artisans used this opportunity to develop expertise in a new craft and establish themselves in it.[102] Especially in workshops established by a European company, there might be senior artisans known as head weavers, 'master reelers', '*patels*' or '*muqaddams*'.[103] It is hard to say to what extent Dutch or English merchants took account of caste rules when setting up *kārkhānas* and appointing chief artisans to run them. Nor can we tell whether those workshops sponsored by the Mughal elites introduced structures of leadership independent of castes and sub-castes. Even so, the strength of these organizations was formidable, and most Indian artisans did not form guilds of the kind observed in the Ottoman Empire or Safavid Iran.[104]

Whatever the social organization of Ottoman and Mughal crafts may have been, rural artisans were on the margins, and often the sources do not reflect them at all. However, fields and villages were at the core of both the Ottoman and the Mughal economies, and rural life will occupy us in the following chapter.

Figure 16 Fabrics drying on the banks of the river Gomti: in Lucknow: traditionally, Lucknow has been famous for its textiles, and although today the city is best known for its heavy industry, the city's embroiderers, both men and women, produce work that is in considerable demand, both within India and abroad.

8

Rural Life in the Indian and Ottoman Environments

The sources, such as they are

We begin with a statement that is well known, but bears repeating nonetheless. Whether archival or literary, documentation is never 'innocent' and directly or indirectly, serves the institution of rule and the aims of the governing elites. This home truth applies to the rural world perhaps even more than to urbanites, for the simple reason that when focusing on villagers and nomads, elites all over the world – including Mughal and Ottoman officialdom – were mainly interested in taxes, taxes, and further taxes, with some concerns about labour services and the security of trade routes thrown in. Once again, historians of Northern India seem to be more conscious of the gaps and partisanship arising from this situation than most scholars studying the Ottoman world.

Villagers being mostly illiterate, their voices appear only insofar as officials or scholars saw fit to record them. Thus, we know far less about the majority population, put differently the peasants and nomads subject to the Ottoman sultans and the Mughal emperors than about the much more limited urban populations of the two empires at issue. However, in both cases, for the sixteenth century we possess a certain amount of tax-related statistical evidence, which in the Ottoman case survives in the original and in the Mughal instance, largely in the documentation collected by Abū' l-Fazl 'Allāmī (see Chapter 7). In addition, there are individual documents, often preserved in private hands, and in Mughal India, literati produced numerous manuals teaching accounting skills to aspiring bureaucrats. While not intended as records of village life, these texts contain much information on collecting taxes from rural dwellers.[1] As for the period between the early 1600s and the 1670s, neither Ottoman nor Mughal archives are especially rich; however, in the following years, especially during the 1700s, in both venues the available material increases quite dramatically, although coverage remains very uneven.

In the Ottoman world, the gradual increase in the number of extant qadi registers during the 1600s and 1700s presumably reflects the tendency of people inhabiting villages close to the qadi's seat to seek formal judicial solutions to rural disputes. In earlier times, they would probably have taken such problems to a respected elder for arbitration. Moreover, as noted, after the mid-1700s the Ottoman centre attempted to 'stay in touch' with its Anatolian and Balkan provinces by encouraging provincial subjects to bring their complaints directly to the seat of the sultans. At least in the surroundings of Istanbul, this policy resulted in the resolution of a fair number of rural disputes by the central administration of the eighteenth century.[2] The resulting paper trail is very valuable for the historian of rural life, yet it would be a mistake to assume that the villages near the sultans' capital were typical of the Ottoman countryside in its entirety. Quite likely, the closeness of the Istanbul market determined cultivation to a certain extent, for in the capital the servitors of the administration possessed a purchasing power by far surpassing that available in provincial venues. Thus, fruits and many vegetables were minor luxuries and therefore more common in the surroundings of the capital city than elsewhere. It is also worth noting that, in most cases the holders of taxation rights complained about peasants, but the converse was quite rare; it's likely that social and political status was often a precondition for getting one's complaint into the record.

In addition, the Ottoman elite always considered peasants better taxpayers than nomads and semi-nomads. Unless the latter caused major difficulties to the village population, the sultan's bureaucrats thus wrote very little about non-sedentary people. However, from the late 1600s onward, documentation increased as the Ottoman central administration tried to settle nomads and semi-nomads in peasant villages, by force if necessary.[3] While the earliest attempts usually failed, Ottoman bureaucrats wrote about them quite a lot, and in the 1700s and especially the 1800s, the administration pushed ever harder to enforce settlement. It is however quite likely that by the late nineteenth century, population increase was at least as important in the settlement of former nomads and semi-nomads as the policies of the central government – if not more so.

In the period under discussion, narrative sources foregrounding peasants are very rare. One of the few examples is the work known as 'Hazz al-Quḥūf' by Yusuf b Muhammad al-Shirbīnī, an Egyptian religious scholar of rural background living in Cairo during the second half of the seventeenth century.[4] According to his own statement, this author had composed a commentary on the verses of a folk poet that he calls Abū Shaduf, who does not appear in any other source. Abd Al Raheim A. Abd Al Raheim is of the opinion that a highly placed contemporary scholar had asked al-Shirbīnī to write a text about the general uncouthness of the peasants, which would ridicule Abū Shaduf's complaints and thus deprive them of any validity. In this fashion, al-Shirbīnī supposedly circumvented the censorship that the Ottoman–Mamluk elite exercised over people writing in Egypt. Gabriel Baer by contrast has defended the opinion that no such censorship existed in the 1600s and that Abū Shaduf is a literary creation of al-Shirbīnī. In the manner common to townsmen in many parts of the world, the author wanted to amuse his urban readers by highlighting the – often 'indecent' – details that accompany pervasive poverty. Apart from the ubiquitous dirt, al-Shirbīnī highlights the unsophisticated food and the absence of any serious religious culture.

If one accepts this interpretation, it becomes unnecessary to seek for 'deeper motivations', which al-Shirbīnī may have had. However, in the last paragraph of his article, Baer has admitted that al-Shirbīnī's text is unique in Arab literary history, especially because of the many ethnographic details that the author has included.

While rejecting the background story that previous scholars have discerned behind al-Shirbīnī's text, Baer concedes that the author probably had reasons for writing that remain unknown, thus showing up the dangers of 'close reading' when very little historical context is available.[5]

As for Northern India, in addition to the materials studied by Irfan Habib, for the reign of Aurangzeb (r. 1658–1707) and the following decades, significant information on rural life comes – once again – from the Rajput Kachhwaha principality of Amber (later: Jaipur, see Chapter 7) and at a later stage, from Jodhpur as well. Given the series of succession crises following Aurangzeb's death, we have noted several times that Mughal governors and dependent princes began to run 'their' territories without much reference to the centre. Especially after the 1739 sack of Delhi by Nādir Shāh, the empire contracted to become a North Indian regional kingdom. It so happens that the surviving archives of the princes of Amber, who as noted in the 1720s had moved their capital to the newly founded town of Jaipur, contain a large quantity of documents relevant to village life.[6] Moreover, S. P. Gupta, who has studied this archive in detail, has concluded that in this as in other matters, the rural governance of the Kachhwaha was very similar to that of their (former) overlords the Mughal emperors. Incidentally, the Jaipur princes remained in close contact with Delhi as long as even a semblance of Mughal power remained. Thus, the practices of the Kachhwaha may serve as a stand-in for those of the later Mughals; and the extant sources reflect a set of practices that historians of rural India call 'the agrarian system'.[7] On the other hand, the eighteenth-century principality of Jodhpur has generated an archive of a rather different kind. For in this locality, the emphasis is on the complaints of villagers, and over-taxation a very frequent topic.[8]

The natural settings

The ecological settings of the many rural societies paying taxes to the Ottoman and Mughal treasuries differed profoundly. By the mid-sixteenth century, the Ottoman Empire reached far into the temperate zone. Within this setting, Hungary and most of the Balkan Peninsula had a continental climate, with cold winters that were especially difficult for cultivators because in the Little Ice Age (1300–1850, with significant local variations), the cold season tended to begin earlier and last longer than in the twentieth century. Inner Anatolia had a continental climate as well, while only the coastal fringes enjoyed the hot summers and mild winters typical of the Mediterranean world. On the eastern 'Greater Syrian' coast of the great inland sea, only a relatively small strip of land was suitable for agriculture of the Mediterranean type, as high mountain chains mostly prevented rains from reaching inland areas, where steppe and desert predominated. Furthermore, only the waters of the Nile made it possible for Egypt to produce the foodstuffs, textiles, and cash dues demanded by the government in Istanbul. Without the annual flooding of the river, the country would have been desert as well. The valleys of the Tigris and Euphrates were far less productive, because a considerable part of the land had already suffered from salinity since the Middle Ages. Moreover, the amount of water carried by the two rivers was highly variable, and in consequence, the agriculture of Iraq was less productive and significant for the government in Istanbul than that of Egypt was.[9] Nejat Göyünç and Wolf Dieter Hütteroth have created a map showing the late sixteenth-century agricultural production of the Euphrates area as far south as the town of Hīt in modern Iraq, showing that cultivators focused on wheat, millet and particularly on cotton. Apart from the hills of Sinjār, where vineyards complemented wheat and barley, there was very little cultivation beyond the immediate vicinity of the river.[10]

In India, cultivation largely depended on the monsoon rains, whose appearance in June–July and withdrawal in September–October determined agricultural possibilities.[11] Thus, western Rajasthan was arid, while the eastern part of this region enjoyed a somewhat longer monsoon period and was thus only semi-arid. Further to the east, where the monsoon arrived yet earlier, lay the region whose climate today's geographers call sub-tropical. Temperature was of importance as well; while the area studied was mostly in the sub-tropical zone, the rich province of Bengal was tropical. In addition, the Mughal Empire contained areas with a mountain climate; but they were probably less important from the revenue collector's point of view. Admittedly, we cannot produce a climate map of Mughal India, drawing the curves that depict the incidence of the seventeenth- or eighteenth-century monsoon, in a manner comparable to the maps available for the country today. Even so, the monsoon must have determined early modern agriculture and cattle breeding.

In the past, observations on climate in the Ottoman context would have been only a preamble without much relevance to the subsequent discussion of rural life; for until recently, very few people showed much interest in the natural world and the climatic and soil-related problems that Ottoman peasants had to cope with. In the view of the present author, this omission was not due to chance. Rather, Ottomanist historians, having read the primary sources produced by the sultan's office-holders, had largely accepted the opinion of the latter, namely that human agency alone determined which projects succeeded and especially, which of them failed. Thus, the administration always could put the blame on a specific person and punish him, gaining legitimacy from the – supposed – protection of the subjects from oppression, while making it clear to officials that the sultan would not tolerate failure. However, as environmental history has now 'arrived' in Ottomanist scholarship as well, significant publications have appeared in recent years, surely with more to come in the near future. Thus, the work of Mehmet Yavuz Erler, Alan Mikhail, Sam White, and Mehmet Kuru has made Ottomanist historians aware of the basic fact that agriculture and stockbreeding closely depended on temperature and rainfall.[12] Though not eager to admit failures and delays, quite often the empire's bureaucrats must have been helpless when drought and prolonged cold wrecked harvests and made routes unpassable.

In the late twentieth century, historical geographers had often assumed that the Eastern Mediterranean region had not suffered the consequences of the Little Ice Age, at least not to the same extent as Northern and Western Europe.[13] However, Sam White and more recently Mehmet Kuru have shown that seventeenth-century Ottoman Anatolia was subject to crippling droughts, with the Central and South Eastern sections of the peninsula especially at risk. Kuru has even proposed that the population expansion of the middle decades of the sixteenth century, which had attracted so much interest in twentieth-century historiography, was mainly a feature of the Central and South Eastern regions, which benefited from the relatively high rainfall of this short but privileged period. When beginning in the 1590s major droughts set in, quite a few people fled the afflicted areas, the survivors often settling in the Aegean coastlands or in Istanbul. Apparently, the desolation of the Anatolian countryside in the seventeenth and eighteenth centuries was not due only to military rebellions and the resultant over-taxation, as scholars had previously assumed, but to climatic causes as well.

Incidentally, we cannot tell to what extent the well-documented tendency of young Anatolian peasants of the years around 1600 to leave their villages, joining the army or else para-military bands, was due to frequent droughts rather than to population increase. We need more studies of the type undertaken particularly by White and Kuru to understand how other parts of the empire experienced climate-induced crisis. Agricultural techniques, including the operation of mills when water was scarce and the – very limited – diffusion of windmills also need more attention than they have attracted to date.[14] Apart from Egypt, a special case, we still do not have much concrete information about the manner in which peasants used the available techniques to make a living despite cold and drought.[15]

Where Mughal India is concerned, Irfan Habib has attempted an overall discussion of the 'stubborn struggle against nature, which the Indian peasant has carried on for thousands of years'.[16] More specifically, he has set out to determine which aspects of Mughal agriculture remained unchanged well into the colonial period and in which respects, production expanded or else contracted.[17] Habib concludes that regarding the Mughal Empire in its entirety, cultivation increased between the epochal dates of 1595 and 1910. In this context, 1595 is a crucial cut-off date – many statistics in the *Ā'īn-i akbarī* refer to just this year (see Chapter 7), while 1910 stands in for the agriculture of the fully-fledged colonial period, put differently the late 1800s and early 1900s.[18] However, agricultural growth largely took place in specific districts (*subah*), particularly Allahabad, Awadh and Bihar, in addition to Berar; in all these regions, expansion was due to the clearance of forests. In the Indus region of the post-Mughal period (today part of Pakistan), a novel system of canals made the expansion of agriculture possible.

Outside the Ganges-Yamuna plain, most of the cultivation practised in the Mughal realm depended exclusively on rainfall, especially the seasonal monsoons. However, in certain years, the monsoons did not provide enough water, or by contrast, the rain, often torrential came at the wrong time and destroyed the crops. Given the ever-present danger of drought, Habib's discussion focuses on water supplies and technologies for making water available in the places where cultivators needed it most. The so-called Persian wheel, a water-lifting device that became widespread in Northern India during the 1500s has been of special interest since its diffusion coincides with the beginning of Mughal rule. Habib's work also discusses the canals dug by Mughal emperors; particularly Shāh Jahān (r. 1628–58) ordered a significant amount of canal building, using the waters of the Yamuna for agricultural purposes. In addition, the new canal supplied his recently founded capital of Shāhjahānabād, today Old Delhi.[19] Furthermore, persons of some wealth, frequently anonymous undertook public works to collect water from perennial or non-perennial watercourses through the construction of dams and canals; the latter sometimes used the beds previously excavated by streams that had changed course or disappeared altogether. Members of the Mughal nobility also sponsored irrigation to obtain water for their gardens, which to the early Mughal emperors were at least as important as their palaces, if not more so (see Chapter 5).[20] While Habib's discussion of the difficult conditions that peasants faced in Northern India includes a special section on famines, especially the disastrous monsoon failure of 1630–2, he does not discuss the possible connection between global climatic changes and the droughts experienced in the subcontinent.[21]

Control of the land: The Ottoman world

In the Ottoman Empire before the mid-nineteenth century, the sultan laid claim to all the arable, grazing land and forest. Therefore, the peasants who farmed his lands, known as *miri*, could only be tenants, with the right to retain their tenures as long as they regularly worked them, and upon their deaths, pass them on to their children. Known as *çift* or *çiftlik* and deemed sufficient for the support of a single-family household (*hane*), this tenure supposedly was equal to the amount of land that a peasant could cultivate with a pair of oxen; and Halil İnalcık has called this set of arrangements the *çift-hane* system.[22] Peasants could not leave their villages without prior permission from the man who possessed the right to collect their taxes, although for the latter official, retrieving people who had settled some distance away must often have been difficult.

According to the letter of the law, Ottoman peasants could not divide their tenures: when there was more than one surviving son, the heirs would have to run the farm together. Admittedly, peasants did not always abide by this rule; and by the later 1500s, many Anatolian villages contained but a few full *çift*s and a large number of so-called 'half farms', to say nothing of even smaller farmsteads. Thus, we cannot assume that peasant families inhabiting the same village were equal in terms of family income, even if some mutual assistance between related households was probably common. Furthermore, it is likely that many of the young men that in the late 1500s and early 1600s joined the sultans' armies as mercenaries did so partly because they were unenthusiastic about working a farm under the orders of an elder brother.

When a peasant died, his son if any, inherited the farm and the rights and duties that went with it, firstly being the obligation to pay tithes (*öşür*) from his produce and a further tax as a counterpart for holding his farm (*resm-i çift*).[23] From the later sixteenth century onward, irregular taxes that the government had at first levied under wartime stress (*avarız*) tended to become regular demands. At least in certain cases, these dues were problematic for peasant households because the amounts imposed were impossible to predict and might coincide with poor harvests.

At the same time, in some provinces regional regulations began to permit daughters to inherit a farm if there were no surviving sons. As a rationale, the sultan's officials wrote that it was unjust to deprive a family of the product of the labour, which its deceased head had put into the fields; but in addition, perhaps there was a concern that family farms needed stabilization at a time of frequent rural exodus.[24] Even so, daughters had to pay a special tax (*resm-i tapu*) if they wished to take over; and grandsons, who could inherit in the absence of surviving sons as well, had the same obligation. While the rules of inheritance specified by Islamic law, which governed personal and freehold property remained immutable over the centuries, the regulations governing the inheritance of peasant tenures on *miri* land changed quite often. Overall, the number of persons who might lay claim to the farm of a deceased relative tended to increase.[25] Thus, over time, the rules governing the inheritance of peasant tenures came to resemble the rules governing freehold property, in conformity with Islamic law.

By the seventeenth century, the peasant inheriting a farmstead in certain sections of the Balkans also inherited a share in the collective debt that his fathers and grandfathers had contracted, usually by borrowing money from a local notable to pay their taxes.[26] The qadis of the region seemingly accepted this practice although it went against the rule, enshrined in Islamic law that the survivors had to settle all debts at the death of either creditor or debtor.

It is possible to interpret at least some of the taxes due from Ottoman peasants as a kind of rent, payable to the sultan, after all the owner of the fields. However, Halil İnalcık has suggested that from a historian's point of view, the story was somewhat different.[27] For the oldest Ottoman records contain references to the so-called seven *kulluk* or 'servitudes', which seem to have been labour services later converted into money. Perhaps many peasants at one point had been serfs, who shook off the disabilities connected with this status as the money economy became more widespread. It is also possible or even probable that the early Ottoman sultans taxed their dependents more lightly than the Balkan lords that had preceded them and favoured the conversion of labour dues into cash payments. In particular, the Habsburg rulers who controlled a sizeable share of Central Europe in the late fifteenth and especially the sixteenth century had a bad reputation for the harsh serfdom that they enforced, which induced some peasants, though Christians, to opt for the sultan as an overlord.[28] At the same time, there must have been countervailing factors. For the small strip of territory in the hands of the Habsburg Emperor – or king of Vienna in Ottoman parlance – had a larger population than the more extensive Ottoman section, at least once the border between the two empires had stabilized.[29] Perhaps the special tax on non-Muslims (*cizye*) cancelled out much of the advantage of being an Ottoman subject: it is hard to be sure.

Given eminent domain on the part of the sultans, only houses inhabited by the subject population, together with gardens, orchards and vineyards, could be private property. In practice, there were some 'grey zones' between sultanic and private ownership rights, at least from the later 1600s onward. On the one hand, in certain parts of Anatolia, the holders of an admittedly limited number of fields claimed that these lands were their private property (*mülk*), although we do not know how this exceptional status had come into being.[30] At the same time, disputes arose about trees that villagers had planted, now declaring the resulting orchards as their freehold property. The central administration sometimes took the position that as long as the new and illegal plantation had not borne any fruit, the tax assignee who felt that the villagers had violated his rights could have the trees uprooted. On the other hand, if the tree/vine was already bearing fruit, the tax-taker could only tax the produce.[31]

While the trees were definitely the property of the person who had planted them, the status of the orchard seems to have been less clear. However, we do find orchards in post-mortem lists of inherited properties, while by contrast the fields worked by the decedents, being the property of the sultan, do not feature at all.[32]

Control of the land, control of the peasants: The Mughal orbit

In the Mughal world, many peasants held their plots in perpetuity, as lifelong tenants rather than as owners in the present-day sense. They could sell or mortgage their plots but had to ensure that cultivation continued.[33] However, the emperors' claim to eminent domain apparently did not feature as prominently in legislation as we observe in the Ottoman Empire, where Şeyhülislam Ebusuud (1490–1574) became famous for asserting the sultans' claims to eminent domain and accommodating them within the framework of Islamic law.[34] Perhaps, the reticence of the emperors of the 1500s and 1600s was due to the availability of much forested land, which groups of peasants led by caste elders might find and cultivate, without much reference to a distant overlord. Put differently, perhaps the forests and brushwood of Northern India were so difficult to penetrate that stridently propounded claims to eminent domain seemed unrealistic.

However, within Indian villages, there was a clear hierarchy between higher-caste members and peasants belonging to the service castes; and market relations probably increased income inequalities.[35] A lower-caste peasant family, even if it did hold land, might be under the obligation to provide for the needs of higher-caste families from the same village, especially when preparations were afoot for the often very elaborate wedding feasts celebrated by members of the higher castes. When expecting guests, the latter might demand further services. In the archival records of Jodhpur, where, as noted complaints appear quite frequently, Nandita Prasad Sahai has located cases of abuse on the part of persons feeling entitled to the services and deference of lower-caste men and women.[36]

In the Mughal world, the emperor assigned the taxes payable from agriculture, often about half of the harvest if we include various payments and cesses supplementary to the main revenue, to military men and courtiers as their holdings (*jagīr*). In the Ottoman world, such high rates of taxation were feasible only in exceptional cases. After all, while in the plains of the Ganges and Yamuna two harvests per year were often possible, in Anatolia and the Balkans, the scarcity of water typically forced peasants to leave the land fallow every second year so that it could collect enough moisture for the next season. Under optimum conditions, two years produced four harvests in the core provinces of the Mughal Empire, but only a single harvest in the Ottoman central territories.

In some provinces of the Mughal Empire, successful members of the caste to which the inhabitants of a given village mostly belonged claimed a position of power and seniority; and their caste fellows accepted this claim. The area over which such a personage, known as *zamīndār* held sway might vary widely, from a few settlements to an entire sub-district (*pargana*). While the Mughal administration made a major effort to ensure the direct access of tax collectors to the taxpayers, especially when Akbar's

Hindu finance minister Tōdar Mal (d. 1589) was in office, this attempt was only partially and/or temporarily successful. For Akbar and Tōdar Mal *zamīndārs* were – or should become – tax collectors in the service of the central government, but enforcing this claim was often impossible, especially in the outlying districts.[37] As a result, *zamīndārs* remained a power in the land long after the empire of the Mughals had disintegrated.[38]

Land revenues, disputed or not, accruing to the elites: The Ottoman case

The sultan's officials assigned peasant taxes to members of the military and administrative apparatus (*askeri*), in particular to the cavalrymen (*sipahis*) who participated in the sultans' campaigns (see Chapter 3). Huri İslamoğlu has suggested that the peasants of sixteenth-century North Central Anatolia, to whom she has devoted an important study, were rarely able to market their products beyond the district level. After all, the central administration had decreed that every judicial circumscription (*kaza*) including the (often very small) central town, was to be self-supporting.

By contrast, the tax-takers regularly marketed grain and other dues collected in kind.[39] While modest *sipahis* consumed a sizeable share of the grain arriving in their storehouses, the holders of larger tax grants (*zeâmet* or *has*) sent most of their takings to market. Governors in particular – who were in their given place for only a short time, and afterward employed retainers or tax farmers to collect outstanding dues – must have preferred cash rather than camel loads of grain. When looking for market orientation in the Ottoman countryside, we therefore need to focus on the assignees of tax revenues rather than on the peasant producers, who rarely travelled further than the district centre, unless the government ordered them to carry their grain to a stopping point where campaigning soldiers could collect it. However, when it came to raw materials for textile manufacture, including the hair of angora goats, the situation might be different. Thus, in the 1570s we find villagers from the Ankara area paying their taxes with coins they had earned from mohair sold to Venice. However, this was quite an exceptional case.[40]

When regarding the tax-collecting process from the villagers' point of view, we need to explain how the small number of *timar*-holders left behind when a campaign was afoot, managed to collect the taxes due to their colleagues and in addition, their own revenues. After all, in many places, settlement was sparse and peasants were likely to disappear into the hills when they heard that the tax collector was due to arrive.

As an explanatory hypothesis, we may assume that there was a layer of local notables active in the Anatolian countryside even in the 1500s, at least a century before their successors, later known as *ayan*, took on a semi-official and – in the 1700s – an official role in provincial administration. Often these notables drew power and prestige from the control of the pious foundations, large and small, which dotted the countryside of Anatolia and the Balkans.[41] While such foundation administrators probably did not have large bodies of armed retainers at their disposal, every household of some prominence must have contained a few such servitors. In addition, the descendants of a well-known saint or public benefactor may often have commanded a good deal of respect; and their support legitimized the demands of many a *timar*-holder unknown to the peasants from whom he demanded taxes. However, we are still waiting for evidence to prove or disprove this hypothesis.

Another thorny question involves the resistance, or at least non-compliance, of peasants when it came to burdensome official demands. In eighteenth-century Jodhpur, the prince often received complaints about oppression that he was to deal with according to the rules of behaviour appropriate for Indian kings (*wajabi*).[42] In a similar vein, the inhabitants of Ottoman villages and small towns turned to the sultan, and around 1600, these complaints were so numerous that Murad III (r. 1574–95) issued lengthy 'justice edicts' (*adâletnâme*) forbidding the most common abuses.[43] Especially egregious were the demands of local administrators who descended upon villages in armed tax collecting campaigns and demanded all sorts of illegal dues to support their mercenaries. Another source of peasant misfortune were the judges who declared that ordinary accidents were in fact killings, for which the people deemed responsible had to pay heavy fines. We can assume that the reactions that James Scott has called 'weapons of the weak', put differently deliberate misunderstandings, foot-dragging, late arrivals and incompetent work, occurred in Ottoman Anatolia, the Balkans or Egypt just as they did in twentieth-century Malaysia. In fact, this situation may explain some of the 'stupidities' that al-Shirbīnī ascribed to Egyptian villagers.[44]

In consequence, Ottoman surveyors were sometimes unable to produce proper records. In the sub-province (*sancak*) of Jerusalem, for instance, Amy Singer has found officials reporting that local peasants refused to take them seriously and only joked about the figures that these outsiders to the village community diligently tried to record.[45] Quite possibly, such problems were not unique to the Jerusalem countryside, but not every harassed official would have admitted his failures in writing. Moreover, the locals might corner an overly aggressive tax collector and give him a good beating – with no witnesses willing to tell the judge what had happened.

Until recently, historians used to assume that armed uprisings of peasant qua peasants did not occur in the Ottoman lands. Rather, when the situation became intolerable, the families that suffered most left their villages to hide out in the hills, or the younger men joined bands of roving mercenaries. However, Sam White has shown that strong protests from the countryside, leading to the cancellation of the sultan's demands did occasionally occur. Not by coincidence, the most effective reactions came from Karaman, an area in Southern Anatolia, where migrant sheep breeding was an important source of livelihood.[46] After all, nomads had arms and horses, which were lacking in many villages.

Land revenues, disputed or not, accruing to the elite in the Mughal world

In the Mughal setting, the central finance administration prepared records showing the putative yields of different crops. After Tōdar Mal's reforms, the rule was that the relevant tax-takers should hand written demands for revenue to village headmen and local *zamīndārs*, to which the latter had to respond with an undertaking, in writing as well that they would hand over the amount of taxes at issue.[47] Thus, Akbar's officials elaborated the regulations previously compiled by the administration of the Afghan king Shēr Shāh in the 1540s, when this ruler had replaced the second Mughal emperor Humāyūn, at that time a refugee at the Safavid court. As however neither Shēr Shāh's records nor those of the Mughal emperors have come down to us, we once again depend on the figures recorded by Akbar's courtier and close associate Abū'l-Fazl (d. 1602).[48] Basing his statements on the many figures collected before 1595, the author furnished average yields per unit of land, distinguishing between three categories: namely, 'good', 'medium', and 'poor'. Shireen Moosvi has suggested that these categories mostly reflected the abundance or scarcity of water. By adding, for each settlement, the quantities of produce harvested in the three categories of land and then dividing the total by three, Shēr Shāh's and later Akbar's finance officials arrived at rather rough estimates of average crop yields. They then assumed that land revenue collected by the emperor amounted to one third of total yield; and this amount of money was what – at least theoretically – the peasants would have had to pay. However, as previously noted, a number of surtaxes augmented the tax load to about half of the crop.

In Akbar's time, Tōdar Mal's finance administration cancelled *jagīrs* for a while, paying the *jagīrdārs* money salaries instead; the aim was to arrive at a more detailed survey of the land and the taxes that it might yield in the future.[49] It is difficult to imagine the cash-strapped Ottoman administration attempting a similar measure. However, the surveying procedure adopted in Akbar's realm somewhat resembles the manner in which Ottoman officials of the sixteenth century calculated the dues recorded in the well-known tax registers of the time (*tahrirs*). For in the sultans' empire, finance officials assumed the existence of three categories of land as well; and they calculated average crop yields for three consecutive years to arrive at putative averages.[50] At the same time, Ottoman surveying was probably more rough-and-ready; for Akbar's officials went so far as to decree that when measuring fields, the men in charge needed to use a bamboo rod, because this material was less likely to extend and contract under the influence of heat and humidity than other rods previously used for this purpose.[51] While refinements of this kind may have been more typical of the Mughal world, historians have found that even in Tōdar Mal's time, officials did not succeed in measuring all peasant land.[52]

Irfan Habib has claimed that the custom of frequently changing the *jagīrs* of Mughal office-holders, which was to prevent the latter from building local power bases (see Chapter 3), resulted in heightened oppression of the peasantry. For, given this arrangement, revenue collectors did not receive income from any particular village for a lengthy period, so that they did not worry about long-term productivity.[53] As Ottoman *timar*-holders were mostly of modest status, the sultans were apparently willing to leave these cavalrymen in place for rather longer periods; even if, as noted, *timar*-holders moved from one assignment to the next as well. Enjoying longer tenures, Ottoman *sipahis* perhaps did not abuse the peasantry to quite the same extent.

However, the villagers, as well as the Ottoman administration faced a serious problem with respect to short-term tax farmers (*mültezim*), who were in office for very few years and thus intent on maximizing revenues without concern for the future. Instituted in 1695, lifelong tax farms (*malikâne*) were to solve this problem, by making the beneficiaries develop an interest in the long-term viability of their tax farms. Supposedly, they would therefore protect the taxpayers from over-exploitation.[54] However, matters developed differently once *malikânes* had become an integral part of the Ottoman finance administration. Members of the sultan's family and persons holding high office, evincing more modest tax farmers now were the only possible bidders for *malikânes*. These persons were unlikely to visit the venues of their tax grants. Instead, they relied on contractors and subcontractors to collect revenues 'on the ground'. Quite often, the latter must have behaved much like many *jagīrdārs* of the late Mughal and post-Mughal periods.[55]

Sharecroppers in both empires

While, in principle, Indian peasants paid their taxes in cash, there were exceptions to this rule; at least in the eighteenth century, certain villagers were sharecroppers who delivered part of their produce to the *jagīrdār.* The latter needed to have merchants at his disposal to take charge of commercialization.[56] In post-Mughal principalities, the authorities sometimes put considerable pressure on merchants to make them assume the risks of marketing the dues in kind delivered by sharecroppers.[57] It would be interesting to find out whether peasants paid higher dues if not marketing their own produce.

In the Ottoman Empire of the 1700s, sharecropping was mostly a feature of landed estates (*çiftliks*) established by local power-holders. These were frequent in certain areas with commercial potential, but legally speaking, entities of dubious status on the margins of the Ottoman land system. While in addition to 'their' sharecroppers, notables holding *çiftliks* sometimes employed a few slaves for year-round work and hired a few migrant labourers at harvest time, plantations and monoculture were untypical.[58]

Recent studies of the expansion of *çiftlik* agriculture and sharecropping in the Balkans by a group of Greek and Turkish scholars have shown that, in this region, agricultural enterprises in the hands of non-peasants increased dramatically in the course of the 1700s. Near Salonika, townspeople often acquired *çiftliks* as an investment; in other places, local magnates, often present or former servitors of the sultan were more active. As the new investors preferred to establish their *çiftliks* on abandoned land, likely the war against the Holy League (1683–99) was responsible for the abundance of vacant land and subsequent spread of *çiftliks*.[59] Market-oriented *çiftliks* mostly supplied the Ottoman military apparatus and the city of Istanbul, rather than growing cash crops for export to Western Europe, the latter distinctly a minority phenomenon.[60] Thus, the classical model derived from re-feudalization and grain monoculture in seventeenth-century Poland, or the plantation economies of Central and South America, is not easily applicable to the Ottoman situation, as some economic historians of the 1950s and 1960s had been rather too eager to assume.[61]

Peasant dues in kind and the Ottoman money economy

Most Ottoman peasants seem to have paid their taxes partly in kind and partly in cash. While *çift* dues and the special tax (*cizye*) levied on non-Muslims were always payable in current coin, especially grain tithes (*öşür, aşar*) were usually due in kind. In addition, peasants needed to find cash to defray the tithes of perishable produce such as fruit or vegetables. In the early 1500s particularly, when markets were few, for peasants to take their own grain to market, or the dues in kind collected by *timar* and *zeâmet*-holders, was often a significant hardship: Carts were rudimentary and the villagers must have had trouble maintaining oxen that were, after all, indispensable for the plough.

In most Ottoman provinces, the grain 'tithe' was higher than one tenth, as an additional quantity of grain paid for the expenses of the tax collector; thus, in sixteenth-century Anatolia it was common practice to demand one eighth of the harvest as tithes.[62] *Timar*-holders, along with their retinues and horses, consumed large quantities of barley; therefore, as long as the *sipahi*s were a major force in the Ottoman army (until the early 1600s and sometimes beyond) significant amounts of grain went from producing taxpayer to consuming tax-taker without passing through the market. Moreover, when in this period mercenaries began to form an increasing percentage of the Ottoman armies they received some of their food through non-market channels as well. For, within the framework of *avarız* and *nüzul* taxation, peasants paid taxes in cash; while, as noted, they had to supply storehouses on the pre-arranged stopping points of the Ottoman armies on their way to the frontiers. Some of these deliveries were in lieu of taxes, and thus unpaid; for others the villagers received 'prices' typically below that current in the local market. Even so, in his study of *avarız* taxation in the South Central Anatolian province of Karaman during the seventeenth century, Süleyman Demirci has concluded that these payments were not particularly burdensome.[63]

On the other hand, this taxation contained hidden costs to the peasant household: the latter had to transport grains over what were often long distances and poor roads, with quite a few oxen perishing on the way and presumably, many carts ruined beyond repair. Camels might be useful for transporting grain, but they were usually too expensive for the peasants to maintain, and at most, wealthier villagers could have rented them. Peasants permitted to hand over money instead of grain, because they lived at great distances from the military roads; or, for other reasons were in a privileged position, as they often paid less than the value of the grain demanded from villages in more accessible locales.[64] Other problems resulted from political conflicts. When unemployed mercenaries scoured the countryside, unarmed or poorly armed peasants risked spoliation by brigands; and as Lütfi Güçer has emphasized, tax collectors often robbed the peasants as well.[65]

From the viewpoint of Ottoman army commanders, by contrast, these drawbacks were probably marginal; and the arrangements for military provisioning worked rather well until the late seventeenth or early eighteenth century. The logistics serving the armies of the sultans usually were of better quality than those current among their European rivals.[66]

Non-market or 'pseudo-market' arrangements also ensured that supplies reached the sultan's court and the city of Istanbul. The expression 'pseudo-market' is appropriate here because some suppliers received pay, but once again at rates far below those current in the open market. Perhaps the major reason for paying for these deliveries at all was that if the administration paid a price – even a minuscule one – those taxpayers who by special privilege were exempt from *avarız* taxation had to deliver the goods demanded like everyone else.[67] The privileged food supply enjoyed by the Istanbul population must have been due to concerns about the security of the sultan and top members of the elite in case of major scarcities. After all, especially from the late 1500s onward, increasing numbers of urban artisans and shopkeepers were at least nominal members of the local military corps (*kul*); and in the 1600s and 1700s, several sultans lost their thrones due to the rebellions of their *kul*.

The downside of these privileges enjoyed by the inhabitants of Istanbul was that peasants and larger farmers had little incentive to grow more than required for subsistence, seed, taxes and obligatory deliveries. When military demand grew dramatically in the second half of the eighteenth century, there was thus no readily expandable source of supply. In addition, producers with some surpluses to sell probably inclined toward clandestine exports of grain, first to Venice and later to the deficit areas of southern France: Exporters paid higher prices.

At the same time, the money taxes that peasants had to defray meant that they needed regular access to markets; and, during the sixteenth century, the latter visibly increased in number. However, it is likely that, when seventeenth-century droughts made field agriculture in the Anatolian uplands quite risky, some of these markets disappeared again, with the peasants moving to the western coastlands where water supplies were more secure. Huri İslamoğlu has proposed that when in the 1500s population grew faster than food supplies peasant families avoided cultivating increasingly marginal soils. Instead, they focused on readily marketable crops including cotton and rice, which allowed them to draw more income from the fields already under cultivation.[68] The same author has suggested that claimants to revenue, including the local notables (*ayan*) that came to control much of the Ottoman countryside in the 1600s and 1700s monopolized the commercialization of the most profitable crops, especially those sold to exporting merchants. Once again, as these exporters paid higher prices than Ottoman customers could afford, control over commercialization was a money-spinner.[69] Thus, most *ayan* did not venture into rural enterprises; and at least in Anatolia, large-scale farming was of limited importance and peasant agriculture continued as the dominant relationship of production.

Mughal peasants, the money economy, and its discontents

As noted several times already, the nobles of the Mughal court and other *jagīr* holders demanded and received their dues in money. Therefore, peasants sold a much larger share of their produce than cultivators in the Ottoman world ever did, and the role of rural merchants was correspondingly more significant.

Differently from the Ottoman governments of the sixteenth to eighteenth centuries, the Mughal emperors did not normally set prices by decree. Certainly, the term *nirkh*, corresponding to the Ottoman *narh*, did exist, but the word normally applied to prices observed in the markets rather than to those decreed by administrative fiat.[70] When the monsoon failed, grain prices might rise to unaffordable levels and many peasants sold their lands and left the region, temporarily or for good. When the Mughal emperor and his administration gave aid to peasants in distress, they typically granted remissions of taxes; when the authorities considered the lost harvests less life-threatening they merely allowed arrears. This latter measure might however cause great problems to cultivators during the following years.[71]

Most importantly, many Indian peasants felt the impact of the market because they were part-time weavers, producing the enormous quantities of cotton cloth that English, Dutch and French merchants exported, especially from Bengal and Gujarat (see Chapter 7). In addition, the Indian market absorbed large quantities of cloth as well, although we cannot measure the extent of domestic trade. Likely, many more textiles found customers in South Asia than merchants could hope to sell abroad.

As for peasant weavers active in the Mughal Empire, in parts of Rajasthan villagers wove during the dry season, when the heat made work in the fields impossible.[72] Put differently, many weavers engaged in agriculture and thus reduced dependence on the orders placed – or not – by exporting merchants. In indigo-producing areas near Agra, peasants operated a cottage industry, leaching the dye out of the stalks of the indigo plant and drying it in preparation for sale.[73] If times were reasonably good, peasants bought ornaments, probably of silver suitable for weddings, which might be saleable in times of distress.[74] Apart from cloth manufacturers, other service-providing villagers depended on the market as well, since they received part of their pay in coin. Apparently, historians of an earlier period have exaggerated the importance of the tradition allotting these people shares in the village grain heap.[75]

Peasants often incurred debts to moneylenders, typically to defray their taxes. Once a peasant household had borrowed money, high rates of interest and – especially the frequent incidence of compound interest – made it almost impossible for debtors to repay. In such cases, peasants, or else their wives and children might become servants to powerful and high-caste individuals living in the region. Such servants received minimal wages, probably due to the large number of people resorting to these arrangements in order to make ends meet.[76] The ties of patronage that linked certain cultivator-artisans to powerful families in the region further enhanced economic inequalities.[77] Due to indebtedness, many peasants lost their status as independent cultivators on an inherited piece of land and with the passage of time, descended into the low status of hereditary servants.

Migrations in the Ottoman rural world

In the Ottoman orbit, the elite tended to assume that the only licit migrations occurred when people moved in obedience to the sultan's orders, who might transfer his peasant or artisan subjects from one province to another according to the political aims of the moment. If not ordered to move, villagers were to remain in their places, for this arrangement greatly facilitated the collection of taxes and thus secured elite revenues.

In fact, peasant mobility throughout the empire was significant, as many provinces had small populations by the standards of today or even of the late nineteenth century. Arable land was often available, although we know very little about stockbreeding and thus, about the possibility of acquiring oxen to draw the plough. On the desert margins, particularly in today's Syria, villages were sustainable only if the Ottoman government protected them. When this aid became unreliable in the late 1500s, most peasants seemingly moved out to escape the exactions of the desert nomads.[78] Perhaps some of these refugees resettled in the Syrian coastlands, largely deserted since the later Middle Ages but revived in Ottoman times.[79]

As noted, drought and/or political insecurity induced many Anatolian peasants in the difficult years before and after 1600 to leave their villages. Hypothetically, some of these people still had contacts in the world of nomads and semi-nomads, as a significant section of the Anatolian farming population were descended from nomads who had arrived in the Seljuk period and settled during the population expansion of the sixteenth century. Moreover, many Anatolian peasants down to the population increase of the later 1900s owned significant flocks and upland pastures from which to feed them. They were thus familiar with the routines of animal husbandry. Given these connections, presumably some of the people facing an increasingly precarious livelihood in their villages could prevail on real or supposed relatives among nomads and semi-nomads to help them constitute a flock, and thus make it possible for a family to enter the life world of migrant sheep breeders.

While migrant herders often escaped registration, it is easier to show that in the Ottoman orbit, some of the escaped villagers set up farms in places remote from their original habitats. Or else they migrated to the towns and cities, where officials ultimately might locate and record them. Probably in places where notables set up their landed estates, especially in the Balkans, people who wanted to avoid service as sharecroppers or agricultural labourers migrated to the less accessible hills or mountains.[80] In some environments, this tendency must have contributed to the survival of villages in the latter locations despite the crises of the 1600s, when by contrast, peasants deserted the lowlands even though they were easier to farm. In other localities, however, the lower-lying land was marshy and therefore less desirable than the uplands – given the limits of our knowledge, we cannot claim that observations valid for Southern Anatolia had the same validity in Thrace.[81]

From the studies undertaken to date, it seems that in Ottoman Anatolia, spontaneous migrations – put differently population movements not due to official commands – mostly resulted from droughts and scarcities. Furthermore, especially during the late sixteenth and early seventeenth centuries, migrations between provinces and moves to Istanbul 'the well-guarded' (*mahruse*) resulted from attacks by the rebellious soldiers known as the Celalis, who plundered anybody unable to find refuge behind fortress walls.[82] Sometimes migrants covered great distances; thus, escapees from Trabzon in North Eastern Anatolia made their way to Crimea. A different kind of migration occurred in the Balkans during the war of 1683–99; in this case, a sizeable number of Serbs who had sided with the Habsburgs when the latter had occupied a large section of the region, migrated to the Austrian and Hungarian territories when the Ottomans regained control.[83] In this case, political considerations, namely the fear of punishment for betraying the sultan's cause were the reason for migration. Other groups of people may have crossed the Ottoman–Habsburg border for other political reasons; but often we know little about their numbers and motivations.

As far as we understand from the limited records at our disposal, the Mughal administration did not assume that officials could or should control migration, if only because in many parts of the empire migration during monsoon failures was necessary for survival. Migration was often a lifesaver in the Ottoman provinces as well; but seemingly, officials did not consider it necessary to write about what would happen if they enforced to the letter the sultan's edicts prohibiting migration without permission from the relevant tax-taker. Pragmatically, they apparently let matters take their course until conditions improved, when they might again attempt to settle people in the places from which they had once fled.[84]

Migrations in northern India

In India, grazing land was scarce, a situation that explains why the Mughal elite had no great opinion of the local horses, and animals deemed of a quality sufficient for the army often were imports from Central Asia or else the Arabian Peninsula. Given the lack of grazing, sheep breeding was also marginal, and the local wool often of poor quality. Migratory groups might rear cattle and transport goods (compare with Chapter 6); as theft of cattle was common, breeders had to be ready to defend their herds. Similar to Anatolian nomads and semi-nomads, who had a reputation for frequently using force against villagers and sometimes even against the sultan's governors, cattle breeders in Mughal India were familiar with the use of arms as well.

Thus, the Jats, who in the Middle Ages apparently made a precarious living as herdsmen, by the eleventh century CE, had come to specialize in warfare. In so doing, they learned new techniques; and some Jats now specialized in doing battle on horseback. Others even armed boats for fighting on the river Indus.[85] Probably due to the many wars linked to the Mongol invasions, and the constant competition for control among the many claimants to the Delhi sultanate, some of the Jats moved eastward, from the Indus valley to the plains of the Ganges and the Yamuna. Apparently, we know very little about the particular reasons for this migration and the subsequent change from stockbreeding to agriculture. However, by the beginning of the Mughal period, the Jats had established settlements in Punjab and others relocated in the central provinces of the empire, becoming part of the local caste hierarchy. When their neighbours began to classify them according to the fourfold Hindu hierarchy of Brahmins (religious specialists), Kshatriyas (warriors), Vaishas (merchants and farmers) and Sudras (servants), the Jats took their places at the bottom of the hierarchy, regarded as servants. However, this lowly ritual status did not reflect their economic position, and perhaps because of their military skills, the Jats in the Ganges–Yamuna area often established themselves as substantial cultivators. At the end of the sixteenth century, Abū'l-Fazl 'Allāmī even recorded a significant number of *zamīndārs* of Jat background, put differently of established local power-holders integrated into the Mughal system, who were now responsible for low-level tax collection.[86] Through long-distance eastward migration, some of the Jats had thus bettered their economic if not their ritual status.

If certain members of a given group had gained recognition as *zamīndārs*, historians of the subcontinent have generally considered that the relevant people were now agriculturalists. Whenever population increased, certain communities that had previously lived by cattle breeding – and by cattle rustling too – needed to find land to settle; and often migration to a site where usable land was available, was the precondition for settlement. In certain cases, former migrant herdsmen might find that service to the Mughal court provided an alternative to agriculture. Thus, a significant part of the population known as Meos, who inhabited the Mewar region and the Arawalli Hills close to Delhi, served the imperial postal system as runners, a job for which they received monetary payment. Other men of the same community worked as imperial guardsmen.[87] Stationed outside the palace, it was their job to protect the latter and see to the execution of imperial commands. Popular opinion claimed that Akbar had allotted them land on which to settle, and Surajbhan Bhardwaj believes that this claim may well be true.[88] Perhaps the Meos had received these allotments because of their services to the Mughal court. If this hypothesis is correct, the movement of Meo settlements from hilltops to the plain, the remnants of some deserted highland villages remaining visible, may be due to the integration of at least some of the inhabitants into the Mughal governing apparatus.[89] However, we do not know whether the abandoned hilltop settlements had been the Meo habitat when they still lived by cattle-rearing and robbery, or whether the people at issue had built them when they first decided to settle down. No solid information seems to be available.

Conclusion: Back to the cash nexus

When taxing peasant produce, Iranian accounting know-how, and the practices of Central Asian rulers, seem to have inspired both Ottoman and Mughal officials. Probably, if the Mughal central archives had not suffered such dramatic losses, the similarities would have been even more apparent. However, the modalities of tax collection depended on marketing opportunities as well, to say nothing of the abundance or else lack of bullion. In the central lands of the mid-sixteenth-century Ottoman Empire, markets grew in number with expanding population; they must have declined once again with the withdrawal of villagers and townspeople from the increasingly arid lands of Central and South-Eastern Anatolia – but we do not have much evidence to prove this latter hypothesis. Seemingly, the documentation on rural markets in the Mughal world is sparse too; it is worth recording that the detailed indexes of the two opus magnums by Irfan Habib and Shireen Moosvi respectively, contain no entries referring to village markets.[90]

As noted (see Chapter 6), there must have been much more gold and silver available in Mughal India than was true of the Ottoman world, and this fact surely limited the market involvement of many Anatolian and Balkan peasants. Ironically, most Ottoman peasants had less contact with the money economy than their Mughal counterparts; on the other hand the notion of self-contained villages with little involvement in the market, adopted by Karl Marx in an early stage of his reasoning had originated in a rather flawed understanding of the Indian situation.[91] By contrast, Irfan Habib has stressed that Mughal revenue demand forced the peasants to sell much of their produce, thus connecting them to the market. At the same time, the village needed to supply its needs from within itself, as the income from sales went to the governing apparatus and did not leave the peasant any significant purchasing power. Therefore, villagers of higher status satisfied most of their needs through customary service and barter.[92] Other historians however think that at least in the 1700s, the money economy penetrated even this latter sphere, as goods circulated not only through patronage relationships but through the market as well.[93] While caste membership was important to the life chances of any peasant, it was only one of the determinants of his/her fate and not the only one. In consequence, it makes sense to compare villages of the Ottoman and Mughal worlds; which, by contrast, if caste had been the only decisive factor, would have had so little in common as to make comparison meaningless.

In Mughal India, the stocks of bullion available to the elite were enormous, due to the regularly incoming payments for exported cotton cloth, silks, spices and other luxuries. The wide availability of bullion made it possible for *jagīrdār*s and the Mughal treasury to insist on receiving most peasant taxes in current coin. Unfortunately, there is little information on prices; but apparently, market conditions, rather than the commands of the central government determined the amounts of money that customers paid for rice, wheat, cotton and other necessities. In the Ottoman world, by contrast, governmental fiat should have determined the prices paid in large sectors of the domestic market; and, in many cases, buyers and sellers obeyed the commands they received. On the subcontinent, peasant indebtedness to merchants and moneylenders seems to have prevented most agriculturalists from benefiting, when their goods were in high demand. When prices increased the owners of (even modest) capital usually profited; this situation was common enough in the Ottoman core provinces as well.

Thus, it does not seem realistic to idealize the situation of villagers in the early 1800s before the mid-century reconstruction of the Ottoman state apparatus, or the pre-colonial period in the Indian case. This sobering fact-of-life will become apparent from a closer study of the 'marginal people' in both societies, namely non-elite women, servants and slaves.

9

On the Margins of Society: Women, Servants, Low-Caste People and Slaves

In many human societies there were and are people that the authorities – and members of the society in question – define as being of low status. Even in today's world, at a time when most people are supposedly citizens rather than subjects, such differences in legal and social status persist – and often the resulting conflicts end in violence. Acknowledging this situation, an election poster put up in Munich during the summer of 2018 said, that we could only call a place 'home' if we enjoyed basic human rights in this venue.[1] Moreover, even in wealthy societies people with physical impediments have to struggle, sometimes successfully and sometimes not, to have their needs taken into account. Evidently, many of their co-citizens do not recognize them as men and women with equal rights.

In the Ottoman and Mughal empires too, large sections of the population were in the disadvantageous position of being a 'second-class subject'. Given the powers of sultan and emperor, the decision of the ruler determined the extent of the privileges that a subject might derive from being a Muslim, or the disadvantages arising from a refusal to profess the religion of the elite. In the Ottoman world, being a Muslim gave people the significant financial advantage of not paying the poll tax (*cizye*). As for the Mughal Empire, the demand for *jizya* was intermittent, as Akbar (r. 1556–1605) abrogated it while Aurangzeb (r. 1658–1707) asserted his commitment to Islam by reinstating it (see Chapter 4). Moreover, in some places and times including early modern Europe, humiliating people not of the dominant religion or denomination might appear meritorious at least to certain members of the relevant society. In the Ottoman context, such people might consider it inappropriate to extend even small everyday courtesies to members of an 'inferior' religion.[2] Travellers sometimes noted that women and children, by definition of low social status, were likely to insult them as strangers and adherents of an 'infidel' religion – elite males did not normally do so.[3] However, differently from many rulers in early modern Europe, neither the Ottoman nor the Mughal monarchs ever tried to make their subjects convert by a massive deployment of state power.

In addition, gender divided society into two parts, with men enjoying many more rights and opportunities than women did. Apart from gender-oriented historians, few scholars appreciate that being female and unrelated to members of the political elite automatically relegated people to a lowly position in society, a 'normal' situation given male privileges throughout the known world. 'Second-class' subjects were thus in a majority, even if we exclude women related to members of the governing elites of the Ottoman and Mughal empires, in any case a limited number. Choosing to forget this home truth, people waxing romantic about the past usually identify with the privileged members of society.

This chapter begins with a discussion of non-elite women, followed by a section on slaves and other servants. As the latter were often females, the two categories overlap. In addition, we will briefly return to the caste system (see Chapters 7 and 8), the major factor in which societies on the subcontinent including the Mughal Empire differed from Ottoman social structures. After all, comparisons involve the highlighting not only similarities but of differences as well. At the same time, we need to retain Jeroen Duindam's warning that differences may conceal underlying similarities.[4] We conclude with a discussion of the female dancers and singers, who in the Mughal world might well be courtesans but still gained some respect due to their art.

Sources on 'the second sex'[5]

Much of the Ottoman evidence on women is due to the labours of the scribes employed by the qadi's courts. The registers compiled by the latter contain sizeable numbers of post-mortem inventories belonging to females, due to the right of inheritance accorded to them by Islamic religious law (*şeriat*, sharia). In addition, Islamic law recognized women as individuals, who retained a legal existence independent from that of their fathers or husbands.[6] These rights occasioned the appearance of female plaintiffs or defendants in the courts of urban qadis, sometimes expressing their demands in person. However, the intervention of male relatives often limited the exercise of women's rights, especially when men claimed to represent their female relatives. Some of them may have had the best interests of their women-folk in mind; in other cases, there is reason for scepticism.

Certain female activities have entered the archives because officials regarded them as 'work'. However, such records were infrequent. Certainly, in all patriarchal societies, many women of the subject classes worked all day cooking, cleaning, sewing and taking care of children and invalids; and, in many places they did agricultural work as well. Normally however, their labour did not qualify as work, but merely as 'something that women do'. Once again, defining women's work out of existence is common enough even today; but for our present purposes, this consideration is important because it explains at least in part why we know so little about females at work in the houses, gardens and fields of the Ottoman and Mughal worlds.

Despite this difficulty, by now a significant body of work deals with women from the Ottoman subject class, resident in Anatolia, the Balkans and particularly the Arab provinces, where archival sources are especially ample.[7] Almost all of the females covered were townspeople – few peasant women ever had the chance of leaving their village for the nearest court of law. Most research available today deals with women's material possessions, their marriages and divorces and on a more general level, their problematic situation before the qadi's court. After all, the latter considered female witness undesirable and the testimony of women was not worth much in comparison to that of males. *Nolens volens*, the courts only accepted female witnesses in cases of which men supposedly knew nothing, such as pregnancy or (still)-birth.

While we possess a limited amount of Ottoman sources for the 1500s, relevant court documents increase substantially during the seventeenth and especially the eighteenth century. Even so, it is often difficult to explain the presence or absence of data in particular cases. Why is there a large body of material on the women, who particularly in Aleppo and Cairo were mothers and wives to urban notables, while we do not have much information on the female relatives of magnates active in Anatolia and the Balkans? After all, in the eighteenth century the latter ran many places in very loose subordination to the Ottoman sultan, and they must have stabilized their positions by intra-elite marriage alliances. A similar discrepancy appears when we study charitable works: Sixteenth-century women from Istanbul's subject population quite often established pious foundations (*vakıf*, pl. *evkaf*). On the other hand, a thorough study of the *evkaf* of the magnate dynasty known as the Karaosmanoğulları, dominant on the Aegean seaboard of eighteenth-century Anatolia, has turned up very few female founders.[8] To date, the reasons for this divergence remain unclear.

Women of the Ottoman subject class, earning money in the market and elsewhere

In every town, a certain number of women worked for a living, or lent out money. After all, presumably not all families could or would support female relatives who had lost their husbands because of death or desertion. Situations of this type must have been frequent, especially in the Ottoman central provinces, where the Hanefi (in South Asia: Hanafī) school of law (*mezheb*) predominated. For, unlike counterparts following other schools of law, Hanefi/Hanafī judges could not divorce women whose husbands had deserted them, but only assign the victims a daily stipend from their husbands' properties – if such funds existed.[9] Very occasionally, modest artisans, such as the blacksmiths working in the sultans' naval arsenal, admitted that their wives needed to earn money, as their own duties at the workplace prevented them from taking care of their families in a timely manner.[10] Dated to 1720, this text, a command by Ahmed III (r. 1703–30), which expressly permitted the women at issue to prepare sheep's trotters for sale, is exceptional. However, women who needed to support their families by their work were probably more common than it appears at first glance.

The Ottoman seventeenth-century traveller Evliya Çelebi (1611–after 1683) offered a tantalizing glimpse of women from Edirne, who attended a parade in Istanbul to sell rosewater, probably manufactured in their hometown.[11] Unfortunately, he did not record how the women travelled the considerable distance between the two cities without losing their money and goods to highway robbers.[12]

While as noted, information on working women is rare and dispersed, we do have some data on towns with significant textile production. In seventeenth-century Ankara, a certain percentage of the looms used for the manufacture of fine fabrics from the hair of locally raised angora goats were not in workshops but in private homes.[13] Likely, in such places women helped the male weavers, not only by spinning, but by preparing the yarn for the looms as well. For sixteenth-century Bursa, we possess a tantalizing document referring to a woman who had taken in a female apprentice to teach her the craft of manufacturing the light silk cloth known as *vale* (see Chapter 7). We only know about the affair because the family fell out with the mistress and terminated the relationship; unfortunately, for us, the dispute concerned the marriage of the girl and had nothing to do with textile production.[14]

In the past, scholars often assumed that, while women embroidered for their homes and families, work for the market was the province of men. In recent years, however, cases have emerged that make this neat division seem simplistic. On liturgical veils used for church services among Orthodox Greeks, made between the late 1500s and the early 1700s, we sometimes encounter the names of women. In addition, these pieces feature dates presumably referring to the completion – or else the donation – of the pieces at issue.[15] Especially intriguing is the work of a craftswoman named Despineta, sometimes called Despineta Argiraia, who in the late seventeenth and early eighteenth centuries, probably lived in the former Istanbul suburb of Beşiktaş, today part of the central city. Pieces with her name have turned up in an Ankara church, some 450 km away from her presumed residence, and even further afield, in the little town of Eğin, today Kemaliye, in Eastern Anatolia. Unfortunately, the archives of the Ecumenical Patriarchate in Istanbul, where more information may be waiting, are still largely unknown and unstudied. The Kemaliye inscription (1723) mentions both the donor and the craftswoman that made the embroidery. In other cases, where only the name of one woman is on record, we cannot exclude the possibility that the inscriptions referred not to the makers but to female donors. However, today's experts believe that the female artists/artisans who had made costly embroideries enjoyed the privilege of signing them with their names.

Most recently, Yıldız Yılmaz has shown that, in the 1700s high-ranking eunuchs in the Ottoman palace sometimes owned embroideries made by palace women.[16] We may wonder whether the patron paid for these goods or whether doing such work for a superior was simply one of the duties of a slave woman serving in the sultan's harem.

Women active in commerce might have been slave dealers. The position of these persons was profoundly ambiguous: On the one hand, male slave dealers always wanted to subordinate the female traders to their direction, and if possible push them out of the business. Given the prevalence of misogyny, these men certainly could count on official support; and in the mid-eighteenth century, the women still active in the slave trade no longer counted as dealers but as mere criers or hawkers.[17] However, a complete elimination of women was problematic, as most slave traders could not have done business without female helpmates. At least, in seventeenth-century Istanbul, many or even most slaves seem to have been female; and, after sale they thus entered the harems of their new owners, where no strange male had access. Therefore, even delivering the slave women to their destinations would have been difficult for a male trader alone. Viewed from a different angle, quite a few female slaves were the property of well-to-do women, who did not attend the public slave market in the downtown *khan/han* known as the Esir Hanı. Therefore, saleswomen must have gone to the houses of the prospective purchasers with a number of saleable girls so that elite women could make their choices.

Other women delivered goods to females of high status, who in many cases did not go out to do their own shopping. In the Ottoman palace of the late sixteenth century, such female merchants, frequently Jewish, had the title of *kira*, derived from Greek and meaning 'lady'. Esperanza Malchi (d. 1600), the *kira* serving Safiye Sultan (d. 1618) achieved high status and exercised a significant degree of informal political power. However, she had the misfortune of belonging to the losing faction in a court intrigue, which also involved soldiers stationed in Istanbul; and she lost her life as a result.[18] Later female traders visiting the sultans' harem kept a lower profile. However, women delivering luxuries to elite harems must have been common enough and presumably, future scholars looking for the relevant documents will be able to find them. The cloth in which such small-scale traders wrapped their wares (*bohça*) has given rise to the Turkish expression *bohçacı kadın* for an inveterate female gossip: some women distributed news and hearsay as well as material goods. In addition, certain women working at home probably needed female intermediaries to deliver their work to a merchant, if their personal circumstances did not allow them to do this job on their own. In eighteenth-century Tunis, for instance, such female intermediaries may have acted for women knitting the fezzes for which the city was famous; only at a later stage of production did male dyers and fullers take over.[19]

In seventeenth-century Kayseri, women who owned some money often lent it out. We do not know whether they demanded interest payments.[20] While Islamic law forbids interest, Ottoman pious foundations routinely contravened the prohibition, merely giving buyers 'a good deal'. This custom may have encouraged some private lenders to do likewise, at least where family members were not at issue. Even so, most women who according to their post-mortem inventories had some money owed to them could only claim the 'deferred dowry' (*mihr-i müeccel*), which their husbands needed to pay when divorcing them, or which the executors had to pay a widow out of the funds left by a deceased husband. If the wife died before her spouse, the woman's *mihr-i müeccel* passed to her heirs. Apparently, some women did profit from the high demand for ready money characteristic of the notoriously cash-poor Ottoman society.

Women with resources and managerial talent might act as administrators of pious foundations, often because they had previously set up these charities from their own funds and stated in the foundation document that they would administer the relevant resources as long as they lived.[21] Certainly, these females often designated male family members to take over after their deaths.[22] On the other hand, many male and female donors stipulated that, once they were dead, their descendants or freed slaves should take over. While certain founders excluded females, there were others who did not have any objections to daughters running their charities if male descendants should fail. In the town of Tokat in Northern Anatolia, during the 1790s – and thus, some thirty years after the end of the period covered here – the revenues belonging to a locally influential pious foundation were under the control of a woman named Şerife Fatma. This person, who claimed descent from the Prophet Muhammad, apparently remained in office for several decades.[23] Thus, her lengthy tenure may well have begun around 1770 and therefore within the period under discussion. In terms of Islamic law, women were perfectly capable of administering pious foundations, although they were probably a small minority among the numerous trustees of these institutions. Administering the resources belonging to the wealthier charities was not just a matter of prestige, but a source of gain as well as many donors had assigned substantial salaries to the people they had placed in charge of their *vakıfs*.

Women of the subject classes in the Mughal and post-Mughal worlds

Where the Mughal world is at issue, most primary and secondary sources concentrate on women from the imperial family. As this chapter deals with females from the subject classes, we have to exclude them. A limited number of documents from post-Mughal principalities do however, concern women from the subject class, often because they were petitioners or occurred in the petitions submitted by their men-folk.[24]

Furthermore, Shireen Moosvi has found and discussed a number of Persian-language documents concerning mid-seventeenth-century women from the merchant city of Surat.[25] Some of the texts in question are marriage contracts (*nikāhnāma*) specifying the four conditions to which the prospective husband must adhere. These texts are especially interesting because the conditions at issue were apparently 'quite commonplace among middle-class Muslims in Surat'.[26] According to the contracts the husband's non-compliance with the first three conditions listed, gave the wife an automatic right to a divorce. Firstly, he was not to take a second wife while married to the first one; thus, in Surat merchant circles, monogamous marriages were desirable and some women – or their families – had the social power to impose them on future husbands. Secondly, the husband promised to abstain from severe beating as long as the woman did not seriously break the law – however, if the man could define the extent of the transgression, this condition may not have provided much protection. The third condition specified that the husband should not leave his wife, or fail to provide for her for a period ranging from six months to three years, depending on the time limit specified in the contract at issue. Thus, obviously, these women must have possessed money of their own, or their families must have agreed to help them if necessary. As for the fourth condition, it specified that the husband must not take a concubine; however, if he did so, the wife did not obtain an automatic divorce but could sell, manumit or give away the slave girl, thus removing her from the husband's reach. Unfortunately, we do not have any records of court cases that may have arisen from the non-fulfilment of the stipulations contained in the Surat marriage contracts.

From the letters of Mary Montagu, who as the linguistically gifted and highly literate wife of a British ambassador socialized with Ottoman elite women of the early eighteenth century, we learn that these persons aimed for monogamy as well, and tried to create a climate in which disapproval of polygamy was the norm.[27]

As owning property was a precondition for female rights and privileges, the studies of Shadab Bano are important because they give us some idea of women's property holding, a topic permitting some comparison with the Ottoman world.[28] The types of resource that a given society permitted – or did not permit – women to control indicate the value placed on the resource in question. For males will often consider things in short supply as essential to the well-being of the family, and for this reason deny them to their women-folk.

We have seen that, from a legal perspective, Muslim women had an advantage as religious law formally accorded them a right to the inheritances of their relatives, although they received only half of the amount allotted to a man in the same degree of relationship to the deceased. Furthermore, the enforcement of this stipulation might depend on the availability of a qadi's court. As for some Hindu laws, they excluded all female relatives apart from the daughters of the deceased; and even the latter received only a fourth of the share to which a son might lay claim. However, rich men might make provision for their daughters during their lifetimes: thus, the jeweller Santidas of Ahmadabad, who counted the emperor Shāh Jahān (r. 1628–58) among his customers, had given a house to his daughter, while gifting the bulk of his property to his son.[29] Especially if there were no male heirs, Hindu women might secure the estates of deceased family members.[30]

The situation became more complex because at least in Gujarat, not only Muslim but also Hindus including women turned to the sharia courts when it suited their purposes.[31] Similarly, in the Ottoman world, Christians and Jews used the qadis' courts in this manner, although churchmen and rabbis fulminated against the practice. Quite a few studies now focus on the 'fine art of forum shopping'.[32]

Apparently, in the Gujarati context too, women from wealthier families were quite aware of the fact that that the sharia focused, not on communities, but on individuals and their personal property. Thus, Islamic law could provide a counterweight against the pressures coming from family members. After all, unless headed by a strong-willed widow, households were under the control of men; and, in a world in which disposing of women through marriage was a significant part of the exercise of power, it was unlikely that the female members of a given household would have much control over family property held in common. As Farhat Hasan has put it, while neither the sharia nor the kinship system was particularly supportive of women, the latter, and other subordinate members of society as well, were quite capable of using these institutions to their own advantage.[33] Even so, we need to remember that this type of resistance to patriarchal demands was possible only if the women at issue came from a household living significantly above subsistence level. Moreover, women could hope to defend their rights to property or a monogamous marriage only if they had access to sources of information. If a family kept a new bride in isolation from the outside world, she would not have known about her sharia-based rights until it was too late.

Presumably, in many cases, the jewellery and other ornaments received at her wedding were a woman's principal source of security. Perhaps for this reason, in Mughal and post-Mughal India merchants of jewellery seemingly played a more important role than such traders could claim in the Ottoman Empire. As for the control of real estate and agricultural lands, conditions varied widely; in some parts of the Mughal Empire, women were co-owners of residential plots or received agricultural land; and documents show them donating and mortgaging these properties. As Moosvi has noted, in this prosperous milieu, at least some women were literate and could thus more easily become aware of their rights.[34]

At the same time, Ottoman women of the subject class were frequently on record when selling real estate as well. Thus, we may wonder whether in both contexts, females might sell these possessions to their male relatives in order to retain the support of their brothers, cousins and uncles in case of divorce, illness or widowhood. Many property cases discussed by Shadab Bano concern Muslims; and while Hasan has found a number of additional records pertaining to Hindu women, the scarcity of evidence makes generalization difficult, even on the regional Gujarati level.

While the contracts and other documents analysed by Shireen Moosvi, Farhat Hasan and Shadab Bano gave the wives of merchants a significant degree of protection, as previously noted, these women belonged to a privileged stratum. Among the poor, males could sell their wives and children into slavery. In Akbar's reign, such sales were illegal but in times of famine, when starving children were on offer in the public streets, Mughal officials tolerated them.[35] Such sales were illicit in the Ottoman lands as well: a text from the reign of Sultan Süleyman (r. 1520–66) referred to Tatars selling their children due to a famine, and threatened to execute anyone who might buy such slaves in defiance of the ruler's prohibition.[36] Otherwise, few documents of this type seem to have surfaced, although famines occurred in the Ottoman world as well. Even if a few more documents concerning such sales were to come up in the future, it is safe to say that parents selling their children into slavery were extremely rare in the period under discussion. However, in the later nineteenth century, sales of Circassian girls to elite harems on the part of their relatives do appear in the record, at least occasionally.[37]

Certainly, it is very risky to deduce the absence of an event or custom from the absence of records, as contemporaries might ignore the occurrences in question for any number of reasons. Even so, it is worth noting that outside observers very hostile to the Ottomans – and they are frequent – fail to mention that husbands and fathers could sell their families into slavery. We may thus conclude that the positions of wives in Mughal India varied widely, while stressing that we only have (a limited amount of) information on a very limited part of the female population. Some of the wealthier Muslim women of Surat could demand rights that Ottoman females did not often achieve, including the right to take a husband's concubine away from him – however, we do not know how often a woman insisting on this clause in her marriage contract soon found herself a divorcee. As for female subjects of the Mughal emperors who were poor and had no families to protect them, in the worst of conditions they risked enslavement. We even find occasional cases of both men and women who sold themselves into slavery; likely, these were often women left without support, an occurrence never mentioned in the Ottoman documentation as known today.[38]

In the post-Mughal ambiance of eighteenth-century Jodhpur, village women from artisan or peasant milieus had value only as potential mothers of children or members of the workforce.[39] Mostly they laboured as drudges without any skills.[40] When no longer able to conceive or do hard work, the fellow villagers of older women were quite likely to chase them away as so-called witches – at least, they did not burn them as might happen in early modern Europe. Remarkably, the low value placed on women meant that quite a few lower-caste males whose wives had left them with their lovers merely wanted monetary compensation for the services that the women would no longer provide. Among these castes, at least in post-Mughal Jodhpur, the ethos at the time differed sharply from the mores of the elites, and the flight of a female was not an infringement of male honour.[41] Thus, it is a serious error to assume that the views then current among people of high caste or elevated status were typical of society as a whole.

While archival documentation on women in the Mughal context is not very ample, artists in the service of the emperors have produced a large number of drawings and miniatures in which women feature prominently. By contrast, depictions of females are infrequent in the Ottoman world. A particularly remarkable example is a seventeenth-century miniature showing a female painter at work in a wealthy Indian harem, sketching the features of a senior woman (see Chapter 2).[42] There does not seem to be any information on how this artist had received her training; perhaps she had learned her skills in her father's workshop as sometimes happened in Renaissance Europe. Exceptionally, miniatures attributed to female artists have survived as well.[43] Due to the greater propensity of artists in the Mughal and post-Mughal worlds to depict women, even when at work, we can juxtapose information provided by Ottoman documents with visual records from India.

To provide some notion of the work done by Indian women, Moosvi has combined miniatures from the Mughal period with observations mostly by British authors describing conditions during the early 1800s. Apparently, some historians of Indian technology assume that the techniques used in everyday life did not change very much during the quarter millennium separating these two sets of records; however, this view is open to debate.[44] As noted, spinning was a woman's job, in India as in the Ottoman world and in early modern Europe. Remarkably, an image published by Moosvi shows a spinning wheel rather than a spindle – in Anatolia on the other hand, spindles were common as late as the 1960s, although spinning wheels were in use as well.[45] In agriculture, Indian women at least occasionally transplanted rice and after the harvest, they cleaned the rice with the help of a hammer worked by foot, a procedure that necessitated the cooperation of two people. Or else they beat the rice in a mortar and pestle – an exhausting job that, however, one person could do on her own. Boiling the rice to get rid of the husks was less laborious, but people considered this procedure suitable only for the poorest qualities.

While, in the Ottoman world, water mills and mills driven by packhorses produced flour, in Mughal India, this work frequently fell to women who worked small hand mills. At least at the present stage of our research, we cannot tell whether this lack of interest in mechanization indicates that women's work had a lower value in Mughal India than it had in the Ottoman context, where after all, population outside of the largest cities was comparatively sparse.

Mughal miniatures also provide evidence on women in the building trades, once again in the numerous chores that did not require special training. Thus, on the construction site of Akbar's new capital Fatehpur Sikri we find them breaking stones and bricks, sieving the material before it went into the limekilns. Other females carried bitumen in large bowls. If our present knowledge is at all reliable, we do not find women on Ottoman construction sites or in most other publicly visible places of work. As an exception to this rule, we can however refer to the observation of Evliya Çelebi that in Cairo, women and girls sold bread on the streets.[46] As nineteenth-century documents record this custom too, we can be sure that Evliya was not just trying to add an exotic touch to his story.[47]

In service: The Ottoman ambiance

Servants in the Ottoman world were often slaves, both male and female. By contrast, free servants are rarely on record; and likely, the distinction between slaves and poor children raised by a better-off family and expected to provide service according to their capacities (*beslemes*), was often blurred, especially if the *besleme* was a girl. From the second half of the sixteenth century onward, contracts by which poor people handed over a child to a family wishing for a young servant occasionally show up in the registers of urban judges. Sometimes the natal family reserved the right to arrange the marriage of the girl at issue, but sometimes the parents seem to have abandoned the child to his/her fate.[48] We may imagine that such scenarios were likely if one parent died, the other remarried, and the stepmother/stepfather had no interest in the child's welfare. Other servants who had trouble holding on to their freedom were liberated slaves who had remained in the households of their former owners; the latter might die, and the new head of the household might want the money that a sale would bring.[49]

Slaves were thus the dominant element in the population; they survived, precariously, through service to others. In recent years, Ottoman slavery, including sales and manumissions has attracted considerable scholarly attention, partly because from the second half of the fifteenth century to the 1600s, many members of the governing elite other than religious scholars had a status akin to being slaves of the sultan. Some scholars view these servitors as 'elite slaves'; but it is debatable whether elite slaves, who are not part of the present discussion, were a subcategory of the overarching category of 'slave', or else a separate category altogether.

However, before boys collected for service to the sultan, as so-called *devşirmes* could become soldiers, they performed coerced manual labour. Shortly after leaving their homes, they served peasants in distant villages, and as we learn from a saint's legend concerning sixteenth-century Bursa, they might well lose their lives even after non-fatal accidents. After all, a boy whose feet had frozen was of no use either on the farm or to the military. Thus, the legend studied by Irène Beldiceanu Steinherr recorded that the peasant for whom the hero of the story had been working would have killed him off after his accident, if it had not been for the protests of the farmwife. As it was, the peasant merely threw the boy out of the house. While waiting for positions to open up among the janissaries, the young men who had survived this treatment (*acemi oğlan*) worked on projects as decided by the sultan. Thus, *acemi oğlan* performed almost forty per cent of the man hours recorded when the Süleymaniye was under construction.[50] Other candidate janissaries helped to supply Istanbul with timber and firewood from North Western Anatolia.

Moreover, in the 1950s to 1980s, when Ottomanist historians became interested in social and economic history, they thought only in terms of taxation, crafts and agricultural production, in addition to the sale of goods in the market. However, when the definition of 'work' in use by historians broadened in the 1990s, historians became more interested in the services performed by slaves.[51] As happened in other historical sub-fields as well, Ottomanist social history at this time dissociated itself from economic history; and thus, the labour of people performing household service became more visible and relevant to historical investigation. Feminist scholars have contributed toward the current interest in slavery as well, as seemingly from the seventeenth century onward, many slaves employed by the sultans' subjects were female. In fact, quite possibly by the 1600s, male slaves were mostly the privilege of the sultans and the highest dignitaries of the empire, except for the residents of border provinces such as Trabzon where raids and counter-raids produced a majority of male slaves.[52]

In broad outlines, the history of slavery in the Ottoman lands began with the sultans' conquests in the Balkan Peninsula during the fourteenth century, when prisoners of war – and people captured in peacetime raids as well – probably wound up on the slave markets of Istanbul and Bursa. By this time, the role of slaves in production was probably of limited importance but even so, more significant than it was to be in later years. Thus, Konstantinos Moustakas has studied fifteenth-century tax registers from present-day rural Greece, which record the presence of so-called *azade* who were probably liberated slaves. Moreover, Halil İnalcık has suggested that the labourers employed in the cultivation of rice, a high-value crop, had originally been servile and only at a later stage, managed to gain the status of 'ordinary' Ottoman peasants.[53] Intriguingly, in parts of South Asia agrestic slavery appeared in connection with rice cultivation too, perhaps because of the hard work and health hazards involved.[54] Even so, as the few surviving records from the late 1300s and early 1400s make little reference to slaves our understanding of their role in agriculture and craft production remains largely hypothetical.

Studying the early history of slavery through the documents surviving in the Bursa qadi registers, Halil Sahillioğlu, in an article that remains fundamental, has shown that the enslaved typically appeared in the registers about five to ten years after their capture.[55] At that moment in the lives of male and female slaves, they might change hands through sale. However, many owners decided to prepare for future manumission, concluding contracts that promised the slave his freedom if he completed a certain task (*mükâtebe*) – in the 1500s, such contracts with females were quite rare. Owners of a favoured slave woman might liberate her in view of marriage, either with her former owner or else with a servant of the household. Others promised to liberate their slave(s) after their deaths, a stipulation (*tedbir*) that forbade any future sale. However, once the owner was dead the heirs might object, claiming that the slave was so valuable that the price that he/she might fetch surpassed the one-third share of the inheritance, which the now deceased owner could dispose of by will. To prevent the sometimes hair-raising court cases arising in such situations, at least in the late 1600s some owners declared that their slaves would be free several weeks or months before their own deaths, with the men or women concerned remaining unaware of their new status as freedmen/freedwomen until the owner had actually died.[56]

Apart from prisoners of war, people captured during raids filled Ottoman slave markets. For on the borders with the Habsburg Empire and Poland, local power-holders on both sides frequently carried off captives for the ransom they might bring. A peculiar branch of trade was the result, with brokers sometimes called in as negotiators.[57] In addition, the three Ottoman provinces of Algiers, Tunis and Tripoli in North Africa, loosely subject to the sultan in Istanbul, possessed sizeable corsair navies. When corsair captains captured a ship subject to a Christian ruler who had not concluded a special treaty with the Algerian, Tunisian or Tripolitanian authorities, the people found on the captured ships mostly ended up as slaves. In this type of undeclared war, the corsairs of Ottoman North Africa were the counterparts to the Knights of Malta, who preyed on Ottoman shipping in much the same way. In the Mediterranean world as well, wealthy men and women might offer large sums of money as ransom. As for the poor, they were unlikely to return home unless their families could assemble enough money from charitable donations to buy their freedom. One fifth of the human booty (*pencik*) belonged to the sultan. As long as the Ottoman navy contained large numbers of galleys, put differently to the later seventeenth century, most of these men must have spent the remainder of their often short lives as galley slaves; in the 1700s, when the navy no longer used galleys, we find them labouring in the naval arsenal.[58] Different from ordinary slave owners, the sultans' administration did not often free its slaves, unless a foreign ambassador arranged for ransoming or the slave had become too old for heavy work.[59]

The fate of Ottoman seamen who had the misfortune of capture by Maltese, Papal, or Tuscan ships was quite similar; they suffered enslavement in Italy, with only prisoners of war taken by Venetians typically repatriated after the end of hostilities.[60] In both the Ottoman orbit and in Catholic and Protestant Europe, conversion to the dominant religion was often a precondition for successful integration into the society in which, much against their will the captives now found themselves.[61] However, there were more 'careers open to talent' in the Ottoman world than in the society of estates typical of early modern Europe, where it was often extremely difficult to rise above the status into which one had been born. For this reason, some ex-captives who could have returned home refrained from doing so. In the late 1600s, the grand vizier Kara Mustafa Paşa (d. 1683) had assembled a household of converted persons from Poland and other European polities; apparently, only the single Spaniard among them fantasized about returning home.[62]

War and the raiding of 'outsider' communities apart, free subjects of the sultans quite often were victims of kidnapping, the captors meaning to sell the person abducted as a slave. While such actions were criminal, Ottoman records show that they were no rarity. Janissaries often raided Wallachia and Moldavia, in present-day Rumania, whose populations became fair game whenever their princes rebelled against their Ottoman overlord. Once the province was back under the sultans' control, such raids should have ceased, but often soldiers out for booty continued to do what they had done in wartime. On a more 'private' level, children and especially girls might become kidnapping victims because once away from their families, they had no one that could testify to their freedom in court. Moreover, if abducted to a province whose language the victims did not speak, they were even less able to defend themselves. Most cases in which the kidnappers successfully abducted and sold a young slave have probably not entered the record at all. Our information comes from cases where the plot failed, usually because the parents managed to retrieve the child before he/she became impossible to trace.[63]

In the period at issue here, Ottoman authors did not question slavery as an institution in the way that Akbar did in his later life; at most, they might make a few critical remarks about the cruelties of slave traders. Thus, Evliya Çelebi had watched the 'production' of eunuchs in Cairo when a certain Kethüda İbrahim Paşa wanted some emasculated African boys to distribute as gifts. The travel writer commented on the high mortality of these unfortunates and the cruelty of the men performing the emasculation. However, he did not say that İbrahim Paşa should take some of the blame, although the latter had ordered the operation in the first place.[64]

Performing service in the Mughal world

Where historians of Mughal India are at issue, there does not seem to be the same intense interest in slavery as we observe among present-day Ottomanists, although the numbers of enslaved Indians were considerable. In fact, Mughal India was in a peculiar situation because slave traders might take people out of the country, while other merchants brought in slaves from abroad. In the Ottoman world by contrast, only the unfortunate victims of war and raiding might become slaves outside the limits of the empire. Otherwise, slaves moved into the sultans' territory rather than out of it.

We will begin with the sale of Indian slaves. While these men and women were not very frequent in Bursa during the late 1400s and early 1500s, they occasionally show up in the registers. Probably the slaves on record were often from Southern India, as the documents refer to the darkness of their skins.[65] In South Asia, however, people did not connect dark skin with low status or slavery, while in the Ottoman Empire Africans often had to assert themselves against people who cited sayings spuriously attributed to the Prophet Muhammad in order to denigrate them.[66]

Larger numbers of Indian slaves went to destinations in Central Asia/Turan. Scott Levy has traced the fates of these men and women, who must have crossed the Hindukush, mostly on foot, before their captors sold the survivors.[67] In addition to people enslaved already while in India, there were unlucky travellers who when on their way between Turan and the subcontinent, had suffered capture and wound up on the slave markets. For Muslim captors, selling Hindu 'infidels' into slavery did not pose any moral problems. Other slaves arrived in Central Asia as royal gifts. Although Akbar has become famous for his prohibition of slave sales, at an unspecified time in his long reign, perhaps before coming to the decision that slavery was wrong, he sent four slaves to the ruler of Bukhara to serve the recipient in his construction projects. Jahāngīr followed his father's example, but on a much larger scale.[68]

Archival documents, especially those establishing pious foundations in Uzbekistan, record Indian slaves working the landholdings of local grandees. Important dervish sheikhs might own 300 to 500 such labourers, who cultivated their large, plantation-like estates; modest property owners possessed at least a few slaves for work in the house and garden. Artisans, especially those with skills in the building crafts were in high demand, as their owners put them to work on mosques and other representative structures, the Bībī Khānum mosque in Samarkand, erected by Timur (1336–1405) being a prime example.[69] There are no numerical data from which we may estimate the numbers of Indian slaves present in Central Asia at any particular point in time. For it seems that Uzbek rulers did not collect the *pencik*; and thus there were no records comparable to those that sometimes turn up in the Ottoman archives.[70] Even so, frequent references to Indian slaves in the surviving documentation show the numbers to have been considerable.[71]

Often the enslaved had lost their freedom due to warfare in India. The elites of the Delhi Sultanate, often immigrants from Central Asia, had already sold many of their captives to the regions from which these high-status persons once had originated, and the Mughal emperors followed the same custom. After certain imperial campaigns, there were so many people for sale, that prices dropped and slave traders from distant places came to replenish their stocks of human wares. Even so, in Central Asia young girls who might become concubines generally fetched high prices; as usual, we have no information about the fates of older women. In the Ottoman world of the 1400s and 1500s as well, slave prices dropped after successful campaigns, when impecunious soldiers rapidly sold their booty to obtain ready money; at such times, even better off villagers might own a slave or two. In the seventeenth century, the Mughal emperors forbade the export of slaves outside of their domains.[72] Unfortunately, it is impossible to tell whether this prohibition had any impact, even temporarily, on the numbers of captives sold to Central Asia. Moreover, the futile attempts of Shāh Jahān to conquer Uzbek Central Asia must have resulted in quite a few stranded soldiers ending up on the slave markets of the cities they had set out to conquer (see Chapter 3).

A few individuals recorded their misadventures. Thus, in the Russian archives there survives the tale of an Indian Muslim merchant captured by slave dealers after trading in Central Asia. So, even being a Muslim was not always a protection, as Sunni captors were quite willing to enslave Shiites. Having changed masters several times, this man finally escaped to Russian territory: presumably, he had given up hope of ever returning home, as the file recording his fate was part of his petition to the tsar, dated 1661, in which he requested permission to convert to Christianity.[73] We do not know how the story ended.

Other slaves, frequently females, had originated in India and reached the harems of the Mughal emperors and nobles in ways that we cannot anymore reconstruct. Male slaves might be eunuchs, often from Bengal, but their number was not very high.[74] In Akbar's harem, many female slaves served the spouses of the ruler and the princesses of the imperial family. When Akbar manumitted the male slaves of his palace, he did not extend this generosity to the women; but in the early seventeenth century, Jahāngīr's consort Nūr Jahān (d. 1645) liberated the female slaves as well. From among the troupers serving the ruler and the male slaves freed earlier on, the palace found husbands for the women aged between twelve and forty years, while the older females could either leave the compound and arrange their own marriages or stay on, presumably as free servants. While we may regard the slaves serving the imperial palace as an exception without much bearing on the overall status of slaves, certain nobles close to the seventeenth-century Mughal court defied Akbar's prohibition of the slave trade and accumulated hundreds of female slaves, some of them (potential) concubines and others servants to the women of status in their respective harems.[75] Taken together, the enslaved concubines and service personnel in these various elite households must have run up to significant totals.

From the outside world, slaves arrived in India as well. We know almost nothing about the dancing girls sold to Indian males that Halil Sahillioğlu has found in the records of Bursa of the 1400s and 1500s, not even their places of origin.[76] The buyers, moneyed men from India, presumably intended to take their human property back to their homeland. Much more frequent were African slaves, some of them imported by the Portuguese and sold in Goa – the town government even built a wall surrounding the settlement that was to prevent the escape of slaves.[77] Subsequently, the Dutch and British East India companies were active in this trade as well. A volume edited by Indrani Chatterjee and Richard Eaton provides an important overview over the slavery question in South Asia, but intriguingly, this work focuses on the Peninsula and there is no chapter on the Mughal Empire.[78] Moreover, certain Indian merchants, based in the Portuguese enclave of Diu from the 1750s onward multiplied the profits they had gained from the exportation of Indian textiles to Africa and the importation of African ivory into the subcontinent, by underwriting the trade in African slaves to Madagascar and the Mascarenes. Admittedly, this involvement belongs in the post-Mughal period as defined here, and involves an area outside the Mughal domains. Even so, it is noteworthy that heavy involvement of Indians in the slave trade was possible even if the number of Africans actually sold in the subcontinent remained limited.[79]

Certain African slaves arrived by way of the Hijaz, where their owners often persuaded them to become Muslims. While military slavery was not in use in the Mughal domains, in Southern India some of these men built successful military careers (see Chapter 3). Thus, Malik 'Ambār (1528–1626), formerly an Abyssinian slave, who in the early 1600s commanded the armies of the Deccan sultanate of Ahmadnagar, for a while, prevented the Mughal conquest of the Deccan. Jahāngīr detested his opponent so much that he had a portrait painted, extant in several versions, which shows him shooting arrows at the head of his dead enemy (see Chapter 2).[80]

Being of low caste in Mughal India

When discussing men and women forced to serve other people, we need to refer to the subordination of lower castes to higher castes, which was/is a basic constituent of society in the subcontinent but for which there was no equivalent in the Ottoman world. In the caste system, supposed 'purity' or 'pollution' counted as important factors in social ranking. By contrast, the effects of this division on economic life are highly controversial, many historians now tending to write economic history with only very limited reference to caste.[81] As for concerns about 'purity': Certainly, the writings on *fütüvvet* or virtuous behaviour in an Islamic sense, popular especially in certain pre-Ottoman and Ottoman artisan milieus, refer to polluting activities including weaving or service at public baths. However, the sultans' administration completely ignored such injunctions. Apart from tavern keeping, which the sultans' officials did regard as a dishonourable activity, they very rarely assumed that any given craft was 'cleaner' than its rivals were.[82]

Among other matters, caste differentiation determined who might eat with whom or who might marry a given person.[83] On one level, caste differences were significant enough to pervade even the social organization of Muslims and Christians, whose religions should have precluded the assumption that certain people were of lower spiritual value on account of their birth. However, while discourses focused on ritual purity and possible pollution by contact with members of lower castes or even outcastes (Dalit), recent historiography has shown that caste boundaries often were much more permeable in real life than in theory. Thus, after he had become a famous king, people readily accepted that Shivaji (d. 1680) who had originally been a Shudra was 'in reality' a Kshatriya.[84]

Given our concern with the lives of commoners, it will suffice to mention the effects that caste differentiation had – or did not have – on the organization of working people. In places where caste councils (*panchayats*) decided disputes among caste members, people submitted contentious economic issues to the decision of the caste elders.[85] Thus, before the colonial period, we do not find the craft guilds so typical of the Ottoman urban scene from the sixteenth century onward.[86] Ghulam A. Nadri has shown the manner in which caste considerations interacted with commercial concerns in the manufacture of textiles, possible export goods destined for – among other places – the Ottoman world (see Chapter 6). In a study of the political economy of Gujarat in the second half of the eighteenth century, the author points out that most of the time, castes and sub-castes did not prevent inter-craft mobility. Thus, when the Khatri weavers found that they had more orders for high-quality cottons than they could fill on their own, they employed adjuncts from another caste known as the Kunbis. The latter soon learned the craft and turned into formidable competitors. Particularly, the Khatris resented that at some time in the mid-1700s, at the very end of the period studied here, the Mughal governor had granted their Kunbi rivals the right to manufacture *saris*, a popular female garment.[87] In 1742, the Khatri weavers refused to deliver cloth to the EIC to protest against the immigration of Muslim weavers; it is difficult to say whether this strike was a purely economic matter or whether religion, status and caste were at issue as well.

Women 'off the straight path' in the Ottoman world

In the Ottoman world as elsewhere, women abandoned by their men-folk might fall into prostitution. However, pertinent evidence is sparse because when compiling the Ottoman qadi registers, the scribes often did not differentiate between 'ordinary' affairs between single people and prostitution.[88] While a cause of great scandal, love affairs must have occasionally occurred, given the large number of unattached young men present in many large cities, and especially in Istanbul. In addition, we may imagine that some clandestine relations came about because a given young person simply disliked the spouse to whom his family had married him or her. Whatever the true story the typical reason for recording extramarital affairs in the qadi registers was the intervention of the neighbours, who might involve the market controller (*muhtesib*), in charge of enforcing morality as well. Typically, the townspeople felt that their quarter would gain a bad reputation if word got around that the inhabitants tolerated women in contact with men who were not their relatives. In addition, these people worried that if there were fights for the favours of such women, they might wind up having to pay the blood money for dead people found in their urban wards, whose killers remained unknown. Sometimes the motive for the complaint was probably the simple suspicion with which people looked at women who were not under the control of any man. Nor can we exclude frustration and envy as motivations.

Studies of court cases have shown that the women concerned in such events normally received notice to leave the town quarter in question, sometimes together with a male relative who had not prevented the scandal from occurring.[89] Sometimes we find references to pimps; even so, the prevailing misogyny often must have prevented the activities of such men, as opposed to the prostitutes whom they exploited, from entering the court registers. Quite often, the women chased out of their town quarters found it difficult to leave and returned after some time, promising to avoid creating annoyances in the future.[90] To date, we have very little evidence from the Ottoman world about women of questionable reputation who excelled as dancers and singers. Did they not exist? Or else, have the authors of the surviving documents merely omitted to mention them?[91]

In the Mughal world: The twilight situation of female musicians and dancers

In Mughal India, by contrast, the situation is complicated because female specialists performed as musicians and dancers, activities, which enjoyed high cultural prestige; but these same women might be courtesans. Mughal miniatures show that female dancers and musicians performed at the celebrations accompanying royal births and weddings – for there is no indication that female impersonators took the places of 'real' girls and women. As Karuna Sharma has expressed it, the line separating dancers from providers of sexual services could be hard to discern.[92] Even so, the Mughal court, as some rulers of the Delhi sultanates before them, distinguished between women who were performing artists and others who were courtesans, although the latter too might use their skills in singing and dancing to enhance the value of the services that they provided.[93] While some women performers seem to have enjoyed a degree of respect and status, none of them apparently merited inclusion in the list of highly regarded musicians recorded by Abū'l-fazl.[94] Elite authors often discussed performers and 'women of the night' in the same breath.

As for wealthy Ottoman households, in the early 1700s at least, the wife of a grand vizier trained young girls as musicians, apparently assuming that her guests would expect performances in an elite household. In the absence of recordings, we know very little about these women.[95] Nor do we know whether the men heading great households ever made their female slaves show their art in front of male guests, for instances at poetry sessions, called *meclis* in the Ottoman context. Such performances seem to have been common enough in elite poetry gatherings organized in the Mughal orbit, here known as *mehfil*.[96] Alternatively, female musicians and dancers may have only provided enjoyment for the elite women of Istanbul. In the Ottoman capital, entertainers showing their art in public seem to have been young boys dressed up as girls.[97]

In Mughal India, by contrast, we know about a dancing girl especially favoured by the pious Princess Jahānārā (1614–81), who noted that the young woman had invented a dance especially for the enjoyment of herself, the royal patron. While the princess was an adept of Islamic mysticism as well, she probably did not think that the presence of a dancing girl in her entourage was 'indecent'.[98] However, enjoying the skills of dancing girls did involve some ambiguity; and Jahānārā's royal brother Aurangzeb (r. 1658–1707) at first limited such performances in the palace to a single day of the week, when the dancers were to be on view briefly and from a distance, then retiring from the scene.[99] In 1669 moreover, the emperor forbade musical performances in the palace altogether, and by implication, dancing as well.[100] With respect to the eighteenth century, probably somewhat beyond the limits of the present study, literary historians have observed that at first courtesans, and later on, respectable elite women as well, gained reputations for their poetry good enough to secure them inclusion in recognized encyclopaedias of poets. Shadab Bano has linked this phenomenon to the increasing frequency with which dancers and singers, even women of questionable reputation, performed at festivities in Indian towns: perhaps this proximity encouraged married women to develop literary skills as well. Sadly, few historians have paid attention to social processes of this type.

In conclusion

In this chapter we have seen that uneven documentation makes comparison even more difficult than usual. At least, it is clear that the gender divide was a fundamental component of social structure both in the Ottoman and in the South Asian realms. Misogyny being so rampant in both realms, we may well ask, what so banal a fact can teach us.

While Mughal miniatures provide some information on the work undertaken by women, where the written word is at issue, we have more data on Ottoman females, due to the relative abundance of qadi registers. As Islamic law gave women (limited) rights of inheritance, females from propertied families might appear before the Ottoman qadi defending their rights to property or even the administration of a pious foundation. It is noteworthy that many of the official documents from South Asia, in which women become visible, seem to originate from Muslim communities. On the other hand, perhaps more information is available on women among the Sikhs, Jains and Hindus – for instance, in the Maratha archives – than we can glean from English-language publications alone.

After all, in the Indian world certain princesses and noble women were highly influential: Admittedly, our concern is with the interface of elite and none-elite; and ruling figures are thus of marginal interest per se. However, records dealing with royal women may contain evidence on their lowly female servants and companions as well.[101] Perhaps going beyond the palace chronicles, for instance into the ample correspondence of Aurangzeb, will provide more diverse evidence on female servants than is available to date.

In the same context, evidence of slavery in the subcontinent may well be more abundant than suspected to date. The (relative) wealth of documentation on Ottoman slaves has become visible only in the last thirty years or so, and the growing body of work on slavery in the Indian Ocean orbit will perhaps inspire scholars familiar with archives on the subcontinent to re-examine this issue. On both the Ottoman and the Mughal/post-Mughal realms, we still have a lot of work to do.

Conclusion

What is the net gain from this attempt to view Ottoman history from a distance, after having mentally placed ourselves in the centres of Mughal power in Northern India? Barring error on the side of the present author, this study is the first attempt to turn around and look at Mughal India from the viewpoint of a historian working on the Ottoman Empire in its mature stage. At a later stage of research, scholars will surely emerge who are equally familiar with the Ottoman and Mughal contexts. For the time being, however, the reader has to live with the Ottomanist *déformation professionelle*, which the present author cannot possibly shake off. Even with this caveat in mind, the present enterprise leaves us with some results that are worth thinking about.

History, historiography, (non-)accommodation and legitimacy

Our discussion has proceeded on three distinct levels: First, there are questions of source use, and especially historiography, which in and of themselves are major issues, inviting more detailed treatment than is possible here. If we assume that humankind has a common history, where should we place the polities and societies governed by the Ottoman sultans and Mughal emperors, moving beyond the simplistic and partisan assumptions prevalent in much of the older secondary literature? While the debates about Feudalism, the Asiatic Mode of Production, and the Islamic City have now passed into the intellectual history of the later 1900s, the underlying concern with the intellectual ordering of human societies and polities retains its validity.

Although the debates about possible Ottoman or Mughal feudalism died down in the course of the 1980s, historians still need to deal with the interactions of elites and their subjects, especially merchants trading over long distances. After all, with the internet taking on an increasing role in business and everyday life during the late twentieth and early twenty-first centuries, interactions between world empires and world-encompassing economic systems, on the one hand, and local communities and mini-economies on the other, have become issues of political importance. Therefore, historians have begun to ask whether such confrontations between global and local concerns were significant in the early modern period as well. While relevant to both Ottoman and Mughal historians, a comprehensive treatment of these issues is unfortunately too large for the modest study presented here.

Second, we have dealt with imperial structures, office-holders, and the political culture generated by these elite figures, put differently, the establishment and maintenance of rule. In this context, the similarities and differences between Anatolian or Balkan society on the one hand, and the socio-political order in Northern India on the other, are especially intriguing. While we have not focused on dynastic ups and downs, it is remarkable that the rule of Bābur (r. in India: 1526–30), who spent his time 'on the move' and whose capital was wherever the conquering monarch happened to be, resembles, to some extent, the arrangement prevailing in Anatolia and the Balkans in the fourteenth and fifteenth centuries. As the principalities established in these areas usually did not survive for very long, most rulers and elites had no occasion to establish fully developed administrations, for which fixed capital cities with offices and archives would have been practical or even necessary. At first, Bābur's kingdom did not seem permanent. For the wars of succession between his several sons allowed Shēr Shāh, an Afghan prince established in northern India, to oust Bābur's son Humāyūn (1530–40, 1555–6) and set up his own kingdom, which he ruled until his death.

Humāyūn could re-found Mughal rule only because he garnered the support of the shah of Iran, a major outside potentate, a solution unavailable to most Anatolian or Balkan princes that had lost their thrones. After all, while Timur reinstated many Anatolian princes during his war against Bayezid I (r. 1389–1402), thus serving as an 'outside support' to these petty rulers, he did not stay in the area long enough to firmly re-establish the polities previously conquered by Sultan Bayezid. Therefore, he could not give any support comparable to that which Shah Tahmāsp (r. 1524–76) provided to Humāyūn.

Expanding the Mughal kingdom into a fully-fledged empire was thus the work of Bābur's grandson Akbar (r. 1556–1605). In a certain sense, the latter's role resembled that of Murad II (r. 1421–44, 1446–51) and Murad's son Mehmed the Conqueror (r. 1444–6, 1451–81), who firmly established Ottoman imperial rule over much of Anatolia and the Balkans. On the other hand, when we focus on the court culture that emerged during Akbar's reign, we might argue that the Mughal emperor of the later 1500s was comparable to Süleyman the Lawgiver/the Magnificent (r. 1520–66). Even if – as previously promised – we avoid establishing parallels between entire reigns of Ottoman sultans and Mughal emperors, the present study has shown that parallels between ruling apparatuses, taxation practices, and the Persianate culture adopted by both courts are very prominent.

While both the Ottomans and the Mughals invoked the notion of conquest as a justification for their rule, by this term they meant different things. In Anatolia and the Balkans, as İnalcık has shown more than half a century ago, the Ottoman takeover meant that some members of the pre-conquest elites joined the sultans' army and administration.[1] Others lost their lives in war or else emigrated. With the exception of certain border provinces, the Ottoman elite thus governed a uniform population of subjects, both Muslim and non-Muslim, which the rulers could tax, move to distant locales (*sürgün*) and if Christian villagers, draft into their armies as *devşirme* boys, whom at least in the 1400s and 1500s the administration regarded as slaves of the sultans. However, the sultan could not sell his subjects as slaves if natural or manmade catastrophes made it impossible for them to pay their taxes. Şeyhülislam Ebusuud (1490–1574) had opined that, if non-Muslim subjects rebelled against an abusive governor, but did not throw off their allegiance to the sultan, it was not permissible to enslave them.[2] Rebellions of the kind envisaged by Ebusuud must have often been due to over-taxation.

With respect to the Mughal world, however, Irfan Habib has claimed that failure to pay the revenue demanded might mean that the delinquent subjects, most of them peasants, ended up on the slave market.[3] Presumably, the Mughal elites considered non-payment of taxes for whatever reason as a sign of rebellion, punishable by enslavement. For this statement, Habib cites the seventeenth-century travel accounts of Francisco Pelsaert and Peter Mundy as primary sources. However, Richard Eaton rejects this claim; in the latter's perspective peasants unable to pay typically escaped into the forests, where the limited forces of the emperors had no chance of tracking them down.[4] On the other hand, prisoners taken during new conquests within India or during the re-conquest of formerly imperial territories after a rebellion might in fact end their lives as slaves in Central Asia. While Akbar and some of his successors had forbidden the sale of captives outside the empire's borders, the practice seems to have continued nonetheless.[5]

Even so, in other respects the Mughal conquests involved more negotiation with pre-conquest power-holders than was typical of the Ottoman world from the sixteenth century onward. After the conquest of the Deccan sultanates, quite a few members of local elites submitted, in the expectation of receiving *jagīr*s as a reward for changing their allegiance. Perhaps their attitude resembled that of the petty Anatolian lords who in the 1300s and 1400s, submitted to the Ottomans on condition that they would continue to receive a share of the local taxes.[6] Moreover, while Aurangzeb conquered most of present-day India, apart from the southern tip of the Peninsula, the Marathas continued to be a powerful force of mobile raiders after the imperial armies had conquered Shivaji's former kingdom, and even the distant province of Bengal suffered from these attacks.[7] While Akbar's administration had tried to make established caste and district headmen (*zamīndār*s) into obedient tax collecting and tax paying subjects, evidently success was partial and temporary.[8] Especially in areas where forest clearance was recent, low-level *zamīndār*s and the villagers loyal to these personages could easily escape into inaccessible territory, similar to peasants unable to pay their taxes. In consequence, the Mughal rulers never governed an even 'more or less' uniform subject population, but rather an agglomeration of local power-holders, great and small, along with the populations that accepted these dignitaries as their immediate rulers.

A major reason for this divergence in the structures of Ottoman and Mughal rule lay in the continuous existence of a 'military labour market' on the subcontinent.[9] The latter allowed part-time, as well as full-time, soldiers to offer their services to the potentate promising them the best conditions, and they could just as easily desert their employer if the latter did not meet their expectations. In the Ottoman world of the 1500s, such situations were less common, although the 'rebellious pashas' of the early 1600s, to use a term coined by İnalcık, hired mercenaries whose behaviour was probably similar.[10] Put differently, the soldiers who fought out the battles between provincial magnates, very common in Anatolia and the Balkans during the eighteenth century, had likely entered the service of their employers after negotiations resembling those then current in South Asia. At the same time, the existence of a centrally controlled infantry of janissaries and palace cavalry, inefficient though these military corps may have been by the 1700s, probably limited the dependence of Ottoman power-holders, including the sultans, on the local variety of the military labour market.

When moving from military and administrative affairs into political discourse, we once again encounter some similarities, but once we look closer, the divergence of legitimizing discourses strikes the eye much more forcefully. While certain sixteenth-century Ottoman sultans seemingly sympathized with millennial ideas and projected notions of special sanctity, this feature was not nearly as prominent in Istanbul as it was at the courts of Humāyūn, Akbar and Jahāngīr. Moreover, the prestige and potential power of dervish saints was greater in the Mughal Empire, perhaps comparable to that enjoyed by Anatolian holy men before the sultans' rule had fully stabilized. While both sultans and emperors needed to be visible to their subjects, in the Ottoman realm, the reason for this requirement was strictly practical: A good ruler had to be available, so that he could take cognizance of the complaints of his subjects.[11] In the Mughal context, this aspect was surely important as well, but in addition, the viewing or visualizing a deity or monarch (*darshan*) had a religious aura probably stronger than the numinous quality surrounding the Ottoman sultan, which admittedly, the latter possessed as well.

When it came to the treatment of non-Muslims as a legitimizing device *vis à vis* the Muslim population, the Ottoman sultans seem to have changed policies in the period following the conquest of the Arab lands (1516–17). Previously, 'accommodation' (*istimalet*) of their non-Muslim subjects had been a priority, with Christians holding *timar*s in Albania and other Christian soldiers guarding Ottoman fortresses.[12] However, once the empire had become a polity in which the majority of subjects were Muslims, other considerations became more important: Particularly, it was now necessary to ensure the allegiance of established Arab religious scholars in Syria and Egypt, for whom *istimalet* may well have seemed an unnecessary and illegitimate concession to the infidels. However, we should not exaggerate the importance of taking *ulema* views into consideration. After all, in a demonstrative gesture, Selim I just after conquering Damascus ordered the embellishment of the grave of Ibn 'Arabī (1165–1240), although he must have known that many local men of religion profoundly disapproved of this mystic.[13] In the long term, continuing warfare against the Habsburgs in Central Europe may have made the Christian population of the Balkans appear as a potential 'fifth column', to whom it would have been imprudent to entrust fortified places, as had been common enough before 1517.

On a different level, religious toleration in the Ottoman world made financial sense, as the head tax (*cizye*) paid by non-Muslims was a significant contribution to the sultans' budgets.[14] Even so, Mehmed IV (r. 1648–67) was willing to downplay this aspect as he made a name for himself by his intense efforts to promote Islamization.[15] Toward the end of the century, however, maximizing *cizye* revenues became important once again, given the war against the Habsburgs and the Holy League (1683–99), Mehmed IV now ordering reforms in *cizye* collection to augment revenues. On the other hand, in the Mughal Empire, the *jizya* did not have the same financial significance, and Akbar's abolishing it was not a major sacrifice for the Mughal treasury. About a century later, Aurangzeb re-imposed the head tax, and in recent historiography, this measure has become a subject of scholarly debate. According to Tapan Raychaudhuri, Aurangzeb hoped that paying the *jizya* would hurt the incomes of wealthy Hindus badly enough that they would consider converting.[16] By contrast, Satish Chandra and Richard Eaton suggest motivations less directly connected to Aurangzeb's religious convictions: In the perspective of these two scholars, re-instituting the *jizya* was a means of mobilizing the adherence of the Empire's Muslims for a fully-fledged campaign in the Deccan, where by the 1670s Mughal power was in crisis.

As an empire ruled by Muslims but with a majority of non-Muslim subjects, quite a few of them armed, the Mughal emperors had little alternative to policies of a kind that the Ottomans called *istimalet*. On the other hand, the emperors had to deal with the criticism of Islamic scholars who opposed compromises they considered non-Islamic.[17] Whichever explanation the reader may accept, filling the treasury, while important, was secondary to religious-cum-political concerns. The reason for this attitude, so different from that of the Ottoman sultans, was surely the much greater tax revenue at the disposal of the Mughal emperors.

The world of the subjects: Traders, artisans and peasants

In economic terms, the major difference between the Ottoman and Mughal worlds was the fact that both Akbar's realm, and the regions later – and briefly – conquered by Aurangzeb, were major exporters of manufactured goods, especially cotton textiles. For the Mughal elites, textile manufactures were a source of revenue, albeit dwarfed by rural dues. Far-flung mercantile networks run by Indians and outsiders distributed these goods abroad and brought back large quantities of silver, which remained in South Asia. After all, the inhabitants imported very few goods, mainly horses suitable for warfare. Famously, Indian textiles found an extensive market in Western and Northern Europe, but customers in Southeast Asia and Africa demanded plain and printed cottons as well. In East Africa, the demand of local rulers for South Asian cottons fuelled the slave trade to the Deccan sultanates, where African slave soldiers were in high demand.[18]

On the other hand, the Ottoman Empire exported only limited quantities of manufactured goods: Some angora-based textiles before and after 1600 had markets in Poland and Venice, some high-quality seventeenth-century silks went to Polish nobles and elite Russians, while traders carried Anatolian carpets to Transylvania and to a lesser extent, to Italy and Western Europe.[19] Agricultural products, including raw cotton and semi-finished products such as leather and cotton thread, were more significant exports than goods destined for the final consumer. Local craftspeople thus worked mostly for local customers, including the gigantic consumers' market of Istanbul.[20] Many Ottoman artisans of the fifteenth to eighteenth centuries produced directly for the markets of their hometowns or nearby cities. Thus, long-distance merchants exercised less control over manufacturers than in the subcontinent, where traders ensured the production of goods saleable on the Ottoman-cum-Arab, Southeast Asian, East African, and European markets.

In the Ottoman world, with few exceptions only the sultan could afford to keep workshops producing for his household alone, and it is surely significant that in the late 1500s, Mustafa 'Âlî thought that these court-affiliated artisans cost more than their services were worth.[21] At some time in the later 1600s, the sultans' senior officials agreed, and the number of court artisans diminished dramatically.[22] On the other hand, in Mughal India a large share of total craft production apparently took place in the ateliers working for the emperor, in addition to those belonging to the households of court nobles and later on, of post-Mughal princes. By contrast, unless new sources emerge that show us a different picture, it is believed that household-based ateliers, maintained by governors and regional power-holders, were uncommon in the Ottoman world.[23]

Admittedly, it is impossible to measure the extent of production sponsored by the imperial court and later sub-Mughal princes. Shireen Moosvi has suggested that two thirds of the money spent on the imperial household of Akbar's time paid for goods produced by the crafts sector. However, the emperor and his male and female servants consumed not only the manufactures of court ateliers, but items procured through the 'regular' market as well, so that the sum of money that Moosvi has computed did not go entirely to the court workshops.[24] Whatever the situation may have been, clearly many artisans not involved in the export trade laboured to fulfil the demands of the emperor and the nobility – to say nothing of the military establishment which, as in other early-modern polities, absorbed much of the productive capacity of the Ottoman and Mughal worlds.

In both empires, merchants built connections through long-distance trade. The work of Stephen Dale, Scott Levy and Arup Banerji has shown that the increasing traffic on the maritime routes to Europe did not cause the decline of the overland trade to Central Asia and Russia, at least not before the late eighteenth century.[25] Moreover, maritime traffic was not a monopoly of European traders, as Gujarati merchants crossed the Indian Ocean, sometimes combining pilgrimage to Mecca with trade and money lending. Thus, South Asian merchants did business in Yemen, the Hijaz, Iran, Southeast Asia and Russia, but on some regions, information is limited indeed. However, a reasonable number of sources is available on Russia, from the late sixteenth century onward.[26]

As for Muslim and non-Muslim long-distance traders subject to the sultans, if they left the Ottoman domains, they were likely to travel westward. With only temporary success, Armenian merchants of the early 1600s tried to establish themselves in Marseilles as importers of raw silk. While the silk had originated in Iran and some of the Armenians were in the service of the shah, others may well have been from Aleppo and thus Ottoman subjects. The French crown had originally tolerated the newcomers to revive the trade of Marseilles, which had suffered greatly from the civil wars of the later sixteenth century. Local merchants however, did not relish the competitors and by mid-century, succeeded in getting rid of them.[27] In addition, Muslim, Jewish and Orthodox traders, all Ottoman subjects, did business in late sixteenth- and early seventeenth-century Venice until the long war over Crete (1645–69) and the series of Veneto-Ottoman conflicts between 1684 and 1718 largely ended the Venetian presence in the Eastern Mediterranean.[28] Other Ottoman traders, both Orthodox and Armenians, were active in eighteenth-century Amsterdam; and a regular caravan moved between Istanbul and the then Polish, now Ukrainian, city of Lwow/Lviv.[29] In the 1700s, Balkan traders, mostly Orthodox as well, did business in Hungary, Vienna and even at the Leipzig fairs.[30]

By contrast, on the eastern fringes of the Ottoman Empire, the activity of Ottoman merchants was more limited. André Raymond has shown that by the 1700s, Cairo merchants rarely ventured beyond Jeddah or Mocha.[31] Even so, Ottoman traders did business in Surat, as attested by a prominent family of the 1700s known as the Chelabis.[32] After about 1600, however, the sultans' officials showed but minimal interest in Ottoman subjects once they had left the territories ruled by their monarch. Archival records are thus scanty, but perhaps Gujarati sources will allow us to fill this gap in the future.

Thus, the tendency of Ottoman traders to value their contacts with western partners is not a novelty of the mid-nineteenth century, but goes back much further. Given the scarcity of timber in Egypt, to many Ottoman merchants the expense of sending a ship into the Indian Ocean in the absence of a Suez Canal must have seemed prohibitive. While this observation may at first glance appear anachronistic, the seventeenth-century Ottoman traveller Evliya Çelebi has commented on the advantages of reviving the Suez Canal of Achaemenid times and on the enormous Indian ships plying the Red Sea in the later 1600s.[33] An Ottoman merchant wishing to enter this market would have encountered formidable competitors, especially since he would have needed to carry out specie – an action that eighteenth-century sultans disapproved of as much as did the kings of France.

Studies of rural life in the Ottoman and Mughal orbits present some similar features: in both realms, the monarchs had ordered the regular registration of village households. In the Ottoman case the documents survive as originals, while with respect to the Mughal world we have to rely on the data presented by Abū'l-Fazl 'Allāmī (1551–1602).[34] Remarkably, the similarity of the source bases makes the differences between the two worlds even more apparent. Certainly, the Nile valley and the Ganges-Yamuna plain resemble one another as, in both cases, agricultural prosperity is a gift of the river(s). Even so, the area fertilized in Northern India is far larger than that watered by the Nile, and in the Ganges-Yamuna region, it was/is often possible to harvest two crops per year. Moreover, much of the wheat and barley consumed by the sultans' armies and navies did not come from Egypt but from the Balkans, where especially in the western regions mountainous terrain made ploughing difficult. As a result, agricultural revenues as calculated at the end of Akbar's reign apparently were almost three times the size of their Ottoman equivalent.[35]

Although the two empires shared a background of Iranian and Central Asian traditions of rule, the organization of landholding was comparable only in broad outlines but differed profoundly with respect to detail. While the Ottoman sultan claimed to be the owner of almost all agriculturally used land (*miri*) and had this fact emphasized in many decrees, the exact status of the land cultivated by most South Asian peasants apparently was not a major topic for Mughal administrators. While these peasants were lifelong tenants similar to their Ottoman counterparts, it is worth noting that Irfan Habib in his great work on Mughal agriculture and taxation did not devote a special chapter to peasant tenure.[36] Most rural taxes were due in money, reflecting the more extensive monetization of the Mughal economy, and Northern Indian tax assignments of the Mughal period (*jagīr*) were always sums of money that the *jagīrdārs* received in cash.[37] By contrast, many revenues collected by Ottoman *timar*-holders were payable in kind.

In both empires, peasant survival was often in danger due to drought. Outside the Ganges-Yamuna plain, the insufficiency or late arrival of the monsoon was a major threat to peasant and artisan survival. Peasant insolvency might result in hereditary servitude to the creditor and his descendants, due to the high interest that made it impossible for most villagers to repay their debts. In the Ottoman world, debt slavery was completely absent. Even so, drought threatened seventeenth-century Central Anatolia too, and although the sultans had decreed that no peasant could move without permission from whomever had the right to collect his taxes, substandard rainfall and the banditry of jobless mercenaries caused widespread abandonment, particularly of the most drought-prone areas.[38] On the other hand, large-scale landholdings (*çiftliks*) producing for the domestic or export market, with a dependent labour force of sharecroppers and labourers, remained a minority phenomenon, especially in Anatolia. As Huri İslamoğlu has put it, rural elites could appropriate the profits from selling peasant produce collected as taxes, so that in many venues, they likely did not have much interest in taking over the management of peasant lands.[39]

The world of the subjects: Women and slaves

The survival of much of the Ottoman archives has allowed scholars to do significant research on people whose doings entered the narrative sources but rarely, especially non-elite women and slaves. For the period under discussion, qadi registers are the most viable source, although even in these local records the appearance of the 'lower orders' is strictly limited.

In the case of non-elite women living in South Asia, Gujarati sources are especially valuable although most of the time they survive only in copies. Originating mostly from Surat, these documents often concerning Muslims, feature women property owners, for Islamic law guarantees females a share in the inheritance of their relatives.[40] Intriguingly, in Surat the practice at the time was to seek out the court most likely to favour the interest of the plaintiff; this procedure, known as 'forum shopping', was customary in the Ottoman world as well and is now a subject favoured by Ottomanist legal historians. Thus, Ottoman Jews might turn to the Muslim qadi of Salonika despite rabbinical prohibitions, while Gujarati Hindus might address their complaints to the Muslim qadi as well.[41] While, as Farhat Hasan has reminded us, the sharia and prevailing kinship systems did not favour females, especially in property disputes, Jewish or Hindu practice might be even less cognizant of women's interests.[42]

In the Ottoman context, whatever information we have typically concerns urban women with some property to leave. After all, in any society, a modicum of control over material resources is a precondition for enjoying status, respect and visibility in the written record. In the Ottoman inheritance registers kept by the qadis' scribes, we find the owners of houses and/or gardens, good-quality textiles, and jewellery, with perhaps some money lent out, at interest or not. In fact, the historiography on Ottoman women began in the 1970s and 1980s with a focus on the 'women and property' issue. Currently, the ways in which females coped with violence and enslavement, attempted to preserve their honour, and fought for a modicum of choice in their marriage partners, have turned into favoured issues.[43] As social historians respond to the concerns of the society in which they live, we can assume, that reactions especially among urban

Turkish women and their male sympathizers against husbands who beat their wives, and especially, against 'honour killings', play a part in these choices.[44]

In the last decade, Ottomanists have focused on slavery, of men and particularly of women. Until the recent past, dependent labour of all types, including slavery, had mainly concerned scholars working on the late Ottoman period, or else of historians of Mediterranean pirates and corsairs. At present, however, they attract 'mainstream' historians of the sixteenth to eighteenth centuries as well. One reason for this upsurge of interest is surely the fact that Ottomanist historians no longer exclude personal service from their definitions of 'work', so that the labour performed by slaves in the homes and gardens of Ottoman elite figures has become a viable topic. Historians concerned with charity and acculturation have been attracted to the – frequent – manumissions of slaves. In terms of primary sources, Ottomanists with an interest in slavery can now work in St Petersburg and access the qadi registers of Crimea, a region where in the 1500s and 1600s, the capture and sale of slaves had considerable economic significance.[45]

South Asia was remarkable for both importing and exporting slaves. Indians, Portuguese, Englishmen and others brought in slaves from Africa, especially numerous in the Peninsula. Other slaves both male and female originated from within the Mughal orbit, as despite official disapproval, parents sometimes sold their children during famines.[46] Even cases of husbands selling their wives are on record. While brief references to slaves are frequent in the secondary literature on Mughal and post-Mughal India, it is difficult to get an idea of the numbers involved. Even so, a few historians continue to work on the problem of slavery.[47]

Crisis and dissolution: Political economy vs. political culture

In the present study, we have not discussed the decline of the Ottoman or Mughal Empire. Determining to what extent the crises that the two polities experienced in the eighteenth century affected the tax paying populations is a delicate task, requiring detailed studies. Unfortunately, with respect to the Ottoman world, these are still in a beginning stage. Traditionally, Ottomanists have emphasized that the pressures from outside opponents, especially the Russian Empire, and later on, France and Great Britain as well, combined with the (proto)-nationalist aspirations of various Balkan peoples to threaten the rule of the sultans. While this statement is most appropriate for the 1800s, recent work has focused on its relevance to the second half of the eighteenth century as well, when the treaty of Küçük Kaynarca (1774) put the grain supply of Istanbul at risk. For, from that point Russian ships were able to enter the Black Sea and in wartime prevent Ottoman ships from reaching Istanbul. In addition, much of the fighting between Ottomans and Russians occurred in Wallachia and Moldavia, destroying harvests and driving peasants from their homes.

For a historian concerned with the interactions of elites and non-elites, one of the major difficulties comes from the fact that most studies relevant to Ottoman 'decline' concentrate on the elites, with ordinary people featuring simply as victims of over-taxation, war, robberies and other misfortunes, from which they had no way of defending themselves. While this view is legitimate up to a point, for our present purposes we need to focus on the agency of the various subject populations. Baki Tezcan has suggested that in the 1600s and 1700s, the coalescing of soldiers and artisans in large Ottoman cities, especially in Istanbul, admittedly endangered military efficiency. On the other hand, this alliance provided a broad spectrum of Muslim urbanites with a say in politics that they had not possessed under sixteenth-century sultans.[48] The reverse side of the coin, however, was that the sizeable non-Muslim population of Istanbul could not possibly achieve these advantages; a fact that may well have encouraged some of the more prosperous Christians and Jews to seek the protection of European consulates.[49]

To mention a different example, we need to know much more about the Ottoman irregular soldiers, who lost their sources of livelihood when raiding across the Habsburg frontier became less and less feasible in the course of the eighteenth century.[50] Away from the borders, mercenaries typically lost their jobs whenever the governor who had hired them lost his. To compound the problem, irregulars, when dismissed after the end of the fighting or even before, often did not receive their full pay. These men showed agency by using the force of their arms to make a living by plunder; thus, it became very difficult for ordinary villagers to feed themselves and produce surpluses for the consumption of armies, court and capital. Tolga Esmer has studied the account of one such mercenary, who fought in diverse wars during the early 1800s – admittedly well beyond the time limits envisaged here – but who legitimized his conduct in a manner surely known in the eighteenth century as well.[51] As throughout the 1700s, literacy in Bulgarian, vernacular Turkish and Arabic became more widespread people produced more texts reflecting the life experiences of a variety of 'ordinary' subjects. Thus, a victim of soldierly violence, the bishop of Vratsa known by his clerical name as Sofroni (1739–1813) has left an account of what happened when the Ottoman state was no longer in a position to supply its armies and the agency of soldiers cum robbers jeopardized future revenues and undermined the loyalties of non-Muslim Balkan subjects. Confronted with demands they could not fulfil, Orthodox subjects in appreciable though still not very large numbers transferred their loyalty to the tsars, as Sofroni did when much against his conscience, he had abandoned his flock and fled to the protection of a Wallachian monastery.[52]

Studies of Mughal decline differ from Ottomanist work, for the simple reason that the Mughal Empire unravelled in the course of the 1700s, while its Ottoman counterpart survived, though in a much weakened state. M. Athar Ali (1925–98) has suggested that in the eighteenth century, European trade hegemonies had a deleterious effect on both empires and even their 'successor states', although the Mughal polity broke up well before the East India Company, or any other European actor, was strong enough to have an impact on the balance of power in India. However, as a careful scholar, he admitted he did not have enough evidence to substantiate this hypothesis.[53]

In M. Athar Ali's perspective, it was probably even more important that the Mughal elites did not grasp the importance of technologic innovations including the clock, the flintlock gun or the telescope. Here we find an analogy with Ottomanist debates on the belated acceptance of printing.[54] It was not that, in Mughal India innovations in technology were completely absent. Irfan Habib has shown the contrary; more recently,

Giorgio Riello has focused on the sophistication of Indian cotton printers, from whom Europeans struggled to learn the arcana of the trade.[55] Even so, the pace of technologic progress in the Mughal world was very slow and this slowness affected key variables including urbanization. For in M. Athar Ali's perspective, cities were not parasites on the rural economy as had been a widespread assumption in the 1970s and 1980s. Rather, he considered that towns and cities might be a safety valve in times of agricultural crisis, a line of thinking that Rajat Datta was to develop later on.[56]

M. Athar Ali thought that, due to European exports Indian luxuries became less available to local magnates, who then engaged in ferocious competition over the limited supplies available. These struggles should have made life difficult for peasants, artisans and traders, at least as much or even more than the high level of official revenue demand. At the same time, in the thinking of Irfan Habib, excessive exploitation by the elite was a key factor in Mughal decline, even if peasant rebellions were not a factor in bringing down the empire.[57] Other historians have concentrated on the so-called *jagīr* crisis: When conquests in the Deccan necessitated generous grants to nobles willing to side with the Mughals, the paradoxical result was that because of this success the resources available for distribution became scarce. More detailed studies have shown that these sources of taxation might be available 'on the ground', but the Mughal administration may not have succeeded in establishing the ties to local aristocrats that would have allowed the central government to dispose of the revenues at issue.[58]

On the other hand, Muzaffar Alam has proposed a different reading; in his study of Awadh and Punjab in the early 1700s, he points out that these regional economies were prospering, a prosperity that allowed Mughal governors to obtain the arms that permitted them to break loose from the imperial centre. In terms of motivation, several of these magnates came to feel that the central power had nothing to offer them, an impression promoting de facto secession while continuing formal acknowledgement of the imperial pre-eminence.

By contrast, in the new Introduction that prefaces the second issuance of Alam's work in 2013, the author focuses not on the political economy, but rather on political-cum-cultural factors.[59] He now foregrounds the fact that the established court nobility, often of Iranian or Central Asian antecedents, was not willing to accommodate, with a good grace, the rise of new Indian elites, who might well have originated in urban commercial or even more modest milieus. To compound the problem, the monarchs, who rapidly succeeded one another after the death of Aurangzeb in 1707, did not develop the personal authority necessary to enforce the compromises now required with newly emergent merchants and other 'upstarts', often emphatically Indian and Hindu. Alam does not agree with the hypothesis of M. Athar Ali; namely, that the Mughals failed to be sufficiently innovative on the cultural level. However, he does consider that the decline of the centre in the early 1700s had something to do with a failure of political culture. Courtly literati were quite ready to denigrate both newly risen competitors and the emperors as persons, while the latter did not develop a viable political response to the demands of the newcomers for recognition and inclusion. Albeit on a different level, Alam thus agrees that in the early 1700s, cultural failure was a crucial reason for the rapid collapse of the social, political and interreligious arrangements undergirding the Mughal regime.

To conclude a conclusion

These arguments have taken us far away from the preoccupations of many if not most Ottomanists. Furthermore, when perusing the present study, the reader will doubtless think of many themes which this book could or should have dealt with but has not. In part, space constraints are at fault. Other reasons include the limited competences, linguistic and otherwise, of the present author. Moreover, when entering a field as an outsider, it is easy to miss crucial historiographical advances. Those who follow will make the necessary revisions . . . .

Timeline

Year	Ottoman Empire	Mughal Empire
1336–1405	Life of Amir Timur/Timur Lenk	Life of Amīr Timur/Timur Lenk
1398		Timur defeats Sultan Mahmūd Tughluq of the Delhi sultanate, massacres population of Delhi
1402	Timur defeats Bayezid II in the battle of Ankara	
1421–44, 1446–51	Reign of Murad II	
1453	Conquest of Constantinople, later (as Istanbul), the capital of the Ottoman Empire	
1481	Ottoman conquest of the Italian town of Otranto, given up the following year after the death of Mehmed II	
1481–1512	Reign of Sultan Bayezid II	
1483–1530		Bābur, descendant of Timur and first ruler of the Mughal dynasty
1512–1520	Reign of Sultan Selim I	
1514	Sultan Selim's victory at Chāldirān over Shah Ismā'īl I (r. 1501–24)	
1516–17	Ottoman conquest of Syria and Egypt	
1520–66	Reign of Sultan Süleyman	
1521	Belgrade conquered by the Ottomans	
1526	Süleyman's victory over Lajos II at Mohacz	Bābur's victory over the Lodi dynasty in the First Battle of Panipat
1527		Bābur's victory at Khanwa over the Rajput ruler Rana Sangra
1529	Süleyman secures the Hungarian throne for his vassal John Zapolya, but fails to take Vienna	
1530–40, 1555–6		Reign of Bābur's son Humāyūn, driven out of India but returned with Safavid support
1533–6	Süleyman's campaign against the Safavids, resulting in the conquest of Iraq	
1538	Ottoman naval victory of Preveza, won by Hayreddin Barbarossa against the combined fleets of Spain, Genova and Venice	

(*continued*)

Year	Ottoman Empire	Mughal Empire
1548–1626		Malik ʿAmbar, who prevented the Mughal conquest of the Nizāmshāhī kingdom for several decades
1556	Russian conquest of the khanate of Astrakhan	Visit of Seydi Ali Reʿis the Ottoman seaman-cum-diplomat, to Humāyūn's and Akbar's court; Second Battle of Panipat, in which Akbar defeats King Hem Chandra Vikramaditya (Hemu), executed after the battle
1556–1605		Reign of Akbar
late 1550s		Bihar Mal, prince of Amber from the Kachhwaha dynasty, submits to Akbar
1570–3	War of the Holy League, the Ottoman Empire conquers Cyprus from Venice	
1572		Akbar's conquest of Gujarat
1576		Mughal possession of Bengal becomes final
1589		Beginning of the Mughal conquest of Kashmir
1600		Mughal conquest of the Nizāmshāhī capital city of Ahmadnagar
1605–27		Reign of Jahāngīr
1627–80		Shivaji Bhonsla, Maratha king since 1674
1628–58		Reign of Shāh Jahān
1645–69	Ottoman–Venetian war over Crete, conquest complete with the taking of Candia in 1669	
1648–87	Reign of Mehmed IV, in whose reign the empire reached its maximum extent	
1658–1707		Reign of Aurangzeb
1664 and 1670		Shivaji Bhonsla twice raids the Mughal port of Surat
1665		Raja Jai Singh Kachhwaha (d. 1667) conquers Shivaji's major fort of Purandhar for Aurangzeb
1683	Failure of the second Ottoman siege of Vienna	
1685		Aurangzeb's conquest of Bijapur
1699	Peace of Karlowitz: the Ottomans lose most of Hungary	

Year	Ottoman Empire	Mughal Empire
from 1707 onward		A sequence of reigns by short-lived and/or ineffective Mughal rulers, beginning with Bahadur Shāh I (r. 1707–12) and Farrukh-Siyar (r. 1713–19)
about and after 1722	Ottoman projects for territorial acquisitions in Iran, particularly Tabriz, in Ottoman hands 1725–29	Fall of Isfahan to the Ghilzai, flight of the shah, end of Safavid rule in Iran
1739		Nādir Shāh plunders Delhi
1742–51		Maratha attacks destabilize the post-Mughal principality of Bengal/Murshidabad
1757		Following a complicated intrigue, the EIC wins the battle of Plassey against Sirāj al-Dawla, acquires taxation rights in Bengal
1759		The EIC takes over the fortress of Surat in the so-called 'Castle revolution'
1761		Third Battle of Panipat, the Afghan ruler Ahmad Shāh Durranī defeats a Maratha army
1768–74	Russo-Ottoman War, lost by the Ottomans	
1774	Peace of Küçük Kaynarca: the Ottomans lose Crimea	

Glossary

O stands for Ottoman terms and **M** for Mughal, sub-Mughal or post-Mughal

Acemi oğlan (O) candidate janissary, waiting for an opening in the janissary corps

Adâletnâme (O) sixteenth- and seventeenth-century 'justice edicts', which forebade the most common abuses against taxpayers

Akçe (O) Ottoman silver coin, much devalued in the late 1500s.

Akıncı (O) irregular troops in Ottoman service, of paramount importance in the conquest of Rumelia, later relegated to the avant-garde that terrified local populations before the main army intervened

Alacha (M) in Bengali usage, a striped silk textile in bright colours, probably with some connection to the 'mixed' or 'striped' fabric known as *alaca* and available in Ottoman markets.

Arasta (O) shop-lined street, usually built 'at one go' and producing rent for a specific pious foundation

Askeri (O) servitors of the sultan, exempt from most taxes. Although '*asker*' means 'soldier', scholar-officials including judges and college teachers were *askeri* as well

Avarız, avarız-ı divaniyye (O) irregular taxes that the late sixteenth-century government levied under wartime stress and which later became regular demands

Ayan (Muslim), or if Christian, **kocabaşı (O)** local notables/magnates. *Ayan* could achieve their position by informal means or benefit from official appointment after local selection; *kocabaşı*s, who functioned as tax collectors, needed an appointment document from the sultan's administration

Baba (O) 'father', a term used for dervish saints as well

Bailo (O) Venetian permanent ambassador in Istanbul

Baraka (M) blessings from a saint

Başmuhasebe (O) central accounting office

Bedestan (O) covered market, usually vaulted and built of stone

Besleme (O) a poor child raised by a better-off family and expected to provide service according to his/her capacities

Beylerbeyi (O) governor of a province, which in the early empire was often very large. Later the sultans instituted smaller provinces, but the old *beylerbeylik*s of Anadolu and Rumeli remained quite extensive

Beylerbeylik (O) province governed by a *beylerbeyi*

Bisat (O, M) term designating salespeople without stands of their own, who spread out their wares on the ground. A variant of this term was in use in Jodhpur

Bohça (O) cloth wrappers protecting valuable goods, sometimes highly decorated

Caravane maritime (O) French or Italian boats carrying goods and people between Ottoman destinations, in the 1700s, often in competition with Ottoman Greek shippers

Çarşı (O) street/quarter devoted to business and craftwork
Çarşı ressamları (O) miniature painters working for the open market and producing more modest items than those destined for the palace. As the painters are anonymous, we do not know whether some of them began to work for the market when their art was no longer of interest to the elite
Chowki (M) checkpoint or police post
Cizye (O) head tax payable by non-Muslims
Çiftlik (O) 1. Farm deemed sufficient for the support of a single-family household. 2. Farmstead in the hands of a non-peasant, operated for profit and/or social prestige
Çift-hane system (O) term introduced by Halil İnalcık for Ottoman peasant tenures: see *hane*
Dam (M) Indian copper coin
Darokha (M) decorated balconies on the outer walls of fortified Mughal palaces, suitable for the public appearances of the emperor
Darshan (M) viewing or visualizing a deity or monarch, an Indian custom adopted by the early Mughal emperors
Defterdar (O) head of the financial administration
Derbend (O) mountain pass, guarded by peasants of privileged status known as *derbendci*
Devşirme (O) levy of Christian peasant boys drafted for the service of the sultan
Dirlik (O) see *timar*
Divān-i ʿamm (M) meeting space in the emperor's palace frequented by large groups of people
Durbar (M) solemn meetings presided over by the emperor, which grandees of the empire needed to attend
Ehl-i hiref (O) artists/artisans in the service of the palace, in receipt of salaries
Ehl-i örf (O) local administrators and their armed servitors
EIC (M) (British) East India Company
Esir, üsera (O) prisoners of war, slaves
Fukara (O) 'the poor', a term used for dervishes as well
Fütüvvetnâme (O) writings inculcating virtuous behaviour, popular especially in certain pre-Ottoman and Ottoman artisan milieus
Gazavat (O) raids, often declared as furthering the spread of Islam
Guruş (O) silver coin, of Spanish *(riyal)* or Dutch *(aslani)* origin. The Ottoman mints of the 1600s and 1700s produced their own (frequently devalued) *guruş*, while many imported coins were of low value as well, to the point of being counterfeit
Han (O) business building with one or two courtyards, for the accommodation of traders and artisans, the rents paid by the users usually supporting a charity
Hane (O) a single-family household, officially deemed the 'building block' of rural society
Hanefi (in South Asia: Hanafi) **(M, O)** Islamic school of law (*madhhab*/*mezheb*)
Has (O) tax assignment worth over 100,000 *akçe*, usually granted to provincial governors and members of the sultan's family
Hil'at-i fahire (O) 'robes of honour', issued by the sultan or a high dignitary
Hul' (O, M) a type of divorce in which the woman pays her husband so that he will

divorce her. As a counterpart, at the least, she foregoes the three-month maintenance that the ex-husband would have had to pay if he unilaterally divorced her. Often the woman hands over some cash as well

Icmâl (O) summary revenue accounts, part of the tax registers known as *tahrir*

Ijāra (M) rural revenues farmed out, presumably to the highest bidder. As the central administration disapproved of tax farming, it permitted *ijāra* only if the contractors committed themselves to restoring abandoned fields. However, contravention was frequent (Habib 1999, pp. 274–75)

Ijāradār (M) a person benefiting from an *ijāra* contract

İrsaliye (O) sum of tax money sent to Istanbul, often from provinces where there were no *timar*s

İstimalet (O) accommodation of non-Muslim subjects by an Islamic ruler

Jagīr (M) large batches of revenue sources assigned by the emperor to commanders and courtiers in exchange for military and administrative services. *Jagīr*s were revocable at the ruler's pleasure and changed hands frequently.

Jagīrdār (M) holder of a *jagīr*

Jizya (M) head tax payable by non-Muslims

Kale (O) citadel, fortress

Kārkhāna (M) an atelier, sponsored by Mughal emperors, as well as sub- and post-Mughal princes or nobles, producing mostly for the households of these dignitaries

Kasaba (O) a small town in both Ottoman and Modern Turkish

Kaza (O) district in which a qadi officiates, smaller than a sub-province (*sancak*)

Khān-i khānān (M) an elevated office at the Mughal court

Kul (O) a servitor of the sultan, tax-exempt and dependent on the ruler to the extent of being a near-slave

Kulluk, yedi (O) 'seven servitudes', early Ottoman labour services later converted into money

Levent (O) mercenary soldier, often in the navy

Madad-i ma'āsh (M) a money grant made to men of religion

Madrasa (*medrese)* **(M, O)** in the Ottoman world, a college of Islamic divinity and law, in the Mughal orbit, often a school training future administrators

Mahalle, mahalla (M, O) an urban ward

Mahruse (O) 'the well-guarded', an attribute used for the possessions of the sultan and especially for cities

Malikâne (O) a term with several meanings, here: a lifetime tax farm

Mandi (M) a low-level market

Mansab (M) high military or civilian offices granted by the Mughal emperors

Mansabdār (M) holders of high Mughal office, responsible for raising armies that they led on Mughal campaigns but whose men were principally loyal to the dignitary that they served (Streusand 2011, p. 208)

Meclis, mahfil (O, M) poetry gatherings, in the Mughal orbit sometimes enhanced by singing and dancing

Mevlevihane (O) lodge of Mevlevi dervishes

Mihr-i müeccel (O) 'deferred dowry': a sum of money, which a husband needed to pay when divorcing his wife. If the husband pre-deceased his wife, the executors had to pay the widow her *mihr-i müeccel*, out of the estate of her deceased husband

Miri (O) fields, meadows and woods whose ultimate owner was the sultan, which peasants used as the monarch's tenants

Mufassal (O) detailed revenue accounts, mostly of the fifteenth and sixteenth centuries, on which the administration based the assignment of *timar*s and *zeâmet*s. For summaries, see *icmâl*

Muhtesib (O) market inspector, in charge of enforcing morality as well

Mükâtebe (O) contract of a slave owner with his/her slave, promising freedom if the slave satisfactorily completed certain tasks. Once concluded, the slave owner could not arbitrarily abrogate the contract

Mülk (O) private property

Mültezim (O) short-term tax farmer

Muraqqa'/murakka (M, O) album containing samples of calligraphy and miniature painting, often in exquisite frames

Nakkaşhane (O) a 'design office' sponsored by the Ottoman court

Narh (O) administratively decreed prices

Nawab (M) the second-in-command to a king or an emperor

Nikāhnāma (M) marriage contracts among Gujarati Muslims, specifying three conditions, whose violation gave the wife an automatic divorce: Firstly, the husband was not to take a second wife while married to the woman mentioned in the contract. Secondly, he promised to abstain from severe beating as long as the woman did not seriously break the law. The third condition specified that the husband should not leave his wife or fail to provide for her for a period ranging from six months to three years, depending on the time limit specified in the contract

Nirkh (M) records of prices sometimes on record in the official documents of Bengal. However, the rulers normally confirmed the prices set by the vendors

Nizâm, later often: **nizâmnâme (O)** formal registration of guild rules

Nizam-ı alem (O) 'world order', in practical terms a rapid succession to the Ottoman throne without prolonged wars among the sultan's sons

Nüzul (O) dues collected to supply storehouses on the pre-arranged stopping points of the Ottoman armies on their way to the frontiers

Öşür, aşar (O) tithe, a tax recognized by Islamic law. In practice, it might amount to more than one tenth, and some Anatolian villages paid a double tithe

Panchayat (M) locally based caste/sub-caste councils

Pargana (M) sub-district

Paytaht (O) the residence of the sultan

Pencik (O) one fifth of all imported slaves, accruing to the sultan

Piastre (O) see *guruş*

Qasbah (M) a small town

Ra'īyatī (M) non-elite taxpayers

Rāhdārī (M) transit dues

Rajput (M) Hindu warriors, some of them fighting as devoted allies of the Mughals and others as their inveterate enemies

Reaya (singular: *raiyyet*) **(O)** non-elite taxpayers
Reaya fukarası (O) the 'poor subjects' of the sultan, a term often used when counselling moderation in tax collection
Resm-i çift (O) tax paid by Muslim peasants as a counterpart for holding their farms
Resm-i tapu (O) a special tax demanded if a person other than the son of a deceased peasant took over his tenure
Sancak (O) banner, sub-province
Sharia, Ottoman Turkish: **şeriat** Islamic religious law
Silsilename (O) here: list of Ottoman sultans, often embellished with portrait miniatures
Sipahi (O) cavalryman, either in the service of the Palace or financed by village taxes, participating in the sultans' campaigns
Sürgün (O) people banished to a site selected by the sultan
Tabor, Wagenburg (O) war tactic used with great success by the Ottomans: carts linked together by chains and defended by soldiers, redoubt from where units could regroup and resume attack
Tahrir, tapu tahrir (O) tax registers, mostly of the fifteenth and sixteenth centuries listing provinces, districts and settlements, along with the taxpayers and at times the tax exempt. Listing a variety of agricultural dues as well, these documents were the basis for the assignment of *timar*s
Tedbir (O) promise, on the part of the owner to liberate a slave after his/her death
Tercüman, dragoman **(O)** professional translator (of varying levels of competence)
Timar, dirlik (O) assignment of taxes of up to 20,000 *akçe.* The assignees had to join the sultans' armies on horseback, together with a number of armed men if their *timar*s were of a certain size (İnalcık n. d.)
Tophane (O) cannon foundry
Uç beğleri (O) 'lords of the marches', semi-independent fighters allied with the sultans in the conquest of the Balkans
Vakfiyye, vakıfname (O) document establishing a pious foundation
Vakıf, plural: **evkaf (O)** pious foundation
Wajabī (M) 'appropriateness', meaning a modicum of justice and willingness to listen to the complaints of the subjects, as well as the moderation of tax demands
Wakala (O) see: *han* (Cairene usage)
Watan jagīr (M) *jagīr* assigned to a prince who having submitted to the Mughals, could keep his ancestral lands as a revenue source for his family. Different from ordinary *jagīrs, watan jagīr*s thus did not change their holders every few years
Yaya, müsellem (O) peasant-soldiers with assigned farms, active in early Ottoman armies
Zamīndār (M) established local power-holder (more or less) integrated into the Mughal system, responsible for low-level tax collection
Zāt (M) personal rank at court, numerically expressed. Under Akbar, a rank of 500 *zāt* defined a person as a noble, in the 1600s, an inflation of *zāt* ranks had occurred and now a man needed 1000 *zāt* to qualify (Richards 1993, p. 63)
Zeâmet (O) assignment of taxes worth from 20,000 to 100,000 *akçe.* The assignees, known as *zâim*s or *subaşı*s, had to join the sultans' armies together with a number of armed followers (İnalcık n. d.)

Notes

Acknowledgements

1 Sabyasachi Bhattacharya ed., *Towards a New History of Work*, (New Delhi: Tulika Books, 2014).

Introduction

1 For some outstanding examples see: İnalcık 2003; Kinra 2016.
2 Duindam 2016, p. 14.
3 Ward Perkins 2006.
4 Bang 2008.
5 Kastritsis 2016.
6 Fromkin 1989.
7 Subrahmanyam 2018b, p. 14.
8 Duindam 2016.
9 See Vatin and Veinstein 2003 for the Ottoman context.
10 Hasan 2004, p. 8.
11 For this reason, Hodgson 1974 uses the term 'Timurī'.
12 Kumar 2007.
13 Subrahmanyam 2005a, 2011 and 2018a. Dale 2010, p. 6 considers this term problematic, but I agree with the arguments of Asher and Talbot 2008.
14 Asher and Talbot 2008, p. 4.
15 Subrahmanyam 2018b, quotation on p. 17.
16 Anand and Dalrymple 2017, pp. 71–83 includes a dramatic account of the 1739 spoliation of Delhi.
17 I have taken this description of Mughal borders from Richards 1993, p. 7, who has recycled a map originally published by Irfan Habib.
18 For recent studies, see Başaran 2014 and A. Yıldız 2017.
19 Subrahmanyam 2005a, Subrahmanyam 2018b, p. 22.
20 Mughul 1974; Farooqi 1988; Özbaran 1994.
21 Casale 2010 and Casale 2013.
22 Farooqi 1988.
23 Ibid.
24 Mughul 1974, p. 123.
25 Casale 2010, p. 121.
26 Alam and Subrahmanyam 2007, pp. 324–7.
27 Vryonis 1971.
28 According to Anooshahr 2009, p. 39, Bābur no longer mentioned his Timurid connection after arriving in India.

29 The term 'Persianate' refers to the fact that the adherents of an originally Iranian tradition or culture might not be ethnic Iranians. See Duindam 2016, p. 273.
30 In analogy to terms like 'classicist' or 'medievalist', we will use 'Ottomanist' for scholars studying the Ottoman Empire during the past century or so.
31 İnalcık 1973; Lowry 2003; Tezcan 2012.
32 Islamoğlu İnan ed. 1987, reprint 2004; Eldem, Goffman and Masters 2005.
33 See for example Esenbel and Chiharu 2003.
34 For the observations of an Indian historian, see Prasad Sahai 2007, p. 35.
35 Subrahmanyam 2005b.
36 Hodgson 1974; Dale 2010; Streusand 2010.
37 Alam and Subrahmanyam 2007; Farooqi 1988 and 2017; Sood 2016.
38 Anooshahr 2009.
39 Hodgson 1974; Dale 2010; Streusand 2010.
40 Matthee and Mashita 2012.
41 Arjomand 2015.
42 This observation is all the more remarkable as it preceded the publication of Raymond 1973–74 and 1984.
43 Hodgson 1974, pp. 111–13; 133.
44 Hodgson 1974, pp. 119–25.
45 Dankoff 2006; Eldem 2013. Fatih Çalışır (Ibn Haldun University, Istanbul) is working on an Ottoman medical man who spent several years in mid-seventeenth-century India.
46 Necipoğlu 1991; Peirce 1993; Hodgson 1974, p. 103.
47 Tosun Arıcanlı organized several of these conferences during his time at Harvard.
48 Subrahmanyam 2018a.
49 Subrahmanyam 2018a, p. 178, referring in part to Kuran 2011.
50 Çizakça and Kenanoğlu 2008.
51 Subrahmanyam 2018a, p. 184.
52 Relevant in the present context: Dale 1994 and Dale 2004.
53 Dale 2010, p. 9.
54 Ibid., p. 8.
55 Ibid., p. 186.
56 Ibid., pp. 185–6 and Anooshahr 2009, p. 3. Anooshahr's most recent work appeared in 2018, too late for inclusion into the present study.
57 Anooshahr 2009, pp. 31–3.
58 Streusand 2011, p. 79.
59 Anooshahr 2009. However, Sultan Süleyman even in old age, led his armies in person. My thanks to Giancarlo Casale for his discussion of periodization. The third stage of monarchy discussed by Anooshahr, presided over by a ruler interested mostly in his private pleasures, will not concern us here.
60 Faroqhi 2012.
61 İşkorkutan 2017.
62 Alam 1998, p. 326.
63 Das Gupta 1979a, reprint 1994, pp. 8–9.
64 Hanna 1998, pp. 34–5 and 65.
65 Banarasidas 2009.
66 Katsiardi-Hering 2008; Serinidou 2008; Kadı 2012.
67 Özel 2016, p. 117 records a decrease of over 60 per cent for the city of Amasya and its surrounding district.
68 Braudel 1979.

69 For an important text, see Moosvi 2008.
70 Tuğ 2012.
71 Prasad Sahai 2006, p. 92; Zilfi 2010.
72 Faroqhi 1984, p. 279.
73 Nazım Hikmet, *Memleketimden İnsan Manzaraları*, edited by Mehmet Fuat, 4 vols. (Istanbul: De Yayınları, 1966), vol. 2, pp. 240–1. There are many editions of this work.

1 Texts in Context: Relating Primary to Secondary Sources

1 Critical historians of modern India often stress that the blanket term 'Hindu' for a set of religious beliefs is of relatively late date; at first, it simply meant 'Indian'.
2 Dale 2010, pp. 1–7.
3 On occasion, where misunderstandings are not likely, I will use the term 'India' instead of South Asia.
4 For exceptions, see S. Yıldız 2005.
5 Apart from Babinger and Üçok 1982, see now http://ottomanhistorians.uchicago.edu/ (Aiming to cover all historians having worked on Ottoman territory, this project is under the direction of Cemal Kafadar (Harvard Univ.), Hakan Karateke and Cornell Fleischer (Chicago Univ.)) (accessed on 27 April 2018).
6 Kinra 2016, p. 117.
7 Aquil 2016.
8 Eldem 2013.
9 Yılmazer n. d. (accessed on 14 October 2016).
10 Brentjes 2012, p. 340.
11 Eren 1960.
12 https://www.britannica.com/biography/Asikpasazade (viewed on 18 October 2016); İnalcık 1994.
13 Piterberg 2002; Tezcan 2002. I have borrowed the term 'Ottoman tragedy' from Gabriel Piterberg.
14 As two examples among many, see Fleischer 1986 and Neumann 1994.
15 Karahasanoğlu 2017.
16 Sarkar reprint 2009, see in addition Chakrabarty 2015 and Truschke n. d.
17 Kinra 2016, pp. 266–81.
18 Ibid., p. 263.
19 Ibid., p. 266.
20 Ibid., pp. 254–8.
21 Ibid., pp. 18–19, 252–3.
22 Kumar 2007.
23 Ibid., p. 9.
24 Kumar ed. 2008.
25 To name just a few examples: Uzunçarşılı's work on the town of Kütahya (1932) was a pioneer, followed by Wittek 1934; Flemming 1964; Akın 1968; Varlık 1974 and others.
26 Sümer 1980.
27 For an overview, see Vryonis 1971.
28 Thapar 2004, pp. 48–52.
29 Ibid., pp. 65–7.
30 Ibid., pp. 196–7.
31 Eaton 2000, pp. 128–32.

32 Subrahmanyam 2011, p. 98. Bangladesh became a separate state in 1971, when the former provinces of East Pakistan seceded from the (West) Pakistani government.
33 Haider 2005.
34 Fleming 1999.
35 http://mustafa-akdag.kimdirkimdir.com/; https://tr.wikipedia.org/wiki/Mustafa_Akda%C4%9F (both accessed on 22 October 2016). Akdağ 1963 is still a starting point of the study of ordinary sixteenth-century Anatolians.
36 This is a slight variation on the title of the seminal book by Davis 1987.
37 Halil İnalcık has studied two of the oldest surviving *tahrirs*, both of them fragments: İnalcık 1954 and 2012.
38 Lowry 1992.
39 Singer 1994, p. 91.
40 Ergene 2002.
41 Davis 1987.
42 For example, Moosvi 2008b and c.
43 Prasad Sahai 2006.
44 Richards 1993, pp. 75–86.
45 Prasad Sahai 2006, p. 153.
46 Subramanian 2016, p. 226.
47 Ibid., pp. 226–7.
48 An example is: İşkorkutan 2017.
49 Ocak 1978.
50 Chakrabarty 2015, pp. 38–132, 241–60.
51 Ibid., pp. 241–50.
52 Ibid., p. 119.
53 Ibid., pp. 121–5.
54 Deshpande 2007; Chakrabarty 2015, p. 158.
55 Nicol 1996.
56 Oikonomidis 1994.
57 Delilbaşı 1989.
58 Zachariadou 1994.
59 Bohn, Gheorghe and Weber 2013.
60 Zachariadou 1983.
61 İnalcık 1991.
62 Fleet 1999.
63 For early correspondence with the sultans, see Bojović 1998.
64 Köprülü 1966.
65 For a bibliography, compare Yıldırım 2007.
66 Mélikoff 1975.
67 Yürekli 2012.
68 Kumar 2007, pp. 192–4.
69 Malekandathil 2014.
70 Kumar 2007, pp. 373–4.
71 Beldiceanu Steinherr 1971; Yıldırım 2007, pp. 149–50.
72 In 2016, Naciye Zeynep Çavuşoğlu (Sabancı University, Istanbul) and Seda Şenvarıcı (Istanbul Bilgi University) both defended MA theses comparing Ottoman and Mughal practices. While Çavuşoğlu has focused on the legitimization of rulers, Şenvarıcı's study dealt with political institutionalization.
73 Subrahmanyam 2005; Hasan 2004; Lal 2005.

74 Peirce 1993.
75 For a recent survey, see Alam and Subrahmanyam 2007.
76 İnalcık 1997.
77 For a discussion of this trope, see Kafadar 2007, p. 11.
78 Barkan reprint 1980; Divitçioğlu 1971; İslamoğlu and Keyder 1987 reprint 2004; Berktay 1987 and 1992.
79 Berktay 1987 and 1992.
80 See the article by Cemil Kocak, written upon Divitçioğlu's death: http://t24.com.tr/haber/prof-sencer-divitcioglunun-basina-gelenler,271382 (accessed on 5 November 2017).
81 İslamoğlu reprint 2007; Wallerstein, Decdeli and Kasaba 1987; İnalcık reprint 1985.
82 Abou-El-Haj 1991, pp. 2–11.
83 This sentence appears toward the beginning of 'The Eighteenth Brumaire of Louis Bonaparte' (1851) https://www.marxists.org/archive/marx/works/1852/18th-brumaire/ch01.htm (accessed on 5 November 2017).
84 A few examples: Mantran 1962 on Istanbul; İnalcık 1960, 1971; and 1997 on Bursa; Göyünç 1969 on Mardin; Faroqhi 1984 on Anatolian towns; Gerber 1988 on Bursa; Goffman 1990 on İzmir; Ergenç 1995 on Ankara and Konya; Yi 2005 on Istanbul; Ergenç 2006 on Bursa; Olnon 2014 on Izmir; Özel 2016 on Amasya; and Kuru 2017 on İzmir.
85 Kütükoğlu 1983; Su. Kumar 2007, p. 285.
86 Akdağ 1963; Özel 2016; Kuru 2017.
87 Kuru 2017.
88 Akdağ 1963.
89 Goffman 1990, pp. 25–49 had emphasized the key role of European trade.
90 Mukhia reprint 2001a, pp. 123–4; Berktay 1987.
91 Mukhia reprint 2001b, p. 42.
92 Ibid., pp. 40–2; Habib 2008; M. Kumar 2017.
93 Richards 1993, pp. 45–6.
94 Habib 1963 and 1999, with many reprints.
95 İslamoğlu İnan 1994.
96 Habib 1999, p. 405.
97 Ibid., pp. 206–8; Alam 1986, p. 6.
98 İnalcık 1975.
99 Kinra 2016, pp. 56–9.
100 Alam 1986, p. 313.
101 This discussion owes a great deal to the comments of Najaf Haider (Jawaharlal Nehru University, New Delhi).

2 The Trouble with Imagery

1 I have taken this title from one of my favourite films, Alfred Hitchcock's 'The Trouble with Harry' (US 1955).
2 Kinra 2016, p. 117.
3 It was on display when I visited the museum in October 2016.
4 Fetvacı 2013, pp. 29–33.
5 As one example among many see Losty, 2016, No. 17 'A Prince and his Mistress in an Embrace' and No. 18 'A Princess seated on a Throne beneath a Tree, with two

female Attendants': https://bl.academia.edu/JeremiahLosty (accessed on 6 November 2016).

6 As examples see Losty 2016, No. 7 'Simurgh Chick' and No. 8 'Tethered Bear'.
7 For a reproduction see Necipoğlu 2007.
8 Öney 2002, pp. 411–28; Arık 2000, pp. 132–50.
9 For an engraving showing the walls of Konya decorated with an eagle and a headless classical statue, see: https://www.google.de/search?q=the+city+walls+of+Konya&num=100&newwindow=1&client=firefox-b-ab&tbm=isch&tbo=u&source=univ&sa=X&ved=0ahUKEwizgc640IDSAhXJ1xQKHR7yD80Q7AkIMw&biw=1600&bih=1052#imgrc=u-lZ1pzECe52FM: (accessed on 8 February 2017).
10 Tezcan 2013.
11 Faroqhi 2012.
12 Dankoff 2006, pp. 71–2.
13 Koch 2002, p. 30.
14 Artan 2006, pp. 419–20.
15 For a few reproductions, compare İnalcık 1973, Ill. No. 40–2 and the recent, postumous publication by Metin And: And 2018.
16 Rothman 2012.
17 Majer 1999; Artan 2006, pp. 431–2.
18 Milstein 1989.
19 Kazan 2010, p. 35.
20 Uluç 2006.
21 Fekete 1960; Tülay Artan is now preparing a comprehensive study of this personage.
22 Chong 2005.
23 Uzunçarşılı 1981–6; Kazan 2010 contains a detailed discussion.
24 İrepoğlu 1999, pp. 38–72 has published some of his poems and, as far as possible, reconstructed his biography.
25 Majer 1999.
26 Koch 2002, p. 29.
27 Orthmann 1996.
28 Peirce 1997 has discussed the deference to palace protocol required from royal women.
29 However, occasionally non-Muslims did work on the decoration of a mosque, draftees from the island of Chios painting the Selimiye in Edirne; compare Necipoğlu 2007, pp. 20 and 23.
30 Soni 2016, pp. 20–7.
31 Soni 2016, p. 33, note 76.
32 See the map in Peck 2014, p. 86 (upper right hand corner).
33 Seyller 2002, pp. 42–3.
34 Chakraverty 2008, p. 52.
35 Aitken 2009.
36 Wright 2008, p. 24.
37 Soni 2016, pp. 52–4.
38 Tanındı 1984.
39 Atıl 1986.
40 Fetvacı 2013, pp. 130–2.
41 Published in Necipoğlu 2000b, pp. 288–9.
42 Artan 2010a and b.
43 Değirmenci 2012.
44 Seyller 2002, pp. 32–43, see p. 39.
45 Wright 2008, p. 39.

46 Chakraverty 2008, p. 30. Lal 2018, pp. 271-2 is of the opinion that the woman depicted was Nūr Jahān On the very limited depiction of females in Rajput and Mughal painting, see Aitken 2002.
47 An eighteenth-century copy of this portrait is in the Taj Mahal Museum, Agra (seen in 2012 and 2015). On the painter Nādira Bānū, see Verma 2009a, p. 123. Natif 2018 has discussed the work of Rukaya Bānū and Nini: Natif 2018, pp. 89–109.
48 Losty 2016, pp. 44–5.
49 İrepoğlu 1999, pp. 180–5.
50 Stchoukine 1966, vol. 2, for example figures No. II, III and XXIX.
51 Hamadeh 2008, plate 1.
52 Hamadeh 2008, plate 2; Artan and Schick 2013.
53 Necipoğlu 2000a.
54 Meyer zur Capellen and Bağcı 2000, pp. 103–4, 120.
55 Reproduced, among other venues, in Seyller 2002, p. 22.
56 Compare the catalogue section in Calza ed. 2012, no. IV.7 and IV.8; Kangal et alii eds. 2000, pp. 222–3.
57 Jahangir, ed. by Thackston, 1999, p. 165.
58 Peirce 1993, pp. 61–2.
59 Necipoğlu 1991, pp. 25–6.
60 Rezavi 2013, p. 72.
61 Meyer zur Capellen and Bağcı 2000, p. 129.
62 Stchoukine 1966, vol. 1, pp. LII–LIII, see the foreign visitors at the extreme left of the gallery; Atıl 1999, p 94.
63 This image exists in two versions, for one of them see Ölçer et alii eds. 2010, pp. 137–8.
64 Relations with the supernatural were confined to texts; for the dreams of Murad III see: Felek ed. 2012.
65 For an example: Bağcı, Çağman, Renda and Tanındı 2006, p. 80.
66 Koch 1997.
67 Koch 2001.
68 Atıl 1999, p. 234.
69 Soucek n. d. This is the generally accepted version of his biography, with which Soucek seems to agree.
70 Soucek 1992; Emiralioğlu 2014.
71 Piri Reis 1935, 2013.
72 Piri Reis 2013, p. 14.
73 Denny 1970.
74 Yurdaydın 1976, Ill. No 9a and 9b.
75 Hagen 2003.
76 https://www.loc.gov/item/2004626120/; https://en.wikipedia.org/wiki/Cedid_Atlas (both accessed on 8 November 2016).
77 Unat 1941; Salzmann 2004, pp. 31–74.
78 Habib 1977. I thank Nonica Datta (Jawaharlal Nehru University, Centre for Historical Studies) for providing a copy of this article.
79 Koch 2012.
80 Halim Khan 2015, pp. 18–20.
81 Ibid., p. 18. See also Soni 2016, pp. 68–73. For a map of Agra, the work of Jaipur artists as well, see Chapter 5.
82 Keskinkılıç 2014: http://www.actaturcica.com/sayi11/VI_I_b_01.pdf (accessed on 5 January 2015). This article contains a photograph of the inscription, which in addition to the original, also survives in an eighteenth-century copy made by Hafız Hüseyin

Ayvansarayî. See: http://www.genelturktarihi.net/genc-osman-ve-sevgili-ati-sisli-kirin-mezari (accessed on 5 January 2015).
83 Artan 2010b.
84 Stchoukine 1966, vol. 2, figure No XXXVI.
85 Kahraman 2015.
86 Recep et alii eds. 2010, pp. 120 and 165.
87 Demiriz 2005; Ayverdi 2006.
88 Welch and Masteller 2004, pp. 96–7.
89 Verma 2009 pp. 45–6.
90 Demiriz 2005, p. 109.
91 Atasoy 1997.
92 Atıl 1999; İşkorkutan 2017. To date, İşkorkutan is the only scholar to have discussed the second set of miniatures depicting the parades of 1720.
93 For a good example, see Bağcı, Çağman, Renda and Tanındı 2006, p. 205.
94 Verma 2009b; for an example see Rezavi 2013, fig. 2.1.
95 Rezavi 2011.
96 Due to the limits of my knowledge, I do not discuss Jewish arts of the book.
97 Layton 1994.
98 Petrovszky 2014; Gratziou 2011. I am grateful to Marinos Sariyannis and especially to the author for supplying me with copies of Gratziou's publications.
99 Gratziou 2011.
100 Kouymjian 2015a, p. 33. For a general overview over Armenian manuscript production see Kouymjian, 2015b. My thanks to Daniel Ohanian (Los Angeles) for directing me to Kouymjian's work.
101 Kouymjian 2015a, p. 29.
102 Guirguis 2008, pp. 74–8.
103 Ibid., p. 91.
104 Ibid., p. 92.
105 Soni 2016.
106 However, the recent publication of the Jaipur holdings (Soni, in Tillotson and Venkateswaran 2016, p. 13) contains only a nineteenth-century chromolithograph of a sample page from this manuscript, rather than a modern photograph.
107 Halim Khan 2015.
108 Ibid. 2015, p. 17.
109 Soni 2016, pp. 24–5.
110 Necipoğlu 2007, p. 17.
111 Raby 2000, p. 148. Hayreddin's portrait was in a Habsburg collection too; today it is on show in the museum of Ambras near Innsbruck/Austria, a dependency of the Kunsthistorisches Museum in Vienna.
112 Wright 2008, p. 39.
113 Cohen 2008; Gagliardi Mangilli 2012.

3 Geopolitical Constraints, Military Affairs and Financial Administration

1 This is the point of a German saying valid in other places too.
2 Dávid 2013, p. 300.

3 Schulze 1978, pp. 364–8.
4 Eickhoff 1988, pp. 329–425.
5 İnalcık 1948; Kurat n. d.
6 Eickhoff 1988, pp. 265–80.
7 Aksan 2007, pp. 95–7.
8 Şehdi Osman Efendi ed. Unat 1941–2, vol. 1, 391.
9 Ragsdale 1988 and many others, listed in the author's footnotes.
10 İnalcık reprint 1998.
11 Calic 2016, pp. 190–7.
12 Başaran 2014, pp. 56–62.
13 Sofroni 2016.
14 Isom-Verhaaren 2011, pp. 114–15.
15 Ibid., pp. 141–7.
16 Eickhoff 1988, pp. 240–64.
17 Bérenger ca 2006: https://francearchives.fr/commemo/recueil-2006/39551 (accessed on 25 January 2018).
18 Lane 1973, pp. 369–74, 407–11.
19 Pedani Fabris 1994b; for a comprehensive discussion of Ottoman corsairs, see Gürkan 2018.
20 Costantini 2001.
21 Davis 1967.
22 Frangakis-Syrett 1992, pp. 215–47.
23 Panzac 2004.
24 Eldem 1999.
25 Sohrweide 1965; Imber 1979.
26 Yurdaydin1976, p. 10.
27 Uzunçarşılı 1972, p. 23.
28 İnalcık 1960; Eaton 2005, pp. 59–77 is a detailed biography of this personage.
29 Casale 2010, p. 121.
30 Ibid., p. 145.
31 Braudel 1966, vol. 1, pp. 510–16.
32 Jahangir 1999, p. 382.
33 Gommans 2002, p. 108.
34 Matthee and Mashita 2012.
35 Richards 1993, pp. 132–3.
36 M. Athar Ali reprint 2006b, pp. 331–2.
37 Richards 1933, p. 133.
38 Maurya 2014, pp. 379–80.
39 Richards 1993, p. 33; Chatterjee 2009, pp. 25–6.
40 Richards 1993, pp. 33–4. I thank Richard Eaton for setting me right on the chronology.
41 Chatterjee 2009, p. 25.
42 Ibid., pp. 26–7.
43 Jasonoff 2005, pp. 28–30.
44 See the map on the frontispiece of Richards 1993.
45 Sarkar 1984, pp. 33–6.
46 Ibid., pp. 40–1.
47 Richards 1993, pp. 32–3.
48 Eaton 2005, pp. 123–4; Omar Ali 2016.
49 Richards 1993, pp. 205–17.

50 Sarkar 1984, pp. 123–4.
51 Compare the map in Richards 1993, p. 206.
52 Richards 1993, pp. 220–3.
53 Ibid., p. 238; Eaton 2005, p. 183.
54 Prakash 1998, pp. 124–5. In the eyes of Indian rulers, European merchants active on the western coast of the Peninsula appeared as another source of problems.
55 Subrahmanyam 1993, p. 85.
56 Ibid., p. 276.
57 Jasonoff 2005, pp. 23–32.
58 Nadri 2009, pp. 16–17.
59 Jasonoff 2005, pp. 30–1.
60 Prakash 2009a.
61 Balabanlilar 2012, pp. 37–70.
62 Anooshahr 2009, p. 41.
63 Tezcan 2013; on the remote (supposed) ancestors of the Ottoman dynasty, see Ogasawara 2017.
64 Hathaway 1997, pp. 46–51; Hathaway 2008, pp. 51–2.
65 Kunt 1983, p. 32; Ménage 1965.
66 Faroqhi 1981.
67 Ménage 1965, p. 212.
68 İnalcık 1997, p. 129.
69 Gommans 2002, p. 82 assumes that the *timar*-holders were of tribal background; but this is a misunderstanding.
70 Gommans 2002, pp. 62–77.
71 Streusand, 2011, pp. 98–101, 206–8.
72 Ibid., p. 85.
73 Veinstein 1983.
74 Dávid 2013, p. 289.
75 Akdağ 1963, p. 83.
76 Afyoncu 2013, p. 162.
77 Gommans 2002, p. 67.
78 Ibid., p. 80; İnalcık 1980.
79 Gommans 2002, p. 39.
80 İnalcık 1985b.
81 Khoury 1997, p. 46. My thanks go to Jane Hathaway for pointing out the importance of political compromise.
82 Raymond 1973–4, pp. 688–709; Yılmaz 2015.
83 Aksan 2007, pp. 48–53, 62–3, 130–5.
84 Jasonoff 2005, pp. 29–30; quotation on p. 29.
85 For one example among many, see Sarkar 1984, p. 193.
86 For example, Sofroni 2016; Sarkar 1984, p. 163.
87 Ágoston 2005, p. 19.
88 Börekçi 2006, p. 438.
89 Seydi Ali Reis ed. Kiremit 1999, pp. 85–90. Here Seydi Ali vividly describes the dangers of the sea and the poor condition of his ships. His decision to return overland was probably caused by the lack of sailors as well; Richards 1993, pp. 57 and 289.
90 From the 1650s to 1703, it seemed as if the administration might permanently move to Edirne, but a rebellion forced Sultan Ahmed III (r. 1703–30) to return to Istanbul.
91 Kunt 2007, pp. 67–8.

92 Ibid., p. 68.
93 İnalcık 1954b.
94 Uzunçarşılı 1972, p. 7.
95 Orhonlu 1974; Fleischer 1986, pp. 180–1.
96 On Podolia: Kołodziejczyk 2004.
97 Gülsoy 2005, pp. 284–5.
98 Uzluk ed. 1958.
99 Faroqhi 1981, pp. 112–13.
100 Adanır reprint 2014, p. 185.
101 Lowry 1986, p. 23.
102 Faroqhi 2005.
103 Kiel 1985, p. 351 and elsewhere; Gradeva 2004.
104 Rozen 2002, pp. 37–9. Rozen emphasizes that not all Jews shared this positive evaluation.
105 Sohrweide 1965.
106 Raychaudhuri 1982, p. 172.
107 Ariel Salzmann has found a relevant song, included in Zarinebaf 2010, pp. 183–6.
108 See Lafi 2018 for a forceful statement of this point.
109 On the scarcity of resources that could serve as *jagīrs*, see Raychaudhuri 1982, p. 178.
110 Chandra reprint 1998, pp. 359–60.
111 Mukhia 2004, p. 38.
112 Ibid., pp. 37–8.
113 Krstić 2013.
114 Anooshahr 2009, pp. 159–60.
115 Streusand 2011, p. 22; Arjomand 2015.
116 Bayerle 1980, pp. 10 and 14.
117 Shaw 1962, pp. 240–9.
118 Richards 1993, pp. 83–5.
119 Faroqhi 2015.
120 Habib 1999, pp. 274–6.
121 İnalcık 1954.
122 The fundamental study is still Uzunçarşılı 1948; see also Fleischer 1986, pp. 312–14. The standard studies of the last thirty to forty years are Tabakoğlu 1985; Cezar 1986; Darling 1996; Sahillioğlu 1999; Genç 2000, the latter two books being collections of articles published earlier on.
123 Sarınay et alii 2010, pp. 146–59.
124 Genç 1975.
125 Seydi Ali Reis ed. Kiremit 1999, p. 122.
126 Raychaudhuri 1982, p. 183.
127 Nadri 2009, p. 13.
128 Raychaudhuri 1982, p. 186.
129 Ibid., p. 186–7.
130 Ibid., p. 175.
131 Ibid., pp. 184, 190–3.
132 Ibid., p. 188.
133 Manucci reprint 1989, p. 111. I am grateful to Richard Eaton for his timely warning.
134 Genç 1995.
135 İnalcık 1969.
136 Darling 2012.

137 Özel 2016; Prasad Sahai 2016.
138 Faroqhi 1992.
139 Mukhia 2004, p. 54.
140 Prasad Sahai 2006, pp. 20–6.
141 Raychaudhuri 1982, p. 190.
142 Faroqhi 2005a.

4 Legitimizing Monarchic Rule Amid Religious and Linguistic Diversity

1 Duindam 2016, pp. 24–5.
2 Moin 2012.
3 Duindam 2016, pp. 27–35; Mukhia 2004, pp. 46–50.
4 Salzmann 2007.
5 Ricci 2005, pp. 76–94.
6 Çizakça 2013, p. 250.
7 Castellan 1991, p. 195.
8 This is the implication of Todorova 2009, pp. 276–81. I am grateful to the author for discussing this issue with me.
9 Pelsaert 1925 (reprint 2011), p. 58.
10 Mukhia 2004, pp. 59–60.
11 Richards 1993, pp. 63–9.
12 İnalcık reprint 1978, originally published in 1964.
13 İnalcık 1973, pp. 3–4.
14 İnalcık reprint 1978, p. 45; İnalcık 1980.
15 In the Introduction to İnalcık 1997, first published in 1994, the author places the term 'decline' in quotation marks; and it does not reoccur in the detailed index of this book.
16 Cantemir 1734.
17 Lewis 1962.
18 Peirce 1993, pp. 1 and 282.
19 Abou-El-Haj 1991, pp. 24–8.
20 İnalcık 1980.
21 Tezcan 2011.
22 Ibid., pp. 197–8.
23 Jane Hathaway, oral communication.
24 Murphey 2008, pp. 1–3.
25 Ibid., p. 41.
26 Ibid., pp. 106–7.
27 Ibid., p. 3.
28 Ibid., pp. 10–11.
29 Fleischer 1986, p. 295.
30 Mukhia 2004, pp. 50–61.
31 Ibid., pp. 56–7.
32 Eaton 1983/2011.
33 Mukhia 2004, p. 52.
34 Fleischer 1986, p. 298; Vatin and Veinstein 2003, pp. 156–7.
35 Çıpa 2017, pp. 1–3.

36 Evliya Çelebi 2006, pp. 229–30.
37 Necipoğlu 2000a.
38 Some of these inventions were a product of cultural exchanges with Renaissance Italy: Necipoğlu 2000a, pp. 38–9.
39 Kangal ed. 2000, pp. 200 and 216–17.
40 Fetvacı 2013, pp. 30–3.
41 Anooshahr 2009, p. 41.
42 Raychaudhuri 1988, p. 172.
43 I thank A. Azfar Moin for sharing his reflections on this question. However, a Pakistani cruise missile goes by the name of Babur: https://economictimes.indiatimes.com/news/defence/pakistan-successfully-test-fires-enhanced-version-of-babur-cruise-missile/articleshow/63765730.cms (accessed on 27 August 2018).
44 Anooshahr 2009, p. 41.
45 Fleischer 1986, p. 285; for the Mughal context, Moin 2012 has stressed the centrality of the astrological notion of being a 'lord of the conjunction'.
46 Necipoğlu 1991, pp. 95–6.
47 Sarıcaoğlu 2001, pp. 47–9; Aynural 2005.
48 Richards 1993, p. 211. The sources used by Sarkar 1984, pp. 129–31, which this historian considers definitive, do not mention the fainting fit. Perhaps the chronicler used by Richards has added this feature to minimize Shivaji's defiance.
49 Tietze ed. 1979, p. 38; Felek 2012, pp. 27–30 discusses the claims of Murad III (r. 1574–95) to spiritual attainment, including the performance of miracles.
50 While Fikret Yılmaz has recently published some very sharp criticisms of Çıpa's work the presumed saintliness of Selim I is not at issue: F. Yılmaz 2018. I thank Tülay Artan for directing me to this publication.
51 Vatin and Veinstein 2003, pp. 353–420. On millennial sovereignty in Iran and India, see Moin 2012.
52 Evliya Çelebi 2006, p. 116.
53 Duran and Gümüşoğlu eds. 2011, pp. 204–9.
54 Antov 2017, p. 85; pp. 71–89. A comparison with Moin 2012 demonstrates the many parallels between heterodox religious practices in Anatolia and Northern India.
55 Antov 2017, p. 240; for visits of sultans to famous religious scholars see Değirmenci 2012, p. 293.
56 Eaton 1993, pp. 22–41.
57 Ibid., p. 83.
58 Moin 2012, pp. 97–125.
59 Subrahmanyam 2005a, p. 126; Moin 2012, p. 139.
60 On other conditions adherents had to fulfil, see Moin 2012, p. 144.
61 Ansari 1988 updated 2011.
62 Rizvi reprint 1995, pp. 232, 250, 284.
63 Wright (ed.) 2008, pp. 226–7. While the dignitary depicted is supposedly a mythical Hindu king, he wears the clothes of a Mughal noble and the album was the property of Prince Salīm, the future emperor Jahāngīr.
64 Amin 2015, see map on p. 15.
65 Ibid., p. 19.
66 Ibid., pp. 9–11.
67 Anooshahr 2009, pp. 44–5.
68 Amin 2015, p. 10.
69 Ibid., pp. 108–14.
70 Ibid., pp. 211–41.

71 Ibid., pp. 122–45.
72 Ibid., pp. 59–72, 160–1, 196–7.
73 Şahin 2010.
74 Çıpa 2017, p. 225.
75 Flemming 1987; Fleischer 2009, pp. 240–3.
76 The name Isa corresponds to Jesus, a figure that in Muslim understanding plays a role in the run-up to the Last Judgement: Subrahmanyam 2005a, p. 112.
77 Subrahmanyam 2005a, p. 120; Moin 2012, p. 108–9.
78 Subrahmanyam 2005a, p. 126.
79 Fleischer 1986, p. 134.
80 Çıpa 2017, pp. 235–6.
81 Özcan 1997.
82 Subrahmanyam 2005a, p. 126.
83 Farooqi 1988; Lal 2005, pp. 211–3.
84 Evliya Çelebi 2005, p. 396.
85 Farooqi 1988; Faroqhi 1994, pp. 55–8.
86 Barbir 1980, pp. 174–8.
87 Faroqhi 1994, pp. 37–9.
88 Erdem 1996, p. 22.
89 Faroqhi 1994, pp. 134–9, Alam and Subrahmanyam 2007, pp. 33–5.
90 Fine 1994, pp. 538, 608–10.
91 Paudice 2006. https://ottomanhistorians.uchicago.edu/en/historian/elia-capsali (accessed on 17 March 2017).
92 See Darling 2012, p. 108, for the Muslim historian Juvaynī's (d. 1283) defence of non-Muslim Mongol rule as a manifestation of justice.
93 Evliya Çelebi ed. Kreutel 1963, pp. 40–1, 161–2.
94 Murphey 2008, pp. 59–60. Murphey uses the striking formula: 'lèse majesté resulting from loss of territory previously held' (p. 59).
95 Veinstein 2005.
96 Ibid.
97 For Bengal, see Chatterjee 2009, p. 224.
98 Tillotson and Venkateswaran eds. 2016, p. 42; Calza ed. 2012, p. 74, Ill. No. 41.
99 Moin 2012, pp. 140–2.
100 Develi ed. 1998, pp. 23–5.
101 Compare the many translated samples in Dankoff 2006.
102 Bojović 1998.
103 Hitzel ed. 1997; Rothman 2012.
104 Pedani Fabris 1994.
105 Ebubekir Ratib ed. Uçman 1999, pp. 91–3.
106 Bağış 1983.
107 Kütükoğlu 1994, pp. 360–6; Selçuk 2015, p. 60.
108 Selçuk 2015.
109 Establet and Pascual 2005, pp. 172–3.
110 Kut and Eldem 2010, p. 69.
111 Eldem 2007.
112 Aynur and Karateke 1995, pp. 71–4; Hamadeh 2008, pp. 87–9.
113 Kuru 2013, p. 592.
114 Seydi Ali Reis 1999, pp. 144–50.
115 Duindam 2016, p. 273, citing a statement by Metin Kunt.

116 Fleischer 1986, pp. 157–8.
117 Chew 1937; Rouillard 1941; Maclean 2004 and 2007.
118 Uluç 2006.
119 Kenderova 2000, p. 76.
120 Eldem 2007.
121 Sarıyıldız 2011; Tuğ 2017.
122 Veinstein 1996.
123 Gul-Badan Begam ed. Beveridge 2011, p. 79. The sole extant manuscript is in Persian.
124 Chatterjee 2009, p. 42.
125 Alam 1998, p. 328.
126 Alam, 2010, p. 54.
127 Zilli 2010, p. 98.
128 Alam reprint 2010.
129 Alam 2010, pp. 41–4.
130 Orthmann 1996.
131 Kinra 2016, pp. 240–85; Fleischer 1986, pp. 154–9.
132 Kinra 2016, pp. 5–6.
133 Ibid., pp. 234–6, 259–75.
134 Truschke 2016, p. 104.
135 Alam 2010, p. 73.
136 Chatterjee 2009, p. 128–9.
137 Alam 2010, p. 54.
138 Ibid., pp. 72–3.
139 Mukhia 2004, p. 53.
140 Stephanov 2018, Introduction shows that the 'father–children' trope did occur in the time of Mahmud II; Faroqhi 2009b.
141 Faroqhi 2007.
142 Murphey 2008, pp. 95–7.
143 Moin 2012, pp. 151–4.
144 See Moin 2012, p. 200 for claims that Akbar was a reincarnation of the Hindu god-king Rama.
145 Mukhia 2004, p. 47.
146 Baer 2008.
147 Philliou 2011, p. 42.

5 Towns and Cities

1 Tillotson and Venkateswaran 2016, pp. 68–73.
2 Koch 1991, pp. 68–9.
3 Asher and Talbot 2008, pp. 15–35.
4 Çulpan 2002, pp. 112–15.
5 Emecen 1992; http://www.islamansiklopedisi.info/dia/ayrmetin.php?idno=050007 (accessed on 26 November 2017).
6 Satish Kumar 2014, p.187.
7 Moosvi 2008d, p. 289; Kumar Singh 2014, p. 541.
8 Bajekal 1990.
9 Singh 2017.
10 Kothiyal 2014, p. 340.

11 Bhukya 2017.
12 Goffman 1990, pp. 36–49.
13 Kafescioğlu 2009, pp. 35–43.
14 Ibid., pp. 53–108.
15 İnalcık 1972.
16 Kafescioğlu 2009, p. 178.
17 İnalcık 2012.
18 For a photograph, compare: http://www.edirnevdb.gov.tr/edirne/kervan_g.html (accessed on 16 July 2018).
19 Abou-El-Haj 1984, p. 86.
20 Bilgin 2006.
21 Öcalan, Sevim and Yavaş 2013, pp. 66–9.
22 For a photograph see http://culturecityistanbul.blogspot.com/2016/12/rustem-pasha-caravanserai.html (accessed on 16 July 2018).
23 Necipoğlu 2005, p. 364.
24 For a biography detailing the pious foundations of this grand vizier, authored by Tayyip Gökbilgin, see: http://tayyibgokbilgin.info/wp-content/uploads/2012/05/Article-103.pdf (accessed on 17 July 2018).
25 Muṣṭafā ʿĀlī ed. Tietze 1979, 1982, vol. 2, pp. 26–7, 144–5.
26 Koch 1991, pp. 110–11.
27 And 2004.
28 For an example see Rezavi 2013, p. 123.
29 Rezavi 2013, pp. 34 and 42.
30 Ray 2015, pp. 302–3
31 Moosvi 2015, pp. 318–22, see p. 322.
32 Koch 1986 and 2005.
33 Koch 2005, pp. 131–4.
34 Ray 2015, pp. 293–4.
35 Koch 1991, p. 68.
36 Faroqhi 1994, pp. 164–6.
37 Evliya 2005, p. 396.
38 Rezavi 2013, p. 19.
39 Truschke 2016, pp. 34–7.
40 Mishra 2014, pp. 264–5.
41 On sultans of the 1800s making donations to non-Muslim religious sites, see Stephanov 2018. In an unpublished MA thesis of 2016 (p.34) Ahmet Tekin has noted that Sultan Ibrahim (r. 1640–48) once had a burnt-down church rebuilt. See: http://www.academia.edu/36664394/OTTOMAN_ISTANBUL_IN_FLAMES_CITY_CONFLAGRATIONS_GOVERNANCE_AND_SOCIETY_IN_THE_EARLY_MODERN_PERIOD (accessed on 12 March 2019)
42 Peri 2001.
43 Ibid.
44 Evliya 2001, p. 14; Göyünç 1970. Malatya has moved to a new site.
45 Faroqhi 1984, p. 42. For a photograph from the 1940s, when the structure was still in existence, see https://www.karamandan.com/Nostalji-Karamanda_Cem_Sultan_Bedesteni-h36854.html (accessed on 19 July 2018).
46 Eski Anadolu Medeniyetleri Müzesi, or Museum of Ancient Anatolian Civilizations, Ankara. Mahmud Paşa was the descendant of a Byzantine noble family established in Serbia, converted to Islam as a young prisoner of war: Stavridis 2001.

47 Koch 1991, p. 90; Trivedi 2014, p. 131.
48 Hamadeh 2008, pp. 38–43.
49 I owe these considerations to the unpublished MA thesis of Ayşe Kaplan (Istanbul Bilgi University 2012) and cordially thank her for her help.
50 Çadırcı 2011, pp. 126–7.
51 Kırlı 2001.
52 Rezavi 2013, p. 46.
53 Ibid., pp. 151–3.
54 Ibid., pp. 28–33.
55 Ibid., p. 2.
56 Kothiyal 2014, p. 339.
57 Imam 2016.
58 Braudel 1982–84 vol. 1, pp. 519–20.
59 Kunt 1983, p. 97.
60 Kuyulu 1992; Nagata 2015.
61 Rezavi 2013, p. 121, Plan 6.1.
62 Ibid., p. 38–9, Plan 2.7.
63 Ibid., pp. 36–7 describes the principal streets.
64 Ibid., p. 79, Plan 4.6.
65 Blake 2016; Tillotson and Venkateswaran 2016, pp. 68–73.
66 Bacqué-Grammont (1981). 'Old' Van, destroyed during World War I is now uninhabited, and the new town is located some distance away.
67 Ergenç 1995, p. 16.
68 Necipoğlu 1991, p. 32
69 Faroqhi 2012.
70 Hamadeh 2008, p. 51.
71 Dale 2004, p. 353.
72 Rezavi 2013, pp. 126–33.
73 Koch 1991, pp. 33–4.
74 Raymond 1984, pp. 5–9.
75 Watenpaugh 2004.
76 Masters 1988, pp. 164–75.
77 Abdelnour 1982.
78 Aigen edited by Tietze, pp. 32–3.
79 Masters 1988, pp. 124–5; Watenpaugh 2004, p. 162.
80 Satish Kumar 2014; Ray 2015.
81 Ray 2015, p. 414.
82 Ibid., p. 423.
83 Ibid., p. 421.
84 Ibid., p. 422.
85 Masters 1988, pp. 124–5.
86 Moosvi 2008e, pp. 132–3. In addition, compare the articles in Keller and Pearson eds. 2015.
87 Subramanian 2015.
88 Panzac 2004.
89 Moosvi 2008b, p. 259.
90 Das Gupta 1994a, 30 refers to the Turkish family known as the 'Chellabies' prominent in Surat during the early 1700s. The mosque founded by this family was still in existence in the 1990s.

91 Kafadar 2007.
92 Seydi Ali's testimony apart, suspect because the author had to compensate for his failure as a naval commander, the evidence found by Casale comes from Portuguese sources: Casale 2010, pp. 104–5, 121–2.
93 Richards 1993, pp. 32–3.
94 Galland 2000, pp. 92–3.
95 Goffman 1990, pp. 36–45; Olnon 2014.
96 Das Gupta 1979a, reprint 1994, p. 8.
97 Kumar Singh 2014, p. 528.
98 Arasaratnam and Ray 1994, pp. 117–218.
99 Subramaniam 2015.
100 Hütteroth 2006, pp. 32–5.
101 Orhonlu 1967, p. 101.
102 Güreşsever Cantay 2016, pp. 78–81.
103 Faroqhi 1984, pp. 61 and 268.
104 Devra 2014, pp. 243–50. The term for lines of camels travelling together was *katar*, and the same word denoted the same thing in the Ottoman context. As for sea-borne trade, the term *naul* (Moosvi 2008b, p. 258) corresponds to Ottoman Turkish *navlun*. Passengers paid *āzūqa* for the provisions they carried, which may have the same root as Turkish *azık* (food taken along while travelling).

In this section, we need to go beyond 1739, as Devra's work only in a few cases provides CE equivalents for the dates on record. Some of the cases cited must have occurred in the late 1700s and early 1800s.
105 Devra 2014, p. 246.
106 Ibid., p. 245.
107 Habib 1999, pp. 230–6 stresses that revenue demand sometimes increased to the point that peasant subsistence was in danger; in consequence, there could not have been any exchanges between townsmen and villages. For a different opinion, see Datta 2014.
108 Braudel 1982–84, vol. 1, pp. 504–58.
109 Chenoy 2014, pp. 159 and 165; Koch 2016, p. 137. Older texts sometimes call Delhi Dār ul-mulk. However, it is strange that the documents translated by Moosvi seemingly contain dates but do not indicate the locations where the emperor had issued his commands: Moosvi 2008b and Moosvi (editor and translator) 2008.
110 http://population.city/india/surat/ (accessed on 6 December 2017).
111 So http://population.city/india/surat/utik Biswas 'Has Gujarat moved on since 2002's riots' accessed through http://www.bbc.com/news/world-asia-india-17200961 (4 December 2017).
112 Faroqhi 1980.

6 Investigating the Business of Merchants

1 Faroqhi 1979.
2 İnalcık 1996, p. 97.
3 Kuran 2011; Çizakça and Kenanoğlu 2008, p. 212.
4 Hanna 1997.
5 Genç 1975.
6 Genç 1987.

7 Kothiyal 2014.
8 Çizakça 1996, pp. 89–116.
9 Ibid., pp. 94–5.
10 Nadri 2009, p. 13.
11 Kadı 2012; Papakostantinou 2008.
12 Masters 1988; on the institutional framework of French Mediterranean trade see Masson 1911.
13 Frangakis-Syrett 1992, pp. 143–54; Eldem 1999.
14 Smyrnelis 2006.
15 Davis 1967.
16 Mather 2011.
17 Cornelissen 2015.
18 Banarasidas tr. by Chowdhury 2009. I am most grateful to Najaf Haider (Jawaharlal Nehru University), who has presented me with a copy of this wonderful book.
19 On the English translation of Ranga Pillai's diary compare: https://archive.org/stream/privatediaryofan01ananuoft/privatediaryofan01ananuoft_djvu.txt (accessed on 7 July 2017).
20 Banarasidas tr. by Chowdhury 2009, pp. 195–7 has a graphic description of people running away from a dignitary known for his brutality.
21 Habib 1963, pp. 273–97.
22 Ibid., pp. 284–5; Nadri 2009, p. 14.
23 İnalcık 1973, pp. 108–18.
24 Richards 1993, pp. 66–93.
25 Bajekal 1990, pp. 91–2 has pointed out that share cropping may have been more common than official sources acknowledge. The records she has studied deal with the mid-eighteenth-century principality of Jaipur.
26 Bajekal 1990, p. 92.
27 Findley 2010.
28 Nadri 2009, pp. 19–21.
29 Findley 2010.
30 Das Gupta 1994a, p. 29.
31 Malekandathil 2013.
32 See Prakash reprint 2012 as one example among many.
33 Nadri 2009, p. 16.
34 Ibid., pp. 13–21.
35 Jasonoff 2006, p. 40.
36 Aktepe 1971; Faroqhi 1984, p. 116; Olnon 2014. I am grateful to the librarians of Leiden University for sending me a copy of this important study.
37 Erim 1991.
38 Salzmann 2004, pp. 139–63 has provided an impressive analysis of the province of Diyarbekir, as it was mostly in the 1700s.
39 İnalcık 1996, p. 110.
40 Pedani Fabris 2008; Stefini 2015; Kafadar 1986.
41 Panzac 1996.
42 Raymond 1991, accessed through: https://books.openedition.org/ifpo/1667 (23 July 2018).
43 Aynural 2001, pp. 9–15 and idem 2005.
44 Bajekal 1991, p. 109.
45 Bajekal 1990, p. 120.
46 İnalcık 1971, p. 213.

47 Çizakça and Kenanoğlu 2008; for a more recent statement of Kuran's position see Kuran 2011, pp. 3–24.
48 Genç 1995.
49 Banarasidas 2009, pp. XXIX and 39.
50 Alam 2000.
51 Banarasidas 2009, p. 45.
52 Ibid., p. 35; Aslanian 2011, pp. 166–201.
53 Banarasidas 2009, p. XXVII (Introduction by Rohini Chowdhury).
54 Ibid., pp. 51 and 69.
55 Ibid., p. 239.
56 For the cultured pearl industry practised in these areas today, see: http://www.biologydiscussion.com/invertebrate-zoology/phylum-mollusca/pearl-fishery-in-india/33001 (accessed on 6 July 2017).
57 Banarasidas 2009, pp. 155 and 167.
58 Ibid., pp. 233–5.
59 Ibid., pp. 155–61.
60 Mehta 1991a.
61 Ibid., pp. 56–7.
62 For an explication of Aurangzeb's actions, who did not destroy Hindu temples out of sheer fanaticism, compare Truschke n. d. (accessed on 14 July 2017).
63 Mehta 1991b, pp. 100–1.
64 Mehta 1991d; Das Gupta 1979a, pp. 94–134; idem 1979b.
65 Raymond 1973–4, vol. I, pp. 294–5, vol II, pp. 410–1.
66 For a photograph compare Kuran 2011, p. 177.
67 Gedikli 1998, pp. 237–60.
68 Raymond 1973–4, vol. II, pp. 414–15.
69 Aslanian 2011, pp. 215–34.
70 Katsiardi-Hering 2008; Kadı 2012.
71 Raymond 1973–4, vol. II, pp. 483–97.
72 For a description and photographs, see https://en.wikipedia.org/wiki/Ampelakia,_Larissa (accessed on 11 July 2017).
73 Serinidou 2008; Katsiardi-Hering 2008.
74 Banarasidas 2009, pp. 57–61.
75 Levi 2016, p. 47.
76 Banerji 2011, pp. 45–66 and 127–37.
77 Ibid., p. 43.
78 Levi 2016, pp. 53–9; Aslanian 2011, pp. 215–34.
79 Braudel 1979, vol. 2, p. 129.
80 Findley 2010.
81 Chowdhury 2016.
82 İnalcık 1970.
83 Barnes 1997: http://www.jameelcentre.ashmolean.org/collection/7/10236/10318 (accessed on 1 July 2017).
84 http://www.jameelcentre.ashmolean.org/collection/7/10236/10319 (accessed on 2 July 2017).
85 http://www.jameelcentre.ashmolean.org/collection/7/10236/10333 (accessed on 1 July 2017).
86 Raymond 1973–74, vol. 1, p. 135 points out that we have few Cairo records on the importation of Indian textiles during the 1700s; however, Arasaratnam 1986, p. 99

refers to Coromandel cottons of the late seventeenth and early eighteenth centuries going to Bandar Abbas and Mocha. Presumably quite a few of the textiles arriving in Mocha ended up in Cairo.

87 http://www.jameelcentre.ashmolean.org/collection/7/10236/10333 (accessed on 1 July 2017).

88 I owe this information to Selçuk Esenbel (Boğaziçi University, Istanbul).

89 https://calicomuseum.org/ and http://nationalcraftsmuseum.nic.in/map_crafts%20museum.htm (both accessed on 2 July 2017).

90 İnalcık 1960, 1970, 1971; Veinstein 1999.

91 Evliya 2007, pp. 270, 335.

92 İnalcık 1960, p. 141; Veinstein 1999; for the dates of the Bahmani/Bahamani dynasty see Sherwani 1960, pp. 924–5 and Abhijit Rajadhyaksha, 'Far East Kingdoms, South Asia: The Bahamani sultanate' http://www.historyfiles.co.uk/KingListsFarEast/IndiaBahamanis.htm (accessed on 10 July 2017).

93 İnalcık 1979–80, pp. 52–4.

94 Ibid., pp. 15 and 53.

95 Parthasarathi 2009a.

96 Riello 2013, pp. 87–186; Berg 1999: admittedly the author is more concerned with Chinese goods; Parthasarathi 2009a.

97 Said 1978.

98 Fukasawa 1987, p. 43.

99 Ali Efendi and Abdurrahim Muhibb Efendi 1998, pp. 220–3.

100 Fukasawa 1987, pp. 39–45.

101 Establet 2017; compare the list of Indian fabrics compiled by Veinstein: Veinstein 1999, pp. 113–15.

102 İnalcık 1970, p. 215.

103 Fukasawa 1987, pp. 46–51.

104 Alam 1994.

105 Kothiyal 2016, p. 144.

106 Bulliet 1975; Faroqhi 1982.

107 For these hopes see: Busbequius 1994, pp. 174–5.

108 Faroqhi 1982; Stoianovich 1960.

109 Kothiyal 2016, pp. 144–5.

110 Ibid., pp. 122–3.

111 Habib 1990, pp. 372–9; Bhukya 2017; for an image, see Braudel 1979, vol. 3, p. 432.

112 Pamuk 2000b.

113 Barkan 1975, which is an abridged translation of an article published in Turkish (Barkan 1970).

114 Pamuk 2000a, pp. 112–30.

115 Given population growth, the prices of foodstuffs increased more rapidly than those of manufactured goods. In consequence, the more prosperous section of the rural population made a profit from the grain and other produce that they sold, but especially the poorer town dwellers suffered quite badly (Pamuk 2000a, p. 129).

116 Sahillioğlu 1999, pp. 30–1.

117 Levi 2016, pp. 121–30.

118 Habib 1988.

119 Prakash 2004, pp. 27–8.

120 Ibid., p. 23.

121 Moosvi 2002; Haider 2002.

122 Prakash 2004, pp. 21–8.
123 Moosvi 2002.
124 Alam 1986, p. 304.
125 Richards 1988, p. 11. In addition, see Richards 1993, pp. 185–204. The preceding paragraph recapitulates Richards' argument.
126 Kunt 1977.
127 Schacht 1964, p. 153.
128 Frangakis-Syrett 1992, p. 103.
129 Prakash 2004, pp. 50–2; Nadri 2009, pp. 1–7.
130 Parthasarathi 2009a, p. 416.
131 Prakash 2009a.
132 Moosvi 2015, pp. 432–3.
133 Genç 1995.
134 Mukherjee 2013; Roy 2016, pp. 137–43.
135 Roy 2016, pp. 199–200.
136 Ibid., pp. 218–21.
137 Ibid., p. 220.
138 Mehta 1991c; Subramanian 2016.
139 Hanna 1997; Kadı 2012.

7 Early Modern Crafts in the Ottoman and Indian Orbits

1 This chapter has greatly benefited from the advice of Rishad Chowdhury, to who I am much obliged.
2 Vanina 2004. I am very grateful to Vijaya Ramaswamy for directing me to this work.
3 Editors of the *Encyclopaedia Britannica* n. d. after 2011.
4 Dalsar 1960, p. 320.
5 Asdrachas et alii 2007, vol. 2, pp. 284–5; Fotopoulos and Delivorrias 1997, pp. 298, 307, 315.
6 Prasad Sahai 2006, p. 90.
7 Tavernier reprint, n. d., vol. 1, p. 97.
8 Aščerić-Todd 2007.
9 Faroqhi 1979.
10 Establet 2015.
11 Kütükoğlu 1983.
12 Uzunçarşılı 1981–6; Kazan 2010; Yaman 2008.
13 Vanina 2004, pp. XVII–XXV provides an overview over the principal primary sources.
14 Halim Khan 2015.
15 Abū'l-fazl (1927–49), vol. 1, pp. 14, 93–102.
16 Raychaudhuri 1982, pp. 266–7.
17 Prasad Sahai 2006.
18 Tavernier reprint, n. d., vol. 1, pp. 42–7, vol. 2, pp. 41–76.
19 Richards 1993, pp. 84–6.
20 Abū'l-fazl 1927–49.
21 Moosvi 2015, p. 5.
22 Ibid., p. 314; Establet 2017.

23 Lowry 1992.
24 Monographs on Ottoman towns, which include at least a chapter or two on artisans, are numerous, for example: Gerber 1988; Ergenç 2006; Wilkins 2010.
25 Shaw 1962; in addition, compare Raymond 1973–4; Tuchscherer 1999; Michel 2005; Hanna 2011; and Mikhail 2011.
26 McGowan 1969.
27 Given the linguistic limits of the present author, there may be studies of which I am not aware.
28 Moosvi 2015, pp. 312–13.
29 Braudel 1979, vol. 1, pp. 418–20.
30 On artists and artisans receiving salaries, compare Uzunçarşılı 1981–6, Mahir 1986, Veinstein 1994, Yaman 2008, Çağman 2016 and Yaman 2018 (the latter focuses on the palace tailors, a separate organization, but includes information on the *ehl-i hiref* too). Veinstein (p. 354) points out that there were a few Christians and Jews among the *ehl-i hiref*, mostly manufacturing weapons.
31 Atasoy and Raby 1989, pp. 96–263.
32 Yaman 2018, p. 20.
33 Tietze 1979, 1982, vol. 1, pp. 61–2 and 155–7.
34 Vanina 2004, pp. 93–114.
35 Bernier reprint 2010, p. 228, Vanina 2004, p. 99.
36 Vanina 2004, p. 100.
37 Halim Khan 2015, p. 2; Abū'l-fazl (1927–49), vol. 1, pp. 93–102.
38 C. A. Bayly 1986, pp. 300–2.
39 Halim Khan 2015, pp. 33–4.
40 Natif 2018, pp. 69–84.
41 Compare the 'Table of Contents' of Halim Khan 2015, page not numbered.
42 Prakash 2012, pp. 114–17.
43 Phillips 2014.
44 Yaman 2008, pp. 32–3.
45 Barkan 1941–2; 1943; 1943; Kütükoğlu 1983.
46 Kütükoğlu 1983, pp. 15–16.
47 Tietze 1979, 1982, vol. 1, pp. 61–2 and 155–7.
48 Kütükoğlu 1983, p. 4.
49 Pamuk 2000b, pp. 67 and 92 (Tables 4.2 and 6.3).
50 Ibid., p. XIV.
51 Vanina 2004, p. 96.
52 Raymond 1973–4, vol. 1, pp. 133–5.
53 İnalcık 1979–80; Parthasarathi 2009a.
54 Wilkins 2010; Ergenç 1995; Gerber 1988; Hanna 2011; Aščerić-Todd 2007. For general overviews, see Faroqhi 2009a and Faroqhi ed. 2015b.
55 S. Bayly 1998, p. 24.
56 Ibid., p. 191. Once again, I thank Rishad Chowdhury for pointing out this argument and directing me to the works of S. and C. A. Bayly.
57 Stein 2002, p. 57.
58 Rishad Chowdhury, personal communication.
59 Yıldırım 2002.
60 Prasad Sahai 2006, pp. 112–15.
61 Yi 2015.
62 C. A. Bayly 1986, pp. 293–4.

63 Ibid., p. 290.
64 Sarıyıldız 2011.
65 Faroqhi 2014.
66 Prasad Sahai 2006, pp. 20–8. For a similar concept in the late Ottoman world, see Stephanov 2018.
67 Linda Darling has authored the most comprehensive study of the many variations of this piece of political wisdom: Darling 2012.
68 Prasad Sahai 2006, p. 2; Darling 2012.
69 Prasad Sahai 2006, pp. 55–60.
70 Kırlı 2001 and later studies by the same author.
71 Toward the end of Akbar's reign, the Mughal Empire had between 100 and 150 million inhabitants, while optimistic estimates assume a population of about 30 million for the Ottoman Empire: Dale 2010, pp. 107–8.
72 Washbrook 2009, p. 185.
73 Ibid., p. 184.
74 Parthasarathi 2002.
75 Barkan 1972 and 1979, vol. 1, pp. 144–56.
76 Faroqhi 1992.
77 Goffman 1990, p. 82.
78 Parthasarathi 2009b.
79 Prakash 2012, pp. 60–5; Prakash 2009b.
80 Establet and Pascual 2005, pp. 312–13.
81 Prakash 2012, p. 65.
82 Vanina 2004, pp. 93–114.
83 Ramaswamy 2013, pp. 84–7.
84 Nadri 2009, pp. 24–33.
85 Papakostantinou 2008, p. 138.
86 Atasoy and Uluç 2012.
87 Habib 2008, pp. 36–46.
88 İnalcık 2011.
89 Dhar n. d.
90 N. Kumar 1988, see particularly pp. 33–9.
91 Pelsaert 2011, p. 7; Tavernier reprint, n. d., vol. 1, p. 97.
92 Pelsaert 2011, p. 7.
93 Kumar 1988, p. 36.
94 Tavernier reprint, n. d., vol. 2, pp.18–19.
95 Jane Hathaway informs me that the Archive of Turkish Oral Narrative/Türk Öyküleri Sandığı of Texas Tech University, Lubbock/Texas (http://aton.ttu.edu/) may contain relevant material.
96 Glassie 1993.
97 Cillov 1949; Doğanalp Votzi 1997 and 2005; Kickinger 2005.
98 Doğanalp Votzi 1997, 2005.
99 Lapidus 1984, pp. 96–102.
100 Abū'l-fazl (1927–49), vol. 1, pp. 15–16, 93–102, 232–9. While hunting falcons are not craft products, the ruler had fixed their prices for the same reason: ibid., pp. 306–7.
101 Mukherjee 2013, p. 26.
102 Nadri 2009, p. 26.
103 Ibid., p. 28.
104 Keyvani 1982.

8 Rural Life in the Indian and Ottoman Environments

1 Habib 1963 and 1999. Many relevant documents appear in the catalogue appended to Habib's work: Habib 1999, pp. 468–81.
2 Faroqhi 2015.
3 Orhonlu 1963.
4 Abd Al Raheim A. Abd Al Raheim 1975; Baer reprint 1982. The translation of the heading is difficult, meaning something like 'the enjoyment of [thinking] heads'. I thank Dr. Daniel Potthast (Ludwig-Maximilians-Universität, Munich) for his suggestion. See Hathaway 2008, p. 175 for a variant translation: 'Brains Confounded by the Ode of Abu Shaduf Expounded.'
5 Baer reprint 1982, p. 37.
6 Gupta 1986.
7 While the title of Irfan Habib's *opus magnum* is '*The agrarian system of Mughal India*' (1963, 1999), Gupta 1986 has chosen the title of '*The agrarian system of eastern Rajasthan*'.
8 Prasad Sahai 2006.
9 Thus, the chapter on the grain trade in Fattah 1997, pp. 139–57 deals only with the period after 1830, although the book as a whole concerns the period from 1745 to 1900.
10 Göyünç and Hütteroth 1997, Map 3b, 'Landwirtschaftliche Produktion'. The maps are missing from many copies of this work currently in circulation.
11 https://www.mapsofindia.com/maps/india/climaticregions.htm (accessed on 5 October 2017).
12 Erler 2010; White 2011; Mikhail 2011; Kuru 2017. Semih Çelik will hopefully turn his recently defended thesis (European University Institute, 2017) into a book as well.
13 Hütteroth 2006. For present-day views, see https://www.britannica.com/science/Little-Ice-Age (accessed on 10 September 2017).
14 Compare however: Bir, Acar and Kaçar 2012.
15 The works of Alan Mikhail particularly Mikhail 2011 are of central importance in this context.
16 Habib 1999, p. 1.
17 For a similar problematic, see the discussion of Moosvi's work in Chapter. 7.
18 Habib 1999, pp. 21–2.
19 Ibid., pp. 34–5.
20 Ibid., p. 39, Balabanlilar 2012, pp. 79–83.
21 Habib 1999, pp. 112–22.
22 İnalcık 1997, pp. 143–54; 174.
23 İnalcık 1973, p. 108.
24 Faroqhi 1984, p. 244.
25 Barkan 1980, pp. 315–16.
26 Gara 2005.
27 İnalcık 1959.
28 Çizakça 2013, p. 250.
29 Dávid 2013, p. 300.
30 Faroqhi 1984, pp. 263–5.
31 Faroqhi 2015a, pp. 17–18.
32 For example, see Barkan 1966, p. 228, No. 36, p. 232, No. 38, and p. 243, No. 40.
33 Mukhia reprint 2001a, p. 119.
34 Düzdağ 1972, pp. 167–71.
35 Habib 1999, p. 138.

36 Prasad Sahai 2006, pp. 124–5 and elsewhere.
37 Richards 1993, pp. 86–7.
38 Ibid., pp. 79–90 treats the institution of the Mughal revenue system under Akbar.
39 İslamoğlu İnan 1994, pp. 70–7, 204.
40 Faroqhi 1984, p. 143.
41 Faroqhi 2008.
42 Prasad Sahai 2006, Chapter 1, pp. 4–5.
43 İnalcık 1965a.
44 Scott 1985.
45 Singer 1994, p. 91.
46 White 2011, pp. 118–19.
47 Richards 1993, p. 85.
48 Moosvi 2015, p. 73.
49 Richards 1993, p. 84.
50 İnalcık 1997, pp. 132–42.
51 Moosvi 2015, p. 99.
52 Ibid., p. 98.
53 Habib 1999, p. 367.
54 Genç 1975.
55 Habib 1999, pp. 367–70.
56 See Habib 1999, p. 277 for an example.
57 Bajekal 1990.
58 See Barkan 1966, p. 291 for an example of a small number of slaves present on a *çiftlik*. However, most of the *çiftlik* owners recorded in this publication did not own any slaves; in addition, see McGowan 1981, p. 72.
59 I owe this information to a set of papers given by Antonis Anastasopoulos, Andreas Lyberatos, Demetrios Papastamatiou, and Yücel Terzibaşoğlu during the 22nd CIÉPO conference, Sofia, September 2018.
60 McGowan 1981, pp. 75–9.
61 Braudel 1972–3, pp. 724–5.
62 İslamoğlu İnan 1994, p. 43.
63 Demirci 2009, p. 122.
64 Güçer 1964, p. 90.
65 Ibid., pp. 22–8.
66 Murphey 1999, pp. 86–7.
67 Aynural 2001, p. 7. On *avarız* in general, see Demirci 2009.
68 İslamoğlu İnan 1994, pp. 157–61.
69 Islamoğlu İnan 1994, pp. 205–8.
70 Gupta 1986, p. 74, note 3.
71 Habib 1999, pp. 290–3.
72 Prasad Sahai 2006, p. 126–7.
73 Habib 1999, pp. 66–7.
74 Prasad Sahai 2016, p. 199.
75 Prasad Sahai 2006, p. 130.
76 Ibid., p. 138–9.
77 Ibid., pp. 132–3; Habib 1999, pp. 85–6.
78 Hütteroth and Abdulfattah 1977, pp. 58–61.
79 Ibid. 1977, p. 86.
80 Akdağ 1963, pp. 250–4; Hütteroth 1968, pp. 202–3.

81 This issue will be the topic of a volume currently in preparation: 'Seeds of Power: Explorations in the Environmental History of the Ottoman Empire,' edited by Onur İnal and Yavuz Köse (Winwick – Cambridgeshire: White Horse Press, planned for 2019).
82 Özel 2016, p. 150 and elsewhere.
83 Rothenberg 1966, pp. 12–13.
84 Faroqhi 1984, pp. 268–71.
85 Choudhary 2016, p. 51.
86 Ibid., pp. 54–7.
87 Bhardwaj 2016, pp. 108–11.
88 Ibid., p. 88.
89 Ibid., p. 90.
90 Habib 1999, pp. 516–47; Moosvi 2015, pp. 451–76.
91 For an anonymous dictionary definition, see 'Asiatic mode of production' in Oxford Reference http://www.oxfordreference.com/view/10.1093/oi/authority.20110803095428735 (accessed on 15 October 2017).
92 Habib 1999, p. 144–5.
93 Prasad Sahai 2006, pp. 129–34.

9 On the Margins of Society: Women, Servants, Low-Caste People and Slaves

1 This poster was an advertisement of the 'Green' party for the Bavarian election of September 2018.
2 Develi ed. 1998, p. 33.
3 Elliot 2004, pp. 116–17.
4 Duindam 2016, p. 14.
5 I have borrowed this title from the classic study by Simone de Beauvoir: *The Second Sex*, see: http://www.nytimes.com/2010/05/30/books/excerpt-introduction-second-sex.html (accessed on 14 December 2017).
6 Tuğ 2012.
7 Compare for example: Meriwether 1999.
8 Canatar 2004, pp. XXXIII–XL; Kuyulu 1992, pp. VII–IX.
9 Meriwether 1999, p. 129.
10 Faroqhi 2002, pp. 167–78.
11 Evliya Çelebi 2006, p. 262.
12 See Fleischer 2008–09 for the misadventures of an Ottoman woman who upon the orders of Sultan Selim I (r. 1512–20) had travelled a short distance on Anatolian roads with a significant sum of money. The sultan wanted to prove that the roads were so secure that such travel was feasible. However, he had been far too optimistic.
13 Faroqhi 1987, pp. 104–6.
14 Dalsar 1960, p. 320.
15 Ballian 2011, p.156. My sincere thanks go to Anna Ballian, who not only gave me this catalogue but also pointed out the importance of the Eğin inscription.
16 Yılmaz 2017.
17 Faroqhi 2002, pp. 245–63.
18 Bornstein-Makovetsky published online: 2010, accessed on 3 January 2018.

19 Valensi 1969.
20 Jennings 1973 and 1975.
21 See: Canatar 2004, pp. XXXIII–XL for a list of the women who had established Istanbul pious foundations between the mid-fifteenth and the late sixteenth centuries.
22 Baer 1984.
23 Duman 1998, p. 204.
24 Prasad Sahai 2006, pp. 35, 89–97.
25 Moosvi reprint 2008c; see Hasan 2004, pp. 71–90 for a broadly based treatment.
26 Moosvi reprint 2008c.
27 Montagu ed. Desai and Jack 1994, p. 72.
28 Bano 2008.
29 Ibid., p. 409.
30 Hasan 2004, p. 85.
31 Ibid., pp. 71–90.
32 Among others, see Ergene 2003.
33 Hasan 2004, p. 89.
34 Moosvi 2008f, p. 153.
35 Bano 2002, p. 320.
36 Binark et alii eds. 1993, p. 640, No. 1478.
37 Toledano 1982, pp. 188–9; Peirce 2014 contains a case of a father selling his daughter.
38 Bano 2001, p. 369.
39 Prasad Sahai 2006, pp. 89–90.
40 Ibid., p. 90.
41 Ibid., p. 91.
42 Chakraverty 2008, p. 30 (many pages not numbered).
43 Natif 2018, pp. 89–109.
44 Moosvi 2008f, p. 138.
45 I saw women with spindles in small towns of western Anatolia when travelling through the area in the 1960s. In the 1970s, antique dealers in Ankara occasionally sold spinning wheels, unfortunately too pricey for my budget.
46 Evliya Çelebi 2007, p. 195.
47 Tucker 1985, p. 81.
48 Faroqhi 1984, p. 279.
49 While we do not have any evidence for the period under discussion, Maloni 2015 has discussed a case of this type for the later nineteenth century.
50 Beldiceanu Steinherr 1961; G. Yılmaz 2009; Barkan 1972–9, pp. 108–31.
51 See Faroqhi 2017 for a survey of the literature, mostly concerning Ottoman domestic slavery. About half of the eighty-odd titles used in this text have appeared in and after the year 2000. Regrettably Sel Turhan 2018 appeared too late for inclusion in the present work.
52 Zilfi 2010. I owe the observations on Trabzon to an unfortunately anonymous oral comment at the 22nd CIÉPO in Sofia (September 2018).
53 Moustakas 2015, İnalcık reprint 1985c, p. 84.
54 I owe this information to a letter from Shadab Banu. Similarly, İnalcık had connected the unpopularity of rice cultivation with the harsh working conditions and the dangers of infection.
55 Sahillioğlu reprint 1999, p. 127. The original appeared in 1985.
56 Faroqhi 2014b.
57 Dávid and Fodor eds. 2007.
58 Marmara 2005; Nalçacı 2015.

59 Heberer von Bretten reprint 1967.
60 Bono 1999.
61 Quakatz 2011.
62 Faroqhi 2005a.
63 Faroqhi 2005b; Sofroni 2016.
64 On Ottoman eunuchs, see Hathaway 2005 and 2018.
65 Sahillioğlu reprint 1999, p. 134.
66 Tezcan 2007.
67 Levy 2002, pp. 62–71.
68 Ibid., p. 64.
69 Ibid., p. 62.
70 On Ottoman *pencik* figures from around 1500, see Sahillioğlu reprint 1999, pp. 132–3.
71 Levy 2002, pp. 62–71.
72 Bano 2002.
73 Levy 2002, p. 64, note 204.
74 Hambly 1974; Bano 2009.
75 Bano 2002.
76 Sahillioğlu reprint 1999, p. 140.
77 Bano 2001, p. 372, note 31.
78 Chatterjee and Eaton eds. 2006.
79 Machado 2009 and 2014.
80 This miniature is now in The Freer-Sackler Collection in Washington DC. https://www.freersackler.si.edu/object/jahangir-shooting-the-head-of-malik-ambar/#object-content (accessed on 30 December 2017). Compare Eaton 2005, p. 121 and Omar Ali 2016.
81 Habib reprint 2010, p. 177.
82 Faroqhi 2009a, p. 30.
83 See the section 'Caste' of the article on 'India' in the *Encyclopedia Brittanica*, online version: authored by Stanley A. Wolpert, Romila Thapar and others: https://www.britannica.com/place/India/Caste#ref487279 (accessed on 30 December 2017).
84 Richards 1993, p. 213.
85 Prasad Sahai 2006, pp. 106–12.
86 Roy 2008.
87 Nadri 2009, pp. 27–8.
88 Sariyannis 2008; for the Istanbul underworld in general see Sariyannis 2006. I have borrowed the expression 'off the straight path' from the title of Semerdjian 2008.
89 Tamdoğan undated.
90 Tamdoğan undated; Semerdjian 2008, pp. 119–29.
91 Compare, however, Sahillioğlu reprint 1999, p. 155 on female slaves trained as dancers and singers and their often very high prices.
92 Sharma 2007, p. 299; she has used a statement by Irfan Habib.
93 Bano 2011, p. 47.
94 Ibid.
95 Montagu 1994, p. 88.
96 Sharma 2007, p. 302.
97 For a relevant miniature by the eighteenth-century artist Levni, see Atıl 1999, p. 159.
98 Sharma 2007, p. 299.

99 Bano 2011, p. 50.
100 Streusand 2011, p. 252.
101 Eaton 2005, p. 177 quotes a statement by Tarabai (1675–1761). If a verbatim quote from this princess survives, perhaps some evidence on her female entourage is extant as well.

Conclusion

1 İnalcık 1954.
2 Düzdağ 1972, p. 101.
3 Habib 1999, p. 370.
4 Richard Eaton, private communication.
5 Levy 2002, p. 66.
6 Barkan reprint 1980.
7 Chatterjee 2009, p. 94.
8 Richards 1993, pp. 82–90.
9 Gommans 2002, pp. 67–98.
10 Barkey 1994, pp. 164–5, 196–7.
11 Murphey 2008, p. 11.
12 Lowry 2003, pp. 97–110.
13 Çıpa 2017, pp. 230–3.
14 İnalcık 1965b.
15 Baer 2008, pp. 185–208.
16 Raychaudhuri 1982, p. 188.
17 Chandra 1969; Richard Eaton, personal communication. My thanks to Richard Eaton for making me aware of Chandra's article.
18 At least in the late 1700s and early 1800s, the exportation of Indian cottons and the importation of African slaves were in close connection: Machado 2009, pp. 77–9. On a smaller scale, this exchange had occurred in earlier periods as well: Eaton 2005, p. 109.
19 On Ottoman luxuries in Europe, currently a very popular topic, see Atasoy and Uluç 2012.
20 Kütükoğlu 1983.
21 Tietze 1979, 1982, vol. 1, pp. 61–2 and 155–7.
22 On this issue, we await the MA thesis by Özge Nur Yıldırım, currently in preparation.
23 For an exception, see Milstein 1989.
24 Moosvi 2015, p. 278.
25 Levy 2002; Dale 2010; Banerji 2011.
26 Dale 1994; Sood 2016, pp. 1–5.
27 Bergasse and Rambert 1954, pp. 64–70.
28 Pedani Fabris 2008.
29 Braudel 1985, vol. 2, 157.
30 Stoianovich 1960.
31 Raymond 1973–4, vol. 1, p. 117.
32 Maloni 2015, p. 277. A merchant named Ahmad Chelabi had surrounded himself with a number of Rumis, thus maintaining his ties to 'the old country'.
33 Faroqhi 1991.
34 Habib 1999 and Gupta 1986. The literature on Ottoman villages based on tax registers is by now enormous, as examples see İslamoğlu İnan 1994 and Singer 1994.

35 Dale 2010, pp. 107–8. Thomas Coryat, who visited India during the reign of Jahāngīr, claimed that the Mughal emperor had 40 million crowns of annual revenues, while those of the Ottoman sultan were no more than 15 million. While the eccentric traveller supposedly had gathered the latter titbit in Istanbul, we have no idea as to his source: Coryat edited by Foster 1921, p. 246. My thanks go to Richard Eaton for pointing out this text.
36 Habib 1999, see the Table of Contents.
37 Richards 1993, pp. 66–71, 85.
38 Özel 2016, p. 150 and elsewhere.
39 İslamoğlu İnan 1994, pp. 172, 243–9.
40 Moosvi reprint 2008c; Hasan 2004, pp. 71–90.
41 Rozen 2018; Hasan 2004, pp. 71–90.
42 Hasan 2004, p. 89.
43 Tuğ 2012.
44 Interestingly, a government-sponsored poster visible in Istanbul a few years ago stated that men who beat women are not 'real' men.
45 For a recent example, see Yaşa 2014.
46 Bano 2001, p. 366.
47 Compare the articles by Shadab Bano.
48 Tezcan 2012.
49 Unfortunately, Zarinebaf 2018 appeared too late for inclusion in this study.
50 Adanır 1982.
51 Esmer 2014.
52 Sofroni 2016.
53 M. Athar Ali 2008, at p. 338.
54 Sabev 2006.
55 While Habib 2008 appeared long after the death of M. Athar Ali, we can assume that the two scholars, who were friends, had had many discussions on this subject. On Indian models for European textile manufacture, see Riello 2009, pp. 337–43.
56 M. Athar Ali 2008, at p. 341; Datta 2014.
57 Habib 1999.
58 Streusand 2011, p. 284.
59 Alam 1986 and 2013. I am grateful to the author for sending me a copy of the new Introduction.

Bibliography

As many source editions contain long introductory essays and certain secondary works have sizeable documentary appendixes, distinguishing the line between the two categories is to some extent arbitrary. A few publications dealing with subjects outside the Ottoman and Mughal orbits appear in the section 'The Ottoman world: Secondary sources' because their number was too small for a separate section.

Studies relevant to both empires

Anooshahr, Ali (2009). *The Ghazi Sultans and the Frontiers of Islam: A Comparative Study of the Late Medieval and Early Modern Periods* (London, New York: Routledge).

Dale, Stephen F. (2010). *The Muslim Empires of the Ottomans, Safavids, and Mughals* (Cambridge: Cambridge University Press).

Hodgson, Marshall (1974). *The Venture of Islam: Conscience and History in a World Civilization* (Chicago: The University of Chicago Press), vol. 3, *The Gunpowder Empires and Modern Times*.

Matthee, Rudi (2011). *Persia in Crisis: Safavid Decline and the Fall of Isfahan* (London: I. B. Tauris).

Robinson, Francis (1997). 'Ottomans-Safavids-Mughals: Shared Knowledge and Connective Systems,' *Journal of Islamic Studies*, 8, 2, 151–84.

Streusand, Douglas (2010). *Islamic Gunpowder Empires: Ottomans, Safavids and Mughals* (Boulder, CO: Westview Press).

Subrahmanyam, Sanjay (2018a). 'Mughals, Ottomans and Habsburgs: Some Comparisons,' in idem, *Empires between Islam and Christianity 1500–1800* (Delhi: Permanent Black and Ashoka University), pp. 149–85.

Subrahmanyam, Sanjay (2018b). 'Introduction: Revisiting Empires and Connecting Histories,' in idem, *Empires between Islam and Christianity 1500–1800* (Delhi: Permanent Black and Ashoka University), pp. 1–25.

The Ottoman World: Primary sources, written and pictorial

Ali Efendi, Moralı Seyyid and Abdurrahim Muhibb Efendi (1998). *Deux Ottomans à Paris sous le Directoire et l'Empire. Relations d'ambassades*, translated by Stéphane Yérasmos (Arles and Paris: Actes Sud).

Atıl, Esin (1986). *Süleymanname: The Illustrated History of Süleyman the Magnificent* (Washington, New York: National Gallery of Art and Harry N. Abrams Inc.).

Atıl, Esin (1999). *Levni and the Surnâme. The Story of an Eighteenth-Century Ottoman Festival* (Istanbul: Koçbank).

Aynur, Hatice and Hakan T. Karateke (1995). *Aç Besmeleyle İç Suyu Han Ahmed'e Eyle Dua: III. Ahmed Devri İstanbul Çeşmeleri* (Istanbul: İstanbul Büyükşehir Belediyesi Kültür İşleri Daire Başkanlığı).

Ayverdi, Ekrem Hakkı (2006). *18. Asırda Lâle*, edited by M. Uğur Derman (Istanbul: Kubbealtı Neşriyatı).

Barkan, Ömer Lütfi (1941–42), (1943), (1943). 'XV. Asrın Sonunda Bazı Büyük Şehirlerde Eşya ve Yiyecek Fiyatlarının Tesbit ve Teftiş Hususlarını Tanzim Eden Kanunlar,' *Tarih Vesikaları*. I/5, 326–40; II/9, 15–40; II/9, 168–77.

Barkan, Ömer Lütfi and Ekrem Ayverdi eds. (1970). *İstanbul vakıfları tahrîr defteri, 953 (1546) tarîhli* (Istanbul: İstanbul Fetih Cemiyeti).

Binark, Ismet et alii eds. (1993). *3 Numaralı Mühimme Defteri (966–68/1558–60)*, 2 vols (Ankara: Başbakanlık Devlet Arşivleri Genel Müdürlüğü) vol. unnumbered: *Özet ve Transkripsiyon*.

Bohn, Thomas M., Adrian Gheorghe and Albert Weber eds. (2014). *Corpus Draculianum – Dokumente und Chroniken zum walachischen Fürsten Vlad der Pfähler: Band 3: Die Überlieferung aus dem Osmanischen Reich: Postbyzantinische und osmanische Autoren* (Wiesbaden/Germany: Harrassowitz).

Bojović, Boško (1998). *Raguse (Dubrovnik) et l'empire ottoman: (1430–1520) ; les actes impériaux ottomans en vieux-Serbe de Murad II à Selim Ier* (Paris: Éditions de l'Association Pierre Belon) (Textes, documents, études sur le monde byzantin, néohellénique et balkanique 3).

Busbequius, Augerius Gislenius (1994). *Legationis turcicae epistolae quatuor*, edited by Zweder von Martels, translated into Dutch by Michel Goldsteen (Hilversum: Verloren).

Canatar, Mehmet ed. (2004). *İstanbul Vakıfları Tahrîr Defteri 1009 (1600) Târîhli* (Istanbul: İstanbul Fetih Cemiyeti).

Cantemir, Demetrius (1734). *The History of the Growth and Decay of the Ottoman Empire*, translated by N. Tindal, 2 vols (London: John James & Paul Knapton).

Delilbaşı, Melek ed. and tr. (1989). *Johanis Anagnostis, 'Selânik (Thessaloniki)'nin Son Zabtı Hakkında Bir Tarih' (Sultan II. Murad Dönemine Ait Bir Bizans Kaynağı)* (Ankara: Türk Tarih Kurumu).

Demiriz, Yıldız (2005). *Osmanlı Kitap Sanatında Doğal Çiçekler* (Istanbul: Yorum Sanat).

Develi, Hayati ed. (1998). *XVIII. Yüzyıl İstanbul Hayatına dair* Risâle-i garîbe (Istanbul: Kitabevi).

Duran, Hamiye and Dursun Gümüşoğlu eds. (2011). *Hünkar Hacı Bektaş Veli Velayetnamesi* (Ankara: Gazi Üniversitesi Yayınları).

Düzdağ, Ertuğrul (1972). *Şeyhülislam Ebusuud Efendi Fetvaları Işığında 16. Asır Türk Hayatı* (Istanbul: Enderun).

Ebubekir Ratib Efendi (1999). *Ebubekir Ratib Efendi'nin Nemçe Sefaretnamesi*, edited by Abdullah Uçman (Istanbul: Kitabevi).

Evliya Çelebi (2001). *Evliya Çelebi Seyahatnâmesi, Topkapı Sarayı Bağdat 305 Yazmasının Transkripsyonu -Dizini*, vol. 1, edited by Orhan Şaik Gökyay et alii (Istanbul: Yapı Kredi Yayınları).

Evliya Çelebi (2005). *Evliya Çelebi Seyahatnâmesi, Topkapı Sarayı Kütüphanesi, Bağdat 306, Süleymaniye Kütüphanesi Pertev Paşa 462, Süleymaniye Kütüphanesi Hacı Beşir Ağa 452 Numaralı Yazmaların Mukayeseli Transkripsyonu Dizini*, vol. 9, edited by Seyit Ali Kahraman, Yücel Dağlı and Robert Dankoff, (Istanbul: Yapı Kredi Yayınları).

Evliya Çelebi (2006). *Evliya Çelebi Seyahatnâmesi, Topkapı Sarayı Bağdat 304 Yazmasının Transkripsyonu -Dizini*, vol. 1, edited by Robert Dankoff, Seyit Ali Kahraman and Yücel Dağlı (Istanbul: Yapı Kredi Yayınları).

Evliya Çelebi (2007). *Evliya Çelebi Seyahatnâmesi, İstanbul Üniversitesi Kütüphanesi Türkçe Yazmalar 5973, Süleymaniye Kütüphanesi Pertev Paşa 462 Süleymaniye Kütüphanesi Hacı Beşir Ağa 452 Numaralı Yazmaların Mukayeseli Transkripsyonu Dizini*, vol. 10, edited by Seyit Ali Kahraman, Yücel Dağlı and Robert Dankoff (Istanbul: Yapı Kredi Yayınları).

Felek, Özgen ed. (2012). *Kitābü'l-Menāmāt: Sultan III. Murad'ın Rüya Mektupları* (Istanbul: Tarih Vakfı Yurt Yayınları).

Fotopoulos, Dionissis and Angelos Delivorrias (1997). *Greece at the Benaki Museum*, translated by John Leatham (Athens: Benaki Museum).

Galland, Antoine (2000). *Le voyage à Smyrne: Un manuscrit d'Antoine Galland (1678)*, edited by Frédéric Bauden (Paris: Chandeigne).

Heberer von Bretten, Johann Michael (reprint 1967). *Aegyptiaca Servitus*, introduction by Karl Teply (Graz: Akademische Druck- und Verlagsanstalt).

İnalcık, Halil (2012). *The Survey of Istanbul 1455 – The Text, English Translation, Analysis of the Text, Documents* (Istanbul: İş Bankası Kültür Yayınları).

Kahraman, Seyit Ali (2015). *Şükufename: Osmanlı Dönemi Çiçek Kitapları* (Istanbul: İstanbul Büyükşehir Belediyesi).

Kangal, Selmin et al. eds. (2000). *The Sultan's Portrait: Picturing the House of Osman* (Istanbul: Türkiye İş Bankası)

Koch, H. A. ed. *Das Kostümbuch von Lambert de Vos: vollstaendige Faksimile-Ausgabe im Originalformat des Codex Ms. or. 9 aus dem Besitz der Staats- und Universitaetsbibliothek Bremen*, 2 vols (Graz/Austria: Akademische Druck- und Verlagsanstalt).

Kołodziejczyk, Dariusz (2004). *Defter-i Mufassal-i Eyalet-i Kamanice: The Ottoman Survey Register of Podolia (ca. 1681)*, (Cambridge, MA: Harvard University Press).

Kreutel, Richard ed. and translator (1963). *Im Reiche des Goldenen Apfels: Des türkischen Weltenbummlers Evliya Çelebi denkwürdige Reise in das Giaurenland und in die Stadt und Festung Wien* (Graz, Vienna, Cologne: Verlag Styria).

Kut, Günay and Edhem Eldem eds. (2010). *Rumelihisarı Şehitlik Dergâhı Mezar Taşları* (Istanbul: Boğaziçi Üniversitesi Yayınları).

Membré, Michele (1993). *Mission to the Lord Sophy of Persia (1539–1542)*, edited and translated by A. H. Morton (London: School of Oriental and African Studies).

Montagu, Lady Mary Wortley (1994). *The Turkish Embassy Letters*, edited by Anita Desai and Malcolm Jack (London: Virago).

Naṣūḥü's-Silāḥī (Maṭrāḳçı) (1976). *Beyān-ı Menāzil-ı Sefer 'Iraḳeyn-i Sulṭān Süleymān Ḫān*, edited by Hüseyin Gazi Yurdaydın (Ankara: Türk Tarih Kurumu).

Öcalan, Hasan Basri, Sezai Sevim and Doğan Yavaş eds. (2013). *Bursa Vakfiyeleri I* (Bursa: Bursa Kültür A. Ş.)

Ölçer, Nazan et alii eds. (2010). *Treasures of the Aga Khan Museum: Arts of the Book and Calligraphy* (Istanbul: Sakip Sabancı Museum).

Piri Reis (1935). *Kitabı Bahriye*, edited by Haydar Alpagut and Fevzi Kurtoğlu (Istanbul: Türk Tarih Kurumu).

Pîrî Reis (2013). *Pîrî Reis Kitab-ı Bahriyye/ Piri Reis's Kitab-ı Bahriyye*, edited by Fikret Sarıcaoğlu (Ankara: T. C. Kültür ve Turizm Bakanlığı).

Recep, Fuat et alii eds. (2010). *İstanbul Kadı Sicilleri: İstanbul Mahkemesi, 24 Numaralı Sicil (H. 1138–1151/M. 1726–1738)* (Istanbul: İSAM).

Sofroni, Vraçalı (2016). *Osmanlı'da bir Papaz: Günahkâr Sofroni'nin Çileli Hayat Hikâyesi 1738–1813*, translated by Aziz Nazmi Şakir (Istanbul: Kitap Yayınevi).

Stchoukine, Ivan (1966). *La peinture turque d'après les manuscrits illustrés*, 2 vols. (Librairie Orientaliste Paul Geuthner), vol. 1 *De Sulaymān Ier à 'Osmān II 1520–1622*, vol. 2 *La peinture turque de Murād III à Muṣṭafā III.*

Tanındı, Zeren (1984), *Siyer-i Nebî: İslâm Tasvir Sanatında Hz. Muhammed'in Hayatı* (Istanbul: Hürriyet Vakfı Yayınları).

Tietze, Andreas ed. and translator (1979, 1982). *Muṣṭafā 'Ālī's Counsel for Sultans of 1581*, vols. 1 and 2 (Vienna: Österreichische Akademie der Wissenschaften).

Uçman, Abdullah ed. (1999). *Ebubekir Ratib Efendi'nin Nemçe Sefaretnamesi* (Istanbul: Kitabevi).

Unat, Faik Reşat (1941). 'Ahmed III. Devrinde Yapılmış bir Önasya Haritası,' *Tarih Vesikaları*, I/2, p. 160, and a map: not numbered.

Unat, Faik Reşat (1941–1942). 'Takriri Şehdi Osman Efendi Sene 1171: Cülûsi Humayun Tebşiri Devleti Rusya'ya Seferidir/Şehdi Osman Efendi Sefaretnamesi,' *Tarih Vesikaları*, 1, 1, 70–80; 1, 2, 156–59; 1, 3, 232–40; 1, 4, 303–20; 1, 5, 340–400.

Uzluk, Feridun Nafız ed. (1958). *Fatih Devrinde Karaman Eyâleti Vakıfları Fihristi: Tapu ve Kadastro Umum Müdürlüğü Arşivindeki Deftere Göre* (Ankara: Vakıflar Umum Müdürlüğü).

The Ottoman World: Secondary sources

Abd Al Raheim A. Abd Al Raheim (October 1975). 'Hazzal-Quḥūf': A New Source for the Study of the Fallāḥīn of Egypt in the XVIIth and XVIIIth Centuries,' *Journal of the Economic and Social History of the Orient*, 18/3, 245–70.

Abou-El-Haj, Rifa'at A. (1984). *The 1703 Rebellion and the Structure of Ottoman Politics* (Leiden: Nederlands Historisch-Archaeologisch Instituut te İstanbul).

Abou-El-Haj, Rifa'at A. (1991). *Formation of the Modern State: The Ottoman Empire, Sixteenth to Eighteenth Centuries* (Albany, NY: SUNY Press).

Adanır, Fikret (1982). 'Heiduckentum und osmanische Herrschaft: Sozialgeschichtliche Aspekte der Diskussion um das frühneuzeitliche Räuberwesen in Südosteuropa,' *Südost-Forschungen*, 41, 43–116.

Adanır, Fikret (reprint 2014). 'The Ottoman Peasantries c. 1360–c. 1860,' in idem, *Balkans: History and Historiography: Selected Studies I* (Istanbul: Eren Publications), pp. 159–220.

Afyoncu, Erhan (2013). 'Zeamet,' in *Türkiye Diyanet Vakfi Islâm Ansiklopedisi*, edited by M. Akif Aydin et alii (Istanbul: Türkiye Diyanet Vakfi), vol. 44, p. 62.

Ágoston, Gábor (2005). *Guns for the Sultan: Military Power and the Weapons Industry in the Ottoman Empire* (Cambridge: Cambridge University Press).

Akdağ, Mustafa (1963). *Celali İsyanları (1550–1603)* (Ankara: Ankara Üniversitesi).

Akın, Himmet (1968). *Aydın Oğulları Tarihi hakkında bir Araştırma* (Ankara: Ankara Dil ve Tarih-Coğrafya Fakültesi.

Aksan, Virginia H. (2007). *Ottoman Wars: An Empire Besieged 1700–1870* (Harlow: Pearson Longman).

Aktepe, Münir (1971). 'İzmir Hanları ve Çarşıları Hakkında Ön Bilgi,' *Tarih Dergisi*, 25, 105–54.

And, Metin (2004). *Osmanlı Tasvir Sanatları: 1 Minyatür* (Istanbul: Türkiye İş Bankası Kültür Yayınları).

And, Metin (2018). *Ottoman Figurative Arts 2: Bazaar Painters*, edited by Tülün Değirmenci and M. Sabri Koz (Istanbul: Yapı Kredi Yayınları).

Anonymous author, http://www.sacred-texts.com/hin/maha/ (accessed on 15 August 2016).

Anonymous author, https://en.wikipedia.org/wiki/Mahabharata#Accretion_and_redaction (accessed on 15 August 2016).

Anonymous author, https://www.google.co.in/webhp?sourceid=chrome-instant&ion=1&espv=2&ie=UTF-8#q=bengali%20language%20number%20of%20speakers (accessed on 15 August 2016).

Anonymous author (n. d., dictionary definition). 'Asiatic mode of production,' in Oxford Reference http://www.oxfordreference.com/view/10.1093/oi/authority.20110803095428735 (accessed on 15 October 2017).

Antov, Nikolay (2017). *The Ottoman 'Wild West': The Balkan Frontier in the Fifteenth and Sixteenth Centuries* (Cambridge: Cambridge University Press).

Arık, Rüçhan (2000). *Kubad Abad: Selçuklu Saray ve Çinileri* (Istanbul: Türkiye İş Bankası Kültür Yayınları).

Arjomand, Saïd Amir (2015). 'HODGSON, MARSHALL GOODWIN SIMMS,' *Encyclopædia Iranica,* online edition, 2015, available at http://www.iranicaonline.org/articles/hodgson-marshall (accessed on 3 September 2018).

Artan, Tülay (2010a). 'Ahmed I's Hunting Parties: Feasting in Adversity, Enhancing the Ordinary,' in *Starting with Food: Culinary Approaches to Ottoman History*, edited by Amy Singer (Princeton, NJ: Markus Wiener Publishers), pp. 93–138.

Artan, Tülay (2010b). 'Ahmed I and 'tuhfetü'l-mülûk ve's-selâtin': A Period Manuscript on Horses, Horsemanship and Hunting,' in *Animals and People in the Ottoman Empire*, edited by Suraiya Faroqhi (İstanbul: Eren Yayıncılık), pp. 235–69.

Artan, Tülay and İrvin Cemil Schick (2013). 'Ottomanizing Pornotopia: Changing Visual Codes in Eighteenth-century Ottoman Erotic Miniatures,' in *Eros and Sexuality in Islamic Art*, edited by Francesca Leoni and Mika Natif (Surrey, England: Ashgate Publishing), pp. 157–207.

Aščerić-Todd, Inez (April 2007). 'The Noble Traders: The Islamic Tradition of "Spiritual Chivalry" (*futuwwa*) in Bosnian Trade Guilds (Sixteenth–Nineteenth Centuries),' *The Muslim World*, 97, 159–73.

Asdrachas, Spyros I. et alii (2007). *Greek Economic History Fifteenth–Nineteenth Centuries*, translated and edited by Doolie Sloman, John Davis and Eftychia D. Liata (Athens/Greece: Piraeus Group Bank, Cultural Foundation).

Aslanian, Sebouh David (2011). *From the Indian Ocean to the Mediterranean: The Global Trade Networks of Armenian Merchants from New Julfa* (Berkeley: University of California Press).

Atasoy, Nurhan and Julian Raby (1989). *Iznik: The Pottery of Ottoman Turkey* (London: Alexandria Press and Laurence King).

Atasoy, Nurhan and Lale Uluç (2012). *Impressions of Ottoman Culture in Europe: 1453–1699* (Istanbul: Armaggan Yayınları and The Turkish Cultural Foundation).

Aubin, Jean (1963). 'Comment Tamerlan prenait les villes,' *Studia Islamica*, 19, 83–122.

Ayalon, Yaron (2015). *Natural Disasters in the Ottoman Empire: Plague, Famine, and Other Misfortunes* (Cambridge: Cambridge University Press).

Aynural, Salih (2001). *İstanbul Değirmenleri ve Fırınları: Zahire Ticareti (1740–1840)* (Istanbul: Tarih Vakfı Yurt Yayınları).

Aynural, Salih (2005). 'The Millers and Bakers of Istanbul,' in *Crafts and Craftsmen of the Middle East: Fashioning the Individual in the Muslim Mediterranean*, edited by Suraiya Faroqhi and Randi Deguilhem (London: I. B. Tauris), pp. 153–94.

Babinger, Franz (1982). *Osmanlı Tarih Yazarları ve Eserleri*, translated with supplementary information by Coşkun Üçok (Ankara: Ministry of Culture and Tourism).

Bacqué-Grammont, Jean-Louis (1981). 'Un plan inédit de Van au XVIIe siècle,' *Osmanlı Araştırmaları*, II, 97–122.

Bacqué Grammont, Jean Louis (1999). 'La fonderie de canons d'Istanbul et le quartier de Tophane. Texte et images commentés, I. La description de Tophane par Evliyâ Çelebi,' *Anatolia Moderna*, 8, 3–42.

Baer, Gabriel (reprint 1982). 'Shirbīnī's Hazz al-Quḥūf and its Significance,' in idem, *Fellah and Townsman in the Middle East: Studies in Social History* (London: Frank Cass), pp. 3–48.

Baer, Gabriel (1984). 'Women and Waqf: An Analysis of the Istanbul *tahrîr* of 1546,' in *Studies in Islamic Society: Contributions in Memory of Gabriel Baer*, edited by Gabriel A. Warburg and Gad G. Gilbar (Haifa: Haifa University Press), pp. 9–28.

Baer, Marc David (2008). *Honoured by the Glory of Islam: Conversion and Conquest in Ottoman Europe* (Oxford: Oxford University Press).

Bağcı, Serpil, Filiz Çağman, Günsel Renda and Zeren Tanındı (2006). *Osmanlı Resim Sanatı* (Istanbul: T. C. Kültür ve Turizm Bakanlığı).

Bağış, Ali Ihsan (1983). *Osmanlı Ticaretinde Gayri Müslimler, Kapitülasyonlar, Beratlı Tüccarlar ve Hayriye Tüccarları (1750–1839)* (Ankara: Turhan Kitabevi).

Ballian, Anna (2011). 'Epitaphios from Eğin/Kemaliye,' in *Relics of the Past: Treasures of the Greek Orthodox Church and the Population Exchange/ The Benaki Museum Collection/ Reliques du passé: Trésors de l'Église orthodoxe grecque et l'Échange de population/ Les collections du Musée Benaki*, exhibition catalogue, edited by Anna Ballian (Athens and Milan: Benaki Museum and Five Continents Editions), pp. 156–7.

Barbir, Karl K. (1980). *Ottoman Rule in Damascus 1708–1758* (Princeton: Princeton University Press).

Barbir, Karl K. (2007). 'One Marker of Ottomanism: Confiscation of Ottoman Officials' Estates,' in *Identity and Identity Formation in the Ottoman World: A Volume of Essays in Honor of Norman Itzkowitz*, edited by Baki Tezcan and Karl K. Barbir (Madison, WI: The Center for Turkish Studies at the University of Wisconsin and The University of Wisconsin Press), pp. 135–46.

Barkan, Ömer Lûtfi (1970). 'XVI. Asrın İkinci Yarısında Türkiye'de Fiyat Hareketleri,' *Belleten* XXXIV, 136, 557–608.

Barkan, Ömer Lütfi (1972–9). *Süleymaniye Cami ve Imareti Inşaatı 1550–57*, 2 vols. (Ankara: Türk Tarih Kurumu).

Barkan, Ömer Lûtfi (1975). '"The Price Revolution" of the Sixteenth Century: A Turning Point in the Economic History of the Near East,' *International Journal of Middle East Studies*, VI, 3–28.

Barkan, Ömer Lütfi (1980). *Türkiye'de Toprak Meselesi* (Istanbul: Gözlem Yayınları).

Barkan, Ömer Lütfi (reprint 1980). 'Türkiye'de "Servaj" Var mıydı?,' in idem, *Türkiye'de Toprak Meselesi* (Istanbul: Gözlem Yayınları), pp. 717–24.

Başaran, Betül (2014). *Between Crisis and Order: Selim III, Social Control and Policing in Istanbul at the End of the Eighteenth Century* (Leiden: Brill).

Bayerle, Gustav (1980). 'The Compromise at Zsitvatorok,' *Archivum Ottomanicum*, 6, 5–53.

Beldiceanu Steinherr, Irène (1961). *Scheich Üftāde der Begründer des Ǧelvetijje Ordens* (Munich: n. p.)

Beldiceanu Steinherr, Irène (1971). 'La Vita de Seyyid 'Alî Sultan et la conquête de la Thrace par les Turcs,' in *Proceedings of the 27th International Congress of Orientalists, Ann Arbor, 1967*, edited by Denis Sinor (Wiesbaden: Harassowitz), pp. 275–6.

Bérenger, Jean (ca. 2006). 'Le traité de Versailles et le renversement des alliances.' https://francearchives.fr/commemo/recueil-2006/39551 (accessed on 25 January 2018).

Berg, Maxine (1999). 'New Commodities, Luxuries and their Consumers in Eighteenth-century England,' in *Consumers and Luxury: Consumer Culture in Europe 1650–1850*, edited by Maxine Berg and Helen Clifford (Manchester University Press), pp. 63–85.

Bergasse, Louis and Gaston Rambert (1954). *Histoire du commerce de Marseille*, vol 4, *Le commerce de Marseille de 1599 à 1660* (Paris: Plon).

Berktay, Halil (1987). 'The Feudalism Debate: The Turkish End: Is "Tax-vs.-Rent" Necessarily the Product and Sign of a Modal Difference?,' *The Journal of Peasant Studies*, 14/3, 291–333.

Berktay, Halil (1992). 'The Search for the Peasant in Western and Turkish History/ Historiography,' in *New Approaches to State and Peasant in Ottoman History*, edited by Halil Berktay and Suraiya Faroqhi, *The Journal of Peasant Studies* (London: Frank Cass), pp. 109–84.

Bilgin, Arif (2006). *Bursa Hassa Harç Eminliği* (Istanbul: Kitabevi).

Bir, Attila, M. Şinasi Acar and Mustafa Kaçar (2012). *Anadolu'nun Değirmenleri* (Istanbul: Yem Yayın).

Bölükbaşı, Ömerül Faruk (2013). *18. Yüzyılın İkinci Yarısında Darphane-i amire* (Istanbul: Istanbul Bilgi University).

Bono, Salvatore (1999). *Schiavi musulmani nell' Italia moderna, Galeotti, vu' cumprà, domestici* (Naples: Edizioni Scientifiche Italiane).

Börekçi, Günhan (2006). 'A Contribution to the Military Revolution Debate: The Janissaries' Use of Volley Fire during the Long Ottoman–Habsburg War of 1593–1606 and the Problem of Origins,' *Acta Orientalia Academiae Scientiarum Hungaricae*, 59, 4, 407–38. https://www.academia.edu/259539/A_Contribution_to_the_Military_Revolution_Debate_The_Janissaries_Use_of_Volley_Fire_during_the_Long_Ottoman-Habsburg_War_of_1593-1606_and_the_Problem_of_Origins (accessed on 26 August 2018).

Bornstein-Makovetsky, Leah (First published online: 2010). 'Malchi (Malkhi) Esperanza,' in *Encyclopedia of Jews in the Islamic World*, Executive Editor Norman A. Stillman. http://referenceworks.brillonline.com/entries/encyclopedia-of-jews-in-the-islamic-world/malchi-malkhi-esperanza-SIM_0014470?s.num=0&s.f.s2_parent=s.f.book.encyclopedia-of-jews-in-the-islamic-world&s.q=esperanza+malchi (Consulted online on 3 January 2018).

Braudel, Fernand (1966). *La Méditerranée et le monde méditerranéen à l'époque de Philippe II*, 2nd edition, 2 vols. (Paris: Armand Colin).

Braudel, Fernand (1979). *Civilisation matérielle, économie et capitalisme,* 3 vols. (Paris: Armand Colin), vol. 2 *Les jeux de l'échange*, vol. 3, *Le temps du monde*.

Braudel, Fernand (1982–5). *Civilization and Capitalism: 15th to 18th Centuries*, 3 vols. translated by Siân Reynolds (New York: Harper and Row) vol. 1 *The Structures of Everyday Life: The Limits of the Possible*, vol. 2 *The Wheels of Commerce*, vol. 3 *The Perspective of the World*.

Brentjes, Sonia (2012). 'The Presence of Ancient Secular and Religious Texts in Pietro della Valle's (1586–1652) Unpublished and Printed Writings,' in *Iran and the World in the Safavid Age*, edited by Willem Floor and Edmund Herzig (London: I.B. Tauris), pp. 327–45.

Bulliet, Richard (1975). *The Camel and the Wheel* (New York: Columbia University Press).

Çadırcı, Musa (2011). *Tanzimat sürecinde Türkiye: Anadolu Kentleri*, edited by Tülay Ercoşkun (Ankara: İmge Kitabevi).

Çağman, Filiz (2016). *Osmanlı Sarayı Tasvir Sanatı* (Istanbul: Masa Yayınları).

Calic, Marie Janine (2016). *Südosteuropa: Weltgeschichte einer Region* (Munich: C. H. Beck).

Camariano, Nestor (1970). *Alexandre Mavrocordato, le Grand Drogman, son activité diplomatique (1673–1709)* (Thessaloniki: Institute for Balkan Studies).

Casale, Giancarlo (2010). *The Ottoman Age of Exploration* (New York: Oxford University Press).

Casale, Giancarlo (2013). 'Seeing the Past: Maps and Ottoman Historical Consciousness,' in *Writing History at the Ottoman Court: Editing the Past, Shaping the Future*, edited by H. Erdem Çıpa and Emine Fetvacı (Bloomington and Indianapolis: Indiana University Press), pp. 80–99.

Castellan, Georges (1991). *Histoire des Balkans XIVe–XXe siècle: Édition augmentée* (Paris: Fayard).

Çelik, Semih (2017). 'Scarcity and Misery at the time of "Abundance beyond Imagination". Climate Change, Famines and Empire-Building in Ottoman Anatolia (c. 1800–1850),' unpublished PhD thesis, European University Institute, Florence-Fiesole.

Cezar, Yavuz (1986). *Osmanlı Maliyesinde Bunalım ve Değişim Dönemi: XVIII. yy'dan Tanzimat'a Mali Tarih* (Istanbul: Alan Yayıncılık).

Chew, Samuel C. (1937). *The Crescent and the Rose: Islam and England during the Renaissance* (Oxford: Oxford University Press).

Chong, Alan (2005). 'Gentile Bellini in Istanbul: Myths and Misunderstandings,' in *Bellini and the East*, edited by Caroline Campbell et alii (London: National Gallery Company Limited), pp. 106–29.

Cillov, Halûk (1949). *Denizli El Dokumacılığı Sanayii* (Istanbul: Istanbul Üniversitesi İktisat Fakültesi).

Çıpa, H. Erdem (2017). *The Making of Selim: Succession, Legitimacy and Memory in the Early Modern Ottoman World* (Bloomington, IN: Indiana University Press).

Çizakça, Murat (1996). *A Comparative Evolution of Business Partnerships: The Islamic World and Europe, with specific reference to the Ottoman archives* (Leiden: E. J. Brill).

Çizakça, Murat (2013). 'The Economy,' in *The Cambridge History of Turkey*, vol. 2, edited by Suraiya Faroqhi and Kate Fleet (Cambridge, New York: Cambridge University Press), pp. 241–75.

Çizakça, Murat and M. Macit Kenanoğlu (2008). 'Ottoman Merchants and the Jurisprudential Shift Hypothesis,' in *Merchants in the Ottoman Empire*, edited by Suraiya Faroqhi and Gilles Veinstein (Leuven: Peeters), Collection Turcica vol. XV, pp. 195–215.

Cornelissen, Marloes (2015). 'The Trials and Tribulations of a Dutch Merchant in Istanbul: Auctions at the Dutch Embassy in the Eighteenth-century Ottoman Capital,' in *Osmanlı İstanbul'u III: III. Uluslararası Osmanlı İstanbulu Sempozyumu Bildirileri*, edited by Feridun Emecen, Ali Akyıldız and Emrah Safa Gürkan, 25–26 Mayıs 2015, İstanbul 29 Mayıs Üniversitesi (Istanbul: İstanbul 29 Mayıs Üniversitesi and İstanbul Büyükşehir Belediyesi), pp. 623–50. Accessed through https://wwwsabanciuniv.academia.edu/MarloesCornelissen (13 May 2017).

Costantini, Vera (2001). 'Il commercio veneziano ad Aleppo nel Settecento,' *Studi Veneziani*, 42, 143–211.

Çulpan, Cevdet (2002). *Türk Taş Köprüleri: Ortaçağdan Osmanlı Devri sonuna kadar* (Ankara: TTK).

Dalsar, Fahri (1960). *Türk Sanayi ve Ticaret Tarihinde Bursa'da İpekçilik* (Istanbul: İstanbul Üniversitesi İktisat Fakültesi).

Dankoff, Robert (2006). *An Ottoman Mentality: The World of Evliya Çelebi* (Leiden: Brill).

Darling, Linda (1996). *Revenue-raising and Legitimacy: Tax Collection and Finance Administration in the Ottoman Empire, 1560–1660* (Leiden: Brill).

Darling, Linda (2012). *A History of Social Justice and Political Power in the Middle East: The Circle of Justice from Mesopotamia to Globalization* (London: Routledge).

Dávid, Géza (2013). 'Ottoman Armies and Warfare, 1453–1603,' in *The Cambridge History of Turkey*, vol. 2, edited by Suraiya Faroqhi and Kate Fleet (Cambridge: Cambridge University Press, 2013), pp. 276–319.

Dávid, Géza and Pál Fodor eds. (2007). *Ransom Slavery along the Ottoman Borders (Early Fifteenth to Early Eighteenth Centuries)* (Leiden: Brill).

Davis, Nathalie Zemon (1987). *Fiction in the Archives: Pardon Tales and Their Tellers in Sixteenth-century France* (Stanford, CA: Stanford University Press).

Davis, Ralph (1967). *Aleppo and Devonshire Square: English Traders in the Levant in the Eighteenth Century* (London, Melbourne and Toronto: Macmillan and Co. Ltd.)

Değirmenci, Tülün (2012). *İktidar Oyunları ve Resimli Kitaplar: II. Osman Devrinde Değişen Güç Sembolleri* (Istanbul: Kitap Yayınevi).

Demirci, Süleyman (2009). *The Functioning of Ottoman* Avârız *Taxation. An Aspect of the Relationship between Centre and Periphery: A Case Study of the Province of Karaman, 1621–1700* (Istanbul: The Isis Press).

Denny, Walter B. (1970). 'A Sixteenth-Century Architectural Plan of Istanbul,' *Ars Orientalis*, 8, 49–63.

Derziotis, Lazaros (2007). *Holy Monastery of Great Meteoron, Transfiguration of Christ the Savior-Holy Meteora: Byzantine Painting, Icons and Frescoes* (Trikala/Greece: Protype Thessalian Editions).

Divitçioğlu, Sencer (1971). *Asya Üretim Tarzı ve Osmanlı Toplumu* (Istanbul: Köz).

Doğanalp-Votzi, Heidemarie (1997). *Der Gerber, der Kulturbringer, Politik, Ökonomie, Zivilisation im osmanischen Vorderasien* (Frankfurt: Peter Lang).

Doğanalp Votzi, Heidemarie (2005). 'Histories and Economies of a Small Anatolian Town: Safranbolu and its Leather Handicrafts,' in *Crafts and Craftsmen of the Middle East, Fashioning the Individual in the Muslim Mediterranean*, edited by Suraiya Faroqhi and Randi Deguilhem (London: I. B. Tauris), pp. 308–37.

Duindam, Jeroen (2016). *Dynasties: A Global History of Power, 1300–1800* (Cambridge: Cambridge University Press).

Duman, Yüksel (1998). 'Textiles and Copper in Ottoman Tokat 1750–1840,' unpublished PhD dissertation, Binghamton University/State University of New York.

Ebel, Kathryn A. (2008). 'Representations of the Frontier in Ottoman Town Views of the Sixteenth Century,' *Imago Mundi*, 60/1, 1–22.

Eickhoff, Ekkehard (2. ed. 1988). *Venedig, Wien und die Osmanen, Umbruch in Südosteuropa 1645–1700* (Stuttgart: Klett-Cotta).

Eldem, Edhem (1999). *French Trade in Istanbul in the Eighteenth Century* (Leiden: Brill).

Eldem, Edhem (2007). 'Urban Voices from Beyond: Identity, Status and Social Strategies in Ottoman Muslim Funerary Epitaphs of Istanbul (1700–1850),' in *The Early Modern Ottomans: Remapping the Empire*, edited by Virginia Aksan and Daniel Goffman (Cambridge: Cambridge University Press), pp. 233–55.

Eldem, Edhem (September 2013). 'Hayretü'l-azime fi intihalati'l-garibe: Voltaire ve Şanizade Mehmed Ataullah Efendi,' *Toplumsal Tarih*, 237, 18–28.

Eldem, Edhem, Daniel Goffman and Bruce Masters (2005). *The Ottoman City between East and West: Aleppo, Izmir and Istanbul* (Cambridge; Cambridge University Press).

Elliot, Matthew (2004). 'Dress Codes in the Ottoman Empire: The Case of the Franks,' in *Ottoman Costumes: From Textile to Identity*, edited by Suraiya Faroqhi and Christoph Neumann (Istanbul: Eren), pp. 103–24.

Emecen, Feridun (1992). 'Balat,' in *TDV İslâm Ansiklopedisi*, vol. 5, pp. 4–7. http://www.islamansiklopedisi.info/dia/ayrmetin.php?idno=050007 (accessed on 26 November 2017).

Emecen, Feridun (n. d.) 'Makbul İbrâhim Paşa,' in *TDV İslâm Ansiklopedisi*. http://www.islamansiklopedisi.info/dia/pdf/c21/c210260.pdf (accessed on 23 September 2018).

Emiralioğlu, Pınar (2014). *Geographical Knowledge and Imperial Culture in the Early Modern Ottoman Empire* (Farnham/Surrey and Burlington, VT: Ashgate).

Erdem, Hakan (1996). *Slavery in the Ottoman Empire and its Demise 1800–1909* (Houndsmills, Basingstoke and New York: Palgrave).

Eren, Meşkûre (1960). *Evliya Çelebi Seyahatnâmesi Birinci Cildinin Kaynakları Üzerinde bir Araştırma* (Istanbul: n.p.)

Ergenç, Özer (1995). *XVI. Yüzyılda Ankara ve Konya: Osmanlı klasik dönemi kent tarihçiliğine katkı* (Ankara: Ankara Enstitüsü Vakfı Yayınları).

Ergenç, Özer (2006). *XVI. Yüzyılın Sonlarında Bursa* (Ankara: Türk Tarih Kurumu).

Ergene, Boğaç (2002). 'Costs of Court Usage in Seventeenth- and Eighteenth-Century Ottoman Anatolia: Court Fees as Recorded in Estate Inventories,' *Journal of Economic and Social History of the Orient*, 45/1, 20–39.

Ergene, Boğaç (2003). *Local Court, Provincial Society and Justice in the Ottoman Empire: Legal Practice and Dispute Resolution in Çankırı and Kastamonu (1652–1744)* (Boston and Leiden: Brill).

Erler, Mehmet Yavuz (2010). *Osmanlı Devleti'nde Kuraklık ve Kıtlık Olayları (1800–1880)* (Istanbul: Libra Yayınları).

Esenbel, Selçuk and Inaba Chiharu (2003). *The Rising Sun and the Turkish Crescent: New Perspectives on the History of Japanese and Turkish Relations* (Istanbul: Bogaziçi University Press).

Esmer, Tolga (2014). 'The Confessions of an Ottoman "Irregular": Self-Representation and Ottoman Interpretive Communities in the Nineteenth Century/ Bir Osmanlı Başıbozuğunun İtirafları: 19. Yüzyıl Osmanlı İmparatorluğu'nda Kişinin Kendini Temsili ve Yorumlayıcı Çevreleri,' *Osmanlı Araştırmaları/The Journal of Ottoman Studies*, 44, 313–40.

Establet, Colette (2015). 'Damascene Artisans around 1700,' in *Bread from the Lion's Mouth: Artisans Struggling for a Livelihood in Ottoman Cities*, edited by Suraiya Faroqhi (New York and Oxford: Berghahn Books), pp. 88–107.

Establet, Colette (2017). 'Consuming Luxurious and Exotic Goods in Damascus around 1700,' in *Living the Good Life: Consumption in the Qing and Ottoman Empires of the Eighteenth Century*, edited by Elif Akçetin and Suraiya Faroqhi (Leiden: Brill), pp. 236–58.

Establet, Colette and Jean-Paul Pascual (2005). *Des tissus et des hommes: Damas vers 1700* (Damascus: Institut Français de Damas).

Farhad, Massumeh and Serpil Bağçı (2010). *Falnama: The Book of Omens* (London: Thames and Hudson Ltd.).

Faroqhi, Suraiya (1979). 'The Life Story of an Urban Saint in the Ottoman Empire,' *Tarih Dergisi*, special issue in honour of İsmail H. Uzunçarşılı, XXXII, 655–78, 1009–18.

Faroqhi, Suraiya (1980a). 'Land Transfer, Land Disputes and *askeri* Holdings in Ankara (1592–1600),' in *Mémorial Ömer Lütfi Barkan*, edited by Robert Mantran (Paris: Bibliothèque de l'Institut Français d'Études Anatoliennes d'Istanbul), pp. 87–99.

Faroqhi, Suraiya (1980b). 'İstanbul'un İaşesi ve Tekirdağ-Rodoscuk Limanı,' *Gelişme Dergisi. İktisat Tarihi Özel Sayısı*, 139–54.

Faroqhi, Suraiya (1981). 'Seyyid Gazi Revisited: The Foundation as Seen Through Sixteenth and Seventeenth-Century Documents,' *Turcica*, XIII, 90–122.

Faroqhi, Suraiya (1982). 'Camels, Wagons, and the Ottoman State,' *International Journal of Middle East Studies*, 14, 523–39.

Faroqhi, Suraiya (1984). *Towns and Townsmen of Ottoman Anatolia, Trade, Crafts, and Food Production in an Urban Setting 1520–1650* (Cambridge: Cambridge University Press).

Faroqhi, Suraiya (1987). *Men of Modest Substance, House Owners and House Property in Seventeenth Century Ankara and Kayseri* (Cambridge: Cambridge University Press, 1987).

Faroqhi, Suraiya (1991). 'Red Sea Trade and Communications as Observed by Evliya Çelebi (1671–72),' *New Perspectives on Turkey*, 5–6, 87–106.

Faroqhi, Suraiya (1992). 'Political Activity among Ottoman Taxpayers and the Problem of Sultanic Legitimation (1570–1650),' *Journal of the Economic and Social History of the Orient*, XXXIV, 1–39.

Faroqhi, Suraiya (1995). 'Merchant Networks and Ottoman Craft Production (16th–17th Centuries)' in idem, *Making a Living in the Ottoman Lands* (Istanbul: The Isis Press), pp. 175–98.

Faroqhi, Suraiya (2002). *Stories of Ottoman Men and Women, Establishing Status Establishing Control* (Istanbul: Eren).

Faroqhi, Suraiya (2005). 'An Orthodox Woman Saint in an Ottoman Document,' in *Syncrétismes et hérésies dans l'Orient seldjoukide et ottoman des XIIIe–XVIIIe siècles, Actes du Colloque du Collège de France octobre 2001*, edited by Gilles Veinstein (Paris: Peeters), pp. 383–94.

Faroqhi, Suraiya (2005a). 'Als Kriegsgefangener bei den Osmanen: Militärlager und Haushalt des Großwesirs Kara Mustafa Paşa in einem Augenzeugenbericht,' in *Unfreie Arbeits- und Lebensverhältnisse von der Antike bis in die Gegenwart*, edited by Elisabeth Herrmann-Otto (Hildesheim, Zurich and New York: Georg Olms Verlag), pp. 206–34.

Faroqhi, Suraiya (2005b). 'Opfer der Gewalt: Einige Fälle von Mord, Raub und Bedrohung in Nordwestanatolien um 1760,' in *Gewalt in der frühen Neuzeit*, edited by Claudia Ulbrich, Claudia Jarzebowski and Michaela Hohkamp (Berlin: Duncker & Humblot), pp. 275–90.

Faroqhi, Suraiya (2007). 'Der osmanische Blick nach Osten: Dürrî Ahmed Efendi über den Zerfall des Safawidenreichs 1720–21,' in *Wahrnehmung des Fremden, Differenzerfahrungen von Diplomaten in Europa (1500–1648)*, edited by Michael Rohrschneider and Arno Strohmeyer (Münster/Germany: Aschendorff), pp. 375–98.

Faroqhi, Suraiya (2008). 'Local Elites and Government Intervention in the Province of Anadolu,' in *The Province Strikes Back: Imperial Dynamics in the Eastern Mediterranean*, edited by Björn Forsen and Giovanni Salmeri (Athens and Helsinki: Foundation of the Finnish Institute in Athens), pp. 65–81.

Faroqhi, Suraiya (2009a). *Artisans of Empire: Crafts and Craftspeople under the Ottomans* (London: I. B. Tauris).

Faroqhi, Suraiya (2009b). 'Refugees and Asylum Seekers on Ottoman Territory in the Early Modern Period,' in *Le monde de l'itinerance en Méditerranée de l'Antiquité à l'époque moderne*, edited by Claudia Moatti and Wolfgang Kaiser (Bordeaux: Ausonius), pp. 643–66.

Faroqhi, Suraiya (2012). 'What Happened in Istanbul Gardens and Beauty Spots? Evliya Çelebi on Religion, Domination and Entertainment,' in *Şehrâyîn: Die Welt der Osmanen, die Osmanen in der Welt. Wahrnehmungen, Begegnungen und Abgrenzungen/ Illuminating the Ottoman World. Perceptions, Encounters and Boundaries. Festschrift Hans Georg Majer*,' edited by Yavuz Köse (Wiesbaden: Harrassowitz Verlag), pp. 121–32.

Faroqhi, Suraiya (2014a). 'Did Cosmopolitanism Exist in Eighteenth-century Istanbul? Stories of Christian and Jewish Artisans,' in *Urban Governance under the Ottomans:*

Between Cosmopolitanism and Conflict, edited by Ulrike Freitag and Nora Lafi (London: Routledge), pp. 21–36.

Faroqhi, Suraiya (2014b). 'Manumission in Seventeenth-century Suburban Istanbul,' in *Mediterranean Slavery Revisited (500–1800) – Neue Perspektiven auf mediterrane Sklaverei (500–1800)*, edited by Stefan Hanß and Juliane Schiel, with assistance from Claudia Schmid (Zurich: Chronos Verlag), pp. 381–401.

Faroqhi, Suraiya (2015a). 'A Study of Rural Conflicts: Gegbuze/Gebze (District of Üsküdar) in the Mid-1700s,' in *Ottoman Rural Societies and Economies*, Halcyon Days in Crete VIII, A Symposium Held in Rethymno, 13–15 January 2012, edited by Elias Kolovos (Rethymno: Crete University Press), pp. 9–34.

Faroqhi, Suraiya ed. (2015b). *Bread from the Lion's Mouth: Artisans Struggling for a Livelihood in Ottoman Cities* (New York and Oxford: Berghahn Books).

Faroqhi, Suraiya (2016). 'Making and Marketing Rough Woollens: From Balkan Looms to Istanbul Shops,' *Turcica*, 47, 99–122.

Fattah, Hala (1997). *The Politics of Regional Trade in Iraq, Arabia, and the Gulf: 1745–1900* (Albany, NY: SUNY Press).

Fekete, Lajos (1960). 'Das Heim eines türkischen Herrn in der Provinz im XVI. Jahrhundert,' *Studia Historica Academiae Scientiarum Hungaricae*, 29/5, 3–30.

Fetvacı, Emine (2013). *Picturing History at the Ottoman Court* (Bloomington and Indianapolis: Indiana University Press).

Fetvacı, Emine and Erdem Çıpa eds. (2013). *Writing History at the Ottoman Court: Editing the Past, Fashioning the Future* (Bloomington and Indianapolis: Indiana University Press).

Fine, John V. A. (1994). *The Late Medieval Balkans: A Critical Survey from the Late Twelfth Century to the Ottoman Conquest* (Ann Arbor: The University of Michigan Press).

Fleet, Kate (1999). *European and Islamic Trade in the Early Ottoman State: The Merchants of Genoa and Turkey* (Cambridge: Cambridge University Press).

Fleischer, Cornell (1986). *Bureaucrat and Intellectual in the Ottoman Empire. The Historian Mustafâ 'Âlî (1541–1600)* (Princeton: Princeton University Press).

Fleischer, Cornell (2008–09). 'Of Gender and Servitude, ca. 1520: Two Petitions of the *kul kızı* of Bergama to Sultan Süleyman,' in *Mélanges en l'honneur du Prof. Suraiya Faroqhi*, edited by Abdeljelil Temimi (Tunis: FTRESI), pp. 143–52.

Fleischer, Cornell (2009). 'Ancient Wisdom and New Sciences: Prophecies at the Ottoman Court in the Fifteenth and Sixteenth Centuries,' in *Falnama: The Book of Omens*, edited by Massumeh Farhad with Serpil Bağçı (London: Thames & Hudson), pp. 231–44.

Fleming, Katherine E. (1999). *The Muslim Bonaparte – Diplomacy and Orientalism in Ali Pasha's Greece* (Princeton: Princeton University Press).

Flemming, Barbara (1964). *Landschaftsgeschichte von Pamphylien, Pisidien und Lykien im Spätmittelalter* (Wiesbaden/Germany: Deutsche Morgenländische Gesellschaft and Kommissionsverlag Franz Steiner).

Flemming, Barbara (1987). 'Sahib-kıran und Mahdi: Türkische Endzeiterwartungen im ersten Jahrzehnt der Regierung Süleymans,' in *Between the Danube and the Caucasus*, edited by György Kara (Budapest: The Academy of Sciences), pp. 43–62.

Frangakis-Syrett, Elena (1992). *The Commerce of Smyrna in the Eighteenth Century (1700–1820)* (Athens: Institute for Asia Minor Studies).

Fromkin, David (1989). *A Peace to End All Peace: The Fall of the Ottoman Empire and the Creation of the Modern Middle East* (New York: Henry Holt).

Fukasawa, Katsumi (1987). *Toilerie et commerce du Levant, d'Alep à Marseille* (Paris: Editions du CNRS).

Gara, Eleni (2005). 'Moneylenders and Landowners: In Search of Urban Muslim Elites in the Early Modern Balkans,' in *Provincial Elites in the Ottoman Empire*, edited by Antonis Anastasopoulos (Rethymno: Crete University Press), pp. 135–47.

Gedikli, Fethi (1998). *Osmanlı Şirket Kültürü: XVI–XVII. Yüzyıllarda Mudarebe Uygulaması* (Istanbul: İz Yayıncılık).

Genç, Mehmet (1975). 'Osmanlı Maliyesinde Malikâne Sistemi,' in *Türkiye İktisat Tarihi Semineri, Metinler – Tartışmalar . . .*, edited by Osman Okyar and Ünal Nabantoğlu (Ankara: Hacettepe Üniversitesi), pp. 231–96.

Genç, Mehmet (1987). 'A Study of the Feasibility of Using Eighteenth-century Ottoman Financial Records as an Indicator of Economic Activity,' in *The Ottoman Empire and the World Economy*, edited by Huri İslamoğlu İnan (Cambridge and Paris: Cambridge University Press and Éditions de la Maison des Sciences de l'Homme), pp. 345–59.

Genç, Mehmet (1994). 'Ottoman Industry in the Eighteenth Century: General Framework, Characteristics and Main Trends,' in *Manufacturng in the Ottoman Empire and Turkey 1500–1950*, edited by Donald Quataert (Albany: SUNY Press), pp. 59–86.

Genç, Mehmet (1995). 'L'économie ottomane et la guerre au XVIIIème siècle,' *Turcica*, 27, 177–96.

Genç, Mehmet (2000). *Osmanlı İmparatorluğunda Devlet ve Ekonomi* (Istanbul: Ötüken).

Gerber, Haim (1988). *Economy and Society in an Ottoman City: Bursa, 1600–1700* (Jerusalem: The Hebrew University).

Glassie, Henry (1993). *Turkish Traditional Art Today* (Indianapolis and Bloomington, IN: Indiana University Press).

Goffman, Daniel (1990). *Izmir and the Levantine World, 1550–1650* (Seattle: University of Washington Press).

Göyünç, Nejat (1969). *XVI. Yüzyılda Mardin Sancağı* (Istanbul: İstanbul Üniversitesi Edebiyat Fakültesi).

Göyünç, Nejat (1970). 'Eski Malatya'da Silâhdar Mustafa Paşa Hanı,' *Tarih Enstitüsü Dergisi*, 1, 63–92.

Göyünç, Nejat and Wolf Dieter Hütteroth (1997). *Land an der Grenze: Osmanische Verwaltung im heutigen türkisch-syrisch-irakischen Grenzgebiet im 16. Jahrhundert* (Istanbul: Eren Publications).

Gradeva, Rossitsa (2004). 'Ottoman Policy towards Christian Church Buildings,' in *Rumeli under the Ottomans, 15th–18th Centuries: Institutions and Communities* (Istanbul: The Isis Press), pp. 339–68.

Gratziou, Olga (2011). 'Illustrated Manuscripts in the Age of the Printed Book,' in *Exploring Greek Manuscripts in the Gennadius Library*, edited by Maria Politi and Eleni Pappa (Princeton, NJ: American School of Classical Studies at Athens and Greek Paleographical Society), pp. 49–57.

Güçer, Lütfi (1964). *XVI. ve XVII. Osmanlı İmparatorluğunda Hububat Meselesi ve Hububattan Alınan Vergiler* (Istanbul: İstanbul Üniversitesi İktisat Fakültesi).

Guirgis, Magdi (2008). *An Armenian Artist in Ottoman Egypt: Yuhanna al-Armani and his Coptic Icons* (Cairo: The American University of Cairo).

Gülsoy, Dr. Ersin (2005). *Girit'in Fethi ve Osmanlı İdaresinin Kurulması* (Istanbul: TATAV).

Gürkan, Emrah Safa (2018). *Sultanın Korsanları: Osmanlı Akdenizi'nde Gazâ, Yağma ve Esaret 1500–1700* (Istanbul: Kronik Kitap).

Güreşsever Cantay, Prof. Dr. Gönül (2016). *Osmanlı Menzil Kervansarayları* (Istanbul: Fatih Sultan Mehmet Vakıf Üniversitesi).

Hagen, Gottfried (2003). *Ein osmanischer Geograph bei der Arbeit. Entstehung und Gedankenwelt von Katib Celebis Ğihannüma* (Berlin: Klaus Schwarz Verlag).

Hamadeh, Shirine (2008). *The City's Pleasures: Istanbul in the Eighteenth Century* (Seattle: University of Washington Press).

Hanna, Nelly (1997). *Making Big Money in 1600: The Life and Times of Isma'il Abu Taqiyya, Egyptian Merchant* (Syracuse, NY: Syracuse University Press).

Hanna, Nelly (2011). *Artisan Entrepreneurs in Cairo and Early-Modern Capitalism (1600–1800)* (Syracuse, NY: Syracuse University Press).

Hathaway, Jane (1997). *The Politics of Households in Ottoman Egypt: The Rise of the Qazdağlıs* (Cambridge: Cambridge University Press).

Hathaway, Jane (2005). *Beshir Agha Chief Eunuch of the Ottoman Imperial Harem* (Oxford: Oneworld Publications).

Hathaway, Jane, with contributions by Karl K. Barbir (2008). *The Arab Lands under Ottoman Rule, 1516–1800* (Harlow/England: Pearson Longman).

Hathaway, Jane (2018). *The Chief Eunuch of the Ottoman Harem: From African Slave to Power Broker* (Cambridge: Cambridge University Press).

Hitzel, Frédéric ed. (1997). *Istanbul et les langues orientales* (Paris: L'Harmattan).
https://www.britannica.com/biography/Asikpasazade (accessed on 18 October 2016).

Hütteroth, Wolf Dieter (1968). *Ländliche Siedlungen im Südlichen Inneranatolien in den letzten vierhundert Jahren* (Göttingen: Selbstverlag des Geographischen Instituts der Universität Göttingen).

Hütteroth, Wolf Dieter (2006). 'Ecology of the Ottoman Lands,' in *The Cambridge History of Turkey*, vol. 3, *The Later Ottoman Empire* edited by Suraiya Faroqhi (Cambridge: Cambridge University Press, 2006), pp. 18–43.

Hütteroth, Wolf Dieter and Kamal Abdulfattah (1977). *Historical Geography of Palestine, Transjordan and Southern Syria in the Late 16th Century* (Erlangen: Palm and Enke).

Imber, Colin (1979). 'The Persecution of Ottoman Shi'ites according to the Mühimme Defterleri, 1565–1585,' *Der Islam*, 56, 2, 245–73.

İnalcık, Halil (1948). 'Osmanlı-Rus Rekabetinin Menşei ve Don-Volga-Kanalı Teşebbüsü, 1569,' *Belleten*, XII, 349–402.

İnalcık, Halil (1953). 'Stefan Duşan'dan Osmanlı İmparatorluğuna: XV. Asırda Rumeli'de Hıristiyan Sipahiler ve Menşeleri,' in *60. Doğum Yılı Münasebetiyle Fuad Köprülü Armağanı*, edited by Osman Turan (Ankara: DTCF Yayınları), pp. 207–48.

İnalcık, Halil (1954). *Hicrî 815 Tarihli Suret-i Defter-i Sancak-ı Arvanid* (Ankara: Türk Tarih Kurumu).

İnalcık, Halil (1954b). 'Ottoman Methods of Conquest,' *Studia Islamica*, II, 104–29.

İnalcık, Halil (1959). 'Osmanlılar'da *Raiyyet Rusumu*,' *TTK Belleten*, XXIII, 92, 575–610.

İnalcık, Halil (1960). 'Bursa and the Commerce of the Levant,' *Journal of the Economic and Social History of the Levant*, 3, 2, 131–47.

İnalcık, Halil (1965a). 'Adâletnâmeler (14 fotokopi ile),' *Belgeler*, II, 3–4, 49–142.

İnalcık, Halil (1965b). 'Djizya II, Ottoman,' in *Encyclopaedia of Islam Second Edition*, edited by P. Bearman, Th. Bianquis, C.E. Bosworth, E. van Donzel and W.P. Heinrichs, vol. 11, *C-G* (Leiden and London: Brill and Luzac), pp. 562–6.

İnalcık, Halil (1969). 'Capital Formation in the Ottoman Empire,' *The Journal of Economic History*, XXIX, 1, 97–140.

İnalcık, Halil (1970). 'The Ottoman Economic Mind and Aspects of the Ottoman Economy,' in *Studies of the Economic History of the Middle East*, edited by M.A. Cook (London: Oxford University Press), pp. 207–18.

İnalcık, Halil (1971). 'Ḥarīr,' in *The Encyclopaedia of Islam, Second Edition*, edited by P. Bearman, Th. Bianquis, C.E. Bosworth, E. van Donzel and W.P. Heinrichs, vol. 3 (London and Leiden: Luzac and Brill), 212–18.

İnalcık, Halil (1973). *The Ottoman Empire: The Classical Age 1300–1600* (London: Weidenfeld and Nicolson).

İnalcık, Halil (1975). 'The Socio-Political Effects of the Diffusion of Fire-Arms in the Middle East,' in *War, Technology and Society in the Middle East*, edited by V. Parry and M. Yapp (Oxford: Oxford University Press), pp. 207–21.

İnalcık, Halil (reprint 1978). 'The Nature of Traditional Society: Turkey,' in idem, *The Ottoman Empire: Conquest, Organization, Economy* (London: Variorum), No. 15.

İnalcik, Halil (1979–80). 'Osmanlı Pamuklu Pazarı, Hindistan ve İngiltere: Pazar Rekabetinde Emek Maliyetinin Rolü,' *Gelişme Dergisi*, special issue *Türkiye İktisat Tarihi Üzerine Araştırmalar*, 1–65.

İnalcık, Halil (1980). 'Military and Fiscal Transformation in the Ottoman Empire, 1600–1700,' *Archivum Ottomanicum*, VI, 283–337.

İnalcik, Halil (reprint 1985). 'Impact of the *Annales* School on Ottoman Studies and New Findings,' in idem, *Studies in Ottoman Social and Economic History* (London: Variorum Reprints), No. IV.

İnalcık, Halil (reprint 1985b). 'The Emergence of Big Farms, çiftliks: State, Landlords and Tenants,' in idem, *Studies in Ottoman Social and Economic History* (London: Variorum Reprints), No. VIII.

İnalcık, Halil (reprint 1985c). 'Rice Cultivation and the *çeltükci-reʿaya* System in the Ottoman Empire,' in idem, *Studies in Ottoman Social and Economic History* (London: Variorum Reprints), No. VI.

İnalcık, Halil (1991). 'Ottoman Galata (1453–1553),' in *Première Rencontre Internationale sur l'Empire Ottoman et la Turquie Moderne*, edited by Edhem Eldem (Istanbul and Paris: Éditions Isis), pp. 17–116.

İnalcık, Halil (1994). 'How to read 'Āshık Pasha-Zāde's History,' in *Studies in Ottoman History in Honour of Professor V. L. Ménage,* edited by Colin Heywood and Colin Imber (Istanbul: The Isis Press), pp. 139–56.

İnalcık, Halil (1996). *Sources and Studies on the Ottoman Black Sea: The Customs Register of Caffa 1487–1489*, edited by Victor Ostapchuk (Cambridge, MA: Harvard University Press).

İnalcık, Halil (1997). 'Selīm I,' in *The Encycloclopaedia of Islam, Second Edition* edited by P. Bearman, Th. Bianquis, C. E. Bosworth, E. v. Donzel, W.P. Heinrichs (Leiden: Brill), vol. IX *San-Sze*, pp. 127–31.

İnalcık, Halil (1997, 1st publication 1994). *An Economic and Social History of the Ottoman Empire, Vol. One 1300–1600* (Cambridge: Cambridge University Press).

İnalcık, Halil (reprint 1998). 'The Question of the Closing of the Black Sea under the Ottomans,' in Halil İnalcık, *Essays in Ottoman History* (Istanbul: Eren), pp. 411–45.

İnalcık, Halil (2003). *Şair ve Patron* (Ankara and Istanbul: Doğu Batı Yayınları).

İnalcık, Halil (2011). *Studies in the History of Textiles in Turkey* (Istanbul: Türkiye İş Bankası Kültür Yayınları).

İnalcık, Halil (2012). 'Istanbul,' in *Encyclopaedia of Islam, Second Edition*, edited by P. Bearman, Th. Bianquis, C.E. Bosworth, E. van Donzel and W.P. Heinrichs. (Consulted online on 2 December 2017). http://dx.doi.org/10.1163/1573-3912_islam_COM_0393. First published on line: 2012; First print edition: ISBN: 9789004161214, 1960–2007

İnalcık, Halil (n. d.). 'Timar,' in *Türkiye Diyânet Vakfı İslâm Ansiklopedisi* online https://islamansiklopedisi.org.tr/timar

İrepoğlu, Gül (1999). Levni: *Nakış Şiir Renk* (Istanbul: Kültür ve Turizm Bakanlığı).

Irsigler, Franz and Arnold Lassotta (1993). *Bettler und Gaukler, Dirnen und Henker: Außenseiter in einer mittelalterlichen Stadt* (Munich: Beck).

İşkorkutan, Sinem Erdoğan (2017). 'The 1720 Festival in Istanbul: Festivity and Representation in the Early Eighteenth-Century Ottoman Empire,' unpublished PhD dissertation, Boğaziçi University Istanbul.

Islamoğlu İnan, Huri ed. (1987, reprint 2004). *The Ottoman Empire and the World Economy* (Cambridge and Paris: Cambridge University Press and Maison des Sciences de l'Homme).

İslamoğlu İnan, Huri (1994). *State and Peasant in the Ottoman Empire: Agrarian Power Relations and Regional Economic Development in Ottoman Anatolia during the Sixteenth Century* (Leiden: Brill).

İslamoğlu, Huri (2007). *Ottoman History as World History* (Istanbul: The Isis Press).

İslamoğlu, Huricihan and Çağlar Keyder (1987, reprint 2004). 'Agenda for Ottoman History,' in *The Ottoman Empire and the World Economy*, edited by Huri İslamoğlu İnan (Cambridge and Paris: Cambridge University Press and Maison des Sciences de l'Homme), pp. 42–62.

Isom-Verhaaren, Christine (2011). *Allies with the Infidel: The Ottoman and French Alliance in the Sixtreenth Century* (London: I. B. Tauris).

Jennings, Ronald C. (1973). 'Loan and Credit in Early 17th Century Ottoman Judicial Records: The Sharia Court of Anatolian Kayseri,' *Journal of the Economic and Social History of the Orient*, XVI, 2–3, 168–216.

Jennings, Ronald C. (1975). 'Women in Early 17th Century Ottoman Judicial Records: The Sharia Court of Anatolian Kayseri,' *Journal of the Economic and Social History of the Orient*, XVIII, 1, 53–114.

Kadı, İsmail Hakkı (2012). *Ottoman and Dutch Merchants in the Eighteenth Century: Competition and Cooperation in Ankara, Izmir, and Amsterdam* (Leiden: Brill).

Kafadar, Cemal (1986). 'A Death in Venice (1575): Anatolian Muslim Merchants Trading in the Serenissima,' *Journal of Turkish Studies*, 10, *Raiyyet Rüsumu, Essays presented to Halil İnalcık*: 191–218.

Kafadar, Cemal (2007). 'A Rome of One's Own: Cultural Geography and Identity in the Land of Rum,' *Muqarnas*, 24, 7–25.

Kafescioğlu, Çiğdem (2007). 'Osmanlı Şehirciliğinde Dönüşüm ve Devamlılık: Onbeşinci Yüzyıl İstanbul'unda Külliye ve Mahalleler,' in *550. Yılında Fetih ve İstanbul* (Ankara: Türk Tarih Kurumu), pp. 177–88.

Kangal, Selmin et alii eds. (2000). *The Sultan's Portrait: Picturing the House of Osman* (Istanbul: Türkiye İş Bankası).

Kaplan, Ayşe (2012). 'From Seasonal to Permanent: A Study of the Effects of *Göç* Tradition on the Bosphorus Shores,' unpublished MA thesis, Istanbul Bilgi University.

Karaca, Zafer (1995). *İstanbul'da Osmanlı Dönemi Rum Kiliseleri* (Istanbul: Yapı Kredi Yaynları).

Karahasanoğlu, Selim (2012). *Kadı ve Günlüğü: Sadreddinzâde Telhisî Mustafa Efendi Günlüğü (1711–1735) Üstüne bir İnceleme* (Istanbul: Türkiye İş Bankası).

Karahasanoğlu, Selim (2017). 'Challenging the Paradigm of the Tulip Age: The Consumer Behavior of Nevşehirli Damad İbrahim Paşa and his Household,' in *Living the Good Life: Consumption in the Qing and Ottoman Empires of the Eighteenth Century*, edited by Elif Akçetin and Suraiya Faroqhi (Leiden: Brill), pp. 134–60.

Kastritsis, Dimitri (2016). 'The Alexander Romance and the Rise of the Ottoman Empire,' in *Islamic Literature and Intellectual Life in Fourteenth- and Fifteenth-Century Anatolia*, edited by A. C. S. Peacock and Sara Nur Yıldız (Würzburg/Germany: Ergon Verlag Würzburg and Orient-Institut Istanbul), pp. 243–84.

Katsiardi-Hering, Olga (2008). 'The Allure of Red Cotton Yarn, and How it Came to Vienna: Associations of Greek Artisans and Merchants Operating between the Ottoman and Habsburg Empires,' in *Merchants in the Ottoman Empire*, edited by Suraiya Faroqhi and Gilles Veinstein (Leuven: Peeters), pp. 97–132.

Kazan, Hilal (2010). *XVI. Asırda Sarayın Sanatı Himayesi* (Istanbul: ISAR Vakfı).

Kenderova, Stoyanka (2000). *Bibliothèques et livres musulmans dans les territoires balkaniques de l'Empire ottoman: Le cas de Samokov (XVIIIe-première moitié du XIXe siècle)* (Strasburg: Université Marc Bloch, Diffusion ANRT/Thèses à la carte).

Keskinkılıç, Esra (January 2014). 'Ata ağıt: Elegy for a Horse,' *Acta Turcica*, VI, 1–2. http://www.actaturcica.com/sayi11/VI_I_b_01.pdf (accessed on 5 January 2015).

Keyvani, Mehdi (1982). *Artisans and Guild Life in the later Safavid Period, Contributions to the Social-economic history of Persia* (Berlin: Klaus Schwarz Verlag).

Khoury, Dina (1997). *State and Provincial Society in the Ottoman Empire: Mosul 1540–1834* (Cambridge: Cambridge University Press).

Kickinger, Claudia (2005). 'Relations of Production and Social Conditions among Coppersmiths in Contemporary Cairo,' in *Crafts and Craftsmen of the Middle East, Fashioning the Individual in the Muslim Mediterranean*, edited by Suraiya Faroqhi and Randi Deguilhem (London: I. B. Tauris), pp. 285–307.

Kiel, Machiel (1985). *Art and Society of Bulgaria in the Turkish Period: A Sketch of the Economic, Juridical and Artistic Preconditions of Bulgarian Post-Byzantine Art* (Hilversum: Verloren).

Kırlı, Cengiz (2001). 'A Profile of the Labor Force in Early Nineteenth-Century Istanbul,' *International Labor and Working Class History*, 60, 125–40.

Köprülü, Mehmet Fuat (1966, reprint 2016). *Türk Edebiyatı'nda İlk Mutasavvıflar* (Istanbul: Alfa Yayıncılık).

Krstić, Tijana (2013). 'Conversion and Converts to Islam in Ottoman Historiography of the Fifteenth and Sixteenth Centuries,' in *Writing History at the Ottoman Court: Editing the Past, Shaping the Future*, edited by H. Erdem Çıpa and Emine Fetvacı (Bloomington and Indianapolis: Indiana University Press), pp.58–79.

Kuban, Doğan et alii (2002). *Selçuklu Çağında Anadolu Sanatı* (Istanbul: YKY).

Küçük, Hülya (2001). *The Role of the Bektāshīs in Turkey's National Struggle* (Leiden: Brill).

Kunt, Metin (1983). *The Sultan's Servants: The Transformation of Ottoman Provincial Government 1550–1650* (New York: Columbia University Press).

Kunt, Metin (2007). 'A Prince Goes Forth (Perchance to Return),' in *Identity and Identity Formation in the Ottoman World: A Volume of Essays in Honor of Norman Itzkowitz*, edited by Baki Tezcan and Karl K. Barbir (Madison, WI: The Center for Turkish Studies at the University of Wisconsin and The University of Wisconsin Press), pp. 63–72.

Kuran, Timur (2011). *The Long Divergence: How Islamic Law Held Back the Middle East* (Princeton: Princeton University Press).

Kurat, Akdes Nimet (n.d.). 'Kazan Hanlığı 1437–1556,' https://www.tarihtarih.com/?Syf=26&Syz=380280&/Kazan-Hanl%C4%B1%C4%9F%C4%B1-(1437-1556)-/-Prof.-Dr.-Akdes-Nimet-Kurat (accessed on 28 January 2018).

Kürkman, Garo (2005). *Toprak, Ateş, Sır: Tarihsel gelişimi, atölyeleri ve ustalarıyle Kütahya çini ve seramikleri* (Istanbul: Suna ve İnan Kıraç Vakfı).

Kuru, Mehmet (2017). 'Locating an Ottoman Port City in the Early Modern Mediterranean: Izmir (1580–1780),' unpublished PhD thesis, University of Toronto.

Kuru, Selim (2013). 'The Literature of Rum: The Making of a Literary Tradition,' in *The Cambridge History of Turkey*, vol. 2, edited by Suraiya Faroqhi and Kate Fleet (Cambridge: Cambridge University Press), pp. 548–92.

Kütükoğlu, Mübahat (1983). *Osmanlılarda Narh Müessesesi ve 1640 Tarihli Narh Defteri* (Istanbul: Enderun Kitabevi).

Kütükoğlu, Mübahat (1994). *Osmanlı Belgelerinin Dili (Diplomatik)* (Istanbul: Kubbealtı Neşriyat).

Kuyulu, İnci (1992). *Kara Osman-oğlu Ailesine Ait Mimari Eserler* (Ankara: T. C. Kültür Bakanlığı).

Lafi, Nora (2018). *Esprit civique et organisation citadine dans l'Empire ottoman (XVe–XX siècles)* (Leiden: Brill).

Lane, Frederic C. (1973). *Venice: A Maritime Republic* (London and Baltimore, MD: The Johns Hopkins University Press).

Lapidus, Ira (1984). *Muslim Cities in the Later Middle Ages* (Cambridge: Cambridge University Press).

Layton, Evro (1994). *The Sixteenth Century Greek Book in Italy, Printers and Publishers for the Greek World* (Venice: The Hellenic Institute of Byzantine and Post-Byzantine Studies).

Lewis, Bernard (1962). 'Ottoman Observers of Ottoman Decline,' *Islamic Studies*, 1, 71–87.

Lowry, Heath (1986). 'Changes in Fifteenth-Century Peasant Taxation: The Case Study of Radilofo,' in *Continuity and Change in Late Byzantine and Early Ottoman Society: Papers Given at a Symposium at Dumbarton Oaks in 1982* (Birmingham, UK and Washington, DC: The University of Birmingham, Dumbarton Oaks), pp. 23–38.

Lowry, Heath (1992). 'The Ottoman *Tahrir Defterleri* as a Source for Social and Economic History: Pitfalls and Limitations,' in idem, *Studies in Defeterology: Ottoman Society in the Fifteenth and Sixteenth Centuries* (Istanbul: The Isis Press), pp. 3–18.

Lowry, Heath (2003). *The Nature of the Early Ottoman State* (Albany, NY: SUNY Press).

Maclean, Gerald (2004). *The Rise of Oriental Travel: English Visitors to the Ottoman Empire 1580–1720* (London: Palgrave Macmillan).

Maclean, Gerald (2007). *Looking East: English Writing and the Ottoman Empire before 1800* (London: Palgrave Macmillan).

Mahir, Bânu (1986). 'Saray Nakkaşhanesinin Ünlü Ressamı Şah Kulu ve Eserleri,' *Topkapı Sarayı Yıllığı*, 1, 113–30.

Majer, Hans Georg (1999). 'Gold, Silber und Farbe: Musavvir Hüseyin, ein Meister der osmanischen Miniaturmalerei des späten 17. Jahrhunderts,' in *Studies in Ottoman Social and Economic Life/Studien zur Wirtschaft und Gesellschaft im Osmanischen Reich*, edited by Raoul Motika, Christoph Herzog and Michael Ursinus (Heidelberg: Heidelberger Orientverlag), pp. 9–42.

Mantran, Robert (1962). *Istanbul dans la seconde moitié du XVIIe siècle: essai d'histoire institutionelle, économique et sociale* (Paris: Maisonneuve).

Marmara, Rinaldo (2005). *İstanbul Deniz Zindanı 1740* (Istanbul: Denizler Kitabevi).

Masson, Paul (1911). *Histoire du commerce français dans le Levant au XVIIIe siècle* (Paris: Librairie Hachette).

Masters, Bruce (1988). *The Origins of Western Economic Dominance in the Middle East: Mercantilism and the Islamic Economy in Aleppo, 1600–1750* (New York: New York University Press).

Mather, James (2011). *Pashas: Traders and Travellers in the Islamic World* (London and New Haven: Yale University Press).

McGowan, Bruce (1969). 'Food Supply and Taxation on the Middle Danube (1568–1579),' *Archivum Ottomanicum*, 1, 139–96.

McGowan, Bruce (1981). *Economic Life in Ottoman Europe: Taxation, Trade and the Struggle for Land* (Cambridge: Cambridge University Press).

Mélikoff, Irène (1998). *Hadji Bektach: Un mythe et ses avatars: Genèse et évolution du soufisme populaire en Turquie* (Leiden, Boston and Cologne: Brill).

Ménage, Victor L. (1965). 'Devshirme,' in *The Encycloclopaedia of Islam, Second Edition*, edited by P. Bearman Th. Bianquis, C.E. Bosworth, E. v. Donzel and W.P. Heinrichs (Leiden and London: Brill, Luzac), vol. II, *C-G*, pp. 210–13.

Meriwether, Margaret (1999). *The Kin Who Count: Family and Society in Ottoman Aleppo 1770–1840* (Austin: The University of Texas Press).

Meyer zur Capellen, Jörg and Serpil Bağcı (2000). 'The Age of Magnificence,' in *The Sultan's Portrait: Picturing the House of Osman*, edited by Semin Kangal et alii (Istanbul: Türkiye İş Bankası), pp. 96–133.

Michel, Nicolas (2005). 'Les artisans dans la ville: Ateliers de tissage et tisserands d'Asyût à la fin du XVIIe siècle, d'après les registres du tribunal du qâdî,' in *Society and Economy in Egypt and the Eastern Mediterranean 1600–1900, Essays in honor of André Raymond*, edited by Nelly Hanna (Cairo and New York, The American University in Cairo Press), pp. 51–97.

Mikhail, Alan (2011). *Nature and Empire in Ottoman Egypt: An Environmental History* (New York: Cambridge University Press).

Milstein, Rachel (1989). *Miniature Painting in Ottoman Baghdad* (Costa Mesa and Santa Ana/Cal: Mazda Publishers) (Bibliotheca Iranica, Islamic Art and Architecture Series 5).

Moustakas, Konstantinos (2015). 'Slave Labour in the Early Ottoman Rural Economy: Regional Variations in the Balkans during the 15th Century,' in *Frontiers of the Ottoman Imagination: Studies in Honour of Rhoads Murphey* (Leiden: Brill) pp. 29–43.

Murphey, Rhoads (1999). *Ottoman Warfare 1500–1700* (London: UCL Press).

Murphey, Rhoads (2008). *Exploring Ottoman Sovereignty: Tradition, Image and Practice in the Ottoman Imperial Household, 1400–1800* (London: Continuum).

Nagata, Yuzo (2015). *Tarihte Âyânlar: Kara Osmanoğulları Üzerine bir İnceleme* (Ankara: Türk Tarih Kurumu).

Nalçacı, Nida Nebahat (2015). *Sultanın Kulları: Erken Modern Dönem İstanbul'unda Savaş Esirleri ve Zorunlu İstihdam* (Istanbul: Verita).

Necipoğlu, Gülru (1991). *Architecture, Ceremonial and Power: The Topkapı Palace in the Fifteenth and Sixteenth Centuries* (Cambridge, MA: The Architectural History Foundation and MIT Press).

Necipoğlu, Gülru (2000a). 'Word and Image: The Serial Portraits of Ottoman Sultans in Comparative Perspective,' in *The Sultan's Portrait: Picturing the House of Osman*, edited by Selmin Kangal et alii (Istanbul: Türkiye İş Bankası), pp. 22–61.

Necipoğlu, Gülru (2000b). 'A Period of Transition,' in *The Sultan's Portrait: Picturing the House of Osman*, edited by Selmin Kangal et alii (Istanbul: Türkiye İş Bankası), pp. 202–95.

Necipoğlu, Gülru (2005). *The Age of Sinan: Architectural Culture in the Ottoman Empire* (London: Reaktion Books).

Necipoğlu, Gülru (2007). 'L'idée de décor dans les régimes de visualité islamiques,' in *Purs décors? Arts de l'Islam, regards du XIXe siècle: Collections des Arts Décoratifs*, edited by Rémi Labrusse (Paris: Les Arts Décoratifs et Musée du Louvre), pp. 10–23.

Neumann, Christoph K. (1994). *Das indirekte Argument. Ein Plädoyer für die Tanẓīmāt vermittels der Historie. Die geschichtliche Bedeutung von Aḥmed Cevdet Paşas Taʾrīḫ* (Münster/Germany: Lit Verlag) (*Periplus Parerga*. Band 1).

Nicol, Donald M. (1996), *The Reluctant Emperor: A Biography of John Cantacuzene, Byzantine Emperor and Monk, c.1295–1383* (Cambridge: Cambridge University Press).

Ocak, Ahmet Yaşar (1978). 'Emirci Sultan ve Zaviyesi,' *Tarih Enstitüsü Dergisi*, 9, 129–208.

Ocak, Ahmet Yaşar (1983). *Bektâşi Menâkıbnâmelerinde İslâm Öncesi İnanç Motifleri* (Istanbul: Enderun Kitabevi).

Ocak, Ahmet Yaşar (2011). *Sarı Saltık: Popüler İslâmın Balkanlardaki Destanî Öncüsü (13. Yüzyıl)* 2nd edition (Ankara: Türk Tarih Kurumu).

Ogasawara, Hiroyuki (2017). 'The Quest for the Biblical Ancestors: The Legitimacy and Identity of the Ottoman Dynasty in the Fifteenth–Sixteenth Centuries,' *Turcica*, 48, 37–64.

Öğün, Tuncay (2006). 'Müsadere (Ottoman period),' in *Türkiye Diyanet Vakfı İslâm Ansiklopedisi* (Istanbul: Türkiye Diyanet Vakfı), vol. 32, pp. 67–68.

Oikonomidis, N. (1994). 'From Soldiers of Fortune to Gazi Warriors: The Tzympe Affair,' in *Studies in Ottoman History in Honour of Professor V. L. Ménage*, edited by Colin Heywood and Colin Imber (Istanbul: The Isis Press), pp. 239–48.

Olnon, Merlijn (2014). '"Brought under the Law of the Land": The History, Demography and Geography of Crossculturalism in Early Modern Izmir, and the Köprülü Project of 1678,' unpublished Ph D thesis, Leiden University.

Öney, Gönül (2002). 'Selçuklu Figür Dünyası,' in *Selçuklu Çağında Anadolu Sanatı*, edited by Doğan Kuban et alii (Istanbul: YKY), pp. 411–28.

Orhonlu, Cengiz (1963). *Osmanlı İmparatorluğunda Aşiretleri İskân Teşebbüsü (1691–1696)* (Istanbul: İstanbul Üniversitesi Edebiyat Fakültesi Yayınevi).

Orhonlu, Cengiz (1967). *Osmanlı İmparatorluğunda Derbent Teşkilatı* (Istanbul: İstanbul Üniversitesi Edebiyat Fakültesi Yayınevi).

Orhonlu, Cengiz (1974). *Osmanlı İmparatorluğu'nun Güney Siyaseti: Habeş Eyaleti* (Istanbul: İstanbul Üniversitesi Edebiyat Fakültesi).

Orhonlu, Cengiz (date unknown). '18. Yüzyılda Osmanlılarda Coğrafya ve Bartınlı İbrahim Hamdi'nin Atlas'ı.' https://www.google.co.in/search?sourceid=chrome-psyapi2&ion=1&espv=2&ie=UTF-8&q=cengiz%20orhonlu%20atlas&oq=cengiz%20orhonlu%20atlas&aqs=chrome..69i57.11779j0j7 (accessed on 7 November 2016).

Özbaran, Salih (1994). *The Ottoman Response to European Expansion: Studies on Ottoman–Portuguese Relations in the Indian Ocean and Ottoman Administration in the Arab Lands during the Sixteenth Century* (Istanbul: The Isis Press).

Özcan, Azmi (1997). *Pan-Islamism, Indian Muslims, the Ottomans and Britain (1877–1924)* (Leiden, New York and Köln: Brill).

Özel, Oktay (2016). *The Collapse of Rural Order in Anatolia: Amasya 1576 to 1643* (Leiden: Brill).

Pamuk, Şevket (2000a). *A Monetary History of the Ottoman Empire* (Cambridge: Cambridge University Press).

Pamuk, Şevket (2000b). *İstanbul ve Diğer Kentlerde 500 Yıllık Fiyatlar ve Ücretler 1469–1998/ 500 Years of Prices and Wages in Istanbul and Other Cities* (Ankara: T. C. Başbakanlık Devlet İstatistik Enstitüsü).

Panzac, Daniel (1996). *Commerce et navigation dans l'Empire ottoman au XVIIIe siècle* (Istanbul: Isis Publications).

Panzac, Daniel (2004). *La caravane maritime: Marins européens et marchands ottomans en Méditerranée (1680–1830)*. (Paris: CNRS Editions).

Papakostantinou, Katerina (2008). 'The Pondikas Merchant Family from Thessaloniki ca. 1750–1800),' in *Merchants in the Ottoman Empire*, edited by Suraiya Faroqhi and Gilles Veinstein (Leuven: Peeters), pp. 133–50.

Paris, Robert (1957). *Histoire du commerce de Marseille*, vol 5, *Le Levant, de 1660 à 1789* (Paris: Plon).

Paudice, Aleida (2006). 'Elia Capsali,' https://ottomanhistorians.uchicago.edu/en/historian/elia-capsali (accessed on 17 March 2018).

Pedani Fabris, Maria Pia (1994a). *In nome del Gran Signore, Inviati ottomani a Venezia dalla caduta di Costantinopoli alla guerra di Candia* (Venezia: Deputacione Editrice).

Pedani Fabris, Maria Pia (1994b). 'I Turchi e il Friuli alla fine del Quattrocento,' *Memorie storiche forogiuliesi*, 74, 203–24.

Pedani Fabris, Maria Pia (2008). 'Between Diplomacy and Trade: Ottoman Merchants in Venice,' in *Merchants in the Ottoman Empire*, edited by Suraiya Faroqhi and Gilles Veinstein (Leuven: Peeters), pp. 3–22.

Peirce, Leslie (1993). *The Imperial Harem, Women and Sovereignty in the Ottoman Empire* (New York and Oxford: Oxford University Press).

Peirce, Leslie (1997). 'Seniority, Sexuality, and Social Order: The Vocabulary of Gender in Early Modern Ottoman Anatolia,' in *Women in the Ottoman Empire: Middle Eastern Women in the Early Modern Era*, edited by Madeline Zilfi (Leiden: Brill).

Peirce, Leslie (2014). 'Honor, Reputation, and Reciprocity,' *European Journal of Turkish Studies* [Online] 18 http://ejts.revues.org/4860 (accessed in January 2019).

Peri, Oded (2001). *Christianity under Islam in Jerusalem: The Question of the Holy Sites in Early Ottoman Times* (Leiden: Brill).

Petrovszky, Konrad (2014). *Geschichte schreiben im osmanischen Südosteuropa: Eine Kulturgeschichte orthodoxer Historiographie des 16. und 17. Jahrhunderts* (Balkanologische Veröffentlichungen 60) (Wiesbaden: Harrassowitz).

Philliou, Christine M. (2011). *Biography of an Empire: Governing Ottomans in an Age of Revolution* (Los Angeles, Berkeley and London: University of California Press).

Phillips, Amanda (2014). 'Ottoman *Hil'at*: Between Commodity and Charisma,' in *Frontiers of the Ottoman Imagination: Festschrift for Rhoads Murphey*, edited by Marios Hadjianastasios (Leiden and Boston: Brill), pp. 111–38.

Piterberg, Gabriel (2002). 'The Alleged Rebellion of Abaza Mehmed Paşa: Historiography and the Ottoman State in the Seventeenth Century,' *International Journal of Turkish Studies*, 8 /1–2, 13–24 (guest editor Jane Hathaway).

Quakatz, Manja (2011). '"Gebürtig aus der Türckey": Zu Konversion und Zwangstaufe osmanischer Muslime im Alten Reich um 1700,' in *Europa und die Türkei im achtzehnten Jahrhundert / Europe and Turkey in the Eighteenth Century*, edited by Barbara Schmidt-Haberkamp (Bonn, Göttingen: V & R unipress), pp. 417–32.

Raby, Julian (2000). 'From Europe to Istanbul,' in *The Sultan's Portrait: Picturing the House of Osman*, edited by Selmin Kangal et alii (Istanbul: Türkiye İş Bankası), pp. 136–63.

Ragsdale, Hugh (1988). 'Evaluating the Traditions of Russian Aggression: Catherine II and the Greek Project,' *The Slavonic and East European Review*, 66, 1, 91–117. http://www.jstor.org/stable/4209687 (accessed on 25 January 2018).

Raymond, André (1973–4). *Artisans et commerçants au Caire, au XVIII*[e] *siècle*, 2 vols. (Damascus: Institut Français de Damas).

Raymond, André (1984). *The Great Arab Cities in the 16th–18th Centuries: An Introduction* (New York and London: New York University Press).

Raymond, André (1991). 'Alep à l'époque ottomane (XVIe–XIXe siècles),' *Revue du Monde musulman et de la Méditerranée*, 62, 93–109. Accessed through: https://books.openedition.org/ifpo/1667 (23 July 2018).

Ricci, Giovanni (2005). *Türk Saplantısı: Yeniçağ Avrupa'sında Korku, Nefret ve Sevgi*, translated by Kemal Atakay (Istanbul: Kitap Yayınevi).

Riello, Giorgio (2009). 'The Indian Apprenticeship: The Trade in Indian Textiles and the Making of European Cottons,' in *How India Clothed the World: The World of South Asian Textiles 1500–1850*, edited by Giorgio Riello and Tirthankhar Roy (Leiden: Brill), pp. 309–46.

Riello, Giorgio (2013). *Cotton: The Fabric that Made the Modern World* (Cambridge: Cambridge University Press).

Rothenberg, Gunther E. (1966). *The Military Border in Croatia 1740–1881: A Study of an Imperial Institution* (Chicago and London: University of Chicago Press).

Rothman, E. Natalie (2012). 'Visualizing a Space of Encounter: Intimacy, Alterity, and Transimperial Perspective in an Ottoman Miniature Album,' *Osmanlı Araştırmaları/The Journal of Ottoman Studies*, XL, 39–80.

Rouillard, Clarence Dana (1941). *The Turk in French History, Thought, and Literature (1520–1660)* (Paris: Boivin).

Rozen, Minna (2002). *A History of the Jewish Community in Istanbul: The Formative Years 1453–1566* (Leiden: Brill).

Rozen, Minna (2018). 'Jamila Ḥarabun and Her (sic) Two Husbands: On Betrothal and Marriage among Ottoman Jews in Sixteenth-century Salonika,' *Journal of Family History*, May 2018 – OnlineFirst Online publication date: 02-May-2018, 1–28. (Accessed on 14 May 2018).

Rubin, Avi (2015). 'The Slave, the Governor and the Judge: An Ottoman Socio-Legal Drama from the Late Nineteenth Century,' in *Society, Law, and Culture in the Middle East: 'Modernities' in the Making*, edited by Dror Ze'evi and Ehud R. Toledano (Warsaw and Berlin: De Gruyter Open Ltd.), pp. 87–103.

Sabev, Orlin (Orhan Salih) (2006). *İbrahim Müteferrika ya da İlk Osmanlı Matbaa Serüveni (1726–1746)* (Istanbul: Yeditepe Yayınları).

Sahillioğlu, Halil (1999). *Studies on Ottoman Social and Economic History* (Istanbul: IRSICA).

Sahillioğlu, Halil (reprint 1999). 'Slaves in the Social and Economic Life of Bursa in the Late 15th and Early 16th Centuries,' in *Studies on Ottoman Social and Economic History* (Istanbul: IRSICA), pp. 105–74.

Şahin, Kaya (2010). 'Constantinople and the End Time: The Ottoman Conquest as a Portent of the Last Hour,' *Journal of Early Modern History*, 14, 317–54.

Said, Edward (1978). *Orientalism* (New York: Pantheon Books).

Salzmann, Ariel (2004). *Toqueville in the Ottoman Empire: Rival Paths to the Modern State* (Leiden: Brill).

Salzmann, Ariel (2007). 'A Travelogue Manqué? The Accidental Itinerary of a Maltese Priest in the Seventeenth-century Mediterranean,' in *A Faithful Sea: The Religious Cultures of the Mediterranean 1200–1700*, edited by Adnan A. Husain and K. E. Flemming (Oxford: Oneworld), pp. 149–72.

Sarıcaoğlu, Fikret (2001). *Sultan I. Abdulhamid: Kendi Kaleminden bir Padişahın Portresi (1774–1789)* (Istanbul: TATAV).

Sarınay, Yusuf et alii (2010). *Başbakanlık Osmanlı Arşivi Rehberi* (Ankara: T.C. Başbakanlık Devlet Arşivleri Genel Müdürlüğü).

Sariyannis, Marinos (2006). '"Neglected Trades": Glimpses into the 17th Century Istanbul Underworld,' *Turcica*, 38, 155–79.

Sariyannis, Marinos (2008). 'Prostitution in Ottoman Istanbul, Late Sixteenth to Early Eighteenth Centuries,' *Turcica*, 40, 37–65.

Sarıyıldız, Gülden (2011). *Sokak Yazıcıları: Osmanlılarda Arzuhaller ve Arzuhalciler* (Istanbul: Derlem Yayınları).

Schacht, Joseph (1964). *An Introduction to Islamic Law* (Oxford: At the Clarendon Press).

Schulze, Winfried (1978). *Reich und Türkengefahr im späten 16. Jahrhundert. Studien zu den politischen und gesellschaftlichen Auswirkungen einer äußeren Bedrohung* (Munich: C. H. Beck).

Scott, James (1985). *Weapons of the Weak: Everyday Forms of Peasant Resistance* (New Haven: Yale University Press).

Sel Turhan, Fatma (2018). *18. Yüzyıl Osmanlı'da Savaş Esirleri: 'Soltat Vasil Istefan, Uzun Boylu Genç Oğlandır'* (Istanbul: Vadiy Yayınları).

Selçuk, İklil (2015). 'Tracing Esnaf in Late Fifteenth-Century Bursa Court Records,' in *Bread from the Lion's Mouth: Artisans Struggling for a Livelihood in Ottoman Cities*, edited by Suraiya Faroqhi (New York and Oxford: Berghahn Books), pp. 51–69.

Semerdjian, Elyse (2008). *'Off the Straight Path': Illicit Sex, Law and Community in Ottoman Aleppo* (Syracuse: Syracuse University Press).

Serinidou, Vassiliki (2008). 'Grocers and Wholesalers, Ottomans and Habsburgs, Foreigners and "Our Own": The Greek Trade Diasporas in Central Europe, seventeenth to nineteenth centuries,' in *Merchants in the Ottoman Empire*, edited by Suraiya Faroqhi and Gilles Veinstein (Leuven: Peeters), pp. 81–96.

Shaw, Stanford J. (1962). *The Financial and Administrative Organization and Development of Ottoman Egypt 1517–1798* (Princeton, NJ: Princeton University Press).

Shehada, Housni Alkhateeb (2010). 'Arab Veterinary Medicine and the "Golden Rules" for Veterinarians According to a Sixteenth-century Medical Treatise,' in *Animals and People in the Ottoman Empire*, edited by Suraiya Faroqhi (Istanbul: Eren), pp. 315–32.

Singer, Amy (1994). *Palestinian Peasants and Ottoman Officials: Rural Administration around Sixteenth-century Jerusalem* (Cambridge: Cambridge University Press).

Smyrnelis, Marie Carmen (2006). *Une société hors de soi: identités et relations sociales à Smyrne aux XVIIIe et XIXe siècles* (Paris-Louvain: Peeters).

Sohrweide, Hanna (1965). 'Der Sieg der Safawiden in Persien und seine Rückwirkungen auf die Schiiten Anatoliens im 16. Jahrhundert,' *Der Islam*, 41, 1, 95–223.

Soucek, Svat (1992). *Piri Reis and Turkish Mapmaking after Columbus* (London: The Nour Foundation).

Soucek, Svat (undated). 'Pīrī Re'īs,' in *The Encyclopaedia of Islam, Second Edition*, edited by P. Bearman, Th. Blanquis, C.E. Bosworth, E.V. Donzel and W.P. Heinrich online version http://referenceworks.brillonline.com/browse/encyclopaedia-of-islam-2 (accessed on 12 January 2017).

Stavridis, Theoharis (2001). *The Sultan of Vezirs: The Life and Times of the Ottoman Grand Vezir Mahmud Paşa Angelovič (1453–1474)* (Leiden: Brill).

Stefini, Tommaso (2015). 'Ottoman Merchants in Dispute with the Republic of Venice at the End of the 16th Century: Some Glances on the Contested Regime of the Capitulations,' *Turcica*, 46, 153–76.

Stephanov, Darin (2018). *Ruler Visibility and Popular Belonging in the Ottomon Empire, 1808–1908* (Edinburgh: Edinburgh University Press).

Stichel, Rudolf W. (1991). 'Das Bremer Album und seine Stellung innerhalb der orientalischen Kostümbücher,' in Lambert de Vos, *Das Kostümbuch von Lambert de Vos: vollstaendige Faksimile-Ausgabe im Originalformat des Codex Ms. or. 9 aus dem Besitz der Staats- und Universitaetsbibliothek Bremen*, 2 vols., edited by H. A. Koch (Graz/Austria: Akademische Druck- und Verlagsanstalt), pp. 31–44.

Stoianovich, Traian (autumn of 1953). 'Land Tenure and Related Sectors of the Balkan Economy, 1600–1800,' *The Journal of Economic History*, 13, 4, 398–411.

Stoianovich, Traian (1960). 'The Conquering Balkan Orthodox Merchant,' *The Journal of Economic History*, XX, 234–313.

Sümer, Faruk (1980). *Oğuzlar (Türkmenler) Tarihleri, Boy Teşkilâtı, Destanları* 3rd edition (Ankara: Ana Yayınları).

Sunar, Mert (2009). '"When Grocers, Porters and Other Riff-raff become Soldiers": Janissary Artisans and Laborers in the Nineteenth-century Istanbul and Edirne,' *Kocaeli Üniversitesi Sosyal Bilimler Enstitüsü Dergisi*, 17, 1, 175–94. Accessed through: https://www.academia.edu/587369/_When_grocers_porters_and_other_riff-raff_become_soldiers_Janissary_Artisans_and_Laborers_in_the_Nineteenth_Century_Istanbul_and_Edirne (20 April 2017).

Tabakoğlu, Ahmet (1985). *Gerileme Dönemine Girerken Osmanlı Maliyesi* (Istanbul: Dergâh Yayınları).

Tamdoğan, Işık (undated). 'Osmanlı Döneminden Günümüz Türkiyesi'ne "Bizim Mahalle"' Osmanlı Araştırmaları/Osmanische Forschungen. http://www.os-ar.com/modules.php?name=Encyclopedia&op=content&tid=501674 (accessed on 4 January 2018).

Tekin, Ahmet (2016). 'Istanbul in Flames: City Conflagrations, Governance and Society in the Early Modern Period,' unpublished MA thesis, İstanbul Şehir Üniversitesi. http://www.academia.edu/36664394/ottoman_istanbul_in_flames_city_conflagrations_governance_and_society_in_the_early_modern_period (accessed in March 2019).

Tezcan, Baki (2002). 'The 1622 Military Rebellion in Istanbul: A Historiographical Journey,' *International Journal of Turkish Studies*, 8 /1–2, 25–43 (guest editor Jane Hathaway).

Tezcan, Baki (2007). 'Dispelling the Darkness: The Politics of "Race" in the Early Seventeenth-century Ottoman Empire in the Light of the Work of Mullah Ali,' in *Identity and Identity Formation in the Ottoman World: A Volume of Essays in Honor of Norman Itzkowitz*, edited by Baki Tezcan and Carl Barbier (Madison, WI: The University of Wisconsin Press), pp. 73–96.

Tezcan, Baki (2012). *The Second Ottoman Empire: Political and Social Transformation in the Early Modern World* (Cambridge: Cambridge University Press).

Tezcan, Baki (2013). 'The Memory of the Mongols in Early Ottoman Historiography,' in *Writing History at the Ottoman Court: Editing the Past, Shaping the Future*, edited by H. Erdem Çıpa and Emine Fetvacı (Bloomington and Indianapolis: Indiana University Press), pp. 23–35.

Todorov, Nikolai (1998). 'The Budget of a Family of Bulgarian Workers in the Mid-19th Century,' in idem, *Society, the City and Industry in the Balkans, 15th to 19th Centuries* (Aldershot, UK, Brookfield, VT, Singapore and Sydney: Ashgate/Variorum), No. IX.

Todorova, Maria (2009). *Bones of Contention: The Living Archive of Vasil Levski and the Making of Bulgaria's National Hero* (Budapest and New York: Central European University Press).

Toledano, Ehud (1982). *The Ottoman Slave Trade and its Suppression* (Princeton: Princeton University Press).

Tuchscherer, Michel (1999). 'Evolution du bâti et des fonctions dans les quartiers commerciaux du Caire à l'époque ottomane,' in *Un centre commercial et artisanal du Caire du XIIIe au XXe siècle: Le Khan al-Khalili et ses environs*, edited by Sylvie Denoix and Jean-Charles Depaule (Cairo: IFAO), pp. 67–96.

Tucker, Judith (1985). *Women in Nineteenth Century Egypt* (Cambridge: Cambridge Unversity Press).

Tuğ, Başak (2012). 'Ottoman Women as Legal and Marital Subjects,' in *The Ottoman World*, edited by Christine Woodhead (Abingdon and New York: Routledge), pp. 362–77.

Tuğ, Başak (2017). *Politics of Honor in Ottoman Anatolia: Sexual Violence and Socio-Legal Surveillance in the Eighteenth Century* (Leiden: Brill).

Uluç, Lale (2006). *Turkman Governors, Shiraz Artisans and Ottoman Collectors: Arts of the Book in 16th Century Shiraz* (Istanbul: İş Bankası Kültür Yayınları).

Uzunçarşılı, İsmail Hakkı (1932). *Bizans ve Selcukiylerle Germiyan ve Osmanoğulları Zamanında Kütahya Şehri* (Istanbul: Devlet Matbaası).

Uzunçarşılı, İsmail Hakkı (1972). *Mekke-i Mükerreme Emirleri* (Ankara: Türk Tarih Kurumu).

Uzunçarşılı, İsmail Hakkı (1981–6). 'Osmanlı Sarayında Ehl-i Hiref (Sanatkârlar) Defteri,' *Belgeler*, 11, 23–76.

Valensi, Lucette (1969). 'Islam et capitalisme: Production et commerce des chéchias en Tunisie et en France aux XVIIIe et XIXe siècles,' *Revue d'histoire moderne et contemporaine*, XVI, 376–400.

Varlık, Mustafa Çetin (1974). *Germiyan-oğulları Tarihi* (Ankara: Atatürk Üniversitesi Yayınları).

Vatin, Nicolas (2001). *Les Ottomans et l'occident (XVe-XVIe siècles)* (Istanbul: The Isis Press).

Vatin, Nicolas and Gilles Veinstein (2003). *Le sérail ébranlé: Essai sur les morts, dépositions et avènements des sultans ottomans, XIV–XIX siècle* (Paris: Fayard).

Veinstein, Gilles (1975). 'Ayân de la région d'Izmir et le commerce du Levant (deuxième moitié du XVIIIe siècle),' *Revue de l'Occident musulman et de la Méditerranée*, XX, 131–46.

Veinstein, Gilles (1983). 'L'hivernage en campagne, talon d'Achille du système militaire ottoman classique. A propos des sipāhī de Roumélie en 1559–1560,' *Studia Islamica*, LXVIII, 109–48.

Veinstein, Gilles (1994). 'A propos des *ehl-i hiref* et du *devşirme*,' in *Studies in Ottoman History in Honour of Professor V. L. Ménage*, edited by Colin Heywood and Colin Imber (Istanbul: The Isis Press), pp. 351–68.

Veinstein, Gilles (2005). 'Le rôle des tombes sacrées dans la conquête ottomane,' *Revue de l'histoire des religions* [online version], 4. Placed online: 18 January 2010 (accessed on 27 April 2018). http://journals.openedition.org/rhr/4228; DOI: 10.4000/rhr.4228

Vryonis, Speros (1971). *The Decline of Medieval Hellenism in Asia Minor and the Process of Islamization from the Eleventh through the Fifteenth Century* (Berkeley, Los Angeles and London: University of California Press).

Wallerstein, Immanuel, Hale Decdeli and Reşat Kasaba (1987 reprint 2004). 'The Incorporation of the Ottoman Empire into the World Economy,' in *The Ottoman Empire and the World Economy*, edited by Huri İslamoğlu İnan (Cambridge and Paris: Cambridge University Press and Maison des Sciences de l'Homme), pp. 88–97.

Ward Perkins, Bryan (2006). *The Fall of Rome: And the End of Civilization* (Oxford and London: Oxford University Press).

Watenpaugh, Heghnar Z. (2004). *The Image of an Ottoman City: Imperial Architecture and Urban Experience in Aleppo in the Sixteenth and Seventeenth Centuries* (Leiden: Brill).

White, Sam (2011). *The Climate of Rebellion in the Early Modern Ottoman Empire* (Cambridge: Cambridge University Press).

Wilkins, Charles (2010). *Forging Urban Solidarities: Ottoman Aleppo 1640–1700* (Leiden: Brill).

Wittek, Paul (1934). *Das Fürstentum Mentesche: Studie zur Geschichte Westkleinasiens im 13.–15. Jh.* (Istanbul: Archäologisches Institut des Deutschen Reiches).

Yaman, Bahattin (2008). *Osmanlı Saray Sanatkârları: 18. Yüzyılda Ehl-i Hiref* (Istanbul: Tarih Vakfı Yurt Yayınları).

Yaman, Bahattin (2018). *Sarayın Terzileri: 16.–18. Yüzyıl Osmanlı Hassa Kıyafeti Birimleri* (Istanbul: Kitap Yayınevi).

Yaşa, Fırat (2014). 'Kırım Hanlığı'nda Köleliğin Sosyal ve Malı Boyutları,' *Gaziantep University Journal of Social Sciences*, 13, 3, 657–69. Accessed on 3 March 2017 through: http://dergipark.gov.tr/download/article-file/223191

Yi, Eunjeong (2005). *Guild Dynamics in Seventeenth-century Istanbul: Fluidity and Leverage* (Leiden: Brill).

Yi, Eunjeong (2015). 'Rich Artisans and Poor Merchants? A Critical Look at the Supposed Egalitarianism in Ottoman Guilds,' in *Bread from the Lion's Mouth: Artisans Struggling for a Livelihood in Ottoman Cities*, edited by Suraiya Faroqhi (New York and Oxford: Berghahn Books), pp. 194–216.

Yıldırım, Onur (Dec. 2002). 'Ottoman Guilds as a Setting for Ethno-Religious Conflict: The Case of the Silk-thread Spinners' Guild in Istanbul,' *International Review of Social History*, 47/3, 407–19.

Yıldırım, Rıza (2007). *Seyyid Ali Sultan (Kızıldeli) ve Velâyetnâmesi* (Ankara: Türk Tarih Kurumu).

Yıldız, Aysel (2012). 'The Anatomy of a Rebellious Social Group: The *Yamak*s of the Bosporus at the Margins of Ottoman Society,' in *Political Initiatives 'From the Bottom Up' in the Ottoman Empire: Halcyon Days in Crete VII, A Symposium Held in Rethymno 9–11 January 2009,* edited by Antonios Anastasopoulos (Rethymno: University of Crete Publications), pp. 291–326.

Yıldız, Aysel (2017). *Crisis and Rebellion in the Ottoman Empire. The Downfall of a Sultan in the Age of Revolution* (London: I. B. Tauris).

Yıldız, Saranur (2005). 'Historiography. xi. Persian Historiography in the Ottoman Empire,' in *Encyclopaedia Iranica,* vol. 12, fasc. 4, 403–411.

Yılmaz, Fikret (2018). 'Selim'i Yazmak,' *Osmanlı Araştırmaları/The Journal of Ottoman Studies*, 51, 297–390. (Review article concerning Erdem Çıpa, *The Making of Selim*).

Yılmaz, Gülay (2009). 'Becoming a Devşirme: The Training of Conscripted Children in the Ottoman Empire,' in *Children in Slavery through the Ages*, edited by Gwyn Campbell, Suzanne Miers and Joseph C. Miller (Ohio: Ohio University Press), pp. 119–34.

Yılmaz, Gülay (2015). 'Blurred Boundaries between Soldiers and Civilians: Artisan Janissaries in Seventeenth Century Istanbul,' in *Bread from the Lion's Mounth: Artisans Struggling for a Livelihood in Ottoman Cities*, edited by Suraiya Faroqhi (New York: Berghahn Books), pp. 175–94.

Yılmaz, Yıldız (2017). 'Cutting a Fine Figure among Pots and Pans: Aghas of the Sultan's Harem in the Eighteenth Century,' in *Living the Good Life: Consumption in the Qing and Ottoman Empires of the Eighteenth Century*, edited by Elif Akçetin and Suraiya Faroqhi (Leiden: Brill), pp. 113–33.

Yılmazer, Ziya (n. d.). 'Şânîzâde Mehmed Atâullah Efendi,' in *TDV İslâm Ansiklopedisi*, vol. 38, pp. 334–36: http://www.tdvia.org/dia/ayrmetin.php?idno=380334 (accessed on 14 October 2016).

Yürekli, Zeynep (2012). *Architecture and Hagiography in the Ottoman Empire: The Politics of Bektashi Shrines in the Classical Age* (Birmingham: Ashgate) (Byzantine and Ottoman Studies). http://www.ashgate.com/isbn/9781409411062 (accessed on 6 January 2018).

Zachariadou, Elizabeth (1983). *Trade and Crusade: Venetian Crete and the Emirates of Menteshe and Aydin (1300–1415)* (Venice: Istituto Ellenico di Studi Bizantini e Post-bizantini di Venezia) (Library of the Hellenic Institute of Byzantine and Post-Byzantine Studies, No. 11).

Zachariadou, Elizabeth A. (1994). 'The Worrisome Wealth of the Čelnik Radić,' in *Studies in Ottoman History in Honour of Professor V. L. Ménage,* edited by Colin Heywood and Colin Imber (Istanbul: The Isis Press), pp. 383–97.

Zarinebaf-Shahr, Fariba (2001). 'The Role of Women in the Urban Economy of Istanbul, 1700–1850,' *International Labor and Working Class History*, 60, 141–52.

Zarinebaf, Fariba (2010). *Crime and Punishment in Istanbul, 1700–1800* (Berkeley, Los Angeles and London: University of California Press).

Zarinebaf, Fariba (2018). *Mediterranean Encounters: Trade and Pluralism in Early Modern Galata* (Los Angeles, Berkeley and London: University of California Press).

Zilfi, Madeline (1993). 'A *medrese* for the Palace: Ottoman Dynastic Legitimation in the Eighteenth Century,' *Journal of the American Oriental Society*, 113.2, 184–91.

Zilfi, Madeline (2010). *Women and Slavery in the Late Ottoman Empire: The Design of Difference* (Cambridge: Cambridge University Press).

Primary sources, written and pictorial: the Mughal world

Abū'l-fazl (1927–49). *ᶜAin-i Ākbarī* (sic) *of Abul-Fazl-i* ᶜĀllamī, 3 vols., translated by H. Blochmann, H. S. Jarrett and revised by Jadunath Sarkar (Calcutta: Royal Asiatic Society of Bengal), vols. 1 and 3.

Banarasidas (2009). *Ardhakathanak (A Half Story)*, translated from the Braj Bhasha by Rohini Chowdhury (Delhi: Penguin Books).

Beach, Milo K., Wheeler M. Thackston and Ebba Koch (1997). *The King of the World: The Padshahnama – An Imperial Mughal Manuscript from the Royal Library, Windsor Castle* (London: Thames and Hudson).

Bernier, François (reprint 2010). *Travels in the Mogul Empire 1656–1668*, translated by Archibald Constable (New Delhi and Chennai: Asian Educational Services).

Calza, Gian Carlo ed. (2012). *Akbar: The Great Emperor of India* (Milano: Skira).

Foster, William ed. (1921) *Early Travels in India 1583–1619* (London: Humphrey Milford, Oxford University Press). https://ia801406.us.archive.org/35/items/earlytravelsini00fostgoog/earlytravelsini00fostgoog.pdf (accessed on 13 August 2018).

Gul-Badan Begam (Princess Rose-Body) (reprint 2011). *The History of Humāyun (sic) (Humāyūn-Nāma)*, translated and annotated by Annette S. Beveridge (Delhi: Low Price Publications).

Haider, Navina Najat and Marika Sardar eds. (2015). *Sultans of Deccan India: Opulence and Fantasy* (New York: The Metropolitan Museum of Art).

Ibn Battuta (1854). *Voyages d'Ibn Batoutah, texte arabe, accompagné d'une traduction*, vol. 2, edited and translated by C. Defrémery and B. R. Sanguinetti (Paris: Imprimerie Impériale).

Jahangir, *The Jahangirnama: Memoirs of Jahangir, Emperor of India*, translated and edited by Wheeler M. Thackston (Washington: Freer Gallery of Art and Arthur M. Sackler Gallery; New York: Oxford University Press, 1999).

Manucci, Niccolao (reprint 1989). *Mogul India 1653–1708 or Storia do Mogor*, translated by William Irvine, 4 vols. (Delhi: Atlantic Publishers and Distributors), vol. 4.

Moosvi, Shireen ed. and translator (2008). 'Problems of Mughal Revenue Administration: Todarmal's original memorandum, March 1582,' in eadem, *People, Taxation and Trade in Mughal India* (New Delhi: Oxford University Press of India), pp. 159–74.

[Pelsaert, Francisco] (2011). *Jahangir's India: The Remonstratie of Francisco Pelsaert, translated by W. H. Moreland and P. Geyl* (Delhi: Low Price Publications).

Seydi Ali Reis, *Seydi Ali Reis: Mir'âtü'l-Memâlik, İnceleme, Metin, Indeks*, edited by Mehmet Kiremit (Ankara: Türk Dil Kurumu, 1999).

Seyller, John et alii eds. (2002). *The Adventures of Hamza, Painting and Storytelling in Mughal India*, (Washington DC and London: Freer Gallery of Art and Arthur M. Sackler Gallery, Smithsonian Institution, in association with Azimuth Editions Limited, London).

Tavernier, Jean-Baptiste (reprint, n. d.). *Travels in India by Jean-Baptiste Tavernier baron d'Aubonne*, translated by V. Ball, 2nd edition edited by William Crooke, 2 vols. (Delhi: Low Price Publications).

Tillotson, Giles and Mrinalini Venkateswaran eds. (2016). *Painting and Photography at the Jaipur Court* (New Delhi: Nyogi Books and Maharaja Sawai Singh II Museum Trust).

Welch, Stuart Cary and Kimberley Masteller eds. (2004). *From Heart, Mind and Hand: Persian, Turkish, and Indian Drawings from the Stuart Cary Welch Collection* (New Haven, CT, London and Cambridge, MA: Yale University Press and Harvard College).

Wright, Elaine et alii (2008). *Muraqqa': Imperial Mughal Albums from the Chester Beatty Library Dublin* (Alexandria, VA: Art Services International).

Secondary sources: The Mughal world

Aitken, Molly Emma (2002). 'Pardah and Portrayal: Rajput Women as Subjects, Patrons, and Collectors,' *Artibus Asiae*, 62/2, 247–80. Accessed through JStor: https://www.jstor.org/stable/pdf/3250267.pdf (30 December 2016).

Aitken, Molly Emma (2009). 'Parataxis and the Practice of Reuse, from Mughal Margins to Mīr Kalān Khān,' *Archives of Asian Art*, 59, 81–103. Accessed through JStor: https://www.jstor.org/stable/40863702?seq=1#page_scan_tab_contents (30 December 2016).

Alam, Ishrat (2000). 'Diamond Mining and Trade in South India in the Seventeenth Century,' *The Medieval History Journal*, 3/2, 291–305.

Alam, Muzaffar (1986). *The Crisis of Empire in Mughal North India: Awadh and the Punjab, 1707–48* (Delhi: Oxford University Press).

Alam, Muzaffar (1994). 'Trade, State Policy and Regional Change: Aspects of Mughal-Uzbek Commercial Relations, C. 1550–1750,' *Journal of the Economic and Social History of the Orient*, XXVII/3, 202–27.

Alam, Muzaffar (2002). 'Aspects of Agrarian Uprisings in North India in the Early Eighteenth Century,' in *The Eighteenth Century in India*, edited by Seema Alavi (Debates in Indian History and Society) (Delhi: Oxford University Press), pp. 84–112.

Alam, Muzaffar (reprint 2010). 'The Pursuit of Persian: Language in Mughal Politics,' in *Exploring Medieval India II, Sixteenth to Nineteenth Centuries: Culture, Gender, Regional Patterns*, edited by Meena Bhargava (Himayatnagar/ Hyderabad: Orient Black Swan), pp. 39–73.

Alam, Muzaffar (2013). 'Introduction,' in *The Crisis of Empire in Mughal North India: Awadh and the Punjab, 1707–48* (Delhi: Oxford University Press), pp. XIII–LXI.

Alam, Muzaffar and Sanjay Subrahmanyam (2007). *Indo-Persian Travels in the Age of Discoveries* (Cambridge: Cambridge University Press).

Ali, M. Athar (reprint 2006a). 'The Passing of the Empire: The Mughal Case,' in idem, *Mughal India: Studies in Polity, Ideas, Society, and Culture*, prefaced by Irfan Habib (Delhi: Oxford University Press), pp. 337–49.

Ali, M. Athar (reprint 2006b). 'The Objectives behind the Mughal Expedition into Balkh and Badakhshan, 1646–47,' in idem, *Mughal India: Studies in Polity, Ideas, Society, and Culture*, prefaced by Irfan Habib (Delhi: Oxford University Press), pp. 327–33.

Ali, Omar (2016). *Malik Ambar: Power and Slavery across the Indian Ocean* (Oxford and New York: Oxford University Press).

Amin, Shahid (2016). *Conquest and Community: The Afterlife of the Warrior Saint Ghazi Miyan* (Chicago and London: The University of Chicago Press).

Anand, Anita and William Dalrymple (2017). *Koh-i-Noor: The History of the World's Most Infamous Diamond* (London: Bloomsbury).

Ansari, A. S. Bazmee (1988, updated 2011). 'Badā'ūnī, 'Abd-al-Qāder,' in *Encyclopedia Iranica*. http://www.iranicaonline.org/articles/badauni-abd-al-qader-b (accessed on 25 March 2018).

Aquil, Raziuddin (2016). 'Hazret-i Delhi: The Making of the Chishti Sufi Centre and the Stronghold of Islam,' in *Essays in Medieval Delhi*, edited by Nirmal Kumar (New Delhi: Research in India Press) (Debates in Indian History Series).

Arasaratnam, Sinappah (1986). *Merchants, Companies and Commerce on the Coromandel Coast 1650–1740* (Delhi: Oxford University Press).

Arasaratnam, Sinappah (1990). 'Weavers, Merchants and Company: The Handloom Industry in South-eastern India 1750–1790,' in *Merchants, Markets and the State in Early Modern India*, edited by Sanjay Subrahmanyam (Delhi: Oxford University Press of India), pp. 190–214.

Arasaratnam, Sinappah and Aniruddha Ray (1994). *Masulipatnam and Cambay: A history of two port- towns 1500–1800* (Delhi: Munshiram Manoharlal).

Asher, Catherine B. and Cynthia Talbot (2008). *India before Europe* (Cambridge: Cambridge University Press).

Bajekal, Madhavi (1990). 'The State and the Rural Grain Market in Eighteenth-century Eastern Rajasthan,' in *Merchants, Markets and the State in Early Modern India*, edited by Sanjay Subrahmanyam (Delhi: Oxford University Press), pp. 90–120.

Balabanlilar, Lisa (2012). *Imperial Identity in the Mughal Empire: Memory and Dynastic Politics in Early Modern South and Central Asia* (New York and London: I. B. Tauris).

Banerji, Arup (2011). *Old Routes: North Indian Nomads and Bankers in Afghan, Uzbek and Russian Lands* (Gurgaon/Haryana: Three Essays Collective).

Bang, Peter (2008). *The Roman Bazaar: A Comparative Study of Trade and Markets in a Tributary Empire* (Cambridge: Cambridge University Press).

Bano, Shadab (2001). 'Slave Markets in Medieval India,' *Proceedings of the Indian History Congress, 61st session,* Kolkata, 365–73.

Bano, Shadab (2002). 'Slave Acquisition in the Mughal Empire, Professor J. S. Grewal Prize Essay,' *Proceedings of the Indian History Congress, 62nd Session, 2001,* Kolkata, 317–24.

Bano, Shadab (2004). 'Women Slaves in Medieval India,' *Proceedings of the Indian History Congress, 65th session,* Bareilly, 314–23.

Bano, Shadab (2008). 'Women and Property in Mughal India,' *Proceedings of the Indian History Congress*, Delhi, pp. 406–15.

Bano, Shadab (2009). 'Eunuchs in Mughal Royal and Aristocratic Establishments,' *Proceedings of the Indian History Congress*, Kolkata, 417–27.

Bano, Shadab (2011). 'Women Performers and Prostitutes in Medieval India,' *Studies in History*, 27, 1, 41–53.

Barnes, Ruth (1997). *Indian Block-Printed Textiles in Egypt: The Newberry Collection in the Ashmolean Museum, Oxford: A Catalogue of Newberry's Block-printed Textiles by Ruth Barnes* (published Oxford, 1997). Accessed through http://www.jameelcentre.ashmolean.org/collection/7/10236/10318 (2 July 2017).

Bayly, Christopher A. (1986). 'Home Industry or *swadeshi*,' in *The Social Life of Things: Commodities in Cultural Perspective*, edited by Arjun Appadurai (Cambridge: Cambridge University Press), pp. 285–322.

Bayly, Susan (1998). *Caste, Society and Politics in India from the Eighteenth Century to the Modern Age* (Cambridge: Cambridge University Press, Cambridge Histories online). Accessed through: https://archive.org/stream/CasteSocietyAndPoliticsInIndiaIn18CenturyIndiaSusanBaylyOUP2008/Caste%2C%20Society%20and%20Politics%20in%20India%20-in%2018%20Century%20IndiaSusan%20Bayly%20OUP%202008_djvu.txt (9 August 2018).

Bhardwaj, Surajbhan (2016). 'Migration, Mobility and Memories: Meos in the Processes of Peasantisation and Islamisation in the Medieval Period,' in *Migrations in Medieval and Early Colonial India*, edited by Vijaya Ramaswamy (Oxford and New York: Routledge), pp. 87–126.

Bhargava, Meena ed. (2010). *Exploring Medieval India: Sixteenth to Eighteenth Centuries*, Vol. II: *Culture, Gender and Regional Patterns* (New Delhi: Orient BlackSwan).

Bhukya, Bhangya (2017). 'The Twilight World of the Caravan: The Regulated Market Economy and the Caravanners in Hyderabad State,' in *Frontiers of Environment: Issues in Medieval and Early Modern India*, edited by Meena Bhargava (Delhi: Orient BlackSwan), pp. 98–127.

Biswas, Soutik (2012). 'Has Gujarat Moved on Since 2002's Riots,' http://www.bbc.com/news/world-asia-india-17200961 (accessed on 4 December 2017).

Blake, Stephen (2016). 'Cityscape of an Imperial Capital: Shahjahanabad in 1739,' in *Essays in Medieval Delhi*, edited by Nirmal Kumar (New Delhi: Research India Press), pp. 261–311.

Buehler, Arthur F. (1996). 'The Naqshbandiyya in Tīmūrid India: The Central Asian Legacy,' *Journal of Islamic Studies*, 7/2, 208–28, http://jis.oxfordjournals.org/content/7/2/208.full.pdf (accessed on 1 September 2016).

Casale, Giancarlo (2009). *The Ottoman Age of Exploration* (New York: Oxford University Press).

Chakrabarty, Dipesh (2015). *The Calling of History: Sir Jadunath Sarkar and His Empire of Truth* (Ranikhet and Delhi: Permanent Black and Ashoka University).

Chakraverty, Anjan (2008). *Indian Miniature Painting* (Delhi: India Crest, Lustre Press, Roli Books).

Chandra, Satish (1969). 'Jizyah and the State in India during the 17th Century,' *Journal of the Economic and Social History of the Orient*, 12, 3, 322–40.

Chandra, Satish (reprint 1998). 'Review of the Crisis of the Jagirdari System,' in *The Mughal State 1526–1750*, edited by Muzaffar Alam and Sanjay Subrahmanyam (Delhi: Oxford University Press), pp. 346–60.

Chatterjee, Indrani and Richard Eaton eds. (2006). *Slavery and South Asian History* (Bloomington and Indianapolis: Indiana University Press).

Chatterjee, Kumkum (2009). *The Cultures of History in Early Modern India: Persianization and Mughal Culture in Bengal* (Oxford and Delhi: Oxford University Press).

Chaudhuri, K. N. (1985). *Trade and Civilization in the Indian Ocean: An Economic History from the Rise of Islam to 1750* (Cambridge: Cambridge University Press).

Chenoy, Shama Mitra (2014). 'Shahjahanabad: A Medieval Indian Experience,' in *Cities in Medieval India*, edited by Yogesh Sharma and Pius Malekandathil (Delhi: Primus Books), pp. 157–80.

Choudhary, Pragyan (2016). 'Social Mobility and Migration among the Jats of Medieval India,' in *Migrations in Medieval and Early Colonial India*, edited by Vijaya Ramaswamy (Oxford and New York: Routledge), pp. 44–64.

Chowdhury, Rishad (2016). 'The Hajj and the Hindi: The Ascent of the Indian Sufi Lodge in the Ottoman Empire,' *Modern Asian Studies*, 50, 6, 1888–1931.

Cohen, Steven (2008). 'Textiles, Dress and Apparel as Depicted in the Albums,' in *Muraqqa': Imperial Mughal Albums from the Chester Beatty Library Dublin* (Alexandria, VA: Art Services International), pp. 178–87.
Dale, Stephen F. (1994). *Indian Merchants and Eurasian Trade 1600–1750* (Cambridge: Cambridge University Press).
Dale, Stephen F. (2004). *The Garden of the Eight Paradises: Babur and the Culture of Empire in Central Asia, Afghanistan and India (1485–1530)* (Leiden: Brill).
Das Gupta, Ashin (1979a, reprint 1994). *Indian Merchants and the Decline of Surat c. 1700–1750,* 2nd edition (Delhi: Manohar).
Das Gupta, Ashin (1979b). 'Indian Merchants and the Red Sea Trade 1700–1725,' in *The Age of Partnership: Europeans in Asia before Dominion*, edited by Blair B. Kling and Michael N. Pearson (Honolulu: The University Press of Hawaii), pp. 123–58.
Datta, Rajat (2014). 'The Rural-Urban Continuum and the Making of a Proto-Industrial Economy in Early Modern India,' in *Cities in Medieval India*, edited by Yogesh Sharma and Pius Malekandathil (Delhi: Primus Books), pp. 83–112.
Deshpande, Prachi (2007). *Creative Pasts: Historical Memory and Identity in Western India, 1700–1960* (New York: Columbia University Press).
Devra, G. S. L. (2014). 'Formation and Growth of Mandis and Chowkis in Western Rajasthan, AD 1700–1830,' in *Cities in Medieval India*, edited by Yogesh Sharma and Pius Malekandathil (Delhi: Primus Books), pp. 243–61.
Dhar, Bidisha (2011). 'Coping with a Changing World: the Artisans of Lucknow c. mid-19th to late 20th Century,' PhD dissertation, Centre for Historical Studies, Jawaharlal Nehru University, New Delhi.
Eaton, Richard (1993). *The Rise of Islam and the Bengal Frontier 1204–1760* (Berkeley: University of California Press).
Eaton, Richard (reprint 2000). 'Temple Desecration and Indo-Muslim States,' in idem, *Essays on Islam and Indian History* (Delhi: Oxford University Press), pp. 94–132.
Eaton, Richard (2005). *A Social History of the Deccan 1300–1761* (Cambridge: Cambridge University Press).
Eaton, Richard M. (1983–2011). 'Abu'l-Fazl Allami,' *Encyclopædia Iranica*, I/3, pp. 287–289; an updated version is available online at http://www.iranicaonline.org/articles/abul-fazl-allami-historian (accessed on 3 March 2018).
Editors of the *Encyclopaedia Britannica* (n. d. after 2011). 'Lucknow,' https://www.britannica.com/place/Lucknow#ref32610 (accessed on 21 September 2018).
Farooqi, Naim R. (1986). 'Mughal–Ottoman Relations: A Study of Political and Diplomatic Relations between Mughal India and the Ottoman Empire 1556–1748,' unpublished PhD dissertation, University of Wisconsin in Madison (obtained through University Microfilms).
Farooqi, Naim R. (1988). 'Moguls, Ottomans and Pilgrims: Protecting the Routes to Mecca in the Sixteenth and Seventeenth Centuries,' *The International History Review*, X, 2, 198–220.
Farooqi, Naim R. (2017). 'An Overview of Ottoman Archival Documents and their Relevance for Medieval Indian History,' *The Medieval History Journal*, 20/1, 192–229.
Faruqui, Munis D. (2012). *The Princes of the Mughal Empire 1504–1719* (Cambridge: Cambridge University Press).
Faruqui, Munis D. (2014). 'Dara Shukoh, Vedanta and Imperial Succession in Mughal India,' in *Religious Interactions in Mughal India*, edited by Vasudha Dalmia and Munis D. Faruqui (Delhi: Oxford University Press), pp. 30–64.

Findley, Ellison Banks (1993). *Nur Jahan: Empress of Mughal India* (Oxford: Oxford University Press).

Findley, Ellison Banks (2010). 'The Capture of Maryam-uz-Zamānī's Ship: Mughal Women and European Traders,' in *Exploring Medieval India II, Sixteenth to Nineteenth Centuries: Culture, Gender, Regional Patterns*, edited by Meena Bhargava (Himayatnagar/Hyderabad: Orient Black Swan) pp. 261–84.

Gagliardi Mangilli, Elisa (2012). 'Akbar the Great: The Emperor's New Clothes; The Evolution of Mughal Costumes in the Contemporary Documentary Sources,' in *Akbar: The Great Emperor of India*, edited by Gian Carlo Calza (Milano Skira), pp. 71–80.

Ghoswami, Chhaya (2016). *Globalization before its Time: The Gujarati Merchants from Kachchh*, Introduction by Gurcharan Das (Gurgaon/India: Penguin/Portfolio).

Gommans, Jos (2002). *Mughal Warfare: Indian Frontiers and High Roads to Empire, 1500–1700* (London and New York: Routledge).

Goswamy, B. N. (2016). *The Spirit of Indian Painting: Close Encounters with 101 Great Works 1100–1900* (London: Thames & Hudson).

Gupta, S. P. (1986). *The Agrarian System of Eastern Rajasthan (c. 1650–c. 1750)* (Delhi: Manohar Publishers and Distributors).

Guy, John (1982). 'Mughal Painting under Akbar: The Melbourne Hamzanama and Akbarnama Paintings,' *Art Journal*, 22: http://www.ngv.vic.gov.au/essay/mughal-painting-under-akbar-the-melbourne-hamza-nama-and-akbar-nama-paintings/ (accessed on 19 August 2016).

Habib, Irfan (1963). *The Agrarian System of Mughal India* (London: Asia Publishing House).

Habib, Irfan (1977). 'Cartography in Mughal India,' in *Medieval India: A Miscellany*, 4 (Aligarh and New York: Aligarh Muslim University and Asia Publishing House), pp. 122–34.

Habib, Irfan (1989). 'A System of Trimetallism in the Age of the "Price Revolution": Effects of the Silver Influx on the Mughal Monetary System,' in *The Imperial Monetary System of Mughal India*, edited by John F. Richards (Delhi: Oxford University Press), pp. 137–70.

Habib, Irfan (1990). 'Merchant Communities in Pre-colonial India,' in *The Rise of Merchant Empires: Long-Distance Trade in the Early Modern World, 1350–1750*, edited by James D. Tracy (Cambridge: Cambridge University Press), pp. 379–96.

Habib, Irfan (1999). *The Agrarian System of Mughal India 1556–1707, Second Revised Edition* (Delhi: Oxford University Press).

Habib, Irfan (2002). 'The Eighteenth Century in Indian Economic History,' in *The Eighteenth Century in India*, edited by Seema Alavi (Debates in Indian History and Society) (Delhi: Oxford University Press), pp. 57–83.

Habib, Irfan (2008). *Technology in Medieval India, c. 650–1750* (Delhi: Tulika Books and Aligarh Historians Society).

Habib, Irfan (reprint 2010). 'Caste in Indian History,' in idem, *Essays in Indian History: Towards a Marxist Perspective* (Delhi: Tulika Books), pp. 161–79.

Habib, Irfan (2011). 'Hindi/Hindwi in Medieval Times: Aspects of Evolution and Recognition of a Language,' in *The Varied Facets of History: Essays in Honour of Aniruddha Ray*, edited by Ishrat Alam and Syeed Eyaz Hussain (Delhi: Primus Books), pp. 104–13.

Haider, Najaf (2002a). 'Global Networks of Exchange, the India Trade and the Mercantile Economy of Safavid Iran,' in *The Growth of Civilizations in India & Iran*, edited by Irfan Habib (Aligarh History Congress and Tulika Books), pp. 189–210.

Haider, Najaf (2002b). 'The Monetary Basis of Credit and Banking Instruments in the Mughal Empire,' in *Money & Credit in Indian History from Early Medieval Times*, edited by Amiya Kumar Bagchi (New Delhi: Tulika Books), pp. 58–83.

Haider, Najaf (2005). 'A "Holi Riot" of 1714: Versions from Ahmedabad and Delhi,' in *Living Together Separately: Cultural India in History and Politics*, edited by Mushirul Hasan and Asim Roy (Delhi: Oxford University Press), pp. 127–44.

Halim Khan, Sumbul (2015). *Art and Craft Workshops under the Mughals: A Study of Jaipur Karkhanas* (Delhi: Primus Books).

Hambly, Gavin (1974). 'A Note on the Trade in Eunuchs in Mughal Bengal,' *Journal of the American Oriental Society*, 94, 1, 125–30.

Hasan, Farhat (2004). *State and Locality in Mughal India: Power Relations in Western India, c.1572–1730* (Cambridge: Cambridge University Press).

Husayn, Iqbal (1999). 'Hindu Shrines and Practices as Described by a Central Asian Traveller in the First half of the Seventeenth Century,' in *Medieval India I: Researches in the History of India 1200–1750*, edited by Irfan Habib (New Delhi: Oxford University Press of India), pp. 141–53.

Imam, Fatima (2016). 'An Imperial Capital or a Camp City? A Review of Bernier's Testimony,' in *Essays in Medieval Delhi*, edited by Nirmal Kumar (New Delhi: Research India Press), pp. 233–60.

Jasonoff, Maya (2006). *Edge of Empire: Conquest and Collecting in the East 1750–1850* (London: Harper Perennial).

Keller, Sara and Michael Pearson eds. (2015). *Port Towns of Gujarat* (Delhi: Primus Books).

Khan, Iqtidar Alam (2010). 'Akbar's Personality Traits and World Outlook: A Critical Reappraisal,' in *Akbar and his India*, edited by Irfan Habib (Delhi: Oxford University Press), pp. 79–96.

Kinra, Rajeef (2016). *Writing Self, Writing Empire: Chandar Bhan Brahman and the Cultural World of the Indo-Persian State Secretary* (Delhi: Primus Books).

Koch, Ebba (1986). 'The Zahara Bagh (Bagh-i Jahanara),' *Environmental Design*, 2, 30–37.

Koch, Ebba (1988). *Shah Jahan and Orpheus: Pietre Dure Decoration and the Programme of the Throne in the Hall of Public Audiences at the Red Fort of Delhi* (Graz: Akademische Druck- und Verlaganstalt).

Koch, Ebba (1991). *Mughal Architecture* (Munich: Prestel Verlag).

Koch, Ebba (1997). *Dara Shikoh Shooting Nilgais: Hunt and Landscape in Mughal Painting* (Washington, DC: Freer Gallery and Arthur M. Sackler Gallery). (Occasional Papers).

Koch, Ebba (2001). 'The Hierarchical Principles of Shah-Jahani Painting,' in eadem, *Mughal Art and Imperial Ideology*, (New Delhi: Oxford University Press), pp. 130–62 (accessed through: https://www.academia.edu/8446252/The_Hierarchical_Principles_of_Shah-Jahani_Painting on 4 January 2017).

Koch, Ebba (2002). 'The Intellectual and Artistic Climate at Akbar's Court,' in *The Adventures of Hamza, Painting and Storytelling in Mughal India*, edited by John Seyller (Washington, DC and London: Freer Gallery of Art and Arthur M. Sackler Gallery, Smithsonian Institution, in association with Azimuth Editions Limited, London), pp. 18–31.

Koch, Ebba (2005). 'The Taj Mahal: Architecture, Symbolism and Urban Significance,' *Muqarnas*, 22, 128–49.

Koch, Ebba (2010). 'The Mughal Emperor as Solomon, Majnun, and Orpheus, or the Album as a Think Tank for Allegory,' *Muqarnas*, 27, 277–311. file:///C:/Users/Suraiya/

Downloads/The_Mughal_Emperor_as_Solomon_Majnun_and.pdf (accessed on 6 November 2016).

Koch, Ebba (2012). 'The Symbolic Possession of the World: European Cartography in Mughal Allegory and History Painting,' *Journal of the Economic and Social History of the Orient*, 55, 547–80.

Koch, Ebba (2016). 'The Delhi of the Mughals Prior to Shahjahabad as Reflected in the Patterns of Imperial Visits,' in *Essays in Medieval Delhi*, edited by Nirmal Kumar (New Delhi: Research India Press), pp. 122–62.

Kolff, Dirk H. A. (1990). *Naukar, Rajput and Sepoy: The Ethnohistory of the Military Labour Market in Hindustan 1450–1850* (Cambridge: Cambridge University Press).

Kothiyal, Tanuja (2014). 'Market Towns in Late Medieval and Early Modern Marwar,' in *Cities in Medieval India*, edited by Yogesh Sharma and Pius Malekandathil (Delhi: Primus Books), pp. 339–65.

Kothiyal, Tanuja (2016). *Nomadic Narratives: A History of Mobility and Identity in the Great Indian Desert,* (Delhi: Cambridge University Press).

Kumar, Mayank (2017). 'Situating the Environment: Settlement, Irrigation and Agriculture in Pre-colonial Rajasthan,' in *Frontiers of Environment: Issues in Medieval and Early Modern India*, edited by Meena Bhargava (Delhi: Orient Blackswan), pp. 167–95.

Kumar, Nita (1988). *The Artisans of Banaras: Popular Culture and Identity, 1880–1986* (Princeton: Princeton University Press).

Kumar, Satish (2014). 'Patna: A Riverine City,' in *Cities in Medieval India*, edited by Yogesh Sharma and Pius Malekandathil (Delhi: Primus Books), pp. 181–207.

Kumar, Sunil (2007). *The Emergence of the Delhi Sultanate 1192–1286* (Ranikhet/India: Permanent Black).

Kumar, Sunil ed. (2008). *Demolishing Myths or Mosques and Temples? Readings on History and Temple Desecration in Medieval India* (Gurgaon/India: Three Essays Collective) (authors: Richard H. Davis, Romila Thapar, Richard Eaton, Finbar B. Flood).

Kumar Singh, Abhay (2014). 'Cambay as Maritime City of Gujarat, AD 1200–1650,' in *Cities in Medieval India*, edited by Yogesh Sharma and Pius Malekandathil (Delhi: Primus Books), pp. 525–73.

Lal, Ruby (2005). *Domesticity and Power in the Early Mughal World* (Cambridge: Cambridge University Press).

Lal, Ruby (2018). *Empress: The Astonishing Reign of Nur Jahan* (New York: W.W. Norton).

Levi, Scott C. (2002). *The Indian Diaspora in Central Asia and its Trade, 1550–1900* (Leiden: Brill).

Levi, Scott C. (2016). *Caravans: Punjabi Khatri Merchants on the Silk Road* (Delhi: Penguin/Portfolio).

Losty, Jeremiah (2016). *Court Paintings from Persia and India 1500–1900* (London: Francesca Galloway).

Machado, Pedro (2009). 'Cloths of a New Fashion: Indian Ocean Networks of Exchange and Cloth Zones of Contact in Africa and India in the Eighteenth and Nineteenth Centuries,' in *How India Clothed the World: The World of South Asian Textiles 1500–1850*, edited by Giorgio Riello and Tirthankhar Roy (Leiden: Brill), pp. 53–84.

Machado, Pedro (2014). *Ocean of Trade: South Asian Merchants, Africa and the Indian Ocean, c. 1750–1850* (Cambridge: Cambridge University Press).

Malekandathil, Pius (2013). 'Indian Trade with Eastern Mediterranean during the Age of Portuguese Commercial Expansion 1500–1650,' in idem, *The Mughals, the Portuguese and the Indian Ocean: Changing Imageries of Maritime India* (Delhi: Primus Books), pp. 107–22.

Malekandathil, Pius (2014). 'Spatial Articulations of a Power Centre: A Study of the Medieval City of Delhi, 1206–1506,' in *Cities in Medieval India*, edited by Yogesh Sharma and Pius Malekandathil (Delhi: Primus Books), pp. 135–56.

Maloni, Ruby (2015). 'Surat in the Seventeenth Century: A Pre-modern Urban Environment,' in *Port Towns of Gujarat*, edited by Sara Keller and Michael Pearson (Delhi: Primus Books), pp. 273–84.

Matthee, Rudi and Hiroyuki Mashita (2012). 'Kandahar iv. From The Mongol Invasion through the Safavid Era,' *Encyclopædia Iranica*, XV/5, pp. 478–84, available online at http://www.iranicaonline.org/articles/kandahar-from-the-mongol-invasion-through-the-safavid-era (accessed on 27 January 2018).

Maurya, Anubhuti (2014). 'A City of Two Settlements: Srinagar in the Seventeenth Century,' in *Cities in Medieval India*, edited by Yogesh Sharma and Pius Malekandathil (Delhi: Primus Books), pp. 367–83.

Mehta, Makrand (1991a). 'Virji Vora: The Profile of an Indian Businessman in the 17th Century,' in idem, *Indian Merchants and Entrepreneurs in Historical Perspective with Special Reference to the Shroffs of Gujarat: 17th to 19th Centuries* (Delhi: Academic Foundation), pp. 53–64.

Mehta, Makrand (1991b). 'Social Base of Jain Entrepreneurs in the 17th Century: Shantidas Zaveri of Ahmedabad' in idem, *Indian Merchants and Entrepreneurs in Historical Perspective . . .* (Delhi: Academic Foundation), pp. 91–113.

Mehta, Makrand (1991c). 'Indian Bankers and Political Change: A Case Study of the Travadis of Surat, c. 1720–c. 1820,' in idem, *Indian Merchants and Entrepreneurs in Historical Perspective. . .* (Delhi: Academic Foundation), pp. 153–70.

Mehta, Makrand (1991d). 'Some Aspects of Surat as a Trading Centre in the 17th Century,' in idem, *Indian Merchants and Entrepreneurs in Historical Perspective . . .* (Delhi: Academic Foundation), pp. 33–52.

Mishra, K. P. (2014). 'Pilgrims, Fairs and Banking,' in *Cities in Medieval India*, edited by Yogesh Sharma and Pius Malekandathil (Delhi: Primus Books), pp. 263–77.

Moin, A. Azfar (2012). *The Millenial Sovereign: Sacred Kingship and Sainthood in Islam* (New York: Columbia University Press).

Moin, A. Azfar (2015). 'Sovereign Violence: Temple Destruction in India and Shrine Desecration in Iran and Central Asia,' *Comparative Studies in Society and History*, 57, 2, 467–96.

Moosvi, Shireen (2002). 'A Note on Interest Rates in the Seventeenth and Early Eighteenth centuries,' in *Money & Credit in Indian History from Early Medieval Times*, edited by Amiya Kumar Bagchi (Delhi: Tulika Books), pp. 84–92.

Moosvi, Shireen (2008a). 'Ecology, Population Distribution and Settlement Pattern in Mughal India,' in eadem, *People, Taxation and Trade in Mughal India* (New Delhi: Oxford University Press of India), pp. 89–102.

Moosvi, Shireen (2008b). 'Mughal Shipping at Surat in the First Half of Seventeenth Century,' in eadem, *People, Taxation and Trade in Mughal India* (New Delhi: Oxford University Press of India), pp. 257–74.

Moosvi, Shireen (2008c). 'Travails of a Mercantile Community: Aspects of Social Life at the Port of Surat (Earlier Half of the Seventeenth Century),' in eadem, *People, Taxation and Trade in Mughal India* (New Delhi: Oxford University Press of India), pp. 275–87.

Moosvi, Shireen (2008d). 'Gujarat Ports and their Hinterland: The Economic Relationship,' in eadem, *People, Taxation and Trade in Mughal India* (New Delhi: Oxford University Press of India), pp. 288–96.

Moosvi, Shireen (2008e). 'Urban Population in Pre-colonial India,' in eadem, *People, Taxation and Trade in Mughal India* (New Delhi: Oxford University Press of India), pp. 119–34.

Moosvi, Shireen (2008f). 'Work and Gender in Mughal India,' in eadem, *People, Taxation and Trade in Mughal India* (New Delhi: Oxford University Press of India), pp. 135–58.

Moosvi, Shireen (2015). *The Economy of the Mughal Empire c. 1595: A Statistical Study* (revised and enlarged edition Delhi: Oxford University Press).

Mughul, Dr. Muhammad Yakub (1974). *Osmanlıların Hint Okyanusu Politikası ve Osmanlı-Hint Müslümanları Münasebetleri* (Istanbul: Fetih Yayınevi).

Mukherjee, Tilottama (2013). *Political Culture and Economy in Eighteenth-Century Bengal: Networks of Exchange, Consumption and Communication* (New Delhi and Hyderabad: Orient Black Swan).

Mukhia, Harbans (reprint 2001a). 'Was there Feudalism in Indian History?,' in Harbans Mukhia, *Perspectives on Medieval History* (New Delhi: Vikas Publishing House Ltd), pp. 91–152.

Mukhia, Harbans (reprint 2001b). 'Communalism and the Writing of Medieval Indian History: A Reappraisal,' in Harbans Mukhia, *Perspectives on Medieval History* (New Delhi: Vikas Publishing House Ltd), pp. 33–45.

Mukhia, Harbans (2004). *The Mughals of India* (Oxford and Malden, MA: Blackwell Publishing).

Nadri, Ghulam A. (2009). *Eighteenth-Century Gujarat: The Dynamics of its Political Economy, 1750–1800* (Leiden: Brill).

Natif, Mika (2018). *Mughal Occidentalism: Artistic Encounters between Europe and Asia at the Courts of India, 1580–1630* (Leiden: Brill).

Orthmann, Eva (1996). *Abd or-Rahim Han-e Hanan (964–1036 / 1556–1627): Staatsmann und Mäzen* (Berlin: Klaus Schwarz Verlag).

Orthmann, Eva (2014). 'Ideology and State Building: Humāyūn's Search for Legitimacy in a Hindu–Muslim Environment,' in *Religious Interactions in Mughal India*, edited by Vasudha Dalmia and Munis D. Faruqui (Delhi: Oxford University Press), pp. 3–29. http://ottomanhistorians.uchicago.edu/ (Accessed on 27 April 2018).

Parthasarathi, Prasannan (2002). 'Merchants and the Rise of Colonialism,' in *The Eighteenth Century in India*, edited by Seema Alavi (Debates in Indian History and Society) (Delhi: Oxford University Press), pp. 199–224.

Parthasarathi, Prasannan (2007). *The Transition to a Colonial Economy: Weavers, Merchants and Kings in South India 1720–1800* (Cambridge: Cambridge University Press).

Parthasarathi, Prasannan (2009a). 'Historical Issues of Deindustrialization in Nineteenth-century South India,' in *How India Clothed the World: The World of South Asian textiles 1500–1850*, edited by Giorgio Riello and Tirthankhar Roy (Leiden: Brill), pp. 415–36.

Parthasarathi, Prasannan (2009b). 'Cotton Textiles in the Indian Subcontinent, 1200–1800,' in *The Spinning World: A Global History of Cotton Textiles, 1200–1850*, edited by Giorgio Riello and Prasannan Parthasarathi (Oxford: Pasold Research Foundation and Oxford University Press), pp. 17–42.

Peck, Lucy (2014). *Fatehpur Sikri: Revisiting Akbar's Masterpiece* (Delhi: Lustre Press, Roli Books).

Prakash, Om (2002). 'The System of Credit in Mughal India,' in *Money & Credit in Indian History from Early Medieval Times*, edited by Amiya Kumar Bagchi (Delhi: Tulika Books), pp. 40–57.

Prakash, Om (2004). *Bullion for Goods: European and Indian Merchants in the Indian Ocean Trade, 1500–1800* (New Delhi: Manohar Publishers).
Prakash, Om (2007). 'Trade and Politics in Eighteenth-century Bengal,' in *The Eighteenth Century in India*, edited by Seema Alavi (Debates in Indian History and Society) (Delhi: Oxford University Press), pp. 136–64.
Prakash, Om (2009a). 'From Market-determined to Coercion-based: Textile Manufacturing in Eighteenth-century Bengal,' in *How India Clothed the World: The World of South Asian Textiles 1500–1850* (Leiden: Brill), pp. 217–52.
Prakash, Om (2009b). 'The Dutch and the Indian Ocean Textile Trade,' in *The Spinning World: A Global History of Cotton Textiles, 1200–1850* (Oxford: Pasold Research Foundation and Oxford University Press), pp. 145–60.
Prakash, Om (reprint 2012). *The Dutch East India Company and the Economy of Bengal 1630–1720* (Delhi: Manohar Publishers).
Prasad Sahai, Nandita (2006). *Politics of Patronage and Protest: The State, Society, and Artisans in Early Modern Rajasthan* (Delhi: Oxford University Press). Online version: http://www.oxfordscholarship.com.0012b22k043f.emedia1.bsb-muenchen.de/view/10.1093/acprof:oso/9780195678963.001.0001/acprof-9780195678963-chapter-1?rskey=ckpYvf&result=2 (Accessed on 14 August 2018).
Prasad Sahai, Nandita (2016). 'From Marwar to Malwa and Back: Artisanal Mobility and Circulation during the Eighteenth Century,' in *Migrations in Medieval and Early Colonial India*, edited by Vijaya Ramaswamy (London, New York and Delhi: Routledge), pp. 193–224.
Rajadhyaksha, Abhijit (1960). 'Far East Kingdoms, South Asia: The Bahamani Sultanate.' http://www.historyfiles.co.uk/KingListsFarEast/IndiaBahamanis.htm (accessed on 10 July 2017).
Ramaswamy, Vijaya (2013). *The Song of the Loom: Weaver Folk Traditions in South India* (Delhi: Primus Books).
Ray, Aniruddha (2015). *Towns and Cities of Medieval India* (Delhi: Oxford University Press).
Raychaudhuri, Tapan (1982). 'The State and the Economy: 1. The Mughal Empire,' in *The Cambridge Economic History of India, vol. 1 c. 1200–c. 1750*, edited by Tapan Raychaudhuri and Irfan Habib (Cambridge: Cambridge University Press), pp. 172–93. There are many reprints, compare: Hyderabad: Orient Black Swan and CUP, 2009.
Rezavi, Syed Ali Nadeem (2011). 'Representations of Middle Class Professionals in Mughal Visual Art,' in *The Varied Facets of History: Essays in Honour of Aniruddha Ray*, edited by Ishrat Alam and Syeed Eyaz Hussain (Delhi: Primus Books), pp. 159–94.
Rezavi, Syed Ali Nadeem (2013). *Fathpur Sikri Revisited* (Delhi: Oxford University Press).
Richards, John F. (1989). 'Introduction,' in *The Imperial Monetary System of Mughal India*, edited by John F. Richards (Delhi: Oxford University Press), pp. 1–12.
Richards, John F. (1993). *The Mughal Empire* (The New Cambridge History of India) (Cambridge: Cambridge University Press).
Rizvi, Saiyid Athar Abbas (reprint 1995). *Muslim Revivalist Movements in Northern India in the Sixteenth and Seventeenth Centuries* (Delhi: Munshiram Manoharlal Publishers).
Roy, Tirthankar (2008). 'The Guild in Modern South Asia,' in *The Return of the Guilds*, edited by Jan Lucassen, Tine de Moor and Jan Luyten van Zanden (Cambridge: Cambridge University Press), pp. 95–120.
Roy, Tirthankar (2016). *The East India Company: The World's Most Powerful Corporation* (Gurgaon/Haryana: Penguin/Portfolio).

Sarkar, Sir Jadunath (1984). *A History of Jaipur c. 1503–1938*, revised and edited by Raghubir Sinh (Himayatnagar/Hyderabad and Jaipur: Orient Longman and Maharaja Sawai Man Singh II Museum).

Sarkar, Sir Jadunath (2009). *A Short History of Aurangzib* (Himayatnagar/Hyderabad: Orient Blackswan).

Sharma, Karuna (2007). 'The Social World of Prostitutes and *Devadasis*: A Study of the Social Structure and its Politics in Early Modern India,' *Journal of International Women's Studies*, 9, 1, 297–310. Available at: http://vc.bridgew.edu/jiws/vol9/iss1/17/ (accessed on 31 December 2017).

Sherwani, H. K. (1960).'Bahmanīs,' in *Encyclopaedia of Islam, Second Edition* edited by P. Bearman, Th. Bianquis, C.E. Bosworth, E. van Donzel and W.P. Heinrichs (Leiden and London: Brill and Luzac), vol. 1, pp. 923–25.

Singh, Chetan (2017). 'Forests, Pastoralists and Agrarian Society in Mughal India,' in *Frontiers of Environment: Issues in Medieval and Early Modern India*, edited by Meena Bhargava (Delhi: Orient Blackswan), pp. 71–97.

Soni, Sonika (2016). 'Glories of the Suratkhana: Two Centuries of Painting at the Jaipur Court,' in *Painting and Photography at the Jaipur Court*, edited by Giles Tillotson and Mrinalini Venkateswaran (New Delhi: Nyogi Books and Maharaja Sawai Singh II Museum Trust), pp. 11–138.

Sood, Gagan (2016). *India and the Islamic Heartlands: An Eighteenth-Century World of Circulation and Exchange* (Cambridge: Cambridge University Press).

Stein, Burton (2002). *A History of India* (Delhi: Oxford University Press).

Stephen, S. Jeyaseela (2011). 'Commercial Ledgers and Books of Accounts of a Tamil Merchant in Pondicherry (AD 1736–69),' in *The Varied Facets of History: Essays in Honour of Aniruddha Ray*, edited by Ishrat Alam and Syeed Eyaz Hussain (Delhi: Primus Books), pp. 205–14.

Subrahmanyam, Sanjay (1990). *The Political Economy of Commerce: South India 1500–1650* (Cambridge: Cambridge University Press).

Subrahmanyam, Sanjay (1992). 'Iranians Abroad: Intra-Asian Elite Migration and Early Modern State Formation,' *The Journal of Asian Studies*, 51.2, 340–63.

Subrahmanyam, Sanjay (1993). *The Portuguese Empire in Asia 1500–1700: A Political and Economic History* (London and New York: Longman).

Subrahmanyam, Sanjay (2005a). 'Sixteenth-century Millenarianism from the Tagus to the Ganges,' in idem, *Explorations in Connected History: From the Tagus to the Ganges* (New Delhi: Oxford University Press), pp. 102–37.

Subrahmanyam, Sanjay (reprint 2005b). 'Violence, Grievance and Memory in Early Modern South Asia,' in idem, *Explorations in Connected History: From the Tagus to the Ganges* (New Delhi: Oxford University Press), pp. 80–101.

Subrahmanyam, Sanjay (reprint 2011). *Explorations in Connected History: From the Tagus to the Ganges* (New Delhi: Oxford University Press).

Subrahmanyam, Sanjay and Christopher A. Bayly (1990). 'Portfolio Capitalists and the Political Economy of Early Modern India,' in *Merchants, Markets and the State in Early Modern India*, edited by Sanjay Subrahmanyam (Delhi: Oxford University Press of India), pp. 242–65.

Subramanian, Lakshmi (2015). 'Piracy and the Northward Coast: Problems of Definition,' in *Port Towns of Gujarat*, edited by Sara Keller and Michael Pearson (Delhi: Primus Books), pp. 163–80.

Subramanian, Lakshmi (2016). *Three Merchants of Bombay: Business Pioneers of the Nineteenth Century*, Introduction by Gurcharan Das (Gurgaon/India: Penguin/Portfolio).

Thapar, Romila (2004). *Somanatha: The Many Voices of a History* (Gurgaon/Haryana: Penguin Books India).

Tillotson, Giles (2012). *Taj Mahal* (Cambridge MA: Harvard University Press).

Trautmann, Thomas R. (2015). *Elephants and Kings: An Environmental History* (Delhi: Permanent Black and Ashoka University).

Trivedi, K. K. (2014). 'Agra City in the Making,' in *Cities in Medieval India*, edited by Yogesh Sharma and Pius Malekandathil (Delhi: Primus Books), pp. 113–32.

Trivedi, K. K. (2017). *Medieval City of Agra* (Delhi: Primus Books).

Truschke, Audrey (2016). *Culture of Encounters: Sanskrit at the Mughal Court* (Gurgaon/Haryana: Penguin Books).

Truschke, Audrey (n. d.). 'Revisiting History: Mughal Emperor Aurangzeb Protected Hindu Temples more often than he Demolished them'; Quartz Media LLC (US): https://qz.com/918425/mughal-emperor-aurangzeb-protected-hindu-temples-more-often-than-he-demolished-them/ (accessed on 14 July 2017).

Vanina, Eugenia (2004). *Urban Crafts and Craftsmen in Medieval India (Thirteenth to Eighteenth Centuries)* (Delhi: Munshiram Manoharlal Publishers).

Veinstein, Gilles (1999). 'Commercial Relations between India and the Ottoman Empire (Late Fifteenth to Late Eighteenth Centuries): A Few Notes and Hypotheses,' in *Merchants, Companies and Trade: Europe and Asia in the Early Modern Era*, edited by Sushil Chaudhury and Marc Morineau (Paris and Cambridge: Maison des Sciences de l'Homme/Cambridge University Press), pp. 95–115.

Verma, Som Prakash (2009a). *Interpreting Mughal Painting: Essays in Art, Society and Culture* (Delhi: Oxford University Press of India).

Verma, Som Prakash (2009b). 'Ordinary Life in Mughal India: A Survey of Mughal Painting,' in idem, *Interpreting Mughal Painting: Essays in Art, Society and Culture* (Delhi: Oxford University Press of India), pp. 157–73.

Verma, Som Prakash (2010). 'Painting under Akbar as Narrative Art,' in *Akbar and his India*, edited by Irfan Habib (Delhi: Oxford University Press of India), pp. 147–160.

Washbrook, David (2009). 'The Textile Industry and the Economy of South India,' in *How India Clothed the World: The World of South Asian Textiles 1500–1850* (Leiden: Brill), pp. 173–92.

Wright, Elaine (2009). 'An Introduction to the Albums of Jahangir and Shah Jahan,' in *Muraqqa': Imperial Mughal Albums from the Chester Beatty Library Dublin* (Alexandria, VA: Art Services International), pp. 38–53.

Zilli, Ishtiyaq Ahmad (reprint 2010). 'Development of Inshā Literature to the End of Akbar's Reign,' in *Exploring Medieval India, Sixteenth to Eighteenth Centuries*, vol. II *Culture, Gender, Regional Patterns*, edited by Meena Bhargava (Hyderabad: Orient BlackSwan), pp. 74–112.

Index